W9-CDY-907

DUNCAN GARWOOD
ABIGAIL HOLE

ROME

CITY GUIDE

INTRODUCING ROME

The Basilica di Santa Maria Maggiore (p105; foreground) and St Peter's Basilica (p137) create a heavenly skyline

History, human genius and the hot midday sun have conspired to make Rome one of the world's most seductive capitals, a city of incomparable beauty and exuberant Mediterranean passion.

It's easy to exaggerate when describing Rome, but this remarkable city really does get into your bloodstream. Not only does it boast an unparalleled cultural legacy, but it's also a pulsating, chaotic modern metropolis, home to almost three million people. History reverberates all around, but everyday life goes on – market workers set up stalls on historic piazzas, scooters scream through medieval alleyways, and stylish drinkers sip cocktails in sexy lounge bars.

But while modern Romans embrace the present, there's no escaping the city's past. The Colosseum and Pantheon remind you of Rome's imperial heyday as *caput mundi* (capital of the world), St Peter's Basilica trumpets Catholic power to the pilgrims lined before it, and works by Michelangelo, Caravaggio, Raphael and Bernini evoke the great artistic upheavals of history. Whichever way you look, you're faced with reminders of the city's unsurpassed pedigree.

Away from the big sights, Rome reveals a quieter, more intimate side. And it's here, among the labyrinthine backstreets and tranquil parks, that you'll discover the city's real charm. It might be a fading ochre-coloured *palazzo* (mansion) or a cat snoozing on an ancient ruin; you might stumble across an undiscovered trattoria or hit upon a once-in-a-lifetime view. Whatever it is, it'll stay with you, etched into your memory and urging you to return.

ROME LIFE

As a visitor, it's often difficult to see beyond Rome's spectacular veneer to the large, modern city that lies beneath. It's a living, breathing capital with all the tensions, difficulties and problems that go with that – problems often exacerbated by the city's ancient infrastructure and huge cultural legacy. Ancient roads might look good to tourists but they're a nightmare to drive down and require constant attention. Similarly, the upkeep of monuments, museums and galleries places a great strain on the city's coffers.

Rome is not a city used to rapid change, but in the mid-noughties it underwent something of a renaissance. Under its bohemian, art-loving former mayor, Walter Veltroni, city hall invested heavily in the arts, sponsoring a series of high-profile cultural events and aggressively promoting tourism. The result was a fanfare of positive publicity and a feel-good factor through the roof.

Things have since calmed down a bit, but Rome remains a city dedicated to spectacle. In May 2009 the city hosted the European Champions League football final, and three months later the world swimming championships were held here. If current mayor Gianni Alemanno has his way, the city will also be staging Formula One motor racing from 2012.

Romans adore their city, and while they're aware that services are often patchy and efficiency is the exception rather than the norm, their good humour is an integral part of the city's appeal. They flock to the festivals, concerts and events that enliven the city's hot summer nights and take great delight in dressing up for an *aperitivo* at the latest 'in' bar.

But it's not all parties and designer chic. Rome has not escaped the ravages of the global credit crunch, and tourist revenue, a mainstay of the city economy, is down. To try and stop the rot, Alemanno has announced plans for a major development in the city's southern reaches, including proposals for an ancient Roman theme park, an aquarium and an overhaul of the Ostia seafront. In the meantime, city life continues much as it always has – commuters struggle against the gridlock, students party in Campo de' Fiori, and politicians hatch their plots in neighbourhood bars and trattorias.

On the Piazza della Rotonda dine under the sky and next to history: the ancient Pantheon (p73)

HIGHLIGHTS

ANCIENT ROME

More than anything, it's the majestic vestiges of Rome's ancient past that set the city apart. No photo can prepare you for your first sight of the Colosseum or the serene majesty of the Palatino.

❶ Colosseum
Rome's great icon is one of the world's great buildings (p62)

❷ Roman Forum
Dream of past glories in the heart of imperial Rome (p67)

❸ Palatino
Home to Romulus and Remus, this is Rome's mythical birthplace (p63)

❹ Bocca della Verità
Put your hand in and test the lie-detecting legend (p71)

❺ Capitoline Museums
Spectacular sculpture stars at the world's oldest museums (p70)

VATICAN CITY

The independent state of the Vatican City might cover less than half a square kilo-metre, but its riches are incalculable. From the awe-inspiring St Peter's Basilica to Michelangelo's Sistine Chapel and the vast Vatican Museums, it boasts some of Europe's most famous masterpieces.

① Sistine Chapel
Feast your eyes on Michelangelo's great masterpiece (p145)

② Piazza San Pietro
Bernini's extraordinary piazza funnels the faithful into St Peter's Basilica (p142)

③ Swiss Guards
They're Swiss, they wear pretty uniforms and they never smile (p137)

④ Michelangelo's Pietà
This moving sculpture is one of Michelangelo's earliest works (p140)

⑤ St Peter's Basilica
All eyes are drawn to the Vatican's towering centrepiece (p137)

⑥ Stanze di Raffaello
A stunning suite of rooms decorated by Raphael and his students (p144)

HISTORIC CENTRE

It's in Rome's romantic centre that you'll find the Rome of your mind's eye: café tables spilling onto baroque piazzas, Renaissance palaces looming over medieval alleyways and cars crunching over cobbled roads. Works of art share the streets with ruins, buskers, tourists and pigeons.

1 Museo dell'Ara Pacis
Augustus' monumental altar is housed in a controversial contemporary museum (p95)

2 Pantheon
This remarkable 1st-century temple is a masterclass in ancient engineering (p73)

3 Piazza Navona
A flamboyant piazza showcasing the best of Roman baroque (p78)

4 Jewish Ghetto
Medieval lanes weave through Rome's atmospheric Jewish Quarter (p83)

5 Elefantino
Bernini's whimsical sculpture of a bemused elephant carrying an ancient obelisk (p76)

6 Campo de' Fiori
A raucous square known for its daily market and noisy nightlife (p81)

7 Piazza del Popolo
Twin churches mark this neoclassical piazza, once the city's northern entrance (p94)

EAST OF THE CENTRE

Hidden in the busy streets east of the historic centre, you'll find two of Rome's most celebrated monuments: the Spanish Steps and Trevi Fountain. Further uphill, dolce vita ghosts haunt Via Vittorio Veneto, and Italy's head of state relaxes on the Quirinale hill.

1 Trevi Fountain
Toss a coin into this landmark fountain and you'll return to Rome (p99)

2 Galleria Nazionale d'Arte Antica – Palazzo Barberini
Sumptuous frescoes, baroque stairwells, Renaissance paintings – you get it all at this superb gallery (p103)

3 Spanish Steps
Take a breather on Rome's most famous perch (p95)

4 Piazza del Quirinale
A good sunset spot, this tranquil piazza fronts Italy's presidential palace (p101)

5 Via Vittorio Veneto
Paparazzi once snapped *dolce vita* stars on this refined boulevard (p104)

1 Museo e Galleria Borghese
Bernini's sculpture took baroque art to new levels (p148)

2 Villa Borghese
The city's green lung cuts a swath through northern Rome (p149)

3 Auditorium Parco della Musica
The hub of Rome's cultural life is Renzo Piano's cutting-edge concert complex (p153)

4 Via Appia Antica
Christians buried their dead in the catacombs under the Appian Way (p122)

5 Terme di Caracalla
These immense ruins reveal the scale of ancient Rome (p119)

6 Basilica di San Giovanni in Laterano
Rome's cathedral has been overawing visitors since the 4th century (p116)

FURTHER AFIELD

The areas to the north and south of the centre are rich in interest. Rome's famous park, Villa Borghese, balloons northwards and eastwards, providing a rare break from the energy-sapping streets. To the south, medieval churches and Roman ruins litter the cityscape.

CONTENTS

Duncan Garwood

When Duncan first visited Rome in 1996 he had no idea that within three years he'd be living there. His Italian adventures began in 1997 when he gave up life as a corporate journalist in southern England and headed off to the Adriatic port of Bari. After an eye-opening two years there, he moved to Rome, just in time to witness the turn of the millennium in Piazza Venezia. He lives with his Italian wife and two kids in the Alban hills, just south of the capital. Since 2002 he has contributed to a raft of Lonely Planet guides to Italy, including the past three editions of this book, *Naples & the Amalfi Coast*, *Sardinia* and *Piedmont*.

For this guide Duncan wrote the following chapters: Introducing Rome, Highlights, Getting Started, Background, Art & Architecture, Neighbourhoods, Festivals & Events, Transport and Directory.

DUNCAN'S TOP ROME DAY

Romans, who know a thing or two about the pleasures of eating, like to breakfast standing at a bar with a cappuccino or espresso and a *cornetto* (croissant). I do too, and I order them at La Tazza d'Oro (p217), a busy café near the Pantheon. It's early morning but there's plenty of life on the streets, particularly on Campo de' Fiori (p81), where the market traders are already hard at work. I sniff around the colourful stalls, picking up some fruit to munch, before heading off to explore the historic centre. I have no particular agenda in mind but I know that at some point I'll end up in Piazza Navona (p78). The streets to the west of the piazza are among Rome's most evocative, and I spend an enjoyable hour or two poking around the antique shops along Via dei Coronari (p79) and the boho boutiques on Via del Governo Vecchio (p80). I also stop off at the Chiostro del Bramante (p79), where I'm delighted to discover that there's an exhibition by Maurizio Savini, a Roman artist known for his pink chewing-gum sculptures. I've agreed to meet a friend for lunch but first we need to decide where. After a flourish of text messages we agree on Da Giggetto (p200), an old-school restaurant in the atmospheric Jewish Quarter. Long lunches make for sleepy afternoons and there's nowhere better for an al fresco siesta than the pretty Villa Celimontana (p116) park, which is where I head next.

After a pleasant snooze I start to feel the heat of the afternoon giving way to the cool of the evening and my energy returning. I've just got time for a quick *aperitivo* before heading out to Pigneto for a gig at the Circolo degli Artisti (boxed text, p227).

Abigail Hole

Chaos, beauty, endless summer, effortless cool, handsome inhabitants, the ice cream of your dreams, and picturebook countryside on your doorstep: Rome fits Abigail's view of an ideal city, and since she visited in 2003 she's never really left. She's married to an Italian, her first son was born in the Eternal City, and her Italian *famiglia* live here. She's written on Rome for various newspapers, magazines and websites, and contributed to Lonely Planet's *Best of Rome*, *Italy*, and *Puglia & Basilicata* guides. A freelance writer, she does her best to divide her time between Rome, London and Puglia. For this guide she updated the Eating, Drinking & Nightlife, Shopping, Sleeping, The Arts, Sports & Activities and Excursions chapters.

Ever since Grand Tourists invaded in the 18th century, Rome has been a major tourist attraction. The city's main gateway is Leonardo da Vinci Airport (aka Fiumicino), although if you're flying with a low-cost European airline you'll probably land at Ciampino. Both airports are well connected with the city centre. Once in town, you'll find the centre is best explored on foot – it's not big, and the streets are wonderfully vibrant.

WHEN TO GO

Rome is a busy year-round destination, although some months are busier than others. The city is at its most enticing in spring, between April and June – the weather is generally good, flowers are blooming and the light is gorgeous. Early autumn (September and October) is another good time. It follows, however, that these months are the busiest of the year and prices are at their highest. Peak rates also apply at Christmas, New Year and Easter.

Visitors are traditionally warned to avoid August, when high temperatures make sightseeing a physical challenge. However, if you can handle the heat, it can be a good time to visit – the city is less chaotic than usual, the festival season is in full swing and prices are more manageable (many hoteliers offer discounts to entice holidaymakers from the sea). The trick to surviving Rome in the heat is to adapt your daily routine so that you avoid the hottest time of the day – go out in the morning, rest up in the early afternoon and head out again around 5.30pm or 6pm.

Note that many small businesses, including some restaurants and hotels, close for two weeks or so in August.

FESTIVALS

Rome's calendar bursts with events ranging from colourful traditional celebrations with a religious and/or historical flavour to performing-arts festivals. Summer and autumn are the best times to catch the top events. For more info, see the Festivals & Events colour spread, p85; for a list of public holidays, see the Directory, p292. Good online resources include www.whatsonwhen.com and www.romacheap.it, which lists upcoming free events.

January
FESTA DI SANT'ANTONIO
Chiesa di Sant'Eusebio, Piazza Vittorio Emanuele II;
Ⓜ Vittorio Emanuele

On 17 January animal-lovers take their pets to be blessed at the Chiesa di Sant'Eusebio in honour of the patron saint of animals.

February
CARNEVALE
In the week before Ash Wednesday, children take to the streets in fancy dress and throw coriandoli (coloured confetti) over each other.

March
MARATONA DI ROMA
www.maratonadiroma.it; Ⓜ Colosseo
Sightseeing becomes sport at Rome's annual marathon. Held in late March, the 42km race starts and finishes near the Colosseum.

April
EASTER
Ⓜ Colosseo & Ottaviano-San Pietro
On Good Friday the pope leads a candlelit procession around the Colosseum. At noon on Easter Sunday he blesses the crowds in Piazza San Pietro.

SETTIMANA DELLA CULTURA
Culture Week; www.beniculturali.it, in Italian
A week of free entry to museums, galleries and otherwise closed sites. Dates change annually so check the website.

ROMA INDEPENDENT FILM FESTIVAL
www.riff.it
A weeklong homage to independent Italian and international film. Venues and dates change annually.

NATALE DI ROMA
Piazza del Campidoglio; 🚌 Piazza Venezia
Rome celebrates its birthday on 21 April with bands on Piazza del Campidoglio and fireworks all around.

MOSTRA DELLE AZALEE

Piazza di Spagna; M Spagna
In late April, the Spanish Steps are lined with thousands of brightly coloured azaleas – a perfect photo occasion.

May

PRIMO MAGGIO

Piazza di San Giovanni, Laterano; M San Giovanni
Rome's May 1 rock concert attracts huge crowds and Italian performers.

FOTOGRAFIA

www.fotografiafestival.it; Palazzo delle Esposizioni; ⬛ Via Nazionale
Contemporary photography comes to Rome. Exhibitions are held in the Palazzo delle Esposizioni between late May and August, and in galleries across the city.

FESTIVAL DELLE LETTERATURE

www.festivaldelleletterature.it; Roman Forum; M Colosseo
Spilling over into June, Rome's Literature Festival presents free readings in the atmospheric Basilica di Massenzio in the Roman Forum. DJs provide backing sounds.

June

ESTATE ROMANA

www.estateromana.comune.roma.it
Between June and September, Rome's big summer festival turns the city into a giant stage. Events range from book fairs to raves and gay parties.

COSMOPHONIES

www.cosmophonies.com; Ostia Antica; ⬛ Ostia Antica
Music, theatre and dance are staged in the ancient theatre at Ostia Antica. The festival is held over two periods: from mid-June to the end of July, and the first two weeks of September.

FESTIVAL INTERNAZIONALE DI VILLA ADRIANA

☎ 06 802 41 281; www.auditorium.com/villaadriana; Villa Adriana, Tivoli; ⬛ Tivoli
The vast ruins of Villa Adriana in Tivoli set the unforgettable stage for the Festival Internazionale di Villa Adriana. Contempo-

rary dance and theatre performances are presented between mid-June and mid-July.

FIESTA CLUB

www.fiesta.it, in Italian; Via Appia Nuova; ⬛ Via Appia Nuova
A festival of Latin American music and culture on the racecourse on Via Appia Nuova. The fun lasts from mid-June to mid-August.

ROMA INCONTRO IL MONDO

www.villaada.org; Laghetto di Villa Ada; ⬛ Via di Ponte Salario
A corner of Villa Ada is turned into a colourful multi-ethnic village between mid-June and early August. Top-quality concerts add to the party vibe.

VILLA CELIMONTANA JAZZ

www.villacelimontanajazz.com; Villa Celimontana; ⬛ Via della Navicella
Ravishing Villa Celimontana sets the scene for high-quality jazz from mid-June to mid-September.

FESTA DI SAN GIOVANNI

M San Giovanni
The birth of St John the Baptist is commemorated on 24 June, particularly around the Basilica di San Giovanni in Laterano.

FESTA DEI SANTI PIETRO E PAOLO

St Peter's Basilica & Basilica di San Paolo fuori le Mura; M Ottaviano-San Pietro & San Paolo
Romans celebrate patron saints Peter and Paul on 29 June, a public holiday. Festivities are centred on St Peter's Basilica and Via Ostiense.

ROCK IN ROMA

www.rockinroma.com; Via Appia Nuova; ⬛ Via Appia Nuova
Dust down the denims for Rome's big rock fest, held from the end of June through to July. Headline acts in 2009 included the Killers, Franz Ferdinand and Motorhead.

July

INVITO ALLA DANZA

www.invitoalladanza.it, in Italian; Teatro Villa Pamphilj, Via di San Pancrazio; ⬛ Via di San Pancrazio
This month-long dance festival draws top-notch international performers to the parklands of Villa Doria Pamphilj.

ROMA ALTA MODA
www.altaroma.it, in Italian
Catwalk models parade designer gear at locations throughout the city during Rome's biannual fashion week.

FESTA DI NOANTRI
www.festadenoantri.it, in Italian; Piazza Santa Maria in Trastevere; 🚊 or 🚋 Viale di Trastevere
Trastevere's annual party takes over the neighbourhood the last two weeks of July.

ROME PRIDE
www.romapride.it, in Italian
An annual festival celebrating gay rights and culture.

GAY VILLAGE
www.gayvillage.it; Piazza Barcellona, EUR; 🚊 Via delle Tre Fontane
Dance to the beat of Rome's premier gay event – a summer-long party of concerts, performances and DJ sets.

August
FESTA DELLA MADONNA DELLA NEVE
Basilica di Santa Maria Maggiore; 🚊 Piazza Santa Maria Maggiore
A 4th-century snowfall is celebrated at the Basilica di Santa Maria Maggiore on 5 August.

FERRAGOSTO
The Festival of the Assumption, 15 August, is celebrated with almost total shutdown as the entire population heads out of town.

September
ROMAEUROPA
www.romaeuropa.net
Rome's premier music and dance festival runs from late September to November.

VIA DELL'ORSO CRAFT FAIR
Piazza Navona; 🚊 Corso Rinascimento
Artisans around Via dell'Orso open studios and workshops to browsers and buyers.

October/November
FESTIVAL INTERNAZIONALE DEL FILM DI ROMA
www.romacinemafest.it; Auditorium Parco della Musica; 🚊 Viale Tiziano

Rome's film festival rolls out the red carpet for Italy's cinema big shots.

VIA DEI CORONARI MOSTRA-MERCATO
Piazza Navona; 🚊 Corso del Rinascimento
In late October, this famous antiques street opens its doors and displays its wares.

FESTIVAL INTERNAZIONALE DI MUSICA E ARTE SACRA
www.festivalmusicaeartesacra.net
Over four days in mid-November, the Vienna Philharmonic Orchestra performs a series of classical concerts in Rome's four papal basilicas.

ROMA JAZZ FESTIVAL
www.romajazzfestival.it; Auditorium Parco della Musica; 🚊 Viale Tiziano
Jazz greats descend on the Auditorium Parco della Musica for three weeks of concerts in November.

December/January
PIAZZA NAVONA CHRISTMAS FAIR
Piazza Navona; 🚊 Corso del Rinascimento
Piazza Navona is taken over by market stalls selling all manner of seasonal goodies (and rubbish).

CAPODANNO
New Year's Eve is celebrated with open-air concerts and fireworks.

COSTS & MONEY
It's pointless to beat about the bush – Rome is expensive. As a visitor, accommodation is going to be your biggest outlay, costing

CASH VS CREDIT CARD
Although credit cards are widely accepted – Visa and MasterCard more than American Express – they are not used nearly as much as in the UK or USA. Many family-run shops, trattorias and *pensioni* don't accept them, or if they do they are reluctant to take them for small purchases. You can often pre-book tickets for major sights with a credit card, but don't assume that this means you can pay with them on the door. In short, it's always best to carry enough cash to cover your immediate expenses. See p294 for more advice on dealing with money.

TOP 10 MONEY-SAVING TIPS

- Look for hotel bargains in the low season, from November to March (excluding the Christmas and New Year period). Many hoteliers also offer discounts in August. For a long sojourn consider a self-catering apartment.
- Visit the Vatican Museums on the last Sunday of the month (but be prepared for queues).
- Time your visit to coincide with Settimana della Cultura (Culture Week; see p16) when all museums are free.
- Look out for free concerts during festivals.
- Fill up on art at Rome's churches – they're all free (see boxed text p63).
- Buy a Roma Pass (see p291) if you want to blitz the sights.
- Carry a water bottle with you so that you can fill up at drinking fountains. Rome's water is perfectly drinkable.
- Lunch on sliced pizza (pizza *a taglio*) or buy picnic provisions from a local market.
- Drink during happy hour – many bars have these in the early evening – and dine on the bar snacks you get with *aperitivo*.
- Avoid the overpriced bars and restaurants around the big tourist sites, such as the Trevi Fountain and St Peter's Basilica. Stand up at the bar to drink coffee rather than sitting down.

anywhere between €90 and €250 for a double room in a three-star hotel. For a high-season bed in a hostel dorm reckon on up to €35. If you're travelling with kids, note that some hotels don't charge for toddlers who bunk up with mum and dad. Obviously, location affects hotel prices with those in the *centro storico* (historic centre) more expensive than those around Stazione Termini. Food costs also vary tremendously. A sit-down pizza with a beer might cost around €15, while a full meal at a city-centre restaurant will set you back at least €25. However, it's perfectly acceptable to mix and match, and order, say, a starter and pasta dish, and forego the main course *(secondo)*.

Museum admission varies from about €6.50 to €14, but many places are free to EU citizens under 18 and over 65, with discounts generally available to students. Some of Rome's

great sights are free to everyone, including the Pantheon, Trevi Fountain, Spanish Steps, and all churches, many of which boast priceless works of art. See the boxed text, p63 for a full list of free sights and details of where you can see works by Michelangelo, Raphael, Caravaggio and Bernini for free.

There are various discount cards available that might or might not save you money – see p291 for more on this. Public transport is fairly cheap, with a day pass costing €4 – see the boxed text, p286 for details.

INTERNET RESOURCES

060608 (www.060608.it) A huge website listing everything from hotels and bars to upcoming events, car parks and public loos.

Auditorium (www.auditorium.com) Get the lowdown on what's going on at the Auditorium Parco della Musica, Rome's vibrant cultural centre. Buy tickets online.

Lonely Planet (www.lonelyplanet.com) Check out the Rome destination guide and swap thoughts on the Thorn Tree forum.

Musei in Comune (www.museiincomuneroma.it) Provides information on 17 important museums, including the Capitoline Museums and the Museo dell'Ara Pacis.

Piccoli Turisti (http://piccolituristi.turismoroma.it) A good planning tool for parents, this colourful site presents kid-friendly itineraries, attractions and services.

Pierreci (www.pierreci.it) A bang-up-to-date site with the latest on exhibitions, monuments and museums. This is the place to book online tickets to the Colosseum and other major sights.

Roma C'è (www.romace.it) Online version of Rome's best weekly listings guide. It's in Italian, but you can download the small English section.

HOW MUCH?

0.5L mineral water €1.50

Slice of pizza €2 to €3.50

Bottle of Peroni beer €1.20 to €5

A coffee €0.70 to €1

A gelato €1.50 to €3.50

Taxi to/from the airport €40 (Fiumicino), €30 (Ciampino)

1L unleaded petrol €1.30

Ticket to the Colosseum €9 (plus possible €3 exhibition supplement)

Double room in a three-star hotel €90 to €250

Souvenir T-shirt €10

ADVANCE PLANNING

You probably won't need a visa, but if you do – see p301 to find out – make sure you get onto it early. Italian bureaucracy is notoriously complex and the wheels turn very slowly.

Accommodation is something else you'd do well to sort out in advance. If you're visiting in high season (spring, Christmas, New Year and Easter), a reservation is essential and you should try to book as early as possible. At other times, it's not absolutely necessary but is still a good idea, especially if you want your first choice of hotel.

Not many sights require you to book in advance although you'll cut down on queuing time by reserving tickets for the Colosseum (p62) and the Vatican Museums (p142). To visit the Museo e Galleria Borghese (p148), one of Rome's most spectacular galleries, you have to book ahead.

Check to see if your visit coincides with any big festivals and events (p16). Upcoming cultural events are listed online at www.060608.it and www.romace.it. Music fans should also consult the concert schedule at the Auditorium Parco della Musica (p153). If you're interested in taking a course, you'll need to do some pre-trip research – see p290 for details of schools and courses on offer.

Unless you have your heart set on a Valentine's Day tête-à-tête or New Year's Eve dinner, you shouldn't have many problems booking a restaurant once you're in town. A phone call a day or two beforehand will usually suffice. However, for the top dining spots, you'll need to reserve in advance; a couple of weeks or so should be sufficient for most places.

Rome Tourist Board (www.turismoroma.it) Rome Tourist Board's comprehensive website with info on sights, accommodation, city tours, transport and much more.

Spotted by Locals (www.spottedbylocals.com/rome) A great blog written by a team of five Romans, with insider tips on the hottest bars, sights and shops.

Vatican (www.vatican.va) Book tickets to the Vatican Museums and check out the pope's liturgical diary on the Holy See's official site.

SUSTAINABLE ROME

A tourist destination for centuries, Rome is bearing up remarkably well. Some of the big monuments are showing signs of wear and tear but after so long in the spotlight that's only to be expected. The question now is: will they last another 2000 years?

The city authorities are taking the problem seriously and in 2008 a bike-sharing scheme was introduced. For a city with no great cycling tradition and one of the highest rates of car ownership in Europe, this was a bold

gesture and the scheme was slow to catch on. However, as the initial problems are dealt with, it is beginning to take hold and as of June 2009 there were 3200 registered users. See p284 for practical details.

As a visitor there's not a huge amount you can do to safeguard Rome's environment but by following a few commonsense guidelines you can minimise your impact.

Respect barriers Most of Rome's archaeological sites are open to the public but there are areas that are off-limits. The reason is usually far from clear but if there's a barrier, bite the bullet and turn around.

Keep the camera under wraps You'd never guess from the amount of flashes going off around you, but many churches and museums ban (flash) photography.

Re-use plastic bottles Fill up with water at the fountains dotted around the centre. The water is drinkable.

Walk Distances in Rome are not huge, and half the fun of Rome is getting lost in its labyrinthine streets.

For more information on environmental issues, see p40.

HISTORY

Rome's history spans three millennia, from the classical myths of vengeful gods to the follies of Roman emperors, from Renaissance excess to swaggering 20th-century fascism. Emperors, popes and dictators have come and gone, playing out their ambitions and conspiring for their place in history.

ANCIENT ROME, THE MYTH

As much a mythical construct as a historical reality, Ancient Rome's image has been carefully nurtured throughout history. Intellectuals, artists and architects have sought inspiration from this skilfully constructed legend, while political and religious rulers have invoked it to legitimise their authority and serve their political ends.

Rome's original mythmakers were the first emperors. Eager to reinforce the city's status as *Caput Mundi* (capital of the world), they turned to writers such as Virgil, Ovid and Livy to create an official Roman history. These authors, while adept at weaving epic narratives, were less interested in the rigours of historical research and frequently presented myth as reality. In the *Aeneid*, Virgil brazenly draws on Greek legends and stories to tell the story of Aeneas, a Trojan prince who arrives in Italy and establishes Rome's founding dynasty. Similarly, Livy, a writer celebrated for his monumental history of the Roman Republic, makes liberal use of mythology to fill the gaps in his historical narrative. But accuracy wasn't considered necessary and Roman officialdom enthusiastically adopted their works as the basis for Rome's history.

Ancient Rome's rulers were sophisticated masters of spin; under their tutelage, art, architecture and elaborate public ceremony were employed to perpetuate the image of Rome as an invincible and divinely sanctioned power. Monuments such as the Ara Pacis (p95), the Colonna di Traiano (p69) and the Arco di Costantino (p63) celebrated imperial glories, while gladiatorial games highlighted the Romans' physical superiority. The Colosseum (p62), the Roman Forum (p67) and the Pantheon (p73) were not only supremely sophisticated feats of engineering, they were also impregnable symbols of Rome's eternal might.

During the Renaissance, a period in which Ancient Rome was hailed as the high point of Western civilisation, these symbols inspired a whole generation of artists and architects. Bramante, Michelangelo and Raphael modelled their work on classical precedents as they helped rebuild Rome as the capital of the Catholic Church.

But more than anyone, it was Italy's 20th-century fascist dictator, Benito Mussolini, who invoked the glories of ancient Rome. Mussolini spared no effort in his attempts to identify his fascist regime with imperial Rome – the term fascism is a derivation of an ancient Roman term, *fascis*, meaning a bundle of rods that officials carried as a symbol of authority. He made Rome's traditional birthday, 21 April, an official fascist holiday, he printed stamps with images of ancient Roman emperors, and he commissioned archaeological digs to unearth further proof of Roman might. His idealisation of the Roman Empire underpinned much of his colonialist ideology.

TIMELINE

753 BC	509 BC	146 BC
If you believe the legend, this is the year in which Romulus kills his twin brother Remus, founds Rome and rapes the Sabine women. Archaeological evidence exists of an 8th-century settlement on the Palatino.	On the death of Tarquinius Superbus, the last of Rome's seven kings, Lucius Junius Brutus founds the Roman Republic, giving birth to the acronym SPQR (Senatus Populusque Romanus; the Senate and People of Rome).	Carthage is razed to the ground at the end of the Third Punic War and mainland Greece is conquered by rampant legionaries. Rome becomes undisputed master of the Mediterranean.

ROMULUS & REMUS, ROME'S LEGENDARY TWINS

The most famous of all Roman legends is the story of Romulus and Remus, the mythical twins who are said to have founded Rome on 21 April 753 BC. Few historians accept the myth as fact, but most acknowledge that the city was founded as an amalgamation of Etruscan, Latin and Sabine settlements on the Palatino (Palatine), Esquilino (Esquiline) and Quirinale (Quirinal) hills. Archaeological discoveries have confirmed the existence of a settlement on the Palatino dating to the 8th century BC.

Romulus and Remus were born to the vestal virgin Rhea Silva after she'd been seduced by Mars. At their birth they were immediately sentenced to death by their great-uncle Amulius, who had stolen the throne of Alba Longa from his brother, and Rhea Silva's father, Numitor. But the sentence was never carried out, and the twins were abandoned in a basket on the banks of the River Tiber. Following a flood, the basket ended up on the northwestern summit of the Palatino (p63), where the babies were saved by a she-wolf and later brought up by a shepherd, Faustulus.

Years later, Remus was arrested for attacking some shepherds on the Aventino and carted off to face the king. Hearing the news, Faustulus told Romulus about his birth and asked him to save Remus. Romulus immediately set off for the Alban palace, where he not only freed his brother but also killed Amulius and reinstated his grandfather Numitor to the throne.

To celebrate, the twins decided to found a city on the site where they'd originally been saved. But they didn't know where this was, so they consulted the omens. Remus, on the Aventino, saw six vultures; his brother over on the Palatino saw 12. The meaning was clear and Romulus began building his new city walls. In a fit of anger Remus jumped over the unfinished walls, shouting; he asked how, if they couldn't keep him out, were they going to keep invaders out? Romulus, by now in a rage himself, killed his brother.

Romulus continued building and soon had a city. To populate it he created a refuge on the Campidoglio, Aventino, Celio and Quirinale hills, to which a ragtag population of criminals, ex-slaves and outlaws soon decamped. However, the city still needed women. Romulus's solution to this problem was to invite everyone in the surrounding country to celebrate the Festival of Consus (21 August). As the spectators watched the festival games, Romulus and his men pounced and abducted all the women, an action known as the Rape of the Sabine Women.

Nowadays, the myth of Rome is used less as a rallying cry and more as an advertising tool – and with some success. However cynical and world-weary you are, it's difficult to deny the thrill of seeing the Colosseum for the first time, or of visiting the Palatino (p63), the hill where Romulus is said to have killed his twin and founded the city in 753 BC.

LEGACY OF AN EMPIRE

Rising out of the bloodstained remnants of the Roman Republic, the Roman Empire was the Western world's first great superpower. At its zenith under Emperor Trajan (r AD 98–117), it extended from Britannia in the north to North Africa in the south, from Hispania (Spain) in the west to Palestina (Palestine) and Syria in the east. Rome itself had more than 1.5 million inhabitants and the city sparkled with the trappings of imperial splendour: marble temples, public baths, theatres, circuses and libraries. Decline eventually set in during the 3rd century and by the latter half of the 5th century Rome was in barbarian hands.

The empire's most immediate legacy was the division of Europe into east and west. In AD 285 the emperor Diocletian, prompted by widespread disquiet across the empire, had split the Roman Empire into eastern and western halves – the west centred on Rome, and the east on Byzantium (later called Constantinople) – in a move that was to have far-reaching consequences. In the west, the fall of the Western Roman Empire in AD 476 paved the way for the emergence

73–71 BC	49 BC	AD 14
Spartacus leads a slave revolt against the Roman dictator Cornelius Sulla. Defeat comes at the hands of Marcus Licinius Crassus and punishment is brutal. Spartacus and 6000 of his followers are crucified along Via Appia Antica.	'Alea iacta est' ('The die is cast'). Julius Caesar leads his army across the River Rubicon and marches on Rome. Victory over Pompey is short-lived as Caesar is murdered five years later.	Augustus dies after 41 years as Rome's first emperor. His reign is peaceful and culture thrives. Not so under his mad successors Tiberius and Caligula, who go down in history for their cruelty.

EMPERORS' WHO'S WHO

Of the 250 or so emperors of the Roman Empire, only a few were truly heroic. Here we highlight 10 of the best, worst and completely mad.

- **Augustus (27 BC–AD 14)** Rome's first emperor. Ushers in a period of peace and security; the arts flourish and many monuments are built, including the Ara Pacis and Pantheon.
- **Caligula (37–41)** Emperor No 3 after Augustus and Tiberius. Remains popular until illness leads to the depraved behaviour for which he is famous. Is murdered by his bodyguards on the Palatino.
- **Claudius (41–54)** Expands the Roman Empire and conquers Britain. Is eventually poisoned, probably at the instigation of Agrippina, his wife and Nero's mother.
- **Nero (54–68)** Initially rules well but later slips into insanity – he has his mother murdered, persecutes the Christians and attempts to turn half the city into a palace. He is eventually forced into suicide.
- **Vespasian (69–79)** First of the Flavian dynasty, he imposes peace and cleans up the imperial finances. His greatest legacy is the Colosseum.
- **Trajan (98–117)** Conquers the east and rules over the empire at its zenith. Back home he revamps Rome's city centre, adding a forum, market place and column, all of which still stand.
- **Hadrian (117–38)** Puts an end to imperial expansion and constructs walls to mark the empire's borders. He rebuilds the Pantheon and has one of the ancient world's greatest villas constructed at Tivoli.
- **Aurelian (270–5)** Does much to control the rebellion that sweeps the empire at the end of the 3rd century. Starts construction of the city walls that bear his name.
- **Diocletian (284–305)** Splits the empire into eastern and western halves in 285. Launches a savage persecution of the Christians as he struggles to control the empire's eastern reaches.
- **Constantine I (306–37)** Although based in Byzantium (later renamed Constantinople in his honour), he legalises Christianity and embarks on a church-building spree in Rome.

of the Holy Roman Empire and the Papal States, while in the east, Roman (later Byzantine) rule continued until 1453 when the empire was finally conquered by rampaging Ottoman armies.

In broader cultural terms, Roman innovations in language, law, government, art, architecture, engineering and public administration remain relevant to this day.

One of the Romans' most striking contributions to modern society was democratic government. Democracy had first appeared in 5th-century BC Athens, but it was the Romans, with their genius for organisation, who took it to another level. Under the Roman Republic (509–47 BC), the Roman population was divided into two categories: the Senate and the Roman people – hence the initials SPQR (Senatus Populusque Romanus; the Senate and People of Rome). Both held clearly defined responsibilities. The people, through three assembly bodies – the Centuriate Assembly, the Tribal Assembly and the Council of the People – voted on all new laws and elected two annual tribunes who had the power of veto in the Senate. The Senate, for its part, elected and advised two annual consuls who acted as political and military leaders. It also controlled the Republic's purse strings and, in times of grave peril, could nominate a dictator for a six-month period.

This system worked pretty well for the duration of the Republic, and remained more or less intact during the empire – at least on paper. In practice, the Senate assumed the Assemblies' legislative powers and the emperor claimed power of veto over the Senate, a move which pretty much gave him complete command, although in such a way as to preserve the façade of Republican government.

AD 64–67	80	285
St Peter and St Paul become martyrs as Nero massacres Rome's Christians. The persecution is a thinly disguised ploy to win back popularity after the emperor is blamed for the fire that ravaged Rome in AD 64.	The 50,000-seat Flavian Amphitheatre, better known as the Colosseum, is inaugurated by Emperor Titus. Five thousand animals are slaughtered in the 100-day games held to celebrate.	In an attempt to control anarchy within the Roman Empire, Diocletian splits it into eastern and western halves. The eastern half is later incorporated into the Byzantine Empire; the western half falls to the barbarians.

THE ROMAN EMPIRE

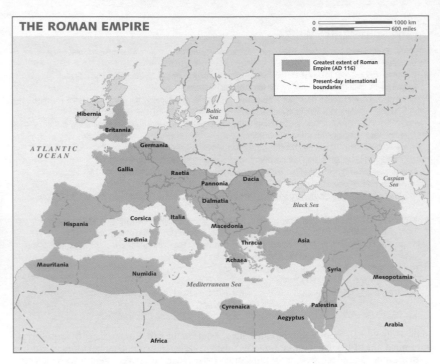

The observance of law was an important element in Roman society. As far back as the 5th century BC, the Republic had a bill of rights, known as the Twelve Tables. This remained the foundation stone of Rome's legal system until Emperor Justinian (r 527–565) produced his mammoth Corpus Iurus Civilis (Body of Civil Law) in 529. This not only codified all existing laws but also included a systematic treatise on legal philosophy. In particular, it introduced a distinction between *ius civilis* (civil law – laws particular to a state), *ius gentium* (law of nations – laws established and shared by states) and *ius naturale* (natural law – laws concerning male-female relationships and matrimony).

But more than the laws themselves, Rome's greatest legacy to the legal profession was the Latin language. Latin was the lingua franca of the Roman Empire and was later adopted by the Catholic Church, a major reason for the language's survival. It is still today one of the Vatican's official languages, and until the 2nd Vatican Council (1962–65) it was the only language in which Catholic Mass could be said. As the basis for modern Romance languages such as Italian, French and Spanish, it provides the linguistic roots to many modern words.

And just as many words lead to Latin, so all roads lead to Rome. The ancient Romans were the master engineers of their day, and their ability to travel quickly was an important factor

476	754	1084
The fall of Romulus Augustulus marks the end of the Western Empire. The end had been on the cards for years: in 410 the Goths sacked Rome; in 455 the Vandals followed suit.	Thanks to a deal between Pope Stephen II and Pepin, king of the Franks, the Lombards are driven out of Italy and the Papal States are created. The papacy is to rule Rome until Italian unification.	Rome is sacked by a Norman army after falling to the Holy Roman Emperor Henry IV. Pope Gregory VII had asked the Normans for protection but they arrived too late to prevent him surrendering.

in their power to rule. The queen of all ancient roads was Via Appia Antica (p122), which connected Rome with the southern Adriatic port of Brindisi. Via Appia survives to this day, as do many of the other ancient roads: Via Aurelia, Via Cassia, Via Flaminia and Via Salaria are among the most important.

CHRISTIANITY & PAPAL POWER

For much of its history Rome has been ruled by the Pope, and today the Vatican still wields immense influence over the city.

The ancient Romans were remarkably tolerant of foreign religions. They themselves worshipped a cosmopolitan pantheon of gods, ranging from household spirits and former emperors to deities appropriated from Greek mythology (Jupiter, Juno, Neptune, Minerva etc). Religious cults were also popular – the Egyptian gods Isis and Serapis enjoyed a mass following, as did Mithras, a heroic saviour-god of vaguely Persian origin, who was worshipped by male-only devotees in underground temples.

Christianity entered this religious cocktail in the 1st century AD, sweeping in from Judaea, a Roman province in what is now Israel and the West Bank. Its early days were marred by persecution, most notably under Nero (r 54–68), but it slowly caught on, thanks to its popular message of heavenly reward and the evangelizing efforts of Sts Peter and Paul. However, it was the conversion of the emperor Constantine (r 306–37) that really set Christianity on the path to European domination. In 313 Constantine issued the Edict of Milan, officially legalising Christianity, and later, in 378, Theodosius (r 379–95) made Christianity Rome's state religion.

By the 4th century, the Church had developed a sophisticated organisational structure based on five major sees: Rome, Constantinople, Alexandria, Antioch and Jerusalem. At the outset, each bishopric carried equal weight but in subsequent years Rome emerged as the senior party. The reasons for this were partly political – Rome was the wealthy capital of the Roman Empire – and partly religious – early Christian doctrine held that St Peter, founder of the Roman church, had been sanctioned by Christ to lead the universal Church.

But while Rome had control of Christianity, the Church had yet to conquer Rome. This it did in the dark days following the fall of the Roman Empire by skilfully stepping into the power vacuum created by the demise of imperial power. And although no one person can take credit for this, Pope Gregory the Great (r 590–604) did more than most to lay the groundwork. A leader of considerable foresight, he won many friends by supplying free bread to Rome's starving citizens and restoring the city's water supply. He also stood up to the menacing Lombards, who presented a very real threat to the city.

It was this threat that pushed the papacy into an alliance with the Frankish kings, an alliance that resulted in the creation of the two great powers of medieval Europe: the Papal States and the Holy Roman Empire. In Rome, the battle between these two superpowers translated into endless feuding between the city's baronial families and frequent attempts by the French to claim the papacy for their own. This political and military fighting eventually culminated in the papacy transferring to the French city of Avignon between 1309 and 1377, and the Great Schism (1378–1417), a period in which the Catholic world was headed by two popes, one in Rome and one in Avignon.

As both religious and temporal leaders, Rome's popes wielded influence well beyond their military capacity. For much of the medieval period, the Church held a virtual monopoly on Europe's

1188	1309	1471
Pope Clement III bows to pressure from newly formed artisans' guilds and recognises Rome as a commune with rights to appoint senators and a prefect.	Fighting between French-backed pretenders to the papacy and the Roman nobility, led by the Orsini family, culminates in Pope Clement V transferring his court to Avignon. Only in 1377 does Pope Gregory XI return to Rome.	The Capitoline Museums are established. The first exhibits are a series of bronzes gifted to the Roman people by Pope Sixtus IV. In 1538 Michelangelo starts work on Piazza del Campidoglio outside the museums.

GLADIATORS

Few images better encapsulate the cruelty and splendour of Ancient Rome than crowds baying for blood at the Colosseum.

Gladiatorial combat originated as part of Etruscan funerary rites and was later adopted in Campania and Lucania (modern-day Basilicata). The first recorded bout in Rome was in 264 BC. By the 1st century BC gladiatorial games had outstripped this funereal context and were being staged by wealthy citizens as a form of politics by display – the greater the spectacle, the greater the sponsor's prestige. Later, these private games *(munera)* gave way to public games *(ludi)* controlled by the state.

Gladiatorial fights were usually staged in the afternoon as part of an all-day spectacle – the morning was given over to animal displays and the lunch break to the execution of condemned criminals. A typical afternoon would involve about 12 pairs of gladiators fighting in bouts of 10 to 15 minutes. Exceptions were rare although often spectacular: Caesar exhibited 320 pairs in 65 BC, and Augustus and Trajan each displayed 5000 pairs on different occasions during their reigns. Bouts, accompanied by music, were not usually to the death *(sine missione)*, as the games' sponsor was required to pay the owner of a killed gladiator one hundred times the gladiator's value. Accidents did happen, though, and gladiators died.

The fate of a defeated gladiator lay in the hands of the presiding sponsor, who would decide on the basis of the crowd's reaction. Traditionally, thumbs up was said to signal life and thumbs down meant death. However, it's not at all clear that this was the case, and many historians believe that thumbs down was the signal to lower weapons and thumbs up was the go-ahead to stab the defeated gladiator in the chest.

Gladiators were prisoners of war, slaves, condemned criminals or volunteers, many of whom were ex-soldiers signing up for a make-or-break period in the arena. It was a tough life, and although only about 10% of gladiators died in the ring, very few lived beyond the age of 30. Only a tiny number made it big – gladiators were allowed to keep any prize money they won – and became celebrities.

Once condemned to a gladiatorial life, recruits were sent to gladiator school where they were assigned roles: *secutores* were armed with a large shield and sword; *retiarii* carried a trident and net; and *thraeces* fought with a scimitar and small shield. To ensure the greatest spectacle, heavily armed gladiators were usually paired with lighter, more nimble opponents.

Part entertainment and part business (vast sums were wagered on the games), gladiatorial games played a key propagandist function. The state-run spectacles were a demonstration of public might, and the use of exotic animals was a tactic to advertise the extent of Rome's reach. Crowd participation in the sentencing of defeated gladiators allowed the people to share in the state's authority over life and death.

The popularity of the games waned in the 3rd century AD and in 399 Emperor Honorius finally banned gladiatorial combat.

reading material (mostly religious scripts written in Latin) and was the authority on virtually every aspect of human knowledge. All innovations in science, philosophy and literature had to be cleared by the Church's hawkish scholars, who were constantly on the lookout for heresy.

Almost 1000 years on and the Church is still a major influence on modern Italian life. In recent years, Vatican intervention in political and social debate has provoked fierce divisions within Italy. A recent case in point was a right-to-die case involving a woman who'd been in a vegetative coma since 1992. In November 2008, the Italian High Court ruled that doctors could cease Eluana Englaro's treatment, something which her father had long maintained was what she wanted. The Church, fearing that this was the first step on the road to euthanasia, bitterly opposed the decision and fought tooth and nail to have it overruled. Public opinion was divided on the subject but Berlusconi's right-wing government sided with the Vatican and at the last minute tried to

1506	1508	1527
Pope Julius II employs 150 Swiss mercenaries to protect him. The 100-strong Swiss Guard, all practising Catholics from Switzerland, are still responsible for the pope's personal safety.	Michelangelo starts painting the Sistine Chapel while down the hall Raphael begins to decorate Pope Julius II's private apartments, better known as the Stanze di Raffaello (Raphael Rooms).	Pope Clement VII takes refuge in Castel Sant'Angelo as Rome is overrun by troops loyal to Charles V, king of Spain and Holy Roman Emperor. The city is sacked in an orgy of looting and violence.

halt proceedings with an emergency decree. This provoked howls of outrage from 'right-to-die' activists and criticism from Italy's Head of State, Giorgio Napolitano, who refused to sign the decree, saying that it was unconstitutional. In the end, the High Court's ruling was carried out and Eluana's treatment was interrupted in February 2009. She died a few days later.

This relationship between the Church and Italy's modern political establishment is a fact of life that dates to the establishment of the Italian Republic in 1946. For much of the First Republic (1946–94), the Vatican was closely associated with the Christian Democrat party (DC, Democrazia Cristiana), Italy's most powerful party and an ardent opponent of communism. The Church, keen to weed communism out of the political landscape, played its part by threatening to excommunicate anyone who voted for Italy's Communist Party (PCI, Partito Comunista Italiano). Today, no one political party has a monopoly on Church favour, and politicians across the spectrum tread warily around Catholic sensibilities. But this reverence is not limited to the purely political sphere; it also informs much press reporting and even law enforcement. In September 2008, Rome's public prosecutor threatened to prosecute a comedian for comments made against the pope, invoking the 1929 Lateran Treaty under which it is a criminal offence to 'offend the honour' of the pope and Italian president. The charge, which ignited a heated debate on censorship and the right to free speech, was eventually dropped by the Italian justice minister.

RENAISSANCE, A NEW BEGINNING

Bridging the gap between the Middle Ages and the modern age, the Renaissance (*Rinascimento* in Italian) was a far-reaching intellectual, artistic and cultural movement. It emerged in 14th-century Florence but quickly spread to Rome, where it gave rise to one of the greatest makeovers the city had ever seen.

The movement's intellectual cornerstone was humanism, a philosophy which focused on the central role of humanity within the universe, a major break from the medieval world view which had placed God at the centre of everything. It was not anti-religious, though. Many humanist scholars were priests and most of Rome's great works of Renaissance art were commissioned by the Church. In fact, it was one of the most celebrated humanist scholars of the 15th century, Pope Nicholas V (r 1447–84), who is generally considered the harbinger of the Roman Renaissance.

When Nicholas became pope in 1447 Rome was not in a good state. Centuries of medieval feuding had reduced the city to a semi-deserted battleground, and the city's bedraggled population lived in constant fear of plague, famine, and flooding (the Tiber regularly broke its banks). In political terms, the papacy was recovering from the trauma of the Great Schism and attempting to face down Muslim encroachment in the east.

It was against this background that Nicholas decided to rebuild Rome as a showcase of Church power. To finance his plans, he declared 1450 a Jubilee year, a tried and tested way of raising funds by attracting hundreds of thousands of pilgrims to the city (in a Jubilee year anyone who comes to Rome and confesses receives a full papal pardon).

Over the course of the next 80 years or so, Rome underwent a complete overhaul. Pope Sixtus IV (r 1471–84) had the Sistine Chapel (p145) built and, in 1471, gifted the people of Rome a selection of bronzes that became the first exhibits of the Capitoline Museums (p70). Julius II (r 1503–13) laid Via del Corso and Via Giulia (p82), and ordered Bramante to rebuild St Peter's Basilica (p137). Michelangelo frescoed the Sistine Chapel and designed the dome of St Peter's, while Raphael inspired a whole generation of painters with his masterful grasp of perspective.

1555	1626	1798
As fear pervades Counter-Reformation Rome, Pope Paul IV confines the city's Jews to the area now known as the Jewish Ghetto. Official intolerance of Rome's Jewry continues on and off until the 20th century.	After more than 150 years of construction, St Peter's Basilica is consecrated. The hulking basilica remains the largest church in the world until well into the 20th century.	Napoleon marches into Rome, forcing the elderly Pope Pius VI to flee. A republic is announced, but it doesn't last long and in 1801 Pius VI's successor Pius VII returns to Rome.

But outside of Rome an ill wind was blowing. The main source of trouble was the longstanding conflict between the Holy Roman Empire, led by the Spanish Charles V, and the Italian city states. This simmering tension came to a head in 1527 when Rome was invaded by Charles' marauding army and subsequently ransacked as Pope Clement VII (r 1523–34) hid in Castel Sant'Angelo (p146).

The sack of Rome, regarded by most historians as the nail in the coffin of the Roman Renaissance, was a hugely traumatic event. It left the papacy reeling and gave rise to the view that the Church had been greatly weakened by its own moral shortcomings. That the Church was corrupt was well known, and it was with considerable public support that Martin Luther pinned his famous 95 Theses to a church door in Wittenberg in 1517, thus sparking off the Protestant Reformation.

The Catholic reaction to the Reformation was all-out. The Counter-Reformation was marked by a second wave of artistic and architectural activity, as the Church once again turned to bricks and mortar to restore its authority. But in contrast to the Renaissance, the Counter-Reformation was a period of persecution and official intolerance. With the full blessing of Pope Paul III, Ignatius Loyola founded the Jesuits in 1540, and two years later the Holy Office was set up as the Church's final appeals court for trials prosecuted by the Inquisition. In 1559 the Church published the *Index Librorum Prohibitorum* (Index of Prohibited Books) and began to persecute intellectuals and freethinkers. Galileo Galilei (1564–1642) was forced to renounce his assertion of the Copernican astronomical system, which held that the earth moved around the sun. He was summoned by the Inquisition to Rome in 1632 and exiled to Florence for the rest of his life. Giordano Bruno (1548–1600), a freethinking Dominican monk, fared worse. Arrested in Venice in 1592, he was burned at the stake eight years later in Campo de' Fiori (p81). The spot is today marked by a sinister statue.

Despite, or perhaps because of, the Church's policy of zero tolerance, the Counter-Reformation was largely successful in re-establishing papal prestige. And in this sense it can be seen as the natural finale to the Renaissance that Nicholas V had kicked off in 1450. From being a rural backwater with a population of around 20,000 in the mid-15th century, Rome had grown to become one of Europe's great 17th-century cities, home to Christendom's most spectacular churches and a population of some 100,000 people.

POWER & CORRUPTION

The exercise of power has long gone hand in hand with corruption. As the British historian Lord Acton famously put it in 1887, 'Power tends to corrupt; absolute power corrupts absolutely.' And no-one enjoyed greater power than Rome's ancient emperors.

Of all Rome's cruel and insane leaders, few are as notorious as Caligula. A byword for depravity, Caligula was hailed as a saviour when he inherited the empire from his great-uncle Tiberius in AD 37. Tiberius, a virtual recluse by the end of his reign, had been widely hated, and it was with a great sense of relief that Rome's cheering population welcomed the 25-year-old Caligula to the capital.

Their optimism was to prove ill-founded. After a bout of serious illness, Caligula began showing disturbing signs of mental instability and by AD 40 had taken to appearing in public dressed as a god. He made his senators worship him as a deity and infamously tried to make his horse, Incitator, a senator. He was accused of all sorts of perversions and progressively alienated

1848	1870	1883
As rebellion sweeps Europe, a popular assembly declares a republic in Rome. Led by Giuseppe Mazzini and Giuseppe Garibaldi, it is eventually defeated by French forces fighting on behalf of Pope Pius IX.	Nine years after Italian unification, Rome falls to Italian troops. The city walls are breached at Porta Pia and Pope Pius IX is forced to cede the city to Italy. Rome becomes the Italian capital.	In the small town of Forlì in Emilia-Romagna, Italy's future dictator Benito Mussolini is born. An ardent socialist, Mussolini rises through the ranks of the Italian Socialist Party.

himself from all those around him. By AD 41 his Praetorian Guard had had enough and on 24 January its leader, Cassius Chaerea, stabbed him to death.

Debauchery on such a scale was rare in the medieval papacy, but corruption was no stranger to the corridors of ecclesiastical power. It was not uncommon for popes to father illegitimate children, and nepotism was rife. The Borgia pope Alexander VI (r 1492–1503) fathered two illegitimate children with the first of his two high-profile mistresses. The second, Giulia Farnese, was the sister of the priest who was to become Pope Paul III (r 1534–59), himself no stranger to earthly pleasures. When not persecuting heretics during the Counter-Reformation, the Farnese pontiff managed to sire four children.

Corruption has also featured in modern Italian politics, most famously in the 1990s Tangentopoli (Kickback City) scandal. Against a backdrop of steady economic growth, the controversy broke in Milan in 1992 when a routine corruption case – accepting bribes in exchange for public works – blew up into a nationwide crusade against corruption.

Led by the 'reluctant hero', magistrate Antonio di Pietro, the Mani Pulite (Clean Hands) investigations exposed a political and business system riddled with corruption. Politicians, public officials and businesspeople were investigated and for once no-one was spared, not even the powerful Bettino Craxi (prime minister between 1983 and 1989), who, rather than face a trial in Italy, fled to Tunisia in 1993. He was subsequently convicted *in absentia* on corruption charges and died in self-imposed exile in January 2000.

Tangentopoli left Italy's entire establishment in shock, and as the economy faltered – high unemployment and inflation combined with a huge national debt and an extremely unstable lira – the stage was set for the next act in Italy's turbulent political history.

Chief among the actors were Francesco Rutelli, a suave media-savvy operator who oversaw a successful citywide cleanup as mayor of Rome (1993–2001), and the charismatic media magnate Silvio Berlusconi, whose three terms as prime minister (1994, 2001–06 and 2008–) have been plagued by judicial problems. His most recent brush with the judiciary came in February 2009 when a British lawyer, David Mills, was sentenced to 4½ years in prison for having accepted a bribe from Berlusconi. Berlusconi himself was not tried thanks to a law his government had passed granting parliamentary immunity to the Italian prime minister and the presidents of the Republic, Senate and Chamber of Deputies.

THE FIRST TOURISTS

As a religious centre Rome has long attracted millions of pilgrims. In 1300 Pope Boniface VIII proclaimed the first Jubilee Year, with the promise of a full pardon for anyone who made the pilgrimage to St Peter's Basilica and the Basilica di San Giovanni in Laterano. Hundreds of thousands came and the Church basked in popular glory. In 2000 some 24 million visitors poured into the city for Pope John Paul II's Jubilee. However, it was in the late 18th and early 19th centuries that Rome's reputation as a tourist destination was born.

The Grand Tour, the 18th-century version of the gap year, was considered an educational rite of passage for wealthy young men from northern Europe and Britain in particular. In the 19th century it became fashionable for young ladies to travel, chaperoned by spinster aunts, but in the late 1700s the tour was largely a male preserve.

The overland journey through France and into Italy followed the medieval pilgrim route, entering Italy via the St Bernard pass and descending the west coast before cutting in to Florence

1922	1929	1944
Some 40,000 Fascists march on Rome. King Vittorio Emanuele III, worried about the possibility of civil war, invites Mussolini to form a government. At 39 Mussolini becomes the youngest ever Italian prime minister.	Keen to appease the Catholic Church, Mussolini signs the Lateran Treaty, thus creating the state of the Vatican City. To celebrate, Via della Conciliazione is bulldozed through the medieval Borgo to Piazza San Pietro.	On 24 March 1944, Nazis shoot 335 Romans at the Fosse Ardeatine cave complex in retaliation for a partisan attack. On 4 June US forces liberate Rome.

and then down to Rome. After a sojourn in the capital, tourists would venture down to Naples, where the newly discovered ruins of Pompeii and Herculaneum were causing much excitement, before heading up to Venice.

Rome, enjoying a rare period of peace, was perfectly set up for this English invasion. The city was basking in the aftermath of the 17th-century baroque building boom, and a craze for all things classical was sweeping Europe. Rome's papal authorities were also crying out for money after their excesses had left the city coffers bare, reducing much of the population to abject poverty.

Thousands came, including Goethe, who stopped off to write his 1817 travelogue *Italian Journey*, and Byron, Shelley and Keats, who all fuelled their romantic sensibilities in the city's vibrant streets. So many English people stayed around Piazza di Spagna (p95) that locals christened the area *er ghetto de l'inglesi* (the English ghetto). Trade in antiquities flourished and local artists did a roaring business producing etchings for souvenir-hungry visitors.

Artistically, rococo was the rage of the moment. The Spanish Steps (p95), built between 1723 and 1726, proved a major hit with tourists, as did the exuberant Trevi Fountain (p99).

top picks

HISTORY BOOKS

- Ancient Rome: The Rise and Fall of an Empire (Simon Baker; 2007) A well-paced, sweeping and easy-to-read history.
- Caesar: The Life of a Colossus (Adrian Godsworthy; 2007) Learn what drove Julius Caesar in this gripping biography.
- The Oxford History of the Roman World (ed John Boardman, Jasper Griffin and Oswyn Murray; 2001) Fascinating essays on literature, arts and politics by leading Oxford historians.
- Rome: The Biography of a City (Christopher Hibbert; 1998) A comprehensive overview of the city's history.
- The Families Who Made Rome: A History and a Guide (Anthony Majanlahti; 2006) An insightful study of Rome's great dynastic families and their contribution to the city.

THE GHOSTS OF FASCISM

Rome's fascist history is a deeply sensitive and highly charged subject. In recent years historians on both sides of the political spectrum have accused each other of recasting the past to suit their views: left-wing historians have accused their right-wing counterparts of glossing over the more unpleasant aspects of Mussolini's regime, while right-wingers have attacked their left-wing colleagues for whitewashing the facts to perpetuate an over-simplified myth of antifascism.

Benito Mussolini was born in 1883 in Forlì, a small town in Emilia-Romagna. As a young man he was an active member of the Italian Socialist Party, rising through the ranks to become editor of the party's official newspaper, *Avanti!* However, service in WWI and Italy's subsequent descent into chaos led to a change of heart and in 1919 he founded the Italian Fascist Party. Calling for rights for war veterans, law and order, and a strong nation, the party won support from disillusioned soldiers, many of whom joined the squads of Blackshirts that Mussolini used to intimidate his political enemies.

In 1921 Mussolini was elected to the Chamber of Deputies. His parliamentary support was limited but on 28 October 1922 he marched on Rome with 40,000 black-shirted followers. The march was largely symbolic but it had the desired effect. Fearful of civil war between the Fascists and Socialists, King Vittorio Emanuele III invited Mussolini to form a government.

1957	1960	1990
Leaders of Italy, France, West Germany, Belgium, Holland and Luxembourg sign the Treaty of Rome in the Palazzo dei Conservatori on the Campidoglio. The treaty officially establishes the European Economic Community.	Rome stages the Olympic Games while Federico Fellini makes his masterpiece *La Dolce Vita* in Cinecittà film studios. At the same time Stanley Kubrick is using Cinecittà to film his Roman epic *Spartacus*.	Football fans tune into Italia 90, the Italian-staged World Cup. The final, won by Germany, is held in Rome's revamped Studio Olympic. Sixteen years later, Italy is to win the 2006 World Cup in Berlin's Olympiastadion.

HOW HISTORY HAS SHAPED ROME

Corrado Augias is one of Italy's best-known journalists and writers. He has lived and worked in Rome, Paris, London and New York, and written more than 20 books, including *The Secrets of Rome: Love & Death in the Eternal City*.

How does Rome compare to London and Paris? Rome's main distinguishing characteristic is the presence of so many historical cultures, from pre-classical Rome to the present day, all superimposed on top of each other. It's a real feature and there are places, such as the Basilica di San Clemente, where you can actually see it.

Another characteristic of Rome is that it's a very southern city. Here you can feel the Mediterranean and the Balkans, as well as the Middle East and North Africa.

What was ancient Rome's legacy to the modern city? On a cultural level, its religiosity. Like the pagan religions of ancient Rome, Roman Catholicism is a religion of external manifestation, a religion which places great emphasis on demonstration rather than internal spiritual thought.

Another legacy is the mix of spirituality and politics. The Roman Emperor was both a spiritual leader – the *Divus Augustus* – and the political head of the Roman Empire. Similarly, the Catholic Church, the true heir to the Roman Empire, is ruled by the Pope – the *Sommo Pontefice* – whose role is based on that of the Roman Emperor.

How has fascism shaped Rome? There are two aspects here. Firstly, fascist architecture and urban design left a positive imprint on the city. The main expression of this is EUR, a quarter which was planned for the 20th anniversary of fascism.

In cultural terms, it's another matter. A few years ago there was a debate in Italy as to whether fascism was an accident of Italian history or a constant. The prevailing theory, which I agree with, is that fascism is a constant of the Italian psyche – although not just of the Italian psyche, also of many other peoples'. In this context, fascism means the idea that you can resolve problems through laws, brutal laws, deluding yourself that they are the solution. For example, today we tackle the problem of illegal immigration by picking the immigrants up and sending them home, which is not only impractical but also inhumane. Mussolini wanted to transform a people of low cultural level into a true European population through the use of force. This is typical of fascist ideology and is a constant temptation of the Italian psyche.

Which historical books would you recommend? My guide to Rome is the *History of the City of Rome in the Middle Ages* by the 19th-century German historian Gregorovius. I'd also recommend Edward Gibbon's *Decline and Fall of the Roman Empire*.

His first government was a coalition of Fascists, nationalists and liberals, but victory in the 1924 elections left him much better placed to consolidate his personal power, and by the end of 1925 he had seized complete control of Italy. In order to silence the Church he signed the Lateran Treaty in 1929, which made Catholicism the state religion and recognised the sovereignty of the Vatican State.

On the home front, Mussolini embarked on a huge building programme: Via dei Fori Imperiali and Via della Conciliazione were laid out; parks were opened on the Oppio hill and at Villa Celimontana (p116); the Imperial Forums (p69) and the temples at Largo di Torre Argentina (p77) were excavated; and the monumental Foro Italico sports complex (p153) and EUR (p128) were built.

Abroad, Mussolini invaded Abyssinia (present-day Ethiopia) in 1935 and sided with Hitler in 1936. In 1940, from the balcony of Palazzo Venezia (p71), he announced Italy's entry into WWII

2001	2005	2008–9
Charismatic media tycoon Silvio Berlusconi becomes prime minister for the second time. His first term in 1994 was a short-lived affair; his second lasts the full five-year course, an almost unheard-of event in Italian politics.	Seriously ill for a long time, Pope John Paul II dies after 27 years on the papal throne. He is replaced by his long-standing ally Josef Ratzinger, who takes the name Pope Benedict XVI.	Berlusconi bounces back for a third term as PM after a two-year spell in opposition. He hosts the G8 summit in July 2009 and faces down lurid press reports about his private life.

to a vast, cheering crowd. The good humour didn't last long, though, as Rome suffered, first at the hands of its own fascist regime, then, after Mussolini was ousted in 1943, at the hands of the Nazis. Rome was liberated from German occupation on 4 June 1944.

But defeat in WWII didn't kill off Italian fascism, and in 1946 hardline Mussolini supporters founded the *Movimento Sociale Italiano* (MSI; Italian Social Movement). For close on 50 years this overtly fascist party participated in mainstream Italian politics, while on the other side of the political spectrum the *Partito Comunista Italiano* (PCI; Italian Communist Party) grew into Western Europe's largest communist party. The MSI was finally dissolved in 1994, when Gianfranco Fini re-branded it as the post-fascist *Alleanza Nazionale* (AN; National Alliance). AN remained an important political player until it was incorporated into Silvio Berlusconi's *Popolo delle Libertà* coalition in 2009.

Outside of the political mainstream, fascism (along with communism) was a driving force behind the domestic terrorism that rocked Italy during the *anni di piombo* (years of lead), between the late 1960s and early 1980s. In these years, terrorist groups emerged on both sides of the ideological spectrum, giving rise to a spate of politically inspired violence. Most famously, the communist Red Brigades kidnapped and killed former PM Aldo Moro in 1978, and the neo-fascist Armed Revolutionary Nuclei bombed Bologna train station in 1980, killing 85 people and leaving up to 200 injured.

In more recent years, extreme right-wing groups have been connected with organised football hooliganism. According to figures released by Italy's Home Ministry in 2009, up to 234 fan groups have been identified as having political ties, of which 61 are said to be closely associated with extreme right-wing movements.

Fascism once again hit the headlines in April 2008 when Gianni Alemanno, an ex-MSI activist and member of AN, was elected mayor of Rome. In his first year in office, Alemanno has had to walk an ideological tightrope as he tries to sell himself as a mayor for everyone. Inevitably, though, his fascist past has aroused discomfort. The sight of supporters hailing his election victory with the fascist salute – something he was quick to distance himself from – did not go down well in many quarters and in September 2008 he infuriated Rome's Jewish community by refusing to condemn fascism as 'absolute evil'. Ironically, two months later he won praise from the community's leader for leading a group of 250 schoolchildren to Auschwitz and urging them never to forget the tragedy of the Holocaust.

ARTS

Rome's arts scene is in pretty good health, all things considered. The credit crunch and cuts in funding have had an impact, and while the current right-wing administration is less culturally minded than its left-wing predecessor, Rome's arts scene remains vibrant.

LITERATURE

A history of authoritarian rule has given rise to a rich literary tradition, encompassing everything from ancient satires to dialect poetry and anti-fascist prose. As a backdrop, Rome has inspired scribes as diverse as Goethe and Dan Brown.

The Classics

Famous for his blistering oratory, Marcus Tullius Cicero (106–43 BC) was the Roman Republic's pre-eminent author. A brilliant barrister, he became consul in 63 BC and subsequently published many philosophical works and speeches. Fancying himself as the senior statesman, Cicero took the young Octavian under his wing and attacked Mark Antony in a series of 14 speeches, the *Philippics*. These proved fatal, though, for when Octavian changed sides and joined Mark Antony, he demanded – and got – Cicero's head.

A contemporary of Cicero, Catullus (c 84–54 BC) cut a very different figure. A passionate and influential poet, he is best known for his epigrams and erotic verse, much of which was inspired by his love for Lesbia.

On becoming Emperor Augustus, Octavian encouraged the arts, and Virgil (70–19 BC), Ovid, Horace and Tibullus all enjoyed freedom to write. Of the works produced in this period, it's

Virgil's rollicking *Aeneid* that stands out. A glorified mix of legend, history and moral instruction, it tells how Aeneas escapes from Troy and after years of mythical mishaps ends up landing in Italy, where his descendants Romulus and Remus eventually found Rome. It also left us with the memorable lines: 'Fortune favours the bold', 'Love conquers all' and 'Time flies'.

Little is known of Decimus Iunius Iuvenalis, better known as Juvenal, but his 16 satires have survived as classics of the genre. Writing in the 1st century AD, he combined an acute mind with a cutting pen, famously scorning the masses as being interested in nothing but 'bread and circuses'. He also issued the classic warning *'quis custodiet ipsos custodes?'* or 'who will guard the guards?'.

The two major historians of the period were Livy (59 BC–AD 17) and Tacitus (c 56–116). Although both wrote in the early days of empire, they displayed very different styles. Livy, whose history of the Roman Republic was probably used as a school textbook, cheerfully mixed myth with fact to produce an entertaining and popular tome. Tacitus, on the other hand, took a decidedly colder approach. His *Annals* and *Histories*, which cover the early years of the Roman Empire, are cutting and often witty, although imbued with an underlying pessimism.

Street Writing & Popular Poetry

Rome's tradition of street writing, which today survives in the form of colourful graffiti art, goes back to the dark days of the 17th century. With the Church systematically suppressing every whiff of criticism, Counter-Reformation Rome was not a great place for budding authors. As a way round censorship, disgruntled Romans began posting *pasquinades* (anonymous messages; named after the first person to have written one) on the city's so-called speaking statues. These messages, often archly critical of the authorities, were sensibly posted in the dead of night and then gleefully circulated around town the following day. The most famous speaking statue, which still today is covered with messages, stands in Piazza Pasquino (p80) near Piazza Navona.

Poking savage fun at the rich and powerful was one of the favourite themes of Gioacchino Belli (1791–1863), one of a trio of poets who made their names writing poetry in Roman dialect. Born poor, Belli started his career with conventional and undistinguished verse, but found the crude and colourful dialect of the Roman streets better suited to his outspoken attacks on the chattering classes.

Carlo Alberto Salustri (1871–1950), aka Trilussa, is the best known of the trio. He, too, wrote social and political satire, although not exclusively, and many of his poems are melancholy reflections on life, love and solitude. One of his most famous works, the anti-fascist poem

---

PIER PAOLO PASOLINI, MASTER OF CONTROVERSY

Poet, novelist and filmmaker, Pier Paolo Pasolini (1922–75) was one of Italy's most important and controversial 20th-century intellectuals. His works, which are complex, unsentimental and provocative, provide a scathing portrait of Italy's postwar social transformation.

Although he spent much of his adult life in Rome, Pasolini had a peripatetic childhood. He was born in Bologna but moved around frequently, and rarely spent more than a few years in any one place. He did, however, form a lasting emotional attachment to Friuli, the mountainous region in northeastern Italy where his mother was from and where he spent the latter half of WWII. Much of his early poetry, collected and published in 1954 as *La meglio gioventù*, was written in Friulano dialect.

Politically he was a communist, but he never played a part in Italy's left-wing establishment. In 1949 he was expelled from the *Partito Comunista Italiano* (PCI; Italian Communist Party) after a gay sex scandal and for the rest of his career he remained a sharp critic of the party. His most famous outburst came in the poem *Il PCI ai giovani*, in which he dismisses left-wing students as bourgeois and sympathises with the police, whom he describes as *'figli di poveri'* (sons of the poor). In the context of 1968 Italy, a year marked by widespread student agitation, this was a highly incendiary position to take.

Pasolini was no stranger to controversy. His first novel *Ragazzi di Vita* (The Ragazzi), set in the squalor of Rome's forgotten suburbs, earned him success and a court case for obscenity. Similarly, his early films – *Accattone* (1961) and *Mamma Roma* (1962) – provoked righteous outrage with their relentlessly bleak depiction of life in the Roman underbelly.

True to the scandalous nature of his art, Pasolini was murdered in 1975. It was originally thought that his death was linked to events in the gay underworld but revelations in 2005 hinted that it might, in fact, have been a politically motivated killing. The case is still open.

All'Ombra (In the Shadow), is etched onto a plaque in Piazza Trilussa, the Trastevere square named in his honour.

The poems of Cesare Pescarella (1858–1940) present a vivid portrait of turn-of-the-20th-century Rome. Gritty and realistic, they pull no punches in describing everyday life as lived by Rome's forgotten poor.

Rome as Inspiration

With its magical cityscape and historic atmosphere, Rome has provided inspiration for legions of foreign authors. In the 18th century the city was a hotbed of literary activity as historians and Grand Tourists poured in from northern Europe. German author Johann Wolfgang von Goethe captures the elation of discovering ancient Rome and the colours of the modern city in his celebrated travelogue *Italian Journey* (1817).

Rome was also a magnet for the English Romantic poets. John Keats, Lord Byron, Percy Bysshe Shelley, Mary Shelley and other writers all spent time in the city. Byron, in a typically over-the-top outburst, described Rome as the city of his soul even though he visited only fleetingly. Keats came to Rome in 1821 in the hope that it would cure his ill health, but it didn't and he died of tuberculosis in his lodgings at the foot of the Spanish Steps (p95).

Later, in the 19th century, American author Nathaniel Hawthorne penned his lumbering classic *The Marble Faun* (1860) after two years in Italy. Taking his inspiration from a sculpture in the Capitoline Museums (p70), Hawthorne uses a murder story as an excuse to explore his thoughts on art and culture.

In recent years it's become fashionable for novelists to use Rome as a backdrop. Dan Brown's thriller *Angels and Demons* (2001) is set in Rome, as is Kathleen A Quinn's love story *Leaving Winter* (2003). Jeanne Kalogridis transports readers back to the 15th century in her historical novel *The Borgia Bride* (2006), a sensual account of Vatican scheming and dangerous passions.

Robert Harris's accomplished fictional biography of Cicero, *Imperium* (2006), is just one of a number of books set in 1st-century Rome. Steven Saylor's *The Triumph of Caesar* (2009) skilfully evokes the passion, fear and violence that hung in the air during Julius Caesar's last days. Similarly stirring is *Antony and Cleopatra* (2008), the last in Colleen McCullough's Masters of Rome series, which centres on the doomed love triangle between Octavian, Mark Antony and Cleopatra.

For a completely different read, *Rome Noir* (2009) is an anthology of short stories by Italy's best-known crime writers. Early reviews have been lukewarm but fans of the genre might enjoy its dark take on the Eternal City.

Politics Fuels the Imagination

A controversial figure, Gabriele D'Annunzio (1863–1938) was the most flamboyant Italian writer of the early 20th century. A WWI fighter pilot and ardent nationalist, he was born in Pescara and settled in Rome in 1881. Forever associated with fascism, he wrote prolifically, both poetry and novels. Of his books, perhaps the most revealing is *Il Fuoco* (The Flame of Life; 1900), a passionate romance in which he portrays himself as a Nietzschean superman born to command.

On the opposite side of the political spectrum, Roman-born Alberto Moravia (1907–90) was banned from writing by Mussolini and, together with his wife, Elsa Morante (1912–85), was

top picks

ROMAN BOOKS

- **Roman Tales** (Alberto Moravia; 1954) A collection of 19 short stories set in Rome's poorest neighbourhoods; in turn honest, funny and tragic.
- **That Awful Mess on Via Merulana** (Carlo Emilio Gadda; 1957) Gadda's great masterpiece combines linguistic experimentation and social criticism.
- **The Ragazzi** (Pier Paolo Pasolini; 1955) Pasolini brilliantly captures the tough reality of Rome's grim postwar suburbs in his first great novel.
- **Three Metres Above the Sky** (Federico Moccia; 1992) He's from the wrong side of the tracks, she's in her last year at school – you can probably guess the rest.
- **The Secrets of Rome: Love & Death in the Eternal City** (Corrado Augias; 2007) Journalist Augias explores his hometown, musing on little-known historical episodes as he goes.

forced into hiding for a year. The alienated individual and the emptiness of fascist and bourgeois society are common themes in his writing. In *La Romana* (The Woman of Rome; 1947) he explores the broken dreams of a country girl, Adriana, as she slips into prostitution and theft.

The novels of Elsa Morante are characterised by a subtle psychological appraisal of her characters and can be seen as a personal cry of pity for the sufferings of individuals and society. Her 1974 masterpiece, *La Storia* (The History), is a tough tale of a half-Jewish woman's desperate struggle for dignity in the poverty of occupied Rome.

Taking a similarly antifascist line, Carlo Emilio Gadda (1893–1973) combines murder and black humour in his classic whodunnit, *Quer Pasticciaccio Brutto de Via Merulana* (That Awful Mess on Via Merulana; 1957). Although the mystery is never solved, the book's a brilliant portrayal of the pomposity and corruption that thrived in Mussolini's Rome.

The Current Crop

Born in Rome in 1966, Niccolò Ammaniti is the king of Rome's literary young guns. In 2007 he won the Premio Strega, Italy's top literary prize, for his novel *Come Dio comanda* (As God Commands), but he's probably best known for *Io Non Ho Paura* (I'm Not Scared; 2001), a soulful study of how a young boy awakens to the fact that his father is involved in a child kidnapping. Striking an altogether different chord, Federico Moccia's brand of romance-lite was raised to cult status after the success of the 2004 film *Tre metri sopra il cielo* (Three Metres Above the Sky), the cinematic version of his 1992 book. Starring the young heart-throb Riccardo Scamarcio, it's a classic tale of romance between ill-suited lovers.

Other Roman writers making a name for themselves include 29-year-old Licia Troisi, whose trio of fantasy novels *Cronache del Mondo Emerso* has sold extremely well in Italy, and Leonardo Columbati, author of *Rio* (2007), a pessimistic tale of lost dreams and dodgy morals set in the cocaine and fast living of mid-1990s London.

CINEMA & TELEVISION

Cinema

The 2008 Cannes film festival was a high point for Italian cinema. Matteo Garrone, a young Roman director, took the Grand Prix for *Gomorra* (Gomorrah), a hard-hitting exposé of the Neapolitan mafia, and Paolo Sorrentino scooped the Special Jury Prize for *Il Divo*, an ice cold portrayal of Giulio Andreotti, Italy's most famous postwar politician. Headlines across the world hailed a new generation of Italian filmmakers.

But once the festival frenzy had cooled, reality returned, and the reality of the Italian film industry is one of cuts and falling box-office returns. Italians continue to make films – in 2008 some 154 were produced, 33 more than in 2007 – but few make it on to the big screen, and

---

MR SPAGHETTI WESTERN

Best known for virtually singlehandedly creating the 'spaghetti western', Sergio Leone (1929–89) is a hero to many. Martin Scorsese, Quentin Tarantino and Robert Rodriguez are among the directors who count him as a major influence, while Clint Eastwood owes him his cinematic breakthrough. Astonishingly, he only ever directed seven films.

The son of a silent-movie director, Leone cut his teeth as a screenwriter on a series of sword-and-sandal epics, before working as assistant director on *Quo Vadis?* (1951) and *Ben-Hur* (1959). He made his directorial debut three years later on *Il Colosso di Rodi* (The Colossus of Rhodes; 1961).

However, it was with his famous dollar trilogy – *Per un pugno di dollari* (A Fistful of Dollars; 1964), *Per qualche dollari in più* (For a Few Dollars More; 1965) and *Il buono, il brutto, il cattivo* (The Good, the Bad and the Ugly; 1966) – that he really hit the big time. The first, filmed in Spain and based on the 1961 samurai flick *Yojimbo*, set the style for the genre. No longer were clean-cut, morally upright heroes pitted against cartoon-style villains; characters were more complex, often morally ambiguous and driven by self-interest.

Stylistically, Leone introduced a series of innovations that were later to become trademarks. Characters were associated with musical themes (brilliantly scored by his longtime collaborator Ennio Morricone – see the boxed text, p39); long silences were accompanied by extreme close-ups and followed by bursts of explosive action; and the Mexican standoff was used, most famously in the three-way shootout at the end of *Il buono, il brutto, il cattivo*.

those that do struggle to compete with the big Hollywood imports.

This is largely down to money. In recent years the government, one of the major financiers of Italian cinema, has been systematically slashing investment – in 2002 by 43%, in 2005 by 35%, in 2009 by 23%. As a result many producers simply can't afford to market their films, and without an effective build-up, few cinemas are prepared to risk screening small-scale Italian films.

Recognising the problem, Rome's mayor, Gianni Alemanno, has called for an 'Italianisation' of Rome's annual film festival. Since it was inaugurated in 2006, the festival has attracted some of Hollywood's biggest names but it has been repeatedly criticised for its failure to showcase homespun talent. This is something Alemanno is keen to redress and his first festival, in 2008, was marked by a noticeable increase in the number of Italian films.

Recent years have also witnessed a renewal of interest in Rome's film-making facilities. Private investment in Cinecittà has lured a number of big-name directors to Rome's legendary studios, including Ron Howard for his 2009 thriller *Angels and Demons*, Mel Gibson for *The Passion of the Christ* (2004), and Martin Scorsese, who had 19th-century New York recreated for his 2002 epic *Gangs of New York*.

Leading the new wave of Roman filmmakers is Matteo Garrone (b 1968), whose *Gomorra* (Gomorrah; 2008) helped seal a reputation already on the up after his 2002 film *L'Imbalsamatore* (The Embalmer). In 2008 he also produced the award-winning comedy *Si Puo Fare*, directed by fellow Roman Giulio Manfredonia (b 1967). Following in Garrone's wake, Emanuele Crialese (b 1965) won plaudits for the 2006 film *Nuovomondo* (Golden Door) and Saverio Costanzo (b 1975) aroused interest for his take of the Israeli-Palestinian conflict in *Private* (2004). Gabriele Muccino (b 1967), director of the 2001 smash *L'Ultimo Bacio* (The Last Kiss), continues to work in Hollywood, where he has twice directed Will Smith, in *The Pursuit of Happyness* (2006) and *Seven Pounds* (2008).

Before Muccino, Rome was generally represented by Carlo Verdone (b 1950) and Nanni Moretti (b 1953). A comedian in the Roman tradition, Verdone has made a name for himself satirising his fellow citizens in a number of bittersweet comedies, which at best are very funny, and at worst are repetitive and predictable. His 1995 film *Viaggi di Nozze* (Honeymoons) is one of his best.

Moretti, on the other hand, falls into no mainstream tradition. A politically active writer, actor and director, his films are often whimsical and self-indulgent. Arguably his best work,

top picks

ROMAN FILMS

- Roma Città Aperta (Rome Open City; Roberto Rossellini; 1945) Filmed on Rome's recently liberated streets, this neorealist masterpiece stars Anna Magnani as a woman desperate to save her lover from the Nazis.
- Ladri di Biciclette (Bicycle Thieves; Vittorio de Sica; 1948) A genuinely moving drama that follows the protagonist's desperate search for his stolen bicycle.
- La Dolce Vita (Federico Fellini; 1960) Anita Ekberg frolics in the Trevi Fountain while Marcello Mastroianni looks on in Fellini's slow-moving classic.
- Mamma Roma (Pier Paolo Pasolini; 1962) Pasolini's second film focuses on the fruitless struggle of a middle-aged prostitute to forge a better life for her teenage son.
- Il buono, il brutto, il cattivo (The Good, the Bad and the Ugly; Sergio Leone; 1966) The most famous of Leone's testosterone-laden spaghetti westerns, featuring a classic Ennio Morricone soundtrack.
- Profondo Rosso (Deep Red; Dario Argento; 1975) A masterclass in terror from the king of Italian horror, this tale of bloody murder paved the way for hundreds of imitations.
- Caro Diario (Dear Diary; Nanni Moretti; 1994) Join Moretti as he scooters around a semi-deserted Rome in the opening episode of this, his most accessible film.
- L'Ultimo Bacio (The Last Kiss; Gabriele Muccino; 2001) Muccino explores the lack of ideals and fears affecting Italy's well-to-do 30-something generation, in a glossy and well-observed film that never entirely convinces.
- Nuovomondo (Golden Door; Emanuele Crialese; 2006) Charlotte Gainsbourg stars in the touching story of Salvatores, an illiterate Sicilian farmer who gives up everything to realise his American Dream.
- Gomorra (Gomorrah; Matteo Garrone; 2008) Based on Roberto Saviano's bestselling book, this gritty film exposes the grim reality behind the Neapolitan Camorra's huge business empire.

Caro Diario (Dear Diary; 1994) earned him best director at Cannes in 1994 – an award that he topped in 2001 when he won the Palme d'Or for *La Stanza del Figlio* (The Son's Room).

However, for the real golden age of Roman film-making you have to turn the clocks back to the 1940s, when Roberto Rossellini (1906–77) produced a trio of neorealist masterpieces. The first and most famous was *Roma Città Aperta* (Rome Open City; 1945), filmed with brutal honesty in the Prenestina district east of the city centre. Vittorio de Sica (1901–74) kept the neorealist ball rolling in 1948 with *Ladri di Biciclette* (Bicycle Thieves), again filmed in Rome's sprawling suburbs.

Federico Fellini (1920–94) took the creative baton from the neorealists and carried it into the following decades. His disquieting style demands more of audiences, abandoning realistic shots for pointed images at once laden with humour, pathos and double meaning. Fellini's greatest international hit was *La Dolce Vita* (1960), starring Marcello Mastroianni and Anita Ekberg.

The films of Pier Paolo Pasolini (1922–75) are similarly demanding. A communist Catholic homosexual, he made films that not only reflect his ideological and sexual tendencies but also offer a unique portrayal of Rome's urban wasteland. See the boxed text, p33, for more on Pasolini.

A contemporary of both Pasolini and Fellini, Sergio Leone (1929–89) struck out in a very different direction – see the boxed text, p35.

Rome's contribution to cinema, however, goes beyond its directors. Its streets, piazzas and *palazzi* have provided a memorable backdrop to numerous films. The 1953 classic *Roman Holiday* highlights a number of Rome's most famous monuments, including the Spanish Steps and the Bocca della Verità, site of a famous scene starring Gregory Peck and Audrey Hepburn. In Federico Fellini's *La Dolce Vita* (1960), Anita Ekberg splashes saucily around the Trevi Fountain, while the Pantheon takes centre stage in Peter Greenaway's arthouse flick *The Belly of an Architect* (1987). More recently, *The Talented Mr Ripley* (1999) featured scenes in Piazza di Spagna, Piazza Navona and the Jewish Ghetto, and *Angels and Demons* (2009) boasts a whole host of Roman sights. Some of these were shot on location but many were recreated on a Hollywood soundstage after the Vatican refused permission for filming at St Peter's Basilica and the Sistine Chapel.

Television

The real interest in Italian TV is not so much what's on the screen as the political shenanigans that go on behind it. Unfortunately, none of this real-life drama translates to on-screen programming, which remains ratings-driven and advert-drenched. Soap operas, quizzes and reality shows are staples and homemade drama rarely goes beyond the tried and tested, with an incessant stream of made-for-TV films on the lives of popes, saints, priests and martyrs. Scantily clad women, known as *veline,* appear in droves, particularly on the interminable variety shows that run on Saturday evenings and Sunday afternoons.

Italian broadcasters are, on the whole, fairly liberal when it comes to sex and violence. However, they don't always get it right; in 2008, RAI (Italy's state broadcaster) fell foul of public opinion with its screening of Ang Lee's gay western *Brokeback Mountain.* Ironically, though, it wasn't the gay love scenes that provoked the anger but the lack of them – they'd been cut from the film. Italy's gay-rights activists screamed discrimination and liberals throughout the country took up the cry of censorship. RAI responded by saying it had all been a simple oversight, that they'd bought the film already edited and had simply forgotten to reinstate the cuts when they screened the film.

For more on TV, see p42.

MUSIC

Rome's music scene is thriving. International orchestras perform to sell-out audiences, jazz greats jam in steamy clubs and rappers rage in underground venues. It wasn't always like this, though, and until relatively recently Rome was considered something of a musical backwater. What changed things was the 2002 opening of Rome's contemporary concert complex, the Auditorium Parco della Musica (p153) and an administration that invested heavily in culture.

Castration & Choral Music

In a city of churches, it's little wonder that choral music has deep roots. In the 16th and 17th centuries, Rome's great Renaissance popes summoned the top musicians of the day to tutor

CLASSICAL MUSIC GUIDE

A well-known journalist and author, Leonetta Bentivoglio has been writing on music, dance and theatre since the early 1980s.

'The Auditorium, with its three halls and open-air arena, has really inspired Rome's music scene, not just in classical music but also rock, pop and ethnic music. Run by the Associazione Santa Cecilia and the Fondazione Musica di Roma, an association created by the Comune di Roma, it has staged many musical events. The Accademia di Santa Cecilia is excellent and has a very well-known musical director, Antonio Pappano. Anyone who loves music should really keep their eye on Santa Cecilia's programme.

'Of the other music associations, one of the most interesting is the Accademia Filarmonica Romana, which puts on high-level performances at the Teatro Olimpico. Another active institution is the Istituto Universitaria Concerti, which does a lot of work with the university and puts on concerts at the university's Aula Magna.

'In terms of composers, Giorgio Batistelli does a lot of musical theatre and is well known abroad. He's innovative and fun. More cerebral is the German-trained Luca Lombardi. Of course, there's Ennio Morricone, who doesn't just do film work but also writes symphonic music, and the great German composer Hans Werner Henze, who lives just outside Rome in Marino Laziale.'

the papal choir. Two of the most famous were Giovanni Pierluigi da Palestrina (c 1525–94), one of Italy's foremost Renaissance composers, and the Naples-born Domenico Scarlatti (1685–1757). Girolamo Frescobaldi (1583–1643), admired by the young JS Bach, was twice an organist at St Peter's Basilica.

The papal choirs, originally composed of priests, were closed to women, and the high parts were taken by *castrati*, boys who had been surgically castrated before puberty to preserve their high voices. Although castration was punishable by excommunication, the Sistine Chapel and other papal choirs contained *castrati* as early as 1588 and as late as the early 20th century. The last known *castrato*, Alessandro Moreschi (1858–1922), known as *il angelo di Roma* (the angel of Rome), was castrated in 1865, just five years before the practice was officially outlawed. He entered the Sistine Chapel choir in 1883 and 15 years later became conductor. He retired in 1913, 10 years after Pius X had banned *castrati* from the papal choirs. Boy sopranos were introduced in the 1950s.

In 1585 Sixtus V formally established the Accademia di Santa Cecilia as a support organisation for papal musicians. Originally it was involved in the publication of sacred music, although it later developed a teaching function, and in 1839 it completely reinvented itself as an academy with wider cultural and academic goals. Today it is one of the world's most highly respected conservatories, with its own orchestra and chorus.

Opera

Rome is often snubbed by serious opera buffs who prefer their Puccini in Milan, Venice or Naples. However, in recent years the city's main opera company, the Teatro dell'Opera di Roma (p236), has upped its standards and performances are enthusiastically followed. The Romans have long been keen opera-goers – it's said that Barberini used to stage spectacular performances in Palazzo Barberini in the 17th century – and in the 19th century a number of important operas were premiered in Rome, including Rossini's *Il Barbiere di Siviglia* (The Barber of Seville; 1816), Verdi's *Il Trovatore* (The Troubadour; 1853) and Giacomo Puccini's *Tosca* (1900).

Tosca not only premiered in Rome but is also set in the city. The first act takes place in the Chiesa di Sant'Andrea della Valle (p82), the second in Palazzo Farnese (p81), and the final act in Castel Sant'Angelo (p146), the castle from which Tosca jumps to her death.

Jazz, Hip-Hop & the Contemporary Scene

Jazz has long been a mainstay of Rome's music scene. Introduced by US troops during WWII, it grew in popularity during the postwar period and took off in the 1960s with the opening of the Folkstudio club. Since then, it has gone from strength to strength and the city now offers some of Italy's finest jazz clubs. Big names to look out for include Enrico Pieranunzi, a

Roman-born pianist and composer, and Doctor 3, whose idiosyncratic sound has earned them considerable acclaim.

Rome also has a vibrant hip-hop scene. Hip-hop, which arrived in the city in the late 1980s and spread via the *centro sociale* (organised squat) network, was originally highly politicised and many early exponents associated themselves with Rome's alternative left-wing scene. But in recent years exposure and ever-increasing commercialisation has diluted this political element and the scene has largely gone mainstream. A key contributor to this evolution was rapper Piotta, whose 1999 hit 'Supercafone' introduced the world to the Roman *coatto* (a working-class tough guy with attitude and bling). For a taste of genuine Roman rap, tune into bands like Colle der Fomento and Cor Veleno, or the ragamuffin outfit Villa Ada Posse.

For something completely different, Vinegar Socks is a local indie-folk quartet that has been making a name for itself on the city's concert circuit.

THEATRE & DANCE

Surprisingly for a city in which art has always been appreciated, Rome has no great theatrical tradition. It has never had a Broadway or West End, and while highbrow imports are greeted enthusiastically, fringe theatre remains something of a novelty. That said, experimental theatre is increasingly finding space in the city's cultural calendar. The annual International Urban Theatre Festival provides a showcase for alternative performers, while the Teatro Cometa Off in Testaccio is making a name for itself as host of the Liberi Esperimenti Teatrali, an annual programme of workshops, laboratories and experimental performances.

Although not strictly speaking a Roman, Dacia Maraini (b 1936) has produced her best work while living in Rome. Considered one of Italy's most important feminist writers, she continues to work as a journalist while her all-women theatre company Teatro della Maddalena stages her 30-plus plays. Some of these, including the 1978 *Dialogo di una Prostituta con un suo Cliente* (Dialogue of a Prostitute with Client), have also played abroad.

Gigi Proietti (b 1940), on the other hand, is pure Roman. A hugely popular writer, performer and director, he combines TV acting with dubbing (he's dubbed Robert De Niro, Richard Burton, Marlon Brando and Dustin Hoffman) and theatre work. He's artistic director of the Teatro Brancaccio and regularly plays to full houses.

Dance is a major highlight of Rome's big autumn festival, RomaEuropa. But while popular, performances rarely showcase homegrown talent, which remains thin on the ground. In fact, Rome's reputation in the world of dance rests more on its breakdancers than its corps de ballet. The city's most celebrated crew is Urban Force, which often represents the capital in national and international competitions and regularly performs live.

Major ballet performances are staged at the Teatro dell'Opera, home to Rome's principal ballet company, the Balletto del Teatro dell'Opera. The company has long had a shaky reputation,

MORRICONE'S MUSIC MAKES CINEMA MAGIC

The success of Sergio Leone's spaghetti westerns (boxed text, p35) owes a huge debt to the music of Ennio Morricone, Rome's best-known modern composer. Although Leone had initially been reluctant to hire his old schoolmate for *Per un pugno di dollari* (A Fistful of Dollars), he relented, opening the door to what would become one of the finest creative partnerships in cinematic history.

Arguably his finest work is the haunting score for *Il buono, il brutto, il cattivo* (The Good, the Bad and the Ugly). A unique orchestration of trumpets, whistles, gunshots, church bells, harmonicas and electric guitars, it was inducted into the Grammy Hall of Fame in 2009.

Born in Rome on 10 November 1928, Morricone studied trumpet, composition and choral music at the Conservatory of Santa Cecilia before graduating to become a successful studio arranger for the Radio Corporation of American (RCA). He worked with Chet Baker and the Beatles before he began his collaboration with Leone in 1964. Since then he's scored up to 500 films and TV series. He's worked with a who's-who of directors, including John Carpenter, Brian De Palma, Quentin Tarantino and Robert Rodriguez.

In 2007 Morricone won an Oscar for Lifetime Achievement after five previous nominations, most notably for *The Mission* in 1986 and *The Untouchables* in 1987.

but under its internationally renowned director, Carla Fracci (b 1936), production standards have improved and its international profile is growing.

See the Festivals & Events section (p85) for details of Rome's arts festivals, and the Arts chapter (p234) for listings of theatre and dance venues.

ENVIRONMENT & PLANNING

Geography as much as history has conspired to make Rome the cluttered chaotic city it is today. The city's most famous geographical feature is its seven hills – the Palatino (Palatine), Campidoglio (Capitoline), Aventino (Aventine), Celio (Caelian), Esquilino (Esquiline), Viminale (Viminal) and Quirinale (Quirinal). Two other hills – the Gianicolo (Janiculum), which rises above Trastevere, and the Pincio, above Piazza del Popolo – were never part of the ancient city.

Rome's hills are not especially high – the city's highest point, Monte Mario, is only 139m – but they make for some tough walking and spectacular views. One of the best vantage points is the top of the Gianicolo (p135), from where it's possible to identify each of the seven hills, although the Viminale and Quirinale are swallowed up by the city sprawl and seem little more than gentle slopes.

Rome's river is the Tiber, which originates in the Tuscan Apennines and flows into the sea at nearby Ostia. An important transport link in ancient times, the Tiber has always been subject to flooding and for much of the city's history was a constant source of worry. Relief only came in 1900 when the river's embankments were raised. However, exceptional rainfall can still threaten the city. In December 2008 heavy rain caused water levels to rise by 5m and the river came extremely close to bursting its banks. Had it done so swaths of northern Rome would have been under water.

GREEN ROME

Like many Italian cities, Rome suffers from serious air pollution. Much of this can be attributed to Romans' love affair with the car (there are an estimated 76 cars per every 100 inhabitants). In an attempt to tackle this auto-dependency, city authorities have extended traffic restrictions to cover much of the centre and introduced car- and bike-sharing schemes – see p20 for further details.

A second front against air pollution was opened in summer 2009, when mayor Gianni Alemanno announced plans for a major investment project in renewable energy sources. Objectives include the generation of 150MW of energy through solar panels and a 50% reduction in CO_2 emissions by 2012.

The Vatican is also a keen advocate of green energy and has announced that it hopes to supply 20% of its energy needs through renewable sources by 2020. It made a good start in 2008, by placing 2400 solar panels on the roof of the 6000-seater Paul IV Auditorium. These provide up to 300 MWh of clean electricity a year and save the equivalent of 80 tonnes of oil. The state has also planted trees in a Hungarian national park to offset its CO_2 emissions.

Recycling is something that many Romans feel ought to be done, but in practice they're making little headway. Part of the problem is a lack of recycling bins, something that AMA, the city's waste management company, addressed in July 2009 by supplying more than 2000 bins for differentiated rubbish. Earlier in the year it had expanded its door-to-door waste collection service to cover up to half of the city's bars and restaurants.

Rome is not the cleanest of cities and many visitors are struck by the amount of graffiti around the place – even Berlusconi commented on it in May 2009, saying that it broke his heart to 'see all the writing on the walls and filth in the streets'. The problem persists but the situation has improved in recent years, thanks in the main to the efforts of the Ufficio Decoro Urbano (Office of Urban Decorum), set up in 2002 to clean up the city.

With the exception of a flourishing cat population, Rome's flora and fauna is largely limited to the city's 14 natural parks, many of which used to belong to Rome's noble families. As they were designed and planted according to the fashion of the day, they generally contain a wide variety of exotic species.

Archaeological sites provide an ideal environment for the *cappero* (caper). In spring it forms cascading, puffy bushes, which in June become masses of pink flowers. You'll see them growing in areas including the Palatino and Terme di Caracalla, and on the Ponte Rotto near the Isola Tiberina.

URBAN PLANNING & DEVELOPMENT

On becoming mayor in April 2008, Gianni Alemanno inherited a vast urban renewal plan from his successor Walter Veltroni. During his time in opposition Alemanno had often spoken out against the plan but as mayor he has backed the ambitious programme, which calls for the construction of 100,000 new houses and flats, 14 new transport corridors (including four metro lines), the creation of 19 parks and a substantial redevelopment of the capital's run-down suburbs.

However, the mayor is not without his own ideas and in March 2009 he unveiled proposals for a massive redevelopment project in the city's southern and eastern suburbs. The plan recommends, among other things, the creation of an aqueduct in EUR, a major revamping of the Ostia seafront and the construction of a Disney-style Ancient Roman theme park. This last proposal, first aired in August 2008, provoked a predictable uproar, with critics saying it would be better to spend money restoring the real Colosseum rather than building a new one, and advocates claiming it would create jobs and be a major boost for tourism.

GOVERNMENT & POLITICS

Italian life is political to degrees that foreigners find difficult to comprehend. Cynicism is deeply ingrained and nothing happens without speculation as to the dark political motives behind it. On an everyday level, the fact that most Romans live in self-managed *condominios* (blocks of

THE POLITICAL LOWDOWN

As a TV journalist working in Rome, Patrizia Notarnicola, 37, is ideally placed to clear up some of the complexities of Roman political life.

Can you explain Rome's local government system? Rome's local government is part of a national system of regional government based on three divisions: the region, the province and the comune. So in the case of Rome, you have the Region of Lazio, which is divided into several provinces, including the Province of Rome, and then the smaller comunes, the most important of which is obviously Rome itself. The president of the region has considerable powers in that he or she receives money from central government and parcels it out to the provinces within the region. But the most important person in Rome is the mayor. A couple of months ago a new law was introduced which granted Rome special status as the capital city. This means that in the future the city will receive more money from central government and that the mayor will have more decision-making powers than his colleagues in other cities. He'll have authority over the upkeep of the city's artistic and cultural heritage, the city's environmental policies, development and civil protection.

On a national level, why do Italian governments last such a short time? Mainly because they're based on coalitions. A new electoral law, passed in 2005, made it possible to vote not only for a party but also for a coalition. So what happens is that political parties which don't necessarily have a lot in common come together to form a coalition for the election. Then when there's a parliamentary debate, disagreements emerge and individual parties decide to vote independently with the result that the government loses its majority and falls. Berlusconi's great strength has been his ability to keep his coalitions together even when they've been rocked by internal disagreements.

What influence does the Church have on Italian political life? The Church has enormous power because it is extremely rich and controls a lot of votes – here many people are Catholic and follow what the Church says. It conditions politics and social life, and even laws on abortion and the *testamento biolgico* (Living Will – a document allowing people to express their wishes regarding future treatment in the case of mental incapacity). For example, I know many politicians who would vote for a *testamento biolgico*, something which the Church is against, but don't for reasons of political convenience.

Is the press free in Italy? The Italian press doesn't have any freedom for one specific reason – that journalists work for publishers who have various interests, including political interests, and who never let you write anything that goes against their interests. But Italians don't really buy newspapers, they just watch TV and it's the TV news that controls politics. The print press is slightly freer but no one really reads the papers.

individually owned flats) gives rise to all sorts of politicking as rival residents seek to outsmart one another at *condominio* meetings.

The top man in Rome is the *sindaco* (mayor), currently Gianni Alemanno, who heads the city's municipal government up on the Campidoglio, the seat of city government since the late 11th century. The mayor leads his appointed *giunta*, a group of councillors called *assessori* who hold ministerial positions as heads of municipal departments. The *assessori* are appointed from the *consiglio comunale*, a body of elected officials much like a parliament.

A former member of the post-fascist Alleanza Nazionale party, Gianni Alemanno stepped into the hot seat in April 2008 after an election campaign dominated by crime and security issues. Ironically, though, Alemanno has had more than his fair share of dealings with the law. In 1981 he was arrested for allegedly beating up a left-wing student and a year later he spent eight months in prison after being accused of throwing a Molotov cocktail at the Soviet Embassy. In both cases all charges were dropped.

His first year on Campidoglio has been surprisingly low-key. So low-key, in fact, that critics have accused him of abandoning the city to its own devices. Naturally, he paints a different picture and highlights his success in reducing crime and bringing the city's finances back into shape after 15 years of free-spending by his left-wing predecessors.

Since 2005 Lazio's regional government has been led by governor Piero Marrazzo, a former TV journalist turned moderate left-wing politician.

A parliamentary republic, Italy is headed by a president (Presidente della Repubblica Italiana), who appoints the prime minister, known as the Presidente del Consiglio. The parliament consists of two houses – a Senate and a Chamber of Deputies, both with equal legislative power.

The president resides in Palazzo del Quirinale (p102), on Rome's Quirinale hill; the Chamber of Deputies sits in Palazzo di Montecitorio (p84), just off Via del Corso; and the Senate sits in Palazzo Madama (p80), near Piazza Navona.

At the time of writing the Italian prime minister was Silvio Berlusconi, leader of the right-wing Popolo della Libertà (People of Freedom) coalition. A colourful and charismatic character, Berlusconi built up a multibillion dollar fortune before entering politics in 1994. Since then he has led three governments (1994–95, 2001–06, and 2008– to date) and courted no end of controversy, much of it focused on his vast media empire.

MEDIA

To discuss the media in Italy is to discuss Silvio Berlusconi, Italy's undisputed TV king. Italian TV is dominated by two networks – RAI, the Rome-based state broadcaster, and Mediaset, Italy's largest private media company – and Berlusconi has interests in both camps. He's the controlling shareholder of Mediaset and as PM wields enormous influence over RAI. This 'conflict of interest' has long aroused debate, both inside and outside of Italy, and is one of the reasons why in 2009 Freedom House, a US-based press watchdog, reduced Italy's freedom of press rating from 'free' to 'partly free'.

In recent years Italy's TV duopoly has come under attack from a third party – Sky Italia, the Italian branch of Robert Murdoch's global corporation. Sky currently controls about 90% of Italy's pay-TV market and continues to market itself aggressively. The upshot has been an undeclared battle for control of Italian TV. In autumn 2008, Berlusconi's government increased tax on pay-TV subscriptions in a move that was widely seen as a direct assault on Sky. Sky responded by running an advertising campaign against the increases and poaching one of RAI's star performers. Then, in June 2009, Berlusconi accused Murdoch of using his global media outlets to run negative stories about him in relation to a call-girl scandal. A month later, RAI and Mediaset clubbed together to announce the launch of TivùSat, a free satellite TV package. It's too early to tell who will prevail but in the meantime international media observers are having a whale of a time watching the media titans battle it out.

For information on Rome's cinema scene and more on Italian TV, see p35.

Rome's publishing sector is dominated by small, independent publishing houses, many of which rely on government contracts or serve specialised markets, such as the academic university sector. But there are some interesting literary publishers, too, including Minimum Fax and Einaudi Stile Libero.

La Repubblica and Il Messaggero are the two major newspapers produced in Rome, along with the popular sports daily, Corriere dello Sport. For more information, see p295.

Rome's alternative media scene is centred on the centri sociali (organised squats), of which there are about 30 in and around town; websites include www.forteprenestino.net and www .spartaco.it, both in Italian. The city also has a lively blogsphere, with any number of local and foreign bloggers. Top sites to look out for include www.06blog.it (in Italian), which covers everything from breaking news to restaurant reviews, and www.eternallycool.net (in English), which highlights all the latest fads and events.

FASHION

The concept of cutting a dash (fare la bella figura) is important to Romans. That means wearing the latest threads, having your hair cut just so and carrying a top-of-the-range cellulare (mobile phone). A cool car, perhaps a Smart or an SUV, also helps. Fashion in Rome is less about making a statement as about fitting in, about toeing the line and being one of the crowd. The result is a uniformity of taste and a widespread conformity to the dictates of the season.

This slavish adherence to style isn't, of course, limited to clothes – the Roman lifestyle is also subject to the fluctuations of fashion. Among recent fads, one of the most popular has been the extended aperitivo (aperitif). Traditionally, an aperitivo is an early-evening warm-up, a pause on the way home or a prelude to a night out. But in its revamped form – dubbed the 'seven eleven' because it's served between 7pm and 11pm – it's become the main event, a full evening of cocktails, buffet food and DJ sounds.

Another successful import (the aperitivo was a habit in many northern Italian cities long before it arrived in Rome) is clothes swapping, or 'swishing', as it's been called. Touted as an ecofriendly way of shopping for free, swapping has been enthusiastically adopted by credit-crunched Rome, and fashionistas have been seen flocking to swap parties to exchange their designer cast-offs.

Rome generally plays second fiddle to Milan in the fashion stakes. Most of Italy's big-name designers are based in Milan and the Milan fashion week is one of the highlights of the European catwalk calendar. However, Rome is fighting back and in recent years it has made a concerted effort to present itself as a showcase for emerging talent. Since 2007, the city's main fashion event, the twice-yearly Alta Moda event (held in January and July), has featured collections by young up-and-coming Italian and international designers.

Rome's two most famous fashion houses are Valentino and Fendi. Celebrated for his trademark evening gowns, usually in red, white or black, Valentino Garavani celebrated 45 years in alta moda (high fashion) with a glamorous 36-hour extravaganza in summer 2007, shortly before announcing his retirement. Fendi, under iconic German designer Karl Lagerfeld, is best known for its leather goods and handbags. Another name to look out for is Laura Biagiotti, who specialises in luxurious knitwear and sumptuous silk separates, often in cream and white.

Ranging from ancient ruins and medieval churches to Renaissance frescoes, baroque sculptures and hulking fascist *palazzi*, Rome's artistic and architectural legacy is unparalleled. The city is home to some of the Western world's most celebrated buildings, and its churches and galleries offer more masterpieces than many midsize countries. Michelangelo, Raphael, Caravaggio and Bernini are among the artists who have stamped their genius on Rome's remarkable cityscape. But it's not all about history. Since the mid-1990s a number of high-profile building projects have drawn the world's top architects to the city and a recent spate of gallery openings has breathed life into the contemporary arts scene.

THE ANCIENTS
ETRUSCAN ROOTS

Etruscan culture was a major influence on early Roman art and architecture. By the 7th century BC the Etruscans were the dominant force on the Italian peninsula with important centres at Tarquinia, Caere (Cerveteri) and Veii (Veio). These city-states were fortified with defensive walls and although little actually remains – the Etruscans generally built with wood and brick, which hasn't aged well – archaeologists have found evidence of aqueducts, bridges and sewers, as well as sophisticated temples. Outside the city walls, Etruscan cemeteries harboured richly decorated stone vaults covered by mounds of earth. Most of what we now know about the Etruscans derives from findings unearthed in these tombs.

The Etruscans placed great importance on their funerary rites and they developed sepulchral decoration into a highly sophisticated art. Elaborate stone sarcophagi were often embellished with a reclining figure or a couple, typically depicted with a haunting, enigmatic smile. A stunning example is the *Sarcofago degli Sposi* (Sarcophagus of the Betrothed) in the Museo Nazionale Etrusco di Villa Giulia (p152). Underground funerary vaults were further enlivened with bright, exuberant frescoes. These frequently represented festivals or scenes from everyday life, with stylised figures shown dancing or playing musical instruments, often with little birds or animals in the background.

The Etruscans were also noted for their bronze work and jewellery. Bronze ore was abundant and was used to craft everything from chariots to candelabras, bowls and polished mirrors. The 5th-century-BC bronze *Lupa Capitolina* (Capitoline Wolf) in the Capitoline Museums (p70) is considered the Etruscans' greatest masterpiece. Etruscan jewellery was unrivalled throughout the Mediterranean. Goldsmiths produced elaborate pieces using sophisticated filigree and granulation techniques that were only rediscovered in the 20th century.

For Italy's best collection of Etruscan art, head to the Museo Nazionale Etrusco di Villa Giulia (p152); to see Etruscan treasures *in situ* head out of town to Cerveteri (p269) and Tarquinia (p270).

ROMAN DEVELOPMENTS

When Rome was founded in 753 BC (if legend is to be believed), the Etruscans were at the height of their power and Greeks colonists were establishing control over southern Italy. In subsequent centuries a three-way battle for domination ensued, with the Romans emerging victorious. Against this background,

top picks

MUSEUMS & GALLERIES

- Museo e Galleria Borghese (p148) Houses the best of Bernini's baroque sculpture and a lot more besides.
- Capitoline Museums (p70) A must for anyone interested in classical sculpture; the star turn is the 5th-century BC *Lupa Capitolina* (Capitoline Wolf).
- Vatican Museums (p142) One of the world's great museums, home to the Sistine Chapel.
- Museo Nazionale Romano: Palazzo Massimo alle Terme (p111) A gem of a museum with fabulous Roman frescoes and wall mosaics.
- Palazzo e Galleria Doria Pamphilj (p93) Artists on show include Raphael, Tintoretto, Titian, Caravaggio, Bernini and Velázquez.

SIGNATURE WORKS – THE ANCIENTS

- Sarcofago degli Sposi (Sarcophagus of the Betrothed) A fine example of Etruscan funerary art in the Villa Nazionale Etrusco di Villa Giulia (p152).
- Apollo Belvedere and Laocoön Two outstanding works of classical sculpture in the Vatican Museums' Museo Pio-Clementino (p143).
- Ara Pacis (p95) One of the great masterpieces of early imperial art.
- Colosseum (p67) Rome's iconic 2000-year old stadium.
- Pantheon (p73) The high point of ancient engineering.

Roman artists and architects borrowed heavily from Greek and Etruscan traditions.

In terms of decorative art, the Roman use of floor mosaics and wall frescoes is derived from Etruscan funerary decoration. By the 1st century BC, floor mosaics were a popular form of Roman home décor. They could be bought readymade in a number of designs or ordered to suit the individual tastes of the purchaser. Typical themes included landscapes, still lifes, geometric patterns or depictions of gods. Wall mosaics, however, were rare, being unaffordable to all but the wealthiest of citizens. In the Museo Nazionale Romano: Palazzo Massimo alle Terme (p111), you'll find a spectacular series of wall mosaics taken from a *nymphaeum* (shrine to water nymphs) at Nero's villa in Anzio, as well as a series of superb 1st-century-BC frescoes from Villa Livia, one of the homes of Augustus' wife Livia Drusilla.

Sculpture was an important element of Roman art, and was largely influenced by Greek styles. In fact, early Roman sculptures were often made by Greek artists or were, at best, copies of imported Greek works. They were largely concerned with the male physique and generally depicted visions of male beauty in mythical settings – the *Apollo Belvedere* and the *Laocoön* in the Vatican Museums' Museo Pio-Clementino (p143) are classic examples.

Over time differences began to emerge between Roman and Greek styles. Roman sculpture lost its obsession with form and began to focus on accurate representation, mainly in the form of sculptural portraits. Anyone who spends time browsing the collections of the Museo Palatino (p63) or the Museo Nazionale Romano: Palazzo Massimo alle Terme (p111) cannot fail to be struck by how lifelike – and often ugly – so many of the marble busts are.

In terms of function, Greek art was all about beauty, harmony and dramatic expression while Roman art was highly propagandistic. From the time of Augustus (r 27 BC–AD 14) onwards Roman art was increasingly used to serve the state, and artists came to be regarded as little more than state functionaries. This new narrative art often took the form of relief decoration recounting the story of great military victories – the Colonna di Traiano (p69) and Ara Pacis (p95) are two stunning examples of the genre. Both are magnificent, monumental works of art designed to exalt the power and might of the Roman Empire.

ANCIENT ARCHITECTURE

Like its later art, ancient Roman architecture was monumental in form and propagandistic in nature. Huge amphitheatres, aqueducts and temples joined muscular and awe-inspiring basilicas, arches and thermal baths in trumpeting the skill and vision of the city's early rulers and the nameless architects who worked for them.

Early Roman works were heavily influenced by Greek styles and techniques. In particular, Republican-era temples were based on Hellenic models. But whereas Greek temples had steps and colonnades on all sides, Roman models had a high podium with steps and columns only at the front, forming a deep porch. Good examples of this include the Tempio di Ercole Vincitore and Tempio di Portunus (p72) near Piazza della Bocca della Verità and, though they're not so well preserved, the temples in the Area Sacra di Largo di Torre Argentina (p77).

SIGNATURE WORKS – EARLY CHRISTIAN

- Catacombe di Priscilla (p154) A catacomb with early Christian frescoes.
- Basilica di Santa Sabina (p118) A striking 4th-century basilica.
- Basilica di Santa Maria Maggiore (p105) One of Rome's four papal basilicas.
- Basilica di Santa Maria in Trastevere (p131) Rome's oldest church dedicated to the Madonna.
- Chiesa di Santa Prassede (p109) Celebrated for its Byzantine mosaics.

THE DOME THAT DEFIES THE EXPERTS

One of the city's must-see sights, the Pantheon is widely regarded as the pinnacle of ancient Rome's architectural achievement. A solid, thick-set temple (now church), it's topped by the largest masonry vault ever built, a structure so sophisticated that no-one is quite sure why it is still standing. Had it been made with modern concrete it would have collapsed under its own weight long ago.

Supported by giant piers hidden in the main hall's 6m-thick walls, the dome was built over a temporary wooden frame onto which increasingly thin layers of concrete were poured: the concrete is 5.9m thick at the base of the dome and 1.5m at the top. This was one of the key tricks used to keep its weight to an absolute minimum.

Weight reduction was the main problem facing the Pantheon's architects. They employed various solutions, of which two were particularly ingenious. One was to circle the dome with five bands of decorative coffers (the rectangular recesses you see on the inside of the dome); the other was to modify the grade of the concrete to ensure that it was lighter at the top than at the base. The Romans invented concrete in the 1st century BC by mixing lime with pozzuolana (volcanic ash from the Campi Flegrei area near Naples) and an aggregate. No-one is exactly sure of the composition used for the Pantheon, but the most credible theory is that heavy basalt was used as the aggregate at the bottom, brick or tufa in the midsection and light pumice at the top.

At the centre of the dome, the 8.7m-diameter oculus serves a dual purpose. Most obviously, it allows light into the building, but it also acts as a compression ring, absorbing and redistributing the huge structural forces centred on the dome's apex.

The Roman use of columns was also Greek in origin, even if they favoured the more slender Ionic and Corinthian columns over the plain Doric pillars. To see examples of all three study the Colosseum (p67), where the columns are Doric at ground level, Ionic in the middle and Corinthian on the top tier.

The early Romans' greatest architectural achievement was in perfecting existing construction techniques and using them on a hitherto unseen scale. They learnt how to build roads and bridges from the Etruscans, and used these skills to create aqueducts and arches that still impress today. The invention of concrete in the 1st century BC was a major breakthrough. Made by mixing volcanic ash with lime and an aggregate, often tufa rock or brick rubble, it was quick to make, easy to use and cheap. Furthermore, it freed architects from their dependence on skilled masonry labour (up to that point construction techniques required stone blocks to be specially cut to fit into each other). Concrete was used to roof vast areas such as the Pantheon (p73), which boasts the largest unreinforced concrete dome in existence (see the boxed text, above), and the huge vaults that covered the baths in the Terme di Caracalla (p119), built in AD 217.

Concrete wasn't particularly attractive, though, and while it was used for heavy-duty structural work it was usually lined with coloured marble and travertine, imported from Greece and North Africa. Brick was also an important material, used both as a veneer and for construction.

As Rome's power grew, so its builders became increasingly audacious. The forums developed into richly decorated public spaces dedicated to civic, religious and commercial activity. You need only look at the Mercati di Traiano (Trajan's Markets; p69) to realise that shopping was an important pursuit in 2nd-century Rome. To the northeast, the 13-hectare Terme di Diocleziano (p112), built in 298, became the largest baths complex in ancient Rome.

EARLY CHRISTIAN

The history of early Christianity is one of persecution and martyrdom. Introduced in the 1st century AD, it was legalised by the emperor Constantine in 313 AD and became Rome's state religion in 378. The most startling reminders of early Christian activity are the catacombs, a series of underground burial grounds built under Rome's ancient roads. Christian belief in the resurrection meant that the Christians could not cremate their dead, as was the custom in Roman times, and with burial forbidden inside the city walls they were forced to go outside of the city. Like the Etruscans, the Christians decorated their burial chambers and you'll find traces of biblical frescoes in the Catacombe di Priscilla (p154) on Via Salaria and the Catacombe di San Sebastiano (p123) on Via Appia Antica. Typical imagery includes Lazarus being raised from the dead, Jesus as the good shepherd, and the early Christian saints – Peter, Paul and Cecilia. Symbols also abound: the dove representing peace and happiness, the anchor or trident symbolising the cross, and the fish in reference to an acrostic from the Greek word for fish (Ichthys) which spells out Jesus Christ, Son of God, Saviour.

CHURCH BUILDING

The Christians began to abandon the catacombs in the 4th century and increasingly opted to be buried in the basilicas that the emperor Constantine was building in the city. Although Constantine was actually based in Byzantium, which he renamed Constantinople in his own honour, he nevertheless financed an ambitious building programme in Rome. The most notable of the many churches that he commissioned is the Basilica di San Giovanni in Laterano (p116). Built between 315 and 324 and reformed into its present shape in the 5th century, it was the model on which many subsequent basilicas were based. Other showstoppers of the period include the Basilica di Santa Maria in Trastevere (p131) and the Basilica di Santa Maria Maggiore (p105).

A second wave of church-building hit Rome in the period between the 8th and 12th centuries. As the early papacy battled for survival against the threatening Lombards, its leaders took to construction to leave some sort of historical imprint. By this time churches were almost universally based on the layout of the Roman basilicas (originally a basilica was a hall for public functions). Typically these were rectangular with a flat roof and a wide nave, flanked on both sides by narrow aisles. A good example is the Basilica di Santa Sabina (p118), which owes much of its current look to the 9th and 13th centuries.

Other churches dating to this period include the Chiesa di Santa Prassede (p109), and the 8th-century Chiesa di Santa Maria in Cosmedin (p71), better known as home to the Bocca della Verità (Mouth of Truth).

The 13th and 14th centuries were dark days for Rome as internecine fighting raged between the city's noble families. While much of northern Europe and even parts of Italy were revelling in Gothic arches and towering vaults, little of lasting value was being built in Rome. The one great exception is the city's only Gothic church, the Chiesa di Santa Maria Sopra Minerva (p77).

MOSAIC DECORATION

In early Christian Rome, mosaic art moved into the public arena and surpassed sculpture as the principal artistic endeavour. Religious themes took over and mosaics were increasingly used to decorate churches – stunning examples include the 4th-century apse mosaic in the Chiesa di Santa Pudenziana (p108) and the wonderful mosaics in the vaulted ambulatory of the Mausoleo di Santa Costanza (p154). Another church celebrated for its mosaics is the Basilica di Santa Maria Maggiore (p105), where the 5th-century works beautifully depict Old Testament biblical stories.

Eastern influences became much more pronounced between the 7th and 9th centuries, when Byzantine styles swept in from the east, leading to a brighter, golden look. Byzantine art tended to de-emphasise the naturalistic aspects of the classical tradition and exalt the spirit over the body, so glorifying God rather than the man or the state. The best examples in Rome are in the Basilica di Santa Maria in Trastevere (p131) and the Chiesa di Santa Prassede (p109), a small 9th-century church built in honour of an early Christian heroine.

In the 13th century the Cosmati family revolutionised the art of mosaic-making by slicing up ancient columns of coloured marble into circular slabs, which they then used to create intricate patterns. You'll find memorable Cosmati work in the Sancta Sanctorum (p117) and the Basilica di San Paolo fuori le Mura (p127).

THE RENAISSANCE

Florence, rather than Rome, is generally regarded as Italy's great Renaissance city. Yet it was in the heady days of the 15th and 16th centuries that Rome embarked on its great makeover, a process that was to recast the city as a centre of avant-garde art and design.

It's impossible to pinpoint the exact year that the Renaissance arrived in Rome, but many claim that it was the election of Pope Nicholas V in 1447 that sparked off the artistic furore that subsequently swept the city. Nicholas believed that as head of the Christian world Rome had a duty to impress, a theory that was eagerly taken up by his successors, and it was at the behest

SIGNATURE WORKS – RENAISSANCE

* Tempietto di Bramante (p135) A small temple epitomising classical harmony.
* Chiesa di Santa Maria del Popolo (p94) One of Rome's earliest and richest Renaissance churches.
* St Peter's Basilica (p137) Rome's greatest basilica is the seat of the Catholic Church.
* Sistine Chapel (p145) Home to Michelangelo's celebrated frescoes.
* La Scuola d'Atene (p145) Raphael's great masterpiece.

of the great papal dynasties – the Barberini, Farnese and Pamphilj – that the leading artists of the day were summoned to Rome.

The Venetian Pope Paul II (r 1464–71) commissioned many works, including Palazzo Venezia (p71), Rome's first great Renaissance *palazzo* (mansion). Built in 1455 when Paul was still a cardinal, it was enlarged in 1464 when he became pope. Sixtus IV (r 1471–84) had the Sistine Chapel (p145) built, and enlarged the Chiesa di Santa Maria del Popolo (p94). But it was under Julius II (1503–13) that the Roman Renaissance reached its peak, thanks largely to a classically minded architect from Milan, Donato Bramante (1444–1514). Considered the high priest of Renaissance architecture, Bramante arrived in Rome in 1499. Here, inspired by the ancient ruins, he developed a refined classical style. His 1502 Tempietto (p135) is a masterpiece of elegance. Similarly harmonious is his beautifully proportioned 1504 cloister at the Chiesa di Santa Maria della Pace (p79) near Piazza Navona.

In 1506 Julius commissioned Bramante to start work on the job that would finally finish him off – the rebuilding of St Peter's Basilica (p137). The fall of Constantinople's Aya Sofya (Church of the Hagia Sofia) to Islam in the mid-14th century had pricked Nicholas V into ordering an earlier revamp, but the work had never been completed and it wasn't until Julius took the bull by the horns that progress was made. Bramante never got to see how his original Greek-cross design was developed, as he died in 1514.

St Peter's Basilica occupied most of the other notable architects of the High Renaissance, including Giuliano da Sangallo (1445–1516), Baldassarre Peruzzi (1481–1536) and Antonio da Sangallo the Younger (1484–1546). Michelangelo Buonarroti (1475–1564) eventually took over the task in 1547 and created the magnificent dome, based on Brunelleschi's design for the Duomo in Florence.

MICHELANGELO & RAPHAEL

Michelangelo was the greatest of all Renaissance men – a painter, sculptor, architect and occasional poet. His masterpieces are legion, but he's perhaps best known for his frescoes in the Sistine Chapel (p145). These he painted over two separate periods: between 1508 and 1512 he worked on the ceiling fresco *Genesis,* widely regarded as the high point of Western artistic achievement; and then between 1536 and 1541 he painted the *Giudizio Universale* (Last Judgment). This latter proved highly controversial. Critics panned Michelangelo for damaging existing wall frescoes to make room for his own work – the chapel had originally been decorated by Pietro Vannucci (Perugino; 1446–1523), Sandro Botticelli (1445–1510), Domenico Ghirlandaio (1449–94), Cosimo Rosselli (1439–1507), Luca Signorelli (c 1445–1523) and Bernadino di Betto (Pinturicchio; 1454–1513) – and the final product caused outrage thanks to the copious quantities of flesh on show.

The human form was a central theme to much Renaissance art, and artists such as Michelangelo and Leonardo da Vinci famously studied human anatomy to perfect their representations. Underlying this trend was the humanist philosophy, the intellectual foundation stone of the Renaissance, which held man to be central to the God-created universe and beauty to represent a deep inner virtue.

The extensive depiction of people in Renaissance art led to great innovations in technique, including a far greater appreciation of perspective. Early Renaissance artists in Florence had made great strides in formulating rules of perspective but they found that the rigid formulae they were experimenting with often made harmonious arrangements of figures difficult. This was precisely the challenge that Raffaello Sanzio (Raphael; 1483–1520) tackled in *La Scuola d'Atene* (The School of Athens; 1510–11) in the Stanze di Raffaello (p144) in the Vatican Museums and the *Trionfo di Galatea* in Villa Farnesina (p134).

Originally from Urbino, Raphael arrived in Rome from Florence in 1508 and went on to become the most influential painter of his generation. A paid-up advocate of the Renaissance exaltation of beauty, he painted many versions of the Madonna and Child, all of which epitomise the Western model of 'ideal beauty' that perseveres to this day.

THE BAROQUE

As the principal motor of the Roman Renaissance, the Catholic Church became increasingly powerful in the 16th century. But with power came corruption and calls for reform. These culminated in Martin Luther's 95 Theses and the far-reaching Protestant Reformation. This hit the Church hard and prompted the Counter-Reformation (1560–1648), a vicious and sustained campaign to get people back into the Catholic fold. In the midst of this great offensive, baroque art and architecture emerged as a highly effective form of propaganda. Stylistically, baroque art is based on a dramatic sense of dynamism, emotion and theatricality; architecturally, it combines spatial complexity with clever lighting and a flamboyant use of decorative painting and sculpture.

One of the first great Counter-Reformation churches was the Jesuit Chiesa del Gesù (p78), designed by the leading architect of the day, Giacomo della Porta (1533–1602). In a move away from the style of earlier Renaissance churches, the mannerist façade has pronounced architectural elements that create a contrast between surfaces and a play of light and shade.

The end of the 16th century and the papacy of Sixtus V (1585–90) marked the beginning of major urban-planning schemes. Domenico Fontana (1543–1607) and other architects created a network of major thoroughfares to connect previously disparate parts of the sprawling medieval city, and decorative obelisks were erected at vantage points throughout Rome. Fontana also designed the main façade of Palazzo del Quirinale (p102), the immense palace that served as the pope's summer residence for almost three centuries. His nephew, Carlo Maderno (1556–1629), also worked on the *palazzo*, when not amending Bramante's designs for St Peter's Basilica.

CARAVAGGIO, BERNINI & BORROMINI

The holy trinity of the Roman baroque was formed by Michelangelo Merisi da Caravaggio (1573–1610), Gian Lorenzo Bernini (1598–1680) and Francesco Borromini (1599–1667).

Born in Milan, Caravaggio was the *enfant terrible* of the late-16th-century art world. A controversial and often violent character, he arrived in Rome around 1590 and immediately set about re-writing the artistic rule books. While his peers and Catholic patrons sought to glorify and overwhelm, he tried to paint nature as he saw it, warts and all. He had no time for 'ideal beauty' and caused uproar with his lifelike portrayal of hitherto sacrosanct subjects – his barefoot depiction of the Virgin Mary in the Madonna dei Pellegrini in the Chiesa di Sant'Agostino (p81) is typical of his audacious approach. However, not even his harshest critics could question his technical virtuosity, and his skilful use of chiaroscuro as a dramatic device.

Bernini and Borromini were much more mainstream in their approach, if no less influential. Two starkly different characters – Naples-born Bernini was smooth and charismatic, while Borromini, from Lombardy, was difficult and depressive – they led the transition from Counter-Reformation rigour to baroque exuberance.

Bernini is perhaps best known for his work in the Vatican. He designed Piazza San Pietro (p142), famously styling the colonnade as 'the motherly arms of the Church', and was chief architect at St Peter's Basilica from 1629. While working on the basilica, he created the baldachin (altar canopy) above the main altar, using bronze stripped from the Pantheon.

SIGNATURE WORKS – BAROQUE

- Chiesa del Gesù (p78) Rome's prototype Counter-Reformation church.
- Madonna dei Pellegrini (p81) Caravaggio's masterpiece hangs in the Chiesa di Sant'Agostino.
- Chiesa di San Carlo alle Quattro Fontane (p102) This Borromini church bears all the hallmarks of his genius.
- Santa Teresa traffitta dall'amore di Dio (p103) Bernini's spectacular depiction of St Teresa lost in religious ecstasy.
- Trionfo della Divina Provvidenza (p103) Pietro da Cortona's celebrated fresco in Palazzo Barberini.

ART & ARCHITECTURE THE BAROQUE

ROCOCO FRILLS

In the early days of the 18th century, as baroque fashions began to fade and neoclassicism waited to make its 19th-century entrance, the rococo burst into theatrical life. Drawing on the excesses of the baroque, it was a short-lived fad but one that left a memorable mark.

The Spanish Steps (p95), built between 1723 and 1726 by Francesco de Sanctis, provided a focal point for the many Grand Tourists who were busy discovering Rome's classical past. A short walk to the southwest, Piazza Sant'Ignazio was designed by Filippo Raguzzini (1680–1771) in 1728 to provide the Chiesa di Sant'Ignazio di Loyola (p84), Rome's second Jesuit church, with a suitably melodramatic setting.

Most spectacular of all, however, was the Trevi Fountain (p99), one of the city's most exuberant and enduringly popular monuments. It was designed in 1732 by Nicola Salvi (1697–1751) and completed three decades later.

Under the patronage of the Barberini pope Urban VIII, Bernini was given free rein to transform the city, and his churches, *palazzi*, piazzas and fountains remain landmarks to this day. However, his fortunes nose-dived when the pope died in 1644. Urban's successor, Innocent X, wanted as little contact as possible with the favourites of his hated predecessor and instead turned to Borromini, Alessandro Algardi (1595–1654), and Girolamo and Carlo Rainaldi (1570–1655 and 1611–91, respectively). Bernini, however, later came back into favour with his magnificent design for the 1651 Fontana dei Quattro Fiumi in the centre of Piazza Navona (p78), opposite Borromini's Chiesa di Sant'Agnese in Agone.

Borromini, the son of an architect and well versed in stonemasonry and construction techniques, created buildings involving complex shapes and exotic geometry. A recurring feature of his designs is the skilful manipulation of light, often obtained by the clever placement of small oval-shaped windows. His most memorable works are the Chiesa di San Carlo alle Quattro Fontane (p102), which has an oval-shaped interior, and the Chiesa di Sant'Ivo alla Sapienza (p80), which combines a complex arrangement of convex and concave surfaces with an innovative spiral tower.

One of the hallmarks of the baroque period was the increased use of painting and sculpture in church design, with works often set in elaborately decorated niches. Bernini perfectly encapsulates this style in his remarkable depiction of *Santa Teresa traffita dall'amore di Dio* (Ecstasy of St Teresa) in the Chiesa di Santa Maria della Vittoria (p103). A brilliant blend of realism, eroticism and theatrical spirituality, it is one of the greatest works of baroque art in Western Europe. Further evidence of Bernini's artistic genius is on show at the Museo e Galleria Borghese (p148), where you can marvel at his ability to make stone-cold marble seem soft as flesh in the *Ratto di Proserpina* (Rape of Persephone), or his magnificent depiction of Daphne transforming into a laurel tree in *Apollo e Dafne* (Apollo and Daphne).

Other important baroque artists include Annibale Carracci (1560–1609), whose frescoes in Palazzo Farnese (p81) are said to equal those of the Sistine Chapel; and Pietro da Cortona (1596–1669), author of the *Trionfo della Divina Provvidenza* (Triumph of Divine Providence) in Palazzo Barberini (p103).

FASCISM, FUTURISM & THE 20TH CENTURY

Rome entered the 20th century in good shape. During the last 30 years of the 19th century it had been treated to one of its periodic makeovers – this time after being made capital of the Kingdom of Italy in 1870. Piazzas were built – Piazza Vittorio Emanuele II (p110), at the centre of a new upmarket residential district, and neoclassical Piazza della Repubblica (p111), over Diocletian's bath complex – and roads were laid. Via Nazionale and Via Cavour were constructed to link the city centre with the new railway station, Stazione Termini, and Corso Vittorio Emanuele II to connect Piazza Venezia with the Vatican. To celebrate unification and pander to the ego of the ruling Savoy family, the Vittoriano monument (p71) was built between 1885 and 1911.

In artistic terms, the early 20th century was marked by the development of two very different movements: futurism, led by the poet Filippo Tommaso Marinetti (1876–1944), and metaphysical painting (*pittura metafisica*), an early form of surrealism.

Often associated with fascism, Italian futurism was an ambitious movement, embracing not only the visual arts but also architecture, music, fashion and theatre. It started with the publication of Marinetti's *Manifesto del futurismo* (Manifesto of Futurism) in 1909, which was backed up a year later by the futurist painting manifesto written by Umberto Boccioni (1882–1916), Giacomo Balla (1871–1958), Luigi Russolo (1885–1947) and Gino Severini (1883–1966). A rallying cry for modernism and a vitriolic rejection of artistic traditions, these manifestos highlighted dynamism, speed, machinery and technology as their central tenets. They were also nationalistic and highly militaristic.

One of the movement's founding fathers, Giacomo Balla (1871–1958) encapsulated the futurist ideals in works such as *Espansione dinamica Velocita'*, one of a series of paintings exploring the dynamic nature of motion, and *Forme Grido Viva l'Italia*, an abstract work inspired by the futurists' desire for Italy to enter World War I. Both paintings are on show at the Galleria Nazionale d'Arte Moderna (p152).

In contrast to the brash vitality of futurism, metaphysical paintings were peopled by mysterious images conjured up from the subconscious world. Its most famous exponent was Giorgio De Chirico (1888–1978), whose visionary works were a major influence on the French surrealist movement. With their stillness and sense of foreboding they often show classical subjects presented as enigmatic mannequin-like figures. Good examples include *Ettore e Andromeda* in the Galleria Nazionale d'Arte Moderna (p152), and *Orfeo Solitario* in the Museo Carlo Bilotti (p152).

SIGNATURE WORKS – FASCISM, FUTURISM & THE 20TH CENTURY

- Futurist collection at Galleria Nazionale d'Arte Moderna (p152) Includes works by futurist founders Giacomo Balla, Umberto Boccioni and Gino Severini.
- Giorgio De Chirico collection at Museo Carlo Bilotti (p152) Eighteen canvases by the maestro of metaphysical painting.
- Palazzo della Civiltà del Lavoro (p128) The square Colosseum, symbol of EUR.
- Foro Italico (p153) An impressive Fascist-era sports complex centred on Rome's Stadio Olimpico.
- Albergo Rosso (p128) A striking example of home-grown Roman architecture.

RATIONALISM, ITALIAN STYLE

Influenced by the German Bauhaus movement, architectural rationalism was all the rage in 1920s Europe. In its international form it advocated an emphasis on sharply defined linear forms, but in Italy it took on a slightly different look, thanks to the influence of the Gruppo Sette, its main Italian promoters, and Benito Mussolini, Italy's fascist dictator. Basically, the Gruppo Sette acknowledged the debt Italian architecture owed to its classical past and incorporated elements of that tradition into their modernist designs. Aesthetically and politically, this tied in perfectly with Mussolini's vision of fascism as the modern bearer of ancient Rome's imperialist ambitions.

A shrewd manipulator of imagery, Mussolini embarked on a series of grandiose building projects, including the 1928–31 Foro Italico sports centre (p153), Via dei Foro Imperiali and the residential quarter of Garbatella (p128). Garbatella, now a colourful neighbourhood in southern Rome, was originally planned as an English-style garden city to house the city's workers, but in the 1920s the project was hijacked by the Fascist regime, which had its own designs. Central to these were innovative housing blocks, known as *alberghi suburbani* (suburban hotels), which were used to accommodate people displaced from the city centre. The most famous of these hotels, the *albergo rosso*, was designed by Inocenzo Sabbatini (1891–1983), the leading light of the Roman School of architecture. This local movement looked to ally modern functionalism with a respect for tradition and a utopian vision of urban development.

Mussolini's most famous architectural legacy is the EUR district (p128) in the extreme south of the city. Built for the Esposizione Universale di Roma in 1942, this strange quarter of wide boulevards and huge linear buildings owes much of its look to the vision of the *razionalisti* (rationalists). In practice, though, only one of their number, Adalberto Libera, actually worked on the project, as by this stage most of the Gruppo Sette had fallen out with the ruling junta. Libera's Palazzo dei Congressi (p128) is a masterpiece of rationalist architecture, but EUR's most iconic building is the 'Square Colosseum', the Palazzo della Civiltà del Lavoro (p128), designed by Giovanni Guerrini, Ernesto Bruno La Padula and Mario Romano.

For much of the postwar period architects in Rome were limited to planning cheap housing

GET THE INSIDE PICTURE

Daughter of a fashion photographer father and a model mother, Valentina Moncada is a major voice in Rome's contemporary arts world. Since 1990 she has run the Valentina Moncada gallery on Via Margutta.

Where can I get a glimpse into Rome's contemporary arts scene? You should go to the Pastificio Cerere in San Lorenzo, where there's a whole scene with artists and galleries, even restaurants. It's been around for a while but it used to be pretty much forgotten and it's only recently that it's been coming up. Then there are a few galleries in Il Pigneto, where Pasolini used to live, and in the Flaminio and Trastevere areas. A few museums have also opened up, like the MAXXI by Zaha Hadid. These places are putting on important exhibitions and it wasn't like that even five years ago.

Are there are any emerging Roman artists on the horizon? There are very few young Italian artists who have hit the big time. But the contemporary art scene is problematic all over the world right now. There are so many artists stepping onto the scene but very few have become stars. Many are making statements but it's difficult to single anyone out.

Where would you take a first-time visitor to Rome? Rome is so rich that first I'd need to know their interests. If it was baroque, I'd take them to Borromini's Chiesa di Sant'Ivo alla Sapienza; if it was medieval Christian art, there are some amazing mosaics at the Chiesa di Santa Prassede. We have some wonderful Renaissance palaces that are still owned by aristocratic families, such as Palazzo Colonna or Palazzo Spada. For Roman art, the Capitoline Museums are simply breathtaking. Also the Palazzo Massimo alle Terme, which is usually empty, has entire rooms given over to mosaics and frescoes. If they were interested in contemporary art and architecture, there's Richard Meier's Ara Pacis. Everybody shouts that it's a scandal, but it's interesting to see people's reactions to it. Or there's the Auditorium Parco della Musica. A lot of Fascist architecture is very beautiful too.

for the city's ever-growing population. Swaths of hideous apartment blocks were built along the city's main arteries, and grim suburbs sprang up on land claimed off local farmers.

The 1960 Olympics heralded a spate of sporting construction, and both Stadio Flaminio (p244) and Stadio Olimpico (p153) date to this period. Pier Luigi Nervi, Italy's master of concrete and a hugely influential innovator, added his contribution in the form of the Palazzetto dello Sport (p128).

MODERN ROME

Rome's recent past has witnessed a flurry of artistic and architectural activity. Modern art galleries have opened across the city and a clutch of superstar architects have completed projects in the city. These include Renzo Piano, Italy's foremost architect; renowned American Richard Meier; Anglo-Iraqi Zaha Hadid; Odile Decq; and Dutch legend Rem Koolhaas. Out in EUR, work is underway on Massimiliano Fuksas' cutting-edge Centro Congressi Italia and a 120m steel-and-glass skyscraper designed by Franco Purini.

The foundations of this building boom date to the early 1990s when the then-mayor Francesco Rutelli launched a major clean-up of the historic centre. As part of the process he commissioned Richard Meier to build a new pavilion for the 1st-century AD Ara Pacis. Predictably, Meier's glass-and-steel Museo dell'Ara Pacis (p95) caused controversy when it was unveiled in 2006. Vittorio Sgarbi, an outspoken art critic and politician, claimed that the American's design was the first step to globalising Rome's unique classical heritage.

SIGNATURE WORKS – MODERN ROME

- Auditorium Parco della Musica (p153) Renzo Piano's audacious concert complex.
- Museo dell'Ara Pacis (p95) Controversial museum housing an ancient Roman altar.
- Museo Nazionale delle Arti del XXI Secolo (p153) A contemporary art gallery designed by Zaha Hadid.
- Museo d'Arte Contemporanea di Roma (p155) An ex-brewery turned modern art museum.
- Palazzo delle Esposizioni (p112) Rome's premier exhibition space.

FUKSAS ON ROME

Born in Rome in 1944, Massimiliano Fuksas is one of the world's top architects. He has worked on projects across the globe, and while he has no signature building as such, his design for the Centro Congressi Italia (currently under construction in EUR) comes as close as any to embodying his futuristic style. A rectangular 30m-high glass shell containing a 3500-sq-m steel-and-Teflon cloud supported by steel ribs and suspended over a vast conference hall, its look is fearlessly modern. Yet it's not without its references to the past: in both scale and form it owes its inspiration to the 1930s rationalist architecture that surrounds it.

How is work progressing on the Centro Congressi Italia? Fine. We have now spent just over a year building the underground foundations. Everybody thinks the most difficult part of this project will be building the glass box with the cloud inside, but what is really difficult is building everything that we have to underground. We will then start work on the parking area and the hotel, and then the main floor, which has a very complex 5m-high ceiling and will cover around 9000 sq m. This will be the great congress hall.

How has the city of Rome influenced your architectural style? I was born in Rome and it has given me so much. I've spent a lot of time in Paris and New York, but the way I see space is really a Roman view of space – in Rome, tiny alleyways open up onto huge spaces which then become narrow spaces again. Rome is a theatrical city, a city for great events where the spirit of baroque lives on. Sunlight and shadow create dramatic contrasts of light and dark on the façades of buildings which change throughout the day. It's also tremendous to see the stratification of the city – Piazza Navona, for example, was built over the Stadio di Domiziano and Piazza Farnese stands over the Pompeo area – and the many interesting styles of architecture, from the classical to the great rationalist works of the 1930s, such as the Foro Italico and the university.

How do you see the relationship between classical and modern architecture in Rome? In fact, there is only one contemporary building in the historic heart of Rome (the Museo dell'Ara Pacis) Of course, there are others in the city – my building is in EUR, and there are works by Zaha (Hadid) and Renzo (Piano) in the Flaminio district, which is a 20th century development. The Museo dell'Ara Pacis was heavily criticised, a huge part of the city was against it, but it is not as bad as everybody described it.

There's a big difference between Rome's beautiful historic centre and the drab suburbs where most Romans actually live. How can architecture bridge the gap between these two realities? If you take the historical centre of Rome there are no more than 127,000 residents. All around this you have something like three million people. I never call this the *periferia* (outskirts) because it is more Rome than Rome, in the sense that the real city is where the people live. I think that to make an interesting space you need what I call a cultural infrastructure, as well as mobility (good-quality public transport) and green space. If you have these things then you really start to have something.

Where would you take a visitor on a whistlestop tour of Rome? There are two main areas: the Vatican, which is really important for its 16th- and 17th-century architectural works, and the historic centre. From the Trevi Fountain you can go through to Piazza di Pietra, and on to the Pantheon, Piazza Navona, Campo de' Fiori and Piazza Farnese, then over to Trastevere. Doing all this you'll see works by people such as Michelangelo, Bernini, Borromini.

Where do you go in Rome to relax and get away from it all? The centre of Rome is always so busy, so full of people, but the Aventino is quiet and very nice. There are some interesting churches and there's a great viewing terrace in a small park full of orange trees (Parco Savello). Beyond that is Piranesi's wonderful piazza, Piazza dei Cavalieri di Malta.

Which Italian architect do you particularly admire? Borromini is very important. You'd really need a trip to Rome just for Borromini's works.

SAINTS GLOSSARY

As befits the world's Catholic capital, Rome is overrun by saints. Roads are named after them, churches commemorate them and paintings portray them in all their righteous glory. Here we list some of the big-name *santi* (saints) that you'll come across in Rome.

Sant'Agnese (d 305, b Rome) Patron saint of virgins and Girl Scouts, St Agnes died a martyr at the age of 13. According to tradition, she was beheaded on Piazza Navona (p78), although not before a last-minute miracle. Just before she was executed her tormentors stripped her naked, only to recoil in amazement as her hair instantly grew to cover her body.

Santa Caterina di Siena (1347–80, b Siena, Tuscany) An avid letter writer – her 300-plus surviving letters are considered masterpieces of early Tuscan literature – St Catherine worked tirelessly to bring the papacy back from Avignon to Rome. She's now mostly buried in the Chiesa di Santa Maria Sopra Minerva (p77), although her head and right thumb are in Siena and her foot is in Venice.

Santa Cecilia (2nd century, b Rome) A popular Roman saint, St Cecilia is the patron of music and musicians. She earned this accolade after singing for three days after her executors botched her beheading. She was buried in the Catacombe di San Callisto (p126) and was later moved to the Basilica di Santa Cecilia in Trastevere (p130).

San Clemente (d 97, b Rome) St Clement was ordained by St Peter and became the fourth pope in 88 AD. He was later banished to the Crimean mines by Trajan and thrown into the Black Sea by guards fed up with his continual preaching. The sea water receded some time later, revealing a tomb miraculously containing his body.

Sant'Elena (c 248–328, b Turkey) St Helena is best known as the mother of Constantine, Rome's first Christian emperor. She traipsed off to the Holy Land in search of the Holy Cross and sent pieces to Rome and Constantinople.

San Giovanni (d c 101) Author of the gospel of St John and the Book of Revelation, St John was a travelling companion of Jesus and friend of St Peter. He was tortured by the emperor Domitian but apparently emerged unscathed from a cauldron of boiling oil. The Basilica di San Giovanni in Laterano (p116) is dedicated to him and St John the Baptist.

San Gregorio (540–604, b Rome) Born into a family of saints, St Gregory made his name as Pope Gregory the Great. He sent St Augustine to convert the Brits, built monasteries and lent his name to a style of liturgical singing – the Gregorian chant. He is the patron saint of choirboys.

Sant'Ignazio di Loyola (1491–1556, b Guipuzcoa, Spain) Although Spanish by birth, St Ignatius Loyola earned his Roman colours by founding the Jesuits in Rome in 1540. He spent his last days in a suite of rooms at the Chiesa del Gesù (p78).

San Lorenzo (c 225–258, b Huesca, Spain) A canny financial manager, St Lawrence safeguarded the assets of the 3rd-century Roman Church when not helping the sick, poor and crippled. His patronage of chefs and cooks results from his indescribably awful death – he was grilled to death on a griddle iron.

San Marco (1st century AD, b Libya) Although a native of Libya and the patron saint of Venice, St Mark is said to have written the second gospel while in Rome. The Basilica di San Marco (p71) stands over the house where he used to stay when in town.

San Matteo (1st century AD, b Ethiopia) As patron saint of bankers, stockbrokers and accountants, St Matthew will have been in much demand recently. A Roman tax collector turned apostle, he is portrayed by Caravaggio in the Chiesa di Luigi dei Francesi (p80).

San Paolo (c 3–65, b Turkey) Saul the Christian hater became St Paul the travelling evangelist after conversion on the road to Damascus. He was eventually decapitated in Rome during Nero's persecution of the Christians. Along with St Peter, he's the capital's patron saint. Their joint feast day, a holiday in Rome, is 29 June.

San Pietro (d 64, b Galilee) One of Rome's two patron saints, St Peter is said to have founded the Roman Catholic Church after Jesus gave him the keys to the Kingdom of Heaven. He was crucified upside down and buried on the spot where St Peter's Basilica (p137) now stands. His head is supposed to be in the Basilica di San Giovanni in Laterano.

Santa Prassede (d 164) Daughter of a Roman senator and sister of fellow saint, St Pudenziana, St Praxedes made her name harbouring Christians in a time of persecution and burying their dead in a well on her family estate.

Santa Pudenziana (d 160) Little is known of the virgin martyr St Pudenziana, except that she was St Praxedes' sister, and that she appears in the apse mosaic in Chiesa di Santa Pudenziana (p108), one of Rome's oldest churches.

San Sebastiano (d c 288, b France) St Sebastian distinguished himself as an officer in Diocletian's imperial army before converting to Christianity. Diocletian wasn't amused and had him tied to a tree and turned into an archery target. He survived only to be beaten to death. He's the patron saint of archers and police officers.

Santa Teresa (1515–1582, b Avila, Spain) The Spanish St Theresa is the subject of Bernini's famous sculpture *Santa Teresa traffitta dall'amore di Dio* (p103). When not founding Carmelite convents or writing mystical literature, she often experienced bouts of religious ecstasy.

ART & ARCHITECTURE, TECHNICALLY SPEAKING

ambulatory – a place to walk in a cloister; also an aisle, often semi-circular, running behind the high altar in a church

apse – a semi-circular or polygonal recess with a domed roof over a church's altar

architrave – the main beam set atop columns

baroque – style of European art, architecture and music of the 17th and 18th centuries

basilica – an oblong hall with an apse at the end of the nave; used in ancient Rome for public assemblies and later adopted as a blueprint for medieval churches

capital – the head of a pillar or column

chiaroscuro – a three-dimensional effect created with contrasting highlights and dark shading; often associated with works by Caravaggio

colonnade – a row of columns supporting a roof or other structure

cornice – a horizontal moulded projection that crowns a building; the upper part of an entablature

cloister – enclosed court attached to a church or monastery; consists of a roofed ambulatory surrounding an open area

crypt – an underground room beneath a church used for services and burials

cupola – a rounded dome forming part of a ceiling or roof

entablature – the part of a classical façade that sits on top of the columns; it consists of an architrave, on top of that is a decorative frieze and the cornice

forum – in ancient Rome, a public space used for judicial business and commerce

fresco – a type of painting done on wet plaster on a wall or ceiling

frieze – a horizontal band, often with painted or sculptural decoration, that sits between the architrave and cornice

futurism – Italian early 20th-century artistic movement which embraced modern technology

loggia – a gallery or room with one side open, often facing onto a garden

nave – the central aisle in a church, often separated from parallel aisles by pillars

neoclassicism – dominant style of art and architecture in the late 18th and early 19th centuries; a return to ancient Roman styles

portico – a porch with a roof supported by columns

perspective – the relationship and proportions of elements in a picture, so that ones that are large and low seem close and those small and high seem far away

rationalism – international architectural style of the 1920s; its Italian form, often associated with fascism, incorporates linear styles and classical references

relief – the projection of a design from a plane surface

Renaissance – European revival of art and architecture based on classical precedents between the 14th and 16th centuries

rococo – ornate 18th-century style of architecture

Romanesque – architectural style used between the 10th and 12th centuries; characterised by vaulting and round arches

stucco – wall plaster used for decorative purposes

trompe l'oeil – a visual illusion tricking the viewer into seeing a painted object as a three-dimensional image

The Roman public appreciated the idea of introducing modern architecture to the city centre, but few were entirely convinced by Meier's design.

Meier won far more acclaim for a second project, his striking Chiesa Dio Padre Misericordioso (p113) in Tor Tre Teste, a dreary suburb east of the city centre. Another religious project that won widespread applause was Paolo Portoghesi's postmodern mosque (p154), opened in 1995 in the upmarket Parioli district.

Back nearer the centre, Renzo Piano's Auditorium Parco della Musica (p153) has had a huge impact on Rome's music and cultural scene. Piano, the man behind the Centre Pompidou in Paris and the New York Times building, is one of two Italian architects who can genuinely claim international celebrity status. The other is Massimiliano Fuksas (see boxed text, p53).

To the southeast of EUR, the Nuovo Fiera di Roma is a vast complex, comprising 14 pavilions and 70,000 sq m of exhibition space. Inaugurated in 2006 and designed by the Rome-based architect Tommaso Valle, its glass-and-steel design makes innovative use of biodegradable materials.

In early 2009, the Rem Koolhaas–designed Città dei Giovani project was finally given the green light after years of bureaucratic delays. Construction has yet to start on the Via Ostiense site but once work is finished Rome's former wholesale markets (Mercati Generali) will have been transformed into a brand-spanking-new arts and retail centre.

THE ARTS SCENE

Rome's contemporary arts scene was given a major boost by the commissioning of two flagship arts centres: the Museo Nazionale delle Arti del XXI Secolo, better known as MAXXI (p153), and the Museo d'Arte Contemporanea di Roma, also known by its acronym, MACRO (p155). Situated a few blocks from Renzo Piano's Auditorium, MAXXI features a striking design by the Anglo-Iraqi architect Zaha Hadid, while MACRO, housed in an ex-brewery, sports a dazzling glass shell and a thrilling rooftop garden.

Elsewhere in the city, an increasing number of galleries and historic *palazzi* are opening their doors to contemporary art. In recent years the Mercati di Traiano (p69), Palazzo Barberini (p103) and the Complesso Monumentale Santo Spirito in Sassia (p146) have hosted exhibitions as part of the annual Road to Contemporary Art fair. A similar event, Art Contemporanea Moderna Roma, showcases Italian and international art at the Palazzo dei Congressi (p128) in EUR.

Rome's principle cultural centre is the neoclassical Palazzo delle Esposizioni (p112), which dishes up everything from Mark Rothko abstracts to sculptures by Costa Rican sculptor Jiménez Deredia and video art by Bill Viola. There are also an increasing number of private galleries, including the Gagosian Gallery (p104) and Valentina Moncada (boxed text, p98) on Via Margutta.

In terms of home-grown talent, Rome's artistic hub is the Pastificio Cerere (p113) in San Lorenzo. A pasta factory turned art studio, it is home to a number of working artists, including Maurizio Savini, celebrated for his sculptures made from pink chewing gum. Street art also thrives, particularly in the suburbs of San Lorenzo, Pigneto and Ostiense, where walls are covered in stencil art, poster work and graffiti.

NEIGHBOURHOODS

top picks

- **Colosseum** (p67) Ancient Rome's great gladiatorial arena.
- **St Peter's Basilica** (p137) The world's second-largest church, testament to artistic genius and Catholic power.
- **Museo e Galleria Borghese** (p148) Rome's finest art gallery.
- **Pantheon** (p73) The capital's best-preserved ancient monument is a masterpiece of Roman architecture.
- **Piazza Navona** (p78) Rome's showcase baroque piazza.
- **Capitoline Museums** (p70) The world's oldest public museums boast magnificent classical sculpture.
- **Vatican Museums** (p142) The Sistine chapel and the Stanze di Raffaello are the highlights.
- **Museo Nazionale Romano: Palazzo Massimo Alle Terme** (p111) See how ancient royalty decorated its villas at this stunning museum.
- **Trevi Fountain** (p99) Throw a coin into Rome's flamboyant fountain to ensure a return to the Eternal City.
- **Palatino** (p63) Birthplace of a city, this is where Romulus killed Remus and founded Rome in 753 BC.

What's your recommendation? www.lonelyplanet.com/rome

The result of 3000 years of ad hoc urban development, Rome can seem an overwhelming prospect. To help you navigate the labyrinth, we've divided the city into 11 manageable chunks.

At the southern end of the city centre, Ancient Rome provides an unforgettable introduction to the city with its thrilling reminders of Rome's mythical past: the Colosseum, the Palatino (Palatine hill), the forums, and Campidoglio (Capitoline hill).

'the Vatican is the world's smallest sovereign state and home to St Peter's Basilica and the Sistine Chapel'

To the northwest, the centro storico (historic centre) is a heady tangle of baroque piazzas, tangled lanes and romantic corners. The Pantheon and Piazza Navona are the star turns but you'll enjoy just strolling the atmospheric streets.

Continuing northwards, you come to Piazza del Popolo at the apex of a triangular area known as the Tridente. From the piazza, three roads – Via del Corso, Via di Ripetta and Via del Babuino – spear south, enclosing a smart district of designer boutiques, swanky hotels and the legendary Spanish Steps.

Rising to the east, the Trevi, Quirinale & Via Veneto neighbourhood boasts Rome's iconic Trevi Fountain and two of the city's most lavish palaces: Palazzo Barberini and Palazzo del Quirinale. Snaking up from Piazza Barberini, Via Vittorio Veneto is haunted by ghosts of *la dolce vita*.

Rome's chaotic transport hub, Stazione Termini, sits at the heart of the Monti, Esquilino & San Lorenzo area. Although not an immediately loveable part of town, this busy district throws up some hidden treasures, including some fine churches and one of Rome's best museums – the Museo Nazionale Romano: Palazzo Massimo alle Terme. On the other side of Termini, San Lorenzo is a student hang-out full of bohemian eateries and popular bars.

To the south, you can branch off the beaten track in the Celio Hill & Lateran neighbourhood, home to the monumental Basilica di San Giovanni in Laterano, and the serene Villa Celimontana park.

Separating the Celio from the River Tiber is Aventino & Testaccio. The tranquil Aventino is a breath of fresh air with its medieval churches and refined streets, while to the east the Terme di Caracalla offer Rome's most awesome ruins. Down by the river, Testaccio is an earthy district known for its nightlife.

Continuing southwards, Via Appia Antica, the ancient Appian Way, heads out of the city through Southern Rome. Beneath this most historic of roads lie the catacombs where the early Christians buried their dead. For something completely different head to EUR, a showcase of Fascist-inspired architecture.

On the east bank of the Tiber, Trastevere & Gianicolo is a wonderfully photogenic neighbourhood. Formerly a bastion of working-class independence, it's now a trendy hang-out full of restaurants, cafés, pubs and pizzerias. Behind it, the Gianicolo hill offers an escape from the heat and hustle below.

Continue north from Trastevere and you come to Vatican City, Borgo & Prati. Independent since 1929, the Vatican is the world's smallest sovereign state and home to St Peter's Basilica and the Sistine Chapel, two of Rome's top attractions, as well as hundreds of overpriced restaurants and souvenir shops.

Back over the river, the highlight of Villa Borghese & Northern Rome is Villa Borghese itself. Rome's most famous park boasts several art galleries (including the must-see Museo e Galleria Borghese), the city zoo and plenty of benches to rest your weary legs.

Public transport makes getting around pretty straightforward, and throughout this chapter we have included the best transport options. For more on transport, see p283.

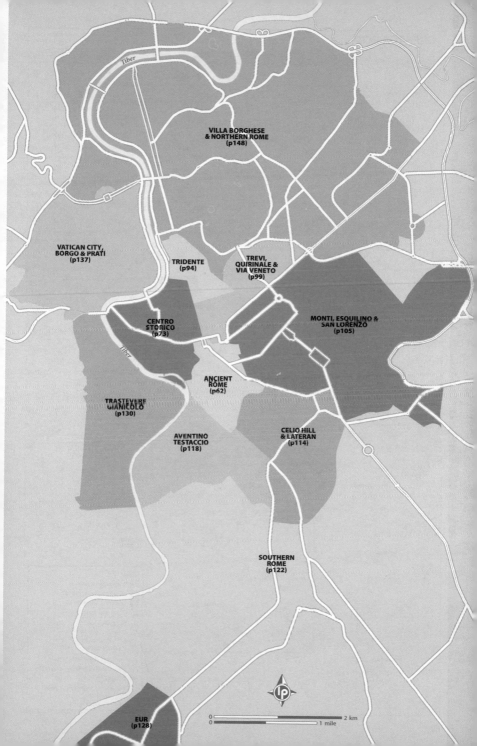

VILLA BORGHESE
& NORTHERN ROME
(p148)

VATICAN CITY,
BORGO & PRATI
(p137)

TRIDENTE
(p94)

TREVI,
QUIRINALE &
VIA VENETO
(p99)

CENTRO
STORICO
(p73)

MONTI, ESQUILINO &
SAN LORENZO
(p105)

ANCIENT
ROME
(p62)

TRASTEVERE
GIANICOLO
(p130)

AVENTINO
TESTACCIO
(p118)

CELIO HILL
& LATERAN
(p114)

SOUTHERN
ROME
(p122)

EUR
(p128)

Tiber

0   2 km
0   1 mile

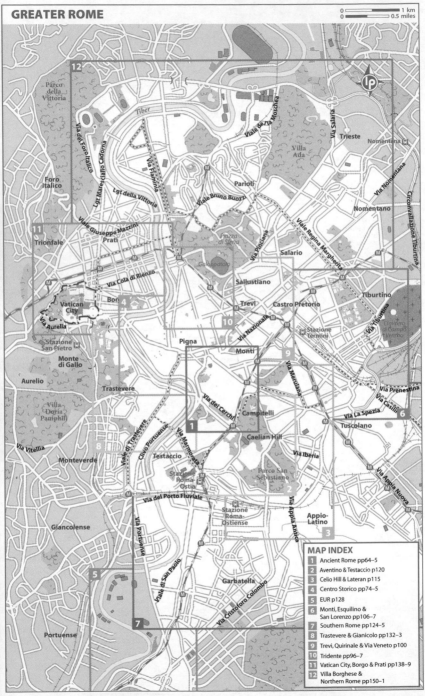

GREATER ROME

MAP INDEX

NEIGHBOURHOODS GREATER ROME

lonelyplanet.com

ITINERARY BUILDER

The table below allows you to plan a day's worth of activities in any area of the city. Simply select which area you wish to explore, and then mix and match from the corresponding listings to build your day. The first item in each cell represents a well-known highlight of the area, while the other items are more off-the-beaten-track gems. For the purposes of our Itinerary Builder, Tridente includes our Trevi, Quirinale & Via Veneto neighbourhood, and Southern Rome includes Celio Hill & Lateran and Aventino & Testaccio.

ACTIVITIES	Sights	Eating	Drinking & Nightlife
Ancient Rome	Colosseum (p62)	San Teodoro (p194)	Oppio Caffè (p217)
	Palatino (p63)	Ara Coeli (p193)	Cavour 313 (p217)
	Capitoline Museums (p70)	La Piazzetta (p194)	
Centro Storico	Pantheon (p73)	La Rosetta (p195)	La Tazza D'Oro (p217)
	Piazza Navona (p78)	Lilli (p197)	Société Lutèce (p219)
	Palazzo e Galleria Doria Pamphilj (p93)	Ditirambo (p198)	Caffè Sant'Eustachio (p219)
Tridente	Trevi Fountain (p99)	Babette (p201)	Stravinkij Bar – Hotel de Russie (p220)
	Museo dell'Ara Pacis (p95)	Edy (p201)	
	Piazza di Spagna (p95)	Palatium (p202)	Gregory's (p221)
Monti, Esquilino & San Lorenzo	Basilica di Santa Maria Maggiore (p105)	La Carbonara (p204)	Ai Tre Scalini (p222)
	Museo Nazionale Romano: Palazzo Massimo alle Terme (p111)	Trattoria Monti (p204)	La Bottega del Caffè (p222)
		Tram Tram (p206)	Solea Club (p223)
	Chiesa di Santa Prassede (p109)		
Southern Rome	Basilica di San Giovanni in Laterano (p116)	Il Bocconcino (p207)	Il Pentagrappolo (p225)
	Terme di Caracalla (p119)	Trattoria Priscilla (p209)	Doppiozeroo (p227)
	Via Appia Antica & the Catacombs (p122)	Trattoria da Bucatino (p208)	Goa (p228)
Trastevere & Gianicolo	Basilica di Santa Maria in Trastevere (p131)	Le Mani in Pasta (p209)	Freni e Frizioni (p229)
	Villa Farnesina (p134)	Da Enzo (p210)	La Meschita (p230)
	Tempietto di Bramante & Chiesa di San Pietro in Montorio (p135)	Bir & Fud (p210)	Ombre Rosse (p230)
Vatican City, Borgo & Prati	St Peter's Basilica (p137)	Dino & Tony (p212)	Castroni (p230)
	Vatican Museums (p142)	Osteria dell'Angelo (p213)	Alexanderplatz (p230)
	Castel Sant'Angelo (p146)	Veranda de l'Hotel Columbus (p212)	
Villa Borghese & Northern Rome	Museo e Galleria Borghese (p148)	Red (p214)	Chioschetto di Ponte Milvio (p231)
	Museo Nazionale Etrusco di Villa Giulia (p152)	Pallotta (p214)	Piper Club (p231)
	Galleria Nazionale d'Arte Moderna (p152)		Brancaleone (p232)

ANCIENT ROME

Drinking & Nightlife p216; Eating p194; Sleeping p249

In a city of extraordinary beauty, Rome's ancient heart exerts a compelling hold. It's here that you'll find the great icons of Rome's past set imperiously against the realities of modern urban life. Buses crammed with commuters thunder past 2000-year-old ruins, while costumed centurions fleece tourists with their grins ever ready for the camera.

There are two focal points: the Colosseum to the east and Campidoglio (Capitoline Hill) to the west. In between lie the forums, on either side of Via dei Fori Imperiali – the more famous Roman Forum to the southwest and the Imperial Forums to the northeast. Now Rome's most famous ruins, the forums were once showpiece examples of cutting-edge urban design, incorporating shops, markets, courts, temples and government buildings. They were dramatic public spaces, richly decorated and grandly scaled. Fascinating as the ruins are, they're not well signposted and it's often difficult to know what you're looking at. To help, get a copy of the Electa *Ancient Rome* map (€3.50) from the Roman Forum ticket office at Largo Romolo e Remo. For a more detailed introduction, Electa also produces a guide, in English, to the *Roman Forum, Palatine and Colosseum* (€8).

top picks

ANCIENT ROME

- Capitoline Museums (p70)
- Colosseum (p67)
- Palatino (opposite)
- Roman Forum (p67)
- Bocca della Verità (p71)

Rising above the Roman Forum, the Palatino is where it all began, where Romulus killed his brother Remus and founded the city in 753 BC. Later it became the Beverly Hills of Ancient Rome, where emperors lived in gilded splendour far removed from the squalor of the city below them.

To the southwest, the Forum Boarium was once Rome's cattle market and river port. Not a lot remains of what must once have been a noisy, smelly part of the capital, and the area is today crisscrossed with busy roads. The one big crowd-puller is the Bocca della Verità, Rome's mythical lie detector.

By public transport the best way to get to Ancient Rome is to take metro line B to Colosseo or one of the frequent buses to Piazza Venezia. There's also a metro station (line B) at Circo Massimo.

COLOSSEUM & PALATINO

COLOSSEUM Map pp64–5

☎ 06 399 67 700; www.pierreci.it; Piazza del Colosseo; admission incl Palatino & Roman Forum adult/EU 18-24yr/EU under 18yr & over 65yr €9/4.50/free plus possible €3 exhibition supplement, audioguides €4.50, videoguides €5.50; ⏰ 8.30am-6.15pm Apr-Aug, to 6pm Sep, to 5.30pm Oct, to 4.30pm mid-end Mar, to 4pm mid-Feb–mid-Mar, to 3.30pm Nov–mid-Feb; Ⓜ Colosseo

A monument to raw, merciless power, the Colosseum (Colosseo) is the most thrilling of Rome's ancient sights. It was here that gladiators met in mortal combat, and condemned prisoners faced wild beasts, in front of baying, bloodthirsty crowds. Two thousand years on and it is Italy's top tourist attraction, which means lengthy queues and long waits – see the boxed text, p67, for tips on avoiding the queues.

Built by Vespasian (r AD 69–79) in the grounds of Nero's vast Domus Aurea (p110) complex, the Colosseum was inaugurated in AD 80. To mark the occasion, Vespasian's son and successor Titus (r AD 79–81) staged games that lasted 100 days and nights, during which some 5000 animals were slaughtered. Trajan (r 98–117) later topped this, holding a marathon 117-day killing spree involving 9000 gladiators and 10,000 animals. For more on gladiators, see the boxed text, p26.

The 50,000-seat arena was originally known as the Flavian Amphitheatre, and although it was Rome's most fearful arena, it wasn't the biggest – the Circo Massimo could hold up to 250,000 people. The name Colosseum, when introduced in medieval times, was not a reference to its size but to the *Colosso di Nerone*, a giant statue of Nero that stood nearby.

The outer walls have three levels of arches, articulated by Ionic, Doric and Corinthian columns. They were originally covered in travertine, and marble statues once filled the niches on the 2nd and 3rd storeys. The upper level had supports for 240 masts that held up a canvas awning over the arena. The 80 entrance arches, known as *vomitoria*, allowed the spectators to enter and be seated in a matter of minutes.

The interior was divided into the arena, *cavea* and podium. The arena had a wooden floor covered in sand to prevent the combatants from slipping and to soak up the blood. It could also be flooded for mock sea battles. Trapdoors led down to underground chambers beneath the arena floor. Animals in cages and sets for the various battles were hoisted onto the arena by a complex system of pulleys.

The *cavea*, for spectator seating, was divided into three tiers: magistrats and senior officials sat in the lowest tier, wealthy citizens in the middle and the plebs in the highest tier. Women (except for vestal virgins) were relegated to the cheapest sections at the top. The podium, a broad terrace in front of the tiers of seats, was reserved for emperors, senators and VIPs.

With the fall of the Roman empire in the 6th century, the Colosseum was abandoned and gradually became overgrown. In the Middle Ages it became a fortress, occupied by two of the city's warrior families, the Frangipani and the Annibaldi. It was later used as a quarry for travertine and marble for Palazzo Venezia, Palazzo Barberini and Palazzo Cancelleria, among other buildings.

ARCO DI COSTANTINO Map pp64–5
Via di San Gregorio; Ⓜ **Colosseo**

The Arco di Costantino (Arch of Constantine) was built in 312 to commemorate Constantine's victory over his rival Maxentius at the Battle of Ponte Milvio (see p153). One of the last great Roman monuments, it is a patchwork of panels from other sculptures – the lower stonework dates from Domitian's reign (AD 81–96) while the eight large medallions depicting hunting scenes are Hadrianic (117–138).

top picks

IT'S FREE

Many of Rome's museums are free to EU citizens under 18 and over 65. If that's you, make sure you have a passport or ID card to prove your age. The following are free to all (but note that while all churches are free, many have small museums and/or excavations that require payment).

- Trevi Fountain (p99)
- Spanish Steps (p95)
- Pantheon (p73)
- Bocca della Verità (p71)
- All churches
- Vatican Museums (p142) On the last Sunday of the month.
- Works by Michelangelo in St Peter's Basilica (p137), Basilica di San Pietro in Vincoli (p110), and Chiesa di Santa Maria Sopra Minerva (p77)
- Works by Raphael in Chiesa di Santa Maria della Pace (p79), Chiesa di Sant'Agostino (p81) and Chiesa di Santa Maria del Popolo (p94)
- Works by Caravaggio in Chiesa di San Luigi dei Francesi (p80), Chiesa di Sant'Agostino (p81) and Chiesa di Santa Maria del Popolo (p94)
- Works by Bernini in St Peter's Basilica (p137), Piazza Navona (p78), Chiesa di Santa Maria del Popolo (p94), Chiesa di Santa Maria della Vittoria (p103) and Chiesa di San Francesco d'Assisi a Ripa (p131)

Between the Colosseum and the arch you can see the brick foundations of an ancient fountain known as the Meta Sudans (Sweating Meta).

PALATINO Map pp64–5
☎ 06 399 67 700; www.pierreci.it; Via di San Gregorio 30; admission incl Museo Palatino, Colosseum & Roman Forum adult/EU 18-24yr/EU under 18yr & over 65yr €9/4.50/free plus possible €3 exhibition supplement, audioguide €4, incl Roman Forum €6; ☉ 8.30am-6.15pm Apr-Aug, to 6pm Sep, to 5.30pm Oct, to 4.30pm mid-end Mar, to 4pm mid-Feb–mid-Mar, to 3.30pm Nov–mid-Feb; Ⓜ Colosseo

The Palatino (Palatine) is a beautifully atmospheric area of leafy gardens, majestic ruins and memorable views. According to legend, it was here that Romulus killed his twin Remus and founded Rome in 753 BC. Archaeological evidence has dated human habitation here to the 8th century BC.

ANCIENT ROME

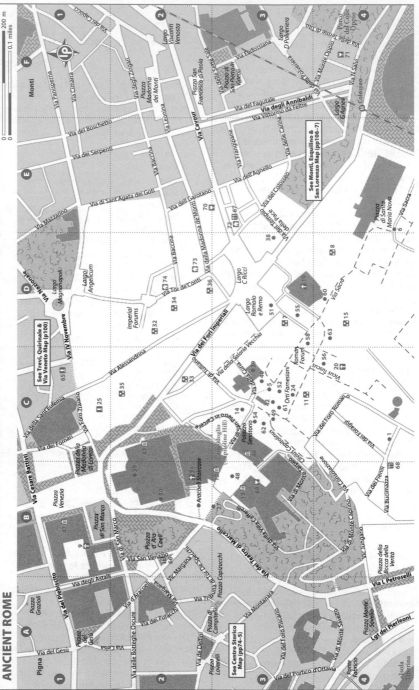

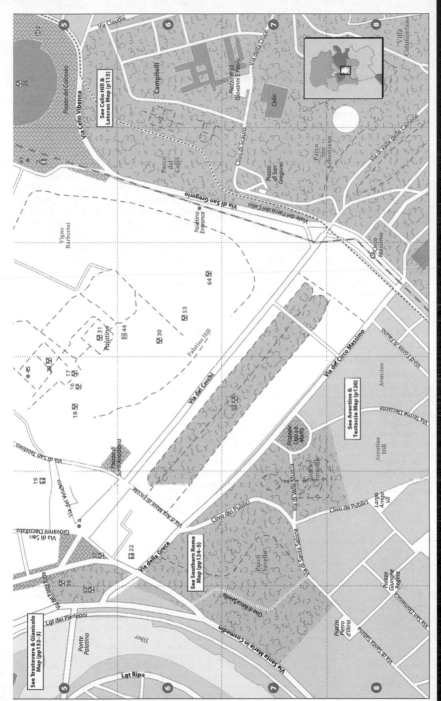

See Celio Hill & Lateran Map (p115)

Campitelli

Celio

See Aventino & Testaccio Map (p120)

See Southern Rome Map (pp124–5)

See Trastevere & Gianicolo Map (pp132–3)

Palatino Entrance

Palatino

Via di San Gregorio

Viale del Parco del Celio

Via Celio Vibenna

Piazza del Colosseo

Via Claudia

Piazza di SS Giovanni e Paolo

Via della Croce

Piazza di San Gregorio

Parco del Celio

Parco San Sebastiano

Via di Valle delle Camene

Villa Celimontana

Circo Massimo

Via di Fonte di Fauno

Via del Circo Massimo

Aventino

Aventino Hill

Via Terme Deciane

Vigna Barberini

Palatino Hill

Via dei Cerchi

Piazza di Sant'Anastasia

Via di San Teodoro

Piazza di Santa Maria della Consolazione

Clivo dei Publicii

Clivo de Publicii

Via di Valle Murcia

Via di Santa Sabina

Largo Arrigo VII

Piazzale Ugo la Malfa

Via della Greca

Via di San Giovanni Decollato

Via del Velabro

Via del Foro Boario

Ponte Palatino

Lgt dei Pierleoni

Lgt Ripa

Tiber

Parco Savello

Via Santa Maria in Cosmedin

Clivo di Rocca Savella

Via di Santa Sabina

Via San Domenico

Piazza Pietro d'Illiria

Piazza Giunone Regina

Sandwiched between the Roman Forum and Circo Massimo, the Palatino was Ancient Rome's poshest neighbourhood. Augustus lived here all his life and successive emperors built increasingly opulent palaces. But after Rome's fall, it fell into disrepair and in the Middle Ages churches and castles were built over the ruins. During the Renaissance, members of wealthy families established gardens on the hill.

Most of the Palatino as it appears today is covered by the ruins of Emperor Domitian's vast complex, which served as the main imperial palace for 300 years. Divided into the Domus Flavia (imperial palace), Domus Augustana (the emperor's private residence) and a *stadio* (stadium), it was built in the 1st century AD.

On entering the complex from Via di San Gregorio, head uphill until you come to the first recognisable construction, the stadio. Adjoining the stadium are the scant remains of the complex built by Septimius Severus, comprising baths (the Terme di Settimio Severo) and a palace (the Domus Severiana).

On the other side of the *stadio* are the ruins of the huge Domus Augustana, the em-

peror's private residence. It was built on two levels, with rooms leading off a *peristilio* (peristyle or garden courtyard) on each floor. You can't get down to the lower level, but from above you can see the basin of a fountain and beyond it rooms that were paved with coloured marble.

In 2007, a mosaic-covered vaulted cavern was discovered beneath here, more than 15m underground. Some believe this to be the Lupercale, a cave believed by ancient Romans to be where Romulus and Remus were suckled by a wolf.

The grey building near the Domus Augustana houses the Museo Palatino (8am-4pm) and its collection of archaeological artefacts. Highlights include a beautiful 1st-century bronze, the *Erma di Canefora,* and a wonderful bust of Giovane Principessa, daughter of Nero's successor Marcus Aurelius.

North of the museum is the Domus Flavia, the public part of Domitian's huge palace complex. The Domus comprised three halls: one to the north; one in the centre, which was the emperor's throne room; and, to the south, a large banqueting hall, or *triclinium,* decorated in coloured

JUMP THE QUEUE

Almost as famous as Rome's great sights are the queues to get into them. The Colosseum and the Vatican Museums, in particular, attract huge crowds in peak seasons. And while there are ways to skip the ticket queues, there's really not much you can do to avoid waiting for the security checks. Queue-busting tips include the following:

Colosseum

- Buy your ticket from the Palatino entrance (about 250m away at Via di San Gregorio 30). Tickets are valid for the Palatino, the Roman Forum and the Colosseum, and there are rarely queues outside the Palatino.
- Get the Roma Pass (see p291), which is valid for three days and a whole host of sites.
- Reserve your ticket online. You can book for the Colosseum at www.pierreci.it (plus booking fee of €1.50).
- If all else fails, join an official English-language tour. These cost €4 on top of the regular Colosseum ticket price.

Vatican Museums

At the Vatican Museums you can pre-book tickets at http://biglietteriamusei.vatican.va/musei/tickets/do?weblang=en&do (plus €4 fee). Otherwise good timing can help: Wednesday mornings are a good bet, as everyone is at the pope's weekly audience at St Peter's; lunchtime is generally better than the morning; and avoid Mondays, when many other museums are shut.

marble. The *triclinium* looked out onto an oval fountain, the remains of which are still clearly visible.

Among the best-preserved buildings on the Palatino is the Casa di Livia, northwest of the Domus Flavia. Home to Augustus' wife Livia, it was built around an atrium leading onto what were once reception rooms, decorated with frescoes of mythological scenes, landscapes, fruits and flowers. In front is the Casa di Augusto (entry in groups of five; ☽ 11am-3.30pm Mon, Wed, Sat & Sun), Augustus' separate residence. Opened to the public in 2008 after years of restoration, the casa boasts superb frescoes.

Next to the Casa di Augusto is the Casa di Romolo (House of Romulus), where it is thought Romulus and Remus were brought up after their discovery by the shepherd Faustulus.

To the northeast of the Casa di Livia is the criptoportico, a 128m tunnel where Caligula is said to have been murdered and which Nero later used to connect his Domus Aurea with the Palatino. Lit by a series of windows, it originally boasted elaborate stucco decorations and is now used to stage temporary exhibitions.

The area west of this was once Tiberius' palace, the Domus Tiberiana, but is now the site of the 16th-century Orti Farnesiani, one of Europe's earliest botanical gardens. Twin pavilions stand at the northern point of the garden, commanding breathtaking views over the Forum below.

CIRCO MASSIMO Map pp64–5
Via del Circo Massimo; Ⓜ Circo Massimo
Now little more than a basin of yellowing grass, the Circo Massimo (Circus Maximus) was Rome's biggest stadium, a 250,000-seater capable of holding a quarter of the city's entire population. The 600m racetrack circled a wooden dividing island with ornate lap indicators and Egyptian obelisks.

Chariot races were held here as far back as the 4th century BC, but it wasn't until Trajan rebuilt it after the AD 64 fire that it reached its maximum grandeur.

THE FORUMS & AROUND

Before venturing into the forums, take a minute to prepare yourself at the I Fori di Roma Centro Espositivo Informativo (☎ 06 679 77 02; Via dei Fori Imperiali; ☽ 9.30am-6.30pm), an information centre dedicated to the area.

ROMAN FORUM Map pp64–5
☎ 06 399 67 700; www.pierreci.it; entrances at Largo Romolo e Remo 5-6 & Via di San Gregorio 30; admission incl Colosseum & Palatino adult/EU 18-24yr/EU under 18yr & over 65yr €9/4.50/free plus possible €3 exhibition supplement, audioguide €4, incl Palatino €6; ☽ 8.30am-6.15pm Apr-Aug, to 6pm Sep, to 5.30pm Oct, to 4.30pm mid-end Mar, to 4pm mid-Feb–mid-Mar, to 3.30pm Nov–mid-Feb; Ⓜ Colosseo
To get the best out of the Roman Forum (Foro Romano) requires effort and imagination. What was once the gleaming heart of the ancient world, a grandiose ensemble

of marble-clad temples, proud basilicas and vibrant public spaces, is now a collection of confusing and badly labelled ruins that can leave you drained and confused. But if you can set your imagination going, there's something undeniably compelling about walking in the footsteps of Julius Caesar and the great emperors of Roman history.

The oldest and most famous of the forums, the Roman Forum grew over the course of 900 years. Originally an Etruscan burial ground, it was first developed in the 7th century BC and expanded to become the centre of the Roman Republic. Its importance declined after the 4th century AD until eventually the site was used as pasture land. In the Middle Ages it was known as the Campo Vaccino (literally 'Cow Field') and was extensively plundered for its stone and marble. During the Renaissance, with the renewed appreciation of all things classical, the forum provided inspiration for artists and architects. The area was systematically excavated in the 18th and 19th centuries, and excavations continue.

As you enter from Largo Romolo e Remo, to your left you'll see the Tempio di Antonino e Faustina, a 2nd-century temple that was transformed into a church in the 8th century; its 10 soaring columns now frame the Chiesa di San Lorenzo in Miranda. To your right, the Basilica Aemilia, built in 179 BC, was a vast 100m-long public hall with a two-storey porticoed façade lined with shops.

At the end of this short path you come to Via Sacra (Sacred Way), the Forum's main thoroughfare. Opposite the Basilica Aemilia stands the Tempio di Giulio Cesare (Temple of Julius Caesar), erected by Augustus in 29 BC on the site where Caesar's body had been cremated 15 years earlier. Head right up Via Sacra to the Curia, the big brick building on the right just after the Basilica Aemilia. Once the meeting place of the Roman Senate, it was rebuilt successively by Julius Caesar, Augustus, Domitian and Diocletian and was converted into a church in the Middle Ages. What you see today is a 1937 reconstruction of Diocletian's Curia. In front of the Curia is the Lapis Niger, a large piece of black marble that covered a sacred area said to be the tomb of Romulus.

At the end of Via Sacra stands the Arco di Settimio Severo (Arch of Septimius Severus). Dedicated to the eponymous emperor and his two sons, Caracalla and Geta, it was built in AD 203 to celebrate victory over the Parthians.

Nearby, at the foot of the Tempio di Saturno, is the Millarium Aureum, which marked the centre of Ancient Rome; from here distances to the city were measured. Built by Augustus in 20 BC, it was originally covered in gold.

On your left are the remains of the Rostrum, an elaborate podium where Shakespeare had Mark Antony make his famous 'Friends, Romans, countrymen…' speech.

The eight granite columns that you see from here are all that remain of the Tempio di Saturno (Temple of Saturn), an important temple that doubled as the state treasury. Behind it, and backing onto the Campidoglio, are (from north to south): the ruins of the Tempio della Concordia (Temple of Concord); the three remaining columns of the Tempio di Vespasiano (Temple of Vespasian); and the Portico degli Dei Consenti, of which 12 columns remain.

Turning round, the Colonna di Foca (Column of Phocus) marks the centre of the Piazza del Foro, the forum's main market and meeting place. To your right are the foundations of the Basilica Giulia, a law court built by Julius Caesar in 55 BC.

To the southeast of the basilica is the Tempio di Castore e Polluce (Temple of Castor and Pollux), also known as the Tempio dei Castori. Built in 489 BC to mark the defeat of the Etruscan Tarquins, it was dedicated to the Dioscuri (or Heavenly Twins). Three Corinthian columns mark the spot.

Behind the temple is the Chiesa di Santa Maria Antiqua, the oldest Christian church in the Forum.

Back towards Via Sacra is the Casa delle Vestali (House of the Vestal Virgins), home of the vestal virgins (see the boxed text, opposite), whose job it was to keep the sacred flame alight in the adjoining Tempio di Vesta.

Once back on Via Sacra turn right and after the Tempio di Romolo (Temple of Romulus), you'll see the vast Basilica di Massenzio on your left. Emperor Maxentius initiated work on the basilica, and Constantine finished it in 315 (it's also known as the Basilica di Costantino). The largest building in the forum, it originally covered an area of approximately 100m by 65m, and was used for business and the administration of justice. Continuing, you come to the Arco di Tito (Arch of Titus), built in AD 81 to celebrate Vespasian's and Titus' victories against Jerusalem.

LIKE A VESTAL VIRGIN

Despite privilege and public acclaim, life as a vestal virgin was no bed of roses.

Every year six physically perfect patrician girls between the ages of six and 10 were chosen by lottery to serve Vesta, daughter of Saturn and goddess of hearth and household. The girls spent their first 10 years in training, learning, among other things, the rudiments of fire preservation – as a fully fledged vestal their most important task was to keep the sacred fire of Vesta burning in the inner chamber of the Tempio di Vesta.

Once fully qualified, the girls faced 10 years of service, during which they were treated as deified beauty queens, appearing at public ceremonies, participating in harvest festivals and taking the seats of honour at the Colosseum.

To round off their 30-year period of service they spent a decade teaching the next generation of vestals. Only after this were they free to marry. Most retired virgins, however, chose to stay on in the Casa delle Vestali (House of the Virgins).

The wellbeing of the state was thought to depend on the cult of Vesta, and, in particular on the vestals' virginity. If a priestess were to lose her virginity she risked being buried alive, since her blood could not be spilled, and the offending man faced death by flogging.

IMPERIAL FORUMS Map pp64–5

Ⓜ Colosseo

The expanse of ruins to the northeast of Via dei Fori Imperiali are known collectively as the Imperial Forums (Fori Imperiali). Constructed between 42 BC and AD 112, they were largely buried in 1933 when Mussolini built Via dei Fori Imperiali. Excavations have since unearthed much of them, but work continues and visits are limited to the Foro di Traiano (Trajan's Forum), accessible through the Museo dei Fori Imperiali (below).

Little that is recognisable remains of the forum except for some pillars from the Basilica Ulpia and the Colonna di Traiano (Trajan's Column), whose minutely detailed reliefs celebrate Trajan's military victories over the Dacians (from modern-day Romania).

To the southeast of Trajan's forum, three temple columns arise from the ruins of the Foro di Augusto (Augustus' Forum), now mostly under Via dei Fori Imperiali. The Foro di Nerva (Nerva's Forum) was also buried by Mussolini's road-building, although part of a temple dedicated to Minerva still stands. Originally, it would have connected the Foro di Augusto to the 1st-century Foro di Vespasiano (Vespasian's Forum), also known as the Forum of Peace.

On the other side of the road, three columns on a raised platform are all that remain of the Foro di Cesare (Caesar's Forum).

MUSEO DEI FORI IMPERIALI Map pp64–5

☎ 06 820 59 127; www.mercatiditraiano.it; Via IV Novembre 94; adult/concession €6.50/4.50, audioguide €3.50; ☾ 9am-7pm Tue-Sun, last entry 6pm; ◘ Via IV Novembre

Elegantly set in Trajan's 2nd-century market complex, this striking museum provides a fascinating introduction to the Imperial Forums with detailed explanatory panels and a smattering of archaeological artefacts. From the main hallway, a lift whisks you up to the Torre delle Milizie (Militia Tower), a 13th-century red-brick tower, and the upper levels of the Mercati di Traiano (Trajan's Markets). These markets, housed in a three-storey semicircular construction, housed hundreds of traders selling everything from oil and vegetables to flowers, silks and spices.

BASILICA DI SS COSMA E DAMIANO
Map pp64–5

▣ 06 699 15 40; Via dei Fori Imperiali; ☾ 8am-1pm & 3-7pm; Ⓜ Colosseo

Backing onto the Roman Forum, this 6th-century basilica incorporates parts of the Foro di Vespasiano (left) and Tempio di Romolo (opposite), visible through the glass wall at the end of the nave. The real reason to visit, though, are the vibrant 6th-century apse mosaics, depicting Christ's second coming. Also worth a look is the huge 18th-century Neapolitan presepio (nativity scene; admission €1 donation; ☾ 10am-1pm & 3-6pm Fri-Sun), in a room off the tranquil 17th-century cloisters.

CARCERE MAMERTINO Map pp64–5

☎ 06 679 29 02; donation requested; ☾ 9am-7pm Apr-Oct, 9am-5pm Nov-Mar; ◘ Piazza Venezia

At the foot of the Campidoglio (Capitoline hill), the small church of San Pietro in Carcere was once a notorious prison (the Mamertine Prison) where prisoners were left to starve in the basement dungeon. St Peter was believed to have been imprisoned here and to have created a miraculous stream of water to baptise his jailers.

CAMPIDOGLIO

Rising above the Roman Forum, the Campidoglio (Capitoline hill) was one of the seven hills on which Rome was founded. An important political and spiritual site, it was considered the true heart of the Roman Republic. At its summit were Rome's two most important temples: one dedicated to Jupiter Capitolinus (a descendant of Jupiter, the Roman equivalent of Zeus) and another (which housed Rome's mint) to Juno Moneta. More than 2000 years on, the hill still wields considerable clout as seat of Rome's municipal government.

PIAZZA DEL CAMPIDOGLIO Map pp64–5
🚇 Piazza Venezia

Designed by Michelangelo in 1538, this graceful piazza is one of Rome's most beautiful. The most dramatic approach is via the Cordonata, the graceful staircase that leads up from Piazza d'Ara Coeli. At the top of the stairs, the piazza is bordered by three palazzi: Palazzo Nuovo to the left, Palazzo Senatorio straight ahead and Palazzo dei Conservatori on the right. Together, Palazzo Nuovo and Palazzo dei Conservatori house the Capitoline Museums (below), while Palazzo Senatorio is home to Rome's city council.

In the centre, the bronze equestrian statue of Marcus Aurelius is a copy. The original, which dates from the 2nd century AD, was in the piazza from 1538 until 1981, when it was moved to Palazzo Nuovo to protect it from erosion.

CAPITOLINE MUSEUMS Map pp64–5
☎ 06 820 59 127; www.museicapitolini.org; Piazza del Campidoglio 1; adult/EU 18-25yr/EU under 18yr & over 65yr €6.50/4.50/free, incl exhibition €9/7/free, incl Centrale Montemartini & exhibition €11/9/free, audioguide €5; ☷ 9am-8pm Tue-Sun, last admission 7pm; 🚇 Piazza Venezia

The world's oldest national museums, the Capitoline Museums date to 1471, when Pope Sixtus IV donated a number of bronze statues to the city, forming the nucleus of what is now one of Italy's finest collections of classical art.

The main entrance is in Palazzo dei Conservatori, where you'll find the original core of the sculptural collection and, on the 2nd floor, an art gallery with a number of important works.

Before you head upstairs, though, take a moment to admire the ancient masonry littered around the ground-floor courtyard, most notably a mammoth head, hand and foot. These all come from a 12m-high statue of Constantine that originally stood in the Basilica di Massenzio in the Roman Forum (p67).

Of the sculpture on the 1st floor, the Etruscan *Lupa Capitolina* (Capitoline Wolf) is the most famous. Standing in the Sala Della Lupa, the 5th-century-BC bronze wolf stands over her suckling wards Romulus and Remus. The statue was given to the Roman people in 1471 by Sixtus IV, which was when the twins were added. Other crowd-pleasers are the *Spinario,* a delicate 1st-century-BC bronze of a boy removing a thorn from his foot, in the Sala dei Trionfi, and Gian Lorenzo Bernini's head of Medusa in the Sala delle Oche.

On the 2nd floor the Pinacoteca contains paintings by such heavyweights as Titian, Tintoretto, Reni, van Dyck and Rubens. The Sala di Santa Petronilla has a number of important canvases, including two by Caravaggio: *La Buona Ventura* (The Fortune Teller; 1595), which shows a gypsy pretending to read a young man's hand but actually stealing his ring, and *San Giovanni Battista* (John the Baptist; 1602), a sensual and unusual depiction of the New Testament saint.

A tunnel links Palazzo dei Conservatori to Palazzo Nuovo on the other side of the square via the Tabularium, ancient Rome's central archive, beneath Palazzo Senatorio.

Palazzo Nuovo is crammed to its elegant rafters with classical Roman sculpture. The real show-stoppers are in the Sala del Gladiatore. These include the *Galata Morente* (Dying Gaul), a Roman copy of a 3rd-century-BC Greek original that movingly depicts the anguish of a dying Frenchman; the 5th-century-BC *Amazzone Ferita* (Wounded Amazon); and a marble *Satiro in Riposo* (Resting Satyr), said to be the inspiration for Nathaniel Hawthorne's novel *The Marble Faun.*

CHIESA DI SANTA MARIA IN ARACOELI Map pp64–5
☎ 06 679 81 55; Piazza del Campidoglio 4; ☷ 9am-12.30pm & 3-6pm; 🚇 Piazza Venezia

Marking the highest point of the Campidoglio, this 6th-century church sits on the site of the Roman temple to Juno Moneta. According to legend it was here that the Tiburtine Sybil told Augustus of the coming birth of Christ, and today the church still has a strong association with the nativity. Its venerated statue of Jesus, the so-called *santo bambino* (holy baby) is, however, a copy. The original, said to have been carved of wood from the garden of Gethsemane, was stolen in 1994 and has never been recovered.

The church has a rich interior, with a Cosmatesque floor and an important 15th-century fresco by Pinturicchio.

PIAZZA VENEZIA

Spread out below the Campidoglio, Piazza Venezia is dominated by Rome's most visible landmark, Il Vittoriano, aka the Altare della Patria.

IL VITTORIANO Map pp64–5

☎ 06 699 17 18; www.ambienterm.arti.beniculturali.it/vittoriano/index.html; Piazza Venezia; admission free; ☹ 10am-4pm Tue-Sun; 🚇 Piazza Venezia

Love it or loathe it, as most locals do, you can't ignore Il Vittoriano, the massive mountain of white marble towering over Piazza Venezia. Known as the Altare della Patria (Altar of the Fatherland), it was begun in 1885 to commemorate Italian unification and honour Vittorio Emanuele II, Italy's first king and the subject of its gargantuan equestrian statue. It also hosts the Tomb of the Unknown Soldier.

Whatever you make of it, there's no denying that the 360-degree views from the top are quite stunning. To get to the top, take the glass lift, Roma del Cielo (adult/concession €7/3.50; ☹ 9.30am-6.30pm Mon-Thu, to 7.30pm Fri-Sun) from the side of the building.

Inside the body of the structure, the Museo Centrale del Risorgimento (☎ 06 679 35 98; Via di San Pietro in Carcere; admission free; ☹ 9.30am-6pm), often referred to as the Complesso del Vittoriano, hosts temporary art exhibitions and has a small collection of military knick-knacks documenting the history of Italian unification.

PALAZZO VENEZIA Map pp64–5

🚇 Piazza Venezia

Built between 1455 and 1464, Palazzo Venezia was the first of Rome's great Renaissance palaces. For centuries it served as the embassy of the Venetian Republic, although its best known resident was Mussolini, who used the vast Sala del Mappamondo as his office and famously made speeches from the balcony overlooking the square.

top picks

VIEWS

Get to the following places for the best views in town:
* Il Vittoriano (left)
* Priorato dei Cavalieri di Malta (p119)
* Gianicolo Hill (p135)
* Dome of St Peter's Basilica (p141)
* Castel Sant'Angelo (p146)
* Pincio Hill Gardens (p95)

Nowadays, the *palazzo* houses the Museo del Palazzo Venezia (☎ 06 699 94 318; Via del Plebiscito 118; adult/concession €4/2; ☹ 8.30am-7.30pm Tue-Sun), with its superb Byzantine and early Renaissance paintings and an eclectic collection of jewellery, tapestries, ceramics, bronze figurines, arms and armour.

BASILICA DI SAN MARCO Map pp64–5

☎ 06 679 52 05; Piazza di San Marco; ☹ 8.30am-noon & 4-6.30pm Mon-Sat, 9am-1pm & 4-8pm Sun; 🚇 Piazza Venezia

The early 4th-century Basilica di San Marco dates stands over the house where St Mark the Evangelist is said to have stayed while in Rome. It has undergone several facelifts over the centuries but in its current form it boasts a Renaissance façade, an 11th-century Romanesque bell tower and a largely baroque interior. The main attraction is the golden 9th-century apse mosaic, which depicts Christ with saints and Pope Gregory IV.

FORUM BOARIUM & AROUND

BOCCA DELLA VERITÀ Map pp64–5

☎ 06 678 14 19; Piazza della Bocca della Verità 18; ☹ 9.30am-5pm; 🚇 Via dei Cerchi

A round piece of marble once used as an ancient manhole cover, the *Bocca della Verità* (Mouth of Truth) is one of Rome's great curiosities. According to legend, if you put your hand in the carved mouth and tell a lie, it will bite your hand off. Apparently, priests used to put scorpions in the mouth to perpetuate the myth, and Roman husbands used it to test their wives' fidelity.

The mouth lives in the portico of the Chiesa di Santa Maria in Cosmedin, one of Rome's most beautiful medieval churches. Originally built in the 8th century, the church was given a major revamp in the 12th century, when the seven-storey bell tower and portico were added and the floor was decorated with Cosmati inlaid marble.

FORUM BOARIUM Map pp64–5
Piazza della Bocca della Verità; 🚌 Via dei Cerchi

Piazza della Bocca della Verità stands on what was once Ancient Rome's cattle market (Forum Boarium). Opposite Chiesa Santa Maria in Cosmedin are two tiny Roman temples dating to the 2nd century BC: the round Tempio di Ercole Vincitore and the Tempio di Portunus, dedicated to the god of rivers and ports, Portunus. Just off the piazza, the Arco di Giano (Arch of Janus) is a four-sided Roman arch that once covered a crossroads. Beyond it is the medieval Chiesa di San Giorgio in Velabro (☎ 06 692 04 534; Via del Velabro 19; ☺ 10am-12.30pm & 4-6.30pm Tue & Fri), a beautiful, atmospheric church, the original 7th-century portico of which was completely destroyed by a Mafia bomb attack in 1993.

CENTRO STORICO

Drinking & Nightlife p217; Eating p195; Shopping p171; Sleeping p250

Bound by the River Tiber on one side and Via del Corso on the other, the tightly packed *centro storico* (historic centre) is the Rome that many visitors come to see. A suggestive area of cobbled alleyways and animated piazzas, baroque churches, chic cafés and Renaissance *palazzi*, it's made for aimless wandering. Even without trying you'll come across some of Rome's great sights: the Pantheon, Piazza Navona and Campo de' Fiori, as well as a host of monuments, museums and churches, many with works by Michelangelo, Raphael, Caravaggio and Bernini. To the south, the Jewish Ghetto has been home to Rome's Jewish community since the 2nd century BC.

The history of the centre goes back to Roman times, when the area around Piazza Navona and the Pantheon was known as the Campus Martius (Field of Mars). A peripheral district full of sports arenas, barracks and temples, it was incorporated into the city proper in the Middle Ages and grew to become the core of Renaissance Rome.

But it's to the baroque 17th century that the area owes most. No two people did more to fashion the face of central Rome than Gian Lorenzo Bernini and his bitter rival Francesco Borromini, whose flamboyant churches, fountains and *palazzi* astound today as they must surely have done 350 years ago.

top picks

CENTRO STORICO

- Pantheon (left)
- Piazza Navona (p78)
- Palazzo e Galleria Doria Pamphilj (p93)
- Museo Nazionale Romano: Palazzo Altemps (p79)
- Chiesa di San Luigi dei Francesi (p80)
- Via Giulia (p82)

But the *centro storico* is not all about history and art – it's also the political heart of modern Italy. Politicians hatch their plots in the hundreds of restaurants, trattorias and cafés that pepper the area, while the two chambers of the Italian parliament sit here and the Presidente del Consiglio (the Italian prime minister) has his official residence in a gracious 17th-century *palazzo*.

The *centro storico* is not a big area and is best explored on foot. Starting from Largo di Torre Argentina, Corso Vittorio Emanuele II heads west towards the River Tiber and the Vatican. To the north are the Pantheon and Piazza Navona; to the south the Jewish Ghetto, Piazza Farnese and Campo de' Fiori.

From Termini, buses 40 and 64 stop at Largo di Torre Argentina and continue down Corso Vittorio Emanuele II. From Barberini metro station (line A), bus 116 stops off at Corso Rinascimento (for Piazza Navona), Piazza Farnese and Via Giulia. Tram 8 connects Largo di Torre Argentina with Trastevere.

PANTHEON & AROUND

PANTHEON Map pp74–5

☎ 06 683 00 230; Piazza della Rotonda; admission free, audioguide €4; ⏲ 8.30am-7.30pm Mon-Sat, 9am-6pm Sun; 🚌 Largo di Torre Argentina

Along with the Colosseum, the Pantheon is one of Rome's major icons. A striking 2000-year-old temple, now a church, it is a truly remarkable monument to the skill of ancient Rome's visionary architects.

In its current form it dates to around AD 120, when Emperor Hadrian built over Marcus Agrippa's original temple (27 BC) – you can still see Agrippa's name inscribed on the pediment. Hadrian's temple was dedicated to the classical gods – hence the name Pantheon, a derivation of the Greek words *pan* (all) and *theos* (god) – but in AD 608 it was consecrated as a Christian church. During the Renaissance it was much studied – Brunelleschi used it as inspiration for his Duomo in Florence – and became an important burial chamber. Today you'll find the tomb of Raphael, alongside those of kings Vittorio Emanuele II and Umberto I.

But more than the décor, it's the scale of the Pantheon that really strikes. The dome, the Romans' most important architectural achievement, was the largest in the world until the 15th century and is still the largest unreinforced concrete dome ever built. Its harmonious appearance is due to a precisely

CENTRO STORICO

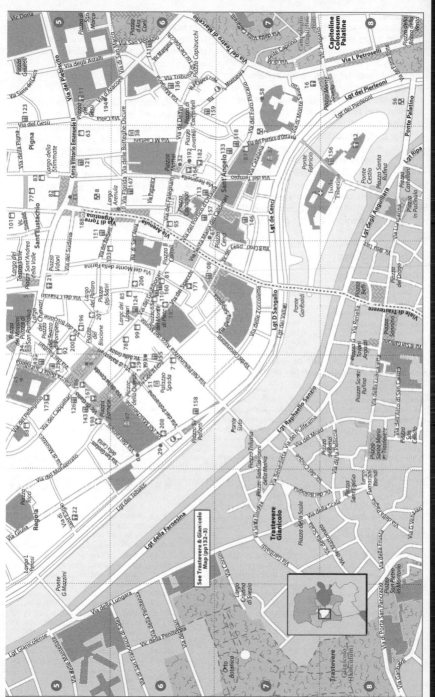

See Trastevere & Gianicolo
Map (pp132–3)

calibrated symmetry – the diameter is exactly equal to the Pantheon's interior height of 43.3m. Light enters through the oculus, an 8.7m opening in the dome that also served as a symbolic connection between the temple and the gods. Rainwater enters but drains away through 22 almost-invisible holes in the sloping marble floor. For more on the dome, see the boxed text, p46.

Somewhat the worse for wear, the exterior is still imposing, with 16 Corinthian columns supporting a triangular pediment. Rivets and holes in the brickwork indicate where the original marble-veneer panels were removed.

Thanks to its consecration as a church in the 7th century, the building was spared the Christian neglect that left other struc- tures to crumble, although it wasn't entirely safe from plundering hands. The gilded-bronze roof tiles were removed and Bernini used bronze from the portico for the baldachin at St Peter's Basilica (p140).

ELEFANTINO Map pp74–5

Piazza della Minerva; Largo di Torre Argentina
A short skip south of the Pantheon stands the Elefantino, a curious and much-loved sculpture of a puzzled elephant carrying a 6th-century-BC Egyptian obelisk. Unveiled in 1667 and designed to glorify Pope Alexander VII, the elephant, symbolising strength and wisdom, was sculpted by Ercole Ferrata to a design by Bernini. The obelisk was taken from the nearby Chiesa di Santa Maria Sopra Minerva.

CENTRO STORICO (pp74–5)

CHIESA DI SANTA MARIA SOPRA MINERVA Map pp74–5

☎ 06 679 39 26; Piazza della Minerva; ⊙ 8am-7pm; 🚌 Largo di Torre Argentina

Built on the site of an ancient temple to Minerva, the Dominican Chiesa di Santa Maria Sopra Minerva is the only Gothic church in Rome, although little remains of the original 13th-century design.

Inside, in the Cappella Carafa (also called the Cappella della Annunciazione), you'll find two superb 15th-century frescoes by Filippino Lippi and the majestic tomb of Pope Paul IV. Left of the high altar is one of Michelangelo's lesser-known sculptures, *Cristo Risorto* (Christ Bearing the Cross; 1520). An altarpiece of the Madonna and Child in the second chapel in the northern transept is attributed to Fra Angelico, the Dominican friar and painter, who is also buried in the church.

The body of St Catherine of Siena, minus her head (which is in Siena), lies under the high altar, and the tombs of two Medici popes, Leo X and Clement VII, are in the apse.

LARGO DI TORRE ARGENTINA Map pp74–5

🚌 Largo di Torre Argentina

A busy transport hub, Largo di Torre Argentina is set around the sunken Area Sacra and the remains of four Republican-era temples. These ruins are off-limits to humans but home to a thriving population of 250 stray cats and a cat sanctuary (☎ 06 687 21 33; www .romancats.com; ⊙ noon-6pm Mon-Sat). To visit

ET TU, BRUTE?

Julius Caesar was stabbed to death on the Ides of March (15 March), 44 BC. As he died he is supposed to have seen his friend Brutus among his killers and uttered the immortal words: 'Et tu, Brute?' ('And you, Brutus?'). This expression, in fact a quote from Shakespeare's play *Julius Caesar*, has since entered the English language as an expression of betrayal.

Caesar's last words have long been the subject of debate. The Roman historian Suetonius is ambiguous on the subject. In his *Lives of the Twelve Caesars* he maintains that Caesar said nothing during the attack but also cites reports that Caesar addressed Brutus in Greek, saying: 'You too, my Child?' Plutarch, writing in his *Lives*, says that Caesar reacts to the sight of Brutus by hiding his head under his toga and silently giving himself up to his assailants.

Caesar was murdered in the Teatro di Pompeo – a vast theatre complex that was hosting Senate meetings after a fire at the Curia. Up to 60 senators were in on the plot, inspired by a desire to save the Roman Republic from Caesar's increasingly dictatorial actions.

the ruins, some of the oldest in Rome, the sanctuary runs a free guided tour at 4pm on Wednesday, Friday and Saturday.

On the piazza's western flank is Rome's premier theatre, the Teatro Argentina (p238), built close to the spot where Julius Caesar was murdered in 44 BC.

CHIESA DEL GESÙ Map pp74–5

☎ 06 69 70 01; www.chiesadelgesu.org; Piazza del Gesù; ☼ 7am-12.30pm & 4-7.45pm; ☒ Largo di Torre Argentina

Rome's most important Jesuit church, the Chiesa del Gesù is a much-copied example of Counter-Reformation architecture. It was built between 1551 and 1584 with money donated by Cardinal Alessandro Farnese.

Although the façade by Giacomo della Porta is impressive, it is the awesome, interior that is the real attraction. Designed by Giacomo Barozzi da Vignola, a pupil of Michelangelo, it's a shimmering ensemble of gold and marble. Of the art on display, the most astounding is the *Trionfo del Nome di Gesù* (Triumph of the Name of Jesus), the swirling, hypnotic vault fresco by Giovanni Battista Gaulli (aka Il Baciccia). Baciccia also painted the cupola frescoes and designed the stucco decoration.

To the left of the main altar is the Cappella di Sant'Ignazio and the tomb of Ignatius Loyola, the Spanish soldier who founded the Jesuits in Rome in 1540. Crafted by Andrea del Pozzo, the tomb, which doubles as an altar, is an opulent marble-and-bronze affair with columns encrusted with lapis lazuli. On top, the terrestrial globe, representing the Trinity, is the largest solid piece of lapis lazuli in the world. On either side are a couple of sculptures whose titles vividly portray the Jesuit ethos: to the left, *Fede che vince l'Idolatria* (Faith defeats

Idolatry); on the right, *Religione che flagella l'Eresia* (Religion Lashing Heresy).

The Spanish saint lived in the church from 1544 until his death in 1556. His private rooms (☼ 4-6pm Mon-Sat, 10am-noon Sun), which contain a masterful trompe l'oeil by Andrea del Pozzo, are just to the right of the main church.

MUSEO NAZIONALE ROMANO: CRYPTA BALBI Map pp74–5

☎ 06 399 67 700; www.pierreci.it; Via delle Botteghe Oscure 31; adult/EU 18-24yr/EU under 18yr & over 65yr €7/3.50/free plus possible €3 exhibition supplement; ☼ 9am-7.45pm Tue-Sun; ☒ Largo di Torre Argentina

The least known of the Museo Nazionale Romano's four museums, the Crypta Balbi provides a fascinating insight into Rome's multilayered past. More than the exhibits, it's the structure of the building itself that's the main interest. It's built around the ruins of medieval and Renaissance structures, themselves set on top of a grand Roman portico and theatre, the Teatro di Balbus (13 BC). You can duck down into the underground excavations before perusing artefacts taken from the Crypta, as well as items found in the forums and on the Oppio and Celio hills.

PIAZZA NAVONA & AROUND

PIAZZA NAVONA Map pp74–5

☒ Corso del Rinascimento

With its ornate fountains, baroque *palazzi* and pavement cafés, Piazza Navona is central Rome's showcase square. Like many of the city's great landmarks, it sits on the site of an ancient monument, in this case the 1st-century-AD Stadio di Domiziano (☎ 06 671 03 819; Piazza Tor Sanguigna 13; admission €3; ☼ by appointment only). This 30,000-seat stadium, remains of which can be seen from Piazza Tor Sanguigna, used to host games – the name Navona is a corruption of the Greek word *agon,* meaning public games. Inevitably, though, it fell into disrepair and it wasn't until the 15th century that the crumbling arena was paved over and Rome's central market transferred here from Campidoglio.

Today interest centres on Bernini's extravagant Fontana dei Quattro Fiumi (Fountain of the Four Rivers). Commissioned by Pope Innocent X and completed in 1651, it depicts the Rivers Nile, Ganges, Danube and Plata, representing the then-known four continents of the world. Legend has it that the figure of the Nile is shielding his eyes from the Chiesa di Sant'Agnese in Agone (☎ 06 681 92 134; www.santagneseinagone.com; ☾ 9.30am-12.30pm & 4-7pm Mon-Sat, 10am-1pm & 4-8pm Sun), designed by Bernini's hated rival, Borromini. In truth, it simply indicates that the source of the Nile was unknown at the time.

The Fontana del Moro at the southern end of the square was designed by Giacomo della Porta in 1576. Bernini added the Moor holding a dolphin in the mid-17th century, but the surrounding Tritons are 19th-century copies. The 19th-century Fontana del Nettuno at the northern end of the piazza depicts Neptune fighting with a sea monster, surrounded by sea nymphs.

The largest building in the square is the elegant Palazzo Pamphilj, built between 1644 and 1650 by Girolamo Rainaldi and Borromini to celebrate Giovanni Battista Pamphilj's election as Pope Innocent X. It is now the Brazilian Embassy.

MUSEO NAZIONALE ROMANO: PALAZZO ALTEMPS Map pp74–5

☎ 06 683 35 66; www.pierreci.it; Piazza Sant'Apollinare 44; adult/EU 18-24yr/EU under 18yr & over 65yr €7/3.50/free plus possible €3 exhibition supplement, audioguide €4; ☾ 9am-7.45pm Tue-Sun; ☒ Corso del Rinascimento

Just north of Piazza Navona, Palazzo Altemps is a gem. A beautiful, late-15th-century *palazzo,* it houses the best of the Museo Nazionale Romano's formidable collection of classical sculpture.

Many of the pieces come from the celebrated Ludovisi collection, amassed by Cardinal Ludovico Ludovisi in the 17th century. Prize exhibits include the 5th-century *Trono Ludovisi* (Ludovisi Throne), a

carved marble throne depicting Aphrodite being plucked from the sea as a newborn babe. It shares a room with two colossal heads, one of which is the goddess Juno and dates from around 600 BC. The wall frieze (about half of which remains) depicts the 10 plagues of Egypt and the Exodus.

Equally impressive is the sculptural group *Galata Suicida* (Gaul's Suicide), a melodramatic depiction of a Gaul knifing himself to death over a dead woman.

The building's baroque frescoes provide an exquisite decorative backdrop. The walls of the Sala delle Prospettive Dipinte are decorated with landscapes and hunting scenes seen through trompe l'oeil windows. These frescoes were painted for Cardinal Altemps, the nephew of Pope Pius IV (r 1560–65) who bought the *palazzo* in the 16th century.

The Egyptian collection from the Museo Nazionale Romano is also housed here, along with the Mattei collection, formerly at Villa Celimontana (the 16th-century estate of the powerful Mattei family).

VIA DEI CORONARI Map pp74–5

☒ Corso del Rinascimento

Named after the *coronari* (rosary-bead sellers) who used to work here, this elegant pedestrian street is famous for its antique shops. A lovely, quiet place for a stroll, it follows the course of the ancient Roman road that connected Piazza Colonna with the River Tiber and was once a popular thoroughfare for pilgrims.

CHIESA DI SANTA MARIA DELLA PACE & CHIOSTRO DEL BRAMANTE Map pp74–5

☎ 06 686 11 56; www.chiostrodelbramante.it; Vicolo dell'Arco della Pace 5; cloisters adult/concession €10/7; ☾ church 9am-noon Mon, Wed & Sat, cloisters 10am-8pm Tue-Fri, 10am-9pm Sat & Sun; ☒ Corso del Rinascimento

Tucked away in the backstreets near Piazza Navona, this small 15th-century church boasts an elaborate porticoed exterior and a minor Raphael fresco *Sibille* (Sibyls). Next door, the Chiostro del Bramante (Bramante Cloisters) is a masterpiece of Renaissance styling, its classic lines providing a marked counterpoint to the church's undulating façade. The cloisters are now used to host art exhibitions and cultural events.

PASQUINO Map pp74–5

Piazza Pasquino; 🚍 Corso Vittorio Emanuele II
A grubby statue covered with tatty bits of paper, the Pasquino is Rome's most famous 'talking statue'. During the 16th century, when there were no safe outlets for dissent, a Vatican tailor named Pasquino began sticking to the statue notes with satirical verses lampooning the church and aristocracy. Others joined in and soon there were talking statues all over town. Even today Romans still leave messages, known as *pasquinade*.

VIA DEL GOVERNO VECCHIO Map pp74–5

🚍 Corso Vittorio Emanuele II
Striking off west from Piazza Pasquino, Via del Governo Vecchio is a lively, atmospheric street full of bohemian boutiques, cheerful eateries and vintage clothes shops. The road, once part of the papal thoroughfare from Palazzo Laterano in San Giovanni to St Peter's Basilica, acquired its name in 1755 when the papal government relocated from Palazzo Nardini at No 39 to Palazzo Madama on the other side of Piazza Navona. Bramante is thought to have lived at No 123.

CHIESA NUOVA Map pp74–5

☎ 06 687 52 89; Piazza della Chiesa Nuova;
⊙ 7.30am-noon & 4.30-7.30pm Mon-Sat, 8am-1pm & 4.30-8pm Sun; 🚍 Corso Vittorio Emanuele II
Something of a misnomer, Chiesa Nuova was built in 1575 as part of a complex to house Filippo Neri's Oratorian order. Originally Neri had wanted a large, plain church, but after his death in 1595 the artists moved in – Rubens painted over the high altar, and Pietro da Cortona decorated the dome, tribune and nave. Neri was canonised in 1622 and is buried in a chapel to the left of the apse.
Next to the church is Borromini's Oratorio dei Filippini and behind it is the Torre dell'Orologio, a clock tower built to decorate the adjacent convent.

MUSEO DI ROMA Map pp74–5

☎ 06 820 59 127; www.museodiroma.it; Piazza di San Pantaleo 10; adult/EU 18-25yr/EU under 18yr & over 65yr €6.50/4.50/free, audioguide €3.50;
⊙ 9am-7pm Tue-Sun; 🚍 Corso Vittorio Emanuele II
Housed in the impressive Palazzo Braschi, the Museo di Roma's eclectic collection of paintings, photographs, etchings, clothes and furniture charts the history of Rome from the Middle Ages to the first half of the

20th century. The *palazzo* itself contains some beautiful frescoed halls, including the extravagant Sala Cinese and the Egyptian-themed Sala Egiziana. Among the paintings, look out for Raphael's 1511 portrait of Cardinal Alessandro Farnese, the future Pope Paul III.

CHIESA DI SANT'IVO ALLA SAPIENZA Map pp74–5

☎ 06 686 49 87; Corso del Rinascimento 40;
⊙ 9am-noon Sun; 🚍 Corso del Rinascimento
Hidden in the porticoed courtyard of Palazzo della Sapienza, the Italian state archive, this tiny church is unique testament to the genius of baroque architect Francesco Borromini. Based on an incredibly complex geometric plan, it combines alternating convex and concave walls with a circular interior topped by a twisted spire. Inside, there's not a lot to see, but it's interesting to note how Borromini uses light to create a sense of spaciousness in such a small area.

PALAZZO MADAMA Map pp74–5

☎ 06 670 62 430; www.senato.it; Piazza Madama 11; admission free; ⊙ guided tours 10am-6pm, 1st Sat of month Sep-Jul; 🚍 Corso del Rinascimento
Seat of the Italian Senate since 1871, Palazzo Madama was originally the 16th-century town house of Giovanni de' Medici. It was enlarged in the 17th century, when the baroque façade was added together with the decorative frieze. The name 'Madama' is a reference to Margaret of Parma, the illegitimate daughter of Charles V, who lived here from 1559 to 1567.

CHIESA DI SAN LUIGI DEI FRANCESI Map pp74–5

☎ 06 68 82 71; Piazza di San Luigi dei Francesi;
⊙ 10am-12.30pm & 4-7pm, closed Thu afternoon; 🚍 Corso del Rinascimento
Church to Rome's French community since 1589, this baroque church boasts no less than three canvases by Caravaggio: *La Vocazione di San Matteo* (The Calling of Saint Matthew), *Il Martiro di San Matteo* (The Martyrdom of Saint Matthew) and *San Matteo e l'Angelo* (Saint Matthew and the Angel), together known as the St Matthew cycle. These were among Caravaggio's earliest religious works, painted between 1600 and 1602, but they are inescapably his, featuring down-to-earth realism and stunning use of chiaroscuro (a three-dimensional

effect created with contrasting highlights and dark shading.

Before you leave the church, take a moment to enjoy Domenichino's colourful 17th-century frescoes of St Cecilia in the second chapel on the right.

CHIESA DI SANT'AGOSTINO Map pp74–5
☎ 06 688 01 962; Piazza di Sant'Agostino; ⏰ 7.45am-noon & 4-7.30pm; 🚌 Corso del Rinascimento

This early Renaissance church is a favourite of soon-to-be mums, who pop in to pay their respects to Jacopo Sansovino's sculpture of the Virgin Mary, the *Madonna del Parto* (1521). The Madonna also features in Caravaggio's *Madonna dei Pellegrini* (Madonna of the Pilgrims; 1604) in the Cappella Cavalletti. Although harmless to modern eyes, this painting caused uproar when it was unveiled in 1604, thanks to its depiction of Mary as barefoot and her two devoted pilgrims as filthy beggars.

Painting almost a century before, Raphael provoked no such scandal with his fresco of *Isaiah*, visible on the third column in the nave.

CAMPO DE' FIORI & AROUND

CAMPO DE' FIORI Map pp74–5
🚌 Corso Vittorio Emanuele II

Noisy and colourful, 'Il Campo' is a major focus of Roman life: by day it hosts a much-loved market, while at night it turns into a raucous open-air pub. For centuries, it was the site of public executions, and in 1600 the philosophising monk Giordano Bruno, immortalised in Ettore Ferrari's sinister statue, was burned at the stake here for heresy.

Many of the streets surrounding Il Campo are named after the artisans who traditionally occupied them: Via dei Cappellari (hatters), Via dei Baullari (trunk makers) and Via dei Chiavari (key makers). Via dei Giubbonari (jacket makers) is still full of clothing shops.

PALAZZO FARNESE Map pp74–5
☎ 06 688 92 818; www.france-italia.it; Piazza Farnese; admission free, under 15yr not admitted; ⏰ 1hr tours depart 3, 4 & 5pm Mon & Thu, by appt only; 🚌 Corso Vittorio Emanuele II

Palazzo Farnese, one of Rome's greatest Renaissance *palazzi*, was started in 1514 by Antonio da Sangallo the Younger, continued by Michelangelo, who added the cornice and balcony, and finished by Giacomo della Porta. Nowadays, it's the French Embassy and open only to visitors who've booked a place on the biweekly guided tour. Visits (with commentary in Italian or French) take in the garden, courtyard and Galleria dei Carracci, home to a series of superb frescoes by Annibale Carracci, said by some to rival the Sistine Chapel. Booking forms can be downloaded from the website and should be sent one to four months before you want to visit. Photo ID is required for entry.

The twin fountains in the square are enormous granite baths taken from the Terme di Caracalla (p119).

A FAMILY AFFAIR

Built in the early 16th century, Palazzo Farnese was the main residence of the all-powerful Farnese dynasty, one of Renaissance Rome's most celebrated families.

Originally landed gentry in northern Lazio, they hit the big time in 1493 when Giulia Farnese became the mistress of Pope Alexander VI. Hardly an official post, it nevertheless gave Alessandro, Giulia's brother, enough influence to secure his election as Pope Paul III (r 1534–49).

Nepotism was a way of life in Renaissance Rome, and a pope in the family was an accepted route to untold wealth. Camillo Borghese (Pope Paul V, r 1605–21) made his nephew, Scipione, a cardinal and gave him the land that is now Villa Borghese (p149); the Sienese banking family, the Chigi, amassed huge fortunes under Pope Alexander VII (r 1655–67), aka Fabio Chigi; and the Pamphilj family enjoyed a 17th-century windfall under their generous kinsman Giovanni Battista Pamphilj, Pope Innocent X (r 1644–55).

Yet of all Rome's great families, only one has a metro station named after it. The Barberini arrived in Rome in the early 16th century, escaping their native Tuscany and a dangerous rivalry with the Florentine Medici. They settled well and in 1623 Maffeo Barberini was elected Pope Urban VIII, opening the floodgates to the usual round of family appointments and extravagant building projects, including the lavish Palazzo Barberini (p103). Some four centuries later the Barberini family still exists, its titular head officially known as the Prince of Palestrina.

PALAZZO SPADA Map pp74–5

☎ 06 683 24 09; www.galleriaborghese.it; Via Capo di Ferro 13; adult/EU 18-25yr/EU under 18yr & over 65yr €5/2.50/free; ☺ 8.30am-7.30pm Tue-Sun; ☒ Corso Vittorio Emanuele II
The central attraction of this 16th-century *palazzo* is Francesco Borromini's famous perspective. What appears to be a 25m-long corridor lined with columns and leading to a hedge and life-sized statue is, in fact, only 10m long. The sculpture, which was a later addition, is actually hip-height and the columns diminish in size not because of distance but because they actually get shorter.

Upstairs, the four-room Galleria Spada houses the Spada family art collection, with works by Andrea del Sarto, Guido Reni, Guercino and Titian.

VIA GIULIA Map pp74–5

☒ Via Giulia
Designed by Bramante in 1508, Via Giulia is a picture-perfect road lined with colourful Renaissance *palazzi* and potted orange trees. At its southern end, the Fontana del Mascherone depicts a 17th-century hippy surprised by water spewing from his mouth. Just beyond it and spanning the road is the ivy-clad Arco Farnese, designed by Michelangelo as part of an ambitious, unfinished project to connect Palazzo Farnese with Villa Farnesina on the opposite side of the Tiber.

Continuing north, on the left, in Via di Sant'Eligio, is Chiesa di Sant'Eligio degli Orefici (☺ 9am-1pm Mon-Fri), the 16th-century goldsmiths' church designed by Raphael.

MUSEO CRIMINOLOGICO Map pp74–5

☎ 06 683 00 234; www.museocriminologico.it; Via del Gonfalone 29; admission €2; ☺ 9am-1pm Tue-Sat plus 2.30-6pm Tue & Thu; ☒ Via Giulia
Check out Rome's dark side at this macabre museum of crime. Housed in a 19th-century prison, its gruesome collection runs the gamut from torture devices and murder weapons to fake Picassos, confiscated smut and the preserved brain of a 19th-century anarchist. You can read up about famous criminal cases and peer into the trunk used in the attempted 1964 kidnap of Israeli spy Mordechai Louk.

CHIESA DI SAN GIOVANNI BATTISTA DEI FIORENTINI Map pp74–5

☎ 06 688 92 059; Via Acciaioli 2; ☺ 7am-12.30pm & 4-7pm; ☒ Via Giulia

This graceful 16th-century church was commissioned by the Medici Pope Leo X as a showcase for Florentine artistic talent. Jacopo Sansovino won a competition for its design, which was then executed by Antonio Sangallo the Younger and Giacomo della Porta, while Carlo Maderno completed the elongated cupola in 1614. Inside the church, the altar is by Borromini, who arranged, on his deathbed, to be entombed here.

A favourite venue for concerts, the church has a 17th-century organ that's played at noon Mass every Sunday.

PALAZZO DELLA CANCELLERIA

Map pp74–5
☎ 06 698 93 491; Piazza della Cancelleria; ☒ Corso Vittorio Emanuele II
Once seat of the Papal Chancellery and now home to the Vatican's highest appeals court, this huge Renaissance *palazzo* was built for Cardinal Raffaele Riario between 1483 and 1513. It's generally closed to the public but you can usually nip through to the courtyard to take a peek at Bramante's glorious double loggia. Next door, and incorporated into the *palazzo*, is the 4th-century Basilica di San Lorenzo in Damaso (☺ 7.30am-noon & 4.30-8pm), one of Rome's oldest Christian churches.

MUSEO BARRACCO DI SCULTURA ANTICA Map pp74–5

☎ 06 682 14 105; Corso Vittorio Emanuele II 166; admission €3; ☺ 9am-7pm Tue-Sun; ☒ Corso Vittorio Emanuele II
One for the specialists, this charming museum boasts a fascinating collection of early Mediterranean sculpture. You'll find Greek, Etruscan, Roman, Assyrian, Cypriot and Egyptian works, all donated to the state by Baron Giovanni Barracco in 1902.

The *palazzo* housing the museum, known as the Piccolo Farnesina, was built for a French clergyman, Thomas Le Roy, in 1523.

CHIESA DI SANT'ANDREA DELLA VALLE Map pp74–5

☎ 06 686 13 39; Corso Vittorio Emanuele II 6; ☺ 7.30am-noon & 4.30-7.30pm Mon-Sat, 7.30am-12.45pm & 4.30-7.45pm Sun; ☒ Corso Vittorio Emanuele II
A must for opera fans, this towering 17th-century church is where Giacomo Puccini

set the first act of *Tosca*. Its most obvious feature is Carlo Maderno's soaring dome, the highest in Rome after St Peter's, but its bombastic baroque interior reveals some wonderful frescoes by Mattia Preti, Domenichino and, in the dome, Lanfranco. Competition between the artists was fierce and legend has it that Domenichino once took a saw to Lanfranco's scaffolding, almost killing him in the process.

JEWISH GHETTO

Centred on lively Via Portico d'Ottavia, the Jewish Ghetto is a wonderfully authentic area studded with artisans' studios, vintage clothes shops, kosher bakeries and popular trattorias.

There have been Jews in Rome since the 2nd century BC, making the city's Jewish community the oldest in Europe. At one point there were as many as 13 synagogues in the city but Titus' victory in Jerusalem in AD 70 changed the status of Jews from citizen to slave. In the 2nd century AD, Romans tended to confuse Jews with the despised monotheistic Christians, making them targets for persecution. Confinement to the ghetto came in 1555 when Pope Paul IV ushered in a period of official intolerance that lasted, on and off, into the 20th century. Ironically, confinement in the ghetto meant that Jewish cultural and religious identity survived intact in Rome.

MUSEO EBRAICO DI ROMA Map pp74–5
☎ 06 684 00 661; www.museoebraico.roma.it; Via Catalana; adult/student/under 10yr €7.50/4/free; ⏰ 10am-6.15pm Sun-Thu & 10am-3.15pm Fri mid-Jun–mid-Sep, 10am-4.15pm Sun-Thu & 9am-1.15pm Fri mid-Sep–mid-Jun; ◻ Lungotevere de' Cenci
The historical, cultural and artistic heritage of Rome's Jewish community is chronicled in this small but engrossing museum. Housed in the city's early-20th-century synagogue, Europe's second largest, it presents harrowing reminders of the hardships experienced by the city's Jewry. Exhibits include copies of Pope Paul IV's papal bull confining the Jews to the ghetto and relics from the Nazi concentration camps.

You can also book a one-hour guided walking tour (adult/student €8/5) of the ghetto at the museum.

PALAZZO CENCI Map pp74–5
Vicolo dei Cenci; ◻ Via Arenula
A veritable house of horrors, Palazzo Cenci was the scene of one of the 16th century's most infamous murders. The victim was the sadistic Francesco Cenci, who was killed by his daughter Beatrice and wife Lucrecia after submitting them to years of abuse. After a long, drawn-out investigation the two perpetrators were beheaded in 1599 on Ponte Sant'Angelo in front of a vast and largely sympathetic crowd. Shelley based his tragedy *The Cenci* on the family, and a famous portrait of Beatrice by Guido Reni hangs in the Galleria Nazionale d'Arte Antica – Palazzo Barberini (p103). It shows a sweet-faced young girl with soft eyes and fair hair.

FONTANA DELLE TARTARUGHE
Map pp74–5
Piazza Mattei; ◻ Via Arenula
This playful 16th-century fountain depicts four boys gently hoisting tortoises up into a bowl of water. Apparently, Taddeo Landini created it in a single night in 1585 on behalf of the Duke of Mattei, who had gambled his fortune away and was on the verge of losing his fiancée. On seeing the fountain, Mattei's father-in-law was so impressed that he relented and let Mattei marry his daughter. The tortoises were added by Bernini in 1658.

AREA ARCHEOLOGICA DEL TEATRO DI MARCELLO E DEL PORTICO D'OTTAVIA Map pp74–5
Via del Teatro di Marcello 44; admission free; ⏰ 9am-7pm summer, to 6pm winter; ◻ Via del Teatro di Marcello
To the east of the ghetto, the Teatro di Marcello is the star turn of this dusty archaeological area. Although originally planned by Julius Caesar, the 20,000-seat theatre was completed by Augustus in 11 BC and named after a favourite nephew, Marcellus. In the 16th century, a *palazzo* was built onto the original building; today this houses some exclusive apartments lived in by a few lucky Romans.

Beyond the theatre, the Portico d'Ottavia is the oldest *quadriporto* (four-sided porch) in Rome. The dilapidated columns and fragmented pediment once formed part of a vast rectangular portico, supported by 300 columns, that measured 132m by 119m. Erected by a builder called Octavius in 146 BC, it was rebuilt in 23 BC by Augustus, who kept the name in honour of his sister Octavia. From the Middle Ages until the late 19th century, the portico housed Rome's fish market.

CHIESA DI SAN NICOLA IN CARCERE
Map pp74–5

☎ 06 683 07 198; www.romeunderground.com; Via del Teatro di Marcello 46; admission church free, excavations donation expected; ☽ 10.30am-6pm; 🚌 Via del Teatro di Marcello

An innocuous-looking building on busy Via del Teatro Marcello, this 11th-century church harbours some fascinating Roman excavations. Beneath the main church you can poke around the claustrophobic foundations of three Republican-era temples, over which the church was built, and the remnants of an Etruscan vegetable market. Marble columns from the temples were incorporated into the church's structure and are still visible today.

ISOLA TIBERINA

The world's smallest inhabited island, the Isola Tiberina (Tiber Island) has been associated with healing since the 3rd century BC, when the Romans adopted the Greek god of healing Asclepius (aka Aesculapius) as their own and erected a temple to him on the island. Today the island is home to the Ospedale Fatebenefratelli.

To reach the Isola Tiberina from the Jewish Ghetto, cross Rome's oldest standing bridge, the 62 BC Ponte Fabricio. Visible to the south of the island are the remains of Ponte Rotto (Broken Bridge), Ancient Rome's first stone bridge, which was all but swept away in a 1598 flood.

CHIESA DI SAN BARTOLOMEO
Map pp74–5

☽ 10.30am-1pm & 3-5.30pm Mon-Sat, 9am-1pm & 6.30-8pm Sun; 🚌 Lungotevere dei Pierleoni

Built on the ruins of the Roman temple to Aesculapius, the Greek god of healing, the island's 10th-century church is an interesting hybrid of architectural styles: the façade is baroque, as is the richly frescoed ceiling, the belltower is 12th-century Romanesque and the 28 columns that divide the interior date to ancient Roman times. Inside, check out the marble wellhead, which is believed to stand over the spring that provided the temple's healing waters.

PIAZZA COLONNA & AROUND

PIAZZA COLONNA Map pp74–5

🚌 Via del Corso

Together with Piazza di Montecitorio, this stylish piazza is Rome's political nerve centre. On its northern flank, the 16th-century Palazzo Chigi (☎ 06 677 93 417; www.governo.it, in Italian; Piazza Colonna 370; admission free; ☽ guided visits 9am-1pm Sat Sep-Jun, booking obligatory) has been the official residence of Italy's prime minister since 1961.

Rising 30m above the piazza, the Colonna di Marco Aurelio was completed in AD 193 to honour Marcus Aurelius' military victories. The vivid reliefs depict scenes from battles against the Germanic tribes (169–173) and, further up, the Sarmatians (174–176). In 1589 Marcus was replaced on the top of the column with a bronze statue of St Paul.

South of the piazza, in Piazza di Pietra, is the Tempio di Adriano. Eleven huge Corinthian columns, now embedded in what used to be the Roman stock exchange, are all that remain of Hadrian's 2nd-century temple.

PALAZZO DI MONTECITORIO Map pp74–5

☎ 06 6 76 01; www.camera.it; Piazza di Montecitorio; admission free; ☽ guided visits 10am-5.30pm, 1st Sun of month; 🚌 Via del Corso

Home to Italy's Chamber of Deputies, this baroque palazzo was built by Bernini in 1653, expanded by Carlo Fontana in the late 17th century and given an Art Nouveau facelift in 1918. Visits take in the palazzo's lavish reception rooms and the main chamber where the 635 deputies debate beneath a beautiful Art Nouveau skyline.

The obelisk outside was brought from Heliopolis in Egypt by Augustus to celebrate victory over Cleopatra and Mark Antony in 30 BC.

CHIESA DI SANT'IGNAZIO DI LOYOLA Map pp74–5

☎ 06 679 44 06; Piazza Sant'Ignazio; ☽ 7.30am-12.30pm & 3-7.15pm; 🚌 Via del Corso

One of Rome's most ornate baroque churches, the 17th-century Chiesa di Sant'Ignazio di Loyola lords it over exquisite Piazza Sant'Ignazio, a small rococo square laid out in 1727 to resemble a stage set. Note the exits into 'the wings' at the northern end and how the undulating surfaces create the illusion of a larger space.

(Continued on page 93)

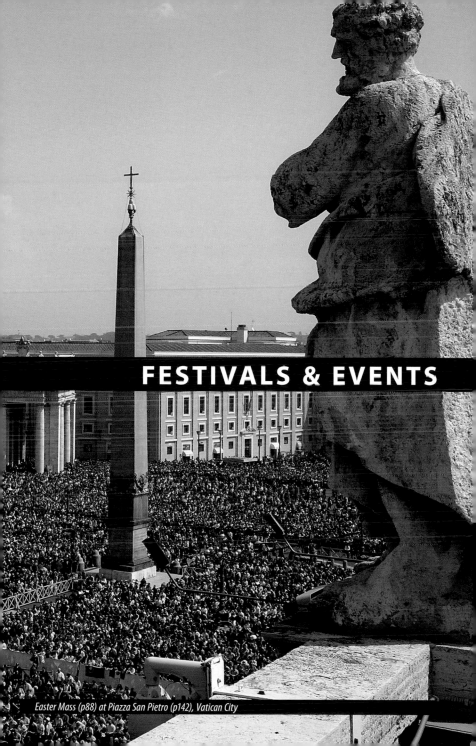

FESTIVALS & EVENTS

Easter Mass (p88) at Piazza San Pietro (p142), Vatican City

In a city celebrated for its past, Auditorium Parco della Musica (p153) represents a cutting-edge present and future

There's never been a better time to enjoy Rome. The city's music and arts scene is flourishing and the festival calendar offers everything from hard rock to jazz, modern art and literature. Here we feature the highlights of the festival year. For a full list of events, see p16.

HOLLYWOOD ON THE TIBER

Now in its fourth year, the Festivale Internazionale del Film di Roma (www.romacinemafest.org) has quickly established itself on the cinema festival circuit. Hollywood A-listers have lent their support, swanning down the red carpet at the Auditorium Parco della Musica (p153), while away from the flashbulbs, industry movers and shakers get down to the real deal in private screening rooms. Rome's film-watching public has also got into the swing of things, attending in ever-increasing numbers.

However, behind the scenes the talk is of politics and cash cuts. Rome's current mayor, Gianni Alemanno, has never been a festival fan, regarding it as little more than an extravagant waste of money. In the run-up to the 2008 mayoral elections he even spoke of cancelling it. He has since softened his line, although not before ordering budget cuts and insisting on a change in focus. With one eye on his electorate – the film industry is a big employer in Rome – he has called for the festival to showcase Italian films rather than highlighting big Hollywood productions. As a result the 2008 festival featured more Italian movies than ever before and the major award, the Marcus Aurelius prize, went to *Resolution 819*, a joint French-Polish-Italian production.

The festival is held in mid-October.

'Terme di Caracalla provides a spellbinding venue for the Teatro dell'Opera's summer season'

ALL OF ROME'S A STAGE

One of Ancient Rome's most memorable sights, the ruins of the Terme di Caracalla (p119) provide a spellbinding venue for the Teatro dell'Opera's summer season (late June to August). The acoustics might not be the city's best but you're unlikely to forget a performance played out against such a backdrop. The programme is traditional, with the emphasis on popular works such as *Swan Lake, Aida, Madame Butterfly* and *Turandot*.

If opera's not your thing, head up the road to Villa Celimontana (www.villacelimontanajazz.com), home to one of Rome's best-loved jazz festivals. Throughout June and August, open-air concerts are held nightly.

Over in the north of the city, Villa Ada stages a boisterous world music festival between mid-June and early August, Roma Incontro Il Mondo (www.villada.org). Headline acts of the 2009 edition included the southern Italian reggae outfit Sud Sound System, Brit

Alexanderplatz (p230), Rome's jazz central station

musician Nitin Sawhney, and Stewart Copeland, drummer of the Police.

The Roman Forum sets a suitably dramatic setting for the Festival delle Letterature (Literature Festival; www.festivaldelleletterature.it), Rome's annual literature festival. Between May and June, big-name authors read and respond to audience questions in the cathedral-like Basilica di Massenzio. Literary genres covered in recent years range from noir to poetry, horror to sci-fi.

CONTEMPORARY VISIONS

For over 20 years, the RomaEuropa festival (www.romaeuropa.net) has been at the forefront of Rome's performing-arts scene. Held between late September and November, it attracts artists, dancers, poets and performers from all over the world, mixing stars with emerging talent, both Italian and foreign. Events range from full-on raves and avant-garde dance performances to installations, multimedia shows, recitals and readings.

Festival stars have come and gone but in recent years Akram Khan, one of Britain's top contemporary dancers, has caused quite a stir. In 2006 he won plaudits for his collaboration with world-renowned ballerina Sylvie Guillem in *Sacred Monsters*, while in 2008 his performance with French actress Juliette Binoche in *In-I* was one of the festival's hottest tickets.

FEAST YOUR EYES FOR FREE

Rome in early spring is a good time for culture vultures on a budget. During the Settimana della Cultura (Culture Heritage Week; www.beniculturali .it/settimanacultura in Italian), admission to public museums and monuments is free, and events are staged throughout the city.

Inaugurated in April 2008, The Road to Contemporary Art (www.romacontemporary.it) provides a showcase for young Italian and international artists. Exhibitions are held in historic sites across the city, including Palazzo delle Esposizioni, Palazzo Barberini and the Mercato di Traiano.

SUMMER FUN

As Romans escape the city for the cool of the coast, Rome's festival season kicks into gear with Estate Romana (www.estateromana.comune.roma.it), which is backed by city hall and sponsors hundreds of events across town.

One such event, Gay Village (www.gayvillage.it), is held between late June and early September. A hugely popular celebration of gay culture, it draws happy crowds and eye-catching performers, including top DJs from London, Paris and Barcelona. There are concerts, film screenings, discos, readings and much more. Venues vary but in 2009 it was held at Piazza Barcellona in EUR.

Pope Benedict XVI greets the faithful gathered on Piazza San Pietro (p142), Vatican City

Traditions run deep in Rome and locals relish their annual celebrations. As befits the capital of the Catholic Church, many have religious origins.

EASTER & VIA CRUCIS

The most important date in the Catholic calendar, Easter is big business in Rome. The Church is at its theatrical best and hundreds of thousands of pilgrims pour into town to witness the whirlwind of events, which kick off with a Mass on Holy Thursday. During the service at the Basilica di San Giovanni in Laterano (p116), the pope washes the feet of 12 priests in imitation of Jesus' gesture at the Last Supper.

The highlight of Good Friday is the solemn candlelit procession around the Colosseum (p67), known as the Via Crucis (Way of the Cross). Led by the crucifix-bearing pope, and broadcast live on Italian TV, it's a re-enactment of Jesus' last walk to Mt Golgotha. Along the way, the faithful stop at each of the 14 stations to say a prayer.

On Easter Sunday all eyes are on the Vatican. In the morning, the pope says Mass at St Peter's Basilica (p137); at noon he delivers his traditional blessing *(urbi et orbi)* from the balcony on Piazza San Pietro (p142).

To get a ticket for Easter Mass is no easy task (contact your home diocese), and almost impossible for non-Catholics. If you can't get one, turn up early and try for standing room on the piazza.

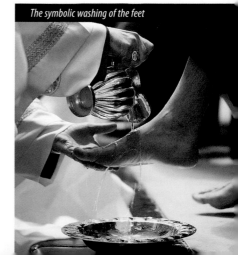

The symbolic washing of the feet

Cardinals walk in the Palm Sunday procession at Piazza San Pietro, Vatican City (p137)

THE SNOW MADONNA

Romans commemorate one of their most unlikely miracles with a floral ticker-tape parade on 5 August. During the Festa della Madonna della Neve (Festival of the Snow Madonna), celebrants re-create a miraculous 4th-century snowfall by releasing thousands of flower petals onto worshippers at the Basilica di Santa Maria Maggiore (p105).

According to legend, the Virgin Mary appeared to Pope Liberius in a dream, in which she instructed him to build a church on the exact spot where he would find snow the following morning. It being August, the chances of snow were remote, but sure enough the next morning (5 August, AD 352) he found

> 'the Virgin Mary appeared to Pope Liberius in a dream and instructed him to build a church'

snow on top of the Esquilino. He obeyed the Madonna, and construction of the Basilica di Santa Maria della Neve (now known as the Basilica di Santa Maria Maggiore) began shortly after.

SAINTS REMEMBERED

The founding fathers of the Christian Church, Pietro (Peter) and Paolo (Paul) are Rome's patron saints. Both were martyred in the 1st century AD and both are celebrated on 29 June. The pope leads a celebratory Mass at St Peter's Basilica (p137) and fireworks are set off at Castel Sant'Angelo (p146). To the south, an all-night market is held on Via Ostiense near the Basilica di San Paolo fuori le Mura (p127), itself built over the site where St Paul was buried. Despite their religious roots, these festivities actually predate Christianity. In Ancient Rome, pagan festivities were held on 29 June to honour Romulus and Remus, Rome's mythical founders.

On 24 June, locals in the San Giovanni district celebrate the birth of San Giovanni (St John the Baptist) by eating stewed snails *(lumache)* – a reference to a legend that tells of witches meeting near the Basilica di San Giovanni in Laterano (p116) to feast on snails during the summer solstice.

One of Rome's most bizarre saints' days is the festival of Sant'Antonio Abate (St Anthony) on 17 January. To commemorate the patron saint of animals, Romans take their pets to be blessed at the Chiesa di Sant'Eusebio (p110) on Piazza Vittorio Emanuele II.

PARTY NIGHTS

Fireworks light up the sky over the cupola of St Peter's Basilica (p137)

Romans have never needed much of an excuse for a party. 'We live on the other side of the river', or 'We're gay', or 'Sod it, let's stay up all night and party' are all reason enough for a good shindig.

ROME ROCKS

Each year, hundreds of thousands of Italians descend on Piazza di San Giovanni in Laterano for the free Primo Maggio (www.primomaggio.com) concert on 1 May. Organised by Italy's trade unions, it kicks off at 4pm and runs until about midnight. You won't recognise many of the acts unless you're up on Italian music, but if you're lucky, you might catch the occasional big-name band.

You shouldn't have much difficulty recognising the stars of Rome's annual rock fest, Rock in Roma (www.rockinroma.com). In 2009, crowds rocked to metal heavyweights Motorhead and Nine Inch Nails, as well as Scottish band Franz Ferdinand and the London-based White Lies.

Capodanno (New Year's Eve) is another good time to catch a gig, with free concerts staged in piazzas throughout Rome. For sedate tunes head for the classical music at Piazza del Quirinale (p101).

WE OTHERS

Although its roots are religious, Trastevere's annual bender, Festa de' Noantri (Festival of We Others, as the locals like to think of themselves), is a two-week binge of eating, drinking, street art and open-air music. Trastevere is always busy, but when festivities kick off in late July, its narrow lanes become almost impenetrable with visitors.

HAPPY BIRTHDAY

Known as the Natale di Roma (Rome's Christmas), Rome's birthday is celebrated on 21 April. Tradition holds that it was on 21 April in 753 BC that Romulus killed his twin Remus and founded Rome on the Palatino (p63). Party central is Piazza del Campidoglio (p70), which is gloriously lit up for the night. Overhead, thousands of fireworks explode in choreographed symphony.

Festivities get under way with the procession of the Madonna del Carmine, a cedar wood statue revered as the protector of the *trasteverini* (Trastevere residents). According to local folklore the Madonna was donated to the Carmelites at the Chiesa di San Crisogono by fishermen who had found her in the Tiber.

ROME PRIDE

Rome's biggest gay day is Roma Pride (www .romapride.it). Culminating in a colourful parade through town, it is preceded by days of events ranging from raves to swimming races and football matches. The 2009 edition, attended by anywhere between 100,000 and a quarter of a million people, depending on who you believe, was preluded by a number of sporting events, including a beach volleyball tournament between gay associations, a table-tennis competition and a footy match between teams of lesbians and assorted VIPs.

CARNIVAL FUN

In Italy, the period preceding Ash Wednesday is known as Carnevale (carnival). Across the city, party-goers let their hair down and children don fancy dress to chuck handfuls of *coriandoli* (coloured confetti) over each other.

Fiesta! (below) adds its bright lights to the big city

Rome's carnival traditions date back to pagan times, namely to the bacchanalian festivities dedicated to the god Saturn. Later, in the 18th century, Carnevale became a big-money earner for the city, as tourists piled in to watch the colourful bedlam of wild-horse races, masked processions, games and feasting.

FIESTA!

Romans get down and dirty at the city's annual celebration of Latin American music and culture, Fiesta! (www.fiesta.it). For two months between mid-June and mid-August, Rome's hippodrome is transformed into a colourful South American village, complete with food stalls, bars, clothes shops and stages. It's a very popular event that attracts huge crowds and big-name performers, including, in recent years, the Costa Rican star Gilberto Santa Rosa and Cuban salsa king Issac Delgado.

Fiesta! (above) brings a slice of Latin America to Rome

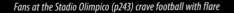

Fans at the Stadio Olimpico (p243) crave football with flare

Games have always excited Roman passions. In ancient times, spectators bayed for blood at the Colosseum, while during the Renaissance Carnevale festivities turned city streets into racetracks. In more recent times, Rome hosted the Olympic Games in 1960 and the World Cup Final in 1990. In 2006 hundreds of thousands of delirious football fans hailed Italy's World Cup–winning team on the Circo Massimo. For more information on sports, see p242.

FOOTBALL RIVALRY

As in the rest of Italy, football is king in Rome. Local loyalties are split between the capital's two Serie A teams, Lazio and Roma, both of whom play at the Stadio Olimpico (p243). The highlight of the season is the biannual derby (p243). A highly charged match, this is preceded by colourful theatrical displays as *ultras* (hardcore fans) try to out-perform their rivals in the opposite stands. To date, Roma has won 58 derbies, Lazio has won 45, and 60 have finished in draws.

ROUND-UP OF THE REST

Five defeats out of five and the wooden spoon in the 2009 Six Nations Tournament marked a low point for Italian rugby, which has struggled to establish itself in football-mad Italy, despite a hard core of support. That said, international matches at the Stadio Flaminio (p244) attract good crowds, especially against Six Nations' opponents in February and March.

Every May, Italy's number-one tennis tournament, the Italian International Tennis Championship, attracts top players to the courts of the Foro Italico (p244). In recent years the golden boy of Spanish tennis, Rafael Nadal, has made the Rome venue his own by winning four out of the past five tournaments.

While tennis aces compete on clay, the world's horse-jumping fraternity decamps to Villa Borghese for the Piazza di Siena showjumping competition (p244), Italy's premier equestrian event.

(Continued from page 84)

The church, built by Jesuit architect Orazio Grassi, boasts an imposing Carlo Maderno façade and a celebrated trompe l'oeil ceiling fresco (the ceiling is in fact completely flat) by Andrea Pozzo (1642–1709) depicting St Ignatius Loyola being welcomed into paradise by Christ and the Madonna. To get the best effect, look up from the small yellow spot on the nave floor.

PALAZZO E GALLERIA DORIA PAMPHILJ Map pp74–5

☎ 06 679 73 23; www.doriapamphilj.it; Via del Corso 305; adult/concession €9/6; ⏲ 10am-5pm, ticket office closes 6.15pm; ⊟ Via del Corso
You wouldn't know it from the grimy grey exterior but this block-sized *palazzo* houses one of Rome's richest private art collections, with works by Raphael, Tintoretto, Brueghel, Titian, Caravaggio, Bernini and Velázquez.

Palazzo Doria Pamphilj dates to the mid-15th century, but its current look was largely the work of the current owners, the Doria Pamphilj family, who acquired it in the 18th century. The Pamphilj's golden age, during which the family collection was started, came during the papacy of one of their own, Innocent X (r 1644–55).

The main picture gallery consists of 10 rooms, chronologically ordered and hung with floor-to-ceiling paintings as per the style of the 16th and 17th centuries. Masterpieces abound, but look out for Titian's powerful *Salomè con la testa del Battista* (Salome with the Head of John the Baptist) and two early works by Caravaggio, *Riposo durante la fuga in Egitto* (Rest During the Flight into Egypt) and *Maddalene Penitente* (Penitent Magdalen). The collection's undisputed star is the Velázquez portrait of an implacable Pope Innocent X, who grumbled that the depiction was 'too real'. In the same room, the *Gabinetto di Velázquez* is Bernini's interpretation of the same subject.

The excellent audioguide (free with your ticket), narrated by Jonathan Pamphilj, brings the place alive with family anecdotes and background information.

CHIESA DI SAN LORENZO IN LUCINA Map pp74–5

☎ 06 687 14 94; Piazza San Lorenzo in Lucina 16; ⏲ 8am-8pm; ⊟ Via del Corso
Little remains of the original 5th-century church that was built here atop an ancient well sacred to Juno. But that shouldn't detract from the very pretty exterior, complete with a Romanesque bell tower and a long 12th-century columned portico. Inside, the otherwise standard baroque décor is elevated by Guido Reni's *Crocifisso* (Crucifixion) above the main altar, and a fine bust by Bernini in the fourth chapel on the southern side. The French painter Nicholas Poussin, who died in 1655, is buried in the church.

TRIDENTE

Drinking & Nightlife p220; Eating p201; Shopping p177; Sleeping p253

To the north of the *centro storico*, this glamorous district has long had a reputation as a bohemian enclave: Keats and Shelley hung out on Piazza di Spagna, Goethe held court on Via del Corso, and *La Dolce Vita* filmmaker Federico Fellini lived on Via Margutta. Nowadays it's the heart of the city's shopping district, full of designer boutiques, fashionable bars and swish hotels.

The area gets its name from the three streets – Via di Ripetta, Via del Corso and Via del Babuino – that arrow out of Piazza del Popolo like a trident's prongs. The piazza, one of Rome's most impressive, is a vast neoclassical showpiece that was once the city's main northern entrance. From its southern flank, Via di Ripetta leads down to the Museo dell'Ara Pacis, a controversial modern museum designed by US architect Richard Meier; and swank Via del Babuino runs down to Piazza di Spagna. The popularity of Piazza di Spagna dates to the 18th century, when it was discovered by travellers on the Grand Tour. Today it's conveniently served by its own metro station, and attracts locals and visitors in equal measure: Roman teenagers pile in on the pull while out-of-towners come to sit on the famous Spanish Steps, which, while always busy, are rarely as colourful as the postcards make out. It's only in early spring that you'll find the famous azaleas lining the steps; for the rest of the year you'll have to make do with exhausted tourists. Piazza di Spagna is also where well-heeled shoppers come to give their credit cards a workout. Via dei Condotti, home to Bulgari, Prada and Armani among others, is the most famous of the area's moneyed shopping strips.

The central of the district's three prongs is Via del Corso, the nearest central Rome has to a main thoroughfare. Lined with flagship department stores, banks and imposing *palazzi*, it swells with tourists, shoppers and schoolkids during the day and quietens considerably at night. Between the late 1400s and the 19th century, Via del Corso was the venue for Rome's traditional pre-Lenten games, which climaxed with a race between riderless horses wired on stimulants and worked into a panic with a barrage of fireworks at the starting line.

By public transport the easiest way to access the area is to take metro line A to Piazza del Popolo (Flaminio) or Piazza di Spagna (Spagna).

top picks

TRIDENTE

- Museo dell'Ara Pacis (opposite)
- Chiesa di Santa Maria del Popolo (right)
- Villa Medici (p98)
- Piazza di Spagna (opposite)

PIAZZA DEL POPOLO & AROUND

PIAZZA DEL POPOLO Map pp96–7

Ⓜ Flaminio

For centuries the sight of public executions, this elegant neoclassical piazza is a superb people-watching spot. It was originally laid out in 1538 to provide a grandiose entrance to the city – at the time, and for centuries before, it was the main northern gateway into the city. Since then it has been extensively altered, most recently by Giuseppe Valadier in 1823. Guarding its southern entrance are Carlo Rainaldi's twin 17th-century baroque churches, Chiesa di Santa Maria dei Miracoli and Chiesa di Santa Maria in Montesanto, while over on the northern flank is the Porta del Popolo, created by Bernini in

1655. In the centre, the 36m-high Egyptian obelisk was moved here from the Circo Massimo in the mid-16th century. To the east are the Pincio Hill Gardens (opposite).

CHIESA DI SANTA MARIA DEL POPOLO Map pp96–7

☎ 06 361 08 36; Piazza del Popolo; ⏰ 7am-noon & 4-7pm Mon-Sat, 8am-1.30pm & 4.30-7.30pm Sun; Ⓜ Flaminio

A magnificent repository of art, this is one of Rome's earliest and richest Renaissance churches. The first chapel was built here in 1099 to exorcise the ghost of Nero, who was secretly buried on this spot and whose malicious spirit was supposed to haunt the area. Some 400 years later, in 1472, it was given a major overhaul by Pope Sixtus IV. Pinturicchio was called in to decorate the pope's family chapel, the Cappella Delle Rovere, and to paint a series of frescoes on the apse, itself designed by Bramante. Also in the apse are Rome's first stained-glass windows, crafted by Frenchman Guillaume de Marcillat in the early 16th century.

Raphael designed the Cappella Chigi, dedicated to his patron Agostino Chigi, but never lived to see it completed. Bernini finished the job for him more than 100 years later, contributing statues of Daniel and Habakkuk. The most famous feature is the 17th-century mosaic of a kneeling skeleton, placed there to remind the living of the inevitable end.

The church's principal calling card is the Cappella Cerasi with its two Caravaggios: the *Conversione di San Paolo* (Conversion of St Paul) and the *Crocifissione di San Pietro* (Crucifixion of St Peter). Of the two, it's the latter that strikes the most, if for nothing other than the brilliant way in which the artist shows the banal awkwardness of the situation. St Peter seems more embarrassed by his position than in pain as three executioners struggle to raise the upturned cross.

PINCIO HILL GARDENS Map pp96–7
Ⓜ Flaminio

Overlooking Piazza del Popolo, the 19th-century Pincio Hill Gardens are named after the Pincl family, who owned this part of Rome in the 4th century. It's quite a climb up from the piazza, but at the top you're rewarded with lovely views over to St Peter's and the Gianicolo hill. From the gardens you can strike off to explore Villa Borghese or head up to the Chiesa della Trinità dei Monti (p98) at the top of the Spanish Steps.

WEST OF VIA DEL CORSO

MUSEO DELL'ARA PACIS Map pp96–7
☎ 06 820 59 127; www.arapacis.it; Lungotevere in Augusta; adult/EU 18-25yr/EU under 18yr & over 65yr €6.50/4.50/free ⊙ 9am-7pm Tue-Sun; 🚌 Lungotevere in Augusta

The first modern construction in Rome's historic centre since WWII, Richard Meier's controversial glass-and-travertine pavilion houses the Ara Pacis Augustae (Altar of Peace), Augustus' great monument to peace and one of the most important works of ancient Roman sculpture. The vast marble altar (it measures 11.6m by 10.6m by 3.6m) was completed in 13 BC and positioned near Piazza San Lorenzo in Lucina, slightly

to the southeast of its current site. The location was calculated so that on Augustus' birthday the shadow of a huge sundial on Campus Martius would fall directly on it.

Over the centuries it fell victim to Rome's avid art collectors, and panels ended up in the Medici collection, the Vatican and the Louvre. However, in 1936 Mussolini unearthed the remaining parts and decided to reassemble them in the present location.

Of the reliefs, the most important depicts Augustus at the head of a procession, followed by priests, the general Marcus Agrippa and the entire imperial family.

MAUSOLEO DI AUGUSTO Map pp96–7
Piazza Augusto Imperatore; 🚌 Piazza Augusto Imperatore

Once one of Ancient Rome's most imposing monuments this is now an unkempt mound of earth, overgrown with weeds and surrounded by unsightly fences. Plans for a revamp have been on the table for some years, but as yet there's no sign of activity.

The mausoleum, which was built in 28 BC, is the last resting place of Augustus, who was buried here in AD 14, and his favourite nephew and heir Marcellus. Mussolini had it restored in 1936 with an eye to being buried here himself.

PIAZZA DI SPAGNA & AROUND

PIAZZA DI SPAGNA & THE SPANISH STEPS Map pp96–7
Ⓜ Spagna

Piazza di Spagna and the famous Spanish Steps (Scalinata della Trinità dei Monti) have been a magnet for foreigners since the 18th century. In the late 1700s the area was much loved by English visitors on the Grand Tour and was known to locals as *er ghetto de l'inglesi* (the English ghetto).

The piazza was named after the Spanish Embassy to the Holy See, although the staircase, designed by the Italian Francesco de Sanctis and built in 1725 with a legacy from the French, leads to the French Chiesa della Trinità dei Monti (p98).

At the foot of the steps, the fountain of a sinking boat, the Barcaccia (1627), is believed to be by Pietro Bernini, father of the more famous Gian Lorenzo. Opposite, Via dei Condotti is Rome's top shopping strip.

To the southeast of the piazza, adjacent Piazza Mignanelli is dominated by the

TRIDENTE

Scale: 0 — 200 m / 0 — 0.1 miles

See Trevi, Quirinale & Via Veneto Map (p100)

See Vatican City, Borgo & Prati Map (pp138–9)

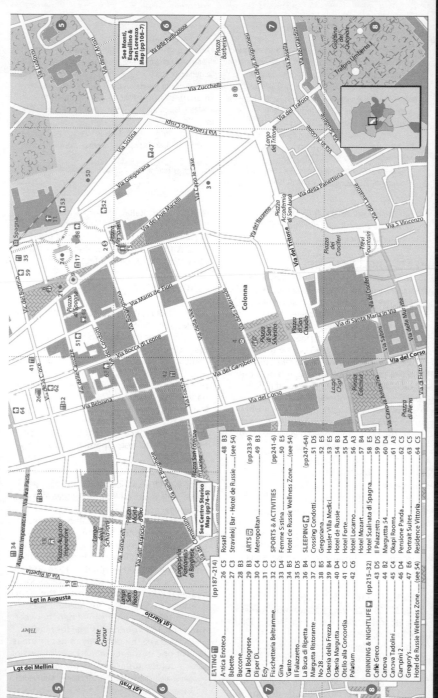

See Monti, Esquilino & San Lorenzo Map (pp106-7)

See Centro Storico Map (pp74-5)

VIA MARGUTTA, THE ARTISTS' STREET

Via Margutta has long been associated with art and artists, and today it is still lined with antique shops and art galleries.

'The street's reputation goes back to the 16th century, when it was declared a tax-free zone for artists', explains Valentina Moncada, owner of the eponymous gallery at Via Margutta 54.

'If you were an artist and a resident, you paid no taxes, so artists came from all over Europe. Also there was Villa Medici nearby and all the winners of the Prix de Rome (a prestigious French art scholarship) would often come down here.'

By the late 1800s, the studio that Valentina's family had established in the mid-19th century had grown into a popular meeting point for visiting artists, writers and musicians.

'A string of important musicians visited including all the Italian opera greats – Puccini, Verdi, Mascagni – as well as the composers Wagner, Liszt and Debussy. The Italian futurists also held their first meetings here and in 1917 Picasso passed by.'

Of the street's more recent residents, the most famous is film director Federico Fellini, who lived at No 110 with his wife Giulietta Masina until his death in 1993.

Colonna dell'Immacolata, built in 1857 to celebrate Pope Pius IX's declaration of the Immaculate Conception.

KEATS-SHELLEY HOUSE Map pp96–7
☎ 06 678 42 35; www.keats-shelley-house.org; Piazza di Spagna 26; adult/6-18yr & over 65yr/under 6yr €4/3/free; ☺ 10am-1pm & 2-6pm Mon-Fri, 11am-2pm & 3-6pm Sat; Ⓜ Spagna
Next to the Spanish Steps, the Keats-Shelley House is where Romantic poet John Keats died in February 1821. He'd come to Rome a year earlier, hoping the Italian climate would improve his failing health, but it didn't, and he died at the age of 25. A year later, fellow poet Percy Bysshe Shelley drowned off the coast of Tuscany. The house is now a small museum crammed with memorabilia relating to the poets and their colleagues Mary Shelley and Lord Byron.

VIA DEI CONDOTTI Map pp96–7
Ⓜ Spagna
A mecca for high-rolling shoppers, this is Rome's smartest shopping strip. At the eastern end, near Piazza di Spagna, Caffè Greco (p221) was a favourite meeting point of 18th- and 19th-century writers. Other top shopping streets in the area include Via Frattina, Via della Croce, Via delle Carrozze and Via del Babuino.

CASA DI GOETHE Map pp96–7
☎ 06 326 50 412; www.casadigoethe.it; Via del Corso 18; adult/student & over 65yr €4/3; ☺ 10am-6pm Tue-Sun; Ⓜ Flaminio
A gathering place for German intellectuals, the Via del Corso apartment where Johann Wolfgang von Goethe whooped it up between 1786 and 1788 is now a lovingly maintained museum. Exhibits include documents

relating to his Italian sojourn and some fascinating drawings and etchings – including a 1982 Andy Warhol portrait of the great man. With advance permission, ardent fans can use the library full of first editions.

CHIESA DELLA TRINITÀ DEI MONTI Map pp96–7
☎ 06 679 41 79; Piazza Trinità dei Monti; ☺ 7am-1pm & 3-7pm Tue-Sun; Ⓜ Spagna
Looming over the Spanish Steps, this landmark church was commissioned by King Louis XII of France and consecrated in 1585. Apart from the great views from outside, it boasts some wonderful frescoes by Daniele da Volterra. His Deposizione (Deposition), in the second chapel on the left, is regarded as a masterpiece of mannerist painting. If you don't fancy climbing the steep steps, there's a lift up from Spagna metro station.

VILLA MEDICI Map pp96–7
☎ 06 6 76 11; www.villamedici.it, in French & Italian; Viale Trinità dei Monti 1; ☺ open for events; Ⓜ Spagna
This striking Renaissance palace has been home to the French Academy since the early 19th century. It was built for Cardinal Ricci da Montepulciano in 1540, but Ferdinando dei Medici bought it in 1576 and it remained in Medici hands until Napoleon acquired it in 1801 and gave it to the French Academy. Its most famous resident was Galileo, who was imprisoned here between 1630 and 1633 during his trial for heresy.

These days, the only way to get inside is to visit one of the regular art exhibitions or take a guided tour of the finely landscaped gardens (adult/concession €8/6; ☺ guided tours in Italian & French Wed, Sat & Sun).

TREVI, QUIRINALE & VIA VENETO

Drinking & Nightlife p221; Eating p203; Shopping p182; Sleeping p255

Rising up the slopes of the Quirinale hill, this fascinating district boasts the famous Trevi Fountain, baroque splendours on the Quirinale and *dolce vita* ghosts along Via Vittorio Veneto.

The Trevi Fountain, one of Rome's most iconic monuments, lies at the centre of a warren of medieval streets near Via del Corso. It's a touristy area, full of tacky souvenir shops, rip-off eateries and crap-hawking streetsellers, but you don't have to go far to escape the crowds; in fact, it's often enough just to step off the main thoroughfares and duck into a quiet sidestreet.

A short but steep climb up from here takes you to the top of the Quirinale, where the atmosphere is quite different. The broad expanse of Piazza del Quirinale and the scale of the adjacent Palazzo del Quirinale lend an imposing sense of space and grandeur. The *palazzo*, now the official residence of Italy's head of state, is the most obvious attraction, but just down the road you'll find a couple of important churches by the twin masters of

top picks

TREVI, QUIRINALE & VIA VENETO

- Trevi Fountain (left)
- Galleria Nazionale d'Arte Antica – Palazzo Barberini (p103)
- Palazzo del Quirinale (p102)
- Galleria Colonna (p101)

Roman baroque, Gian Lorenzo Bernini and Francesco Borromini. For one of Europe's greatest works of baroque art, continue northeast to the Chiesa di Santa Maria della Vittoria, home of Bernini's extraordinary *Santa Teresa traffita dall'amore di Dio* (Ecstasy of St Teresa).

Other artistic hotspots in the area include the lavish Galleria Colonna and the Galleria Nazionale d'Arte Antica – Palazzo Barberini, a fabulous gallery containing works by a who's who of Renaissance and baroque artists.

Snaking its way up from Piazza Barberini to the Villa Borghese park, Via Vittorio Veneto is a graceful tree-lined street with a glamorous past. This was the one time hub of *la dolce vita*, where film stars, models and intellectuals would preen and parlay in front of the hovering paparazzi. It has since lost much of its sheen, although it remains an impressive sight with its towering hotels and expensive pavement cafés.

The area's principal gateway is the metro station on Piazza Barberini (line A, Barberini), from where you can walk down Via del Tritone to the Trevi Fountain. Otherwise, regular buses run up and down Via del Tritone. For the Quirinale, your best bet is either to walk up from the Trevi Fountain or from Via Nazionale.

TREVI FOUNTAIN TO THE QUIRINALE

TREVI FOUNTAIN Map p100

Piazza di Trevi; 🚇 Via del Tritone
Immortalised by Anita Ekberg's dip in *La Dolce Vita*, the Trevi Fountain (Fontana di Trevi) is Rome's largest and most famous fountain. The flamboyant baroque ensemble was designed by Nicola Salvi in 1732 and depicts Neptune's chariot being led by Tritons with sea horses – one wild, one docile – representing the moods of the sea. The water comes from the *aqua virgo*, a 1st-century-BC underground aqueduct, and the name Trevi refers to the *tre vie* (three roads) that converge at the fountain.

The famous custom is to throw a coin into the fountain, thus ensuring your return to the Eternal City. According to the same tradition if you throw in a second coin you'll fall in love with an Italian, while a third will have you marrying him or her. And in case you were wondering, the €3000 or so that is thrown away on an average day is hoovered up and donated to charity.

TIME ELEVATOR Map p100

☎ 06 977 46 243; www.time-elevator.it; Via dei Santissimi Apostoli 20; adult/under 12yr €12/9; ☷ 10.30am-7.30pm; 🚇 Piazza Venezia
Just off Via del Corso, the Time Elevator cinema is ideal for armchair sightseers. There are three programs, but the one to see is *Time Elevator Rome,* a 45-minute trip through 3000 years of Roman history. Shows kick off every hour, and children and adults alike will love the panoramic screens, flight-simulator

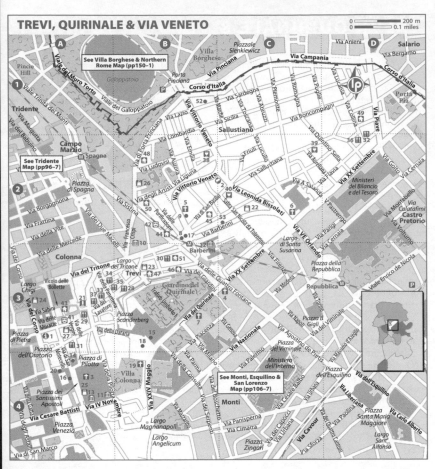

TREVI, QUIRINALE & VIA VENETO

technology and surround-sound system. Note that children under five aren't admitted and anyone who suffers from motion sickness should probably give it a miss.

BASILICA DEI SANTI APOSTOLI Map p100
☎ 06 69 95 71; Piazza dei Santissimi Apostoli; ☼ 7am-noon & 4-7pm; 🚌 Via IV Novembre
This much-altered 6th-century church is dedicated to the apostles James and Philip, whose relics are in the crypt. Its most obvious attraction is the portico with its Renaissance arches and the two-tier façade topped by 13 towering figures. Inside, the flashy baroque interior was completed in 1714 by Carlo and Francesco Fontana. Highlights include the ceiling frescoes by Baciccia and Antonio Canova's grandiose tomb of Pope Clement XIV.

Surrounding the basilica are two imposing baroque *palazzi*: at the end of the square, Palazzo Balestra, which was given to James Stuart, the Old Pretender, in 1719 by Pope Clement XI, and opposite, Palazzo Odelscalchi, with its impressive Bernini façade.

MUSEO DELLE CERE Map p100
☎ 06 679 64 82; www.museodellecereroma.com; Piazza dei Santissimi Apostoli 67; admission €7; ☼ 9am-8pm; 🚌 Via IV Novembre
Madame Tussaud's it ain't, but Rome's waxworks museum does at least provide some light-hearted relief from all the highbrow culture around you. The museum's collection, said to be the world's third largest, comprises more than 250 figures, ranging from Barak Obama to Snow White, Franc-

TREVI, QUIRINALE & VIA VENETO

esco Totti and a whole cast of popes, poets, politicians and murderers.

GALLERIA COLONNA Map p100

☎ 06 678 43 50; www.galleriacolonna.it; Via della Pilotta 17; adult/under 10yr & over 60yr €10/8; ⏰ 9am-1pm Sat, closed Aug; 🚌 Via IV Novembre
The only part of Palazzo Colonna open to the public, this opulent 17th-century gallery houses the Colonna family's private art collection. It's not the capital's largest collection but with works by Salvatore Rosa, Guido Reni, Guercino and Annibale Carracci, it's well worth the ticket price.

The gallery's six rooms are crowned by glorious ceiling frescoes, all dedicated to Marcantonio Colonna, the family's greatest

ancestor, who defeated the Turks at the naval Battle of Lepanto in 1571. Works by Giovanni Coli and Filippo Gherardi in the Great Hall, Sebastiano Ricci in the Landscapes Room and Giuseppe Bartolomeo Chiari in the Throne Room commemorate his efforts. Of the paintings on display, Annibale Carracci's *Mangiafagioli* (The Bean Eater) is generally considered the outstanding masterpiece. Note also the cannonball lodged in the gallery's marble stairs, a vivid reminder of the 1849 siege of Rome.

PIAZZA DEL QUIRINALE Map p100

🚌 Via Nazionale
A wonderful spot to enjoy a glowing Roman sunset, this bare and uneven

MIRACULOUS MADONNAS

Overlooking Vicolo delle Bollette, a tiny lane near the Trevi Fountain, there's a small, simple painting of the Virgin Mary. This is the *Madonna della Pietà*, one of the most famous of Rome's *madonnelle* (small madonnas). There are estimated to be around 730 of these roadside madonnas in Rome's historic centre, most placed on street corners or outside historic *palazzi*. Many were added in the 16th and 17th centuries, but their origins date to pagan times when votive wall shrines were set up at street corners to honour the Lares, household spirits believed to protect passers-by. When Christianity emerged in the 4th century AD, these shrines were simply rededicated to the religion's new icons.

The subject of much popular devotion, they are shrouded in myth. The most famous legend dates to 1796 when news of a French invasion is said to have caused 36 *madonnelle*, including the *Madonna della Pietà*, to move their eyes and some even to cry. A papal commission set up to investigate subsequently declared 26 madonnas to be officially miraculous.

As well as food for the soul, the madonnas also provided a valuable public service. Until street lamps were introduced in the 19th century, the candles and lamps that lit up the images were the city's only source of street lighting.

top picks

FOR CHILDREN

- Colosseum (p67)
- Villa Borghese (p149)
- Bioparco (p149)
- Time Elevator (p99)
- Museo della Civiltà Romana & Planetario (p129)
- Catacombe di San Callisto (p126)
- Capuchin Cemetery (p104)
- Museo delle Cere (p100)
- Explora – Museo dei Bambini di Roma (p153)
- Cinema dei Piccoli (p149)

piazza marks the summit of the Quirinale hill. The obelisk in the centre was moved here from the Mausoleo di Augusto (p95) in 1786 and is flanked by 5.5m statues of Castor and Pollux reining in a couple of rearing horses.

It's not much of a show, but if you're in the neighbourhood on a Sunday you can catch the weekly changing of the guard (6pm in summer, 4pm the rest of the year). More dramatic by far is the classical-music concert staged here on New Year's Eve.

PALAZZO DEL QUIRINALE Map p100

☎ 06 4 69 91; www.quirinale.it; Piazza del Quirinale; adult/over 65yr €5/free; ☻ 8.30am-noon Sun mid-Sep–mid-Jun; 🚇 Via Nazionale
Flanking Piazza del Quirinale, this immense *palazzo* served as the papal summer residence for almost three centuries until the keys were begrudgingly handed over to Italy's new king in 1870. Since 1948, it has been home of the Presidente della Repubblica, Italy's head of state.

Pope Gregory XIII (r 1572–85) originally chose the site for his holiday home and over the course of the next 150 years the top architects of the day worked on it: Domenico Fontana designed the main façade, Carlo Maderno built the chapel, and Bernini was responsible for the *manica lunga* (long sleeve), the austere wing that runs the length of Via del Quirinale.

On the other side of the piazza, the palace's former stables, the Scuderie Papali al Quirinale (☎ 06 399 67 500; www.scuderiequirinale.it; Via XXIV Maggio 16; ☻ depends on exhibition), is now a magnificent exhibition space.

CHIESA DI SANT'ANDREA AL QUIRINALE Map p100

☎ 06 474 08 07; Via del Quirinale 29; ☻ 8.30am-noon & 3.30-7pm Mon-Sat, 9am-noon & 4-7pm Sun; 🚇 Via Nazionale
It's said that in his old age Bernini liked to come and enjoy the peace of this late-17th-century church, regarded by many as one of his greatest. Faced with severe space limitations, he managed to produce a sense of grandeur by designing an elliptical floor plan with a series of chapels opening onto the central area. The opulent interior, decorated with polychrome marble, stucco and gilding, was much appreciated by Pope Alexander VII, who used it while in residence at the Palazzo del Quirinale.

CHIESA DI SAN CARLO ALLE QUATTRO FONTANE Map p100

☎ 06 488 31 09; Via del Quirinale 23; ☻ 10am-1pm & 3-6pm Mon-Fri, 10am-1pm Sat, noon-1pm Sun; 🚇 Via Nazionale
It might not look it, with its filthy façade and unappealing location, but this tiny church is a masterpiece of Roman baroque. It was Borromini's first church and bears all the hallmarks of his genius. The elegant curves of the façade, the play of convex and concave surfaces, the dome illuminated by hidden windows, all combine to transform a minuscule space into a light, airy interior.

The church, completed in 1641, stands at the road intersection known as the Quattro Fontane, after the late-16th-century fountains on its four corners, representing Fidelity, Strength and the Rivers Arno and Tiber.

ROME'S VERSAILLES

If Napoleon had had his way, the Palazzo del Quirinale would have been Rome's Versailles. Journalist and author Corrado Augias explains:

'Napoleon actually chose Rome as his second capital after Paris. He wanted Versailles at Paris and the Palazzo del Quirinale – incidentally, Rome's greatest and most beautiful palace – in Rome. He set artists and architects to prepare it for him and sent down furniture from Paris. In the end he never came and when he was defeated in 1815 the popes took the *palazzo* back for themselves.'

BATTLE OF THE BAROQUE GIANTS

Born within a year of each other, the two giants of Roman baroque hated each other with a vengeance. Gian Lorenzo Bernini (1598–1680), suave, self-confident and politically adept, was the polar opposite of his great rival Francesco Borromini (1599–1677), a solitary and peculiar man who often argued with clients and once had a man beaten half to death.

Their paths first crossed at St Peter's Basilica. Borromini, who had been working as an assistant to Carlo Maderno, a distant relative and the basilica's lead architect, was furious when Bernini was appointed to take over the project on Maderno's death. Nevertheless he stayed on as Bernini's chief assistant and actually contributed to the design of the baldachin – a work for which Bernini took full public credit. To make matters worse, Bernini was later appointed chief architect on Palazzo Barberini, again in the wake of Maderno, and again to Borromini's disgust.

Over the course of the next 45 years, the two geniuses competed for commissions and public acclaim. Bernini flourished under the Barberini pope Urban VIII (r 1623–44) and Borromini under his Pamphilj successor Innocent X (r 1644–1655), but all the while their loathing simmered. Borromini accused Bernini of profiting from his (Borromini's) talents while Bernini claimed that Borromini 'had been sent to destroy architecture'. Certainly, both had very different views on architecture: for Bernini it was all about portraying an experience to elicit an emotional response, while Borromini favoured a more geometrical approach, manipulating classical forms to create dynamic, vibrant spaces.

Of the two, Bernini is generally reckoned to have had the better of the rivalry. His genius was rarely questioned and when he died he was widely regarded as one of Europe's greatest artists. Borromini, on the other hand, struggled to win popular and critical support and after a life of depression committed suicide in 1677.

CHIESA DI SANTA MARIA DELLA VITTORIA Map p100

☎ 06 482 61 90; Via XX Settembre 17; ☺ 8.30am-noon & 3.30-6pm Mon-Sat, 3.30-6pm Sun; Ⓜ Repubblica

Stuck on a busy road junction, this modest and not particularly enticing church is an unlikely setting for one of the great works of European art – Bernini's extravagant and sexually charged *Santa Teresa traffitta dall'amore di Dio* (Ecstasy of St Teresa). In the last chapel on the left, this daring sculpture depicts Teresa, engulfed in the folds of a flowing cloak, floating in ecstasy on a cloud while a teasing angel pierces her repeatedly with a golden arrow. Watching the whole scene from two side balconies are a number of figures, including Cardinal Federico Cornaro, for whom the chapel was built. It's a stunning work, bathed in soft natural light filtering through a concealed window. Go in the afternoon for the best effect.

PIAZZA BARBERINI & VIA VENETO

PIAZZA BARBERINI Map p100

Ⓜ Barberini

More a traffic thoroughfare than a place to linger, this noisy square is named after the Barberini family, one of Rome's great dynastic clans (see the boxed text, p81). In the centre, the Bernini-designed Fontana del Tritone (Fountain of the Triton) depicts the sea-god Triton blowing a stream of water

from a conch while seated in a large scallop shell supported by four dolphins. Bernini also crafted the Fontana delle Api (Fountain of the Bees) in the northeastern corner, again for the Barberini family, whose crest featured three bees in flight.

GALLERIA NAZIONALE D'ARTE ANTICA – PALAZZO BARBERINI Map p100

☎ 06 225 82 493; www.galleriaborghese.it; Via delle Quattro Fontane 13; adult/EU 18-25yr/EU under 18yr & over 65yr €5/2.50/free plus €1 reservation fee; ☺ 9am-7.30pm Tue-Sun, ticket office closes 7pm; Ⓜ Barberini

A must for anyone into Renaissance and baroque art, this sumptuous gallery is housed in one of Rome's most spectacular *palazzi*. Commissioned by the Barberini pope Urban VIII in 1623, it was worked on by a who's-who of 17th-century architects, including Carlo Maderno, Gian Lorenzo Bernini and Francesco Borromini – check out their rival staircases within the building. Pietro da Cortona painted the breathtaking fresco *Trionfo della Divina Provvidenza* (Triumph of Divine Providence), in the main 1st-floor salon, between 1633 and 1639.

The gallery, on the 1st floor, contains a superb selection of 16th- to 17th-century works, including paintings by Raphael, Caravaggio, Guido Reni, Bernini and Holbein.

Highlights include Raphael's lovely *La Fornarina* (The Baker's Girl), a portrait of his mistress who worked in a Trastevere bakery; the luminous *Annunziazione*

(Annunciation) by Filippo Lippi; Guido Reni's *Ritratto di Beatrice Cenci* (Portrait of Beatrice Cenci); and Hans Holbein's famous *Ritratto di Enrico VIII* (Portrait of Henry VIII), painted on the day Henry married Anne of Cleves. Caravaggio fans will delight in his gruesome *Giuditta taglia la testa a Oloferne* (Judith Beheading Holofernes; c 1597–1600), and *Narcisso* (Narcissus; c 1571–1610).

CHIESA DI SANTA MARIA DELLA CONCEZIONE Map p100

☎ 06 487 11 85; Via Vittorio Veneto 27; admission by donation; ⏰ 9am-noon & 3-6pm Fri-Wed; Ⓜ Barberini

There's nothing special about this 17th-century church but dip into the Capuchin cemetery below and you'll be gobsmacked. Everything from the picture frames to the light fittings is made of human bones. Between 1528 and 1870 the resident Capuchin monks used the bones of 4000 of their departed brothers to create the mesmerising and macabre display. There's an arch crafted from hundreds of skulls, vertebrae used as fleurs-de-lys, and light fixtures made of femurs.

VIA VITTORIO VENETO Map p100

Ⓜ Barberini

Curving up from Piazza Barberini to Villa Borghese, Via Vittorio Veneto is the spiritual home of *la dolce vita*. The atmosphere of Fellini's Rome has long gone, and the street today, while still impressive, is largely given over to tourism. Luxury hotels occupy many of the towering streetside *palazzi* while waistcoated waiters stand on the tree-lined pavement, tempting passers-by into their overpriced restaurants. The huge building on the right as you walk up is the US embassy.

GAGOSIAN GALLERY Map p100

☎ 06 420 86 498; www.gagosian.com; Via Francesco Crispi 16; admission free; ⏰ 10.30am-7pm Tue-Sat; Ⓜ Barberini

Since it opened in 2007, the Rome branch of Larry Gagosian's contemporary art empire has hosted the big names of modern art: Cy Twombly, Damien Hirst and Lawrence Weiner, to name a few. The gallery, which was designed by Roman architect Firouz Galdo and Englishman Caruso St John, offers 750 sq m of exhibition space in a stylishly converted 1920s bank, complete with a theatrical neoclassical colonnaded façade.

Drinking & Nightlife p221; Eating p204; Shopping p183; Sleeping p256

Cutting a swath through the eastern half of central Rome, this busy quadrant stretches up the Esquilino hill to Stazione Termini, Rome's main transport hub, and beyond to San Lorenzo. It's a large and cosmopolitan area with something for everyone: there's the cheap Termini district with its bargain-basement shops and budget *pensioni* (guesthouses), there's Monti with its village vibe and kooky boutiques, and there's the student enclave of San Lorenzo. You'll find cheap drinking dens and critically acclaimed restaurants, monumental basilicas and fabulous museums.

Although the Esquilino covers a large chunk of east-central Rome, the term is popularly used to describe the scruffy area around Stazione Termini and Piazza Vittorio Emanuele II. Once a smart residential development, today this is the capital's most multicultural neighbourhood, the closest Rome has to a Chinatown.

Heading downhill, the busy and unlovely Via Cavour leads down to the dishy Monti district. Sandwiched between Via Cavour and Via Nazionale, this was the ancient city's notorious Suburra slum – a sleazy red-light district and the childhood home of Julius Caesar – but is now a charming neighbourhood of hidden eateries, bohemian shops and cool bars.

Art lovers will have their work cut out on the Esquilino. Near Termini the Museo Nazionale Romano: Palazzo Massimo alle Terme displays stunning classical art, while the streets around Piazza Santa Maria Maggiore harbour some of Rome's finest medieval churches, including the towering Basilica di Santa Maria Maggiore. Down near the Colosseum, the underground chambers of the Domus Aurea are all that's left of Nero's huge palace complex.

For a break from classical and religious art, head over to San Lorenzo, a lively student quarter east of Termini. Long a hotbed of radical activity – in the 1920s the area's predominantly working-class population took to the streets against the Fascists – it was one of the few parts of Rome to be bombed in WWII. It doesn't have a lot to see unless you're a fan of graffitied walls or flyover architecture, but after dark it's one of the capital's hippest areas. A quick tram ride to the southeast, Pigneto is one of the city's up-and-coming areas. House prices are rising and its bars and funky offbeat shops attract a regular crowd of artists and fashion-conscious urbanites.

Termini is the city's main transport hub, with metro connections to Piazza della Repubblica (Repubblica, line A) and Via Cavour (Cavour, line B) and regular buses down to Via Nazionale.

top picks

MONTI, ESQUILINO & SAN LORENZO

- Museo Nazionale Romano: Palazzo Massimo alle Terme (p111)
- Basilica di San Pietro in Vincoli (p110)
- Chiesa di Santa Prassede (p109)
- Chiesa di Santa Maria della Vittoria (p103)
- Basilica di Santa Maria Maggiore (left)
- Domus Aurea (p110)

ESQUILINO

BASILICA DI SANTA MARIA MAGGIORE Map pp106–7

☎ 06 698 86 800; Piazza Santa Maria Maggiore; ⏰ 7am-7pm; 🚌 Piazza Santa Maria Maggiore

One of Rome's four patriarchal basilicas, this monumental church stands on the summit of the Esquilino hill, on the spot where snow is said to have miraculously fallen in the summer of AD 358. To commemorate the event every 5 August thousands of white petals are released from the basilica's coffered ceiling.

Although the huge interior retains its original 5th-century structure, the basilica has been much altered over the centuries: the 75m belfry, the highest in Rome, is 14th-century Romanesque; Ferdinand Fuga's 1741 façade is baroque, as is much of the sumptuous interior; and the nave floor is a fine example of 12th-century Cosmati paving. The main draws are the 5th-century mosaics in the triumphal arch and nave. You'll need a pair of binoculars to do them justice, but if you can see that high, they depict various Old Testament scenes. The

MONTI, ESQUILINO & SAN LORENZO

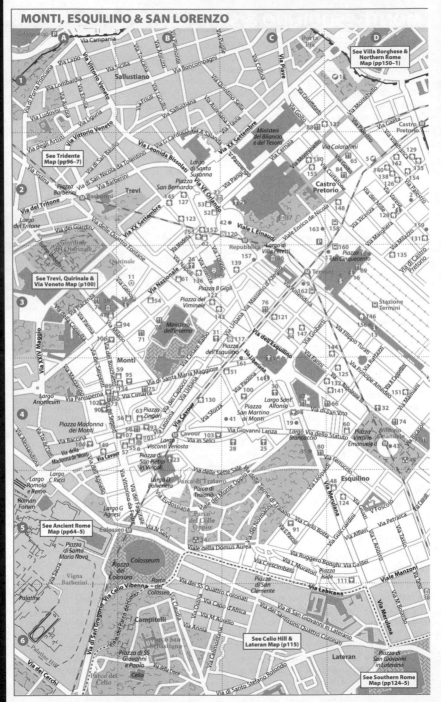

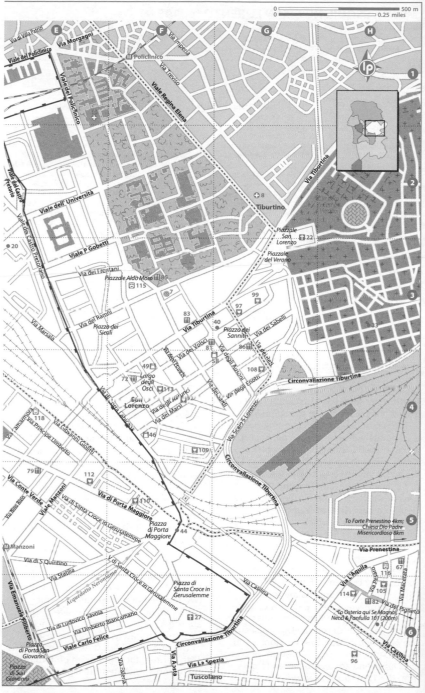

MONTI, ESQUILINO & SAN LORENZO (pp106–7)

central image in the apse, signed by Jacopo Torriti, dates from the 13th century and represents the coronation of the Virgin Mary.

The baldachin (canopy) over the high altar is elaborately decorated with gilt cherubs; the altar itself is a porphyry sarcophagus, which is said to contain the relics of St Matthew and other martyrs. Note the plaque to the right of the altar marking the spot where Gian Lorenzo Bernini and his father Pietro are buried. Steps lead down to the *confessio* (a crypt in which relics are placed) where a statue of Pope Pius IX kneels before a reliquary containing a fragment of Jesus' manger.

The sumptuously decorated Cappella Sistina was built by Domenico Fontana in the 16th century and contains the tombs of Popes Sixtus V and Pius V. Opposite is the flamboyant Cappella Paolina Borghesiana, erected in the 17th century by Pope Paul V. The *Madonna col Bambino* (Madonna and Child) panel above the altar, surrounded by lapis lazuli and agate, is believed to date from the 12th to 13th centuries.

Through the souvenir shop on the right-hand side of the church is a museum (adult/child €4/2; ☯ 9am-6pm) with a rather motley collection of religious artefacts. More interesting is the upper loggia (☎ 06 698 86 802; €5; ☯ guided tours by reservation only), where you'll find some wonderful 13th-century mosaics.

CHIESA DI SANTA PUDENZIANA

Map pp106–7

☎ 06 481 46 22; Via Urbana 160; ☯ 8.30am-noon & 3-6pm; Ⓜ Cavour

This, the church of Rome's Filipino community, boasts a sparkling 4th-century apse mosaic, the oldest of its kind in Rome. An enthroned Christ is flanked by two female figures who are crowning St Peter and St Paul; on either side of them are the apostles dressed as Roman senators. Unfortunately, you can only see 10 of the original 12 apostles, as a barbarous 16th-century facelift lopped off two of them and amputated the legs of the others.

MONTI, ESQUILINO & SAN LORENZO (pp106–7)

CHIESA DI SANTA PRASSEDE Map pp106–7
☎ 06 488 24 56; Via Santa Prassede 9a;
🕑 7.30am-noon & 4-6.30pm; 🚍 Piazza Santa Maria Maggiore

Famous for its brilliant mosaics, this 9th-century church is dedicated to St Praxedes, an early Christian heroine who hid Christians fleeing persecution and buried those that she couldn't save in a well. The position of the well is now marked by a marble disc on the floor of the nave.

The mosaics, produced by artists that Pope Paschal I had brought in specially from Byzantium, bear all the hallmarks of their eastern creators, with bold gold backgrounds and a marked Christian symbolism. The apse mosaics depict Christ flanked by saints Peter, Pudentiana and Zeno on the right, and Paul, Praxedes and Pope Paschal on the left. All the figures have golden halos except for Paschal, whose head is shadowed by a blue nimbus to indicate that he was still alive at the time. Further treasures await In the heavily mosaiced Cappella di San Zenone, including a piece of the column to which Christ was tied when he was flogged – it's in the glass case on the right.

MUSEO NAZIONALE D'ARTE ORIENTALE Map pp106–7
☎ 06 469 74 832; www.museoorientale.it; adult/concession/EU under 18yr & over 65yr €6/3/free;
🕑 9am-2pm Tue-Fri, 9am-7.30pm Sat & Sun;
Ⓜ Vittorio Emanuele

Rome's little-known but impressive National Museum of Oriental Art offers a welcome break from all the ruins, Michelangelos and Caravaggios that litter the rest of the city. Its comprehensive collection of Near and Far Eastern artefacts runs the gamut from 15th-century Kubachi ceramics to painted Tibetan fans and intricate Nepalese textiles. Among the oldest pieces are finds from Shahr-i Sokhta, a city in eastern Iran dating to the 4th millennium BC, and a series of ceramic vases and terracotta figurines from an Iron Age necropolis in northwestern Pakistan.

CHIESA DI SAN MARTINO AI MONTI
Map pp106–7

☎ 06 487 31 66; Viale del Monte Oppio 28;
🕑 7.30am-noon & 4-7pm; Ⓜ Cavour

In the 3rd century this was already a place of worship – Christians would meet here, in what was then the home of a Roman named Equitius. In the 4th century, after Christianity was legalised, a church was constructed and subsequently rebuilt in the 6th and 9th centuries. It was then completely transformed by Filippo Gagliardi in the 1650s. Of note are Gagliardi's frescoes of the Basilica di San Giovanni in Laterano before it was rebuilt in the mid-17th century and St Peter's Basilica before it assumed its present 16th-century look.

CHIESA DI SANTA LUCIA IN SELCI
Map pp106–7

☎ 06 482 76 23; Via in Selci 82; 🕑 9.30-10.30am Sun; Ⓜ Cavour

A small church best known for its 17th-century Borromini interior, Chiesa di Santa Lucia in Selci dates to some time before the 8th century. It's not open to the public, except for Mass on Sunday morning, but if you ring the bell and ask the resident nuns nicely they'll probably let you in.

BASILICA DI SAN PIETRO IN VINCOLI
Map pp106–7

☎ 06 488 28 65; Piazza di San Pietro in Vincoli 4a; 🕑 8am-12.30pm & 3.30-7pm Apr-Sep, 8am-12.30pm & 3-6pm Oct-Mar; Ⓜ Cavour

Pilgrims and art lovers flock to this 5th-century church for two reasons: to marvel at Michelangelo's macho sculpture of Moses and to see the chains that bound St Peter when he was imprisoned in the Carcere Mamertino (p69).

The church was built in the 5th century specially to house these shackles, which had been sent to Constantinople after the saint's death but were later returned as relics. They arrived in two pieces and legend has it that when they were reunited they miraculously joined together. They are now displayed under the altar.

To the right of the altar, Michelangelo's colossal *Moses* (1505) forms the centrepiece of Pope Julius II's unfinished tomb. On either side of the prophet are statues of Leah and Rachel, probably completed by Michelangelo's students. Moses, who sports a magnificent waist-length beard

and two small horns sticking out of his head, has been studied for centuries, most famously by Sigmund Freud in a 1914 essay *The Moses of Michelangelo*. The horns were inspired by a mistranslation of a biblical passage: where the original said that rays of light issued from Moses' face, the translator wrote 'horns'. Michelangelo was aware of the mistake, but he gave Moses horns anyway.

Despite the tomb's imposing scale, it was never completed – Michelangelo originally envisaged 40 statues but he got sidetracked by the Sistine Chapel, and Pope Julius was buried in St Peter's Basilica.

DOMUS AUREA Map pp106–7

☎ 06 399 67 700; www.pierreci.it; Viale della Domus Aurea; 🕑 closed for restoration; Ⓜ Colosseo

A monumental exercise in vanity, the Domus Aurea (Golden House) was Nero's great gift to himself. Built after the fire of AD 64 and named after the gold that covered its façade, it was a huge palace complex covering much of the Palatino (Palatine), Oppio (Oppian) and Celio (Caelian) hills. Its grounds, which included an artificial lake, covered up to a third of the city.

It's estimated only around 20% remains of the original complex – Nero's successors attempted to raze all trace of his megalomania. Vespasian drained the lake and built the Colosseum, Domitian built a palace on the Palatino, and Trajan constructed a baths complex on the Oppio using the Domus Aurea as a foundation. This is the area that is currently being excavated. The baths and underlying ruins were abandoned by the 6th century. During the Renaissance, artists (including Ghirlandaio, Perugino and Raphael) lowered themselves into the ruins in order to study the frescoed grottoes and to doodle on the walls. All of them later used motifs from the Domus Aurea frescoes in their work.

PIAZZA VITTORIO EMANUELE II
Map pp106–7

Ⓜ Vittorio Emanuele

Laid out in the late 19th century as the centrepiece of an upmarket residential district, Rome's biggest square is a noisy, brash affair surrounded by speeding traffic, porticoes and bargain stores. Within the fenced-off central section are the ruins of Trofei di Mario, once a fountain at the end of an aqueduct.

In the northern corner, the Chiesa di Sant'Eusebio (☯ 8.30-9.30am & 6.15-7.15pm Mon-Sat, 8.30-11.30am & 6.15-7.45pm Sun) is popular with pet-owners who bring their animals to be blessed on St Anthony's feast day (17 January). The square itself hosts cultural festivals throughout the year and an outdoor film festival in the summer.

PORTA MAGGIORE Map pp106–7
Piazza di Porta Maggiore; 🚃 Porta Maggiore
Porta Maggiore was built by Claudius in AD 52. Then, as now, it was a major road junction under which passed the two main southbound roads, Via Prenestina and Via Labicana (modern-day Via Casilina). The arch supported two aqueducts – the Acqua Claudia and the Acqua Aniene Nuova – and was later incorporated into the Aurelian Wall.

CHIESA DI SANTA CROCE IN GERUSALEMME Map pp106–7
☎ 06 701 47 69; www.basilicasantacroce.com; Piazza di Santa Croce in Gerusalemme 12; ☯ 7am-1pm & 2-7.30pm; 🚃 Piazza di Porta Maggiore
One of Rome's seven pilgrimage churches, the Chiesa di Santa Croce in Gerusalemme was founded in 320 by St Helena, mother of Emperor Constantine. It takes its name from the Christian relics, including a piece of Christ's cross and St Thomas' doubting finger, that St Helena brought to Rome from Jerusalem. The relics are housed in a chapel at the end of the left-hand aisle. Of particular note are the lovely 15th-century Renaissance apse frescoes representing the legends of the Cross.

MUSEO STORICO DELLA LIBERAZIONE Map pp106–7
☎ 06 700 38 66; www.viatasso.eu; Via Tasso 145; admission free; ☯ 9.30am-12.30pm Tue-Sun & 3.30-7.30pm Tue, Thu & Fri; Ⓜ Manzoni
Now a small museum, Via Tasso 145 was the headquarters of the German SS during the Nazi occupation of Rome (1943–44). Members of the resistance were interrogated, tortured and imprisoned in the cells and you can still see graffiti scrawled on the walls by condemned prisoners. Exhibits, which include photos, documents and improvised weapons, chart the events of the occupation with particular emphasis on the persecution of the Jews, the underground resistance and the Fosse Ardeatina massacre (p126).

PIAZZA DELLA REPUBBLICA & AROUND

PIAZZA DELLA REPUBBLICA Map pp106–7
Ⓜ Repubblica
Flanked by grand neoclassical colonnades, this landmark piazza was laid out as part of Rome's post-unification makeover. It follows the lines of the semicircular *exedra* (benched portico) of Diocletian's baths complex (p112) and was originally known as Piazza Esedra. In the centre, the Fontana delle Naiadi aroused puritanical ire when it was unveiled by architect Mario Rutelli in 1901. The nudity of the four naiads or water nymphs, who surround the central figure of Glaucus wrestling a fish, was considered too provocative.

MUSEO NAZIONALE ROMANO: PALAZZO MASSIMO ALLE TERME Map pp106–7
☎ 06 399 67 700; www.pierreci.it; Largo di Villa Peretti 1; adult/EU 18-24yr/EU under 18yr & over 65yr €7/3.50/free plus possible €3 exhibition supplement, audioguide €4; ☯ 9am-7.45pm Tue-Sun; Ⓜ Termini
Often overshadowed by the city's better-known museums, this is a real highlight, a stunning, light-filled museum spilling over with spectacular classical art.
The ground and 1st floors are given over to sculpture from the 2nd century BC to the 5th century AD. This is all about glorification of Rome's early leaders – check out the depiction of Augustus as Pontifex Maximus in Sala V on the ground floor. In the same room, don't miss the marble frieze from

top picks

MUSEUMS & GALLERIES

- Museo e Galleria Borghese (p148)
- Vatican Museums (p142)
- Museo Nazionale Romano: Palazzo Massimo Alle Terme (above)
- Capitoline Museums (p70)
- Galleria Nazionale d'Arte Antica – Palazzo Barberini (p103)
- Palazzo e Galleria Doria Pamphilj (p93)
- Museo dell'Ara Pacis (p95)
- Museo Nazionale Romano: Palazzo Altemps (p79)
- Museo Nazionale Etrusco di Villa Giulia (p152)
- Galleria Nazionale d'Arte Moderna (p152)

the Basilica Aemilia in the Roman Forum (p67), which depicts scenes from the origin of Rome. In Sala VI next door, the 5th-century BC *Niobide degli Horti Sallustiani* (Niobide from the Gardens of Sallust) depicts one of the 14 children of Niobe. According to legend, all 14 were killed by Apollo and Artemis in retaliation for Niobe insulting their mother Leto.

More gems, including a ravaged, voluptuous *Afrodite* from Villa Adriana (p278) at Tivoli, are found on the 1st floor, but the sensational mosaics and frescoes on the 2nd floor blow everything else away. These include richly coloured paintings from an Augustan-era villa, including *cubicula* (bedrooms) frescoes with religious, erotic and theatre subjects, and landscape paintings from the *triclinium* (dining room).

Stealing the limelight, though, are the garden paintings (dating from 20–10 BC) from Villa Livia, one of the homes of Augustus' wife Livia Drusilla. Excavated in the 19th century, these stunning frescoes depict an illusionary garden with all the plants in full bloom. The room in which they were originally painted was probably a summer *triclinium*, a large living and dining area built half underground to provide protection from the heat.

The museum also boasts a stunning collection of inlaid marble and mosaics, including (in Sala VII) the surviving wall mosaics from a *nymphaeum* (shrine to the water nymph) at Nero's villa in Anzio.

MUSEO NAZIONALE ROMANO: TERME DI DIOCLEZIANO Map pp106–7

☎ 06 399 67 700; www.pierreci.it; Viale Enrico de Nicola 78; adult/EU 18-24yr/EU under 18yr & over 65yr €7/3.50/free plus possible €3 exhibition supplement, audioguide €4; ⏰ 9am-7.45pm Tue-Sun; Ⓜ Termini

Over the road from Piazza dei Cinquecento are the remains of the Terme di Diocleziano (Diocletian's Baths), Ancient Rome's largest baths complex, which covered about 13 hectares and could hold up to 3000 people. It was completed in the early 4th century but fell into disrepair after invaders destroyed the feeder aqueduct in about 536.

The ground and 1st-floor galleries contain a large collection of vases, amphorae and household objects in terracotta and bronze. Among the highlights are three stunning terracotta statues of seated female figures that were found in Ariccia,

southeast of Rome. The extensive 2nd-floor galleries contain artefacts (mainly burial objects such as jewellery and domestic items) dating from the 11th to 6th centuries BC.

Outside, Michelangelo's elegant cloister is lined with classical sarcophagi, headless statues and huge sculptured animal heads, thought to have come from the Foro di Traiano (p69).

To the north, the Aula Ottagona (Piazza della Repubblica; admission free; ⏰ 9am-2pm Mon-Sat, 9am-1pm Sun), which is often closed due to staff shortages, houses yet more Roman sculpture.

CHIESA DI SANTA MARIA DEGLI ANGELI Map p106–7

☎ 06 488 08 12; www.santamariadegliangeliroma .it; Piazza della Repubblica; ⏰ 7am-6.30pm Mon-Sat, 7am-7.30pm Sun; Ⓜ Repubblica

This hulking basilica occupies what was once the central hall of Diocletian's baths complex. It was originally designed by Michelangelo, but only the great vaulted ceiling remains from his plans. Today the chief attraction is the 18th-century double meridian in the transept, one tracing the polar star and the other telling the precise time of the sun's zenith (sunlight enters through a hole to the right of the window above the entrance to the church's right wing). Until 1846, this sundial was used to regulate all Rome's clocks.

CHIESA DI SAN PAOLO ENTRO LE MURA Map pp106–7

☎ 06 488 33 39; www.stpaulsrome.it; cnr Via Nazionale & Via Napoli; ⏰ 9am-2pm Mon-Fri, 8.30am-7pm Sun; ◻ Via Nazionale

With its stripy neo-Gothic exterior and prominent position, Rome's American Episcopal church is something of a landmark. Inside, the unusual 19th-century mosaics, designed by the Birmingham-born Edward Burne-Jones, feature the faces of his famous contemporaries. In his representation of *The Church on Earth,* St Ambrose (on the extreme right of the centre group) has JP Morgan's face, and General Garibaldi and Abraham Lincoln (wearing a green tunic) are among the warriors. In the small garden outside there are a number of modern sculptures.

PALAZZO DELLE ESPOSIZIONI
Map pp106–7

☎ 06 399 67 500; www.palazzoesposizioni.it, in Italian; Via Nazionale 194; ⏰ depends on exhibition; ◻ Via Nazionale

This huge neoclassical palace is Rome's premier cultural centre. Boasting cathedral-scale exhibition spaces, art labs, a bookshop, café and restaurant, it hosts everything from multimedia events and art exhibitions to concert performances, film screenings and conferences. Blockbuster events have included a Mark Rothko retrospective, a photo exhibition dedicated to Bruce Chatwin and a celebration of Charles Darwin's centenary. In various former lives, the *palazzo* served as HQ for the Italian Communist Party, a mess for allied servicemen, a polling station and even a public loo.

SAN LORENZO & BEYOND

BASILICA DI SAN LORENZO FUORI LE MURA Map pp106–7
☎ 06 49 15 11; Piazzale San Lorenzo; ☯ 8am-noon & 4-6.30pm; ☒ Piazzale del Verano
The only one of Rome's major churches to have suffered bomb damage in WWII, the Basilica of St Lawrence Outside the Walls is one of Rome's four patriarchal basilicas. An atmospheric, tranquil place, it's a hotchpotch of rebuilds and restorations. The original church was constructed in the 4th century over St Lawrence's burial place, but rebuilt 200 years later. Subsequently a nearby 5th-century church was incorporated, resulting in the church you see today. The nave, portico and much of the decoration date to the 13th century.

Highlights are the Cosmati floor and the frescoed portico, depicting events from St Lawrence's life. The remains of St Lawrence and St Stephen are in the church crypt beneath the high altar. A pretty barrel-vaulted cloister contains inscriptions and sarcophagi and leads to the Catacombe di Santa Ciriaca, where St Lawrence was initially buried.

CIMITERO DI CAMPO VERANO
Map pp106–7
☎ 06 492 36 349; Piazzale del Verano; ☯ 7.30am-6pm Apr-Sep, 7.30am-5pm Oct-Mar; ☒ Piazzale del Verano

The city's largest cemetery dates to the Napoleonic occupation of Rome between 1804 and 1814, when an edict ordered that the city's dead must be buried outside the city walls. Between the 1830s and the 1980s virtually all Catholics who died in Rome (with the exception of popes, cardinals and royalty) were buried here. If you are in the area, it is worth a look for its grand tombs, although try to avoid 2 November (All Souls' Day), when thousands of Romans flock to the cemetery to leave flowers on the tombs of loved ones.

PASTIFICIO CERERE Map pp106–7
☎ 06 454 22 960; www.pastificiocerere.com; Via degli Ausoni 7; ☯ 3-7pm Mon-Fri; ☒ Via Tiburtina
This hub of Rome's contemporary art scene started life as a pasta factory in 1905. Abandoned in 1960, it came to prominence as home of the Nuova Scuola Romana (New Roman School), a group of six artists who set the nation's art scene alight in the early 1980s. More than 30 years on and a new generation of artists has moved in, including Maurizio Savini, famous for his pink chewing gum sculptures. To visit the complex, email the Fondazione del Pastificio Cerere via the website, specifying which studios you'd like to visit.

CHIESA DIO PADRE MISERICORDIOSO off Map pp106–7
☎ 06 231 58 33; www.diopadremisericordioso.it; Via Francesco Tovaglieri 147; ☯ 7.30am-12.30pm & 3.30-7.30pm; ☒ Via Francesco Tovaglieri
Rome's first minimalist church, this startling white Richard Meier creation is a classic of contemporary design. Built out of concrete, stucco, travertine and 976 sq m of glass, it is flanked on one side by three graduated concrete shells, while on the other side a four-storey atrium connects the church with a community centre.

Drinking & Nightlife p224; Eating p207; Shopping p184; Sleeping p261

One of Rome's original seven hills, the Celio rises to the south of the Colosseum. A good place to escape the crowds, it's near enough to the action to be accessible but far enough away to offer a break from the city's frenetic noise.

In imperial times this was a smart residential district, home to wealthy nobles and politicians. Less pampered were the four-legged residents of the local zoo, who were kept here in preparation for their 15 minutes in the Colosseum. At the top of the Celio, Villa Celimontana is a lush park with well-tended lawns and pretty flower beds. For most of the year it's a serene spot, but in summer it bursts into life as host of the Villa Celimontana jazz festival.

Nearby, and buried under one of the area's many medieval churches, are the Roman houses where the apostles John and Paul are supposed to have lived. Underground treasures also await at the Basilica di San Clemente, a 12th-century church built atop a 2nd-century pagan temple (among other things).

The focal point of the largely residential Lateran district is its monumental cathedral, the Basilica di San Giovanni in Laterano. This is Rome's cathedral, even though it's not technically Roman property – the Vatican has extraterritorial authority over it, and as such it belongs to the independent Vatican state. Apart from the basilica and the Scala Santa, a staircase said by believers to be the one that Jesus walked up in Pontius Pilate's palace in Jerusalem, there's not a great deal to see around here. There is, however, a lively clothes market on Via Sannio that can be fun to browse through.

San Giovanni is served by its own metro station (San Giovanni), although it's perfectly possible to walk up to the basilica from the Colosseum by way of Via di San Giovanni in Laterano. The Celio is a short uphill walk from Via di San Gregorio.

top picks

CELIO HILL & LATERAN

- Basilica di San Clemente (p116)
- Chiesa di SS Quattro Coronati (p116)
- Basilica di San Giovanni in Laterano (p116)
- Scala Santa & Sancta Sanctorum (p117)

CELIO

CHIESA DI SAN GREGORIO MAGNO
Map p115

☎ 06 700 82 27; Piazza di San Gregorio 1; ⏱ 8.30am-12.30pm & 3-6.30pm; Ⓜ Circo Massimo

You have to ring the bell for admission to this looming church, which is built on the site where Pope Gregory the Great is said to have dispatched St Augustine to convert the British to Christianity. Originally it was the pope's family home but in 575 he converted it into a monastery. It was rebuilt in the 17th century and the interior was given a baroque facelift a century later.

Inside, the stately 1st-century-BC marble throne in the Cappella di San Gregorio is believed to have been St Gregory's personal perch. Outside, in the grounds to the left of the church are three impressively frescoed chapels: the Cappella di Santa Silvia, the Cappella di Sant'Andrea and the Capella di Santa Barbara.

CHIESA DI SS GIOVANNI E PAOLO
Map p115

☎ 06 700 57 45; Piazza di SS Giovanni e Paolo; ⏱ 8.30am-noon & 3.30-6pm Mon-Thu; Ⓜ Colosseo or Circo Massimo

While there's little of interest at this much-tweaked 4th-century church, the Roman houses that lie beneath it are fascinating. According to tradition, the apostles John and Paul lived in the Case Romane (☎ 06 704 54 544; www.caseromane.it; adult/12-18yr & over 65yr/under 12yr €6/4/free; ⏱ 10am-1pm & 3-6pm Thu-Mon) before they were beheaded by Constantine's anti-Christian successor, Julian. There's no direct evidence for this, although research has revealed that the houses were used for Christian worship. There are more than 20 rooms, many of them richly decorated. Entry is to the side of the church on Clivo di

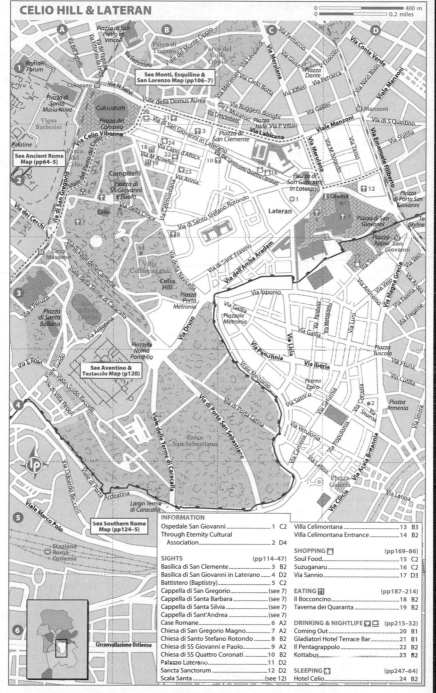

CELIO HILL & LATERAN

0 ——————— 400 m
0 ——————— 0.2 miles

INFORMATION
Ospedale San Giovanni 1 C2
Through Eternity Cultural
Association 2 D4

SIGHTS (pp114–47)
Basilica di San Clemente 3 B2
Basilica di San Giovanni in Laterano 4 D2
Battistero (Baptistry) 5 C2
Cappella di San Gregorio ....(see 7)
Cappella di Santa Barbara ....(see 7)
Cappella di Santa Silvia ....(see 7)
Cappella di Sant'Andrea ....(see 7)
Case Romane 6 A2
Chiesa di San Gregorio Magno 7 A2
Chiesa di Santo Stefano Rotondo 8 B2
Chiesa di SS Giovanni e Paolo 9 A2
Chiesa di SS Quattro Coronati 10 B2
Palazzo Lateranense 11 D2
Sancta Sanctorum 12 D2
Scala Santa ....(see 12)

Villa Celimontana 13 B3
Villa Celimontana Entrance 14 B2

SHOPPING (pp169–86)
Soul Food 15 C2
Suzuganaru 16 C2
Via Sannio 17 D3

EATING (pp187–214)
Il Bocconcino 18 B2
Taverna dei Quaranta 19 B2

DRINKING & NIGHTLIFE (pp215–32)
Coming Out 20 B1
Gladiatori Hotel Terrace Bar 21 B1
Il Pentagrappolo 22 B2
Kottabus 23 B2

SLEEPING (pp247–64)
Hotel Celio 24 B2

115

Scauro. Guided tours are available in English on request.

VILLA CELIMONTANA Map p115

🕐 7am-sunset; 🚌 Via della Navicella

With its lawns and colourful flower beds, this leafy walled park is a wonderful place to escape the crowds and enjoy a summer picnic. Romantic couples can seek out shady corners while parents can earn goodwill by letting their loved ones loose at the playground. At the centre of the park is a 16th-century villa that was once owned by the Mattei family but now houses the Italian Geographical Society. Each summer the park stages a much-loved jazz festival (see p87).

CHIESA DI SANTO STEFANO ROTONDO Map p115

☎ 06 704 93 717; Via di Santo Stefano Rotondo 7; admission by reservation; 🕐 9.30am-12.30pm Tue-Sun & 3-6pm Tue-Sat; 🚌 Via della Navicella

'Such a panorama of horror and butchery no man could imagine in his sleep, though he were to eat a whole pig, raw, for supper.' So wrote Charles Dickens after seeing the 16th-century frescoes at this otherwise tranquil church. The X-rated images graphically depict the various ways in which martyrs were killed in early Christendom.

The church, one of Rome's oldest, dates to the late 5th century, although it was subsequently altered in the 12th and 15th centuries.

CHIESA DI SS QUATTRO CORONATI
Map p115

☎ 06 704 75 427; Via dei Santissimi Quattro Coronati 20; 🕐 church 6.15am-8pm Mon-Sat, 6.45am-12.30pm & 3-7.30pm Sun, Cappella di San Silvestro & cloisters 9.30am-noon & 4.30-6pm Mon-Sat, 9-10.40am & 4-5.45pm Sun; 🚌 or 🚃 Via Labicana

This brooding 4th-century church, rebuilt as a fortified convent after it was destroyed during the 1084 Norman sack of Rome, is dedicated to four Christian sculptors who were killed by Diocletian for refusing to make a statue of a pagan god. As a result, it's still revered by stone-cutters and masons. The most famous feature is the Cappella di San Silvestro and its well-preserved 13th-century frescoes depicting the story of the Donation of Constantine, a famous document by which Constantine ceded control of Rome and the West to the papacy. The donation, in fact a document

forged by the Vatican, was allegedly presented to Sylvester after the devout priest cured the emperor of leprosy.

Also of interest are the beautiful 13th-century cloisters and garden off the northern aisle (ring the bell for admission).

BASILICA DI SAN CLEMENTE Map p115

☎ 06 774 00 21; www.basilicasanclemente.com; Via di San Giovanni in Laterano; admission church/excavations free/€5; 🕐 9am-12.30pm & 3-6pm Mon-Sat, noon-6pm Sun; Ⓜ Colosseo

This fascinating basilica provides a vivid glimpse into Rome's multilayered past: a 12th-century basilica built over a 4th-century church, which, in turn, was constructed over a 2nd-century pagan temple and 1st-century Roman house. Beneath everything are foundations dating to the Roman Republic.

The medieval church features a marvellous 12th-century apse mosaic depicting the *Trionfo della Croce* (Triumph of the Cross), with 12 doves symbolising the apostles and a crowd of bystanders including the Madonna, St John, St John the Baptist and other saints. Though stunning, it's eclipsed by the Renaissance frescoes in the Chapel of St Catherine, which recount scenes from the life of the saint, who was strapped to a wheel and tortured to death (hence the circular firework named after her). The 4th-century church below, the *basilica inferiore*, was mostly destroyed by Norman invaders in 1084, but some faded 11th-century frescoes remain, illustrating the life of St Clement.

Follow the steps down another level and you'll find yourself walking an ancient lane leading to the Roman house and a dark temple of Mithras, which contains an altar depicting the god slaying a bull. Beneath it all, you can hear the eerie sound of a subterranean river, running through a Roman Republic–era drain.

LATERAN

BASILICA DI SAN GIOVANNI IN LATERANO Map p115

☎ 06 698 86 433; Piazza di San Giovanni in Laterano 4; 🕐 7am-6.30pm; Ⓜ San Giovanni

For a thousand years this monumental cathedral was the most important church in Christendom. Founded by Constantine in 324 AD, it was the first Christian basilica to be built in Rome and, until the late 14th century, was the pope's main place of worship. The Vatican still has extraterritorial authority over it, despite it being Rome's official cathedral and the pope's seat as Bishop of Rome.

Surmounted by 15 colossal statues – Christ with St John the Baptist, John the Evangelist and the 12 Apostles – Alessandro Galilei's huge white façade is a mid-18th-century example of late-baroque classicism, designed to convey the infinite authority of the Church. The bronze doors were moved here from the Curia (p67) in the Roman Forum, while to their right the Holy Door is only opened in Jubilee years.

The interior has been revamped on numerous occasions, although it owes much of its present look to Francesco Borromini, who was called in by Pope Innocent X to redecorate it for the 1650 Jubilee. Among other things, Borromini added the sculptural frames around the funerary monuments in the aisles and, above them, his trademark oval windows.

But elements of earlier interiors survive, including the delightful 15th-century mosaic floor and the Gothic baldachin over the papal altar. At the top of the baldachin is a reliquary that supposedly contains the heads of St Peter and St Paul. Below, a double staircase leads to the confessio, which houses pieces of what's thought to be St Peter's wooden altar table, used by 1st- to 4th-century popes.

The fresco behind the first pillar of the right-hand aisle is an original, if rather incomplete, Giotto. While admiring it, cock your ear towards the next pillar, where a monument to Pope Sylvester II (r 999–1003) is said to sweat and creak when the death of a pope is imminent.

To the left of the altar, the beautiful cloister (admission €2; 🕙 9am-6pm) was built in the 13th century. The twisted columns were once completely covered with inlaid marble mosaics, remnants of which can still be seen.

Guided tours of the basilica are available through the Mater et Caput association (☎ 06 698 86 392; adult/concession €5/3; 🕙 on request).

PALAZZO LATERANO & BATTISTERO
Map p115

Piazza San Giovanni in Laterano; admission battistero free; 🕙 battistero 7.30am-12.30pm & 4-7.30pm
Flanking Piazza San Giovanni in Laterano is Domenico Fontana's 16th-century Palazzo Laterano. Part of the original 4th-century basilica complex, it was the official papal residence until the popes moved to the Vatican in 1377. Today it houses the diocese of Rome.

Just around the corner is the fascinating octagonal battistero (baptistry). Built by Constantine in the 4th century, it served as the prototype for later Christian churches and bell towers. The chief interest, apart from the architecture, are the decorative mosaics, some of which date back to the 5th century.

SCALA SANTA & SANCTA SANCTORUM Map p115
☎ 06 772 66 41; Piazza di San Giovanni in Laterano 14; admission Scala/Sancta €3.50/free, Sancta & Cappella San Silvestro €5; 🕙 Scala 6.15am noon & 3.30-6.45pm Apr-Sep, 6.15am-noon & 3-6.15pm Oct-Mar, Sancta Sanctorum 10.30-11.30am & 3-4.30pm Apr-Sep, 10.30-11.30am & 3-4pm Oct-Mar, closed Wed am & Sun year-round; Ⓜ San Giovanni
Boasting a genuinely spiritual atmosphere, the Scala Santa is said to be the staircase that Jesus walked up in Pontius Pilate's palace in Jerusalem. It was brought to Rome by St Helena in the 4th century, and is considered so sacred that you can only climb it on your knees, saying a prayer on each of the 28 steps. At the top of the stairs, and accessible by two side staircases if you don't fancy the knee-climb, is the Sancta Sanctorum (Holy of Holies), once the pope's private chapel. A spectacular sight, it's richly decorated with stunning mosaics and frescoes, the best of which depict the life of St Sylvester in the Cappella San Silvestro.

AVENTINO & TESTACCIO

Drinking & Nightlife p226; Eating p208; Shopping p184; Sleeping p261

Encompassing the refined slopes of the Aventino, the most southerly of Rome's seven hills, and the earthy streets of riverside Testaccio, this wedge of south central Rome offers everything from ancient ruins to medieval churches, busy markets and hip clubs.

The Aventino, now one of the capital's most sought-after residential areas, is an elegant and contemplative part of town. The most atmospheric street is Via di Santa Sabina, where you'll find a number of medieval churches, including the magnificent Basilica di Santa Sabina, and a beautiful walled orange garden, the Parco Savello. At the end of the road, the Piazza dei Cavalieri di Malta boasts a famous keyhole view of St Peter's.

There are various routes up to the Aventino but the nicest is via the pedestrian-only Clivo di Rocca Savelli from Via Santa Maria in Cosmedin by the river. At the top turn right for Via di Santa Sabina or left for Via di Valle Murcia, which takes you past the Roseto Comunale, a beautiful public rose garden, down to the Circo Massimo.

top picks

AVENTINO & TESTACCIO

- Basilica di Santa Sabina (below)
- Piazza dei Cavalieri di Malta (opposite)
- Cimitero Acattolico per gli Stranieri (opposite)
- Terme di Caracalla (opposite)

At the foot of the Aventino, between Via Marmorata and the River Tiber, Testaccio is one of the city's most authentic areas, its inhabitants a kind of Roman cockney. Traditionally working-class, it has kept much of its earthy character – the city's top offal restaurants are here (offal is a Roman speciality) and the local market is considered one of Rome's best – despite the onslaught of clubs and pubs that have transformed it into a nightlife mecca (see p226). There are few must-see sights around here, although the Protestant Cemetery is well worth an hour or so of your time.

To the east of Testaccio, the mammoth ruins of the Terme di Caracalla are one of the neighbourhood's highlights. They're not the easiest to get to, but they really do merit the effort – they're magnificent, easily on a par with anything in the city.

Getting round the Aventino and Testaccio is mostly a case of walking. For the Aventino, you can walk up from the Lungotevere Aventino or from the metro station at Circo Massimo (line B), although this route is considerably longer. One stop further down the line, Piramide is the best stop for Testaccio.

AVENTINO

BASILICA DI SANTA SABINA Map p120

☎ 06 5 79 41; Piazza Pietro d'Illiria 1; ☉ 6.30am-12.45pm & 3-7pm; ⊒ Lungotevere Aventino

A genuinely spiritual spot, this solemn basilica was founded by Peter of Illyria in around AD 422. It was enlarged in the 9th century and again in 1216, just before it was given to the newly founded Dominican order – look out for the mosaic tombstone of Muñoz de Zamora, one of the order's founding fathers, in the nave floor. A 20th-century restoration returned it to its original look.

One of the few surviving 4th-century elements are the basilica's cypress-wood doors. They feature 18 carved panels depicting biblical events, including one of the oldest Crucifixion scenes in existence.

It's quite hard to make out in the top left, but it depicts Jesus and the two thieves although, strangely, not their crosses.

Inside, the three naves are separated by 24 Corinthian columns, which support an arcade decorated with a faded red-and-green frieze. The fluted columns, custom-made for the church rather than plundered from the city's ruins, were the first ever made in Rome to support arches. Light streams in from high nave windows that were added in the 9th century, along with the carved choir, pulpit and bishop's throne.

Behind the church is a garden and a meditative 13th-century cloister.

PARCO SAVELLO Map p120

Via di Santa Sabina; ☉ dawn-dusk; ⊒ Lungotevere Aventino

Known to Romans as the Giardino degli Aranci (Orange Garden), this pocket-sized park is a romantic haven. Grab a perch at the small panoramic terrace and watch the sun set over the Tiber and St Peter's dome. In summer, theatre performances are sometimes staged among the perfumed orange trees.

PIAZZA DEI CAVALIERI DI MALTA
Map p120

Via di Santa Sabina; 🚌 **Lungotevere Aventino**
At the southern end of Via di Santa Sabina, this peaceful little square takes its name from the Cavalieri di Malta (Knights of Malta), who have their Roman headquarters here, in the Priorato dei Cavalieri di Malta. Although it's closed to the public, the priory offers one of Rome's most charming views: look through the keyhole and you'll see the dome of St Peter's perfectly aligned at the end of a hedge-lined avenue.

CHIESA DI SAN SABA Map p120
☎ 06 645 80 133; Piazza Gian Lorenzo Bernini 20; ☀ 8am-noon & 4-7pm Mon-Sat, 9.30am-1pm & 4-7.30pm Sun; 🚌 or 🚊 Viale Aventino
With its leafy walled garden, 13th-century porch and beautiful Cosmati work, this picturesque church is worth a quick detour. Of particular note are the 13th-century frescoes in the left-hand nave, including one of three naked girls in bed. Legend has it that these girls were saved from a life of prostitution by St Nicholas, who threw three stockings filled with gold up to their bedroom. St Nicholas is better known as Santa Claus and this story is the origin of the Christmas-stocking tradition.

TERME DI CARACALLA Map p120
☎ 06 399 67 700; Viale delle Terme di Caracalla 52; admission incl Mausoleo di Cecilia Metella & Villa del Quintili adult/EU 18-24yr/EU under 18yr & over 65yr €6/3/free, audioguide €4; ☀ 9am-7.15pm Tue-Sun Apr-Aug, to 7pm Sep, to 6.30pm Oct, to 5.30pm mid-end Mar, to 5pm mid-Feb–mid-Mar, to 4.30pm Nov–mid-Feb, to 2pm Mon year-round; 🚇 Circo Massimo
The remnants of Caracalla's vast 3rd-century baths complex are among Rome's most awe-inspiring ruins. Spread over 10 hectares, the original leisure centre could hold up to 1600 people and included *caldaria* (hot rooms), a lukewarm *tepidarium*, a swimming pool, gymnasiums, libraries,

shops and gardens. Between 6000 and 8000 people were thought to use them every day. Underground, hundreds of slaves sweated in the 9.5km of tunnels, tending to the complex plumbing systems.

Begun by Antonius Caracalla and inaugurated in AD 217, the baths were used until 537, when the Visigoths smashed their way into Rome. Excavations in the 16th and 17th centuries unearthed important sculptures, many of which found their way into the Farnese family art collection.

Opera fans will enjoy the spectacular performances staged in the ruins in summer (see p235).

TESTACCIO

CIMITERO ACATTOLICO PER GLI STRANIERI Map p120
☎ 06 574 19 00; Via Caio Cestio 5; voluntary donation €2; ☀ 9am-5pm Mon-Sat, 9am-1pm Sun; 🚇 Piramide
Despite the busy roads that surround it, Rome's 'Non-Catholic Cemetery for Foreigners' (aka the Protestant Cemetery) is a surprisingly restful place. As the traffic thunders past, you can wander the lovingly tended paths contemplating Percy Bysshe Shelley's words: 'It might make one in love with death to think that one should be buried in so sweet a place.' And so he was, along with fellow Romantic poet, John Keats, and a whole host of luminaries, including Antonio Gramsci, the revered founder of the Italian Communist Party.

PIRAMIDE DI CAIO CESTIO Map p120
🚇 Piramide
Sticking out like, well, an Egyptian pyramid, this distinctive landmark stands in the Aurelian Wall at the side of a massive traffic junction. A 36m-high marble-and-brick tomb, it was built for Gaius Cestius, a 1st-century-BC magistrate, and some 200 years later was incorporated into the Aurelian fortification near Porta San Paolo. The surrounding area is today known as Piramide.

MONTE TESTACCIO Map p120
☎ 06 06 08; Via Galvani 24; adult/concession €3/1.50; ☀ by appointment; 🚌 Via Marmorata
The sight of bloodthirsty carnival games in the Middle Ages, this artificial hill is made almost entirely of smashed amphorae. Between the 2nd century BC and the 3rd

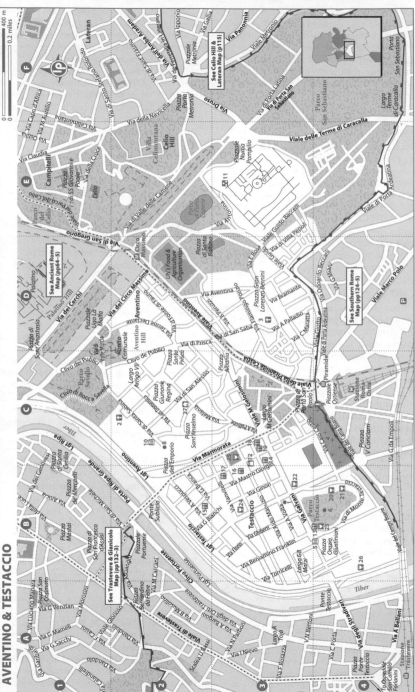

AVENTINO & TESTACCIO

NEIGHBOURHOODS **AVENTINO & TESTACCIO**

AVENTINO & TESTACCIO

century AD, Testaccio was Rome's river port. Supplies of wine, oil and grain were transported in huge terracotta amphorae which, once emptied, were dumped in the river. When the Tiber became almost un-navigable as a consequence, the pots were smashed and the pieces stacked methodically in a pile, which over time grew into a large hill – Monte Testaccio. Visits are by guided tour only.

MACRO FUTURE Map p120

☎ 06 574 26 47; www.macro.roma.museum; Piazza Orazio Giustiniani 4; admission free; ☾ 4pm-midnight Tue-Sun; Ⓜ Piramide
Housed in Rome's ex-slaughterhouse, MACRO's second gallery (the main one is in northern Rome – see p155) serves up contemporary art in two cavernous industrial halls. Recent shows have featured Sean Scully, the Italian futurists and the Russian AES+F collective.

SOUTHERN ROME

Drinking & Nightlife p227; Eating p209

Southern Rome is an extensive and multifaceted neighbourhood that comprises three distinct areas: Via Appia Antica, famous for its catacombs; trendy Via Ostiense; and EUR, Mussolini's futuristic building development.

Heading southeast from Porta San Sebastiano, Via Appia Antica (the Appian Way) is one of the world's oldest roads and a much-prized Roman address. It's a beautiful part of town, with crumbling ruins set in jewel-green fields and towering umbrella pines lining the horizon. But the catacombs are the main reason for visiting – some 300km of underground tunnels used as burial chambers by the early Christians. You can't visit all 300km but three major catacombs (San Callisto, San Sebastiano and Santa Domitilla) are open for guided exploration.

top picks

SOUTHERN ROME

- Basilica & Catacombe di San Sebastiano (opposite)
- Basilica di San Paolo Fuori Le Mura (p127)
- Capitoline Museums at Centrale Montemartini (p128)
- Mausoleo delle Fosse Ardeatine (p126)
- Palazzo della Civiltà del Lavoro (p128)

Via Ostiense presents a very different picture. Busy and traffic-clogged, it runs through one of the capital's hippest districts. Disused factories and warehouses harbour hundreds of restaurants, pubs, clubs and bars, while the city's former wholesale food markets, the Mercati Generali, wait to be converted into a cultural centre. Specific sights are thin on the ground but the Capitoline Museums at Centrale Montemartini contain superb classical statuary, and the Basilica di San Paolo fuori le Mura is the world's third-largest church. Over the road, the character-filled Garbatella district merits exploration for its original architecture and colourful buildings.

In the city's extreme southern reaches, EUR is a world apart. Built by Mussolini as a showcase for his Fascist regime, it's an Orwellian quarter of wide boulevards and linear buildings (now largely used by banks and government ministries) like nowhere else in Rome. Students of modern architecture will not want to miss it.

Southern Rome is very spread out and difficult to explore on foot. Fortunately, there are good public-transport connections. Metro line B runs to Piramide, Garbatella, Basilica San Paolo, EUR Palasport and EUR Fermi; and there are bus connections to Porta San Sebastiano (118, 218 and 714), Via Ostiense (23 and 716) and Via Appia Antica (118, 218 and 660).

VIA APPIA ANTICA & THE CATACOMBS

Known to the ancients as *regina viarum* (queen of roads), Via Appia Antica (the Appian Way) is named after Appius Claudius Caecus, the consul who laid the first 90km section in 312 BC. It was subsequently extended in 190 BC to reach Brindisi, some 540km away on the southern Adriatic coast.

Although it's now one of the capital's most exclusive neighbourhoods, its past is macabre. In 71 BC Spartacus and 6000 of his rebel army were crucified here, and in ensuing centuries Rome's early Christians came here to bury their dead.

There are several information points in the area, including the Appia Antica Regional Park Information Point (☎ 06 513 53 16; www.parcoappiaantica .org; Via Appia Antica 58-60; ⊙ 9.30am-1.30pm & 2-5.30pm Mon-Sat, 9.30am-5.30pm Sun, closes 4.30pm daily in winter), where you can buy a map of the park and hire bikes (per hour/day €3/10). The park authorities organise a series of free guided tours on Sunday mornings – see the website for the latest programme. In addition, a number of local associations run visits, including the Cooperativa Darwin (www.cooperativa darwin.it), which organises group tours (€8 on foot, €12 by bike) in English, French, Spanish and German.

On Sundays a long section of the road is closed to traffic, but be warned that this is when locals and tourists arrive by the coachload. On weekdays there are fewer tourists, but walking or cycling along the road can be dangerous due to the number of cars zooming past.

To get to Via Appia Antica you can catch bus 218 from Piazza San Giovanni in Laterano, bus 660 from the Colli Albani metro station on line A, or bus 118 from the Piramide station on line B. Alternatively, the Archeobus (p296) departs from Termini every 40 minutes.

BASILICA & CATACOMBE DI SAN SEBASTIANO Map pp124–5

☎ 06 785 03 50; www.catacombe.org; Via Appia Antica 136; basilica free, catacombs adult/7-15yr/under 7yr €6/3/free; ☽ basilica 8am-1pm & 2-5.30pm daily, catacombs 9am-noon & 2-5pm Mon-Sat, closed mid-Nov–mid-Dec; ☒ Via Appia Antica

Before you duck into the catacombs, take a moment to explore the 4th-century basilica on top. Much altered over the years, it is dedicated to St Sebastian, who was martyred and buried here in the late 3rd century. In the Capella delle Reliquie you'll find one of the arrows used to kill him and the column to which he was tied. On the other side of the church is a marble slab with Jesus' footprints. (For the whole story, see p126).

The Catacombe di San Sebastiano were the first catacombs to be so called, the name deriving from the Greek kata (near) and kymbas (cavity), because they were located near a cave. During the persecutory reign of Vespasian, they provided a safe haven for the remains of St Peter and St Paul and later became a popular pilgrimage site. The first level is now almost completely destroyed, but frescoes, stucco work and epigraphs can be seen on the 2nd level. There are also three perfectly preserved mausoleums and a plastered wall with hundreds of invocations to Peter and Paul, engraved by worshippers in the 3rd and 4th centuries.

VILLA DI MASSENZIO Map pp124–5

☎ 06 780 13 24; www.villadimassenzio.it; Via Appia Antica 153; adult/EU 18-25yr/EU under 18yr & over 65yr €3/1.50/free; ☽ 9am-1pm Tue-Sat; ☒ Via Appia Antica

The outstanding feature of Maxentius' enormous 4th-century palace complex is the Circo di Massenzio, Rome's best-preserved ancient racetrack – you can still make out the starting stalls used for chariot races. The 10,000-seat arena was built by Maxentius around 309, but he died before ever seeing a race here.

Above the arena are the ruins of Maxentius' imperial residence, most of which are covered by weeds. Near the racetrack, the Mausoleo di Romolo (also known as the Tombo di Romolo) was built by Maxentius for his son Romulus. The huge mausoleum was originally crowned with a large dome and surrounded by an imposing colonnade, in part still visible.

MAUSOLEO DI CECILIA METELLA Map pp124–5

☎ 06 399 67 700; www.pierreci.it; Via Appia Antica 161; incl Terme di Caracalla & Villa dei Quintili adult/EU 18-24yr/EU under 18yr & over 65yr €6/3/free; ☽ 9am-7.15pm Apr-Aug, to 7pm Sep, to 6.30pm Oct, to 5.30pm mid-end Mar, to 5pm mid-Feb–mid-Mar, to 4.30pm Nov–mid-Feb, closed Mon year-round; ☒ Via Appia Antica

Dating to the 1st century BC, this great drum of a mausoleum encloses a burial chamber (built for the daughter of the consul Quintus Metellus Creticus) that is now roofless. The walls are made of travertine and the rather sorry-looking interior is decorated with a sculpted frieze featuring Gaelic shields, ox skulls and festoons. In the 14th century it was converted into a fort by the Caetani family, who used to threaten passing traffic into paying a toll.

Beyond the tomb is a picturesque section of the actual ancient road, excavated in the mid-19th century.

VILLA DEI QUINTILI Map pp124–5

☎ 06 399 67 700; www.pierreci.it; Via Appia Nuova 1092, also accessible from opposite Via Appia Antica 292 Sat & Sun Apr-Oct; admission incl Terme di Caracalla & Mausoleo di Cecilia Metella adult/EU 18-24yr/EU under 18yr & over 65yr €6/3/free; ☽ 9am-7.15pm Apr-Aug, 9am-7pm Sep, 9am-6.30pm Oct, 9am-5.30pm mid-end Mar, 9am-5pm mid-Feb–mid-Mar, 9am-4.30pm Nov–mid-Feb, closed Mon year-round; ☒ Via Appia Nuova

Set on lush green fields between Via Appia Antica and Via Appia Nuova, this vast 2nd-century villa was the luxury abode of two brothers who were consuls under Emperor Marcus Aurelius. Alas, the splendour of the villa was to be the brothers' downfall – in a fit of jealousy, Emperor Commodus had them both killed, taking over the villa for himself. The highlight is the well-preserved baths complex with a pool, caldarium (hot room) and frigidarium (cold room). There's also a small display of

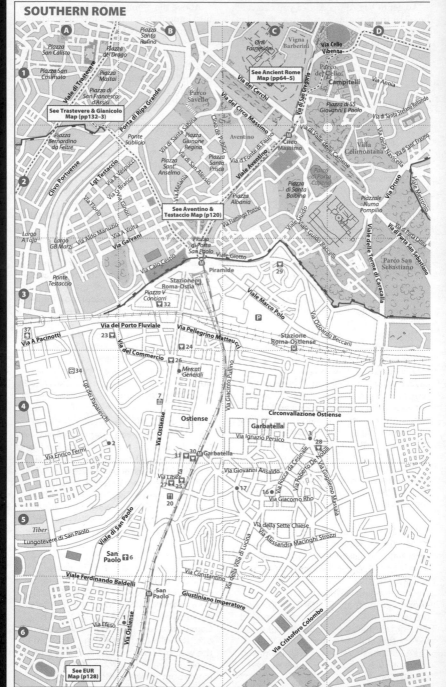

See Ancient Rome Map (pp64–5)

See Trastevere & Gianicolo Map (pp132–3)

See Aventino & Testaccio Map (p120)

See EUR Map (p128)

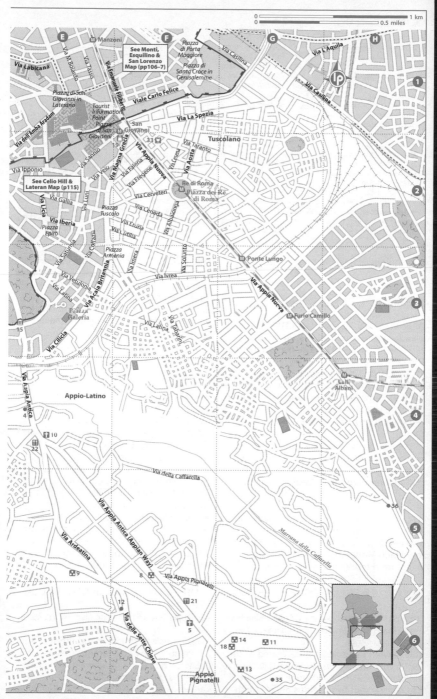

See Monti, Esquilino & San Lorenzo Map (pp106–7)

See Celio Hill & Lateran Map (p115)

Manzoni

Piazza di Porta Maggiore

Piazza di Santa Croce in Gerusalemme

Via L'Aquila

Via Casilina

Via Casilina

Via Labicana

Via M Boiardo

Via Tasso

Via Emanuele Filiberto

Viale Carlo Felice

Via La Spezia

Piazza di San Giovanni in Laterano

Via dell'Amba Aradam

Tourist Information Point

Piazza di San Giovanni

San Giovanni

33

Via Magna Grecia

Via Sannio

Via Veto

Via Appia Nuova

Via Faleria

Via Fregene

Via Leesa

Via Aosta

Via Taranto

Tuscolano

Via Ipponio

Via Gallia

Via Lima

Via Cerveteri

Via Cerveteri

Via Ceneda

Via Albacona

Re di Roma

Piazza dei Re di Roma

Via Iberia

Piazza Tuscolo

Via Eturia

Via Ligia

Piazza Epiro

Via Utilia

Via Solunto

Via Imera

Ponte Lungo

Piazza Armenia

Via Coltazia

Via Saturnia

Via Vetulonia

Via Ivrea

Via Appia Nuova

Via Latina

Via Acaia Britannia

Piazza Galeria

Via Clidia

Via Latina

Via Taburini

Furio Camillo

Via A Appia Antica

Appio-Latino

10

22

Via della Caffarella

36

Via Appia Antica (Appian Way)

Via Ardeatina

9

8

Via Appia Pignatelli

Marrana della Caffarella

Lodi Albani

12

21

Via delle Sette Chiese

5

14

18

11

13

Appio Pignatelli

35

SOUTHERN ROME (pp124–5)

archaeological bits and bobs found in the vicinity.

CATACOMBE DI SAN CALLISTO
Map pp124–5

☎ 06 513 01 580; Via Appia Antica 110 & 126; www.catacombe.roma.it; adult/6-15yr/under 6yr €6/3/free; ☽ 9am-noon & 2-5pm Thu-Tue, closed Feb; ⊜ Via Appia Antica
These are the largest, most famous and busiest of Rome's catacombs. Founded at the end of the 2nd century and named after Pope Calixtus I, they became the official cemetery of the newly established Roman Church. In the 20km of tunnels explored to date, archaeologists have found the tombs of 500,000 people and seven popes who were martyred in the 3rd century. The patron saint of music, St Cecilia, was also buried here, though her body was later removed to the Basilica di Santa Cecilia in Trastevere (p130). When her body was exhumed in 1599, over 1000 years after her death, it was apparently perfectly preserved, as depicted in Stefano Moderno's softly contoured sculpture, a replica of which is here.

MAUSOLEO DELLE FOSSE ARDEATINE
Map pp124–5

☎ 06 513 67 42; Via Ardeatina 174; admission free; ☽ 8.15am-3.30pm Mon-Fri, to 4.45pm Sat & Sun; ⊜ Via Appia Antica
This moving mausoleum is dedicated to the victims of Rome's worst WWII atrocity. Buried here, outside the Ardeatine Caves, are 335 Italians shot by the Nazis on 24 March

1944. Following the massacre, ordered in reprisal for a partisan attack, the Germans used mines to explode sections of the caves and bury the bodies. After the war, the bodies were exhumed, identified and reburied in a mass grave at the site, now marked by a huge concrete slab and sculptures.

At the site there is also a tiny museum dedicated to the Italian resistance to the German occupation.

CATACOMBE DI SANTA DOMITILLA
Map pp124–5

☎ 06 511 03 42; Via delle Sette Chiese 283; adult/6-15yr/under 6yr €6/3/free; ☽ 9am-noon & 2-5pm Wed-Mon, closed Jan; ⊜ Via Appia Antica
Among Rome's largest and oldest, these catacombs stretch for about 17km. They were established on the private burial ground of Flavia Domitilla, niece of Emperor Domitian and a member of the wealthy Flavian family. They contain Christian wall paintings and the underground Chiesa di SS Nereus e Achilleus, a 4th-century church dedicated to two Roman soldiers who were martyred by Diocletian.

CHIESA DEL DOMINE QUO VADIS?
Map pp124–5

Via Appia Antica 51; ☽ 8am-6pm; ⊜ Via Appia Antica
This pint-sized church marks the spot where St Peter, while fleeing Rome, met a vision of Jesus going the other way. When Peter asked: 'Domine, quo vadis?' ('Lord, where are you going?'), Jesus replied 'Venio Roman

iterum crucifigi' ('I am coming to Rome to be crucified again'). Reluctantly deciding to join him, Peter tramped back into town where he was immediately arrested and executed, as portrayed in Caravaggio's *Crocifissione di San Pietro* (Crucifixion of St Peter) in the Chiesa di Santa Maria del Popolo (p94). In the centre of the aisle are copies of two holy footprints supposed to belong to Christ; the originals are up the road in the Basilica di San Sebastiano (p123).

PORTA SAN SEBASTIANO Map pp124–5

☎ 06 704 75 284; www.museodellemuraroma.it; Via di Porta San Sebastiano 18; adult/EU 18-25yr/EU under 18yr & over 65yr €3/1.50/free; ☽ 9am-2pm Tue-Sun; 🚇 Porta San Sebastiano

Marking the start of Via Appia Antica, the 5th-century Porta San Sebastiano is the largest of the gates in the Aurelian Wall. It was originally known as Porta Appia but took on its current name in honour of the thousands of pilgrims who passed under it on their way to the Catacombe di San Sebastiano (p123). During WWII, the Fascist Party secretary Ettore Muti lived here and today it houses the Museo delle Mure, a modest museum illustrating the history of the wall. It's worth a quick look, if for nothing else than the chance to walk along the top of the walls.

OSTIENSE, SAN PAOLO & GARBATELLA

Heading south from Stazione Roma-Ostia, Via Ostiense takes you into a trendy area of converted warehouses, clubs and hidden sights.

BASILICA DI SAN PAOLO FUORI LE MURA Map pp124–5

☎ 06 698 80 800; Via Ostiense 190; ☽ 6.45am-6.30pm; Ⓜ San Paolo

The biggest church in Rome after St Peter's (and the world's third-largest) stands on the site where St Paul was buried after being decapitated in AD 67. Built by Constantine in the 4th century, it was largely destroyed by fire in 1823 and much of what you see today is a 19th-century reconstruction.

However, some treasures survived the fire, including the 5th-century triumphal arch, with its heavily restored mosaics, and the gothic marble tabernacle over the high altar. This was designed in about 1285 by Arnolfo di Cambio together with another artist, possibly Pietro Cavallini. To the right of the altar, the elaborate Romanesque paschal candlestick was fashioned by Nicolò di Angelo and Pietro Vassalletto in the 12th century and features a grim cast of animal-headed creatures. St Paul's tomb is in the nearby confessio.

Looking upwards, doom-mongers should check out the papal portraits beneath the nave windows. Every pope since St Peter is represented and legend has it that when there is no room for the next portrait, the world will fall. There are eight places left.

The stunning 13th-century Cosmati mosaic work in the cloisters (admission free; ☽ 9am-1pm & 3-6pm) of the adjacent Benedictine abbey also survived the 1823 fire. The octagonal and spiral columns supporting the elaborate arcade are arranged in pairs and inlaid with beautiful colourful mosaics.

WORLD OF THE DEAD

Rome's catacombs were built as communal burial grounds. The earliest date back to the 1st century AD and were used mainly by the city's Jewish community. Christian catacombs were added from the 2nd century onwards.

Burial was a problem for Rome's early Christians. Belief in the Resurrection meant that they couldn't cremate their dead, as was the custom at the time, while convention meant that they needed somewhere out of the way to dispose of their bodies. Making matters worse, Roman law banned burial within the city walls. The solution was to head out of town and start digging in the soft tufa rock beneath Via Appia Antica, where a number of converted Christians already had family tombs.

The catacombs remained a popular burial site until Constantine legalised Christianity in 313. After this the Christians increasingly opted to bury their dead near the basilicas being built in the city. This became common practice under Theodosius, who made Christianity the state religion in 394. Further decline set in when marauding barbarians began ransacking the catacombs in the 5th century, forcing the popes to take the remaining relics, including the heads of St Peter and St Paul, inside the city walls. The catacombs were abandoned and largely forgotten until a 16th-century farmer stuck his hoe into a 'world of the dead'.

Since the mid-19th century more than 30 catacombs have been discovered in the Rome area.

CAPITOLINE MUSEUMS AT CENTRALE MONTEMARTINI Map pp124-5

☎ 06 06 08; Via Ostiense 106; adult/EU 18-25yr/EU under 18yr & over 65yr €4.50/2.50/free, incl Capitoline Museums €8.50/6.50/free; ⓨ 9am-7pm Tue-Sun; ⓜ Via Ostiense

This fabulous outpost of the Capitoline Museums (p70) is a treat. Housed in a former power station, it boldly juxtaposes classical sculpture against diesel engines and giant furnaces. The collection's highlights are in the Sala Caldaia, where a giant furnace provides a suitably impressive backdrop. Two of the most beautiful pieces are the *Fanciulla Seduta* sitting with her elbow resting on her knee, and *Musa Polimnia* gazing dreamily into the distance. At the far end of the room is the milky-white *Venus Esquilina* from the 1st century BC, discovered on the Esquilino in 1874.

QUARTIERE GARBATELLA Map pp124-5

ⓜ Garbatella

A favourite location for TV and filmmakers, Quartiere Garbatella is a wonderfully atmospheric district with its own idiosyncratic look. It was originally conceived as a workers' residential quarter but in the 1920s the Fascists hijacked the project and used the area to house people displaced by construction work in the city centre. Many people were moved into *alberghi suburbani* (suburban hotels), big housing blocks designed by Innocenzo Sabbatini, the leading light of the 'Roman School' of architecture. The most famous, Albergo Rosso (Piazza Michele da Carbonara) is typical of the style. Other trademark buildings are the Scuola Cesare Battisti on Piazza Damiano Sauli and Teatro Palladium on Piazza Bartolomeo Romano.

EUR

One of the few planned developments in Rome's history, EUR was built for an international exhibition in 1942, and although war intervened and the exhibition never took place, the name stuck – Esposizione Universale di Roma (Roman Universal Exhibition) or EUR. There are few museums but the area's appeal (or lack of it) lies in its spectacular rationalist architecture. It's not to everyone's taste but the style is beautifully expressed in a number of distinctive *palazzi*, including the iconic Palazzo della Civiltà del Lavoro, the Chiesa Santi Pietro e Paolo (Church of St Peter & Paul; Map p128; Piazzale Santi Pietro e Paolo), the Palazzetto dello Sport

(Map p128; Piazzale dello Sport), and the wonderful Palazzo dei Congressi (Congress Centre; Map p128; Piazza JF Kennedy). The area is still a focus for development, with Massimiliano Fuksas' cutting-edge Nuvola ('cloud') congress centre being built here, and mayor Gianni Alemanno hoping the area may host Formula 1 racing in 2012.

For further online information, Italian speakers can log onto www.romaeur.it.

PALAZZO DELLA CIVILTÀ DEL LAVORO Map p128

Quadrato della Concordia; ⓜ EUR Magliana

Dubbed the Square Colosseum, the Palace of the Workers is EUR's architectural icon, a rationalist masterpiece clad in gleaming white travertine. Designed by Giovanni Guerrini, Ernesto Bruno La Padula and

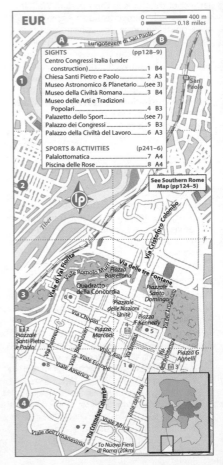

EUR

0 — 400 m
0 — 0.18 miles

SIGHTS	(pp128-9)
Centro Congressi Italia (under construction)	1 B4
Chiesa Santi Pietro e Paolo	2 A3
Museo Astronomico & Planetario	(see 3)
Museo della Civiltà Romana	3 B4
Museo delle Arti e Tradizioni Popolari	4 B3
Palazetto dello Sport	(see 7)
Palazzo dei Congressi	5 B3
Palazzo della Civiltà del Lavoro	6 A3

SPORTS & ACTIVITIES	(p241-6)
Palalottomatica	7 A4
Piscina delle Rose	8 A4

See Southern Rome Map (pp124-5)

NEIGHBOURHOODS SOUTHERN ROME

Mario Romano, and built between 1938 and 1943, it consists of six rows of nine arches, rising to a height of 50m. According to some, these numbers are a homage to the project's Fascist patron, with the six rows reflecting the six letters of Benito and the nine arches the nine letters of Mussolini. The *palazzo* is currently undergoing restoration and will house a new multi-media museum when it reopens.

MUSEO DELLA CIVILTÀ ROMANA & PLANETARIO Map p128

☎ 06 06 08; Piazza G Agnelli 10; adult/EU 18-25yr/EU under 18yr & over 65yr €6.50/4.50/free, incl Museo Astronomico & Planetario €8.50/6.50/free; ⏱ 9am-2pm Tue-Sat, 9am-1.30pm Sun; Ⓜ EUR Fermi

The pick of EUR's museums, this sure-fire kid-pleaser was founded by Mussolini in 1937 to glorify imperial Rome. A hulking place with huge echoing halls, it contains a number of intriguing displays, including a giant-scale re-creation of 4th-century Rome.

For something completely different, learn about the night sky at the on-site Museo Astronomico & Planetario (Astronomy Museum & Planetarium; www.planetarioroma.it; ☎ 06 06 08; adult/6-18yr/under 6yr €6.50/4/free; ⏱ 9am-2pm Tue-Fri, 9am-7pm Sat & Sun).

MUSEO DELLE ARTI E TRADIZIONI POPOLARI Map p128

☎ 06 592 61 48; Piazza Marconi 8; adult/concession €4/2; ⏱ 9am-6pm Tue-Fri, 9am-8pm Sat & Sun; Ⓜ EUR Palasport

You might well have to wake up the ticket-seller at this sleepy museum dedicated to folk art and rural tradition. Not one of Rome's great museums, it's nevertheless more interesting than it sounds, with an eclectic collection of agricultural and artisan tools, clothing, musical instruments and a room full of carnival costumes and artefacts.

TRASTEVERE & GIANICOLO

Drinking & Nightlife p229; Eating p209; Shopping p184; Sleeping p261

Trastevere is one of central Rome's most vivacious neighbourhoods, an outdoor circus of ochre *palazzi*, ivy-clad façades and photogenic lanes, peopled with a bohemian cast of tourists, travellers, students and street sellers. In the midst of the daily mayhem, locals make themselves heard by shouting jokes at each other in thick *romanesco*, the Roman dialect.

The area was originally a working-class district separated from the city proper by the River Tiber – hence its name, a derivation of the Latin *trans Tiberium*, meaning 'over the Tiber'. However, as the city grew, Trastevere was slowly enveloped by urban development and it is today very much a part of Rome's cityscape. Despite this, Trastevere-born Romans (known as *trasteverini*) like to think of themselves as being different, as being *noantri* (we others), and even have their own festival (p90) to prove it.

top picks

TRASTEVERE & GIANICOLO

- Basilica di Santa Maria in Trastevere (opposite)
- Villa Farnesina (p134)
- Basilica di Santa Cecilia in Trastevere (below)
- Tempietto di Bramante (p135)
- Orto Botanico (p135)

But times change, and Trastevere is changing with them. Accommodation in the area is increasingly being targeted by wealthy foreigners and prices are rising. Many old-timers are struggling to keep up with sky-high rents and some have been forced to call it a day and move to the cheaper suburbs.

To a visitor, however, the area is a delight. There aren't a huge number of must-see sights, but the Basilica di Santa Maria in Trastevere is one of Rome's most charming churches, and Villa Farnesina boasts superb frescoes by Raphael. To the east, on the quieter side of Viale di Trastevere, the Basilica di Santa Cecilia is the last resting place of Santa Cecilia, the patron saint of music.

But it's after dark that Trastevere really comes into its own. Its narrow alleyways heave late into the night as Romans and tourists flock to the pizzerias, trattorias, bars and cafés that pepper its atmospheric lanes.

Rising above Trastevere, the Gianicolo (Janiculum hill) is a lovely, romantic spot with some superb city views and a tranquil atmosphere. Students of architecture will not want to miss Bramante's Tempietto, one of the city's great Renaissance buildings.

You can reach Trastevere on foot via the Ponte Sisto footbridge from the *centro storico*, or by taking tram 8 from Largo di Torre Argentina. From Termini, bus H runs to Viale di Trastevere. The easiest way to get to the Gianicolo is to follow Via Garibaldi from near Porta Settimiana; it's a steep 15-minute walk. Alternatively, walk up the steps from Via G Mameli or take bus 870 from Piazza delle Rovere.

EAST OF VIALE DI TRASTEVERE

BASILICA DI SANTA CECILIA IN TRASTEVERE Map pp132–3

☎ 06 589 92 89; Piazza di Santa Cecilia 22; admission basilica/Cavallini fresco/crypt free/€2.50/2.50 ☼ basilica & cypt 9.30am-12.30pm & 4-6.30pm, Cavallini fresco 10.15am-noon Mon-Sat, 11.15am-12.15pm Sun; ☐ or ☒ Viale di Trastevere
The last resting place of St Cecilia, the patron saint of music, this basilica stands on the site of an earlier 5th-century church, itself built over the house where Cecilia was martyred in AD 230. Below the altar, Ste-

fano Moderno's delicate sculpture shows exactly how her miraculously preserved body was found when it was unearthed in the Catacombe di San Callisto (p126) in 1599.

In the right-hand nave the Cappella del Caldarium, complete with two works by Guido Reni, marks the spot where the saint was allegedly tortured. But the basilica's pride and joy is the spectacular 13th-century fresco in the nun's choir. Although there are only fragments remaining, you can see enough of Pietro Cavallini's *Giudizio Universale* (Last Judgment) to realise what an outstanding work it must once have been.

Beneath the church, via the elaborately decorated crypt, you can visit the excavations of several Roman houses, one of which might have belonged to St Cecilia.

CHIESA DI SAN FRANCESCO D'ASSISI A RIPA Map pp132–3 ·

☎ 06 581 90 20; Piazza di San Francesco d'Assisi 88; ◷ 7am-noon & 4-7pm Mon-Sat, 7am-1pm & 4-7.30pm Sun; ▣ or ▤ Viale di Trastevere
The overriding reason to visit this otherwise unexceptional church is to gasp at one of Bernini's most daring works. The *Beata Ludovica Albertoni* (Blessed Ludovica Albertoni; 1674) is a work of highly charged sexual ambiguity showing Ludovica, a Franciscan nun, in a state of rapture as she reclines, eyes shut, mouth open, one hand touching her breast.

St Francis of Assisi is said to have stayed in the church for a period in the 13th century and you can still see the rock that he used as a pillow.

WEST OF VIALE DI TRASTEVERE

BASILICA DI SANTA MARIA IN TRASTEVERE Map pp132–3

☎ 06 581 48 02; www.santamariaintrastevere.org; Piazza Santa Maria in Trastevere; ◷ 7.30am-8pm; ▣ or ▤ Viale di Trastevere
This ravishing basilica is said to be the oldest church in Rome dedicated to the Virgin Mary. According to legend it was built in the early 3rd century over the spot where a fountain of oil miraculously sprang from the ground. Its current Romanesque form, complete with belltower and mosaiced façade, is the result of a 12th-century revamp. The portico came later, added by Carlo Fontana in 1702.

Inside it's the golden 12th-century mosaics that stand out. In the apse, look out for the dazzling depiction of Christ and his mother flanked by various saints and, on the far left, Pope Innocent II holding a model of the church. Beneath this is a series of six mosaics by Pietro Cavallini (c 1291) illustrating the life of the Virgin.

Other features to note include the 21 Roman columns, some plundered from the Terme di Caracalla (p119); the wooden ceiling designed in 1617 by Domenichino; and, on the right of the altar, a spiralling Cosmati candlestick, placed on the exact spot where the oil fountain is said to have sprung. The last chapel on the left-hand side, the Cappella Avila, is also worth a look for its stunning 17th-century dome.

PIAZZA SANTA MARIA IN TRASTEVERE Map pp132–3

▣ or ▤ Viale di Trastevere
Trastevere's focal square is a prime people-watching spot. By day it's full of mums with strollers, chatting locals and guidebook-toting tourists; by night it's the domain of foreign students, young Romans and out-of-towners, all out for a good time.

The fountain in the centre of the square is of Roman origin and was restored by Carlo Fontana in 1692.

BRAMANTE, THE ARCHITECT'S ARCHITECT

One of the most influential architects of his day, Donato Bramante (1444–1514) was the godfather of Renaissance architecture. His peers Michelangelo, Raphael and Leonardo da Vinci considered him the only architect of their era equal to the ancients.

Born near Urbino, he originally trained as a painter before taking up architecture in his mid-30s in Milan. Here he met Leonardo da Vinci, who was to remain a lifelong friend and influence, and worked on a number of prestigious church projects.

However, it was in Rome that he enjoyed his greatest success. Working for Pope Julius II, he developed a monumental style that while classical in origin was pure Renaissance in its expression of harmony and perspective. The most perfect representation of this is his Tempietto (p135), a small but much-copied temple. His original designs for St Peter's Basilica (p137) also revealed a classically inspired symmetry with a Pantheon-like dome envisaged atop a Greek-cross structure.

A rich and influential architect, Bramante was also an adept political operator, a ruthless and unscrupulous manipulator who was not above badmouthing his competitors. It's said that he talked Pope Julius II into giving up a pharaonic tomb project (p110) that Michelangelo had been commissioned for, and that he encouraged Julius to give Michelangelo the Sistine Chapel contract in the hope that it would prove the undoing of the young Tuscan artist.

TRASTEVERE & GIANICOLO

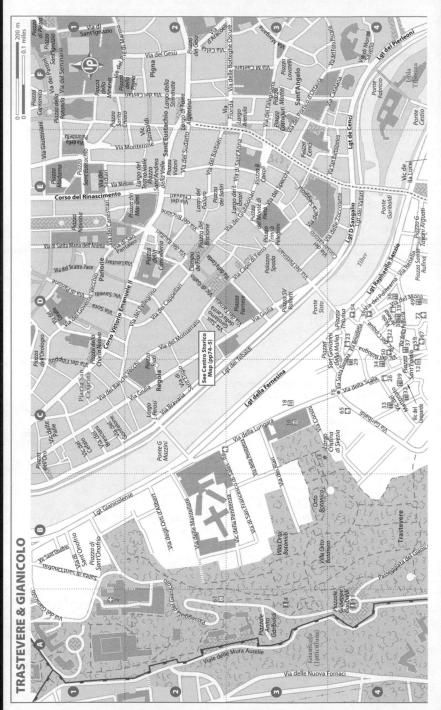

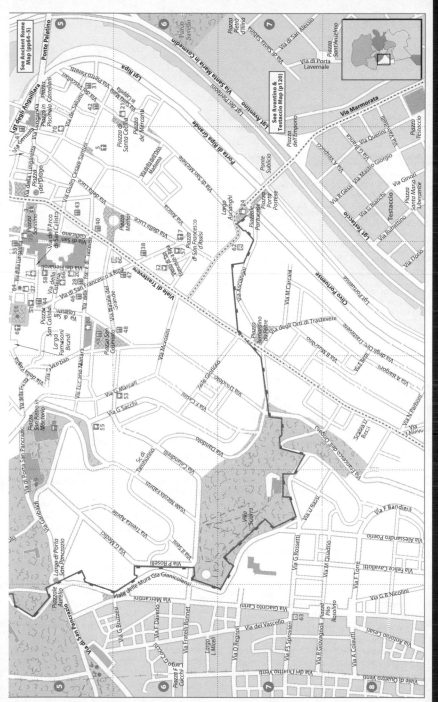

See Ancient Rome Map (pp64–5)

Ponte Palatino

See Aventino & Testaccio Map (p120)

Via Marmorata

TRASTEVERE & GIANICOLO (pp132–3)

MUSEO DI ROMA IN TRASTEVERE
Map pp132–3

☎ 06 820 59 127; www.museodiromaintrastevere
.it; Piazza Sant'Egidio 1b; adult/EU 18-25yr/EU
under 18yr & over 65yr €3/1.50/free; ☺ 10am-8pm
Tue-Sun; 🚊 or 🚋 Viale di Trastevere
Trastevere's traditions and folklore are
celebrated at this small museum. The
1st-floor permanent collection comprises
several re-creations of everyday scenes
from 19th-century Trastevere, and a small
selection of watercolours depicting communal life. It's all very kitsch but the kids
might enjoy it and it's done well. The
downstairs rooms are often used to stage
temporary exhibitions.

PORTA SETTIMIANA Map pp132–3

🚊 Lungotevere della Farnesina (Piazza Trilussa)
Resembling a crenellated keep, Porta
Settimiana marks the start of Via della
Lungara, the 16th-century road that connects Trastevere with the Borgo. It was built
in 1498 by Pope Alexander VI over a small
passageway in the Aurelian Wall and later
altered by Pope Pius VI in 1798.

From Porta Settimiana, Via Santa Dorotea
leads to Piazza Trilussa, a popular evening
hang-out, and Ponte Sisto, which connects
with the centro storico.

VILLA FARNESINA Map pp132–3

🚊 06 680 27 268; Via della Lungara 230; adult/14-
18yr/under 14yr & over 65yr €5/4/free; ☺ 9am-
1pm Mon-Sat; 🚊 Lungotevere della Farnesina
(Piazza Trilussa)
A must for fans of Renaissance art, this
gorgeous 16th-century villa features some
awe-inspiring frescoes by Sebastiano del
Piombo, Raphael and the villa's original
architect, Baldassare Peruzzi. Peruzzi was
commissioned to build the villa by the
powerful banker Agostino Chigi but in 1577
bankruptcy forced the Chigis to sell it to
the Farnese family, after whom it is named.

The most famous frescoes are in the
Loggia of Cupid and Psyche on the ground
floor. Although they are generally attributed to Raphael, the great man did
little more than design the frescoes for his
assistants to paint. Apparently he was so
besotted with his mistress, who worked in a

nearby bakery, that he couldn't concentrate on his work. He did, however, find time to paint the *Trionfo di Galatea* (Triumph of Galatea) in the room of the same name.

On the 1st floor, Peruzzi's dazzling frescoes in the Salone delle Prospettive are a superb illusionary perspective of a colonnade and panorama of 16th-century Rome.

GALLERIA NAZIONALE D'ARTE ANTICA DI PALAZZO CORSINI
Map pp132–3

☎ 06 688 02 323; www.galleriaborghese.it; Via della Lungara 10; adult/EU 18-25yr/EU under 18yr & over 65yr €4/2/free; ☻ 8.30am-7.30pm Tue-Sun; ⊜ Lungotevere della Farnesina (Piazza Trilussa)

Housing part of Italy's national art collection (the rest is in Palazzo Barberini, p103), the 16th-century Palazzo Corsini has a distinguished history. Michelangelo, Erasmus and Bramante all stayed here but the *palazzo* is most readily associated with Queen Christina of Sweden, who took up residency in 1662 and entertained a steady stream of lovers in her richly frescoed bedroom.

Gallery highlights include Van Dyck's superb *Madonna della Paglia* (Madonna of the Straw), Murillo's *Madonna col bambino* (Madonna and Child), and a typically haunting Caravaggio, *San Giovanni Battista* (St John the Baptist), in Room 3. The paintings of the Bologna school in Room 7 also catch the eye, with works by Guido Reni, Agostino and Annibale Carracci, Giovanni Lanfranco and Guercino.

GIANICOLO

It's difficult to imagine now, but in 1849 the Gianicolo was the scene of fierce fighting, as a makeshift army under Giuseppe Garibaldi defended Rome against French troops sent to restore papal rule. Garibaldi is commemorated with a massive monument in Piazzale Giuseppe Garibaldi, while his Brazilian-born wife, Anita, gets her own equestrian monument about 200m away in Piazzale Anita Garibaldi.

The Gianicolo is a superb viewpoint with sweeping panoramas over Rome's rooftops.

ORTO BOTANICO Map pp132–3

☎ 06 499 17 107; Largo Cristina di Svezia 24; adult/6-11yr & over 60yr €4/2; ☻ 9am-6.30pm Mon-Sat Apr–mid-Oct, 9.30am-5.30pm Mon-Sat mid-Oct–Mar; ⊜ Lungotevere della Farnesina (Piazza Trilussa)

ROME'S OPTICAL ILLUSIONS

Aptly for such a theatrical city, Rome contains some magical visual tricks. There's Borromini's perspective-defying corridor at Palazzo Spada (p82); Andrea Pozzo's amazing trompe l'oeil at the Chiesa di Sant'Ignazio di Loyola (p84) and the secret keyhole view from Piazza dei Cavalieri di Malta (p119). Strangest of all is the view of St Peter's Dome from Via Piccolomini near Villa Doria Pamphilj (p136). Here the dome looms, filling the space at the end of the road, framed by trees. But the really curious thing is that as you move towards the cupola it seems to get smaller rather than larger as the view widens.

Formerly the private grounds of Palazzo Corsini (left), Rome's 12-hectare botanical gardens are a great place to unwind. Plants have been cultivated here since the 13th century, but in their present form, the gardens were established in 1883. They now boast up to 8000 species, including some of Europe's rarest plants. You will find an avenue of palms, a garden with 300 types of medicinal plants (Giardino dei Semplici), a collection of cacti, and an aroma garden (Giardino degli Aromi).

TEMPIETTO DI BRAMANTE & CHIESA DI SAN PIETRO IN MONTORIO
Map pp132–3

☎ 06 581 39 40; www.sanpietroinmontorio.it; Piazza San Pietro in Montorio 2; ☻ church 8am-noon & 3-4pm Mon-Fri, tempietto 9.30am-12.30pm & 4-6pm Tue-Sun Apr-Sep, 9.30am-12.30pm & 2-4pm Tue-Sun Oct-Mar; ⊜ Via Garibaldi

Considered the first great building of the High Renaissance, Bramante's sublime Tempietto (Little Temple; 1508) stands in the courtyard of the Chiesa di San Pietro in Montorio, on the spot where St Peter is said to have been crucified. It's a small building but its classically inspired design (a circular interior surrounded by a columned peristyle and topped by a proportionally perfect dome) beautifully captured the Renaissance *zeitgeist*. More than a century later, in 1628, Bernini added a staircase. Bernini also contributed a chapel to the adjacent church, the last resting place of Beatrice Cenci (see p83).

FONTANA DELL'ACQUA PAOLA
Map pp132–3

Via Garibaldi; ⊜ Via Garibaldi

Just up from the Chiesa di San Pietro in Montorio, this monumental white fountain was built in 1612 to celebrate the restoration of a 2nd-century aqueduct that supplied (and still supplies) water from Lago di Bracciano, 35km to the north of Rome. Four of the fountain's six pink-stone columns came from the façade of the old St Peter's Basilica, while much of the marble was pillaged from the Roman Forum. The large granite basin was added by Carlo Fontana in 1690.

VILLA DORIA PAMPHILJ Map pp132–3

🕙 dawn-dusk; 🚌 Via di San Pancrazio

Rome's largest park is a great place to escape the relentless city noise. Once a vast private estate, it was laid out around 1650 for Prince Camillo Pamphilj, nephew of Pope Innocent X. At its centre is the prince's summer residence, the Casino del Belrespiro, and its manicured gardens and citrus trees. It's now used for official government functions.

VATICAN CITY, BORGO & PRATI

Drinking & Nightlife p230; Eating p211; Shopping p185; Sleeping p263

The Vatican, the world's smallest sovereign state (a mere 0.44 sq km), sits atop the low-lying Vatican hill just a few hundred metres west of the River Tiber. Centred on the domed bulk of St Peter's Basilica and Piazza San Pietro, it is the capital of the Catholic world, a spiritual superpower whose law is gospel to the world's one billion Catholics.

Established under the terms of the 1929 Lateran Treaty, the Vatican is the modern vestige of the Papal States, the papal fiefdom that ruled Rome until Italian unification in 1861. As part of the agreement, signed by Mussolini and Pope Pius XI, the Holy See was also given extraterritorial authority over a further 28 sites in and around Rome, including the basilicas of San Giovanni in Laterano (p116), Santa Maria Maggiore (p105) and San Paolo fuori le Mura (p127), the catacombs (p122), and the pope's summer residence at Castel Gandolfo (p279).

top picks

VATICAN CITY, BORGO & PRATI

- Michelangelo's Pietà in St Peter's Basilica (p140)
- Stanze di Raffaello (p144)
- Sistine Chapel (p145)
- Castel Sant'Angelo (p146)
- Piazza San Pietro (p142)

As an independent state, the Vatican has its own postal service, newspaper, radio station and army. The flamboyantly dressed Swiss Guards (all practising Catholics from Switzerland) were first used by Julius II in 1506 to defend the Papal States against invading armies and today they are still responsible for the pope's personal security.

The Vatican's current look is the culmination of more than 1000 years of chipping and chopping. The Leonine walls date to 846 when Leo IV had them put up after a series of Saracen raids, while the Vatican palace, now home to the Vatican Museums and the Sistine Chapel, was originally constructed by Eugenius III in the 12th century. Subsequent popes extended it, fortified it and decorated it according to their political and artistic needs.

Between the Vatican and the river lies the cobbled, medieval district of the Borgo (before Mussolini bulldozed through Via dei Conciliazione, all the streets around St Peter's were like this), while to the north Prati is a graceful residential area popular with media types (Radiotelevisione Italiana – RAI – has its headquarters here).

The easiest way to get to the Vatican is to take metro line A to Ottaviano-San Pietro. Alternatively, catch bus 40 or 64 from Termini.

VATICAN CITY
St Peter's Basilica

In a city of churches, none can hold a candle to St Peter's Basilica (Basilica di San Pietro; Map pp138–9; ☎ 06 698 83 731; www.vatican.va; Piazza San Pietro; admission free, audioguides €5; ☉ 7am-7pm Apr-Sep, 7am-6pm Oct-Mar; Ⓜ Ottaviano-San Pietro), Italy's biggest, richest and most spectacular church. A monument to centuries of artistic genius, it's also a mecca for millions of tourists and on peak days it can attract more than 20,000 visitors. If you want to get in remember to dress appropriately – that means no shorts, miniskirts or bare shoulders.

The first basilica was built by Constantine in the 4th century. Standing on the site of Nero's stadium, the Ager Vaticanus, where St Peter is said to have been buried, it was consecrated in AD 326. Like many early churches, it eventually fell into disrepair and it wasn't until the mid-15th century that efforts were made to restore it, first by Pope Nicholas V and then, rather more successfully, by Julius II. In 1506 Bramante came up with a design for a basilica based on a Greek-cross plan, with a central dome and four smaller domes. In the ensuing construction, Bramante attracted great criticism for destroying the old basilica and, with it, many precious Byzantine mosaics and frescoes.

It took more than 150 years to complete the new basilica. Bramante, Raphael, Antonio da Sangallo, Michelangelo, Giacomo della Porta and Carlo Maderno all contributed, but it is generally held that St Peter's owes most to Michelangelo, who took over the project in 1547 at the age of 72 and was responsible for the great dome.

The façade and portico were designed by Carlo Maderno, who inherited the project after Michelangelo's death. He was also instructed

VATICAN CITY, BORGO & PRATI

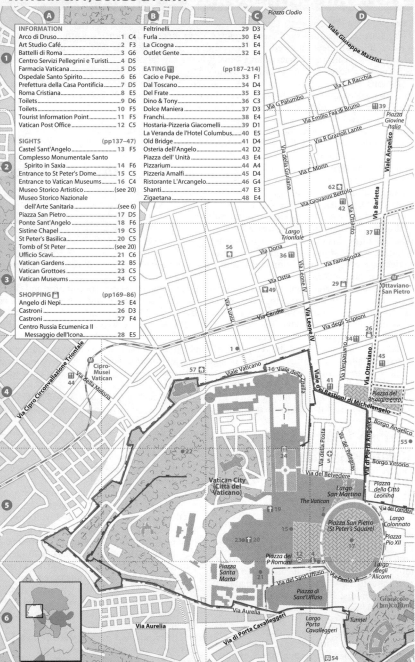

INFORMATION	
Arco di Druso	1 C4
Art Studio Café	2 F3
Battelli di Roma	3 G6
Centro Servizi Pellegrini e Turisti	4 D5
Farmacia Vaticana	5 D5
Ospedale Santo Spirito	6 E6
Prefettura della Casa Pontificia	7 D5
Roma Cristiana	8 E5
Toilets	9 D6
Toilets	10 F5
Tourist Information Point	11 F5
Vatican Post Office	12 C5

SIGHTS	(pp137–47)
Castel Sant'Angelo	13 F5
Complesso Monumentale Santo Spirito in Saxia	14 F6
Entrance to St Peter's Dome	15 C5
Entrance to Vatican Museums	16 C4
Museo Storico Artistico	(see 20)
Museo Storico Nazionale dell'Arte Sanitaria	(see 6)
Piazza San Pietro	17 D5
Ponte Sant'Angelo	18 F6
Sistine Chapel	19 C5
St Peter's Basilica	20 C5
Tomb of St Peter	(see 20)
Ufficio Scavi	21 C6
Vatican Gardens	22 B5
Vatican Grottoes	23 C5
Vatican Museums	24 C5

SHOPPING	(pp169–86)
Angelo di Nepi	25 E4
Castroni	26 D3
Castroni	27 F4
Centro Russia Ecumenica II Messaggio dell'Icona	28 E5

Feltrinelli	29 D3
Furla	30 E4
La Cicogna	31 E4
Outlet Gente	32 E4

EATING	(pp187–214)
Cacio e Pepe	33 F1
Dal Toscano	34 D4
Del Frate	35 E3
Dino & Tony	36 C3
Dolce Maniera	37 D3
Franchi	38 E4
Hostaria-Pizzeria Giacomelli	39 D1
La Veranda de l'Hotel Columbus	40 E5
Old Bridge	41 D4
Osteria dell'Angelo	42 D2
Piazza dell' Unità	43 E4
Pizzarium	44 A4
Pizzeria Amalfi	45 D4
Ristorante L'Arcangelo	46 G4
Shanti	47 E3
Zigaetana	48 E4

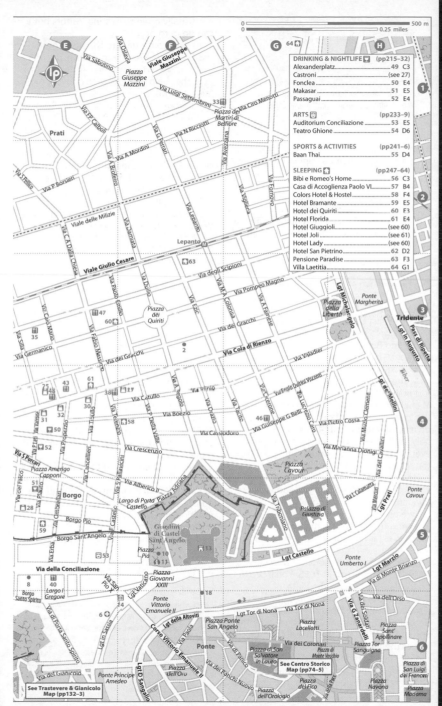

DRINKING & NIGHTLIFE (pp215–32)
Alexanderplatz............................ 49 C3
Castroni ....(see 27)
Fonclea 50 E4
Makasar 51 E5
Passaguai 52 E4

ARTS (pp233–9)
Auditorium Conciliazione 53 E5
Teatro Ghione 54 D6

SPORTS & ACTIVITIES (pp241–6)
Baan Thai...................................... 55 D4

SLEEPING (pp247–64)
Bibi e Romeo's Home 56 C3
Casa di Accoglienza Paolo VI.......... 57 B4
Colors Hotel & Hostel 58 F4
Hotel Bramante 59 E5
Hotel dei Quiriti 60 F3
Hotel Florida 61 E4
Hotel Giugqioli.......................(see 60)
Hotel Joli ....(see 61)
Hotel Lady ....(see 60)
Hotel San Pietrino 62 D2
Pensione Paradise 63 F3
Villa Laetitia............................... 64 G1

THE WORLD'S BIGGEST CHURCH – NEARLY

Contrary to popular opinion, St Peter's Basilica is not the world's largest church – the Basilica of Our Lady of Peace in Yamoussoukro on the Ivory Coast is bigger. Bronze floor plates in the central aisle indicate the respective sizes of the 14 next-largest churches.

to lengthen the nave towards the piazza, effectively altering Bramante's original Greek-cross plan to a Latin cross.

Free English-language guided tours of the basilica are run from the Vatican tourist office, the Centro Servizi Pellegrini e Turisti (p300), at 9.45am on Tuesday and Thursday and at 2.15pm every afternoon between Monday and Friday.

INTERIOR

The cavernous 187m-long interior covers more than 15,000 sq m and contains spectacular works of art, including three of Italy's most celebrated masterpieces: Michelangelo's Pietà, the breathtaking dome and Bernini's famous baldachin (canopy). The following describes an anticlockwise tour of the basilica.

At the beginning of the right aisle, just inside the Porta Santa (Holy Door), Michelangelo's hauntingly beautiful Pietà sits in its own chapel behind a panel of bullet-proof glass. Sculpted when he was only 25 (in 1499), this is the only work he ever signed – his signature is etched into the sash across the Madonna's breast.

Nearby, the red porphyry disk on the floor inside the main door marks the spot where Charlemagne and later Holy Roman Emperors were crowned by the pope.

Paying tribute to a woman whose reputation was far from holy, Carlo Fontana's monument to Queen Christina of Sweden is dedicated to the Swedish monarch who converted to Catholicism in 1655. You'll see it on a pillar just beyond the Pietà.

Moving down the aisle you come to the Cappella del Santissimo Sacramento, a small chapel decorated in sumptuous baroque style. The iron grille separating the chapel from the rest of the basilica was designed by Borromini; the gilt bronze ciborium above the altar is by Bernini; and the altarpiece, *The Trinity*, is by Pietro da Cortona. The chapel's

not usually open to passing visitors but you can go in to pray.

As you continue into the heart of the basilica, your eyes are inevitably drawn towards Bernini's spectacular baldachin over the main altar. However, take a moment to look up at Michelangelo's dome 119m above your head. Based on Brunelleschi's design for the Duomo in Florence, the towering cupola is supported by four solid stone piers, named after the saints whose statues adorn their Bernini-designed niches – Longinus, Helena, Veronica and Andrew – and decorated with reliefs depicting the *Reliquie Maggiori* (Major Relics): the lance of St Longinus, which he used to pierce Christ's side; the cloth of St Veronica, which bears a miraculous image of Christ; and a piece of the True Cross, collected by St Helena, the mother of Emperor Constantine.

At the base of the Pier of St Longinus, to the right as you face the high altar, is a famous bronze statue of St Peter, believed to be a 13th-century work by Arnolfo di Cambio. Much loved by pilgrims, its right foot has been worn down by centuries of kisses and caresses. On the Feast Day of St Peter and St Paul (29 June), the statue is dressed in papal robes.

To the right of the pier is the Cappella Gregoriana, built by Gregory XIII from designs by Michelangelo. Part of a marble column from the old basilica was placed here in 1578; the painting on it, the *Madonna del Soccorso* (Madonna of Succour), can still be made out.

Two notable works in the closed-off right transept are the monument of Clement XIII, one of Canova's most famous works, and the garish Altare della Navicella mosaic, based on a painting by Lanfranco.

Dominating the centre of the basilica is Bernini's 29m-high baldachin. Supported by

THE FACE IN THE BALDACHIN

The frieze on Bernini's baldachin contains a hidden narrative that begins at the pillar to the left, if your back is facing the entrance. As you walk clockwise around the baldachin note the woman's face carved into the frieze of each pillar, at about eye level. On the first three pillars her face seems to express the increasing agony of childbirth; on the last one, it's replaced by that of a smiling baby. The woman was a niece of Pope Urban VIII who gave birth as Bernini worked on the baldachin.

four spiral columns and made with bronze taken from the Pantheon, it stands over the high altar, which itself sits on the site of St Peter's grave. The pope is the only priest permitted to serve at the high altar. In front, the Confessione, built by Carlo Maderno, is where St Peter was originally buried.

Behind the altar in the tribune at the end of the basilica, the Throne of St Peter (1665) is the centrepiece of Bernini's extraordinary Cathedra Petri. In the middle of the elaborate gilded-bronze throne, supported by statues of saints Augustine, Ambrose, Athanasius and John Chrysostom, is a wooden seat, which was once thought to have been St Peter's but in fact dates to the 9th century. Above, rays of yellow light shine through a gaudy window, framed by a gilded mass of golden angels and in whose central pane flies a dove (representing the Holy Spirit).

To the right of the throne, Bernini's monument to Urban VIII depicts the pope flanked by the figures of Charity and Justice.

Moving to the left aisle, in the left transept behind the Pier of St Veronica, the Cappella della Colonna is decorated with figures of angels with garlands of flowers. Above the tomb of St Leo the Great is a particularly fine relief by the baroque sculptor Alessandro Algardi. Opposite it, under the next arch, is Bernini's last work in the basilica, the monument to Alexander VII.

About halfway down the left aisle, the cupola of the Cappella Clementina is named after Clement VIII (d 1605), who had Giacomo della Porta decorate it for the Jubilee of 1600. Beneath the altar is the tomb of St Gregory the Great, and above it a mosaic representing the Miracolo di San Giorgio (Miracle of St George) by Andrea Sacchi. To the left is a classical monument to Pope Pius VII by Thorvaldsen.

Particularly charming is the monument to Leo XI by Alessandro Algardi in the next arch. Beyond it, the richly decorated Cappella del Coro was created by Giovanni Battista Ricci to designs by Giacomo della Porta; Bernini designed the elegant choir stalls. The chapel is usually locked but it's worth sticking your nose through the gate to get a good look. The monument to Innocent VIII by Antonio Pollaiuolo (in the next aisle arch) is a re-creation of a monument from the old basilica.

Continuing back towards the front of the basilica, the Cappella della Presentazione contains two of St Peter's most modern works: on the right of the altar a monument to John XXIII by Emilio Greco, and to the left a monument to Benedict XV by Pietro Canonica. Under the next arch are the so-called Stuart monuments. On the right is the monument to Clementina Sobieska, wife of James Stuart, by Filippo Barigioni, and on the left is Canova's superb monument to the last three members of the Stuart clan, the pretenders to the English throne who died in exile in Rome.

DOME

St Peter's Basilica; admission with/without lift €7/5; ✕ 8am-6pm Apr-Sep, 8am-5pm Oct-Mar
Entry to the dome is to the far right of the basilica. A small lift takes you halfway up but it's still a long climb to the top (320 steps to be exact). Press on and you're rewarded with some stunning views over Rome. It's well worth the effort, but bear in mind that it's a long and tiring climb and not recommended for those who suffer from claustrophobia or vertigo.

MUSEO STORICO ARTISTICO

Treasury of St Peter's; St Peter's Basilica; adult/child & student €6/4; ✕ 9am-6.15pm Apr-Sep, 9am-5.15pm Oct-Mar
The sacristy entrance (halfway down the left aisle) leads to the Museo Storico Artistico (Treasury of St Peter's), which has sacred relics and priceless artefacts. Highlights include a tabernacle by Donatello; the Colonna Santa, a 4th-century Byzantine column from the earlier church; the 6th-century Crux Vaticana (Vatican Cross), a gift of Emperor Justinian II; and the massive 15th-century bronze tomb of Sixtus IV by Pollaiuolo.

TOMB OF ST PETER

admission €10, booking obligatory
Excavations beneath the basilica have uncovered part of the original church and what archaeologists believe is the tomb of St Peter. In 1942 the bones of an elderly, strongly built man were found in a box hidden behind a wall covered by pilgrims' graffiti. After more than 30 years of forensic examination, in 1976 Pope Paul VI declared the bones to be those of St Peter.

The excavations can only be visited on a 90-minute guided tour. To book you'll need to email the Ufficio Scavi (Excavations Office; ☎ 06 698 85 318; scavi@fsp.va) as early as possible.

VATICAN GROTTOES

admission free; ☉ 9am-6pm Apr-Sep, 9am-5pm Oct-Mar

Extending beneath the basilica, the Vatican Grottoes contain the tombs of numerous popes, including John Paul II, whose simple sepulchre contrasts with many of the flamboyant monuments in the basilica above, and several huge columns from the original 4th-century basilica. The entrance is through the right side of the portico.

Piazza San Pietro

One of the world's great public spaces, Bernini's piazza (Map pp138–9; M Ottaviano-San Pietro) was laid out between 1656 and 1667 for Pope Alexander VII.

Seen from above, it resembles a giant keyhole with two semicircular colonnades, each consisting of four rows of Doric columns, encircling a giant ellipse that straightens out to funnel believers into the basilica. The effect was deliberate – Bernini described the colonnades as representing 'the motherly arms of the church'. The 25m obelisk in the centre was brought to Rome by Caligula from Heliopolis in Egypt and later used by Nero as a turning post for the chariot races in his circus.

The scale of the piazza is dazzling: at its largest it measures 340m by 240m; there are 284 columns and, on top of the colonnades, 140 saints. In the midst of all this the pope seems very small as he delivers his weekly address at noon on Sunday.

Vatican Museums

Visiting the Vatican Museums (Musei Vaticani; Map pp138–9; ☎ 06 698 84 947; www.vatican.va; Viale Vaticano; adult/6-18yr & student/under 6yr €14/8/free, last Sun of the month free; ☉ entry 9am-4pm & closing 6pm Mon-Sat, entry 9am-12.30pm & closing 2pm last Sun of month; M Ottaviano-San Pietro) is an unforgettable experience that requires strength, stamina and patience. You'll

need to be on top of your game to endure the inevitable queues – if not for a ticket then for the security checks – and enjoy what is undoubtedly one of the world's great museum complexes.

Founded by Pope Julius II in the early 16th century and enlarged by successive pontiffs, the museums are housed in what is known collectively as the Palazzo Apostolico Vaticano. This massive 5.5-hectare complex consists of two palaces – the Vatican palace nearest St Peter's and the Belvedere Palace – joined by two long galleries. On the inside are three courtyards: the Cortile della Pigna, the Cortile della Biblioteca and, to the south, the Cortile del Belvedere.

You'll never manage to explore the whole complex in one go – you'd need several hours just for the highlights – so it pays to be selective. There are several suggested itineraries, or you can go it alone and make up your own route. Each gallery contains priceless treasures, but for a whistlestop tour get to the Pinacoteca, the Museo Pio-Clementino, Galleria delle Carte Geografiche, Stanze di Raffaello (Raphael Rooms) and the Sistine Chapel.

On the whole, exhibits are not well labelled, so consider hiring an audioguide (€7) or buying the *Guide to the Vatican Museums and City* (€10). There are also authorised guided tours (adult/concession €30/25), bookable on the Vatican's online ticket office (boxed text, p67).

The museums are well equipped for visitors with disabilities: there are four suggested itineraries, lifts and specially fitted toilets. Wheelchairs can also be reserved in advance – fax 06 698 85 433. Parents with young children can take prams into the museums.

MUSEO GREGORIANO PROFANO, MUSEO PIO-CRISTIANO & MUSEO MISSIONARIO-ETNOLOGICO

The Museo Gregoriano Profano contains classical statuary, including sculpture found

---

PAPAL AUDIENCES

At 11am on Wednesday, the pope addresses his flock at the Vatican (in July and August he does so in Castel Gandolfo, p279). For free tickets go to the ticket office of the Prefettura della Casa Pontificia through the bronze doors under the colonnade to the right of St Peter's. You can apply on the Tuesday before the audience or, at a push, on the Wednesday morning. Alternatively, download the application form from the Vatican website (www.vatican.va/various/prefettura/en/biglietti_en.html) and send it by fax or post to the Prefettura della Casa Pontificia (fax 06 698 85 863; Prefecture of the Papal Household, 00120 Vatican City State). Give contact details of the hotel you're staying at so that an arrangement can be made for delivery or collection of your tickets.

When he is in Rome, the pope also blesses the crowd in Piazza San Pietro on Sundays at noon. No tickets are required.

BOOKING ONLINE

Pre-booking a ticket to the Vatican Museums doesn't necessarily mean you'll avoid all queues – even with a ticket you must still pass the security checks – but it'll almost certainly save you time, especially if visiting in peak periods (Easter, Christmas, spring, early summer). You can reserve tickets through the Vatican's online ticket office (http://biglietteriamusei.vatican .va/musei/tickets/do?weblang=en&do), although you'll have to pay a €4 booking fee. On payment you'll receive email confirmation which you should print out and present, along with a valid ID card or passport, at the museum entrance.

in the Terme di Caracalla (p119). Greek pieces date from the 5th and 4th centuries BC, and Roman sculpture from the 1st to the 3rd centuries AD.

The Museo Pio-Cristiano is dedicated to early Christian antiquities. The collection of relics salvaged from the catacombs and carved sarcophagi was founded by Pius IX in 1854 and moved here from the Palazzo Laterano in 1970.

The Museo Missionario-Etnologico exhibits ethnological and anthropological artefacts brought back by missionaries from Africa, the Americas, Asia and the Middle East.

PINACOTECA

Inaugurated in 1932, the papal picture gallery boasts some 460 paintings, with works by Fra Angelico, Filippo Lippi, Benozzo Gozzoli, Federico Barocci, Guido Reni, Guercino, Nicholas Poussin, Van Dyck and Pietro da Cortona. There are several canvases by Raphael, who has a room to himself. Look out for the *Madonna di Foligno* (Madonna of Folignano) and his last painting, the magnificent *La Trasfigurazione* (Transfiguration), which was completed by his students after he died in 1520. Other highlights include Giotto's *Polittico Stefaneschi* (Stefaneschi Triptych); Giovanni Bellini's *Pietà;* Leonardo da Vinci's unfinished *San Gerolamo* (St Jerome); and Caravaggio's *Deposizione* (Deposition from the Cross).

MUSEO GREGORIANO EGIZIO

Pope Gregory XVI founded the Egyptian Museum in 1839 to hold pieces taken from Egypt during Roman times. The collection is small but there are some fascinating

exhibits, including the *Trono di Rameses II,* part of a statue of the seated king, and hieroglyphic inscriptions dating to around 2600 BC. In Room II, you'll find some vividly painted wooden sarcophagi from around 1000 BC and a couple of mummies that will titillate the macabre-minded. On one you can see a hole where the left eye should be – it was probably removed so that the brain could be extracted before mummification.

MUSEO PIO-CLEMENTINO

Housed in the Belvedere Palace, the Museo Pio-Clementino showcases some spectacular classical statuary, including the peerless *Apollo Belvedere* and the 1st-century *Laocoön,* both in the Cortile Ottagono (Octagonal Courtyard).

To the left as you enter the courtyard, the *Apollo Belvedere* is a 2nd-century Roman copy of a 4th-century-BC Greek bronze. A beautifully proportioned representation of the sun god Apollo, it's considered one of the great masterpieces of classical sculpture. Nearby, the *Laocoön* depicts a muscular Trojan priest and his two sons in mortal struggle with two sea serpents. When the statue was unearthed on the Esquilino in 1506, Michelangelo and Giuliano da Sangallo confirmed that it was the same sculpture that had been cited by Pliny the Elder some 1500 years earlier.

Back inside, the Sala degli Animali is filled with sculptures of all sorts of creatures and some magnificent 4th-century mosaics. Continuing through the sala you come to the Galleria delle Statue, which have several important classical pieces; the Sala delle Buste, which contains hundreds of Roman busts; and the Gabinetto delle Maschere, named after the floor mosaics of theatrical masks.

In the Sala delle Muse (Room of the Muses), the *Torso Belvedere* is another must-see. A Greek sculpture from the 1st century BC, it was found in Campo de' Fiori and was much admired by Michelangelo and other Renaissance artists.

The next room, the Sala Rotonda (Round Room) contains a number of colossal statues, including the gilded-bronze figure of *Ercole* (Hercules), and an exquisite floor mosaic featuring sea monsters and battles between Greeks and centaurs. The enormous basin in the centre of the room was found at Nero's Domus Aurea (p110) and is made out of a single piece of red porphyry stone.

MUSEO CHIARAMONTI

This museum is effectively the long corridor that runs down the lower east side of the Belvedere Palace. Its walls are lined with thousands of statues representing everything from immortal gods to playful cherubs and ugly Roman patricians. Near the end of the hall, off to the right, is the Braccio Nuovo (New Wing), which contains a famous sculpture of Augustus and a statue depicting the Nile as a reclining god covered by 16 babies (representing the number of cubits the Nile rose when it flooded).

MUSEO GREGORIANO ETRUSCO

On the upper level of the Belvedere (off the 18th-century Simonetti staircase), the Etruscan Museum contains artefacts unearthed in the Etruscan tombs of southern Etruria (now northern Lazio), as well as a collection of Greek vases and Roman antiquities. Of particular interest is the *Marte di Todi* (Mars of Todi), a full-length bronze statue of a warrior dating from the 4th century BC, in the Sala dei Bronzi.

Magnificent views of Rome can be had from the last room at the end of this wing (through the Sala delle Terracotte). From here you can also get a glimpse down the full drop of Bramante's 16th-century spiral staircase, which was designed so that horses could be ridden up it.

GALLERIA DEI CANDELABRI & GALLERIA DEGLI ARAZZI

By the time you reach these two galleries you're in the home stretch, well on the way to the Stanze di Raffaello and, beyond that, the Sistine Chapel.

Originally an open loggia, the Galleria dei Candelabri is packed with classical sculpture, including several elegantly carved marble candelabras that give the gallery its name.

The corridor continues through to the Galleria degli Arazzi (Tapestry Gallery) and its 10 huge tapestries. The tapestries opposite the windows were designed by students of Raphael and woven in Brussels in the 16th century. On the other side, the 17th-century tapestries were woven at the Barberini workshop.

GALLERIA DELLE CARTE GEOGRAFICHE

One of the unsung heroes of the Vatican Museums, the 175m-long Map Gallery is hung with 40 huge topographical maps. They were all created between 1580 and 1583 for Pope Gregory XIII, and were based on drafts by Ignazio Danti, one of the leading cartographers of his day.

Next to the Map Gallery is the Appartamento di San Pio V, containing some interesting Flemish tapestries, and the Sala Sobieski, named after the enormous 19th-century canvas on its northern wall (depicting the victory of the Polish King John III Sobieski over the Turks in 1683). These rooms lead into the magnificent Stanze di Raffaello.

STANZE DI RAFFAELLO

Even in the shadow of the Sistine Chapel, the Stanze di Raffaello (Raphael Rooms) stand out. The four rooms were part of Pope Julius II's private apartment and in 1508 he commissioned the 25-year-old Raphael to decorate them.

But while they carry his name, not all the rooms were completed by Raphael: he painted the Stanza della Segnatura (Study) and the Stanza d'Eliodoro (Waiting Room), while both the Stanza dell'Incendio (Dining Room) and the Sala di Costantino (Reception Room) were decorated by students following his designs.

The Sala di Costantino is the first room you come to. Finished by Giulio Romano in 1525, five years after Raphael's death, it was used for official functions and decorated to highlight the triumph of Christianity over paganism. This theme is evident in the huge *Battaglia di Costantino contro Maxentius* (Battle of the Milvian Bridge), in which Constantine, Rome's first Christian emperor, defeats his rival Maxentius.

Leading off this *sala* are two rooms that are not traditionally counted as Raphael

top picks

VATICAN MUSEUMS

- Genesis by Michelangelo (opposite)
- Giudizio Universale by Michelangelo (opposite)
- La Scuola d'Atene by Raphael (right)
- Apollo Belvedere & Laocoön by unknown (p143)
- Marte di Todi by unknown (above)

rooms: the Sala dei Chiaroscuri, featuring a Raphael-designed ceiling, and the tiny Cappella di Niccolo V, Pope Nicholas V's private chapel. The superb frescoes here were painted by Fra Angelico around 1450 and depict the lives of St Stephen (upper level) and St Lawrence (lower level).

The Stanza d'Eliodoro, which was used for private audiences, was painted between 1512 and 1514. It takes its name from the painting on the main wall to the right of the entrance, the Cacciata d'Eliodoro (Expulsion of Heliodorus from the Temple). An allegorical work, it tells the story of Heliodorus being killed as he tries to make off with booty stolen from the Temple in Jerusalem; the allusion, however, is to Julius II's military victory over foreign powers.

To the left of this is the Messa di Bolsena (Mass of Bolsena), showing Julius II paying homage to the relic of a 13th-century miracle at the lake town of Bolsena (see p273). Next is Incontro di Leone Magno con Attila (Encounter of Leo the Great with Attila) by Raphael and his school, and on the fourth wall the Liberazione di San Pietro (Liberation of St Peter). This depicts St Peter being freed from prison but is actually an allusion to Pope Leo's imprisonment after the Battle of Ravenna.

The Stanza della Segnatura is named after the Segnatura Gratiae et Iustitiae, the Vatican court that sat here in the 16th century. Here you'll find Raphael's masterpiece, La Scuola d'Atene (The School of Athens), featuring philosophers and scholars gathered around Plato and Aristotle. The lone figure in front of the steps is believed to be Michelangelo, while the figure of Plato is said to be a portrait of Leonardo da Vinci, and Euclide (in the lower right) is Bramante. Raphael also included a self-portrait in the lower right corner (he's the second figure from the right). Opposite is La Disputa del Sacramento (Disputation on the Sacrament), also by Raphael.

The last of Raphael's four rooms, the Stanza dell'Incendio, was completed during Leo X's papacy and is largely dedicated to the glory of his namesakes Leo III and Leo IV. The most famous work, Incendio di Borgo (Fire in the Borgo), depicts Leo IV extinguishing a fire by making the sign of the cross. The ceiling was painted by Raphael's master, Perugino.

From Raphael's rooms, stairs lead to the Appartamento Borgia, decorated with frescoes by Bernardino Pinturicchio and the Vatican's collection of modern religious art.

SISTINE CHAPEL

The one place in the Vatican Museums that not one of the 4.5 million annual visitors wants to miss is the Sistine Chapel (Cappella Sistina). Home to two of the world's most famous works of art – Michelangelo's Genesis (Creation) on the barrel-vaulted ceiling and the Giudizio Universale (Last Judgment) – this 15th-century chapel is where the papal conclave is locked to elect the pope.

The chapel was originally built in 1484 for Pope Sixtus IV, after whom it is named, but it was Julius II who commissioned Michelangelo to decorate it in 1508. Initially the artist was reluctant – he had little painting experience and he regarded himself as a sculptor – but Julius prevailed and over the next four years (1508–12) Michelangelo decorated the entire 800-sq-m ceiling. To do so, he designed a curved scaffolding system that allowed him to work standing up, albeit in an awkward backward-leaning position, and employed a steady stream of assistants to help with the plaster work (producing frescoes involves painting directly onto wet plaster).

The frescoes down the middle of the ceiling represent nine scenes from the book of Genesis: God Separating Light from Darkness; Creation of the Sun, Moon and Planets; Separation of Land from Sea; Creation of Adam; Creation of Eve; Temptation and Expulsion of Adam and Eve from the Garden of Eden; Noah's Sacrifice; The Flood; and the Drunkenness of Noah.

Michelangelo painted these in reverse order, providing critics with a remarkable illustration of his artistic development: the first, the Drunkenness of Noah (nearest the Giudizio Universale) is much more formal than his later works at the other end of the ceiling.

The most famous scene is the image of the Creation of Adam, where God points his index figure at Adam, bringing him to life. God's swirling red cape surrounds a group of people, said to represent the generations to come. In the Temptation and Expulsion of Adam and Eve from the Garden of Eden, Adam and Eve are shown (on the left) taking the forbidden fruit from Satan, represented by a snake with the body of a woman coiled around a tree.

The main scenes are framed by ignudi, athletic male nudes, with which Michelangelo celebrates the male figure. Next to them, on the lower curved part of the vault, separated by trompe l'oeil cornices, are large figures of

Hebrew prophets and pagan sibyls. These muscular, powerful figures – especially the Delphic and Libyan sibyls – are among the most striking and dramatic images on the ceiling.

Pope Clement VII commissioned Michelangelo to paint the end wall 22 years after he finished the ceiling, although it was Clement's successor Paul III who actually chose the subject matter, the Last Judgement. From the outset it was a controversial project. Uproar broke out when two frescoes by Perugino were destroyed to prepare the wall – it had to be replastered so that it tilted inwards to protect it from dust – and when it was unveiled in 1541, its dramatic, swirling mass of predominantly naked bodies provoked outrage. Some years later Pope Pius IV had Daniele da Volterra, one of Michelangelo's students, add fig leaves and loincloths to the many nudes. Supporters, however, considered it one of Michelangelo's best works, surpassing all the other paintings in the chapel, including his own ceiling frescoes.

Whatever the technical judgment, there's no denying its ambition. Paul III wanted a powerful image to act as a warning to Catholics to toe the line during the Reformation (then sweeping Europe) – and that's exactly what he got. Depicting the souls of the dead being torn from their graves to face the wrath of God, it's a work of highly charged emotion that was said by some to reflect Michelangelo's tormented faith. Judge for yourself by examining his self-portrait on the shroud held by St Bartholomew, to the right of Christ.

The walls of the chapel were also painted by important Renaissance artists, including Botticelli, Domenico Ghirlandaio, Pinturicchio and Luca Signorelli. These magnificent late-15th-century frescoes represent events in the lives of Moses (to the left, looking at the *Giudizio Universale*) and Christ (to the right).

Particularly beautiful is Botticelli's *Temptation of Christ* and the *Cleansing of the Leper* (the second fresco on the right). Ghirlandaio's *Calling of Peter and Andrew* (the third fresco on the right) includes among the crowd of onlookers portraits of prominent contemporary figures, while Perugino's superbly composed *Christ Giving the Keys to St Peter* (the fifth fresco on the right) includes a self-portrait – the fifth figure from the right.

VATICAN LIBRARY

Founded by Nicholas V in 1450, the Vatican Library (Biblioteca Apostolica Vaticana), contains more than 1.5 million volumes, including illuminated manuscripts, early printed books, prints, drawings and coins. Selected items from the collection are displayed in the Salone Sistino.

Vatican Gardens

Visits to the Vatican Gardens (Giardini del Vaticano; Map pp138–9; http://biglietteriamusei.vatican.va; adult/child incl entry to Vatican Museums €30/25; ☽ guided tours 9.30am Mon, Tue, Thu & Fri; Ⓜ Ottaviano-San Pietro) are by two-hour guided tour only, for which you'll need to book at least a week in advance. The perfectly manicured gardens contain fortifications, grottoes, monuments and fountains dating from the 9th century to the present day.

BORGO

Overshadowed by Castel Sant'Angelo, this quarter retains a low-key medieval charm despite batteries of restaurants, hotels and pizzerias.

COMPLESSO MONUMENTALE SANTO SPIRITO IN SAXIA Map pp138–9

☎ 06 683 52 433; www.giubilarte.it; Borgo Santo Spirito 1; adult/concession €7.50/6; ☽ guided tours 10am & 3pm Mon; 🚌 Piazza Pia

Originally an 8th-century lodging for Saxon pilgrims, this ancient hospital complex was established by Pope Innocent III in the late 12th century. Three hundred years later Sixtus IV added an octagonal courtyard and two vast frescoed halls, known collectively as the Corsia Sistina (Sistine Ward). A further highlight is the 16th-century Palazzo del Commendatore, where the central courtyard features a gracious double loggia.

Just round the corner, the Museo Storico Nazionale dell'Arte Sanitaria (Map p138–9; ☎ 06 678 78 64; www2.comune.roma.it/artesanitaria; Lungotevere in Sassia 3; adult/concession €2.60/1.60; ☽ 10am-noon Mon, Wed & Fri) continues the medical theme with a ghoulish collection of medical instruments, curiosities and anatomical models.

CASTEL SANT'ANGELO Map pp138–9

☎ 06 681 91 11; Lungotevere Castello 50; adult/EU 18-25yr €5/3; ☽ 9am-7pm Tue-Sun; 🚌 Piazza Pia

With its chunky round keep, this castle is an instantly recognisable landmark. Originally a mausoleum for the emperor Hadrian, it was converted into a papal fortress in the 6th century and named after an angelic vision that Pope Gregory had in 590. Thanks to a secret 13th-century passageway to the Vatican palaces, it provided sanctuary to many popes in times of danger, including Clemente VII who holed up here during the 1527 Sack of Rome.

Its upper floors boast lavishly decorated Renaissance interiors, including, on the 4th floor, the beautifully frescoed Sala Paolina. Two stories further up, the terrace, immor-talised by Puccini in his opera *Tosca,* offers great views over Rome.

PONTE SANT'ANGELO Map pp138–9
📢 **Piazza Pia**

Hadrian built the Ponte Sant'Angelo across the River Tiber in 136 to provide an approach to his mausoleum, but it was Bernini who brought it to life with his angel sculptures in the 17th century. The three central arches of the bridge are part of the original structure; the end arches were restored and enlarged in 1892–94 during the construction of the Lungotevere embankments.

VILLA BORGHESE & NORTHERN ROME

Drinking & Nightlife p231; Eating p214; Shopping p186; Sleeping p264

Boasting the capital's most famous park and a number of fascinating museums, Northern Rome is largely given over to business and housing. Many Italian companies have their headquarters here and Parioli (the district to the north of Villa Borghese) is Rome's poshest neighbourhood.

The obvious starting point is the Villa Borghese park. Popular with joggers and picnickers, this green oasis counts the city zoo, Rome's largest modern art gallery and a stunning Etruscan museum among its myriad attractions. But its pièce de résistance is the Museo e Galleria Borghese, one of Rome's top galleries and home to a stunning collection of Bernini sculpture.

Marking the park's western flank, Via Flaminia shoots northwards from Piazza del Popolo,

top picks

VILLA BORGHESE & NORTHERN ROME

- Museo e Galleria Borghese (below)
- Museo Nazionale Etrusco di Villa Giulia (p152)
- Galleria Nazionale d'Arte Moderna (p152)
- Auditorium Parco della Musica (p153)
- Basilica di Sant'Agnese fuori le Mura & Mausoleo di Santa Costanza (p154)

along the path of an ancient Roman road. It's not an especially inspiring street but it does access two of Rome's most important modern buildings: Renzo Piano's extraordinary Auditorium Parco della Musica and Zaha Hadid's contemporary art gallery, MAXXI. Continue up the road and you come to Ponte Milvio, a bridge popular with starstruck lovers and scene of a decisive Roman battle in 312. Over the river, and to the west, the Stadio Olimpico is Rome's impressive football stadium.

On the eastern side of Villa Borghese, Via Salaria, the old Roman *sale* (salt) road, is now the heart of a smart residential and business district. Among the embassies and town houses, you'll come across a pocket of exuberant Art Nouveau buildings in an area known as Coppedè. Beloved as they are today, these *palazzi* were much maligned in their day, and Coppedè, the architect who designed many of them, killed himself in despair.

To the north of Via Salaria, the vast Villa Ada park expands northwards; to the south, Via Nomentana traverses acres of housing as it heads out of town. On Via Nomentana, Villa Torlonia is a captivating park, and the Basilica di Sant'Agnese fuori le Mura claims Rome's oldest Christian mosaic.

To get to Villa Borghese, you can walk up from Spagna metro station to the top of Via Vittorio Veneto, from where it's a short hop away. Alternatively take bus 116, 52 or 53 from Via Vittorio Veneto near Barberini metro station. Tram 3 trundles down Via Flaminia, and there are regular buses along Via Nomentana and Via Salaria.

VILLA BORGHESE & AROUND

MUSEO E GALLERIA BORGHESE
Map pp150–1

☎ 06 3 28 10; www.galleriaborghese.it; Piazzale Scipione Borghese 5; adult/EU 18-25yr/EU under 18yr & over 65yr €8.50/5.25/2, audioguides €5; ⏰ 8.30am-7.30pm Tue-Sun, prebooking necessary; 🚌 Via Pinciana

If you only have time (or inclination) for one art gallery in Rome, make it this. Housing the 'queen of all private art collections', it provides the perfect introduction to Renaissance and baroque art. To limit numbers, visitors are admitted at two-hourly intervals, so call to prebook, and enter at an allotted entry time, but trust us, it's worth it.

The collection, including works by Caravaggio, Bernini, Botticelli and Raphael, was formed by Cardinal Scipione Borghese (1579–1633), the most knowledgeable and ruthless art collector of his day. It's housed in the Casino Borghese, the neoclassical look of which is the result of a 17th-century revamp of Scipione's original villa.

The villa is divided into two parts: the ground-floor museum, with its superb sculptures, intricate Roman floor mosaics and fab frescoes; and the upstairs picture gallery.

On the ground floor, things get off to a cracking start in the entrance hall, decorated with 4th-century floor mosaics of fighting gladiators and a *Satiro Combattente* (Fighting Satyr) from the 2nd century.

High on the wall is a gravity-defying bas-relief, *Marco Curzio a Cavallo*, of a horse and rider falling into the void, by Pietro Bernini (Gian Lorenzo's father).

Sala I is centred on Antonio Canova's daring depiction of Napoleon's sister, Paolina Bonaparte Borghese, reclining top-less as *Venere Vincitrice* (Victorious Venus; 1805–08).

But it's Gian Lorenzo Bernini's spectacular sculptures – flamboyant depictions of pagan myths – that really steal the show. Just look at Daphne's hands morphing into leaves in the swirling *Apollo e Dafne* (1622–25) in Sala III, or Pluto's hand pressing into the seemingly soft flesh of Persephone's thigh in the *Ratto di Proserpina* (Rape of Persephone; 1621–22) in Sala IV.

Caravaggio, one of Cardinal Scipione's favourite artists, dominates Sala VIII. You'll see a dissipated-looking *Bacchus* (1592–95); the strangely beautiful *La Madonna dei Palafenieri* (Madonna with Serpent; 1605–06); and *San Giovanni Battista* (St John the Baptist; 1609–10), probably Caravaggio's last work. Then there's the much-loved *Ragazzo col Canestro di Frutta* (Boy with a Basket of Fruit; 1593–95); and the dramatic *Davide con la Testa di Golia* (David with the Head of Goliath; 1609–10): Goliath's severed head is said to be a self portrait.

With works representing the best of the Tuscan, Venetian, Umbrian and northern European schools, the picture gallery upstairs offers a wonderful snapshot of European Renaissance art.

In Sala IX don't miss Raphael's extraordinary *La Deposizione di Cristo* (Christ Being Taken Down from the Cross; 1507), and his charming *Dama con Liocorno* (Young Woman with Unicorn; 1506). In the same room is the superb *Adorazione del Bambino* (Adoration of the Christ Child; 1495) by Fra Bartolomeo and Perugino's *Madonna con Bambino* (Madonna and Child; first quarter of the 16th century).

Next door, Correggio's erotic *Danae* (1530-31) shares wall space with a willowy Venus, as portrayed by Cranach in his *Venere e Amore che Reca Il Favo do Miele* (Venus and Cupid with Honeycomb; 1531).

Moving on, Sala XIV boasts two self-portraits of Bernini – one as a young man in 1623 and one painted in 1635 – and Sala XVIII contains two significant works by Reubens: *Pianto sul Cristo Morto* (Lamentation over the Dead Christ; 1602) and

top picks

MUSEO E GALLERIA BORGHESE

- Ratto di Proserpina, by Gian Lorenzo Bernini
- Apollo e Dafne, by Gian Lorenzo Bernini
- Venere Vincitrice, by Antonio Canova
- Ragazzo col Canestro di Frutta, by Caravaggio
- Amor Sacro e Amor Profano, by Titian

Susanna e I Vecchioni (Susanna and the Elders; 1605-07). However, the highlight is Titian's early masterpiece, *Amor Sacro e Amor Profano* (Sacred and Profane Love; 1514) in Sala XX.

VILLA BORGHESE Map pp150–1

www.villaborghese.it; entrances at Piazzale San Paolo del Brasile, Piazzale Flaminio & Via Raimondi; ☼ dawn-dusk; 🚊 Porta Pinciana

Cardinal Scipione Borghese's 17th-century playground is now a ravishing park with shaded avenues, hedged walks, flowerbeds, gravel paths and roads. The English-style Giardino del Lago (Map pp150–1) is a late 18th-century creation, as is Piazza di Siena (Map pp150–1), an amphitheatre used for Rome's top equestrian event in May.

Bike hire is available at various points, including Via delle Belle Arti, near the Galleria Nazionale d'Arte Moderna. Bank on about €5/10 per hour/day.

Near the park's southern entrance (Piazzale San Paolo del Brasile), the Cinema dei Piccoli (Map pp150–1; ☎ 06 855 34 85; www.cinemadeipiccoli.it; Viale delle Pineta 15; tickets €5) is the world's smallest cinema. Housed in a curious chalet-style building, it screens kids' films most afternoons – check the website for details.

BIOPARCO Map pp150–1

☎ 06 360 82 11; www.bioparco.it, in Italian; Viale del Giardino Zoologico 1; adult/child over 1m & under12yr/child under 1m €10/8/free, incl reptile house €12.50/10.50/free; ☼ 9.30am-6pm Apr-Oct, 9.30am-5pm Nov-Mar; 🚊 Bioparco

A tried and tested kid-pleaser, Rome's zoo hosts a predictable collection of animals on a far-from-inspiring 18-hectare site. Quite frankly there are better ways to spend your money, but if your kids are driving you bonkers or you're crying out for a break from classical art, it's a thought.

VILLA BORGHESE & NORTHERN ROME

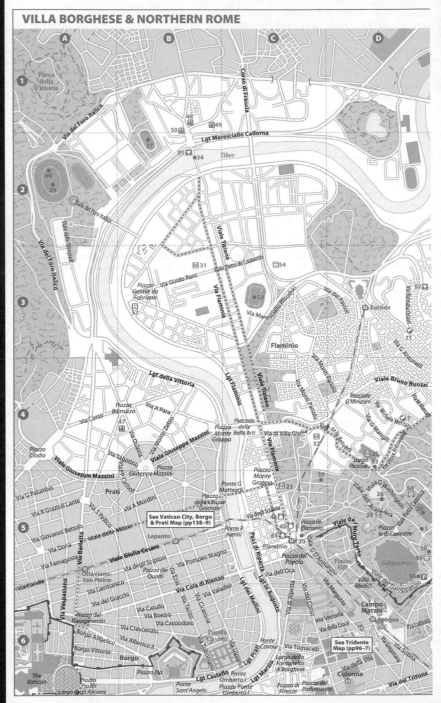

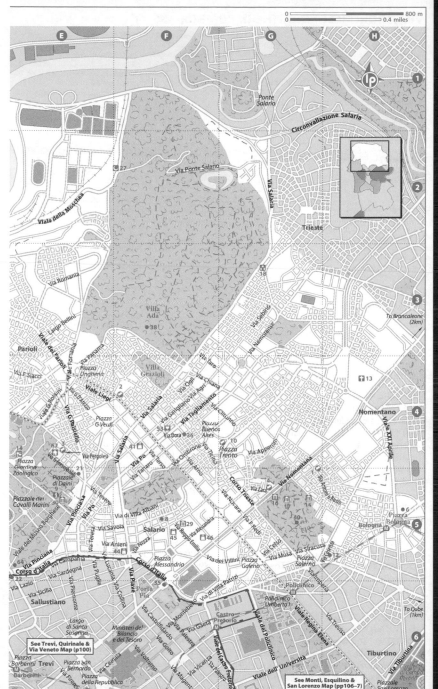

0 _____ 800 m
0 _____ 0.4 miles

E   F   G   H

1

2

3

4

5

6

Circonvallazione Salaria

Ponte
Salario

Trieste

To Broncaleone
(2km)

Via Ponte Salario

Via Salaria

Viale della Moschea

Villa
Ada

Parioli

Largo Bellini

Viale dei Parioli

Via F. Slacci

Via Ghisleri

Piazza
Ungheria

Villa
Grazioli

Via Panama

Via Romania

Nomentano

Via XXI Aprile

Via Salbina

Via Namogoun

Via Taro

Via Ogt

Via Chiana

Via Gargliano

Via Agri

Via Tigliamento

Via Chiumbo

Via Appenini

Viale Liegi

Piazza
G Verdi

Via G Paisiello

Via Paisiello

Piazza
Buenos
Aires

Piazza
Trento

Via Salaria

Via Pergolesi

Via Dora

Via Po

Via Tevere

Via Po

Via Ombrone

Via Metauro

Via Aniene

Via di Villa Albani

Piazzale
di Daini

Piazza
Giardino
Zoologico

Piazzale dei
Cavalli Marini

Viale del Museo Borghese

Via Pinciana

Salario

Via Savoia

Via Nizza

Via Anieni

Corso Trieste

Via Nola

Via Frejus

Via Zara

Via Nomentana

Via Celso

Via Musa

Via Siracusa

Via Cirene

Piazza
Solerno

Bologna

Piazza
Bologna

Piazza
Galeno

Piazza
Alessandria

Via dei Villini

Via Catanzaro

Via di Villa Patrizi

Corso d'Italia

Via Pinciana

Corso d'Italia

Via Campania

Via Sardegna

Via Lazio

Via Sicilia

Via Pinciana

Via Lucania

Via Piave

Via Puglie

Via Collina

Sallustiano

Largo
di Santa
Susanna

Piazza
Barberini

Trevi

Barberini

Piazza San
Bernardo

Piazza San
Bernardo

Piazza
della Repubblica

Ministeri del
Bilancio
e del Tesoro

Via Castelfidardo

Via Montebello

Via Palestro

Via Gaeta

Via Vicenza

Via Magenta

Via Goito

Via Volturno

Via Cernaia

Porta
Pia

Castro
Pretorio

Viale del Castro Pretorio

Viale del Policlinico

Policlinico
Umberto I

Policlinico

Via Regina Elena

Viale dell'Università

Via Tiburtina

Via Tiburtina

Tiburtino

Piazzale
San Lorenzo

To Qube
(1km)

27

13

18

38

2

53

36

41

10

63

3

14

21

29

45

46

44

30

35

22

64

16

80

6

See Trevi, Quirinale &
Via Veneto Map (p100)

See Monti, Esquilino &
San Lorenzo Map (pp106–7)

151

VILLA BORGHESE & NORTHERN ROME (pp150–1)

MUSEO CARLO BILOTTI Map pp150–1

☎ 06 820 59 127; www.museocarlobilotti.it; Viale Fiorello La Guardia; adult/EU 18-25yr/EU under 18yr & over 65yr €4.50/2.50/free; ⊗ 9am-7pm Tue-Sun; ⓖ Porta Pinciana

The art collection of billionaire cosmetics magnate Carlo Bilotti is stylishly housed in the Orangery of Villa Borghese. It's a small collection (only 22 pieces), but it's interesting and well presented with explanatory panels in English and Italian. Paintings range from a Warhol portrait of Bilotti's wife and daughter to 18 works by Giorgio de Chirico (1888–1978), one of Italy's most important 20th-century artists. There's also a fine selection of landscapes by Alessandro Poma (1874–1960).

GALLERIA NAZIONALE D'ARTE MODERNA Map pp150–1

☎ 06 322 98 221; www.gnam.arti.beniculturali .it; Viale delle Belle Arti 131, entrance for visitors with disabilities at Via Antonio Gramsci 73; adult/EU 18-25yr/EU under 18yr & over 65yr €10/8/free; ⊗ 8.30am-7.30pm Tue-Sun; ⓖ Piazza Thorvaldsen

Often overlooked, the GNAM is definitely worth a visit. Here, in a vast *belle époque* palace, you'll find works by some of the most important exponents of modern Italian art. There are canvases by the *macchiaioli* (the Italian Impressionists) and futurists Boccioni and Balla, as well as several impressive sculptures by Canova and major works by Modigliani and De Chirico. International artists are also represented, with works by Degas, Cezanne, Kandinsky, Klimt, Mondrian, Pollock and Henry Moore.

The gallery's charming courtyard café is the perfect place to catch up on what you've just seen.

MUSEO NAZIONALE ETRUSCO DI VILLA GIULIA Map pp150–1

☎ 06 322 65 71; www.ticketeria.it; Piazzale di Villa Giulia 9; adult/EU 18-25yr/EU under 18yr & over 65yr €4/27free; ⊗ 8.30am-7.30pm Tue-Sun; ⓖ Viale delle Belle Arti

If you're planning to visit Lazio's Etruscan sites (see p269 and p270), or even if you're not, this is the ideal place to bone up on Etruscan history. Italy's finest collection of Etruscan treasures is considerately presented in Pope Julius III's 16th-century pleasure palace.

Exhibits, many of which came from burial tombs in the surrounding Lazio region, range from bronze figurines and black *bucchero* tableware to temple decorations, terracotta vases and a dazzling display of sophisticated jewellery.

Must-sees include a polychrome terracotta statue of *Apollo*, the 6th-century BC *Sarcofago degli Sposi* (Sarcophagus of the Betrothed), and the *Euphronios Krater*, a celebrated Greek vase that was returned to Italy in 2008 after a 30-year tug of war between the Italian government and New York's Metropolitan Museum of Art.

FLAMINIO

AUDITORIUM PARCO DELLA MUSICA
Map pp150–1

☎ 06 802 41 281; www.auditorium.com; Viale Pietro de Coubertin 10; guided tours adult/over 65yr/under 26yr €9/7/5; ☿ 11am-6pm Mon-Sat, 10am-6pm Sun, tours depart hourly 11.30am-4.30pm Sat & Sun, by arrangement Mon-Fri; ☒ or ☒ Viale Tiziano
Rome's premier concert complex is not what you'd expect. Designed by Renzo Piano and inaugurated in 2002, it consists of three grey pod-like concert halls set round a 3000-seat amphitheatre and the remains of a 300 BC Roman villa, discovered shortly after construction work began. The complex also boasts one of the capital's best-stocked CD and music bookshops. Guided tours cover the concert halls, amphitheatre (known as the *cavea*) and enormous foyer area, itself home to a small archaeology museum. For more on the Auditorium, see p234.

EXPLORA – MUSEO DEI BAMBINI DI ROMA
Map pp150–1

☎ 06 361 37 76; www.mdbr.it; Via Flaminia 82; adult/3-12yr/under 3yr €6/7/free; ☿ visits depart 10am, noon, 3pm & 5pm Tue-Sun Sep-Jul, noon, 3pm & 5pm Tue-Sun Aug; Ⓜ Flaminio
Rome's only dedicated kids' museum, Explora is aimed at the under-12s. It's set up as a miniature town where children can play at being grown-ups. With everything from a doctor's surgery to a TV studio, it's a hands-on, feet-on, full-on experience that your nippers will love. *And* it runs on solar power.

In order to control the number of visitors, all visits are limited to 1¾ hours, with entry times as detailed above. Booking is advisable on weekdays, essential on weekends.

MUSEO NAZIONALE DELLE ARTI DEL XXI SECOLO (MAXXI)
Map pp150–1

☎ 06 321 01 81; www.maxxi.parc.beniculturali.it; Via Guido Reni 2f; admission free; ☿ 10am-7pm Tue-Sun; ☒ Via Flaminia
Housed in a former army barracks, and built to an avant-garde design by Anglo-Iraqi architect Zaha Hadid, MAXXI (National Museum of 21st-century Art) is due to open in 2010. Until then it is being used to host temporary exhibitions, with past events including a study of art on the internet and a video projection by Serbian performance artist Marina Abramovic. When it eventually opens its doors, there will be a permanent collection dedicated to contemporary art and architecture as well as space for more experimental events.

PONTE MILVIO Map pp150–1
☒ Ponte Milvio
A pretty pedestrian footbridge, Ponte Milvio was the scene of one of the great events in Roman history: Constantine's defeat of Maxentius in 312. These days, it's a favourite with love-struck teenagers who come here to leave padlocks chained to the railings as a sign of their undying *amore*.

The bridge was first built in 109 BC to carry Via Flaminia over the Tiber and survived intact until 1849, when Garibaldi's troops blew it up to stop advancing French soldiers. Pope Pius IX had it rebuilt a year later. On the northern end, the tower Torretta Valadier is sometimes used to stage art exhibitions.

FORO ITALICO Map pp150–1
Viale del Foro Italico; ☒ Lungotevere Maresciallo Cadorna
At the foot of Monte Mario, the Foro Italico is an impressive Fascist-era sports complex. Designed by the architect Enrico Del Debbio, it remains much as it was originally conceived. A 17m-high marble obelisk, inscribed with the words 'Mussolini Dux', stands at the beginning of a broad avenue leading down to the Stadio dei Marmi, a running track surrounded by 60 marble nudes, and the Stadio Olimpico, Rome's 70,000-seater football stadium. The latter was a later addition, built in 1960 for the Olympic Games and revamped for the 1990 World Cup. It's now home to Rome's two football teams.

NOMENTANO

PORTA PIA Map pp150–1

Piazzale Porta Pia; 🚌 Via XX Settembre

An imposing crenellated structure, the Michelangelo-designed Porta Pia was the scene of bitter street-fighting in 1870 as Italian troops breached the adjacent walls to wrest the city from the pope and claim it for the nascent kingdom of Italy.

The concrete monstrosity just inside the city walls is the British Embassy. Opposite it is Villa Paolina, the residence of Napoleon's sister Paolina Bonaparte between 1816 and 1824 and now the French embassy to the Holy See.

VILLA TORLONIA Map pp150–1

Via Nomentana 70; 🕙 dawn-dusk; 🚌 Via Nomentana

Full of towering pine trees, atmospheric palms and scattered villas, this splendid 19th-century park once belonged to Prince Giovanni Torlonia (1756–1829), a powerful banker and landowner. His large neoclassical villa, the Casino dei Principi, later became the Mussolini family home (1925–43) and, towards the end of WWII, Allied headquarters (1944–47). These days it's used to stage temporary exhibitions.

MUSEI DI VILLA TORLONIA Map pp150–1

☎ 06 820 59 127; www.museivillatorlonia .it; adult/EU 18-25yr/EU under 18yr & over 65yr Casino Nobile €4.50/2.50/free, Casino delle Civette €3/1.50/free, both €6.50/3/free; 🕙 9am-7pm Tue-Sun Apr-Sep, to 5.30pm Tue-Sun Mar & Oct, to 4.30pm Tue-Sun Nov-Feb; 🚌 Via Nomentana

With its oversized neoclassical façade – designed by Giuseppe Valadier – Casino Nobile makes quite an impression. Inside, in the luxuriously decorated interior, you can admire the Torlonia family's fine collection of sculpture, period furniture and paintings.

To the northeast, the much smaller Casina delle Civette is a bizarre mix of Swiss cottage, Gothic castle and twee farmhouse decorated in Art Nouveau style. Built between 1840 and 1930, it is now a museum dedicated to stained glass. Alongside the house's original windows, which include works by leading Italian artist Duilio Cambelotti, there are more than 100 designs and sketches for stained glass, decorative tiles, parquetry floors and woodwork.

The main ticket office is just inside the Via Nomentana entrance to the park.

BASILICA DI SANT'AGNESE FUORI LE MURA & MAUSOLEO DI SANTA COSTANZA Map pp150–1

☎ 06 861 08 40; Via Nomentana 349; 🕙 7.30am-noon & 4-7.30pm; 🚌 Via Nomentana

It's well worth searching out this intriguing medieval religious complex. In the 7th-century Basilica di Sant'Agnese fuori le Mura look out for the golden apse mosaic depicting St Agnes standing on the flames that failed to kill her. According to tradition, the 13-year-old Agnes survived the pyre only to be beheaded on Piazza Navona (p78) and buried in the catacombs (guided visit adult/concession €6/3; 🕙 closed Sun morning & Nov) beneath this church.

Across the convent courtyard is the 4th-century Mausoleo di Santa Costanza, built for Constantine's daughters, Constance and Helen. The squat circular building has a dome supported by 12 pairs of granite columns and a vaulted ambulatory decorated with beautiful 4th-century mosaics, said by some to be Christendom's oldest.

SALARIO & BEYOND

CATACOMBE DI PRISCILLA Map pp150–1

☎ 06 862 06 272; http://web.tiscali.it/catacombe _priscilla; Via Salaria 430; guided visit adult/7-15yr/ under 7yr €6/3/free; 🕙 8.30am-noon & 2-5pm Tue-Sun Sep-Jul; 🚌 Via Salaria

Stretching for some 13km, these creepy catacombs boast the oldest known image of the Madonna, dated at early 2nd century. Something of high-society burial ground – several popes were buried here between 309 and 555 – they retain quite a lot of their original decoration. Particularly impressive is the Cappella Greca funerary chapel with its fine stucco decoration and some well-preserved late-3rd-century biblical frescoes.

MOSCHEA DI ROMA Map pp150–1

Rome's Mosque; ☎ 06 808 21 67; Viale della Moschea; admission free; 🕙 9-11.30am Wed & Sat; 🚌 Viale della Moschea

To the northwest of Villa Ada, Paolo Portoghesi's vast postmodernist mosque sits amid the greenery of the posh Parioli district. One of Europe's largest mosques (it extends for some 30,000 sq m), it was paid for by the Saudi royal family and inaugurated in 1995, 11 years after the first stone was laid. It's open daily for Muslims to pray and on Wednesday and Saturday mornings for visitors. Note that visits are suspended in August, during Ramadan and on Italian and Islamic holidays.

MUSEO D'ARTE CONTEMPORANEA DI ROMA (MACRO) Map pp150-1
☎ 06 671 070 400; www.macro.roma.museum; admission €1; Via Reggio Emilia 54; ⏰ 9am-7pm Tue-Sun; 🚃 Via Nizza

Along with MAXXI (p153), this is Rome's flagship contemporary art museum. Exhibits, which include works by all of Italy's important post-WWII artists, are displayed in what was once a brewery, itself an important example of industrial design. The new-look museum retains much of the building's original structure but sports a sexy steel-and-glass finish thanks to a recent revamp by trendy French architect Odile Decq. Collection highlights include abstract paintings by Achille Perilli, 1960s Pop Art by Tano Festa and works by artists from the Nuova Scuola Romana. Temporary exhibitions showcase emerging international talent.

QUARTIERE COPPEDÈ Map pp150-1
🚃 or 🚊 Viale Regina Margherita

Best entered from the corner of Via Tagliamento and Via Dora, this compact quarter is a mesmerising mishmash of Tuscan turrets, Liberty sculptures, Moorish arches, Gothic gargoyles, frescoed façades and palm-fringed gardens, all designed by little-known Florentine architect Gino Coppedè between 1913 and 1926. At its heart is whimsical Piazza Mincio and the Fontana delle Rane (Fountain of the Frogs), a modern take on the better known Fontana delle Tartarughe in the Jewish Ghetto (p83).

VILLA ADA Map pp150-1
entrances at Via Salaria & Via Ponte Salario; 🚃 Via Salaria

If you're in this neck of the woods and you need a breather, Villa Ada is the place. A big rambling park with wooded paths, lakes and lawns, it was once the private property of King Vittorio Emanuele III. Outdoor concerts are held here in summer as part of the Roma Incontro il Mondo festival.

WALKING TOURS

Ancient Rome

1 Il Vittoriano More than the Colosseum, more than the forums or Palatino, it's this vast hulk of white marble (p71) that dominates Ancient Rome's cityscape. Dedicated to Vittorio Emanuele II, unified Italy's first king, it's uniformly disliked but boasts spectacular views.

2 Piazza del Campidoglio Considered by many to be Rome's most beautiful square, Michelangelo's stunning piazza (p70) sits atop the Campidoglio. In ancient times this was the spiritual heart of Rome, home to two of the capital's most important temples; nowadays, it hosts the Capitoline Museums and the headquarters of the Rome city council.

3 Capitoline Museums Dating to 1471, these are the world's oldest public museums (p70). Their collection of classical sculpture, one of Rome's finest, is housed in the two *palazzi* that face each other over the square: Palazzo dei Conservatori and Palazzo Nuovo.

WALK FACTS

Start Il Vittoriano (🚌 Piazza Venezia)
End Palatino (Ⓜ Colosseo)
Distance 1.5km
Duration Three hours
Fuel stop Caffè Capitolino (p216)

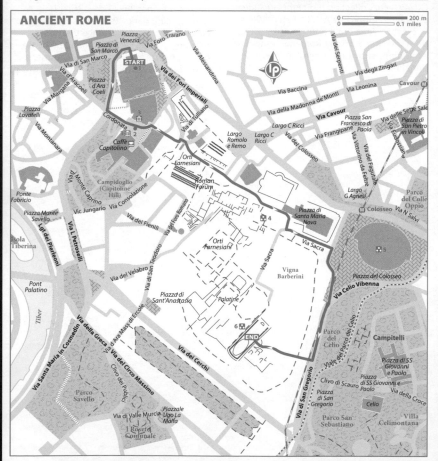

ANCIENT ROME

Inside, the tasty Caffè Capitolino supplies good coffee and views over the forums.

4 Roman Forum Rome's most famous ruins (p67) once constituted the epicentre of world power. If you can imagine it, this is where senators, consuls and emperors met to plot the course of the Roman empire and where virgins coyly fuelled the flames of the vestal fire.

5 Colosseum One of Italy's top tourist attractions, the Colosseum (p67) is an electrifying sight, its tiered stands towering over armies of queuing visitors. A spectacular feat of Roman engineering, the 50,000-seat stadium was inaugurated by Emperor Titus in AD 80.

6 Palatino According to legend the Palatino (p63) is where Romulus killed his twin and founded Rome in 753 BC. An evocative and atmospheric area of giant ruins, this was Ancient Rome's most exclusive neighbourhood, home to the cream of imperial society.

Centro Storico

1 Piazza Colonna Rome's political heart, this elegant square (p84) is dominated by the 30m-high Colonna di Marco Aurelio and flanked by the 17th-century Palazzo Chigi, official residence of the Italian prime minister. Continue to Piazza di Montecitorio for the equally impressive seat of the Chamber of Deputies, the 17th-century Palazzo di Montecitorio (p84).

2 Pantheon Ancient Rome's best-preserved monument, the Pantheon (p73) was built in 27 BC, modified by Hadrian in the 2nd century AD and consecrated as a Christian church in 608. Make sure to look up and admire the largest masonry vault ever built.

3 Chiesa di Santa Maria Sopra Minerva A short walk from the Pantheon, this 13th-century church (p77) is one of the few examples of Gothic architecture in Rome. Inside there's a minor Michelangelo; outside there's Bernini's much-loved Elefantino (p77).

WALK FACTS

Start Piazza Colonna (🚌 Via del Corso)
End Piazza Farnese (🚌 Corso Vittorio Emanuele II)
Distance 2km
Duration Two hours
Fuel stop Caffè Sant'Eustachio (p219)

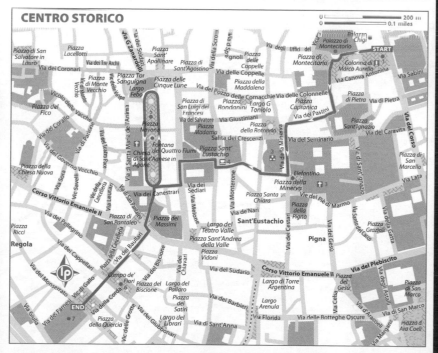

CENTRO STORICO

NEIGHBOURHOODS WALKING TOURS

4 Caffè Sant'Eustachio En route to Piazza Navona, stop at this café (p219) for a coffee. Reckoned by many to be the best in the capital, the espresso is short and creamy with a rich, deep aftertaste.

5 Piazza Navona Baroque central, Piazza Navona (p78) is central Rome's showpiece square. Here, among the street artists, tourists and pigeons, you can compare the two giants of Roman baroque – Bernini, creator of the Fontana dei Quattro Fiumi, and Borromini, responsible for the Chiesa di Sant'Agnese in Agone.

6 Campo de' Fiori On the other side of Corso Vittorio Emanuel II, the busy road that bisects the *centro storico,* life centres on Campo de' Fiori (p81). By day this noisy square stages a colourful fruit 'n' veg market; by night it transforms into a raucous open-air pub, beloved of foreign students and lusty Romans.

7 Palazzo Farnese The focal point of refined Piazza Farnese is this magnificent Renaissance palazzo (p81), home to the French Embassy and some of the city's finest frescoes, said by some to rival those of the Sistine Chapel. To see them, though, you'll need to book well in advance.

Trastevere & Gianicolo

1 Basilica di Santa Cecilia in Trastevere
Musicians can pay homage to their patron saint on the very spot where she was martyred in 230. St Cecilia lived and died in a house buried beneath a 5th-century church, on top of which the current basilica (p130) stands. Her headless body lies in a tomb under the main altar.

2 Piazza Santa Maria in Trastevere Right in the action, this laid-back piazza (p131) is a prime people-watching spot. Grab yourself a drink from the Bar San Calisto (p229) then hang out with the tourists, students, diners and drinkers who converge here every night. The square's fountain is a 17th-century renovation of a Roman original.

WALK FACTS
Start Basilica di Santa Cecilia in Trastevere (🚌 or 🚋 Viale di Trastevere)
End Orto Botanico (🚌 Via della Lungara)
Distance 2km
Duration 2½ hours
Fuel stop Bar San Calisto (p229)

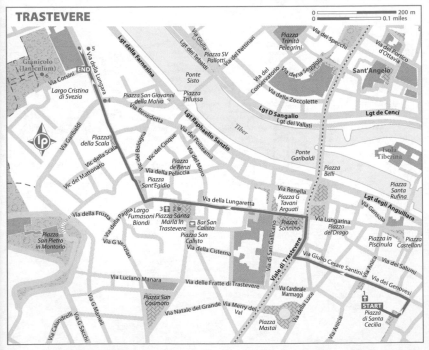

TRASTEVERE

3 Basilica di Santa Maria in Trastevere

Said to be the oldest church (p131) dedicated to the Virgin Mary in Rome, this gem is Trastevere's most important sight. It was originally built in the 3rd century, but it's best known for its stunning gold mosaics, which were added some 900 years later in the 12th century.

4 Porta Settimiana

Guarding Trastevere's northern entrance, Porta Settimiana (p134) was built in the late 15th century and modified 300 years later in 1798. Leading off north, Via della Lungara was laid down in the 16th century to connect Trastevere with the Vatican.

5 Villa Farnesina

Just outside Porta Settimiana, Villa Farnesina (p134) was one of Rome's first great Renaissance palaces. Built in the early 16th century and later bought by the powerful Farnese family, it features some superb frescoes by Raphael, including his acclaimed work, the *Trionfo di Galatea* (Triumph of Galatea).

6 Orto Botanico

Laid out on the slopes of the Gianicolo, Rome's 19th-century botanical gardens (p135) are a lovely, low-key place to unwind. Amateur botanists will have their work cut out identifying the 8000 plant species on display across the 12-hectare site.

Vatican City, Borgo & Prati

1 Castel Sant'Angelo

A squat drum of a castle, this landmark monument (p146) was built as a mausoleum for Hadrian in the 1st century AD. Later converted into a fort, it famously served as a refuge for Pope Clement VII during the 1527 sack of Rome. Admire great views over a coffee at the upstairs bar.

2 Via della Conciliazione

Lined with imperious Fascist buildings, Via della Conciliazione is the dramatic approach road to Piazza San Pietro and St Peter's Basilica. Mussolini had it bulldozed through the area's tightly

---

WALK FACTS

Start Castel Sant'Angelo (🚌 Piazza Pia)
End Vatican Museums (Ⓜ Ottaviano-San Pietro)
Distance 2km
Duration All day
Fuel stop Dino & Tony (p212)

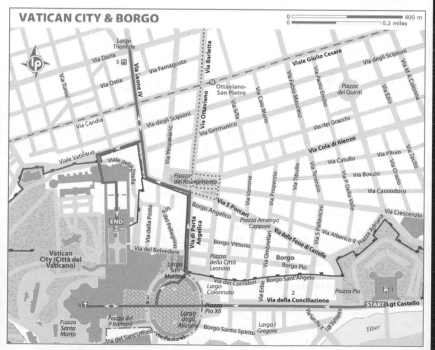

VATICAN CITY & BORGO

packed medieval streets to celebrate the signing of the Lateran Treaty in 1929.

3 Piazza San Pietro One of the world's great urban spaces, Piazza San Pietro (p142) was designed by baroque maestro Gian Lorenzo Bernini in the mid-17th century. Flanked by two semicircular colonnades, it measures 340m by 240m at its largest, and is surrounded by 284 columns and 140 saints.

4 St Peter's Basilica From the instantly recognisable façade to the unbelievably lavish interior, everything about St Peter's Basilica (p137) is designed to awe. Highlights include the *Pietà*, carved by Michelangelo when he was only 25, and Bernini's towering baldachin over the main altar. Overhead, Michelangelo's dome is one of the great feats of Renaissance engineering.

5 Dino & Tony One of the few genuine trattorias in this touristy area, Dino & Tony (p212) serves authentic Roman food at honest prices. The antipasti are memorable and the service is gruff and friendly.

6 Vatican Museums Worth a walking tour in their own right, the Vatican Museums (p142) are vast. Once you're in, and you'll need to be patient as the queues are notoriously long, you'll find yourself face to face with one of the world's great art collections. Save energy for the last stop, the Sistine Chapel (p145).

Southern Rome

1 Mausoleo di Cecilia Metella A short walk from the bus stop at the intersection of Via Cecilia Metella and Via Appia Antica brings you to this imposing 1st-century-BC mausoleum (p123). Built for the daughter of Quintus Metellus Creticus, it was incorporated into the castle of the Caetani family in the early 14th century.

2 Circo di Massenzio In the 4th century AD this open area of rolling grass and towering pine trees was a spectacular 10,000-seat arena (p123) with a chariot racetrack. In the same complex are the ruins of the Tomba di Romolo, built by Maxentius for his son, and the remains of Maxentius' imperial palace.

3 Basilica & Catacombe di San Sebastiano The 4th-century basilica (p123) was built over the catacombs where the apostles Peter and Paul were originally buried, and on the spot where St Sebastian was martyred.

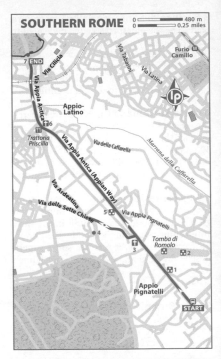

SOUTHERN ROME

WALK FACTS

Start Corner of Via Appia Antica and Via Cecilia Metella ((M) Colli Albani, then (bus) 660 to its final stop)
End Porta San Sebastiano ((M) Piramide)
Distance 4.2km
Duration Three hours
Fuel stop Trattoria Priscilla (p209)

The catacombs are the main attraction but the basilica's worth a quick look, if for nothing other than a glimpse of the marble imprint of Jesus' foot.

4 Mausoleo delle Fosse Ardeatine This is a moving monument (p126) to the victims of Italy's worst WWII atrocity – on 24 March 1944, 335 people were shot here by the Nazis in reprisal for a partisan attack. To get here, go left down Via delle Sette Chiese, then left into Via Ardeatina and after about 100m you'll see the mausoleum on your right.

5 Catacombe di San Callisto If you're doing this walk on a Sunday, you'll find the Catacombe di San Sebastiano closed. Don't worry, though, as these, Rome's largest, most famous, and busiest catacombs (p126), are a fine alternative. To date archaeologists have unearthed some 500,000 bodies, including seven popes, in 20km of tunnels.

6 Chiesa del Domine Quo Vadis? It was here that St Peter is supposed to have met a vision of Jesus and asked *'Domine, quo vadis?'* ('Lord, where are you going?'). Note that to get to this tiny church (p126) you have to walk against the traffic along a section of road that has no pavement.

7 Porta San Sebastiano About 700m beyond the Chiesa del Domine Quo Vadis?, this 5th-century city gate (p127) marks the start (or end – all roads lead *to* Rome, not *from* it) of Via Appia Antica. The largest and most impressive of the gates in the Aurelian Wall,

it houses a small museum illustrating the history of the wall.

Villa Borghese & Northern Rome

1 Museo e Galleria Borghese Home to what's hailed as the 'queen of all private art collections', this gallery (p148) is one of Rome's

WALK FACTS

Start Museo e Galleria Borghese (🚌 Via Pinciana)
End MAXXI (🚌 or 🚊 Via Flaminia)
Distance 3.5km
Duration Four hours
Fuel stop A picnic at Piazza di Siena

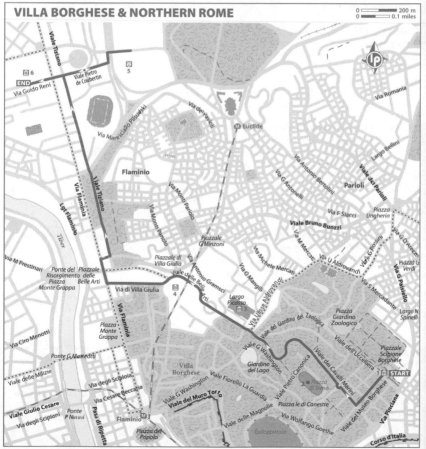

VILLA BORGHESE & NORTHERN ROME

must-see sights. The Bernini sculpture on display here is quite staggering and the rich painting collection includes works by Caravaggio, Botticelli and Raphael. Remember to book your tickets in advance.

2 Piazza di Siena This 18th-century arena (p149) is used to stage Rome's top showjumping event in May. For the rest of the year, it's a good place to flop and regain your strength. Bring your own picnic and watch the impromptu footy games and lunchtime joggers.

3 Galleria Nazionale d'Arte Moderna For a change of period, Rome's premier modern art gallery (p152) is the obvious choice. Get past the neoclassical bombast of the exterior and you'll discover an excellent collection, with works by the Italian *macchiaioli* painters, early-20th-century futurists and a host of international artists.

4 Museo Nazionale Etrusco di Villa Giulia Italy's finest collection of Etruscan treasures is housed in this beautiful Renaissance villa (p152) on the edge of Villa Borghese. Highlights include a terracotta statue of Apollo and the 6th-century-BC *Sarcofago degli Sposi*, taken from a tomb in Cerveteri.

5 Auditorium Parco della Musica A striking example of contemporary architecture, Rome's principal concert complex (p153) has become something of a city icon since it opened in 2002. With its distinct Renzo Piano design and 3000-seat amphitheatre, it is the focus of the city's music scene and regularly stages concerts by world-class musicians.

6 Museo Nazionale delle Arti del XXI Secolo (MAXXI) Designed by Anglo-Iraqi architect Zaha Hadid, the National Museum of 21st-Century Art (p153) is one of Rome's top contemporary-arts galleries. It houses a permanent collection of works by national and international artists and regularly hosts events and temporary exhibitions.

Rome's Baroque Beauty

1 Piazza Navona Dive straight into Rome's baroque heartland at this buzzing piazza (p78). In the centre is the Fontana dei Quattro Fiumi, a flamboyant fountain by Gian Lorenzo Bernini. To the side, the Chiesa di Sant'Agnese in Agone was designed by Bernini's hated rival Francesco Borromini.

2 Chiesa di Sant'Ivo alla Sapienza Regarded as one of Borromini's greatest achievements, this tiny church (p80) is a study in baroque architecture. The combination of convex and concave surfaces, the complex geometric design, the clever use of lighting – they're all here. Topping everything is a unique twisted spire.

3 Chiesa di San Luigi dei Francesi Hidden away in the streets east of Piazza Navona, this church (p80) harbours three, yes three, paintings by Caravaggio, the *enfant terrible* of the 16th-century art world. Highlighting his trademark *chiaroscuro* and his naturalistic approach to religious subjects, they're in the front chapel to the left of the altar.

4 Chiesa di Sant'Ignazio di Loyola This ornate baroque church (p84) boasts a wonderfully showy interior and a celebrated ceiling fresco by Andrea Pozzo. Outside, the piazza is a stunning example of rococo town planning – note how the curved façades make the piazza seem larger than it actually is.

5 Piazza del Quirinale The towering obelisk rising out of this uneven piazza (p101) marks the home of the president of the Italian Republic, Palazzo del Quirinale (p102). The palazzo, built by a band of big-name baroque architects, was commandeered by the Italian state after unification. The resident pope was not happy.

6 Via del Quirinale Flanking the Palazzo del Quirinale, this not particularly enticing street boasts two gems: Bernini's Chiesa di Sant'Andrea al Quirinale (p102) and, further on, Borromini's Chiesa di San Carlo alle Quattro Fontane (p102). The latter, although in dire need of a wash, is considered Borromini's best.

7 Chiesa di Santa Maria della Vittoria You'd never know it from outside, but this small church (p103) holds one of the greatest works of European baroque – Bernini's *Santa Teresa trafitta dall'amore di Dio* (Ecstasy of St Teresa). Oozing sexual ambiguity, it depicts St Teresa lost in religious rapture as she's pierced by an angel's arrow.

8 Galleria Nazionale d'Arte Antica – Palazzo Barberini A magnificent art gallery (p103) housed in one of Rome's great dynastic *palazzi*. Students of the baroque shouldn't miss the *Trionfo della Divina Provvidenza*

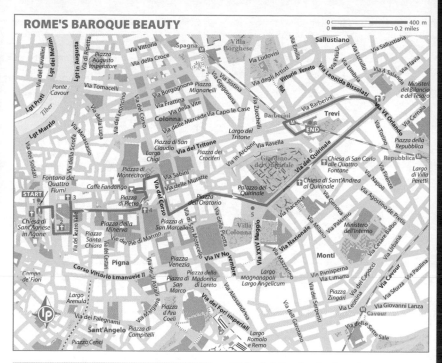

0 ———— 400 m
0 ———— 0.2 miles

WALK FACTS

Start Piazza Navona (🚌 Corso del Rinascimento)
End Galleria Nazionale d'Arte Antica (Ⓜ Barberini)
Distance 3km
Duration Four hours
Fuel stop Caffè Fandango (p217)

(Triumph of Divine Providence), a spectacular fresco by Pietro da Cortona.

Fellini's Rome

1 Via Vittorio Veneto Sweeping down from Villa Borghese, this smart, tree-lined street (p104) was the favourite of the beau monde that Fellini satirises in *La Dolce Vita* (1960). Film buffs will note that the on-screen version is flat – this is because Fellini had it completely reconstructed at Cinecittà film studios.

2 Trevi Fountain Rome's largest and most famous fountain (p99) is where Anita Ekberg teasingly splashes in *La Dolce Vita*. According to tradition, if you toss a coin into the fountain, you'll return to Rome. Consequently, tourists throw in about €3000 a day.

3 Via dei Condotti Bikers charge up Rome's top shopping strip (p98) in the exhilarating night ride at the end of *Roma* (1972). These days it's closed to traffic, so you'll have to get your kicks ogling the jewellery at Bulgari and the bags at Prada.

4 Piazza di Spagna Foreigners flock to this piazza (p95) to hang out on the Spanish Steps. In the film *Roma*, the steps are overrun by flute-playing, free-loving hippies in various stages of undress; in real life you'll find them covered by flirting teenagers, out-of-breath tourists and street hawkers.

5 Via Margutta Until his death on 31 October 1993, Fellini lived with his wife Giulietta Masina at Via Margutta 110. Elegant and low-key, this tranquil and picturesque street (p98) exudes an air of moneyed bohemia with its colourful façades, fancy galleries and tasteful eateries.

6 Piazza del Popolo Just round the corner from Fellini's home, this showy neoclassical piazza (p94) is where Marcello and Maddalena discuss Rome, life and love in *La Dolce Vita*. Grab a table at Canova (p220), Fellini's favourite

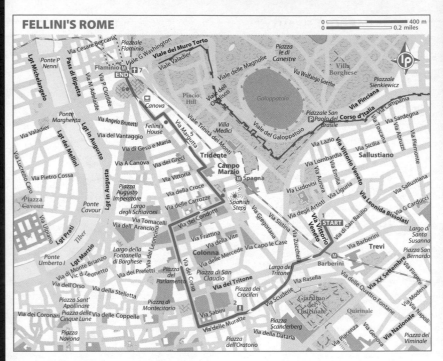

FELLINI'S ROME

WALK FACTS

Start Via Vittorio Veneto (**M** Barberini)
End Chiesa di Santa Maria del Popolo (**M** Flaminio)
Distance 2.5km
Duration Three hours
Fuel stop Canova (p220)

café, and while away the hours over an *aperitivo* (aperitive).

7 Chiesa di Santa Maria del Popolo

Brought up as a Catholic, Fellini often included religious imagery in his films. The Chiesa di Santa Maria del Popolo (p94), built on the site where Nero is supposed to have been buried, is one of Rome's oldest and richest Renaissance churches. Inside, you'll find works by Raphael, Bernini and Caravaggio, as well as Rome's oldest stained-glass windows.

Baths, Basilica, Circus & Cemetery

1 Terme di Caracalla Escape the crowds amid the skeletal ruins of Caracalla's massive

3rd-century baths complex (p119). In its heyday this structure could accommodate as many as 1600 people in its heated pools, baths, gyms, libraries, shops and gardens. Opera fans should make sure to catch a summer performance.

2 Circo Massimo Now a browning basin of worn grass, the Circus Maximus (p67) was ancient Rome's largest stadium, with a 600m racetrack and a capacity of up to 250,000 people. Chariot races and battle recreations were held here while the Roman emperors looked down from their palaces on the nearby Palatino (p63).

3 Parco Savello A small but beautiful park (p118) on the top of the Aventino hill. Known as the Giardino degli Aranci (Orange Garden), it's a lovely, perfumed place to hang out and enjoy views over the Tiber to St Peter's Basilica.

4 Basilica di Santa Sabina Originally built in the 5th century, this august Dominican basilica (p118) boasts one of the oldest and strangest depictions of the crucifixion (they forgot the crosses!). Inside, the 24 Corinthian

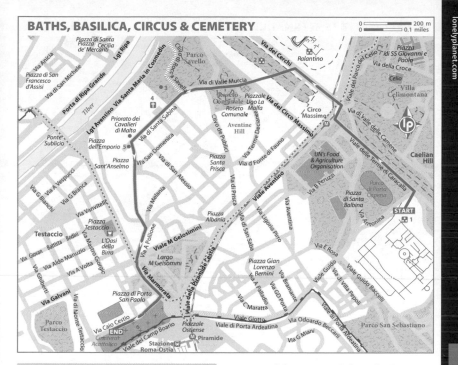

BATHS, BASILICA, CIRCUS & CEMETERY

WALK FACTS

Start Terme di Caracalla (Ⓜ Circo Massimo)
End Cimitero Acattolico per gli Stranieri
(Ⓜ Piramide)
Distance 3km
Duration Three hours
Fuel stop L'Oasi della Birra (p226)

---

columns were custom-made for the church and were the first ever constructed to support an arched arcade.

5 Piazza dei Cavalieri di Malta At the southern end of Via di Santa Sabina, this ornamental neoclassical piazza (p119) is perfect for Peeping Toms. Look through the keyhole of the Priorato dei Cavalieri di Malta and you'll see the dome of St Peter's perfectly positioned at the end of a row of hedges.

6 Cimitero Acattolico per gli Stranieri Looking over a 1st-century-BC pyramid and a 21st-century road junction, Rome's Protestant Cemetery (p119) is a surprisingly tranquil and relaxing place. Noise from the passing traffic might occasionally seep through, but

you won't hear a squeak from the Romantic poets Shelley and Keats, both of whom are buried here.

Romancing the Eternal City

1 Gianicolo Give in to the romance of the moment as you admire the sweeping views from the Gianicolo hill (p135) above Trastevere. As you make the steep climb down, take time to visit the Tempietto di Bramante (p135), a small but perfectly formed masterpiece of Renaissance architecture.

2 Via Giulia On the other side of the river, Via Giulia (p82), designed by Bramante in 1508, is the perfect picture of Roman beauty with its orange trees and refined Renaissance *palazzi*. At the southern end, ivy cascades down from the Michelangelo-designed Arco Farnese and water streams from the 17th-century Fontana del Mascherone.

3 Palazzo Farnese This elegant piazza is dominated by the sublime Renaissance façade of Palazzo Farnese (p81), the current seat of the French Embassy. Over the way, the twin fountains were originally huge baths at the Terme di Caracalla.

165

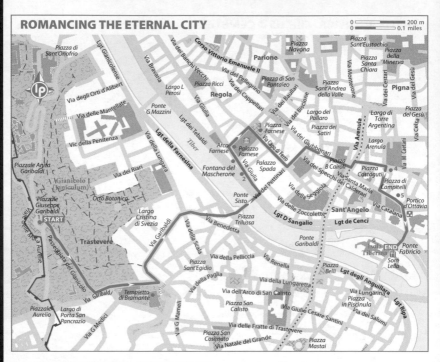

ROMANCING THE ETERNAL CITY

WALK FACTS

Start Gianicolo (🚌 Via Garibaldi)
End Isola Tiberina (🚌 Lungotevere dei Pierleoni)
Distance 2.5km
Duration 2½ hours
Fuel stop Sora Lella (p200)

4 Fontana delle Tartarughe A veritable
monument to the power of love, this playful 16th-century fountain (p83) was made to
save the Duke of Mattei's prospective marriage. Having gambled his fortune away, the
luckless duke needed to impress his future
father-in-law, so he had the fountain made
in a single night.

5 Via Portico d'Ottavia Indulge your inner
child at the cake shops along this street. The
central strip of the Jewish Ghetto (p83) is lined
with popular eateries and the remains of the
Portico d'Ottavia (p83), a huge *quadriporto* (four-
sided porch) that was for centuries Rome's
main fish market.

6 Isola Tiberina Cross Rome's oldest
standing bridge to get to the world's smallest inhabited island. Isola Tiberina (p84) has long
been associated with healing and is still today
home to one of the capital's hospitals. For a
romantic evening to remember book a table
at Sora Lella (p200), the island's celebrated restaurant.

Literary Footsteps

1 Villa Medici Described by Henry James
as 'the most enchanting place in Rome',
Villa Medici (p98) has been home to the French
Academy since 1801. Writers, artists and
musicians have stayed here, including Galileo, who was imprisoned here for three years
in the 17th century while he was tried for
heresy.

2 Keats-Shelley House A temple to Romantic poetry and the poets who wrote it,
this is the house (p95) where John Keats died
in 1821. It boasts an extensive collection of
memorabilia and manuscripts belonging
to Keats and fellow poets Shelley and Lord
Byron.

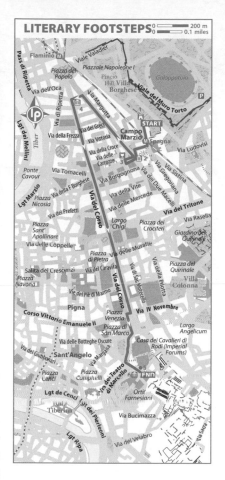

LITERARY FOOTSTEPS

lonelyplanet.com

WALK FACTS

Start Villa Medici (Ⓜ Spagna)
End Capitoline Museums (🚎 Piazza Venezia)
Distance 3km
Duration Three hours
Fuel stop Caffè Greco (p221)

3 Caffè Greco Casanova, Goethe, Wagner, Keats, Byron, Shelley and Baudelaire are among the cultural heavyweights who used to hang out at this historic café (p221). Little of its bohemian character remains, although it does maintain a certain class with gilt mirrors and uniformed staff.

4 Casa di Goethe Like many literary big guns of the 18th century, Goethe spent time in Rome. This, the apartment (p98) where he lived between 1786 and 1788, is now a small museum with a comprehensive library of first editions and an unlikely portrait by Andy Warhol.

5 Piazza del Campidoglio It was on Piazza del Campidoglio (p70), while gazing over the ruins of the Roman Forum (p67) in 1764, that Edward Gibbon first thought of writing a history of the Roman Empire. The result was his six-volume magnum opus, *The Decline and Fall of the Roman Empire*.

6 Capitoline Museums Nathaniel Hawthorne is said to have been so inspired by an ancient statue he saw at the Capitoline Museums (p70) that he used it as the basis for his novel, *The Marble Faun*.

top picks

- Ai Monasteri (p175)
- Confetteria Moriondo & Gariglio (p173)
- Sermoneta (p179)
- TAD (p178)
- Bottega di Marmoraro (p181)
- Arsenale (p175)
- Lorenza Ambrosetti (p186)
- Porta Portese(p185)
- Artigiani Pellettieri – Marco Pelle/di Clemente (p181)
- Volpetti (p184)

What's your recommendation? www.lonelyplanet.com/rome

SHOPPING

Fiercely unique, Rome's shops, studios and boutiques make retail therapy diverting enough to distract you from the incredible cityscape. Wander the backstreets and you'll find yourself glancing into dusty workshops: you'll see framers, ironmongers, furniture restorers and basket weavers. Meandering down medieval streets, jewel-like boutiques and tempting wine shops and delicatessens will lure you into overfilling your luggage. It's not to say that there are no chain stores in Rome, but the city is still dominated by the individual shop: the family-run bakery, and tiny stores specialising in a single item, such as gloves, hats or tights. There's also an attractive lack of malls – because of the difficulties in constructing new buildings in the city centre, shopping centres tend to be on the edge of town.

Italy's reputation for quality is deserved, and Rome is a splendid place to shop for designer clothes, shoes and leather goods. Long viewed as secondary to Milan, Rome is nevertheless no fashion slouch. Valentino chose to show his 45th-anniversary *haute couture* collection here, and local heroes Fendi opened their seven-storey, neoclassical flagship store in the glorious Palazzo Fendi in 2005. The grid of streets around Via dei Condotti and Piazza di Spagna is high-fashion central: even if you can't afford to buy, it's worth a gape.

There is also a wonderful array of small designers selling one-off, hand-made outfits, places to buy made-to-measure shoes, and work-of-art jewellery and leather goods. Foodstuffs are, of course, the tops, and heavenly temples to food abound – delis, bakeries, *pasticcerie* and chocolate shops. Designer homewares are another Italian speciality, and many shops focus on covetable stainless-steel kitchenware, glass baubles and super-sleek interior design.

While prices here are not as steep as they are in, say, London or Paris, they're still not cheap. To grab a bargain, you should try to time your visit to coincide with the *saldi* (sales). Winter sales run from early January to mid-February and summer sales from July to early September.

Most shops accept credit cards and many accept travellers cheques. Note that you're required by Italian law to have a *ricevuta* (receipt) for your purchases (see p298).

SHOPPING AREAS

Big-name designer boutiques glitter and gleam in the grid of streets between Piazza di Spagna and Via del Corso (Map p172). The great Italian and international names are represented, as well as many more off-centre designers, selling clothes, shoes, accessories and dreams. The immaculately clad high-fashion spine is Via dei Condotti, but there's also lots of high fashion in Via Borgognona, Via Frattina, Via della Vite and Via del Babuino.

Downsizing a euro or two, Via Nazionale (Map pp106–7), Via del Corso (Map p172), Via dei Giubbonari (Map pp74–5) and Via Cola di Rienzo (Map pp138–9) are good for midrange clothing stores, with some interesting small boutiques set amid the chains.

Best for cutting-edge designer boutiques and vintage clothes is the wonderful Via del Governo Vecchio (Map pp74–5), a central yet bohemian street that runs from a small square just off Piazza Navona towards the river. Other great places to discover one-off boutiques are Via del Pellegrino and around Campo de' Fiori (Map pp74–5). Via del Boschetto and Via dei Sol-

dati (Map pp106–7) in the Monti area are great for browsing unique designers and jewellery makers, antique sellers and artists. Head to San Lorenzo for edgy, unique arts and crafts, with little boutiques turning out some stunning works of art. You can look up some of these at Made in San Lorenzo (www.madeinsanlorenzo.it in Italian).

For antiques shopping, Via dei Coronari (Map pp74–5), Via Margutta (Map p172), Via Giulia (Map pp74–5) and Via dei Banchi Vecchi (Map pp74–5) are the best places to look. The prices are high but so is the quality.

OPENING HOURS

Many larger shops now open 9am to 7.30pm (or 9.30am to 8pm) Monday to Saturday; some also open on Sundays, typically 11am to 1pm and 4pm to 7pm. However, traditional opening hours – 9am to 1pm and 3.30pm to 7.30pm (or 4pm to 8pm) Monday to Saturday – are still adhered to by many family-run places. Small boutiques might not open until 10am and afternoon hours might also be shortened. Many shops are closed on Monday mornings and for at least two weeks in August. Hours often change in summer, with more places closing at lunchtime and opening later in the evening.

If opening hours are given with a review, it's because they differ from these norms.

CENTRO STORICO
PANTHEON & AROUND

ALBERTA GLOVES Map pp74–5 Accessories
☎ 06 678 57 53; Corso Vittorio Emanuele II 18;
🚌 Corso Vittorio Emanuele II
It must be glove: from elbow-length silk for a grand premiere to crochet for your first communion; from tan-coloured driving gloves for touring the Alps to black fingerless numbers for kinky nights out; from fur-lined kid to polkadots, this crammed, tiny shop has gloves for every conceivable occasion.

FELTRINELLI Map pp74–5 Books
☎ 06 688 03 248; Largo di Torre Argentina 5;
🚌 or 🚊 Largo di Torre Argentina
The bookstores of Italy's most famous bookseller (and publisher) dot the capital. This one has a wide range of books (in Italian) on art, photography, cinema and history, as well as an extensive selection of Italian literature and travel guides in various languages, including English. There's also a small English books section and a café. Other Feltrinelli bookshops are at Galleria Alberto Sordi (Map p100; ☎ 06 677 55 001; Piazza Colonna 31), Viale Giulio Cesare 88 (Map pp138–9; ☎ 06 37 72 411) and Via VE Orlando 81 (Map pp106–7; ☎ 06 487 01 71), where you'll also find the international branch (see p183).

HERDER BUCHHANDLUNG
Map pp74–5 Books
☎ 06 679 46 28; Piazza di Montecitorio 117;
🚌 Via del Corso
Herder Buchhandlung is a historic German bookshop that specialises in theological

top picks

SHOPPING STRIPS

- Via del Governo Vecchio (Map pp74–5) For vintage and independent fashion.
- Via del Pellegrino (Map pp74–5) Lots of small boutiques, jewellers and antique shops.
- Via dei Condotti (Map p172) All the big-name designers; window displays are works of art, and shoppers are entertaining too.
- Via del Boschetto (Map pp106–7) Small independent boutiques specialising in fashion, jewellery and ephemera.
- Via del Corso (Map p172 & Map pp96–7) Head here for big-names and chains, Italian and otherwise.

and philosophical works. But even students of Kant like a break, and you'll find Harry Potter, a small selection of Penguin books in English and some children's books.

DAVIDE CENCI Map pp74–5 Clothing
☎ 06 699 06 81; Via di Campo Marzio 1-7; 🚌 Via del Corso
For a look that discreetly whispers old money (think blazers, slacks and brogues in summer; tweed and flannels in winter) head to Davide Cenci, which carries a selection of impeccable top Italian and international labels (Ralph Lauren, Tod's, Hogan, Ballantyne, Pucci) and own-brand tailoring for men, women and children.

TARTARUGHE Map pp74–5 Clothing
☎ 06 679 22 40; Via del Piè di Marmo 17; 🚌 or 🚊 Largo di Torre Argentina
Tartarughe sells grown-up clothes that are pleasingly frivolous. Designer Susanna Liso's outfits include tops that are whispers of chiffon, multicoloured dresses and knitwear,

HOLY SOCKS!

South of the Pantheon, a string of ecclesiastical shops has clerics from all over the world trying out ceremonial capes for their swish factor, eyeing up lecterns and stocking up on suitably stern undies. If you want an icon or a pair of (glorious!) cardinal's socks (available in poppy red or ecclesiastical purple), Via dei Cestari is where to head, though bear in mind that idle browsing is not the done thing. Ghezzi (Map pp74–5; ☎ 06 686 97 44; Via dei Cestari 32-33) is the least daunting of the shops, but if nothing but the pope's tailors will do, try Anniable Gamarelli (Map pp74–5; ☎ 06 680 13 14; Via di Santa Chiara 34). For a life-sized statue of the Virgin Mary or a host of smaller icons, try Statuaria – Arte Sacra (Map pp74–5; ☎ 06 679 37 53; Via dei Cestari 2). Over near St Peter's, try Centro Russia Ecumenica il Messaggio dell'Icona (Map pp138–9; ☎ 06 689 66 37; Borgo Pio 141), which sells original painted icons, some glinting with real gold leaf.

SHOPPING - AROUND PIAZZA DI SPAGNA & VIA DEL CORSO

0 — 80 m

SHOPPING - AROUND PIAZZA DI SPAGNA & VIA DEL CORSO

strikingly cut jackets and coats, and novel accessories in stone, glass and perspex.

CONFETTERIA MORIONDO & GARIGLIO Map pp74–5   Food
☎ 06 699 08 56; Via del Piè di Marmo 21-22; ☻ 9am-7.30pm Mon-Sat Oct-Apr; 🚌 or 🚊 Largo di Torre Argentina

Roman poet Trilussa dedicated several sonnets to this shop, and you can see why. It's no ordinary sweetshop, but a bygone temple of bonbons. Rows of handmade chocolates and sweets (more than 80 varieties) lie in ceremonial splendour in old-fashioned glass cabinets. Moriondo and Gariglio were Torinese cousins who moved to Rome after the unification of Italy, and many of the chocolates are handmade to their original recipes.

DE SANCTIS Map pp74–5   Homewares
☎ 06 688 06 810; Piazza di Pietra 24; ☻ 10am-1.30pm Mon-Sat, 3.30-7.30pm Mon & Wed-Sat; 🚌 Via del Corso

De Sanctis – in business since 1890 – is full of impressive southern Italian ceramics, with sunbursts of colour decorating candleholders, vases, tiles, urns and plates.

SPAZIO SETTE Map pp74–5   Homewares
☎ 06 688 04 261; Via dei Barbieri 7; 🚌 or 🚊 Largo di Torre Argentina

Even if you don't buy any of the designer homewares at Spazio Sette, it's worth popping in to see the funky modern furniture set against 17th-century frescoes. Formerly home to a cardinal, the *palazzo* (mansion) now houses a three-floor shop full of quality furniture, kitchenware, tableware and gifts.

CREPIDA Map pp74–5   Shoes
☎ 06 686 17 33; Via Arco della Ciambella; 🚌 or 🚊 Largo di Torre Argentina

Join the queues of Romans-in-the-know at this tiny shop tucked behind Largo Argentina. Here you can get custom-made shoes at off-the-peg prices; that is, €250 for a pair of boots, €135 for a pair of shoes. They take about 10 days to make.

SCIÙ SCIÀ Map pp74–5   Shoes
☎ 06 688 06 777; Via di Torre Argentina 8; 🚌 or 🚊 Largo di Torre Argentina

Low key Sciù Scià sells its own range of handmade ladies' shoes and multicoloured suede bags. The vibe is sensible yet chic,

classic with a twist. The leather is buttersoft and the quality excellent.

AS ROMA STORE Map pp74–5   Sportswear
☎ 06 692 00 642; Piazza Colonna 360; 🚌 Via del Corso

AS Roma, one of Rome's two football teams, is continually strapped for cash. Boost the team's coffers by buying a replica shirt or a Roma key ring at this, one of their official club shops, which also sells game tickets.

BARTOLUCCI Map pp74–5   Toys
☎ 06 691 90 894; Via dei Pastini 98; 🚌 Via del Corso del Rinascimento

You can't miss this woodtastic toy shop, where everything's crafted in pine by the Bartolucci family (often you can see work being done in the shop). It's guarded by a cycling Pinocchio and a full-sized wooden motorbike, and within are ticking clocks, rustic cars, planes and more Pinocchios than you've ever seen in your life.

CLOTHING SIZES

Women's clothing

Aus/UK	8	10	12	14	16	18
Europe	36	38	40	42	44	46
Japan	5	7	9	11	13	15
USA	6	8	10	12	14	16

Women's shoes

Aus/USA	5	6	7	8	9	10
Europe	35	36	37	38	39	40
France only	35	36	38	39	40	42
Japan	22	23	24	25	26	27
UK	3½	4½	5½	6½	7½	8½

Men's clothing

Aus	92	96	100	104	108	112
Europe	46	48	50	52	54	56
Japan	S		M	M		L
UK/USA	35	36	37	38	39	40

Men's shirts (collar sizes)

Aus/Japan	38	39	40	41	42	43
Europe	38	39	40	41	42	43
UK/USA	15	15½	16	16½	17	17½

Men's shoes

Aus/UK	7	8	9	10	11	12
Europe	41	42	43	44½	46	47
Japan	26	27	27½	28	29	30
USA	7½	8½	9½	10½	11½	12½

Measurements approximate only; try before you buy

PIAZZA NAVONA & AROUND

CASALI Map pp74–5 — Antiques
☎ 06 678 35 15; Via dei Coronari 115; 🚍 Corso Vittorio Emanuele II

Via dei Coronari's shops mostly specialise in antique furniture or marble, but Casali deals in antique prints, many delicately hand-coloured. The shop is small but the choice is not, ranging from 16th-century botanical manuscripts to €3 postcard prints of Rome.

COMICS BAZAR Map pp74–5 — Antiques
☎ 06 688 02 923; Via dei Banchi Vecchi 127-128; 🚍 Corso Vittorio Emanuele II

Not a comic in sight – this attic-like treasure-trove is crammed to its rafters with antiques. Wade through the lamps that hang everywhere like jungle creepers and you'll find furniture dating from the 19th century to the 1940s, including a large selection of Viennese furniture by Thonet. You might even find the shopkeeper hidden away among it all.

NARDECCHIA Map pp74–5 — Antiques
☎ 06 686 93 18; Piazza Navona 25; 🚍 Corso del Rinascimento

You'll be inviting people to see your etchings after a visit to Nardecchia, where the range encompasses everything from 18th-century etchings of Rome by Giovanni Battista Piranesi to more affordable 19th-century panoramas.

LIBRAIRIE FRANÇAISE DE ROME
Map pp74–5 — Books
☎ 06 683 07 598; Piazza di San Luigi dei Francesi 23; 🚍 Corso del Rinascimento

top picks

SECRETS

- Società Abbigliamento Rappresentanze Tessuti (Sart) (opposite)
- Lorenza Ambrosetti (p186)
- Artigiani Pellettieri – Marco Pelle/di Clemente (p181)
- Crepida (p173)
- Le Tele di Carlotta (left)

This French bookshop nestles next to France's church in Rome, the Chiesa di San Luigi dei Francesi (p80). Browse through the literature, fiction, nonfiction, general interest and children's books before popping into the church to see the paintings by Caravaggio.

LIBRERIA BABELE Map pp74–5 — Books
☎ 06 687 66 28; Via dei Banchi Vecchi 116; 🚍 Corso Vittorio Emanuele II

Rome's only gay and lesbian bookshop, Libreria Babele has helpful staff who can fill you in on the scene, and a well-stocked selection of books, magazines and videos, some of which are in English.

LIBRERIA SORGENTE Map pp74–5 — Books
☎ 06 688 06 950; Piazza Navona 90; 🚍 Corso del Rinascimento

Fancy some literature and nonfiction books in Spanish or Portuguese? Check out Libreria Sorgente, next door to the Spanish Istituto Cervantes.

BEST CHEAP & CHIC TOUR

Balance the books while stocking up on divine Italian style with this handy tour of some of Rome's best-value hotspots. Starting in chi-chi Tridente, buy well-priced quality leather goods (handbags, wallets and so on) at Fatta Fabbrica Italiana (FFI) (p179) or Furla (p179). Women could then update their look at a branch of Ethic (p177), an imaginative, reasonable women's chainstore, and men and women can scour the rails for gems at Discount dell'Alta Moda (p186). And, girls, did you check out Dal Co´ (www.dalco-roma.com; Via Vittoria) famous for its handmade shoes? Step away from the window: they might be chic, but cheap they're not. But there's no need to give up on the dream: head instead to Crepida (p173), close to Largo Argentina, where even misers might be tempted by made-to-measure shoes. Or, if you want the latest in ready-made shoes, scurry to over to Borini (p177) close to Il Campo, or make a detour to the outlet for Fausto Santini (p181) on Via Cavour. Beautifully shod, meander over to Bartolucci (p173), close to Piazza Navona, to find a handcarved wooden toy – with many pieces under €10. Find lovely unguents at monkish prices at Ai Monasteri (opposite) and then get to the Jewish Ghetto for a wonderful mish-mash of bargain Italian homewares at Leone Limentani (p177).

Hop on a bus or the Metro and head to the area around St Peter's, where you can find icons galore for your mantel at Centro Russia Ecumenica il Messaggio dell'Icona (p171) and more fashion bargains at Outlet Gente (p186).

ARSENALE Map pp74–5 — Clothing

☎ 06 686 1380; Via del Governo Vecchio 64;
🚇 Corso Vittorio Emanuele II

Arsenale is a watchword with cool Roman women: the warehouse-like shop is very NYC, and the look is edgy Italian chic. Roman designer Patrizia Pieroni opened Arsenale over 15 years ago, but it still feels cutting edge. Clothes are interestingly structured, in luscious fabrics, and the shoes are hot, too.

LUNA & L'ALTRA Map pp74–5 — Clothing

☎ 06 688 04 995; Via del Governo Vecchio 105;
🚇 Corso Vittorio Emanuele II

A must-stop on any Roman fashionista trail, this It Shop set in a 1600 *palazzo* stocks a finely selected array of Issey Miyake, Dries Van Noten, Gaultier and so on, with a carefully judged selection of accessories.

AI MONASTERI Map pp74–5 — Cosmetics

☎ 06 688 02 783; Corso del Rinascimento 72;
🚇 Corso del Rinascimento

This apothecary-like, wonderfully scented shop sells herbal essences, spirits, soaps, balms, and liqueurs, all created by monks and beautifully packaged. To boost your love life try the Elixir d'Amore (Elixir of Love), though quite why monks are expert at this is anyone's guess.

CASAMARIA Map pp74–5 — Cosmetics

☎ 06 683 30 74; Via della Scrofa 71; 🚇 Corso del Rinascimento

It looks like any old *profumerie* (perfume shop), but it's been plying its trade for almost a century and stocks all the leading cosmetic brands and hundreds of lesser-known names. Straining shelves line the shop like an old fashioned pharmacy, while the knowledgeable staff show admirable athleticism in scaling the towering ladders.

OFFICINA PROFUMO FARMACEUTICA DI SANTA MARIA NOVELLA
Map pp74–5 — Cosmetics

☎ 06 687 96 08; Corso del Rinascimento 47;
🚇 Corso del Rinascimento

Step in for the scent of the place, if nothing else. This bewitching shop – the catchily named Roman branch of one of Italy's oldest pharmacies – sells exquisite lotions and potions under a Murano-glass chandelier. It was founded in Florence in 1612 by the Dominican monks of Santa Maria Novella,

TAXES & REFUNDS

Non-EU residents who spend more than €155 at shops with a 'Tax Free for Tourists' sticker are entitled to a tax rebate. You'll need to fill in a form in the shop and get it stamped by customs as you leave Italy. For more details, see p298.

and many of its cosmetics are based on original 17th-century herbal recipes.

LE TELE DI CARLOTTA
Map pp74–5 — Embroidery

☎ 06 689 2585; Via dei Coronari 228; ⏰ 10.30am-1pm & 3.30-7.30pm; 🚇 Corso Vittorio Emanuele II

This tiny little sewing box of a shop is a delicate concoction of hand-embroidered napkins, bags and antique pieces of jewellery, ranging from 19th century to 1930s. You can have pieces embroidered on request, if you have enough time in Rome. Heirlooms in the making.

SOCIETÀ ABBIGLIAMENTO RAPPRESENTANZE TESSUTI (SART)
Map pp74–5 — Fabric

☎ 06 687 64 49; www.sart1947.it; Largo della Fontanella di Borghese 19; 🚇 Via del Corse

In a gentleman's quest for sartorial splendour, when only the finest Italian cloth will do, the address to know is SART, hidden away off the courtyard of a grand *palazzo* that also houses Rome's venerable hunting club. Walk through the porter's office and you'll find the entrance to the right of the courtyard. There are rolls of lavish wools, linens and cottons, and you can pick up cashmere jumpers to complete your look.

ALDO FEFÈ Map pp74–5 — Gifts

☎ 06 688 03 585; Via della Stelletta 20b; 🚇 Corso del Rinascimento

Started by the owner's father in 1932, this tiny arched workshop produces beautifully handpainted paper. Products include wrapping paper, little chests of drawers, writing paper, picture frames and photo albums, among other things.

RETRO Map pp74–5 — Homewares

☎ 06 681 92 746; www.retrodesign.it; Piazza del Fico 20; 🚇 Corso del Rinascimento

Design buffs, prepare to swoon over the rainbow rows of 1950s and '60s glassware,

Bakelite jewellery, Pop Art carpets, vintage designer furniture and iconic chairs.

TEMPI MODERNI Map pp74–5 · Jewellery
☎ 06 687 70 07; Via del Governo Vecchio 108; 🚌 Corso Vittorio Emanuele II
Tempi Moderni is packed with wow-factor: quality vintage costume jewellery, wonderful '20s and '30s Bakelite pieces, Art Nouveau and Art Deco trinkets, Pop Art bangles, 19th-century resin brooches, and pieces by couturiers such as Chanel, Dior and Balenciaga. Plus you can mix and match with the fine array of vintage designer clothing.

AL SOGNO Map pp74–5 Toys
☎ 06 686 41 98; Piazza Navona 53; 🕙 10am-10pm; 🚌 Corso del Rinascimento
Even from outside you know that Al Sogno is more than your average toy shop, with elaborate window displays featuring elegant Edwardian dolls. Inside is an expensive wonderland, the mezzanine floor straining under the weight of dolls and stuffed animals. The don't-touch atmosphere is best suited to well-behaved little darlings.

BERTÈ Map pp74–5 Toys
☎ 06 687 50 11; Piazza Navona 107-111; 🚌 Corso del Rinascimento
On Piazza Navona, this is one of Rome's great toy shops, an emporium specialising in wooden dolls and puppets, but with a great mishmash of other stuff, from tractors to pushchairs, and doll houses to tea sets. Perfect for pre-/post-sightseeing bribes.

CITTÀ DEL SOLE Map pp74–5 Toys
☎ 06 688 03 805; Via della Scrofa 65; 🚌 Corso del Rinascimento
Città del Sole is a parent's dream, a treasure-trove of imaginative toys created to stretch the growing mind rather than numb it. From well-crafted wooden trains to insect investigation kits, here you'll find toys to (with any luck) keep your children occupied for hours. Other branches are at Via Buonarroti 6 (Map pp106–7; ☎ 06 489 30 292), near Piazza Vittorio Emanuele II, and at Piazza San Cosimato 39 (Map pp132–3; ☎ 06 583 10 429) in Trastevere.

OMERO & CECILIA Map pp74–5 Vintage Clothing
☎ 06 683 35 06; Via del Governo Vecchio 110; 🚌 Corso Vittorio Emanuele II

In this historic street of vintage shops, this is a wonderful tunnel of a place, stashed full of leather bags, '70s velvet coats, tweed jackets, '60s Italian dresses and so on. It's a browser's heaven.

VESTITI USATI CINZIA
Map pp74–5 Vintage Clothing
☎ 06 686 17 91; Via del Governo Vecchio 45; 🚌 Corso Vittorio Emanuele II
Cinzia remains one of the best vintage shops on this street, owned by a former costume designer. There are jackets (in leather, denim, corduroy and linen), slouchy boots, screen-printed T-shirts, vintage skirts and suede coats, and you can snap up vintage designer sunglasses.

CAMPO DE' FIORI & AROUND

IBIZ – ARTIGIANATO IN CUOIO
Map pp74–5 Accessories
☎ 06 683 07 297; Via dei Chiavari 39; 🚌 Corso Vittorio Emanuele II
In this pint-sized workshop, Elisa Nepi and her father craft exquisite, well-priced leather goods, including bags, belts and sandals, in simple but classy designs and myriad colours.

MONDELLO OTTICA Map pp74–5 Accessories
☎ 06 686 19 55; Via del Pellegrino 97-98; 🚌 Corso Vittorio Emanuele II
If you're in Rome, you need shades. A sparkling white temple of sunglasses, Mondello Ottica has frames by leading designers, including Anne et Valentin, l.a.Eyeworks, Cutler and Gross, and the Belgian designer Theo. Prescription glasses can be ready the same day.

LIBRERIA DEL VIAGGIATORE
Map pp74–5 Books
☎ 06 688 01 048; Via del Pellegrino 78; 🚌 Corso Vittorio Emanuele II
If Rome is only a stop on your Grand Tour, this beguiling bookshop is a must. Small but world-encompassing, it's crammed with guides and travel literature in various languages and has a huge range of maps, including hiking maps.

DADADA Map pp74–5 Clothing
☎ 06 681 39 162; Via dei Giubbonari 55; 🚌 Corso Vittorio Emanuele II

Every young Roman fashionista will make a stop at Dadada, for its funky cocktail dresses that can be dressed up or down, bright print summer frocks and eclectic coats. There's a mix of designers, prices are midrange, and there's another branch at Via del Corso 500.

BORINI Map pp74–5 — Shoes
☎ 06 687 56 70; Via dei Pettinari 86-87; Ⓡ Via Arenula

Those in the know pile into this unglitzy shop, run by the Borinis since 1940, to try on the cool, candy-coloured shoes. Whatever is fashionable this season, be it wedges or winklepickers, Borini will have it, at reasonable prices and in a cover-every-eventuality rainbow palette.

LOCO Map pp74–5 — Shoes
☎ 06 688 08 216; Via dei Baullari 22; Ⓑ Corso Vittorio Emanuele II

Shoe fetishists should hotfoot it to Loco. More a trendsetter than fashion follower, it's small, but big in attitude, with an interesting mix of original shoes by international and Italian designers.

POSTO ITALIANO Map pp74–5 — Shoes
☎ 06 686 93 73; Via dei Giubbonari 37a; Ⓡ Via Arenula

Reasonably priced Posto Italiano has an always-beguiling collection of women's shoes; it provides a showcase for a number of emerging Italian designers while also stocking more established brands.

ETHIC Map pp74–5 — Women's Clothing
☎ 06 683 01 063; Piazza B Cairoli 11-12; ☺ 10am-8pm Tue-Sat, noon-8pm Sun & Mon; Ⓡ Via Arenula

This hint-of-boho place is an Italian clothing chain, with retro-influenced, original, bold designs – tribal silver jewellery, military-style coats, long suede boots and cute twinsets. It's an eclectic mix in interesting colours, fabrics and designs. Plus, it's reasonably priced. There are loads of branches around town.

JEWISH GHETTO

MORESCO OTTICA Map pp74–5 — Accessories
☎ 06 688 05 079; Via dei Falegnami 23; Ⓡ Via Arenula

Blink and you'll miss Moresco, a tiny optician's stocking frames by many major

labels – Gucci, Chanel, Persol, Web and Luxottica to name a few. You can have your eyes tested and the friendly proprietor will organise prescriptions in a couple of hours.

LEONE LIMENTANI Map pp74–5 — Homewares
☎ 06 688 06 686; basement, Via del Portico d'Ottavia 47; Ⓡ Via Arenula

Family-run for seven generations, Leone Limentani has a huge, rambling choice of kitchenware and tableware, expensive porcelain and knick-knacks, crockery, cutlery and crystal, all at bargain prices.

TRIDENTE
PIAZZA DI POPOLO & AROUND

BORSALINO Map p172 — Accessories
☎ 06 32650838; Piazza del Popolo 20; Ⓜ Flaminio

Italians really cut a dashing figure in a hat, but don't fret, you can learn. Borsalino is *the* Italian hatmaker, favoured by 1920s criminal Al Capone, Japanese Emperor Hirohito, and Humphrey Bogart. Think fedoras, pork-pie-styles, felt cloches and woven straw caps.

ALINARI Map p172 — Antiques & Books
☎ 06 679 29 23; Via Alibert 16; Ⓜ Spagna

This is the oldest photographic business in the world. The Florentine Alinari brothers founded their enterprise in 1852, and produced more than one million plate-glass negatives in their lifetimes. At their Rome shop you can buy beautiful prints of their work depicting the city in the 19th century, as well as some meaty coffeetable books on photography.

ANIMALIER E OLTRE Map p172 — Antiques
☎ 06 320 82 82; Via Margutta 47; ☺ 10am-1.30pm & 3.30-7.30pm Wed, Fri & Sat, 10am-7.30pm Tue, Thu & Fri; Ⓜ Spagna

This basement appears to be full of the cast-offs of an eccentric, aristocratic family, with bric-a-brac, curios, antiques and unique furniture. Wrought-iron furniture and leather sofas sit alongside a selection of animal-shaped antiques that includes reproductions of 19th-century French *animalier* sculptures.

IL MARE Map p172   Books

☎ 06 361 20 91; Via di Ripetta 239; ⏲ 9.30am-7.30pm Mon-Sat; Ⓜ Flaminio

Ahoy there. Specialising in everything *mare* (sea) related, this friendly bookshop has maritime books in Italian, English and French, nautical charts, binoculars, pirate flags, model yachts, posters, Lonely Planet guidebooks, videos and CD-ROMs

TAD Map p172   Department Store

☎ 06 326 95 131; Via del Babuino 155a; Ⓜ Flaminio/Spagna

TAD is a cutting-edge conceptual department store that sells an entire lifestyle. Here you can buy designer clothes by Chloë, Balenciaga, and more, have a haircut, buy scent and flowers, and furnish your apartment with wooden daybeds and Perspex dining chairs. Don't forget to pick up hip soundtracks to your perfect life from the CD rack. The serene courtyard café is the perfect ladies-who-lunch pitstop, offering appropriately stylish Italian-Asian morsels.

ARTEMIDE Map p172   Homewares

☎ 06 360 01 802; Via Margutta 107; Ⓜ Flaminio

For lamps that light up the world of interior design, head to Artemide. Whether moon-like white globes, or lamps that are so minimalist you hardly notice them till you clock the price tag, this is light as art.

FLOS Map p172   Homewares

☎ 06 320 76 31; Via del Babuino 84-85; ⏲ 3-7pm Mon, 10am-7pm Tue-Sat, 10am-2pm Sun; Ⓜ Spagna

Since its founding in 1962, light design house Flos has been responsible for a firmament of design classics, including Marc Newson's Helice aluminium floor lamp and many Philippe Starck designs. The look varies from primary-coloured plastic to steely and sleek.

MAURIZIO GROSSI Map p172   Homewares

☎ 06 360 01 935; Via Margutta 109; Ⓜ Flaminio

Do you have an obelisk gap? Here's your chance to fill it. Maurizio Grossi is part gallery, part shop, with an eccentric collection of classy repro marble sculptures and busts, including copies of various famous statues. From busts of Julius Caesar to deceptive bowls of sculpted figs and apricots, there's something for every home, from mansion to bedsit.

WEST OF VIA DEL CORSO

TEICHNER Map p172   Food

☎ 06 687 14 49; Piazza San Lorenzo in Lucina; 🚌 Via del Corso

This is one of Rome's many temples to food, so wander in, inhale the delicious scents and select from cheese, hams, pickles, pestos and so on. There are also a select few ready dishes, such as aubergine (eggplant) *parmigiana*.

LAVORI ARTIGIANI ROMANI (LAR) Map p172   Homewares

☎ 06 687 81 75; Via del Leoncino 29; 🚌 Via del Corso

Lamps have been created here by this artisan family business since 1938, in materials such as wood, brass and parchment. Their creations look like vintage finds – from great white cylinders to metallic cubist sculptures. If you want to design a lamp, these are the people to talk to.

MERCATO DELLE STAMPE Map p172 Market

Largo della Fontanella di Borghese; ⏲ 7am-1pm Mon-Sat; 🚌 Piazza Augusto Imperatore

The Mercato delle Stampe (Print Market) is well worth a look if you're a fan of vintage books and old prints. Squirrel through the permanent stalls and among the tired posters and dusty back editions, and you might turn up some interesting music scores, architectural engravings or chromolithographs of Rome.

MESSAGGERIE MUSICALI Map p172   Music

☎ 06 679 81 97; Via del Corso 123; 🚌 Via del Corso

Rome's music megastore has CDs spread over three floors, with everything from easy listening to opera, jazz and pop, plus a well-stocked magazine section (everything from *Q* to *Hello!*) and a ticket agency.

L'OLFATTORIO Map p172   Perfume

☎ 06 361 23 25; Via di Ripetta 34; ⏲ 3.30-7.30pm Tue-Sat; Ⓜ Flaminio

Those with a nose will adore this place. It's like a bar, but with perfume instead of drinks, with scents made by names such as Artisan Parfumeur, Diptyque, Les Parfums de Rosine and Coudray. The bartender will guide you through different combinations of scents to work out your ideal fragrance. Exclusive handmade French perfumes are available to buy. Smellings are free but you should book ahead.

TOD'S Map p172 · Shoes
☎ 06 682 10 066; Via della Fontanella di Borghese 56; 🚇 Via del Corso
The trademark of Tod's is its rubber-studded loafers (the idea was to reduce those pesky driving scuffs), perfect weekend footwear for kicking back at your country estate. This flagship store showcases top-of-the-range casual shoes and expensive leather accessories.

ENOTECA AL PARLAMENTO
Map p172 · Wine
☎ 06 687 34 46; Via dei Prefetti 15; 🚇 Via del Corso
A delectable mingling of scents – wine, chocolate, fine meats and cheeses – greets you as you enter this stately, old-fashioned shop, an empire of taste, walled with wine. Try some caviar tartines while sampling the wines, and consult the helpful staff for advice.

PIAZZA DI SPAGNA & AROUND

FATTA FABBRICA ITALIANA (FFI)
Map p172 · Accessories
☎ 06 691 90 882; Via Vittoria 53; 🚇 Spagna
In a Pop Art range of colours, FFI offers classic-looking bags in canvas or leather that offer Italian quality at affordable prices. The multi-pocketed and zipped little purses are handy for facilitating that reorganisation of your life that's on the to do list.

FRANCESCO BIASIA Map p172 · Accessories
☎ 06 679 27 27; Via dei Due Macelli 62; 🚇 Spagna
If you want an 'it' bag without the 'it' price tag, try slipping a Francesco Biasia over your shoulder. His designs are superb. They come in blacks, browns and bright colours, and with original detailing that sets them apart.

FURLA Map p172 · Accessories
☎ 06 692 00 363; Piazza di Spagna 22; 🚇 Spagna
Simple, good-quality bags in soft leather and a brilliant array of colours is why the handbagging hordes keep flocking to Furla, where all sorts of accessories, from sunglasses to shoes are made. The many other branches include Via Tomacelli 136 (Map p172; ☎ 06 687 82 30), Via Nazionale 54-55 (Map pp106–7;

☎ 06 487 01 27) and Via Cola di Rienzo 226 (Map pp138–9; ☎ 06 687 45 05).

SERMONETA Map p172 · Accessories
☎ 06 679 19 60; Piazza di Spagna 61; 🚇 Spagna
Buying leather gloves in Rome is a rite of passage for some, and this is the shop to do it. At Rome's most famous glove-seller, choose from a kaleidoscopic range of quality leather and suede gloves with linings in silk and cashmere. An expert assistant will size up your hand in a glance. Just don't expect them to smile.

ANGLO-AMERICAN BOOKSHOP
Map p172 · Books
☎ 06 679 52 22; Via della Vite 102; 🚇 Spagna
Particularly good for university reference books, the Anglo-American is well stocked and well known. It has an excellent range of literature, travel guides, children's books and maps, and if it hasn't got a book you want, you can order it.

LION BOOKSHOP Map p172 · Books
☎ 06 326 54 007; Via dei Greci 33-36; 🚇 Spagna
This fabulous, long-running, peaceful English bookshop has English-speaking staff and is well stocked with classics, travel guides and the latest reads. There's a particularly good children's section.

DOLCE & GABBANA Map p172 · Clothing
☎ 06 699 24 999; Via dei Condotti 51-52; 🚇 Spagna
Domenico & Stefano keep the it-crowd looking fabulous, smart and sexy with their seductive and never-shy takes on fashion. Think slinky trouser suits, leopard-skin underwear and gangsters' molls, Scarlett Johansson and red-carpet dressing. Their D&G diffusion line is around the corner on Piazza di Spagna.

FENDI Map p172 · Clothing
☎ 06 69 66 61; Largo Goldoni 420; 🚇 Spagna
A temple to subtly blinging accessories, this multi-storey Art Deco building is the Fendi mothership. The look is old-style glamour, with beautiful and distinctively Fendi products – expensive but not glitzy, chic but not faddy. Fendi is famous for fur and leather products. There are branches at Via della Fontanella di Borghese 48 (Map p172; ☎ 06 683 92 037) and Via Borgognona 36 (Map p172; ☎ 06 69 66 61).

GALLO Map p172 — Clothing
☎ 06 360 02 174; Via Vittoria 63; ☯ 10am-2pm & 3.30-7.30pm Mon-Thu, 10am-7.30pm Fri & Sat; Ⓜ Spagna

Gallo is one of Italy's most venerable and luxurious stocking manufacturers, and this small store is stripier than a Missoni-wearing tiger. There are horizontally striped knee socks, children's clothes and very soft tights, all adored by chic Romans. Fine knit cotton bikinis are true originals.

GIANNI VERSACE Map p172 — Clothing
☎ 06 678 05 21; Via Bocca di Leone 23 & 26-27; Ⓜ Spagna

Not one for shrinking violets, Versace is sexy, theatrical and fierce. Founded by Gianni and, after his murder, directed by his sister Donatella, Versace offers clothes that will get you noticed, especially if you're just popping out for a loaf of bread.

JUST CAVALLI Map p172 — Clothing
☎ 06 679 22 94; Piazza di Spagna 82-83; Ⓜ Spagna

Leopard print, jungle-glitz, glamour and excess: these head-turning designs can only be Roberto Cavalli. For threads that are flamboyant, intrinsically Italian and perfect for a party, head here.

LAURA BIAGIOTTI Map p172 — Clothing
☎ 06 679 50 40; Via Borgognona 43; Ⓜ Spagna

Exquisite creations from cashmere and silk shimmer in the window of this breathtaking place. Worship in this beautifully lit shop (once a theatre), which displays the magical creations of this venerable Roman designer, the 'Queen of Cashmere'.

PRADA Map p172 — Clothing
☎ 06 679 08 97; Via dei Condotti 92-95; Ⓜ Spagna

Worn by the devil, as well as the chicest Italian folk, Prada scarcely needs an introduction. This two-floor store offers shoes, accessories, bags and clothes to create a look that's creative, retro-tinged and impeccable. Nearby is Miu Miu (Map p172; Via del Babuino 91), the funky sister label overseen by Miuccia Prada.

SALVATORE FERRAGAMO
Map p172 — Clothing
☎ 06 678 11 30; Via dei Condotti 73-74; Ⓜ Spagna

Star shoemaker Salvatore shod Hollywood stars in the '20s before setting up shop in Italy in the '30s, and creating both the Roman sandal and the wedge heel. This is where to look if you're after perfect-fit classics in unconventional materials, as well as fabulously glamorous clothing (beautifully cut men's suits are just along the road at number 66).

VALENTINO Map p172 — Clothing
☎ 06 673 94 20; Via dei Condotti 13; Ⓜ Spagna

The watchword for old-school glamour and elegance. Valentino himself might have retired but the label still carries on his dedication to beautifully cut, red, white and black, red carpet–ready outfits. Men head to Bocca di Leone 16.

THOROUGHLY FENDI

Adele Casagrande opened a small leather and fur workshop on Rome's Via del Plebiscito in 1918, and her marriage to Edoardo Fendi in 1925 saw the birth of a brand name. Such was the quality of the work that the shop caused an immediate buzz. In 1932 the Fendis opened another bigger shop and atelier on Via Veneto, and word began to spread beyond Rome.

The couple's five daughters, Paola, Anna, Franca, Carla and Alda, all joined the family business, and in 1964 the family opened the first of several future Fendi shops on Via Borgognona. Then full of artisans, the street became one of Rome's most enduringly elegant catwalks.

In 1965, Fendi began to work with the emerging Paris-based designer Karl Lagerfeld, who created the iconic FF logo, and more than 40 years on, Lagerfeld is still the brand's creative director.

Closely collaborating with the Fendi sisters, Lagerfeld launched the first ready-to-wear fur collection in 1969, shaping fur into light, wearable styles in a way that had never been seen before. Nowadays Fendi is one of the few design houses consistently to work with fur. Naomi Campbell was infamously fired from her position as a People for the Ethical Treatment of Animals spokesperson in 1997 for wearing fur at a Fendi fashion show.

In 1994, Silvia Venturini Fendi, Anna's daughter, became accessories creative director, creating an arm-candy icon in the famous Fendi Baguette. Not at all bread-shaped, but easy to carry under the arm, this bag was partly responsible for kickstarting the It-bag phenomenon of the lavish 1990s.

By 2007, the company had been taken over by the French luxury goods line LVMH, but it still has a unique identity, with stores in places as varied as Houston and Hong Kong, and Carla and Silvia Fendi remain involved.

TEBRO Map p172 Department Store

☎ 06 687 34 41; Via dei Prefetti; Ⓜ Spagna

An old-style department store that has kept wealthy locals in linen, socks, ties, swimwear and underwear for over 140 years. You can even have sheets made to measure for your yacht.

FOCACCI Map p172 Food

☎ 06 679 12 28; Via della Croce 43; 🕒 8am-8pm Mon-Fri, 8am-3pm Sat; Ⓜ Spagna

One of several smashing delis along this pretty street, this is where to buy cheese, cold cuts, smoked fish, caviar, pasta and olive oil as well as wines.

FRATELLI FABBI Map p172 Food

☎ 06 679 06 12; Via della Croce 27; Ⓜ Spagna

A small but flavour-packed delicatessen, this is a good place to pick up all sorts of Italian delicacies – fine cured meats, buffalo mozzarella from Campania, *parmigiano reggiano,* olive oil, *porchetta* from Ariccia – as well as Iranian caviar.

BULGARI Map p172 Jewellery

☎ 06 679 38 76; Via dei Condotti 10; Ⓜ Spagna

If you have to ask the price, you can't afford it. Luckily, the sumptuous window displays mean you can admire the world's finest jewellery without spending a *centesimo*.

ARTIGIANI PELLETTIERI – MARCO PELLE/DI CLEMENTE Map p172 Leather

☎ 06 361 34 02; Via Vittoria 15, int 2; Ⓜ Spagna

Ring the bell at this unassuming doorway and hurry up flights of stairs to a family-run leather workshop that feels like it hasn't changed for decades. The elderly artisans create belts (€70 to €100), watch straps (€40 to €90), bags, picture frames, travel cases, and other such elegant stuff. You can take along a buckle or watch to which you want a belt or strap fitted.

BRIGHENTI Map p172 Lingerie

☎ 06 679 14 84; Via Frattina 7-10; Ⓜ Spagna

You can imagine Sophia Loren popping into this elegant old-fashioned boutique for a well-structured something. Brighenti specialises in star-style luxurious lingerie (think frothy ruffled playsuits and lace-adorned slippers) and sensational too-good-to-get-wet swimming costumes.

LA PERLA Map p172 Lingerie

☎ 06 699 41 933; Via dei Condotti 78; Ⓜ Spagna

Give your life an injection of va-va-voom with lingerie from La Perla, Italy's most luxurious lingerie brand. Lace-trimmed silk bras, negligees that you'll want to dive into and high-heeled fluffy slippers – it's time to indulge your inner movie star.

BOTTEGA DI MARMORARO
Map p172 Marble

Via Margutta 53b; Ⓜ Flaminio

A particularly charismatic hole-in-the-wall shop, lined with marble carvings, where you can get marble tablets engraved with any inscription you like (€15). Peer inside at lunchtime and you might see the *marmoraro* cooking a pot of tripe for his lunch on the open log fire.

AVC BY ADRIANA V CAMPANILE
Map p172 Shoes

☎ 06 699 22 355; Piazza di Spagna 88; Ⓜ Spagna

Roman designer Campanile started with a small shop in Parioli, and nowadays her heels stalk the city. You can see why: AVC's shoes and boots are covetably wearable, stunningly chic and practical – and not insanely priced. There are several other branches, including one in Galleria Alberto Sordi (Map p100; ☎ 06 678 34 84).

FAUSTO SANTINI Map p172 Shoes

☎ 06 678 41 14; Via Frattina 120; Ⓜ Spagna

Rome's best-known shoe designer, Fausto Santini is famous for his beguilingly simple, architectural shoe designs. Colours are beautiful, quality impeccable. For bargains and previous seasons' designs, check out the outlet store at Via Cavour 106 (Map pp106–7; ☎ 06 488 09 34), near the Basilica di Santa Maria Maggiore.

MADA Map p172 Shoes

☎ 06 679 86 60; Via della Croce 57; Ⓜ Spagna

Blink-and-you'll-miss-it Mada is one of those shops that transcends fashion, supplying supremely elegant, beautifully made shoes (€210 to €380) to discerning, stylish women of all ages. Pure old-school Italian quality.

MAXMARA Map p172 Women's Clothing

☎ 06 679 36 38; Via Frattina 28; Ⓜ Spagna

Maxmara is a very Italian label, suffused with classic, understated, elegant style, ideal for

top picks

WOMEN'S SHOES

- Borini (p177)
- AVC (p181)
- Mada (p181)
- Crepida (p173)
- Posto Italiano (p177)

creating the *bella figura*: colours are neutral and simple, cuts elegant, and fabrics luxurious. Branches include Via dei Condotti 17 (Map p172; ☎ 06 692 21 04) and Via Nazionale 28 (Map pp106–7; ☎ 06 488 58 70). Max & Co (Map p172; ☎ 06 678 79 46; Via dei Condotti 46) offers a younger, funkier range at not-so-designer prices.

MISSONI Map p172   Women's Clothing
☎ 06 679 25 55; Piazza di Spagna 78; Ⓜ Spagna
When Ottavio the Dalmatian tracksuit-maker and Rosita, from a shawl-making dynasty in Varese, fell in love, a fashion legend was born. The couple began to create the striped knitwear that today is instantly recognisable. Today the company is still family run, and its hippy chic never goes out of fashion.

MOSCHINO Map p172   Women's Clothing
☎ 06 678 11 44; Via Borgognona; Ⓜ Spagna
Irreverent and fun, Moschino juxtaposes interesting details with unusual shapes, colours and fabrics to create a fresh and inimitable style. Note that the younger line, Cheap & Chic, is hardly cheap.

TREVI, QUIRINALE & VIA VENETO

TREVI FOUNTAIN TO THE QUIRINALE

LIBRERIA GIUNTI AL PUNTO
Map p100   Books
☎ 06 699 41 045; Piazza dei Santissimi Apostoli 59-65; Ⓨ 10am-8pm Mon-Sat May-Oct, 9.30am-7.30pm Mon-Sat Nov-Apr, 10.30am-1pm & 4-7.30pm Sun year-round; 🚌 Piazza Venezia
The 'Straight to the Point' children's bookshop is an ideal place to distract your kids. Large, colourful and well stocked, it has

thousands of titles in Italian and a selection of books in French, Spanish, German and English, as well as a good range of toys, from play dough to puzzles.

LA RINASCENTE Map p172   Department Store
☎ 06 679 76 91; Largo Chigi 20; 🚌 Via del Corso
La Rinascente is a stately, upmarket department store, with a particularly buzzing cosmetics department, all amid Art Nouveau interiors. There's a second store at Piazza Fiume (Map pp150–1; ☎ 06 841 60 81).

VIGNANO Map p100   Hats
☎ 06 679 51 47; Via Marco Minghetti; 🚌 Via del Corso
Piled high with head candy, Vignano opened in 1873 and sells top hats, bowlers and deerstalkers, as well as hacking jackets, to a princely clientele, as if nothing much has changed since it first opened its doors. The owners open when they feel like it (don't venture here before 11am).

GALLERIA ALBERTO SORDI
Map p100   Shopping Centre
Piazza Colonna; Ⓨ 10am-10pm; 🚌 Via del Corso
This elegant stained-glass arcade appeared in Alberto Sordi's 1973 classic, *Polvere di Stelle,* and has since been renamed for Rome's favourite actor, who died in 2003. It's a serene place to browse stores such as Zara, AVC, Feltrinelli, Coccinelle, Gusella and the Bridge, and there's an airy café ideal for a quick coffee break.

PIAZZA BARBERINI & VIA VENETO

BRIONI Map p100   Clothing
☎ 06 48 58 55; Via Barberini 79-81; Ⓜ Barberini
James Bond (aka Pierce Brosnan), Clark Gable, Cary Grant and John Wayne have all got themselves suited and booted at venerable Brioni, all polished wood and gold leaf. Unsurprisingly, looking like Bond isn't cheap: reckon on more than €2000 for a suit, or around €1300 for a silk skirt.

UNDERGROUND Map p100   Market
☎ 06 360 05 345; Ludovisi underground car park, Via Francesco Crispi 96; Ⓨ 3-8pm Sat & 10.30am-7.30pm Sun 2nd weekend of the month Sep-Jun; Ⓜ Barberini
This monthly market indeed takes place underground, in a subterranean car park

near Villa Borghese. There are more than 150 stalls selling everything from antiques and collectables to clothes and toys.

MONTI, ESQUILINO & SAN LORENZO

MONTI

GUSTO ITALIA Map pp106–7   Food
☎ 06 478 23 700; Via Leonina 76; Ⓜ Cavour
Angelo Biagi is the charmingly enthusiastic force behind this small, well-stocked deli. He sells homemade pasta and many other delicious items – try the fantastic Sicilian pesto.

LA BOTTEGA DEL CIOCCOLATO
Map pp106–7   Food
☎ 06 482 14 73; Via Leonina 82; Ⓨ 9.30am-7.30pm Oct-Aug; Ⓜ Cavour
This is a magical world of scarlet walls and old-fashioned glass cabinets set into black wood, with irresistible smells wafting in from the kitchen and rows of lovingly homemade chocolates on display.

I VETRI DI PASSAGRILLI
Map pp106–7   Glassware
☎ 06 474 70 22; www.ivetridipassagrilli.it; Via del Boschetto 94; Ⓜ Cavour
Domenico Passagrilli has had his workshop for more than 25 years, specialising in fusion glassware – creating beautiful artworks through heating glass and moulds in a kiln. Each of the organic-seeming pieces – plates, lamps, tiles and window panes – is unique, and he also restores stained glass.

FABIO PICCIONI Map pp106–7   Jewellery
☎ 06 474 16 97; Via del Boschetto 148; Ⓜ Cavour
A sparkling Aladdin's Cave of decadent one-of-a-kind jewellery, with trinkets that would look perfect on the Moulin Rouge set. This is the domain of artisan Fabio Piccioni, who recycles old trinkets to create remarkable Art Deco–inspired jewellery.

MISTY BEETHOVEN
Map pp106–7   Sensual Stuff
☎ 06 488 18 78; Via degli Zingari 12; Ⓜ Cavour
Slinky gets kinky: diamante handcuffs, to-die-for shoes, mirror-brooches, lickable body paint. Misty Beethoven is a divine confection, with all sorts of naughty-but-nice

items, set amid shiny black walls and under a lavish chandelier made entirely of biros.

LE GALLINELLE Map pp106–7   Vintage Clothing
☎ 06 488 10 17; Via del Boschetto 76; Ⓜ Cavour
With a tiled floor and marble counter, this well-known boutique used to be a butcher's shop. Now, instead of slabs of meat, the hooks suspend new and reworked vintage women's clothes. There's a sewing machine busy at the back, and selected items can be made for you on the spot, in a choice of colours.

ESQUILINO

BOOKÀBAR Map pp106–7   Books
☎ 06 489 13 361; Via Milano 15-17; 🚌 Via Nazionale
In Firouz Galdo–designed, cool, gleaming white rooms, Bookàbar – the bookshop attached to Palazzo delle Esposizioni – is just made for browsing. There are books on art, architecture and photography, DVDs, CDs, vinyl, children's books, and gifts for the design-lover in your life.

MAS Map pp106–7   Department Store
☎ 06 446 80 78; Via dello Statuto 11; Ⓜ Vittorio Emanuele
Glorious MAS (Magazzino allo Statuto) is a multistorey temple of trash, practical goods, thermal vests, bags, watches, pants and the kitchen sink, all piled high and at bargain prices – you can pick up a hat here for a couple of euro, or a pair of silk pyjamas for €5 (just don't expect them to last forever).

PIAZZA DELLA REPUBBLICA & AROUND

FELTRINELLI INTERNATIONAL
Map pp106–7   Books
☎ 06 482 78 78; Via VE Orlando 84; Ⓜ Repubblica
The international branch of Italy's ubiquitous bookseller has a splendid collection of books in English, plus Spanish, French, German and Portuguese. You'll find everything from recent-release bestsellers to dictionaries, travel guides, DVDs and an excellent assortment of maps.

MEL BOOKSTORE Map pp106–7   Books
☎ 06 488 54 05; Via Nazionale 254-255; Ⓜ Repubblica
Mel's, on three floors, has a good range of Italian literature, reference books and travel

guides, as well as CDs, half-priced books (general-fiction paperbacks), a cheery children's section and a few books in English and French.

ORIGINAL FANS LAZIO
Map pp106–7   Sportswear
☎ 06 648 26 688; Via Farini 34; 🚇 Piazza Santa Maria Maggiore
Ever since Lazio won Serie A in 2000, Rome's first (or second, depending on your allegiances) football team has done little except negotiate with banks to stave off financial disaster. Fans can show their support by buying shirts, scarves, hats and tickets here.

SAN LORENZO & BEYOND
LA GRANDE OFFICINA
Map pp106–7   Jewellery
☎ 06 445 03 48; Via dei Sabelli 165B; ☼ 10.30am–7.30pm Mon–Fri; 🚇 Via Tiburtina
Under dusty workshop lamps, husband-and-wife team Giancarlo Genco and Daniela Ronchetti turn everything from old clock parts and Japanese fans into beautiful work-of-art jewellery. Head here for something truly unique.

CLAUDIO SANÒ Map pp106–7   Leather
☎ 06 446 92 84; www.claudiosano.it; Largo degli Osci 67A; ☼ 10am–1pm & 4.30–8pm Mon–Sat; 🚇 Via Tiburtina
Claudio Sano creates gleaming moulded works of art in leather that are beautiful, witty and surreal, such as a briefcase with a keyhole through it, another with a bite taken out of it, and a handbag in the shape of a fish. They're not cheap, but masterpieces seldom are.

CELIO HILL & LATERAN
SUZUGANARU Map p115   Clothing
☎ 06 704 91 719; Via di San Giovanni in Laterano 206; ☼ 10am–1pm Tue–Sat, 4–8pm Mon–Fri, closed Aug; 🚇 Colosseo
Suzuganaru's men's and women's boutiques sit side by side, selling whimsical, individual clothes that you won't find anywhere else. Photographer-designer Marcella Manfredini makes some of the women's clothes in the shop, and there are dresses in unusual prints and accessories such as bright lacquer bangles. Next door the men's clothes are lower key but equally hip.

VIA SANNIO Map p115   Market
☼ 8am–1pm Mon–Sat; 🚇 San Giovanni
This morning market in the shadow of Porta San Giovanni, near the basilica, is awash with wardrobe staples. It has a good assortment of new and vintage clothes, shoes at bargain prices, and a good range of jeans and leather jackets.

SOUL FOOD Map p115   Music
☎ 06 704 52 025; Via di San Giovanni in Laterano 192; 🚇 Colosseo
Hate Records (www.haterecords.com) present rare vintage vinyl to make every true funkster's heart beat faster: rock, punk, '60s garage, jazz, rockabilly, glam. You name it, they've got it, plus retro band T-shirts, fanzines and other ace groupie clobber.

AVENTINO & TESTACCIO
VOLPETTI Map p120   Food
☎ 06 574 23 52; www.volpetti.com; Via Marmorata 47; 🚇 or 🚋 Via Marmorata
Volpetti strides like a colossus among Rome's delis. You'll find everything from smelly cheese to fresh homemade pasta, olive oils, vinegar, salami, veggie pies, wine and grappa. Helpful staff will guide you through your choice and you can also order online.

CALZATURE BOCCANERA Map p120 Shoes
☎ 06 575 68 04; Via Luca della Robbia 36; 🚇 or 🚋 Via Marmorata
This old-fashioned Testaccio shoe store stocks big designer names at big designer prices. With a great range of men's and women's footwear, here you'll find Tod's, Gucci, Prada and D&G, among others. It's particularly worth a look at sale time.

TRASTEVERE & GIANICOLO
EAST OF VIALE DI TRASTEVERE
LA CRAVATTA SU MISURA
Map pp132–3   Accessories
☎ 06 581 66 76; Via Santa Cecilia 12; 🚇 or 🚋 Viale di Trastevere
With ties draped over the wooden furniture, this inviting shop resembles the study of an absent-minded professor. But don't be fooled: these guys know their ties. Only

the finest Italian silks and English wools are used in neckwear made to customers' specifications. At a push, a tie can be ready in a few hours.

PORTA PORTESE Map pp132–3   Market
☎ 7am-1pm Sun; 🚌 or 🚊 Viale di Trastevere
To see another side of Rome head to this mammoth flea market. With thousands of stalls selling everything from rare books to spare bike parts, from Peruvian shawls to iPods, it's crazily busy and a lot of fun. Keep your valuables safe and wear your haggling hat.

WEST OF VIALE DI TRASTEVERE

LUMIERES Map pp132–3   Antiques
☎ 06 580 36 14; Vicolo del Cinque 48; 🚌 Piazza Trilussa
Cut a swath through the metallic stalks that have all but taken over this delightfully unpretentious shop and you'll discover a large collection of antique lamps, ranging from Art Nouveau and Art Deco to 1950s.

ALMOST CORNER BOOKSHOP
Map pp132 3   Books
☎ 06 583 69 42; Via del Moro 45; 🚌 Piazza Trilussa
This is how a bookshop should look: a crammed haven full of rip-roaring reads, with every inch of wall space containing English-language books and travel guides. There's an excellent selection of contemporary novels and bestsellers as well as more obscure titles. If you can't find what you want, the English-speaking staff will order it in.

BIBLI Map pp132–3   Books
☎ 06 588 40 97; Via dei Fienaroli 28; ☎ 5.30pm-midnight Mon, 11am-midnight Tue-Sun; 🚌 or 🚊 Viale di Trastevere
On an artsy Trastevere street, Bibli is a buzzing warren that manages to be a bookshop, cultural centre and café, with a little courtyard and delectable cakes. A great place to pass a pleasant hour or two browsing, it regularly hosts poetry readings and book presentations. There's a limited selection of books in English. There's *aperitivo* (€8, 6.30pm to 8pm), lunchtime buffet (€10, 12.30pm to 3.30pm) and brunch (12.30pm Saturday and Sunday) for peckish intelligentsia.

TEMPORARY LOVE Map pp132–3   Clothing
☎ 06 583 34 772; Via di San Calisto 9; ☎ 11am-8pm Tue-Sun; 🚌 or 🚊 Viale di Trastevere
Backstreet boutique-gallery Temporary Love collaborates with artists to create limited-edition men's and women's bags and edgy threads – from where-did-you-get-that T-shirts to hand-painted totes. There are five collections/exhibitions a year, and they've worked with France's Serge Uberti and local street-art hero Sten.

OFFICINA DELLA CARTA Map pp132–3   Gifts
☎ 06 589 55 57; Via Benedetta 26b; 🚌 Piazza Trilussa
A perfect present pitstop, this tiny workshop produces attractive hand-painted paper-bound boxes, photo albums, recipe books, notepads, photo frames, diaries and charming marionette theatres.

ROMA-STORE Map pp132–3   Perfume
☎ 06 581 87 89; Via della Lungaretta 63; 🚌 or 🚊 Viale di Trastevere
With no sign, Roma-Store is an enchanting perfume shop crammed full of deliciously enticing bottles of scent, including lots of unusual brands as well as English Floris, Italian Aqua di Parma and French Etat Libre d'Orange.

SCALA QUATTORODICI
Map pp132–3   Women's Clothing
☎ Via della Scala 13-14; ☎ 10am-1.30pm Tue-Sat & 4 8pm Mon-Sat; 🚌 Piazza Trilussa
Make yourself over a la Audrey Hepburn with these classically tailored clothes in beautiful fabrics – either made-to-measure or off-the-peg. Pricey (a frock will set you back €600 or so) but oh so worth it.

VATICAN CITY, BORGO & PRATI

CASTRONI Map pp138–9   Food
☎ 06 687 43 83; Via Cola di Rienzo 196; ☎ 8am-8pm; Ⓜ Ottaviano-San Pietro; ☒
This Aladdin's cave of a gourmet food shop (as well as marron glaces, sweets, and so on, it sells Vegemite and baked beans to homesick expats) also houses a top-notch café (see p230). There are smaller branches at Via Ottaviano (Map pp138–9), Via Flaminio 28 (Map pp150–1) and Via Nazionale 71 (Map pp106–7).

DISCOUNT DESIGN

Discount designer outlets are big business here – helping to achieve the all-important *bella figura* (beautiful look). Discount dell'Alta Moda (Map p172; ☎ 06 361 37 96; Via Gesù e Maria 14; Map p100; ☎ 06 482 7790; Via dei Serviti 27; ☎ 06 478 25 672; Via Agostino de Pretis 87) sells big names at knock-down prices (around 50% off) and is well worth a rummage. Outlet Point (Map p172; ☎ 06 325 04 661; Via Vittoria 11), in Spagna, sells De Carlis, a typical Roman high-fashion label, with prices at 50% to 60% off, including cashmere and cocktail dresses. You can also buy discount brands such as Chloe, Prada, Marni and Jill Sander, at Outlet Gente (Map p138–9; ☎ 06 689 26 72; Via Cola di Rienzo 246), the less expensive relation to Gente's main store in Via del Babuino. Fashion fiends on a budget might want to schlep out to Castel Romano Designer Outlet (off Map p60; ☎ 06 50 50 050), around 20km south of Rome, which has over 100 shops selling names such as Dolce & Gabbana, Salvatore Ferragamo and Valentino, with prices reduced from 30% to 70%. You can book a shuttle bus (☎ 06 373 50810) from your hotel (€23 return).

ANGELO DI NEPI

Map pp138–9   Women's Clothing

☎ 06 322 48 00; Via Cola di Rienzo 267; 🚇 Piazza del Risorgimento

Roman designer Nepi adores rich colour, and combines Italian cut and style with rich Indian fabrics: sumptuous reds, shocking pinks, intricate embroidery and heavy silk to make you as pretty as a peacock. You'll find other branches at Via dei Giubbonari 28 (Map p74–5; ☎ 06 689 30 06) and Via del Babuino 147 (Map p172; ☎ 06 360 42 99).

VILLA BORGHESE & NORTHERN ROME

LIBRERIA L'ARGONAUTA

Map pp150–1   Books

☎ 06 854 34 43; Via Reggio Emilia 89, Nomentano; 🚇 Via Nizza

Off the main tourist trail, this travel bookshop is a lovely place to browse. The serene atmosphere and shelves of travel literature can easily spark daydreams of far-off places. Staff are friendly and happy to let you drift around the world in peace.

LORENZA AMBROSETTI

Map pp150–1   Ceramics

☎ 06 440 29 80; Via Reggio Emilia 11; ⏱ 10am-12.30pm & 4-7pm Mon-Fri; 🚇 Via Nomentana

This unprepossessing little shop, just along the street from MACRO (see p155), harbours wonderful wares. Senora Ambrosetti sells tiles created from ancient and historic designs, from 15th-century Spanish to 1970s Sicilian and more. The tiles are still made by artisans. The polished, almost leather-like terracotta flooring at the Galleria Doria

Pamphilj came from here. The average cost is around €70 per sq m.

BORGO PARIOLI MARKET

Map pp150–1   Market

☎ 06 855 27 73; Via Tirso 14-Via Metauro 21, Parioli; ⏱ 9am-8pm Sat & Sun 1st 3 weekends of the month; 🚊 Viale Regina Margherita

Parioli is Rome's most expensive residential area, and its weekend market is a hot date on the capital's monthly shopping calendar. Among the often-expensive bric-a-brac, you'll find original jewellery and accessories from the 1950s onwards, silverware, paintings, antique lamps and old gramophones.

PONTE MILVIO

Map pp150–1   Market

Ponte Milvio, Flaminio; ⏱ 9am-sunset 1st Sun of the month, closed Aug; 🚇 Ponte Milvio

The scene of a famous battle in AD 312, the 2nd-century-BC Ponte Milvio is now the scene of a great monthly antique market along the riverbank. On the first Sunday of every month stalls spring up along the Lungotevere Capoprati (between the Ponte Milvio and Ponte Duca d'Aosta) laden with antiques and collectable clobber.

GOODY MUSIC

Map pp150–1   Music

☎ 06 361 09 59; Via Cesare Beccaria 2; Ⓜ Flaminio

This is where DJs go to stock up on tunes, with a trainspotting collection of hip-hop, nu-jazz, deep and funky house, hardstyle and rare grooves, on vinyl and CD. Staff are knowledgeable, and you can also buy equipment and T-shirts to make you look the part.

top picks

- **Agata e Romeo** (p204)
- **Bir & Fud** (p210)
- **Glass Hostaria** (p210)
- **L'Archangelo** (p211)
- **La Rosetta** (p195)
- **Open Colonna** (p205)
- **Osteria Sostegno** (p195)
- **Pizzeria da Baffetto** (p196)
- **Trattoria Monti** (p204)
- **Veranda de l'Hotel Columbus** (pp211)

In *Un Americano a Roma* (An American in Rome; 1954), Roman actor Alberto Sordi wants to be an American. He comes home to a bowl of his mamma's pasta, but rejects it, trying instead to eat bread with milk before spitting it out. The power of pasta is too strong. Exasperated, he says, 'Maccarone, why are you looking at me? You provoke me and I shall destroy you!' A black-and-white photo of Sordi forking the spaghetti into his mouth is probably a more commonly reproduced image than that of the Sistine Chapel.

Any Roman worth their salt would surely do the same. This is a city that lives to eat, rather than eats to live. There is an obsession with the best seasonal ingredients, and markets overflow with produce fresh from the fields of Lazio. Traditional Roman cooking is rustic and deceptively simple, and like many other Italian cuisines, born of careful use of the ingredients available – making use of the cheaper cuts of meat, like *guanciale* (pig's cheek), and greens that could be gathered wild from the fields.

The city's conservatism might be measured by its menus, on which belly-warming old favourites are always top of the pots. But nowadays there are ever-increasing Michelin-starred and *cucina creativa* (creative cooking) eateries, where inventive chefs do clever things with Roman staples – adding new ingredients and cooking them in delicate, witty ways. There are also new incarnations of the trattoria (neighbourhood restaurant), which use the faithful formula (gingham tablecloths, old friends on the menu) but offer innovative cuisine and scholarly wine lists. Ethnic restaurants are more prevalent these days, though in Rome Italian food remains king. Even the way people eat is changing. Hip young Romans do brunch, and turn *aperitivo* (early-evening snacks and drinks) into a replacement for dinner (but don't tell their parents).

However, the old stalwart trattoria is still where every Roman returns, and some of the city's most memorable culinary experiences are to be had enjoying home-cooked food served by a shuffling matriarch. The favourite casual meal remains the gloriously simple pizza, with Rome's signature wafer-thin, bubbling-topped pizzas slapped down on tables by waiters on a mission.

COOKING COURSES

Check out the Città di Gusto (City of Taste; Map pp124–5; ☎ 06 551 12 21; www.gamberorosso.it; Via Enrico Fermi 161), a six-storey shrine to food created by Italian foodie organisation Gambero Rosso (www.gamberorosso.it). It has cooking courses starring Rome's top chefs, a wine bar, pizza workshop, cookbook shop and the Teatro del Vino for demonstrations, tastings and lessons. For taste-sensation culinary events featuring the best in local produce, there's Rome's Slow Food movement (www.slowfoodroma.com).

Cookery writer Diane Seed (*The Top One Hundred Pasta Sauces*) runs her Roman Kitchen (Map pp74–5; ☎ 06 678 57 59; www.italiangourmet.com) several times a year from her kitchen in the Palazzo Doria Pamphilj. There are one-day, two-day, three-day and week-long courses costing €200 per day and €1000 per week, and a Tuesday market visit and class for €180.

For more information on courses, see p290.

DOS & DON'TS

- Brush up when eating out; Italians dress relatively smartly at most meals.
- Bite through hanging spaghetti rather than slurping it up.
- Pasta is eaten with a fork (not fork and spoon).
- It's OK to eat pizza with your hands.
- In an Italian home you may *fare la scarpetta* (make a little shoe) with your bread and wipe plates clean of sauces.
- If invited to someone's home, traditional gifts are a tray of *dolci* (sweets) from a *pasticceria* (pastry shop), a bottle of wine or flowers.
- At restaurants, leave a tip: anything from 5% in a pizzeria to 10% in a more upmarket place. At least round up the bill.
- Don't be surprised to see *pane e coperto* (bread and cover charge; €1 to €5 per person) added to your bill.

SEASONAL CALENDAR

Although nowadays you can, of course, get some produce year round, Rome's kitchens still remain true to what is best for the time of year. Check this calendar to see what's in season.

Spring

- Spring is prime time for lamb, perfect roasted with potatoes – *agnello al forno con patate*. Sometimes it's described as *abbacchio* (Roman dialect for lamb) *scottadito* ('hot enough to burn fingers').
- May and June are favourable fishing months, and thus good for cuttlefish and octopus, as well as other seafood.
- March to April is the best season for *carciofo alla giudia* (Jewish-style artichoke), when the big round artichokes from Cerveteri appear on the table (smaller varieties are from Sardinia).
- Grass-green *fave* (broad beans) are eaten after a meal in the countryside, best accompanied by some salty *pecorino* cheese. A big day for doing this is May 1.
- It's also time to tuck into *risotto con asparagi di bosco* (rice with woodland asparagus), as asparagus comes into its prime.
- You'll see two types of courgette on Roman market stalls; the familiar dark-green kind, and the lighter green, fluted *zucchine romanesche* (Roman courgette), usually with the flowers still attached – these orange petals, deep-fried, are a delectable feature of Roman cooking.
- This the time to visit Nemi in the Castelli Romani, to eat its famous wild strawberries.

Summer

- *Tonno* (tuna) comes fresh from the seas around Sardinia; *linguine ai frutti di mare* and *risotto alla pescatora* are good light summer dishes.
- Summertime is *melanzane* (aubergine) time: tuck into them grilled as antipasti or fried and layered with rich tomato sauce in *melanzane alla parmagiana*, or try *melanzane e peperoni stufati* (stuffed aubergine and peppers).
- Summer is the season for leafy greens, and Rome even has its own lettuce, the sturdy, flavourful *lattuga romana*. It's usually eaten in a fresh green or mixed salad, dressed simply with olive oil, vinegar and salt.
- Tomatoes are at their full-bodied finest – it's the ideal moment for a light *spaghetti al pomodoro* (with fresh tomatoes and basil).
- Seductive heaps of *pesche* (peaches) and *albicocche* (apricots) dominate market stalls.
- Luscious, succulent, fleshy *fichi* (figs) begin in June, perfect with some salty *proscitto crudo* (cured ham).

Autumn

- *Alla cacciatora* (hunter-style) dishes are sourced from Lazio's hills, with meats such as *cinghiale* (boar) and *lepre* (hare).
- Fish is also good in autumn; you could try fried fish from Fiumicino, such as *triglia* (red mullet), or mixed small fish, such as *alici* (anchovies).
- Autumn also equals mushrooms – the meaty porcini, *galletti* and *ovuli*.
- *Broccoletti* (also called *broccolini*), a cross between broccoli and asparagus, appears at Roman markets as summer begins to fade; it's often served fried with *aglio* (garlic) and *olio* (olive oil).
- Other autumnal vegetables include cauliflower and *spinaci* (spinach), while aubergine, peppers and tomatoes continue.
- *Cicoria selvatica* (wild chicory) has dark-green leaves and a bitter taste, and is at its best sautéed with spicy pepper and garlic.
- Heaping the markets are *uva* (grapes), *pere* (pears) and *meloni* (melon).
- Nuts are now in season, and creamy *nocciola* (hazelnut) and *marron* (chestnut) will be adorning ice-cream cones all over the city.

Winter

- Winter is the ideal time to eat dishes with *ceci* (chickpeas) and minestrone, as well as herb-roasted *porchetta di Ariccia* (pork from Ariccia).
- *Puntarelle* ('little points' – Catalonian chicory), a green only found in Lazio, is a delicious, slightly bitter winter green, often tossed with a dressing of anchovy, garlic and olive oil.
- *Finnochio* (fennel) is a favourite winter vegetable, eaten in salads or on its own.
- *Broccolo Romanesco* (Roman broccoli) looks like a cross between broccoli and a cauliflower.
- Markets are piled high with *aranci* (oranges) and *mandarini* (mandarins), their brilliant orange set off by dark-green leaves.
- In February, look out for *frappé* (strips of fried dough sprinkled with sugar), eaten at carnival time.

HISTORY

Petronius wrote a satirical account of the banquet of the newly wealthy Trimalchio in the 1st century AD, which fixed in the collective consciousness that ancient Romans ate dormice seasoned with poppies and honey. But the basics of Roman cuisine have remained the same throughout history, resting on the availability of local ingredients: olives, olive oil, pulses, cured pork, lamb, offal, vegetables, wild greens, *pecorino* cheese, ricotta, wood-baked bread, pasta and fish. Innards yes, mice no.

In the past, butchers who worked in the city abattoir were often paid in meat as well as money. But they got the cuts that the moneyed classes didn't want, the offal, and so they developed ways to cook them – usually extremely slowly, to develop the flavour and disguise their beginnings. The Roman staple *coda alla vaccinara* translates as 'oxtail cooked butcher's style'.

The growing numbers of pilgrims from the 14th century onwards meant a proliferation of taverns and *osterie* (neighbourhood inns), which usually specialised in one dish and *vino della casa* (house wine). The arrival of the potato and tomato from the New World in the 16th century didn't have an immediate impact, though obviously the Romans did eventually start to use these novel vegetables.

Deep-frying is a staple of *cucina ebraico-romanesca* (Roman-Jewish cooking), and dates to the period between the 16th and 19th centuries when the Jews were confined to the city's ghetto. To add flavour to their limited ingredients – those spurned by the rich, such as courgette (zucchini) flowers – they began to fry everything from mozzarella to *baccalà* (salted cod). Grand Tourists (rich pilgrims, in search of Art rather than God) arrived in the 18th century, and *osterie* began to get more sophisticated. Pizza only arrived post-WWII, introduced by southern migrants. The 1980s saw the development of *cucina creativa,* more experimental ways of cooking. Sometimes this was a simple twist, such as adding a different ingredient to a traditional recipe or using a different kind of pasta with a traditional sauce.

CELEBRATING WITH FOOD

In Rome, as in the rest of Italy, food is an intrinsic part of any celebration. Rites-of-passage celebrations all involve sumptuous spreads that are often laid on as much to impress as to enjoy, as anyone who has eaten

CLOSED IN AUGUST?

Most eateries close for at least a week in August, but the timings vary from year to year. We have listed here where restaurants close for the whole month. With others it's advisable to ring first in August to check that everyone hasn't gone to the beach.

their way through a nine-course wedding banquet can testify.

Festivals in Italy usually have ancient roots – when Christianity came along, many were just adapted to the new figurehead. The biggest festivals are Natale (Christmas), Pasqua (Easter) and Carnevale (the period leading up to Ash Wednesday, the first day of Lent). The classic way to celebrate any feast day is to precede it with a day of eating *magro* (lean) to prepare for the overindulgence to come. On Vigilia (Christmas Eve), for example, tradition dictates that you eat little during the day and have a fish-based dinner as a prelude to the excesses of the 25th. Many special days have dishes associated with them: on Ferragosto (Feast of the Assumption; 15 August) Romans eat *pollo e peperoni* (chicken with peppers).

Most festivals have some kind of food involved, but many of them have no other excuse than food. These are called *sagre* (feasting festivals) and are usually celebrations of local specialities such as hazelnuts, wine and sausages.

ON THE MENU
Home Comforts

Roman favourites are all comfort foods that are deceptively simple and remarkably tasty. In the classic Roman comedy *I Soliti Ignoti* (Big Deal on Madonna Street; 1958) inept thieves break through a wall to burgle a safe, but find themselves in a kitchen by mistake, and console themselves by cooking *pasta e ceci* (pasta with chickpeas). Such iconic dishes, including *carbonara, amatriciana* and *cacio e pepe,* are on almost every menu. In creative restaurants, chefs often take these classics and cook them with a new twist. Check out the boxed texts opposite and on p192 to guide you through the Roman menu. You can also look for what's in season at the market in the boxed text, p189.

When in Rome...

Most entrenched in culinary tradition is the Jewish Ghetto area, with its hearty Roman-Jewish cuisine, including deep-fried delights and spectacular takes on the artichoke, while, for the heart (and liver, and brains) of the *cucina Romana*, head to Testaccio, a traditional working-class district, clustered around the city's former slaughterhouse. This proximity led to the area specialising in offal – a major feature of Roman cooking. Here try pasta with *pajata*, made with the entrails of young veal calves, considered a delicacy since they contain the mother's congealed milk. If you see the word *coratella* in a dish, it means you'll be eating lights (lungs), kidneys and hearts. Often the offal is cooked with *carciofi* (artichokes), which cuts its richness and leaves the palate refreshed. At other times tomato is used, and the expression *in umido*, while normally meaning cooked in a broth, in Lazio tends to mean cooked in a tomato-scented broth.

Seafood can be excellent in Rome; it's fished locally in Lazio. There are lots of dedicated seafood restaurants, usually upper-range places with delicate takes on fish such as sea

LOCAL FAVOURITES

Many of these staples are found on menus citywide – they're not all Roman in origin, but they're close to Roman hearts.

- abbacchio al forno – lamb (in Roman dialect) roasted with rosemary and garlic, usually accompanied by rosemary-roasted potatoes
- agnello alla cacciatore – lamb 'hunter style' with onion and fresh tomatoes
- baccalà – salt cod, often served deep fried in the Roman-Jewish tradition
- bresaola – wind-dried beef, a feature of Roman-Jewish cuisine, served as a replacement for prosciutto
- bruschetta – from the Roman dialect *bruscare*, meaning 'roast over coals', this is a simple culinary masterpiece: grilled bread rubbed with garlic, splashed with olive oil and sprinkled with salt, most commonly then topped by tomatoes
- bucatini all'amatriciana – pasta with tomato sauce, onions, pancetta, cheese and chilli; originated in Amatrice, a town east of Rome, it's an adaptation of *spaghetti alla gricia* – a daring Amatrice cook added tomatoes
- cacio e pepe – piping-hot pasta topped with freshly grated *pecorino romano* (a sharp, salty, sheeps' milk cheese), ground black pepper and a dash of olive oil
- carciofi alla giudia – 'Jewish-style' artichokes deep fried and pressed to look something like a flower – the heart is soft and succulent, the leaves taste like delicious crisps
- carciofi alla romana – artichokes boiled with oil, garlic and mint
- coda alla vaccinara – literally 'tail cooked butcher's style' – a dish developed when abattoir workers received the cheapest cuts of meat and performed alchemy on them
- fiori di zucca – courgette (zucchini) flowers, usually stuffed with mozzarella and anchovies and fried
- involtini – thin slices of veal or beef, rolled up with sage or sometimes vegetables and mozzarella
- minestra di arzilla con pasta e broccoli – Roman-Jewish dish served only at the most traditional restaurants: skate soup with pasta and broccoletti
- pagliata – traditional Roman dish (*pajata* in dialect) made using the intestines of a suckling calf
- pasta e ceci – pasta with chickpeas, warms the cockles in winter; eat when you're in need of the culinary equivalent of a cuddle
- pizza bianca – 'white pizza' – unique to Rome, a plain pizza brushed with salt, olive oil and often rosemary. In many bakeries and cafés you can buy this split and filled with something to make a sandwich. A classic construction-worker's lunch is *pizza bianca* stuffed with mortadella, glugged down with white wine.
- porchetta – a hog roasted by a *porchettaro* (*porchetta* chef) on a spit with herbs and an abundance of *finocchio selvatico* (wild fennel). The best comes from Ariccia, in the hills around Rome.
- saltimbocca alla romana – the deliciously named 'leap in the mouth', in which sparing amounts of prosciutto and sage are used to spark up veal
- spaghetti alla carbonara – gorgeous, barely there sauce of egg, cheese and *guanciale* (cured pig's cheek). The egg is added raw, and stirred into the hot pasta to cook it. Why '*carbonara*'? Some say it's because it was the coal workers' favourite, others claim it's after the specks of black pepper that complete the dish.
- spaghetti alla gricia – pasta with *pecorino* cheese, black pepper and pancetta; comes from the town of Griciano (northern Lazio)
- stracciatella – humble chicken broth given a lift by the addition of Parmesan and whisked egg
- supplì – rice balls, like large croquettes. If they contain mozzarella, they're called *supplì a telefono* because when you break one open, the cheese forms a string like a telephone wire between the two halves.
- trippa alla romana – tripe cooked with potatoes, tomato and mint and sprinkled with *pecorino* cheese, a typical Saturday-in-Rome dish.

bass, skate and tuna. According to the culinary calendar, which was initiated by the Catholic Church to vary the nutrition of its flock, fish is eaten on Friday, and *baccalà* (salted cod) is often eaten with *ceci* (chickpeas), usually on Wednesday.

Thursday is the day for gnocchi (dumplings). The traditional Roman recipe uses semolina flour and makes heavy gnocchi, but you can also find the typical gnocchi with potatoes, usually served with a *ragù* (sauce), which in Rome (unlike, say, Bologna) contains more tomatoes than meat.

Dolci (desserts) tend to be the same at every trattoria: tiramisu, *pannacotta* ('cooked cream', with added sugar and cooled to set) and so on, but for a traditional Roman *dolce* you should look out for ricotta cakes – with chocolate chips or cherries or both – at a local bakery. Many Romans eat at a restaurant and then go elsewhere for a gelato and a coffee to finish off the meal.

WHERE TO EAT

Eateries are divided into several categories. A *tavola calda* (hot table) offers cheap, pre-prepared pasta, meat and vegetable dishes. Quality is usually reasonable while atmosphere takes a back seat. In Ostia Antica (p268)

you can see the *tavola calda*'s ancient ancestor, a *thermopile* complete with frescoed menu.

A *rosticceria* sells cooked meats but often has a larger selection of takeaway food. There are also takeaway pizza joints serving ready *pizza al taglio* (by the slice). When it's good, it's very good.

You can eat well at many *enoteche,* ie wine bars that usually serve snacks (such as cheeses or cold meats) and some hot dishes.

For a full meal you'll want a trattoria, an *osteria* (neighbourhood inn), a *ristorante* (restaurant), or a pizzeria. The difference between them is now fairly blurred. Traditionally, trattorias were family-run places that offered a basic, affordable local menu, and there are still lots of these around. Some have been updated, and may have traditional looks, but offer hip takes on tradition with longer wine lists and creative cookery – places such as Ditirambo (p198), Tram Tram (p206) and Matricianella (p200). *Ristoranti*, however, offer more choice and smarter service, and are more expensive.

A pizzeria will, of course, serve pizza, but many also offer a full menu including antipasti, pasta, meat and vegetable dishes. They're often only open in the evening. Most Romans will precede their pizza with a starter of bruschetta or mixed fried things (zucchini flowers, potato, olives etc) and wash it all down with beer.

PASTA DIRECTORY

Here's a non-exhaustive guide to some of the pastas you're likely to encounter in Rome.

- bucatini – means 'little holes'; it's classically Roman, and holds a hearty sauce well. It's thicker than spaghetti and has a tiny hole through its centre, so that the pasta cooks evenly. If you're eating *bucatini* in a restaurant, even if you're dining with the pope, it's permissible to tuck your napkin into your collar, such is the splash factor.
- cappelletti – meat-filled little parcels, usually cooked in broth. The name means 'little hats' – check out the shape.
- farfalle – means 'butterflies'. Rather like the bowties they resemble, they go with almost anything, but, unlike bowties, they're particularly good in salads.
- fettucine – 'little ribbons' are superb with meat sauces, and are often made fresh
- fusilli – 'little spindles': versatile corkscrew-shaped pasta
- linguine – 'little tongues': flattened, narrow noodles that are sublime with seafood
- orecchiette – 'little ears' are native to the south of Italy but popular in Rome. The dough is made from hard wheat flour and water. They hold a sauce well and are most often paired with *broccoletti* or *ragù* (sauce).
- pappadelle – from the verb *pappare*, meaning 'to gobble up'. These wider, flatter fettucine are particularly divine with rich meat and game sauces.
- penne – 'pens' because they resemble the quill of a fountain pen
- ravioli – fresh pasta envelopes, often filled with spinach and ricotta
- rigatoni – big sturdy tubes with ridges: *riga* means 'straight line'. Traditionally served with – vegetarians look away now – *pagliata* (veal or lamb intestines).
- spaghetti – *spago* means 'twine': best served with thin or oily sauces, such as *alle vongole* (with clams)
- strozzapreti – the proximity of the Vatican might have inspired this popular, thick, ropelike shape: 'priest-strangler'
- trofie – this thin twisted pasta is from Liguria but is popular in Rome
- vermicelli – 'little worms': long strands that are skinnier than spaghetti

CREAMY OR FRUITY, THAT IS THE QUESTION

Eating gelato is as much part of Roman life as the morning coffee – try it and you'll understand why. The city has some of the world's finest ice-cream shops – it's all come a long way since Nero snacked on snow mixed with fruit pulp and honey.

No-one's quite sure where ice cream originated, but credit is usually given to the Arabs, said to have developed techniques for freezing fruit juices and to have made the first sorbets. The word sorbet probably derives from the Arab word *scherbet*, meaning 'sweet snow', or from *sharber*, meaning 'to sip'. When the Arabs invaded Sicily they brought their food with them and the fame of their frozen drink began to spread.

Fast forward to the Renaissance and 16th-century Florence, where two cooks made ice-cream history. The first, Ruggeri, was a chicken farmer who made it to the culinary big time thanks to a sorbet he made for Catherine Medici. The second, Bernardo Buontalenti, was a well-known architect who stunned the gastronomic establishment by producing a frozen dessert based on zabaglione (a dessert of whipped egg yolks, sugar and sweet wine) and fruit.

Both are considered founding fathers of Italy's gelato culture, which, while it's one of the country's most successful exports, is best experienced first-hand. You'll usually be asked if you want *panna* (cream) with your ice cream. A good call is *si*.

In the lion days of summer, another Roman treat is *grattachecca* – a crushed-ice sensation, drowned in a fruity syrup of your choice. It'll cool you down on a sultry night, and is the perfect accompaniment to a riverside stroll. There are several stands around the central bridges over the River Tiber.

The following are all shining stars of the ice-cream scene, but a rule of thumb for elsewhere is to check the colour of the pistachio: ochre-green = good, bright-green = bad. Most places open from around 8am to 1am, though hours are shorter in winter. Prices range from around €1.50 to €3.50 for a *cona* (cone) or *coppetta* (tub).

- **Alberto Pica** (Map pp74–5; ☎ 06 688 06 153; Via della Seggiola; ⓡ Via Arenula) The original Mr Pica worked for Giolitti (below), and this is a historic Roman gelataria, open since 1960. In summer, it offers flavours such as *fragoline di bosco* (wild strawberry) and *petali di rosa* (rose petal), but rice flavours are specialities year-round (resembling frozen rice pudding – yum).

- **Al Settimo Gelo** (Map pp150–1; ☎ 06 372 55 67; Via Vodice 21a; ☽ Tue-Sun; ⓡ Piazza Giuseppe Mazzini) The name's a play on 'seventh heaven' and it's not a far-fetched title for one of Rome's finest, with a devotion to the best possible natural ingredients – pistachios from Bronte, almonds from Avola and so on. Try the Greek ice cream or cardamom made to an Afghan recipe.

- **Ara Coeli** (Map pp64–5; ☎ 06 679 50 85; Piazza d'Ara Coeli 9; ⓡ Piazza Venezia) Close to the base of the Campidoglio, Ara Coeli offers more than 40 flavours of excellent organic ice cream, semicold varieties, Sicilian granita and yoghurt.

- **Fiocco di Neve** (Map pp74–5; ☎ 06 6/8 60 25; Via del Pantheon 51; ⓡ or ⓡ Largo di Torre Argentina) Tiny place, grumpy staff, natural colours – this has all the hallmarks of a good Roman gelateria. Romans come to the 'Snowflake', near the Pantheon, when they're in the mood for something creamy. Zabaglione is the speciality.

- **Fior di Luna** (Map pp132–3; ☎ 06 645 61 314; Via della Lungaretta 96; ⓡ or ⓡ Viale di Trastevere) A busy little Trastevere hub that serves up natural seasonal handmade ice cream and sorbet.

- **Gelateria Giolitti** (Map pp74–5; ☎ 06 699 12 43; Via degli Uffici del Vicario 40; ⓡ Corso del Rinascimento) This started as a dairy in 1900 and still keeps the hordes happy with succulent sorbets and creamy combinations. Gregory Peck and Audrey Hepburn swung by in *Roman Holiday* and it used to deliver marron glacé to Pope John Paul II.

- **Il Caruso** (Map p100; Via Collina 15; ☽ 11am-midnight; ⓡ Corso del Rinascimento) Spot Il Caruso by the gelato-licking hordes outside. It only does a few flavours, but to perfection. Try the incredibly creamy pistachio.

- **La Fonte della Salute** (Map pp132–3; ☎ 06 589 74 71; Via Cardinale Marmaggi 2-6; ⓡ or ⓡ Viale di Trastevere) It might not be quite the 'fountain of health' of the name, but the fruit flavours are so delicious they must surely be good for the soul.

- **Mondi** (Map pp150–1; ☎ 06 333 64 66; Via Flaminia Vecchia 468; ☽ 6.30am-midnight Tue-Sun; ⓡ or ⓡ Viale di Trastevere) Historic *pasticceria*-gelataria serving *fantastico* flavours such as raspberry and chocolate, chocolate and orange peel, and *fragoline di bosco*.

- **Old Bridge** (Map pp138–9; ☎ 06 397 23 026; Via dei Bastioni di Michelangelo 5; Ⓜ Ottaviano-San Pietro) Ideal for a pre- or post-Vatican pick-me-up, this tiny parlour has been cheerfully dishing up huge portions of delicious ice cream for over 20 years. Try the chocolate or pistachio, and, go on, have a dollop of cream.

- **Palazzo del Freddo di Giovanni Fassi** (Map pp106–7; ☎ 06 446 47 40; Via Principe Eugenio 65; ☽ noon-12.30am Sat, 10am-midnight Sun, noon-midnight Tue-Thu; Ⓜ Vittorio Emanuele) A great back-in-time barn of a place, sprinkled with marble tabletops and vintage gelato-making machinery, Fassi offers fantastic classic flavours, such as *riso* (rice), pistachio and *nocciola* (hazelnut). The granita, served with dollops of cream, deserves special mention.

- **San Crispino** Via della Panetteria 42 (Map p100; ☎ 06 679 39 24; Ⓜ Barberini); Piazza della Maddalena 3 (Map pp74–5; ⓡ Largo Argentina) Possibly the world's best gelato. *What?* You want a cone? The delicate, strictly natural and seasonal flavours are served only in tubs (cones would detract from the taste).

top picks

BEST-VALUE EATS

- Bir & Fud (p210) Divine pizzas at rock-bottom prices.
- Cacio e Pepe (p213) Keeps Romans queuing around the block.
- Da Enzo (p210) You: gloriously sated. Your wallet: barely lighter.
- Da Lucia (p211) Pure Trastevere soul food.
- Enoteca Corsi (p196) Central, atmospheric & cheap.
- Forno di Campo de' Fiori (p199) If angels made *pizza al taglio* (sliced), it would taste like this.
- La Veranda de l'Hotel Columbus (p212) Top-of-the-range frescoed wonder, with a lunch menu for €35.
- Open Colonna (p205) Lunch at super-chef Antonello Colonna's restaurant for only €15.
- Pizzeria da Baffetto (p198) The full-on, delicious, noisy pizza experience – yours for peanuts.
- Sora Margherita (p200) A ghetto-fabulous local Roman-Jewish kitchen.

VEGETARIANS & VEGANS

Panic not, vegetarians, you can eat well in Rome, with the choice of bountiful antipasti, pasta dishes, *insalati* (salad), *contorni* (side dishes) and pizzas. There are a couple of extremely good vegetarian restaurants, and some of the more creative restaurants have greater choice of vegetarian dishes.

Be mindful of hidden ingredients not mentioned on the menu – for example, steer clear of anything that's been stuffed (like courgette flowers, often spiced up with anchovies) or check that it's *senza carne o pesce* (without meat or fish). Note that to many Italians vegetarian means you don't eat red meat.

Vegans are in for a tougher time. Cheese is used universally, so you must specify that you want something *'senza formaggio'* (without cheese). Also remember that *pasta fresca*, which may also turn up in soups, is made with eggs. The safest bet is to self-cater or try a dedicated vegetarian restaurant, which will always have some vegan options.

SELF-CATERING

For deli supplies and wine, shop at *alimentari*, which generally open from 7am to 1.30pm and 5pm to 8pm daily except Thursday afternoon and Sunday (during the summer months they will often close on Saturday afternoon instead of Thursday). See also the boxed text, p212.

You can stock up at the small supermarkets dotted around town:

Conad (Map pp106–7; Stazione Termini)

DeSpar (Map pp74–5; Via Giustiniani 18b-21) Near the Pantheon.

DeSpar (Map pp74–5; Via Nazionale 212-213) Near Pantheon.

Dì per Dì (Map pp96–7; Via Vittoria) Near Spanish Steps.

Sir (Map pp106–7; Piazza dell'Indipendenza 28)

Todis (Map pp132–3; Via Natale del Grande 24) In Trastevere.

ANCIENT ROME

Ancient Rome has a few superb restaurants, and if you're near the Colosseum or the Forum, you can also head to nearby Celio Hill & Lateran (p207), to the southwest, or Monti (p204), just north of Via Cavour. It's always good to follow a recommendation around a major tourist haunt, as these areas have an unfair share of overpriced, underwhelming eateries.

SAN TEODORO Map pp64–5   Ristorante €€
☎ 06 678 09 33; Via dei Fienili 49-50; meals €70;
Mon-Sat; Via del Teatro di Marcello
Upmarket San Teodoro has a welcoming, arched interior, but eating outside is best. The restaurant offers sophisticated takes on traditional dishes, and is known for its tasty seafood creations, including baked sea bass coated in artichokes. Chocolate, ricotta and ice cream appear in various guises for dessert. The wine list is impressive.

LA PIAZZETTA Map pp64–5   Ristorante €€
☎ 06 699 16 40; Vicolo del Buon Consiglio 23a;
meals €35; M Colosseo
Molto simpatico, on a tiny medieval lane, this tucked-away, informal yet classy restaurant has a fabulous antipasti buffet and equally impressive *primi* (first courses) and *secondi* (second courses) – try the yolky carbonara. A dessert-sampler buffet means

PRICE GUIDE

The pricing in this chapter refers to the average cost of a meal that includes *primo* (first course), *secondo* (second course) and *dolce* (dessert).

€	under €25
€€	€25 to €50
€€€	over €50

EAT AS THE ROMANS DO

For *colazione* (breakfast), most Romans head to a bar for a cappuccino and *cornetto* – a croissant filled with *cioccolata* (chocolate), *marmellata* (marmalade) or *crema* (custard cream).

The main meal of the day is *pranzo* (lunch), eaten at about 1.30pm. Many shops and businesses close for three to four hours every afternoon to accommodate the meal and siesta that follows. On Sundays *pranzo* is sacred.

Cena (dinner), eaten any time from about 8.30pm, is usually a simple affair, although this is changing as fewer people make it home for the big lunchtime feast.

A full Italian meal consists of an antipasto (starter), a *primo piatto* (first course), a *secondo piatto* (second course) with an *insalata* (salad) or *contorno* (vegetable side dish), *dolci* (sweet), fruit, coffee and *digestivo* (liqueur). When eating out, however, you can do as most Romans do, and mix and match: order, say, a *primo* followed by an *insalata* or *contorno*.

you don't have to face a difficult decision between puddings.

CENTRO STORICO

Around Piazza Navona, Campo de' Fiori and the Pantheon you'll find an array of eateries, including some of the capital's best restaurants (both contemporary and traditional Roman). Again, beware of overpriced tourist traps. The atmospheric Jewish Ghetto is famous for its unique Roman-Jewish cooking.

PANTHEON & AROUND

LA ROSETTA Map pp74–5   Seafood €€€
☎ 06 686 10 02; Via della Rosetta 8–9; meals €110, grand tasting menu €170; ☺ Mon-Sat, closed 3 wks Aug; ☒ or ☒ Largo di Torre Argentina; ☒
Some say this is Rome's best fish restaurant; others say it's the best in Italy. Whichever it is, if you dislike fish, look elsewhere, because vegetarians and carnivores are not catered for. Chef Massimo Riccioli's dishes are often startlingly simple – there's nothing complex about *spaghetti con calamaretti* (pasta with baby squid) – but they're prepared with genius. Outside you glimpse the Pantheon but it's better inside amid yellow hues and white tablecloths. Bookings are essential, and it's more affordable at lunch.

IL BACARO Map pp74–5   Ristorante €€
☎ 06 687 25 54; Via degli Spagnoli 27; meals €50; ☺ lunch Mon-Fri, dinner Mon-Sat; ☒ Corso del Rinascimento; ☒
Book ahead, as Il Bacaro, tucked away on a bijou piazza, is the size of a postage stamp and always busy. It might be small but it's perfectly formed. The meat dishes are hearty, the wine list ample and the *primi* imaginative – try the *spaghetti con gamberi, porcini, pecorino e tartufo* (spaghetti with

prawns, porcini mushrooms, cheese and truffles). Summer seating spills out under a vine-covered pergola.

OSTERIA SOSTEGNO Map pp74–5   Osteria €€
☎ 06 679 38 42; Via della Colonnelle 5; meals €45; ☒ or ☒ Largo di Torre Argentina; ☒
Here you have stumbled on a well-kept secret. It's intimate, a favourite of journalists and politicians, with simple yet excellent dishes such as *lasagnetto al forno con punte di asparagi* (little lasagne with asparagus heads). There's a charming tiny covered terrace. Nearby is similarly splendid Ristorante Settimio (Map pp74–5; ☎ 06 678 96 51; Via della Colonnelle 14; meals €45), run by the same family.

LA CANTINA DI NINCO NANCO
Map pp74–5   Ristorante €€
☎ 06 681 35 558; Via Pozzo delle Cornacchie 36; meals €40; ☒ or ☒ Largo di Torre Argentina; ☒
This rustic cellar specialises in cooking from Lucania – the Basilicata region in the south of Italy, a mountainous area that produces delicious salami and cheeses, as well as dishes such as *baccalà in guazzetto di cipolla pomodori e patate* (cod with onion, tomato and potato sauce).

MACCHERONI Map pp74–5   Trattoria €€
☎ 06 683 07 895; Piazza delle Coppelle 44; meals €40; ☒ or ☒ Largo di Torre Argentina; ☒
Maccheroni feels almost like a scene from a film – there's something so artily styled about its vintage interior, with its spotless tablecloths, bottle-lined walls and strands of garlic. On set is a mix of well-off locals, from families to chic city slickers, keeping it busy even on a Monday night. The menu is stalwartly traditional, with delicious favourites such as *carciofo alla Romana* (artichoke Roman style).

ARMANDO AL PANTHEON
Map pp74–5   Trattoria €€

☎ 06 688 03 034; Salita dei Crescenzi 31; meals €40; ⊗ lunch & dinner Mon-Fri, lunch Sat, closed Aug; 🚇 or 🚊 Largo di Torre Argentina; ⊠
Family-run trattoria (since 1961) Armando's is a wood-panelled, inviting, authentic institution close to the Pantheon. Always busy, it's fed the likes of philosopher Jean-Paul Sartre and footballer Pelé. It specialises in traditional Roman fare, so if it's *baccalo alla Pizzaiola*, it's Friday. Other dishes are available all week, such as *ravioli al tartufo nero* (ravioli with black truffle). To finish try the homemade cakes. Book ahead.

OBIKÀ
Map pp74–5   Mozzarella Bar €€

☎ 06 683 26 30; Piazza di Firenze; meals €30; ⊗ noon-11.30pm; 🚇 Via del Corso; ⊠
This sleek place resembles a sushi joint, but with mozzarella rather than fish. The name means 'here it is' in Neapolitan dialect, and the white stuff arrives fresh daily at 8am. Try the *burrata* (mozzarella-like cheese filled with cream). There's a good brunch. Ancient-meets-modern décor mixes columns and an underlit floor. *Aperitivo* (7pm to 9pm) costs €8.

RICCIOLI CAFÉ
Map pp74–5   Seafood €€

☎ 06 682 10 313; Via delle Coppelle 13; sushi €3-35; ⊗ 9am-1am; 🚇 Corso del Rinascimento
The brainchild of Rome's sultan of seafood, La Rosetta's Massimo Riccioli (see p195), this perennially chic oyster bar and restaurant specialises in seafood, mostly raw. There's superfresh sushi and sashimi, oysters (from Brittany) and a range of Mediterranean shellfish. Eat on blue-velvet banquettes under twisted modernist chandeliers, or casually snack in the Pop Art bar.

ENOTECA CORSI
Map pp74–5   Wine Bar €

☎ 06 679 08 21; Via del Gesù 87; meals €20; ⊗ lunch Mon-Sat; 🚇 or 🚊 Largo di Torre Argentina
Merrily worse for wear, family-run Corsi is a genuine old-style Roman eatery. The look is rustic – bare wooden tables, paper tablecloths, wine bottles – and the atmosphere one of controlled mayhem. The menu, chalked up on a blackboard, contains homely dishes using good, fresh ingredients, such as *melanzane parmigiana*. It follows the culinary calendar, so if it's gnocchi, it's Thursday.

GREEN T
Map pp74–5   Chinese €€

☎ 06 679 86 28; Via del Piè di Marmo 28; dishes €7-20; 🚇 or 🚊 Largo di Torre Argentina
It's unusual to find good Chinese food in Rome, and this elegant place is something entirely different: a tearoom and boutique, serving street food, meat and fish dishes, as well as a selection of sushi.

ZAZÁ
Map pp74–5   Pizzeria €

☎ 06 688 01 357; Piazza San'Eustachio 49; pizza slice around €3; ⊗ 9am-10pm Mon-Sat; 🚊 Via Arenula
Handily sandwiched between Piazza Navona and the Pantheon, this hole-in-the-wall *pizza al taglio* (pizza by the slice) place hits the spot with its highly digestible pizza – the base is made using extra-virgin olive oil and is risen for up to 60 hours. The finishing touch? Succulent, all-organic toppings.

PIZZA FLORIDA
Map pp74–5   Pizzeria €

☎ 06 688 03 236; Via Florida 25; pizza slice around €2; ⊗ 9am-10.30pm Mon-Sat; 🚊 Via Arenula
Run by the friendly Fiori family, fantastic Florida offers delicious slices of pizza with fresh toppings, such as fontina cheese, bacon and chilli.

PIAZZA NAVONA & AROUND

L'ALTRO MASTAI
Map pp74–5   Ristorante €€€

☎ 06 683 01 296; Via G Giraud; meals €110, 7-course tasting menu €95; ⊗ dinner Tue-Sat, closed Aug; 🚇 Corso Vittorio Emanuele II
A graceful, special-occasion place, L'Altro Mastai has an interior that manages to be both grand and intimate. Service is fabulous and Fabio Baldassare's cooking is innovative yet always well balanced, with dishes such as *filetto di merluzzo nero con litchi, mostarda di limone e cipolla di Tropea glassata* (fillet of black cod with lychees, lemon mustard and glazed Tropea onion).

CASA BLEVE
Map pp74–5   Wine Bar €€

☎ 06 686 53 70; Via del Teatro Valle 48-49; meals €45; ⊗ Tue-Sat, closed Aug; 🚇 or 🚊 Largo di Torre Argentina
While away an afternoon in this stately, column-lined courtyard roofed with stained glass. It's ideal for a romantic and epicurean assignation accompanied by sublime wine and cheeses (mature or fresh, such as mozzarella and *burrata),* cold cuts, and *carpaccio* (thin slices of raw beef).

CAMPANA Map pp74–5   Ristorante €€

☎ 06 687 52 73; Vicolo della Campana 18; meals €35; 🕑 12.30-3pm & 7.30-11pm Tue-Sun; 🚌 or 🚋 Largo di Torre Argentina; 😡

Venerable neighbourhood Campana is apparently the oldest trattoria in Rome, and features gleaming white linen table-cloths, wooden, bottle-laden counters and inviting arrays of antipasti. Local families out for a treat are here to be served fresh fish and traditional Roman dishes such as *saltimbocca alla Romana con funghi* ('leap in the mouth' veal Roman style) by proficient, black-waistcoated waiters.

CUL DE SAC Map pp74–5   Wine Bar €€

☎ 06 688 01 094; Piazza Pasquino 73; meals €30; 🕑 noon-4pm & 6pm-12.30am Mon-Sat; 🚌 Corso Vittorio Emanuele II

A fabulous little *enoteca*, just off Piazza Navona, with a tiny terrace and nar-row, pine- and bottle-lined interior. The knowledgeable, swift waiters pass about delicious cold meats and cheeses, and moreish mains: try the delicate *involtini* (veal rolls). There's a phone-directory-sized wine list. Book ahead in the evening.

LILLI Map pp74 5   Trattoria €€

☎ 06 686 19 16; Via Tor di Nona 23; meals €25; 🕑 1-3pm & 8-11pm Tue-Sun; 🚌 Corso del Rinascimento

Close to the river, but only five minutes' walk from Piazza Navona, this is a find, in a cobbled cul de sac undiscovered by the hordes. It's frantically busy at lunch, with diners digging into beautifully turned-out traditional Roman grub such as *spaghetti alla gricia* (spaghetti with *pecorino* cheese, black pepper and pancetta), surrounded by framed engravings and under wood beams.

DA FRANCESCO

Map pp74–5   Trattoria, Pizzeria €€

☎ 06 686 40 09; Piazza del Fico 29; pizzas €6-9, meals €24; 🚌 Corso Vittorio Emanuele II

Gingham, paper tablecloths, frazzled, jovial waiters, groaning plateloads of pasta, tasty pizza: this quintessential Roman kitchen has character coming out of its ears, and tables and chairs spilling out onto the pretty piazza. Rock up early or queue. No credit cards.

ALFREDO E ADA Map pp74–5   Trattoria €

☎ 06 687 88 42; Via dei Banchi Nuovi 14; meals €20; 🕑 dinner Mon-Fri; 🚌 Corso Vittorio Emanuele II

Find a seat at this tiny brick-arched and wood-panelled place, with its spindly marble-topped tables, and then eat what Ada puts in front of you (there's no menu). It'll be simple tasty staples like pasta with tomato sauce and *salsiccia con fagioli* (sausage with beans). Dessert comes from Ada's legendary biscuit tin.

DA TONINO Map pp74–5   Trattoria €

☎ 06 687 70 02; Via del Governo Vecchio 18; meals €15-20; 🕑 Mon-Sat; 🚌 Corso Vittorio Emanuele II

You'll be hard-pressed to find a cheaper place for a sit-down meal in central Rome. Unsigned Tonino's is a wonderfully low-key place with yellowing pictures hanging on white walls, and it's always packed. There's no menu: the waiter will reel off the choices – rib sticking Roman staples, such as hearty *pasta alla gricia*.

LA FOCACCIA Map pp74–5   Pizzeria €

☎ 06 688 03 312; Via del Pace 11; pizzas €7.50-9.50; 🕑 12.30pm-12.30am; 🚌 Corso del Rinasci-mento; 😡

Hotfoot it to one of the few outside tables at this unsigned pizzeria, facing the beauti-ful Chiostro del Bramante, or settle for a place in the surprisingly large interior. As well as great bruschetta, the wood-fired pizzas and breads and delicate fresh pastas, and desserts are worth leaving space for.

LO ZOZZONE Map pp74–5   Panini €

☎ 06 688 08 575; Via del Teatro Pace 32; reg/large pizza bianca €3/5; 🕑 Mon-Sat; 🚌 Corso del Rinascimento

The affectionately named 'dirty one' is sparklingly clean, and growing smarter by the year, with tables inside and out. It also has some of Rome's best *panini*. Pay at the register for a *pizza bianca,* then ask for it to be stuffed with your belly's desire at the bar.

CHIOSTRO DEL BRAMANTE CAFFÈ

Map pp74–5   Café €

☎ 06 688 09 035, ext 26; Via della Pace; dishes €6-12; 🕑 10am-7.30pm Tue-Sun; 🚌 Corso del Rinascimento

A well-kept secret: a footfall from Piazza Navona, you can have a drink and snack (or a €30 Sunday brunch) on salads, *friselli* (Pugliese dried bread, reconstituted with water and loaded with toppings), and so on (€6 to €12), all while making use of the wi-fi, in the peaceful Renaissance splendour of Bramante's cloister, which hosts regular contemporary art installations.

PIZZERIA DA BAFFETTO

Map pp74–5   Pizzeria €

☎ 06 686 16 17; Via del Governo Vecchio 114; pizzas €6-9; ⏱ 6.30pm-midnight; 🚌 Corso Vittorio Emanuele II

Da Baffetto offers some of Rome's best pizzas, served in typical wham-bam style. To partake, join the queue and wait for the bustling waiters to squeeze you in – you may have to share a table. To start, try the tasty fried things – courgette flowers, olive ascolane and so on – before moving onto the pizzas, bubbling hot from the wood-fired oven, and as Roman as it gets.

PIZZERIA LA MONTECARLO

Map pp74–5   Pizzeria €

☎ 06 686 18 77; Vicolo Savelli 11-13; pizzas €4.50-8; ⏱ noon-3pm & 6.30pm-1am Tue-Sun; 🚌 Corso Vittorio Emanuele II

La Montecarlo, another true Roman pizzeria full of raucous charm, is ideal for sightseers exploring the *centro storico* (historic centre), but is also crammed with pizza-hungry locals. Expect thin, wood-charred pizzas, paper tablecloths, milling queues and turbocharged waiters.

VOLPETTI ALLA SCROFA

Map pp74–5   Pizzeria €

☎ 06 688 06 335; Via della Scrofa 31; dishes €2-8; ⏱ 7am-8.45pm Mon-Sat, 9am-8.45pm Sun; 🚌 Corso del Rinascimento

Volpetti offers scrumptious pizza, *pizza rustica* and pastries to take out, as well as a selection of top-notch daily *tavola calda* delights (eat in or takeaway). This is also a glorious deli (see p184).

CAMPO DE' FIORI & AROUND

VINERIA ROSCIOLI SALUMERIA

Map pp74–5   Wine Bar €€€

☎ 06 687 52 87; Via dei Giubbonari 21; meals €50; ⏱ Mon-Sat; 🚇 Via Arenula

Walk in and swoon over the mingled aromas. This traditional deli is a temple to food, with olive oils, cheeses (around 450 varieties), Italian and Spanish hams etc to buy. It's packed at meal times, when you can dine deliciously in the *molto chic* interior (think exposed brick arches and contempo-

rary paintings). Dishes include fresh pastas and beef tartare, and the wine list has some 1100 labels (900 Italian, 200 French).

DITIRAMBO Map pp74–5   Trattoria €€

☎ 06 687 16 26; Piazza della Cancelleria 72; meals €35; ⏱ lunch Tue-Sun, dinner daily; 🚌 Corso Vittorio Emanuele II; Ⓥ

Welcoming new-wave trattoria Ditirambo has a rustic look, excellent wine list and innovative cuisine. The menu changes according to what's fresh at the market, and the chef uses organic produce whenever possible. Among the delicate, sophisticated dishes, there's a good choice for vegetarians, with dishes such as wholewheat lasagne with artichokes and *pecorino*. Finish up with a divine tiramisu. It's unpretentious and popular, so book ahead.

RENATO E LUISA Map pp74–5   Trattoria €€

☎ 06 686 96 60; Via dei Barbieri 25; meals €35; ⏱ 8.30pm-midnight Tue-Sun; 🚌 Via Arenula

A favourite among vivacious young Romans, this backstreet new-style trattoria, in a traditional wood-beamed room, is always thronged. Renato's cooking is delicate and complex, with a buttery French twist, resulting in delectable dishes such as *millefoglie di baccalà e patate* (1000 layers of cod and potatoes).

GRAPPOLO D'ORO Map pp74–5   Trattoria €€

☎ 06 687 16 26; Piazza della Cancelleria 72; meals €35; ⏱ Mon-Sat; 🚌 Corso Vittorio Emanuele II

More contemporary looking than nearby Ditirambo, this is a similarly informal, stylish eatery among the sometimes lacklustre options around il Campo. The food is creative without being over-designed, and includes old favourites such as *spaghetti alla carbonara* (among the best in Rome, according to local foodie bible *Gambero Rosso*).

OSTERIA AR GALLETTO

Map pp74–5   Osteria €€

☎ 06 686 17 14; Piazza Farnese 102; meals €35; ⏱ Mon-Sat; 🚌 Corso Vittorio Emanuele II

You wouldn't expect there to be anywhere reasonably priced on Piazza Farnese, one of Rome's loveliest outdoor rooms, but this long-running *osteria* is the real thing, with good, honest Roman food, a warm local atmosphere and dazzlingly set exterior tables. Roasted chicken is the house speciality (*galletto* means little rooster), but the roasted lamb is just as fine.

SERGIO ALLA GROTTE
Map pp74–5   Trattoria €€

☎ 06 686 42 93; Vicolo delle Grotte 27; meals €30; ⏰ 12.30-3.30pm & 7.30pm-1am Mon-Sat; 🚌 Via Arenula

A flower's throw from the Campo, Sergio's is a textbook Roman trattoria: chequered tablecloths, bustling waiters, steaming plateloads of pasta, and not a frill in sight. A loyal following enjoys classic hearty Roman pastas – *cacio e pepe, carbonara, amatriciana* – and large steaks grilled over hot coals. In the summer there are tables outside on the cobbled, ivy-hung lane.

THIEN KIM Map pp74–5   Vietnamese €€
☎ 06 683 07 832; Via Giulia 201; meals €25; ⏰ dinner Mon-Sat; 🚌 Via Arenula

Rome's lone Vietnamese restaurant is fortunately a winner. The dimly lit interior reveals few Eastern trappings, but the food is authentically delicious, if adapted a little for Italian tastes. To start there's an excellent Green Paradise Island soup (a broth of vegetables, prawns and pork scented with ginger, lemon grass and celery); mains include spicy fried fish in *nuoc nam* (fish sauce).

FILETTI DI BACCALÀ
Map pp74–5   Trattoria €

☎ 06 686 40 18; Largo dei Librari 88; fillet €5; ⏰ 5-10.40pm Mon-Sat; 🚌 Via Arenula

On a pretty, scooter-strewn piazza, this tiny, stuck-in-time institution serves classic cod and chips, without the chips (the name means 'fillet of cod'). You can have crispy battered veggies instead, such as *puntarella* (chicory) salad or crisp-fried courgette flowers.

FORNO DI CAMPO DE' FIORI
Map pp74–5   Pizzeria €

☎ 06 688 06 662; Campo de' Fiori 22; pizza slices from €2; ⏰ 7.30am-2.30pm & 4.40-8pm Mon-Sat; 🚌 Corso Vittorio Emanuele II

Obscenely good, direct-from-the-oven *pizza al taglio* keeps this place permanently packed. The *pizza bianca* – white pizza with olive oil, rosemary and salt – is divine, the *pizza rossa* ('red' pizza, with olive oil, tomato and oregano) sublime, and the *pizza patata* (with potato and rosemary) and *pizza pommidorini* (with cherry tomatoes) are heavenly.

ANTICO FORNO ROSCIOLI
Map pp74–5   Bakery €

☎ 06 686 40 45; Via dei Chiavari 34; ⏰ 7.30am-8pm Mon-Fri, 7.30am-2.30pm Sat, closed Sat in Aug; 🚌 Via Arenula

Not the renowned delicatessen and wine bar (opposite), but the bakery around the corner, this place lives up to the culinary standards of its brother enterprise and has delicious pizza by the slice (the *pizza bianca* is legendary) as well as irresistible cakes. Perfect for putting together a picnic.

JEWISH GHETTO

PIPERNO Map pp74–5   Ristorante €€€
☎ 06 688 06 629; Via Monte de' Cenci 9; meals €55; ⏰ 12.40-2.20pm Tue-Sun, 7.40-10.20pm Tue-Sat; 🚌 Via Arenula

Veritable Roman-Jewish Piperno is formal without being stuffy, a wood-panelled restaurant of the old school, where white-clad waiters serve some of Rome's best deep-fried food, including *filetti di baccalà, carciofi alla giudia* (Jewish-style artichokes) or *fiori di zucca ripieni e fritti* (cheese-and-anchovy-stuffed courgette flowers). It might feel odd to ask the waiter for *palle del Nonno* ('grandpa's balls'), but cast aside your qualms and try the delicious ricotta and chocolate puffs. Booking is essential for Sunday.

VECCHIA ROMA Map pp74–5   Ristorante €€€
☎ 06 686 46 04; Piazza Campitelli 18; meals €50; ⏰ Thu-Tue, closed 3 weeks Aug; 🚌 Via del Teatro di Marcello

On a picturebook cobbled corner, impeccably groomed waiters sport white jackets, the antipasti buffet wows, candles light the outdoor terrace, celebrities sparkle and politicians scheme. The menu changes with the season, offering fabulous salads in summer, 101 things to do with polenta in winter and lots of top-drawer pastas and risottos year-round.

LA TAVERNA DEGLI AMICI
Map pp74–5   Trattoria €€

☎ 06 699 20 637; Piazza Margana 37; meals €45; ⏰ lunch Tue-Sun, dinner Mon-Sat; 🚌 Piazza Venezia

Favoured by politicians from the nearby Democratici di Sinistra headquarters, this sits on a quintessential ivy-draped piazza on the edge of the Jewish Ghetto. It serves consistent classics like *saltimbocca alla romana* ('leap in the mouth' veal with sage), plus delicious fish and homemade desserts. There's also an excellent wine list.

DA GIGGETTO Map pp74–5   Trattoria €€

☎ 06 686 11 05; Via del Portico d'Ottavia 21-22; meals €40; ⏱ Tue-Sun; 🚇 Piazza B Cairoli
The atmospheric ghetto, rustic interiors, white-jacketed waiters, Roman-Jewish cooking – who needs more? Celebrate all things fried by tucking into the marvellous *carciofi alla giudia* and follow on with delicious *calamari* (fried squid). In the warmer months, fight your way to an outside table under the shadow of the ruins of the Portico d'Ottavia. For budgeteers, there's Giggetto 2 (☎ 06 647 60 369; Via S Angelo in Pescheria 13-14; meals €20; ⏱ Wed-Mon), a simple café behind its parent restaurant, which serves tasty traditional dishes (including *carciofo alla Romana*), homemade desserts, a tourist menu at €14, and extremely drinkable wine at €8 per bottle.

SORA MARGHERITA Map pp74–5   Trattoria €€

☎ 06 687 42 16; Piazza delle Cinque Scole 30; meals €25; ⏱ lunch Tue-Sun & dinner Fri & Sat winter, lunch Mon-Fri & dinner Fri summer, closed Aug; 🚇 Via Arenula
No-frills Sora Margherita started as a cheap kitchen for hungry locals, but word has spread. Expect dog-eat-dog queues; cheap, hearty pasta; Roman-Jewish dishes (such as ricotta tart); and a rowdy Roman atmosphere. Service is prompt and you're expected to be likewise. It's closed weekends in summer as, according to the sign, '*tutti al mare*' (everyone's at the beach).

BOCCIONE Map pp74–5   Pasticceria €

☎ 06 687 86 37; Via del Portico d'Ottavia 1; ⏱ 8am-7.30pm Sun-Thu, 8am-3.30pm Fri; 🚇 Piazza B Cairoli
You'll spot this tiny and ancient Jewish bakery by the queue. The burnished cakes erupt fruit and sultanas, and specialities include ricotta cake with chocolate flakes and cherries, marzipan amaretto biscuits, and *mostacciolo romano* (a kind of sweet biscuit) – all served by authentically grumpy elderly ladies.

LA DOLCEROMA Map pp74–5   Bakery €

☎ 06 689 21 96; Via del Portico d'Ottavia 20; pastries €2.50-5; ⏱ 8am-8pm Tue-Sat, 10am-1.30pm Sun; 🚇 Piazza B Cairoli

Breathe in the sweet baking smells of Sweet Rome, which specialises in strudel, Sacher torte, carrot cake, pumpkin pie (October and November only), pastries, muffins and cookies. It also has splendid ice cream, and everything's made on the premises.

ISOLA TIBERINA

SORA LELLA Map pp74–5   Ristorante €€€

☎ 06 686 16 01; Via Ponte Quattro Capi 16; meals €55; ⏱ Mon-Sat; 🚌 or 🚇 Viale di Trastevere; ✖
You can't beat the romance of Sora Lella's setting, on the River Tiber's tiny island. Ring the doorbell to gain entrance to this timeless institution, named after the much-loved Roman TV star (the owner's mother), and family-run since 1940. The classic Roman menu has some twists, such as an amazing aubergine *parmigiana* with added nuts, ricotta and honey.

PIAZZA COLONNA & AROUND

OSTERIA DELL'INGEGNO

Map pp74–5   Ristorante, Vegetarian €€€
☎ 06 678 06 62; Piazza di Pietra 45; meals €45; ⏱ Mon-Sat; 🚇 Via del Corso; ✖ Ⓥ
A casual yet chic restaurant, the 'Osteria of Intelligence' is a favourite of Italian politicians and their glamorous entourages. Eat inside at brightly painted tables, or outside in the charming square overlooking the Tempio d'Adriana. Food has a suitably intelligent twist, with dishes such as *garganelli con fave piselli e carciofi* (homemade pasta with broad beans, peas and artichokes).

MATRICIANELLA Map pp74–5   Trattoria €€

☎ 06 692 02 132; Via del Leone 2/4; meals €40; ⏱ Mon-Sat; 🚇 Via del Corso
Tucked near Piazza di San Lorenzo in Lucina, this popular, chic trattoria, with gingham tablecloths and chintzy murals, also has some streetside seating on the quiet cobbled lane. The cooking is simple, delicious and largely Roman-Jewish. Romans go crazy for the delectable fried antipasti, the artichoke *alla giudia* (fried, Jewish style), the meatballs and the Jewish-style stew. Booking is essential.

GINO Map pp74–5   Trattoria €€

☎ 06 687 34 34; Vicolo Rosini 4; meals €30; ⏱ Mon-Sat; 🚇 Via del Corso

top picks

PIZZA

- Pizzeria da Baffetto (p198)
- Dar Poeta (p211)
- Pizzarium (p213)
- Bir & Fud (p210)
- Forno di Campo de' Fiori (p199)

Oh, Gino! Surely the perfect trattoria: quaint, busy and buzzing, dishing out well-executed staples such as *rigotoni alla gricia* and meatballs under gaudily painted vines. It's hidden away down a narrow lane close to parliament, and perennially packed by gossiping politicians. No credit cards.

PIZZERIA AL LEONCINO
Map pp74–5   Pizzeria €

☎ 06 686 77 57; Via del Leoncino 28; pizza €6-8.50; ⏰ Thu-Tue, dinner only Sat & Sun; 🚌 Via del Corso
It can be difficult to source a cheap meal in this upmarket area, which is why Leoncino gets a round of applause. A boisterous neighbourhood pizzeria with a wood-fired oven, it has two small rooms, cheerful décor and gruff but efficient waiters who will serve you an excellent Roman-style pizza and ice-cold beer faster than you can say 'delizioso'.

TRIDENTE

Rome's designer shopping district may be fashionista heaven, but it retains a neighbourhood feel, albeit a wealthy one. Lots of classy cateries are sandwiched between the boutiques.

PIAZZA DEL POPOLO & AROUND

DAL BOLOGNESE Map pp96–7   Ristorante €€€
☎ 06 361 14 26; Piazza del Popolo 1; meals €55; ⏰ Tue-Sun; Ⓜ Flaminio; 🔀
The moneyed and models mingle at this historically chic restaurant. Dine inside surrounded by wood panelling and exotic flowers, or outside, people-watching with views over Piazza del Popolo. As the name suggests, Emilia-Romagna dishes are the name of the game; everything is good, but try the tagliatelle with truffles, tuna tartare, or the damn fine fillet steak.

MARGUTTA RISTORANTE
Map pp96–7   Vegetarian €€

☎ 06 678 60 33; Via Margutta 118; meals €50; Ⓜ Spagna or Flaminio; 🔀 Ⓥ
Vegetarian restaurants in Rome are rarer than parking spaces, and this airy art gallery/restaurant is an unusually chic way to eat your greens. Most dishes are excellent, with offerings such as artichoke hearts with potato cubes and smoked provolone cheese. There's an impressive wine list and staff are friendly and bilingual. Best value is the Saturday/Sunday buffet brunch (€15/25). It also offers a four-course vegan menu (€30).

BABETTE Map pp96–7   Vegetarian €€
☎ 06 321 15 59; Via Margutta 1; meals €45; ⏰ closed Aug; Ⓜ Spagna or Flaminio; 🔀 Ⓥ
You're in for a feast at Babette's, in a chic yet unpretentious warehouse-like interior of exposed brick walls and vintage painted signs. Food is delicious, with a sophisticated, creative twist (think *tortiglioni* with courgette and pistachio pesto), and the wine list is short but super. There's a daily buffet (€10 Tuesday to Friday, €25 weekends).

LA BUCA DI RIPETTA
Map pp96–7   Ristorante €€

☎ 06 321 93 91; Via di Ripetta 36; meals €40; Ⓜ Flaminio; 🔀
Popular with actors and directors from the district, who know a good thing when they see it, this value-for-money foodie destination offers robust Roman cuisine. Try the *zuppa rustica con crostini do pane aromatizzati* (country-style soup with rosemary-scented bread) or the *matolino do latte al forno alle erbe con patate* (baked suckling pork with potatoes) and you'll be fuelled either for more sightseeing or for a lie down.

EDY Map pp96–7   Trattoria €€
☎ 06 360 01 738; Vicolo del Babuino 4; meals €40; ⏰ Mon-Sat; Ⓜ Spagna; 🔀
Edy's high-ceilinged, intimate interior is peppered with paintings, and it feels like the classy neighbourhood restaurant it is. Despite the tourist-central location, it caters to mainly Italian clientele, and food, such as *linguine al broccoletti,* is delicious. There are a few outside tables on the cobbled street.

OSTERIA DELLA FREZZA

Map pp96–7   Osteria €€

☎ 06 322 62 73; Via della Frezza; meals €40;
🚌 Piazza Augusto Imperatore

Part of the 'Gusto (below) complex, della Frezza is trendy yet simple, with white-tiled, photo-covered walls and a monochrome look. It's part *osteria*, part *enoteca* and part tapas bar. As well as selections of meat or cheese, you can order *cichetti* (mini-helpings) of pasta, meat and fish dishes on the menu, such as *tortelli di baccalà* (cod in pasta wraps) and fried ricotta.

BUCCONE Map pp96–7   Wine Bar €€

☎ 06 36 12 154; Via di Ripetta 19; meals €25;
Ⓜ Flaminio

Step inside, under the faded gilt and mirrored sign, and feel like you've gone back in time. Once a coach house, then a tavern, in the 1960s this building became Buccone, furnished with 19th-century antiques and lined with around 1000 Italian wines as well as a good selection of international tipples. It's perfect for a light meal, with salads, cured meats, cheeses, *torta* (cakes) etc.

'GUSTO Map pp96–7   Pizzeria, Ristorante €

☎ 06 322 62 73; Piazza Augusto Imperatore 9;
pizza €7-11; 🚌 Piazza Augusto Imperatore

If Terence Conran were Italian, he might have dreamed up 'Gusto, once a mould-breaking warehouse-style gastronomic complex. It's still buzzing after all these years, and is a great place to sit on the terrace and eye up the new Richard Meier-designed Ara Pacis museum (p95). Go for the Neapolitan-style pizzas rather than the restaurant fare, which receives mixed reports. There's a recommended brunch (weekends) and lunchtime buffet. Around the corner, No 28 (dishes €14-26; ✹ 8am-2am) is a café-cocktail bar bearing the same hallmarks of industrial chic and interesting cuisine.

PIAZZA DI SPAGNA & AROUND

OSTERIA MARGUTTA Map pp96–7 Trattoria €€€

☎ 06 323 10 25; Via Margutta 82; meals €60;
Ⓜ Spagna; ✹

The epitome of a picturesque trattoria, theatrical Osteria Margutta is colourful inside and out: inside combines blue glass,

rich reds and fringed lampshades, while outside flowers and ivy cover the quaint entrance (snap up a terrace table in summer). Plaques on the chairs testify to the famous thespian bums they have supported. The menu combines classic and regional dishes, with fish served fresh on Tuesday, Friday and Saturday; desserts are homemade, and there's a top wine list.

IL PALAZZETTO Map pp96–7   Ristorante €€€

☎ 06 699 341 000; Via del Bottino 8; meals €55;
✹ noon-3.30pm & 7.30-10.30pm, bar open from 4pm, closed Aug; Ⓜ Spagna; Ⓥ

Despite its sumptuous deep-red interior, this restaurant's spangling jewel is the sun-trap shaded terrace hidden at the top of the Spanish Steps. It's perfect for a glass of *prosecco* (sparkling wine) and a salad or pasta dish on a sunny day. Dinner menus are set to impress (tasting menu €55, vegetarian menu €50), and the *palazzo* also houses the wine academy (p290). It's also open as a wine bar from 4pm.

FIASCHETTERIA BELTRAMME

Map pp96–7   Trattoria €€

Via della Croce 39; meals €45; Ⓜ Spagna

With a tiny dark interior and high ceilings, Fiaschetteria (meaning 'wine-sellers') is a discreet, intimate, stuck-in-time place with a short menu and no telephone. Expect fashionistas with appetites digging into traditional Roman dishes (*pasta e ceci* and so on).

OTELLO ALLA CONCORDIA

Map pp96–7   Trattoria €€

☎ 06 679 11 78; Via della Croce 81; meals €35;
✹ Mon-Sat; Ⓜ Spagna; ✹

A perennial favourite, Otello is a haven near the Spanish Steps. Outside dining is in the vine-covered courtyard of an 18th-century *palazzo*, where, if you're lucky, you can dine in the shadow of the wisteria-covered pergola. Food is tasty and fairly priced, with an ample selection of antipasti, pastas and *secondi*.

PALATIUM Map pp96–7   Wine Bar €€

☎ 06 692 02 132; Via Frattina 94; meals €35;
✹ Mon-Sat, closed Aug; 🚌 Via del Corso; ✹

Conceived as a showcase of Lazio's bounty, this sleek *enoteca* close to the Spanish Steps serves excellent local specialities, such as *porchetta* (pork roasted with herbs), artisan cheese, and delicious salami, as well as an impressive array of Lazio wines (try lesser-known drops such as Aleatico).

ANTICA ENOTECA Map pp96–7 Wine Bar €€
☎ 06 679 08 96; Via della Croce 76b; meals €25; 11am-1am; M Spagna;

Local shoppers and shopkeepers pack this much-loved wine bar, full of frescoes and 19th-century fittings. Plonk yourself at the long wood-and-brass counter and take your pick from the wine list and antipasti, or plunge into the back room for decent pasta or pizza.

GINA Map pp96–7 Café €
☎ 06 678 02 51; Via San Sebastianello 7a; snacks €8-12; 11am-8pm; M Spagna;

Around the corner from the Spanish Steps, this is an ideal place to drop once you've shopped. Comfy white seats are strewn with powder-blue cushions, and it gets packed by a Prada-clad crowd, gossiping and flirting over sophisticated salads and perfect *panini*.

TREVI, QUIRINALE & VIA VENETO

You have to take care choosing a restaurant around the Trevi Fountain, as there are a lot of unexciting just-for-tourist restaurants. But some gems sparkle among the stones – follow this guide and you can't go wrong. There are some splendid restaurants around the presidential palace and parliament – Italian politicians are a discerning bunch when it comes to dining out.

TREVI FOUNTAIN TO THE QUIRINALE

AL PRESIDENTE
Map p100 Seafood €€€
☎ 06 679 73 42; Via Arcione 95; meals €50; Tue-Sun; Via del Tritone

Al Presidente is a discreet, greenery-shrouded place that whispers class, under the walls of the presidential palace. Its sophisticated air is matched by the seafood-centred menu. Innovative dishes include *baccalà* whisked into polenta and grilled, and *trippa di coda di rospo* (tripe of angler-

fish tail), but it also does a lipsmacking *pasta all'amatriciana*.

LE TAMERICI Map p100 Seafood €€
☎ 06 692 00 700; Vicolo Scavolino 79; meals €40; Mon-Sat; Via del Tritone

Tucked-away Le Tamerici impresses with its wine list and range of digestifs, as well as with its classy food, including light-as-air homemade pasta. A great place to settle for an epicurean lunch, in two intimate rooms with bleached-wood beamed ceilings.

NANÀ VINI E CUCINA Map p100 Trattoria €€
☎ 06 691 90 750; Via della Panettaria 37; meals €40; Tue-Sun; Via del Tritone

An appealing and simple trattoria, specialising in Neopolitan flavours. Eat in the high-ceilinged interior, under huge brass pipes, overlooking the open kitchen, or outside on the *piazzetta*. Try *la carne tenenera scaloppina Nanà*, cooked simply in white wine, and other southern dishes.

VINERIA CHIANTI Map p100 Wine Bar €€
☎ 06 678 75 50; Via del Lavatore 81-82; meals €35; Via del Tritone

This pretty ivy-clad wine bar is bottle-lined inside, with watch-the-world-go-by streetside seating in summer. Cuisine is Tuscan, so the beef is particularly good, but it also serves up imaginative salads, and pizza in the evenings.

ANTICO FORNO Map p100 Panini €
☎ 06 679 28 66; Via delle Muratte 8; panini €2.50; 7am-9pm; Via del Tritone

A mini-supermarket opposite the Trevi Fountain, this busy place has a well-stocked deli counter where you can choose a filling for your freshly baked *panino* or *pizza bianca*, plus an impressive selection of focaccia and pizza.

DA MICHELE Map p100 Pizzeria €
☎ 349 252 53 47; Via dell'Umiltà 31; pizza slices from €2; 8am-5pm Mon-Fri, to 8pm summer; Via del Corso

A handy address in Spagna district: buy your fresh, light and crispy *pizza al taglio*, and you'll not only have a delicious lunch on the move, but also save your cents so you can – perhaps – afford that designer outfit.

PIAZZA BARBERINI & VIA VENETO

COLLINE EMILIANE Map p100   Ristorante €€

☎ 06 481 75 38; Via degli Avignonesi 22; meals €45; ☺ Tue-Sat, Sun lunch, closed Aug; Ⓜ Barberini; 🐾

This welcoming, tucked-away restaurant just off Piazza Barberini flies the flag for Emilia-Romagna, the well-fed Italian province that has gifted the world Parmesan, balsamic vinegar, bolognese sauce and Parma ham. On offer here are delicious meats, homemade pasta, rich *ragùs,* and desserts worthy of a moment's silence.

SANTOPADRE Map p100   Ristorante €€

☎ 06 474 54 05; Via Collina 18; meals €30; ☺ from 8pm; Ⓜ Termini

Plastered with photos of horses and jockeys, this little neighbourhood restaurant is a local favourite that's been cooking up Roman faves such as *pasta alla gricia, involtini* and *trippa alla Romana* since 1946. The antipasti is delicious – think delicate marinated vegetables and melt-in-the-mouth meatballs.

MONTI, ESQUILINO & SAN LORENZO

Monti, north of the Colosseum, has some wonderful choices. An ancient slum, it's one of Rome's most interesting up-and-coming districts, with intimate bars, *enoteche,* restaurants and boutiques.

Around Stazione Termini it's hard to find a good restaurant as most cater only to tourists, but there are a few, and this area contains Rome's best ethnic eats.

MONTI

LA CARBONARA Map pp106–7   Ristorante €€

☎ 06 482 51 76; Via Panisperna 214; meals €25; ☺ Mon-Sat; Ⓜ Cavour

Favoured by the infamous Ragazzi di Panisperna, a group of young physicists, including Enrico Fermi, who constructed the first nuclear reactor and atomic bomb. He was probably inspired by La Carbonara's delicious fried potato. Another speciality is the eponymous carbonara, though the restaurant is so-named because the first

owner married a coal seller. The interior is covered in graffiti – tradition dictates that diners should leave their mark in a message on the wall.

CIURI CIURI Map pp106–7   Pasticceria €

☎ 06 454 44 548; Via Leonina 18; snacks around €2; ☺ 10am-midnight; Ⓜ Cavour

A Sicilian ice-cream and pastry shop where you can pop by for delectable homemade sweets such as *cannoli* (a type of pastry), cassata and *pasticini di mandorla* (almond pastries), all available in moreish bite-sized versions, and created using the freshest of ingredients. There are also rib-sticking *arancini* (fried rice balls).

IL GURU Map pp106–7   Indian €

☎ 06 474 41 10; Via Cimarra 4-6; dishes €4-9; ☺ 7.30pm-midnight; Ⓜ Cavour

Il Guru is lined with embroidered drapes and elaborate statuettes, and has a few outdoor tables on the cobbled street. The tandooris are prepared in a proper tandoori oven, the curries and vegetables are tasty and the setting is suggestive, albeit of Rome rather than Rajasthan.

ESQUILINO

AGATA E ROMEO Map pp106–7   Ristorante €€€

☎ 06 446 61 15; Via Carlo Alberto 45; meals €100, tasting menu €110-130, paired with wine €170; ☺ Mon-Fri; Ⓜ Vittorio Emanuele

A match made in heaven: Agata's food and Romeo's wine cellar (see boxed text, p206). This pioneering restaurant nowadays has more rivals, but still wields culinary clout. Agata specialises in innovating around traditional dishes, and presentation is sumptuous. Frequent crowd-pleasers include a delicate take on *coda alla vaccinara* (oxtail) and *filetto di tonno con semi di sesamo* (tuna fillet with sesame seeds). Her *millefoglie* (*millefueilles;* literally 'thousand leaves', small iced cakes made of puff pastry, filled with jam and cream) are legendary.

TRATTORIA MONTI Map pp106–7   Trattoria €€

☎ 06 446 65 73; Via di San Vito 13a; meals €35; ☺ lunch & dinner Tue-Sat, lunch Sun; Ⓜ Vittorio Emanuele; 🐾

The Camerucci family runs this elegant, brick-arched place, offering top-notch traditional cooking from the Marches region, with an unusual menu that includes lots of daily specials. Expect wonderful fried things, delicate pastas and ingredients such as *pecorino di fossa* (sheeps' cheese aged in caves), goose, swordfish, sultanas, mushrooms and truffles. Try the speciality egg-yolk *tortelli* pasta. Desserts are delectable, including apple pie with zabaglione that's worthy of a postcard home. Word has spread, so book ahead.

AFRICA Map pp106–7 African €€
☎ 06 494 10 77; Via Gaeta 26-28; meals €25; ☺ Tue-Sun; Ⓜ Castro Pretorio
Spurn cutlery and dig in with your hands at this ethnic veteran, serving up authentic Ethiopian and Eritrean grub in technicolour *mesobs* (traditional Ethiopian woven baskets) – you can sample spicy stews and delicious *sambusas* (fried savoury pastries).

TRIMANI Map pp106–7 Wine Bar €
☎ 06 446 96 30; Via Cernaia 37b; ☺ 11.30am-3pm & 5.30pm-12.30am Mon-Sat; Ⓜ Termini; ⚹
Part of the Trimani family's wine empire (their shop just round the corner stocks about 4000 international labels), this is a great, unpretentious place, with knowledgeable, multilingual staff. It's Rome's biggest wine bar and has a vast selection of Italian regional wines as well as an ever-changing food menu, with dishes ranging from potato and sausage pie to oysters. Book ahead to take one of the regular wine-tasting courses.

LA GALLINA BIANCA Map pp106–7 Pizzeria €
☎ 06 474 37 77; Via A Rosmini 9; pizzas €7-9.50; ☺ noon-3pm & 6pm-midnight; Ⓜ Termini; ⚹
The 'White Hen' is a friendly, handy pizzeria amid the minefield of tourist trash around Termini, serving thick-crust Neapolitan pizzas made from slow-risen dough. It's large and airy, decorated in cool pale blue and old wood, with shaded outside seating on a not-too-busy street.

INDIAN FAST FOOD Map pp106–7 Indian €
☎ 06 446 07 92; Via Mamiani 11; curries €5.50-7.50; ☺ 11am-4pm & 5-11.30pm; Ⓜ Vittorio Emanuele
Formica tables, Hindi hits, neon lights, chapatti and naan, lipsmacking samosas and bhajis, and a simple selection of main curry dishes: you could almost imagine yourself in India in this authentic joint.

PANELLA L'ARTE DEL PANE
Map pp106–7 Pizzeria €
☎ 06 487 24 35; Via Merulana 54; pizza slices €2.50-5; ☺ 8am-2pm & 5-8pm Mon-Wed & Fri, 8am-2pm Thu, 8am-2pm & 4.30-8pm Sat, 8.30am-2pm Sun; Ⓜ Vittorio Emanuele
With a sumptuous array of *pizza al taglio*, *supplì*, focaccia and fried croquettes, this is a great lunch stop, where you can sip a glass of chilled *prosecco* while eying up gastronomic souvenirs from the deli.

PIAZZA DELLA REPUBLICA & AROUND

OPEN COLONNA Map pp106–7 Pizzeria €€
☎ 06 478 22 641; Via Milano 9a; meals €55; ☺ noon-midnight; 🚌 Via Nazionale; ⚹
Spectacularly set at the back of Palazzo delle Esposizioni, superchef Antonello Colonna's restaurant is tucked on a mezzanine floor under an extraordinary glass roof (wow factor before you've had a bite). The cuisine is new Roman: innovative takes on traditional dishes, cooked with wit and flair. The best thing of all? There's a more basic but still impressive fixed two-course lunch for €15, and Saturday and Sunday brunch at €28, served in the larger downstairs room, so you can live the life without splashing the cash.

DOOZO Map pp106–7 Japanese €
☎ 06 481 56 55; Via Palermo 51; sushi €6-10; ☺ dinner Tue-Sun, lunch Tue-Sat; 🚌 Via Nazionale; ⚹
If you're in the mood for something different, Doozo (meaning 'welcome') is a completely Zen restaurant bookshop gallery that offers tofu, sushi, *soba* (buckwheat noodle) soup and other Japanese delicacies, plus beer and green tea. On the street parallel to noisy Via Nazionale, it's a little oasis, particularly the small garden.

DA RICCI Map pp106–7 Pizzeria €
☎ 06 488 11 07; Via Genova 32; pizzas €8; ☺ 7pm-midnight Tue-Sun; 🚌 Via Nazionale; ⚹
In a tranquil, cobbled cul-de-sac a step away from smoggy Via Nazionale, Rome's oldest pizzeria started life as an *enoteca* in 1905, and its wood-panelled interior feels like it hasn't changed much since. The sign says Est! Est!! Est!!! – Da Ricci's other name (after its white wine from the north

of Lazio). Pizzas are thick-based Neapolitan style (though you can get thin-based if you like), and work best with lots of toppings.

SAN LORENZO & BEYOND

In San Lorenzo, the vibrant boho student area east of Termini, you'll find an enticing mix of extraordinarily good restaurants and dirt-cheap pizzerias.

TRAM TRAM Map pp106–7   Trattoria €€
☎ 06 49 04 16; Via dei Reti 44; meals €40; ☷ Tue-Sun; ⊜ Via Tiburtina; ☒
This trendy yet old-fashioned, lace-curtained trattoria takes its name from the

---

FROM TRATTORIA TO MICHELIN STAR

Award-winning chef-sommelier Mariantonietta Caraccio, daughter of chef Agata Parisella and sommelier Romeo Caraccio, tells us about the development of Roman cuisine and the story of the family restaurant Agata e Romeo (p204), one of Rome's pioneering gourmet kitchens.

I understand the restaurant started in 1890; what's its history? My grandmother was in the kitchen and my grandfather in the dining room. It was a simple trattoria. My mother used to help her mother in the kitchen, and she says that she started to do the *bigné* (cream-filled pastries) when she was 12. They were five brothers and sisters, but my mother was the only one helping – because she loves to cook. Little by little my parents took over, and in time, they made some changes. Before there were no tablecloths. Downstairs was just a storage room. My mother went to school, and my father qualified as a sommelier (previously he was studying medicine), and after he finished they made the wine cellar. Then, in 1997 we took the Michelin Star.

You must remember the restaurant as part of your childhood. My mum tells me I grew up in the kitchen. I don't know when I learned to cook. For me it's not something that I learned, it's natural. I specialise in desserts, but I also studied wine.

Can you tell us something about Lazio wine? Lazio is a small region for the production of wine. We have good wine but nothing so important. In the last 15 years, there are a lot of producers doing good stuff, but still there is nothing crazy.

If you don't know anything of the Lazio wine, you could try Frascati. Before, this was the wine for drunk people – it was cheap and no good at all, but it has become much better. It's a nice wine made from a mix of white grapes. Then, there is Falesco, an incredible wine, one of the few known outside Lazio – you won't find other Lazio wines in other regions, but you will find this one.

How would you describe Roman cuisine? It's a strong taste, because we eat a lot of the interior parts, especially lamb. So, if someone doesn't like this idea, there may be a psychological barrier to trying it. But then when you try, it's really good.

Traditional Roman cuisine is heavy; many people don't want to eat it like that anymore. What my mother does is tries to cook it in a gentle way, without too much seasoning. For example, in the traditional Roman cuisine, if you eat oxtail, the oxtail is big and on the bone. So my mum cooks the oxtail in the same way, but then she debones it, so it's much more delicate and there is no need to dirty your hands.

How has the cuisine scene changed in Rome? Well, when we started this restaurant, the cuisine in Rome was terrible. People used to say, if they wanted to eat good cuisine they'd go to the north of Italy. But lately it has changed a lot. There are a lot of new restaurants, with a younger crowd, where they serve a lot of wine by the glass. Before, you couldn't even think about wine by the glass. Previously, I couldn't speak to anybody about wine, because we couldn't speak the same language. Now I have plenty of friends who are doing the sommelier course or going for tastings. In Rome we have one of the most important branches of the Associazione Italiana Sommelier (www.sommelier.it), which is the best sommelier school.

Haven't Italians long been interested in food? In food yes, but not always in good food. The typical Roman customer is the one who wants to go out and eat a lot, and not pay too much money. They go out and eat lots of fish, and a great big heap of pasta. But lately this has changed. Romans are going out and expecting less food on their plate, and of better quality.

Where can you eat the real traditional Roman cuisine? In Rome we have a strong Roman-Jewish culture. Mostly Roman dishes are of Jewish origin, like the *carciofi alla giudia* (deep-fried artichoke 'Jewish-style') and so, to eat the true Roman cuisine, go to the ghetto.

trams that rattle past outside and offers traditional dishes, with a focus on rustic southern specialities such as *orecchiette alla Norma* (ear-shaped pasta with fried aubergine, tomato, basil and ricotta) and divine Pugliese comfort food *riso cozze patate* (rice, mussels and potatoes).

SAID Map pp106–7 Ristorante €€
☎ 06 446 92 04; Via Tiburtina 135; meals €35; 🚊 Via Tiburtina; 🔀
To experience San Lorenzo at its chicest, head to Said, housed in a 1920s chocolate factory. It includes a glorious chocolate shop, selling delights like Japanese pink-tea pralines, and a stylish restaurant-bar specialising in chocolate-tinged dishes, like *sformatino B-Said di cavolfiore e cioccolato* (cauliflower mousse with chocolate) – great talking points, if not always entirely successful. There's *aperitivo* from 7pm to 9pm.

SUSHIKO Map pp106–7 Japanese €€
☎ 06 443 40 948; Via degli Irpini 8; sushi menus from €35; 🕒 1-2.30pm Tue-Sat & 8pm-midnight Mon-Sat 🚊 Via Tiburtina; 🔀
This nondescript San Lorenzo lane is an unlikely place to find Rome's best sushi, but here it is, with the freshest fish served up as sushi and sashimi, plus rolls, tempura and teppanyaki. It's tiny, with only five tables and 10 places at the bar, so book ahead. It makes financial sense to go set menu rather than à la carte. A glass of sake costs €3.50.

POMMIDORO Map pp106–7 Trattoria €€
☎ 06 445 26 92; Piazza dei Sanniti 44; meals €35; 🕒 Mon-Sat, closed Aug; 🚊 Via Tiburtina; 🔀
Throughout San Lorenzo's metamorphosis from down-at-heel working-class district to down-at-heel bohemian enclave, Pommidoro has remained the same. A much-loved local institution, it's a century-old trattoria, with high star-vaulted ceilings, a huge fireplace and outdoor conservatory seating. It was a favourite of controversial film director Pier Paolo Pasolini, and contemporary celebs stop by – from Nicole Kidman to Fabio Cappello – but it's an unpretentious place with superb-quality traditional food, specialising in magnificent grilled meats.

FORMULA UNO Map pp106–7 Pizzeria €
☎ 06 445 38 66; Via degli Equi 13; pizzas from €5; 🕒 6.30pm-1.30am Mon-Sat; 🚊 Via Tiburtina
As adrenaline-fueled as its name: at this basic, historic San Lorenzo pizzeria, under whirring fans, waiters zoom around delivering tomato-loaded bruschetta, fried courgette flowers, *suppli al telefono* and bubbling thin-crust pizza, to eternal crowds of feasting students.

BOCCA DI DAMA Map pp106–7 Bakery €
☎ 06 443 41 154; Via dei Marsi 2-6; 🕒 11am-8pm Tue-Sat, 11am-1.30pm & 4-8pm Sun; 🚊 Via Tiburtina; 🔀
The 'Mouth of a Woman' (named after a traditional almond cake) is a lovely little patisserie/café run by creative types – think cakes as art. Huge windows overlook the street, and you can tuck into divine little cupcakes topped with blueberries or delicate little sugar carrots, or exquisite bonbons with names like *bacio dell'architetto* (the architect's kiss).

CELIO HILL & LATERAN
There are a few splendid choices in the grid of streets on Celio Hill, conveniently close to the Colosseum and San Giovanni.

TAVERNA DEI QUARANTA
Map p115 Trattoria €€
☎ 06 700 05 50; Via Claudia 24; meals €30; 🕒 Mon-Sat; Ⓜ Colosseo
Off the main tourist track but near the Colosseum, this airy trattoria is run by gentle staff and offers simple Roman cooking, with delicious daily pasta specials, tasty bruschetta and *arostocini* (beef kebabs). There's some outside seating on the leafy yet busy street.

IL BOCCONCINO Map p115 Osteria €€
☎ 06 770 79 175; Via Ostilia 23; meals €30; 🕒 Thu-Tue, closed Aug; Ⓜ Colosseo
Visited the Colosseum and *need* lunch in a local rustic trattoria? Try 'the little mouthful'. Its gingham tablecloths, outdoor seating and cosy interior look like all the others in this area, but it serves up excellent traditional pasta and other dishes, such as *insalata di finocchi arance e olive* (fennel, orange and olive salad) and *saltimbocca alla romana* ('leap in the mouth' veal with sage).

DETOUR: PIGNETO

A short trip east of San Lorenzo, Pigneto has undergone a rapid recent metamorphosis, from working-class ghetto to hip boho hangout, with a main drag dotted by bars and restaurants. The low-rise houses, small-town feel and lavish graffiti all add to the atmosphere, and there are some great places to eat.

- **Primo** (Map pp106–7; ☎ 06 701 38 27; Via del Pigneto 46; meals €35; ☼ Tue-Sun; ☒ ☒ Circonvallazione Casilina; ☒) Flagship of the new scene in Pigneto, Primo is the chicest restaurant in the 'hood. The kitchen mixes creative and classics, the buzz is palpable, and the setting is shabby chic, with pale-grey walls, hexagonal tiled floors and lights dangling on long wires.
- **Antichi Sapori** (Map pp106–7; ☎ 06 703 00 298; Via Macerata 87; meals €25; ☼ Tue-Sun; ☒ ☒ Via Prenestina; ☒) As traditional as they come, this is a little arched restaurant that gets packed by Pigneto-ites after no-nonsense Roman cuisine. Specialities include *carbonara*, *amatriciana* and *cacio e pepe*, and heavier *cacciatora* (hunter-style) dishes in winter, and there are some pavement tables.
- **Osteria Qui Se Magna!** (off Map pp106–7; ☎ 06 27 48 03; Via del Pigneto; meals €25; ☼ Mon-Sat; ☒ Via Casilina) This neighbourhood secret is a buzzing, gay-friendly *osteria*, serving cheap, scrumptious platefuls of *pasta all'amatriciana* and *puntarealla*, to loud, loving-it locals. Book at weekends.

AVENTINO & TESTACCIO

Testaccio is a traditionally working-class enclave, once famous for its abattoir. Thus most of its restaurants specialise in the *quinto quarto* (fifth quarter, or the insides of the animal), though they are also good for other dishes if you think offal is awful. Today Testaccio is famous for its nightclubs and bars – for more on these see p226.

CHECCHINO DAL 1887
Map p120   Ristorante €€
☎ 06 574 63 18; Via di Monte Testaccio 30; meals €45; ☼ Tue-Sat, closed Aug; ☒ or ☒ Via Marmorata; ☒
A pig's whisker from the city's former slaughterhouse, Checchino is a Roman institution, one of the grander restaurants specialising in offal, from calf heads to pig trotters. Run by the fifth generation of the Mariani family, it has risen from humble roots to become one of the city's most vaunted eateries, attracting a well-to-do clientele of local regulars and curious foreigners. For those who can't stomach the Roman soul food there's more standard seasonal fare.

DA FELICE Map p120   Trattoria €€
☎ 06 574 68 00; Via Mastro Giorgio 29; meals €30; ☼ Tue-Sun; ☒ or ☒ Via Marmorata; ☒
Cantankerous former owner Felice used to vet every client on sight, but nowadays you can book ahead without worrying about whether your face will fit at this Testaccio institution. A makeover has seen

it turn all post-industrial chic, but the menu, recited at your table, remains resolutely Roman. Try the glorious *tonnarelli cacio e pepe*, mixed in front of you, and the steaks. For those who love offal, there's also some buttery Roman soul food, and the tiramisu gets top marks.

TRATTORIA DA BUCATINO
Map p120   Trattoria €€
☎ 06 574 68 86; Via Luca della Robbia 84; meals €25; ☼ Tue-Sun; ☒ or ☒ Via Marmorata
This intimate, neighbourhood place is hugely popular. Ask for a table upstairs (with wood panels, chianti bottles and a mounted boar's head) or outside, as downstairs has less atmosphere. The *bucatini all'amatriciana* is a must, the meat-filled cannelloni is another winner, and meaty *secondi* are also excellent, but do try to save room for a homecooked dessert.

PIZZERIA REMO Map p120   Pizzeria €
☎ 06 574 62 70; Piazza Santa Maria Liberatrice 44; pizzas €6; ☼ dinner Mon-Sat; ☒ or ☒ Via Marmorata
Not a place for a romantic tête-à-tête, Pizzeria Remo is one of the city's most popular pizzerias, busy with noisy hordes of young Romans. The mixed fried appetisers are scrumptious, and the pizzas are thin Roman classics, with toppings loading the crisp, charred base. Place your order by ticking your choices on a sheet of paper slapped down by an overstretched waiter. Expect to queue.

VOLPETTI PIÙ Map p120 — Tavola Calda €

☎ 06 574 43 06; Via A Volta 8; ☺ Mon-Sat; ☐ or
☐ Via Marmorata

One of the few places in town where you can sit down and eat well for less than €15, Volpetti Più is a sumptuous *tavola calda,* offering an opulent choice of pizza, pasta, soup, meat, vegetables and fried nibbles. It adjoins Volpetti's to-die-for deli.

SOUTHERN ROME

The increasingly fashionable southern neighbourhoods of Ostiense and Garbatella have some good restaurants, and you can also eat well in a rural setting close to Via Appia Antica.

VIA APPIA ANTICA & THE CATACOMBS

RISTORANTE CECILIA METELLA
Map pp124–5 — Ristorante €€

☎ 06 511 02 13; Via Appia Antica 125; meals €35;
☺ Tue-Sun; ☐ Via Appia Antica; ☒

Near the catacombs of San Callisto, the outside seating here is great, set on a low hill under a vine canopy and with glimpses of the jewel-green countryside. Inside resembles a wedding-reception room, but it's attractive enough, and the food is reasonable too – the grilled meats are recommended.

TRATTORIA PRISCILLA
Map pp124–5 — Trattoria €€

☎ 06 513 63 79; Via Appia Antica 68; meals €25;
☺ Mon-Sat; ☐ Via Appia Antica; ☒

Set in a 16th-century former stable, this intimate family-run trattoria has been feeding hungry travellers along the Appian Way for over 100 years, serving up traditional *cucina Romana,* so think *carbonara, amatriciana* and *cacio e pepe.*

OSTIENSE, SAN PAOLO & GARBATELLA

DA ENZO Map pp124–5 — Trattoria €€

☎ 06 574 13 64; Via Ostiense 36; meals €25;
☺ Mon-Sat; Ⓜ Piramide

With just a few tables, this is a classic Roman family-run trattoria that's been here for around 50 years. The chef used to cook at the parliament, and now feeds the

workers from the nearby market. The fresh pasta is good, the sausage super, and the tiramisu feathery light.

HOSTARIA ZAMPAGNA
Map pp124–5 — Trattoria €€

☎ 06 574 23 06; Via Ostiense 179; meals €25;
☺ Mon-Sat; ☐ Via Ostiense

The trendification of Via Ostiense – with ever-growing numbers of bars and clubs in its side streets – has thankfully bypassed this humble trattoria. As for the past 80 years, you sit down to good hearty food prepared according to the city's weekly calendar. It's all splendid: try *spaghetti alla carbonara, alla gricia* or *all'amatriciana,* then tuck into tripe, beef or *involtini.*

TRASTEVERE & GIANICOLO

Traditionally working-class and poor, now chic and pricey, picturesque Trastevere has a huge number of restaurants, trattorias, cafés and pizzerias. The better places dot the maze of side streets, and it pays to be selective, as many of the restaurants are bog-standard tourist traps. But it's not just tourists here – Romans like to eat in Trastevere too. Find the right spot and you'll have a meal to remember.

EAST OF VIALE DI TRASTEVERE

LA GENSOLA Map pp132–3 — Ristorante €€

☎ 06 581 63 12; Piazza della Gensola 15; meals €45; ☺ closed Sun Jul & Aug; ☐ or ☐ Viale di Trastevere; ☒

Tucked away close to Isola Tiberina, this tranquil, classy, yet unpretentious trattoria thrills foodies with food that has a Sicilian slant and emphasis on seafood, including an excellent tuna tartare, linguine with fresh anchovies and divine *zuccherini* (tiny fish) with fresh mint. Waiters are knowledgeable and quirky, and divine liqueurs mean you finish on a high.

LE MANI IN PASTA Map pp132–3 — Ristorante €€

☎ 06 581 60 17; Via dei Genovesi 37; meals €40;
☺ lunch daily, dinner Tue-Sun; ☐ or ☐ Viale di Trastevere; ☒

Popular and lively, this rustic place has an open kitchen that serves up delicious fresh pasta dishes such as *fettucine con ricotta e pancetta.* The grilled meats are great too.

DA ENZO Map pp132–3 · Trattoria €€

☎ 06 581 83 55; Via dei Vascellari 29; meals €30;
Mon-Sat; Piazza Sonnino
This authentic, snug dining room with rough yellow walls and lots of character serves up great Roman meals with whatever is in season. You can start with bruschetta with *burrata,* and go on to *rigatoni cacio e pepe* followed by *abbacchio al forno* (roasted lamb) and other such Roman classics, finishing off with a tiramisu before staggering home. There's a tiny terrace on the quintessential cobbled street.

BIR & FUD Map pp132–3 · Pizzeria €

Via Benedetta 23; meals €25; 6.30pm-12.30am, to 2am Fri & Sat, closed Aug; or Viale di Trastevere
This orange-and-terracotta, vaulted pizzeria wins plaudits for its amazingly good pizzas, crostini and delicious fried things (potato, pumpkin etc) and has a micro brewery on site. Chef Gabriele Bonci of the wonderful Pizzarium (p213) is consultant here. Save room for dessert. Book ahead.

JAIPUR Map pp132–3 · Indian €

☎ 06 580 39 92; Via di San Francesco a Ripa 56; curries €5-12; Tue-Sun & dinner Mon; or Viale di Trastevere; V
Jaipur is a cut above most other Indian restaurants in Rome and has an airy interior covered in Indian paintings to get you in the mood. Popular with young Romans and foreign students, it specialises in northern Indian cooking, with a large selection of vegetarian and tandoori dishes as well as old friends like *tikka masala* and *rogan josh.*

PANATTONI Map pp132–3 · Pizzeria €

☎ 06 580 09 19; Viale di Trastevere 53; pizzas €6-8.80; 6.30pm-1am Thu-Tue; or Viale di Trastevere;
Panattoni is nicknamed *l'obitorio* (the morgue) because of its marble-slab tabletops. Thankfully the similarity stops there. This is one of Trastevere's liveliest pizzerias, with paper-thin pizzas, a clattering buzz, testy waiters, streetside seating and fried starters (specialities are *supplì* and *baccalà*).

SISINI Map pp132–3 · Pizzeria €

Via di San Francesco a Ripa 137; pizza slices from €2; 9am-10.30pm Mon-Sat, closed Aug; or Viale di Trastevere

Locals love this *pizza al taglio* in Trastevere, and you'll need to jostle with them to make it to the counter. Here, simple styles reign supreme – try the *margherita* or *marinara* – and the *supplì* and roast chicken are tip-top too.

WEST OF VIALE DI TRASTEVERE

GLASS HOSTARIA Map pp132–3 · Ristorante €€€

☎ 06 583 35 903; Vicolo del Cinque 58; meals €55; Piazza Trilussa;
In quaint Trastevere, the modernist modishness of this place stands out. But it's about content, not just style – Glass offers Trastevere's most sophisticated dining. The wine list and creative Italian cuisine are impressive – with imaginative dishes such as *pesce bianco arrosto su piselli, asparagi bianchi, daikon e aria di sale* (white fish roasted with pea sauce, white asparagus, salmon eggs and salt cloud).

PARIS Map pp132–3 · Ristorante €€

☎ 06 581 53 78; Piazza San Calisto 7; meals €45; Tue-Sat, lunch Sun, closed 3 wks Aug; or Viale di Trastevere;
Nothing to do with Paris (it's the name of the founder), this is an old-school Roman restaurant set in a 17th-century building, and it's the best place outside the Ghetto to sample Roman-Jewish cuisine, such as delicate *fritto misto con baccalà* (deep-fried vegetables with salt cod) and *carciofi alla giudia* (Jewish-style artichokes), as well as Roman dishes such as just-right *rigatoni alla carbonara* (pasta with egg and bacon sauce). There's a sunshaded terrace.

ALLE FRATTE DI TRASTEVERE

Map pp132–3 · Trattoria €€
☎ 06 583 57 75; Via delle Fratte di Trastevere 50; meals €30; Thu-Tue; or Viale di Trastevere;
A warm, welcoming trattoria with chirpy paintings, frothy curtains, delicious food and outside seating, Alle Fratte is a hit with savvy priests, busy businesspeople and grateful tourists, who enjoy substantial, tasty platefuls of Roman classics washed down with the very quaffable house wine.

LA BOTTICELLA Map pp132–3 · Trattoria €€

☎ 06 581 47 38; Vicolo del Leopardo 39a; meals €35; 6pm-midnight Mon, Tue & Thu-Sat, noon-3pm Sun; Piazza Trilussa

On a quiet Trastevere backstreet, La Botticella offers pure Roman cooking, outside under the lines of flapping washing, or inside in the picture-lined salon. Menu stalwarts include tripe and *rigatoni alla paiata* (pasta with calf's intestines), but there are less demanding dishes, such as an excellent *spaghetti all'amatriciana* and *fritto alla botticella (*deep-fried vegetables). There's even a children's menu.

DA LUCIA Map pp132–3   Trattoria €
☎ 06 580 36 01; Vicolo del Mattonato 2; meals €20-25; ☽ Tue-Sun; 🚊 Piazza Trilussa
Eat beneath the fluttering knickers of the neighbourhood at this terrific trattoria, frequented by hungry locals and ravenous tourists. On a cobbled backstreet that is classic Trastevere, it serves up a cavalcade of Roman specialities including *trippa all romana* (tripe with tomato sauce) and *pollo con peperoni* (chicken with peppers), as well as bountiful antipasti.

DA AUGUSTO Map pp132–3   Trattoria €
☎ 06 580 37 98; Piazza de' Renzi 15; meals €20; ☽ lunch & dinner Mon-Sat Sep-Jul; 🚊 Piazza Trilussa
For a homely Trastevere feast, plonk yourself at one of Augusto's rickety tables and prepare to enjoy some true Mama-style cooking. The hardworking waiters dish out hearty platefuls of *rigatoni all'amatriciana* and *stracciatella* (clear broth with egg and Parmesan) among a host of Roman classics, accompanied by carafes of wine, and they'll scribble the bill on the paper tablecloth.

DA OLINDO Map pp132–3   Trattoria €
☎ 06 581 88 35; Vicolo della Scala 8; meals €20; ☽ Mon-Sat; 🚌 or 🚊 Viale di Trastevere; 🍴
One of Trastevere's old-style basic kitchens, this is your classic family affair, where the menu is short and the atmosphere is lively. Cuisine is robust, portions are huge. Expect *baccalà con patate* on Fridays and gnocchi on Thursdays, but other dishes – such as *coniglio all cacciatore* (rabbit, hunter-style) or *polpette al sugo* (meatballs in sauce) – whichever day you like.

DAR POETA Map pp132–3   Pizzeria €
☎ 06 588 05 16; Vicolo del Bologna 46; pizzas €7; ☽ from 6.30pm; 🚊 Piazza Trilussa; 🍴
Dar Poeta, a breezy, cheery pizzeria hidden away in an atmospheric side street, prof-

fers some of Rome's best pizza. The base is somewhere between wafer-thin Roman and Neapolitan comfort food, and the slow-risen dough apparently makes it easier to digest. There are also great bruschettas and salads, and it's famous for its unique ricotta and Nutella calzone. Expect to queue, elbows at the ready.

PIZZERIA IVO Map pp132–3   Pizzeria €
☎ 06 581 70 82; Via di San Francesco a Ripa 158; pizzas €6; ☽ Wed-Mon; 🚌 or 🚊 Viale di Trastevere; 🍴
One of Trastevere's most famous pizzerias, Ivo's has been slinging pizzas for some 40 years, and still the hungry come. With the TV on in the corner and the tables full, Ivo's a noisy and vibrant place where the crispy, though not huge, pizzas are made with conventional toppings (exceptions include an unorthodox gorgonzola and apple combo) and the waiters fit the gruff-and-fast stereotype.

VALZANI Map pp132–3   Pasticceria €
☎ 06 580 37 92; Via del Moro 37; cakes €3; ☽ 10am-8pm Wed-Sun, 3-8pm Mon & Tue, closed Jul & Aug; 🚌 or 🚊 Piazza Sonnino
The speciality of this humble cake shop, opened in 1925 and not redecorated since, is the legendary *torta sacher*, the favourite cake of Roman film director Nanni Moretti. But there are also chocolate-covered *mostaccioli* (biscuits), Roman *pangiallo* (honey, nuts and dried fruit – typical of Christmas) and Roman *torrone* (nougat).

FORNO LA RENELLA Map pp132–3   Pizzeria €
☎ 06 581 72 65; Via del Moro 15-16; pizza slices from €2; ☽ 9am-1am; 🚊 Piazza Trilussa
The wood-fired ovens at this historic Trastevere bakery have been firing for decades, producing a delicious daily batch of pizza, bread and biscuits. Piled-high toppings (and fillings) vary seasonally. Popular with everyone from skinheads with big dogs to elderly ladies with little dogs.

VATICAN CITY, BORGO & PRATI

Beware, hungry tourists: there are unholy numbers of overpriced, mediocre eateries around the Vatican and St Peter's, aimed at the thousands who pass through here each day and need somewhere to flop and refuel. It's worth making the extra effort to find somewhere listed in this guide, as there are fabulous places amid the follies.

North of the Vatican is Prati, an upmarket, largely residential district and location of the RAI TV headquarters. It has some excellent, interesting restaurants catering to wining and dining media lovelies.

LA VERANDA DE L'HOTEL COLUMBUS
Map pp138–9   Ristorante €€€

☎ 06 687 29 73; Borgo Santo Spirito; meals €70; 🚇 Piazza del Risorgimento

It's worth eating here if only for the setting, a wonderful hall frescoed by Pinturicchio, but the food is spectacular too, the product of creative takes on Italian ingredients by the Italo-Argentinian chef. It's an ideal place for an extravagant lunch (think beef fillet with foie gras) between all that high-calibre sightseeing, especially as they offer a lunch menu (*primo, secondo,* half

top picks

MARKETS

Rome's fresh-produce markets are a fabulous feature of the city's foodscape. Go to see what's in season and enter the fray with the neighbourhood matriarchs. The markets operate from around 7am to 1.30pm, Monday to Saturday.

Rome's most famous markets:

- **Campo de' Fiori** (Map pp74–5; 🚇 Corso Vittorio Emanuele II) The most picturesque, but also the most expensive. Prices are graded according to the shopper's accent.
- **Nuovo Mercato Esquilino** (Map pp106–7; Via Lamarmora; Ⓜ Vittorio Emanuele) One of Rome's cheapest markets and the best place to find exotic herbs and spices.
- **Piazza dell' Unità** (Map pp138–9; 🚇 Piazza del Risorgimento) Near the Vatican, perfect for stocking up for a picnic.
- **Piazza San Cosimato** (Map pp132–3; 🚇 or 🚋 Viale di Trastevere) Trastevere's neighbourhood market, still the business with foodstuffs.
- **Testaccio** (Map p120; Piazza Testaccio; 🚇 or 🚋 Via Marmorata) The most Roman of all. Sharpen your elbows and admire the queuing techniques of the elderly. It's noted for its excellent quality and good prices.

bottle mineral water, a glass of wine and coffee) for €35.

RISTORANTE L'ARCANGELO
Map pp138–9   Trattoria €€€

☎ 06 321 09 92; Via Giuseppe Gioachino Belli 59-61; meals €55; 🕑 closed lunch Sat & Sun; Ⓜ Ottaviano-San Pietro; 🗓

Prati harbours some of Rome's best *ristoranti,* and l'Arcangelo is a twinkling jewel in the crown. It proffers innovative cooking – twists on classics and stunningly fresh ingredients – served in traditional, wood-panelled surroundings, and is usually dotted with famous or almost-famous politicians and celebrities.

DEL FRATE Map pp138–9   Wine Bar €€

☎ 06 323 64 37; Via degli Scipioni 122; meals €40; 🕑 lunch & dinner Mon-Fri, dinner Sat & Sun; Ⓜ Ottaviano-San Pietro; 🗓

Locals love this upmarket wine shop, and it's a great escape from the Vatican. The high-ceilinged yet small brick-arched rooms have wooden tables and bottle-lined walls. There's a prestigious wine list, and dishes on offer include some delicious *crudo* (raw) dishes, such as beef tartare, as well as melt-in-the-mouth pastas, accompanied by homemade bread.

DINO & TONY Map pp138–9   Trattoria €€

☎ 06 397 33 284; Via Leone IV 60; meals €35; 🕑 Tue-Sun, closed Aug; Ⓜ Ottaviano-San Pietro

Tony stirs the pots, Dino delivers the songs, punchlines and mammoth portions of Roman soul food. It's famous for its *amatriciana* and *pasta alla gricia,* if you get past the mighty antipasti. Belt loosened, you might be able to finish with the signature *granita di caffè* (coffee with crushed ice and at least an inch of whipped cream). No credit cards.

DAL TOSCANO Map pp138–9   Trattoria €€

☎ 06 397 25 717; Via Germanico 58-60; meals €35; 🕑 Tue-Sun, closed Aug; 🚇 Piazza Giuseppe Mazzini; 🗓

Carnivores will adore Dal Toscano, an old-fashioned Italian ristorante that serves top-notch Tuscan food, with an emphasis on superb cuts of meat. Start with the hand-cut Tuscan prosciutto, then try the melt-in-your-mouth *piccata di vitello* (veal scaloppini with lemon sauce) or *bistecche alla Fiorentina* (Florentine-style steak). Book ahead.

ZIGAETANA Map pp138–9   Ristorante €€

☎ 06 321 23 42; Via Cola di Rienzo 263; meals €30, pizza €7.50-10; ⌚ 12.30pm-11pm Sun-Thu, 12.30pm-midnight Fri & Sat; Ⓜ Ottaviano-San Pietro

A huge, arched cellar, this has a funky contemporary feel, but has been family run since early last century. The paintings on the walls and inscription around the fireplace were painted by impecunious artists in exchange for food during the 1930s, and the owner has poems written by Trilussa that were given as payment for meals. And you can see why, as the food is good, including great antipasti, pizzas and pastas.

OSTERIA DELL'ANGELO

Map pp138–9   Trattoria €

☎ 06 372 94 70; Via Giovanni Bettolo 24; meals €20, menus €25-30; ⌚ lunch Tue-Fri, dinner Mon-Sat, closed 2 weeks Aug; Ⓜ Ottaviano-San Pietro

Having hung up his boots, former rugby player Angelo runs a neighbourhood trattoria that's hugely popular (making a reservation is a must), with paper cloths on solid wooden tables, burly fresh-from-the-scrum waiters, photos of Angelo's sporting heroes and a sociable atmosphere. The huge set menu features a mixed antipasti, a robust Roman-style pasta, salad and a choice of hearty main courses including everything from tripe to beef to rabbit. To finish, you're offered lightly spiced biscuits to dunk in sweet dessert wine. The price includes bread, wine and water. No credit cards.

CACIO E PEPE Map pp138–9   Trattoria €

☎ 06 321 72 68; Via Avezzana 11; meals €20; ⌚ Mon-Sat; 🚌 Piazza Giuseppe Mazzini

Romans flock for the home cooking at this humble trattoria, with gingham-clad tables spreading across the pavement in all directions. They'll even put up with freezing winter temperatures to sit outside and dig into great steaming bowls of *cacio e pepe* – the this-morning-fresh bucatini slicked with buttery cheese and pepper.

HOSTARIA-PIZZERIA GIACOMELLI

Map pp138–9   Pizzeria €

☎ 06 372 59 10; Via Emilio Faá di Bruno 25; pizzas from €6; ⌚ Tue-Sat; Ⓜ Ottaviano-San Pietro; 🐕

This neighbourhood restaurant has them queuing around the block for thin and crispy Roman pizzas. The décor is nothing

fancy (high ceilings, lots of photos), but the reliably good food, from the crostini to the spicy diavola pizza, has locals voting with their feet. There's also some in-demand outside seating under striped awnings.

SHANTI Map pp138–9   Indian, Pakistani €

☎ 06 324 49 22; Via Fabio Massimo 68; dishes €5-13; Ⓜ Ottaviano-San Pietro; 🐕

Deservedly popular, this small Indian and Pakistani restaurant has delicately spiced dishes (tandooris, dhals and the like) served in an appealing setting – intimate and softly lit, with lots of intricately carved wood and eastern decoration.

PIZZERIA AMALFI Map pp138–9   Pizzeria €

☎ 06 397 33 165; Via dei Gracchi 12; pizzas €5-9.50; Ⓜ Ottaviano-San Pietro; 🐕

With a yolk-yellow interior featuring murals of the Bay of Naples, you could imagine yourself in Campania, digging into the house pizzas – of course the Neapolitan, thick-crust variety. They're justly popular, and it's always busy, with some sunny streetside tables too. Finish with a creamy crème brûlée.

FRANCHI Map pp138–9   Delicatessen €

☎ 06 687 46 51; Via Cola di Rienzo 198; panini €2.50-4; Ⓜ Ottaviano-San Pietro

Franchi is a longstanding foodie landmark, and great for a swift lunch or snack, or to stock up on stuff to take home. Assistants in white jackets work with a dexterity that only comes with years of practice, slicing hams, cutting cheese, weighing olives and preparing *panini*. There's also wine, vegetables conserved in oil, and truffles. Ready-made dishes include poached salmon, baked *melanzane parmigiana* or *zucchini a la Barese* (Bari-style courgette), to take away or eat at stand-up tables. Locals swear by its fried dishes, such as *supplì*.

PIZZARIUM Map pp138–9   Pizzeria €

☎ 06 397 45 416; Via della Meloria 43; pizza slices €2; Ⓜ Ottaviano-San Pietro; 🐕

Another contender for Rome's best *pizza al taglio,* this unassuming place is the baby of chef Gabriele Bonci, and offers the most superbly digestible fluffy base and crisp crust topped by intensely flavoursome toppings (slice around €2 to €3), made from the freshest seasonal delights. Eat standing up, and wash it down with a chilled beer.

DOLCE MANIERA Map pp138–9 Pasticceria €
☎ 06 375 17 518; Via Barletta 27; ☻ 24hr;
Ⓜ Ottaviano-San Pietro
This 24-hour bakery in a basement next to the British School supplies much of the neighbourhood with breakfast. Head here for cheap-as-chips, delicious *cornetti* (croissants), slabs of pizza, *panini* and an indulgent array of cakes.

VILLA BORGHESE & NORTHERN ROME

Rome's wealthy northern suburbs are speckled with fine restaurants, and there's a cluster around the happening nightlife district of Ponte Milvio (see Drinking, p215).

FLAMINIO

RED Map pp150–1 Fusion €€
☎ 06 806 91 630; Viale Pietro de Coubertin 30; meals €45; 🚇 or 🚊 Viale Tiziano, or shuttle bus M from Stazione Termini; 🌐
Everyone from Josè Saramango to Lou Reed have eaten at snazzy Red, in Renzo Piano's Auditorium Parco della Musica. It's

a glamorous, loungey place with a sexy red interior. The food is duly creative yet thoroughly Roman, with dishes such as *risotto d'astice fave con pecorino di fossa* (rice with broad beans and sheep's milk cheese). There's also *aperitivo* (€10).

PONTE MILVIO

PALLOTTA Map pp150–1 Pizzeria €
☎ 06 333 42 45; Piazzale Ponte Milvio 22; pizza €5-8; ☻ Thu-Tue; 🚌 Ponte Milvio
The Pallotta family has been running this pizzeria for generations. It serves great pizzas, plus the usual fried things and barbecued meats, swiftly, and the leafy garden gives it a special atmosphere. It's an icon of unpretentious quality in this yuppie area.

IL GIANFORNAIO Map pp150–1 Bakery €
Piazzale Ponte Milvio 35; pizza slice €1-2; ☻ 10am-2am Jun-Oct, to 8pm Nov-May; 🚌 Ponte Milvio
A busy bakery that opens late and does fantastic *pizza al taglio,* thin and crispy, with a tang of tomato against a soft creamy mozzarella. The *foccacine bianche* (mini white pizzas) are also exceedingly moreish.

DRINKING & NIGHTLIFE

top picks

- Ai Tre Scalini (p222)
- Caffè Sant'Eustachio (p219)
- Freni e Frizioni (p229)
- Il Baretto (p230)
- La Bottega del Caffé (p222)
- La Tazza d'Oro (p217)
- Necci (boxed text, p227)
- Ombre Rosse (p230)
- Salotto 42 (p217)
- Société Lutèce (p219)

There's no city with better backdrops for a drink. You can sip a cocktail overlooking the Roman Forum or crack open the Campari watching the light bounce off baroque fountains. Often the best way to enjoy nightlife in Rome is to wander from restaurant to bar, getting happily lost down picturesque cobbled streets and being awestruck by ancient splendour.

Rome, like most cities, is a collection of districts, all with their particular character. For more on Rome's different areas, see the boxed text, p224. In cutting-edge club terms, the city's no Berlin or London, but there's still plenty of after-dark fun to be had.

Most people dress up to go out – the *bella figura* (looking good) is important. The majority of locals spend evenings looking beautiful, checking each other out, partaking of the odd ice cream, and not getting drunk – that would be most unseemly. However, this is changing and certain areas – particularly those popular with a younger crowd – can get rowdy with tipsy teens (for example, around Campo de'Fiori and parts of Trastevere).

And smart isn't the only way to go. Rome's flip side is a surprising alternative underbelly, centred on left-wing *centri sociali* (organised squats; see the boxed text, p226), grungy squatter arts centres that often have live music, and where dressed-down is the look.

Up-for-it Romans tend to eat late, then drink at bars before heading off to a club at around 1am. It can be difficult to get around, as some places are far-flung – despite drink-and-drive rules, most locals drive, hence the alarming road-accident statistics.

For a drink you can choose from myriad charming bars, *enoteche* (wine bars) and pubs. Bars range from spit-and-sawdust (no décor but the beer is cheap) to designer places for the exquisitely dressed. The *enoteca* was where the old boys from the neighbourhood used to drink rough local wine poured straight from the barrel. Times have changed: nowadays they tend to be sophisticated if still atmospheric places, offering Italian and international vintages, delicious cheeses and cold cuts. Pubs are based on the Irish or British model and look almost like the real thing, but populated with better-groomed people.

Some of the more popular nightclubs have a whimsical door policy, and men will often find themselves turned away. At many clubs both men and women will have to dress up to get in or fit in. Often admission is free, but drinks are expensive. Cocktails can cost from €10 to €15, but you can drink much more cheaply in the studenty clubs of San Lorenzo, Pigneto and the *centri sociali*.

For listings check *Trovaroma* (an insert in daily newspaper *La Repubblica*) on Thursday and *Roma C'è* on Wednesday, both of which have a short English section, or the English-language *Wanted in Rome* magazine, published every second Wednesday. Also, in bars and cafés look out for the free nightlife listings in monthly *Zero* (www.zero.eu). For alternative and techno events try http://romastyle.info/, while www.musicaroma.it lists concerts in Rome. To book live-music tickets see the local listings publications, try Comune di Roma (www.060608.it), or contact the ticketing agency Orbis (Map pp106–7; ☎ 06 482 74 03; Piazza dell'Esquilino 37).

Major concerts are held indoors or outdoors at the Auditorium della Musica (p234), with an incredible programme of pop, world and jazz music stars. Large concerts also take place at Rome's sports stadiums, Stadio Flaminio (Map pp150–1; www.federugby.it; ☎ 06 368 57 309; Viale Maresciallo Pilsudski) and Stadio Olimpico (p243). For smaller venues, see the listings in this chapter.

Friends in Rome (www.friendsinrome.com) is a social organisation that offers a chance to mingle with an international crowd – a mix of expats, locals and out-of-towners – and find out about the local social scene. The friendly organisers arrange regular social events, including *aperitivi* evenings and film showings.

ANCIENT ROME

In Ancient Rome there are several places in which to drink in the fabulous views. You can't beat a cocktail as the sun goes down on the empire.

CAFFÈ CAPITOLINO Map pp64–5   Café
☎ 06 326 51 236; Capitoline Museums, Piazza del Campidoglio 19; ☺ 9am-midnight Tue-Sat, to 8.30pm Sun, to 5pm Mon; 🚍 Piazza Venezia; ✖
This well-kept secret of a café is a lovely spot to take a break from the wonders of

SUMMER VS WINTER

From around mid-June to mid-September, many nightclubs and live-music venues close, some moving to EUR, Fregene or Ostia. Summer is prime time for outdoor concerts, including the wonderful Roma Incontra il Mondo (www.villaada .org), featuring world music in lakeside gardens. Fiesta (www.fiesta.it) is a Latin-American dance feast in a 7000-sq-m venue close to Via Appia Nuova, beyond Cinecittà. The area around the Isola Tiberina throngs with life nightly during the Lungo er Tevere...Roma, which sprouts bars, stalls and an open-air cinema. The Estate Romana festival (see the boxed text, p234) is a huge, all-encompassing collection of festivals.

This chapter supplies venues' regular hours, but be aware that in winter bars often close earlier in the evening, particularly in areas where the norm is to drink outside.

the Capitoline Museums and relax with a drink or a snack – the food's nothing special, but the views from the rooftop terrace are stupendous. You don't even need a museum ticket; you can enter from the street entrance to the right of the Palazzo dei Conservatori.

OPPIO CAFFÈ Map pp64–5   Café
☎ 06 474 52 62; Via delle Terme di Tito 72;
⊙ 7.30am-2.30am; Ⓜ Colosseo; ⊠
A glass-and-metal exposed-brick café-bar, Oppio has fabulous views of the Colosseum from the outside tables. It's a great place for a beer, cocktail or *aperitivo* (€10; 5pm to 10pm), and has regular live music, plus DJs playing lounge, jazz and house, and wine tasting on Thursday evenings.

CAVOUR 313 Map pp64–5   Wine Bar
☎ 06 678 54 96; Via Cavour 313; ⊙ 10am-2.30pm & 7.30pm-12.30am, closed Aug; Ⓜ Cavour; ⊠
Handy for the Colosseum and Forum, wood-panelled, intimate wine-bar Cavour 313 attracts everyone from actors to politicians to tourists. Sink into its publike cosiness and while away hours over some sensational wine (over 1200 labels on offer), cold cuts, cheeses, *carpacci* or daily specials.

CENTRO STORICO

The *centro storico* (historic centre) is home to a couple of nightlife centres: the area around Piazza Navona, with a number of elegant bars and clubs catering to the beautiful, rich and stylish (and sometimes all three); and the rowdier area around Campo de' Fiori, where the clientele is younger and the drinking is heavier. This is where people tend to congregate after football games. The *centro storico* also harbours Rome's best cafés.

PANTHEON & AROUND

CAFFÈ FANDANGO Map pp74–5   Bar
☎ 06 454 72 913; Piazza di Pietra 32; ⊙ 11am-2am; ⊠ Via del Corso; ⊠
Owned by the Fandango film company, this is a buzzing, arty little labyrinth in black, white and red. There's live music from Tuesday to Thursday (classical and pop) and frequent film showings. A beer costs €5, and *aperitivo* (6.30pm to 9pm) is €12.

CIRCUS Map pp74–5   Bar
☎ 06 976 19 258; www.circusroma.com; Via della Vetrina 8; ⊙ 10am-2am Tue-Sun; ⊠ Via del Corso; ⊠
A great little new café-bar, tucked around the corner from Piazza Navona, this is a funky, informal place to lounge and chat, with DJs on Friday, art exhibitions, and lots of books to browse through. Popular with American students from the nearby school.

SALOTTO 42 Map pp74–5   Bar
☎ 06 678 58 04; Piazza di Pietra 42; ⊙ Tue-Sun; ⊠ Via del Corso; ⊠
Facing 11 weathered Corinthian columns – what remains of Tempio di Adriana – this is a slinky, glamorous little bar, attracting a slinky, glamorous crowd. Run by an Italian-Swedish couple, it's as close as you'll get to a sitting-room experience in the city centre – think designer armchairs, sleek sofas and coffee-table books.

LA TAZZA D'ORO Map pp74–5   Café
☎ 06 679 27 68; Via degli Orfani 84-86; ⊙ 8am-8pm Mon-Sat; ⊠ Via del Corso
Head here for caffeine heaven. A busy, stand-up café with burnished 1940s fittings, this has some of the best coffee in the capital. In summer, a cooling must is the speciality, *granita di caffè*, a crushed-ice,

HOW TO DO COFFEE

To do as the Romans do, you have to be precise about your coffee needs. For an espresso (a shot of strong black coffee), ask for *un caffè*; if you want it with a drop of hot/cold milk, order *un caffè macchiato* ('stained' coffee) *caldo/freddo*. Long black coffee (as in a weaker, watered-down version) is known as *caffè lungo* (an espresso with more water) or *caffè all'american* (a filter coffee). If you fancy a coffee but one more shot will catapult you through the ceiling, you can drink *orzo*, made from roasted barley but served like coffee.

Then, of course, there's the cappuccino (coffee with frothy milk, served warm rather than hot). If you want it without froth, ask for a *cappuccino senza schiuma;* if you want it hot, ask for it *ben caldo*. Italians drink cappuccino only during the morning and never after meals; to order it after 11am would be, well, foreign. In summer *cappuccino freddo* (iced coffee with milk, usually already sugared), a *caffè freddo* (iced espresso) or *granita di caffè* (frozen coffee, usually with cream) top the charts. A *caffè latte* is a milkier version of the cappuccino with less froth and *latte macchiato* is even milkier (warmed milk 'stained' with a spot of coffee). A *caffè corretto* is an espresso 'corrected' with a dash of grappa or something similarly strong.

There are two ways to drink coffee in a Roman bar-café: you can either take it standing up at the bar, in which case pay first at the till and then, with your receipt, order at the counter; or you can sit down at a table and enjoy waiter service. In the latter case you'll pay up to double what you'd pay at the bar.

sugared coffee served with a generous dollop of cream top and bottom. If you just want cream on either the top/bottom, ask for *solo sopra/sotto*.

MISCELLANEA Map pp74–5   Pub
Via delle Paste 110a; 🕑 **noon-3am;** 🚍 **Via del Corso**
American students and their fans love to hang at this down-at-heel pub-bar, tucked near the Pantheon. It has spindly tables and chairs on the cobbled street, while inside has TV screens showing sport and a dingy, informal atmosphere, with conviviality fuelled by reasonably priced beer and cheap dishes and pizzas (€6).

TRINITY COLLEGE Map pp74–5   Pub
☎ **06 678 64 72; Via del Collegio Romano 6;** 🕑 **noon-2.30am;** 🚍 **Via del Corso;** 🔀
A big lively pub just off busy Via del Corso, Trinity College has an ample selection of imported beers and bar food, and a few outdoor tables. It gets packed to overflowing at weekends, when men might have trouble getting past the bouncers.

PIAZZA NAVONA & AROUND

BAR DELLA PACE Map pp74–5   Bar
☎ **06 686 12 16; Via della Pace 5;** 🕑 **8.30am-2am;** 🚍 **Corso Vittorio Emanuele II;** 🔀
Inside, Bar della Pace is gilded baroque and mismatched wooden tables; outside, locals and tourists strike poses over their Campari against a backdrop of ivy. The perfect people-watching spot.

CRUDO Map pp74–5   Bar
☎ **06 683 89 89; Via degli Specchi 6;** 🕑 **12.30-4pm & 6pm-midnight, to 2am Fri & Sat;** 🚍 **Corso Vittorio Emanuele II;** 🔀
Crudo is an easygoing yet uber-chic bar and restaurant that's a great place for a designer drink, whether it's a mojito (courtesy of the award-winning mixologist) or a vegetable shake. The interior is arty, with streaky walls and flickering projections, the clientele is tasty, and the atmosphere NYC cool. The lunch buffet (12.30pm to 3pm) and *aperitivo* (7pm to 10pm) cost €10.

ETABLÌ Map pp74–5   Bar
☎ **06 976 16 694; Vicolo delle Vacche;** 🕑 **6pm-2am Tue-Sun;** 🚍 **Corso del Rinascimento;** 🔀
Italo-Chilean-owned Etablì is a rustic-chic bar-café-restaurant in an airy 16th-century building, strewn with antique Provençal furniture. It's a laidback place, with an eclectic soundtrack – think the Who and Jimi Hendrix. Roman lovelies float in to have a drink or coffee, read the paper, have *aperitivi* and use the wi-fi.

LES AFFICHES Map pp74–5   Bar
☎ **06 686 89 86; Via Santa Maria dell'Anima 52;** 🕑 **8pm-2am Mon-Sat;** 🚍 **Corso del Rinascimento**
Once the boho-favourite 'Stardust', but the name-and-management change doesn't seem to have made much difference. The hep cats in cool hats are postcard-home handsome and hang out in the cobbled street as well as in the cramped red-and-black rooms inside, and there's occasional live music at *aperitivo* o'clock (early evening).

SOCIÉTÉ LUTÈCE Map pp74–5 Bar

☎ 06 683 01 472; Piazza di Montevecchio 17; ⏲ 6.30pm-2am Tue-Sat, closed 2 weeks Aug; 🚃 Corso Vittorio Emanuele II; ✖

A group of Turin trendsters opened Société Lutèce, and like their other venture in Trastevere, Freni e Frizioni (p229), it's among Rome's hippest bars. Think grungy and art-school (expect Joy Division and hair-raising bass) rather than dressed-up and glitzy. The music's genuinely funky, the *aperitivo* is lavish, and the crowds spill out onto the piazza.

CAFFÈ SANT'EUSTACHIO Map pp74–5 Café

☎ 06 686 13 09; Piazza Sant'Eustachio 82; ⏲ 8.30am-1am; 🚃 Corso del Rinascimento

A small stand-up place with some of Rome's best coffee, this is always three deep at the bar. The famous *gran caffè* is created by beating the first drops of espresso and several teaspoons of sugar into a frothy paste, then adding the rest of the coffee on top. It's superbly smooth and guaranteed to put zing into your sightseeing. Specify if you want it *amaro* (bitter) or *poco zucchero* (with a little sugar).

GRAN CAFFÈ LA CAFFETTIERA

Map pp74–5 Café

☎ 06 679 81 47; Piazza di Pietra 65; ⏲ 8am-9pm Mon-Fri, from 9am Sat; 🚃 Via del Corso; ✖

This stately café is famous for its Neapolitan cakes – try the *babà* (sponge cake soaked in rum) for something special, and the southern staple *rustici* (cheese-and-tomato-filled pastry puffs) for something savoury. Sit in the elegant Art Deco interior, or outside, where you can watch life on the

square, overlooked by the ancient Tempio di Adriano.

LA MAISON Map pp74–5 Club

☎ 06 683 33 12; www.lamaisonroma.it; Vicolo dei Granari 4; ⏲ 11pm-4am Wed-Sun Oct-May; 🚃 Corso Vittorio Emanuele II; ✖

Chandeliers and long, low banquettes provide a sexy backdrop for a see-and-be-seen crowd, who flirt and frolic to a soundtrack of poppy tunes and commercial house. It's smooth, mainstream and exclusive, yet more fun than you might expect. Entrance is free, if you can get past the door police, but drinks are €10 to €15 a throw. It gets busy by 2am.

CAMPO DE' FIORI & AROUND

FEMME Map pp74–5 Bar

☎ 06 686 48 62; Via del Pellegrino 14; ⏲ Tue-Sun; 🚃 Corso Vittorio Emanuele II; ✖

Entering this silver-seated modernist bar, with its funky sounds, is rather like wandering into a Calvin Klein advert, with uber-cool gilded youth everywhere you look. The splendid *aperitivo,* from 7pm to 9pm, is almost worth losing one's cool over.

CAFFÈ FARNESE Map pp74–5 Café

☎ 06 688 02 125; Via dei Baullari 106; ⏲ 7am-2am; 🚃 Corso Vittorio Emanuele II

We're with Goethe, who thought Piazza Farnese one of the world's most beautiful squares. Judge for yourself from the vantage of this unassuming café. On a street between Campo de' Fiori and Piazza Farnese, it's ideally placed for whiling away

TIME FOR WINE

There's nothing like a chilled, light white wine on a summer's day. It might be forgettable but it's sublimely refreshing. Most of the house white you'll guzzle in Rome will be from the Castelli Romani area to the southeast of Rome, centred on Frascati and Marino. It arrives by truck: robust and honest, usually mixed from Trebbiano and Malvasia grapes.

However, as Italian wine producers have raised their game to face international competition, so Lazio's winemakers have joined the fray. New production techniques have led to a lighter, drier wine that is beginning to be taken seriously. Frascati Superiore is now an excellent tipple, Castel de Paolis' Vigna Adriana wins plaudits, while the emphatically named Est! Est!! Est!!!, produced north of Rome in Montefiascone, is becoming increasingly drinkable.

Although whites dominate Lazio's production – 95% of the region's Denominazione di Origine Controllata (DOC; the second of Italy's four quality classifications) wines are white – there are a few notable reds worth dipping into. Falesco produces the excellent Montiano, blended from Merlot grapes, while Torre Ercolana from Anagni is another opulent red. To try any wines from Lazio, Palatium (p202) is the place.

Of course, you're not confined to local wine. Rome is full of *enoteche* (wine bars) with knowledgeable staff, proffering wines from all over this beautiful country, as well as from abroad. Some of these are listed in the Eating (p187) and Shopping (p169) chapters.

top picks

CLUBS

- Circolo degli Artisti (p227)
- Goa (p228)
- Rashomon (p228)
- Rialtosantambrogio (right)
- Villaggio Globale (p226)

the early afternoon hours. Try the secret-recipe *caffè alla casa* (house coffee).

IL GOCCETTO   Map pp74–5   *Wine Bar*
☎ 06 686 42 68; Via dei Banchi Vecchi 14; ☽ 11.30am-2pm & 5.30pm-midnight Mon-Sat, closed Aug; 🚌 Corso Vittorio Emanuele II
Join the cast of regulars at the bar at this old-style *vino e olio* (wine and oil) shop, and imbibe delicious drops by the glass, accompanied by tasty snacks (cheeses, salamis, crostini etc) and large helpings of neighbourhood banter.

L'ANGOLO DIVINO   Map pp74–5   *Wine Bar*
☎ 06 686 44 13; Via dei Balestrari 12; ☽ 10am-2.30pm & 5pm-2am Mon-Sat; 🚌 Corso Vittorio Emanuele II; 🖧
A hop and a skip from the busy *campo* lies another *vini e olio* shop, somewhat updated, yet on the go since 1946. It's an oasis of genteel calm, with an ample wine list and delectable bites. It's ideal for a quiet glass of wine, a nibble of cheese or a light meal.

TAVERNA DEL CAMPO   Map pp74–5   *Wine Bar*
☎ 06 687 44 02; Campo de' Fiori 16; ☽ 8am-2am Tue-Sun; 🚌 Corso Vittorio Emanuele II
A breakfast bar for the *campo's* market traders, the Taverna metamorphoses into a hip drinking haunt during the day, almost merging with Vineria next door. Grab an outside table to watch the human traffic.

VINERIA REGGIO   Map pp74–5   *Wine Bar*
☎ 06 688 03 268; Campo de' Fiori 15; ☽ 8.30am-2am; 🚌 Corso Vittorio Emanuele II; 🖧
The coolest bar on the *campo,* this has a small, bottle-lined, cosy interior and outside tables as well, and attracts *fighi* (cool) Romans like bees to a honey pot. A *birra media* costs €4.50.

JEWISH GHETTO

BARTARUGA   Map pp74–5   *Bar*
☎ 06 689 22 99; Piazza Mattei 9; ☽ 3pm-12.30am Mon-Thu, 5pm-2am Fri & Sat; 🚌 Via Arenula; 🖧
As perkily baroque as the turtle-adorned fountain it faces, this velvet-lined, chandelier-slung bar is a theatrical choice for a theatrical crowd. The soundtrack is loungey and jazzy, the mood relaxing and chatty.

RIALTOSANTAMBROGIO
Map pp74–5   *Social Centre*
☎ 06 681 33 640; www.rialto.roma.it; Via Sant'Ambrogio 4; ☽ varies; 🚌 Via Arenula
In the Jewish Ghetto, this ancient courtyard-centred building is Rome's most central *centro sociale* (social centre), with an art-school vibe and an edgy programme that's open to all, with theatre, exhibitions and art-house cinema, plus seriously kicking club nights and gigs – central Rome's best. In summer it hosts outdoor events at Casa del Parco (www.valledeicasali.com) in Monteverde.

VIA DEL CORSO & AROUND

CIAMPINI   Map pp74–5   *Café*
Piazza di San Lorenzo in Lucina; ☽ 7.30am-9pm; 🚌 Via del Corso
The graceful, traffic-free square of San Lorenzo is an ideal stop for an al fresco coffee among the well-heeled folk of the neighbourhood. Bring your big sunglasses and little dog. Sitting outside is pricey, so remember it's an investment and settle. The gelato is also tip-top.

TRIDENTE
PIAZZA DEL POPOLO & AROUND

STRAVINKIJ BAR – HOTEL DE RUSSIE
Map pp96–7   *Bar*
☎ 06 328 88 70; Via del Babuino 9; Ⓜ Flaminio
Can't afford to stay at the celeb-magnet Hotel de Russie (see p253)? Then splash out on a drink at its enchanting bar, set in the courtyard, with sunshaded tables overlooked by terraced gardens. Impossibly romantic in the best *dolce vita* style, it's perfect for a cocktail and some posh snacks.

ROSATI Map pp96–7 — Café

☎ 06 322 58 59; Piazza del Popolo 5; 🕑 7.30am-11.30pm; Ⓜ Flaminio; 🔀

Rosati, overlooking the vast disc of Piazza del Popolo, was once the hang-out of the left-wing chattering classes. Authors Italo Calvino and Alberto Moravia used to drink here while their right-wing counterparts went to the Canova (Map pp96–7; ☎ 06 361 22 31; Piazza del Popolo 16; 🕑 8am-midnight; 🔀) over the square. Today tourists are the main clientele, and the views are as good as ever.

PIAZZA DI SPAGNA & AROUND

CAFFÈ GRECO Map pp96–7 — Café

☎ 06 679 17 00; Via dei Condotti 86; 🕑 10am-7pm Mon & Sun, 9am-7.30pm Tue-Sat; Ⓜ Spagna; 🔀

Caffè Greco opened in 1760 and retains the look: penguin waiters, red flock and gilt mirrors. Casanova, Goethe, Wagner, Keats, Byron, Shelley and Baudelaire were all regulars. Now it's fewer artists and lovers and more shoppers and tourists. Prices reflect this, unless you do as the locals do and have a drink at the bar.

CANOVA TADOLINI Map pp96 7 — Café

☎ 06 321 10 702; Via del Babuino 150a/b; 🕑 9am-10.30pm Mon-Sat; Ⓜ Spagna; 🔀

In 1818 sculptor Canova signed a contract for this studio that agreed it would be forever preserved for sculpture. The place is still stuffed with statues, and it's a unique experience to sit among the great maquettes and sup an upmarket tea or knock back some wine and snacks.

CIAMPINI 2 Map pp96–7 — Café

☎ 06 681 35 108; Via della Fontanella di Borghese; 🕑 8am-9pm May-Oct; Ⓜ Spagna

Hidden away close to the top of the Spanish Steps, this graceful café has a garden-party vibe, with green wooden latticework surrounding the outside tables. There are lovely views over the backstreets behind Spagna, and the ice cream is renowned (particularly the truffle).

GREGORY'S Map pp96–7 — Live Music

☎ 06 679 63 86; www.gregorysjazz.com; Via Gregoriana 54d; admission €5; 🕑 8pm-2am Tue-Sun Sep-Jun; Ⓜ Barberini/Spagna; 🔀

If it were a tone of voice, it'd be husky: unwind in the downstairs bar then unwind some more on squashy sofas upstairs to some slinky live jazz, with quality local performers. Gregory's is a popular hang-out for local musicians.

TREVI, QUIRINALE & VIA VENETO

PIAZZA BARBERINI & VIA VENETO

DONEY H CLUB Map p100 — Bar

☎ 06 470 82 805; Via Vittorio Veneto 141; 🕑 8am-2am; Ⓜ Barberini; 🔀

A former *dolce vita* hang-out on Via Vittorio Veneto, the Doney is the best place to go in search of the contemporary equivalent in this no-longer-it zone. Housed in the plush Westin Excelsior Hotel, its outdoor section is like a sitting room on the street, ideal for smoking your fat cigar, sipping a cocktail, and eyeing up the other wealthy out-of-towners. It heats up around *aperitivo* time. There's a DJ Friday and Saturday nights.

MOMA Map p100 — Café

☎ 06 420 11 798; Via di San Basilio; 🕑 7am-11pm Mon-Sat; Ⓜ Barberini

Molto trendy: this café-restaurant is a real find. It's sleekly sexy and popular with workers from nearby offices. There's a small stand-up café downstairs, with a nice little deck outside where you can linger longer over coffee and delicious *dolcetti*. Upstairs is a *cucina creativa* restaurant (meals €50).

MONTI, ESQUILINO & SAN LORENZO

The Monti area, north of the Colosseum, is splendid for *aperitivo*, a meal, or after-dark drinks, with lots of charming candlelit *enoteche* and even a couple of bar-clubs to lengthen your evening.

If you want to keep it real, head down to San Lorenzo, the student district, packed with pubs, bars, clubs and some surprisingly chic restaurants. Hordes of students pack the piazza beside Arco degli Aurunci on balmy weekends – it's *the* place to drink take-out booze and listen to the didgeridoo.

top picks

WINE BARS

Here's a list of some of Rome's most divine wine bars. You'll notice some of them are listed in the Eating chapter, because they're also particularly good for food.

- Ai Tre Scalini (right)
- Antica Enoteca (p203)
- Casa Bleve (p196)
- Cul de Sac (p196)
- Il Tiaso (p227)
- La Barrique (right)
- La Meschita (p230)
- Palatium (p202)
- Trimani (p205)
- Vineria Reggio (p220)

MONTI

BOHEMIEN Map pp106–7 Bar
☎ 328 173 01 58; Via degli Zingari 36; ⏰ 6pm-2am Wed-Sun; Ⓜ Cavour
This little bar lives up to its name, and feels like something you might stumble on in Left-Bank Paris: small, with mismatched chairs and tables and an eclectic, fittingly boho crowd drinking wine by the glass or cups of tea.

ICE CLUB Map pp106–7 Bar
☎ 06 978 45 581; www.iceclubroma.it; Via Madonna dei Monti 18; ⏰ 6pm-2am; Ⓜ Colosseo; Ⓧ
Novelty value is what the Ice Club, most tempting in summer, is all about. Pay €15 (you get a free vodka cocktail served in a glass made of ice), put on a thermal cloak and mittens, and enter the bar, in which everything is made of ice (temperature: -5 degrees C). Most people won't chill here for long – the record is held by a Russian (four hours).

LA BOTTEGA DEL CAFFÉ Map pp106–7 Café
☎ 06 474 15 78; Piazza Madonna dei Monti 5; ⏰ 8am-2am; Ⓜ Cavour
Ideal for frittering away a morning, lunch, afternoon or evening, this appealing café-bar has greenery-screened tables out on the captivatingly pretty Piazza Madonna dei Monti with its fountain. As well as drinks, it serves lipsmacking snacks, from simple pizzas to cheeses and salamis.

GALLERIA DEI SERPENTI Map pp106–7 Club
☎ 06 487 22 12; Via dei Serpenti 32; admission around €5; ⏰ varies; Ⓜ Cavour; Ⓧ
A kooky, hidden-away place in Monti, this is a hip gallery-club that hosts some nights to remember, from the monthly mod mashup the Right Track (vinyltastic, featuring northern soul and boogaloo) to in-the-know electronica sessions. Check listings to see what's coming up.

CHARITY CAFÉ Map pp106–7 Live Music
☎ 06 478 25 881; Via Panisperna 68; www.charitycafe.it; ⏰ 6pm-2am; Ⓜ Cavour
Think narrow space, spindly tables, dim lighting and a laidback vibe: this is a place to snuggle down and listen to some slinky live jazz. Supremely civilised, relaxed, untouristy and very Monti.

AI TRE SCALINI Map pp106–7 Wine Bar
☎ 06 489 07 495; Via Panisperna 251; ⏰ noon-1am Mon-Fri, 6pm-1am Sat & Sun; Ⓜ Cavour
It's almost obligatory to visit everyone's favourite enoteca before or after dining at La Carbonara (p204). 'The Three Steps' is always packed, with crowds spilling out into the street. Apart from a tasty choice of wines, it also sells the damn fine Menabrea beer, brewed in northern Italy. If you've missed out on dinner, you can tuck into a heart-warming array of cheeses, salami, and dishes such as *porchetta di Ariccia con patate al forno* (roasted Ariccia pork with roast potatoes).

AL VINO AL VINO Map pp106–7 Wine Bar
☎ 06 48 58 03; Via dei Serpenti 19; ⏰ 9.30am-2.30pm & 5.30pm-12.30am Sun-Thu, to 1.30am Fri & Sat; Ⓜ Cavour; Ⓧ
A studiously rustic, vine-decorated place, mixing ceramic tabletops and contemporary paintings, this is an attractive spot to linger over a fine collection of wines, particularly *passiti* (sweet wines). The other speciality is *distillati* – grappa, whisky and so on. And of course there are snacks too, including some Sicilian delicacies.

LA BARRIQUE Map pp106–7 Wine Bar
☎ 06 478 25 953; Via del Boschetto 41b; ⏰ 1-3pm & 7pm-1.30am Mon-Fri, 7pm-1.30am Sat; Ⓜ Cavour; Ⓧ
A dark and cool, softly lit, bottle-lined *enoteca,* La Barrique offers excellent French and Italian wines – including many by

the glass – and 120 types of Champagne, divinely accompanied by *bruchettine* (little bruschettas) and *crostone*.

ESQUILINO

DRUID'S DEN Map pp106–7 | Pub
☎ 06 488 02 58; Via San Martino ai Monti 28; ⏱ 5pm-1.30am; Ⓜ Cavour; ✕
An Irish nook of a pub, the Druid's Den attracts a crowd of young expats and Roman Anglophiles. It meets all your Irish pub needs: the atmosphere is convivial, the walls are wood-panelled, Celtic paraphernalia is everywhere, Guinness is on tap, and it shows all the big games.

FIDDLER'S ELBOW Map pp106–7 | Pub
☎ 06 487 21 10; Via dell'Olmata 43; ⏱ 5pm-2am; 🚆 Via Cavour; ✕
Near the Basilica di Santa Maria Maggiore, the granddaddy of Rome's Irish pubs sticks to the formula that has served it so well over the last 25 years or so: Guinness, darts, crisps, and football and rugby showing when there's a big game on, attracting a mix of Romans, expats and tourists.

FINNEGANS Map pp106–7 | Pub
☎ 06 474 70 26; Via Leonina 66; Ⓜ Cavour
At first glance this seems like an Irish pub anywhere in the world, but look closer and it has some Italian twists – the clientele are well-groomed expats and fresh-faced Romans, and you can order Bellinis as well as Guinness. It's Irish-run and shows all the big football and rugby games.

HANGAR Map pp106–7 | Club
☎ 06 488 13 971; Via in Selci 69; ⏱ 10.30pm-2.30am Wed-Mon, closed 3 weeks Aug; Ⓜ Cavour
A gay landmark for more than 20 years, Hangar is friendly and welcoming, and attracts locals and out-of-towners, especially at weekends and on Monday nights for the weekly porn screenings. Feeling frisky? Head to the dark room.

SAN LORENZO & BEYOND

SOLEA CLUB Map pp106–7 | Bar
☎ 328 925 29 25; Via dei Latini 51; ⏱ 9am-2am; Ⓜ Vittorio Emanuele; ✕
With vintage sofas, chairs, and cushions on the floor, this has the look of a chill-out room in a decadent baroque mansion, and is full of San Lorenzo hipsters lounging all over the floor, drinking the mean mojitos. Fun.

ARCO DEGLI AURUNCI
Map pp106–7 | Café-Bar
☎ 06 445 44 25; Via degli Aurunci 42; ⏱ 8am-2am; 🚆 Via dei Reti; ✕
On the corner of San Lorenzo's most happening piazza, this is a relaxed place for a drink and some snacks (mixed plate of salami and cheeses €14). The interior is airy, with warm orange walls, brick arches and blown-up photos, and there's occasional live music.

DIMMIDISÍ Map pp106–7 | Club
☎ 06 446 18 55; Via dei Volsci 126B; ⏱ 6pm-2am Thu-Mon Sep-May; 🚆 Via dei Reti; ✕
Fronted by lavish murals, this intimate, small-scale white-walled loft of a club is devoted to new music: jazz, soul, dub, electronica and breakbeat. There are regular DJs and it's a good place to see live bands.

ESC ATELIER OCCUPATO Map pp106–7 | Club
Via dei Volsci 159; ⏱ 11pm-4am; 🚆 Via dei Reti; ✕
The 'occupied studio', having been evicted from its previous squat, now has a brand-new home, with 500 capacity, hosting gigs such as French hip hop artist Keny Arcana. Admission and drinks are cheap.

LIAN CLUB Map pp106–7 | Club
☎ 347 650 72 44; Via degli Enotri 6; admission varies; ⏱ 8.30pm-2am, Oct–mid-Jun; 🚆 Via dei Reti; ✕
Brick-arched Lian Club is an intimate place to see up-and-coming local bands and is friendly, relaxed and fun. Entrance is usually €5 (free if you've eaten here) and drinks are cheap too.

MAX'S BAR Map pp106–7 | Club
☎ 06 702 01 599; Via Achille Grandi 3a; admission varies; ⏱ 10.30pm-3.30am Thu-Sun; Ⓜ Vittorio Emanuele
Max is a gay Rome institution, and its unthreatening, welcoming vibe, backed by a hip-wiggling soundtrack of commercial house, is what has endeared it to so many men for so long.

LOCANDA ATLANTIDE
Map pp106–7 | Live Music
☎ 06 447 04 540; www.locandatlantide.it; Via dei Lucani 22b; ⏱ 9pm-2am Oct-Jun; Ⓜ Vittorio Emanuele; ✕

Come, tickle Rome's grungy underbelly, and descend into this cavernous place, decked in retro junk, packed with attitude-free alternative crowds, and with an always entertaining programme of everything from experimental theatre to DJ-spun electro. It's good to know that punk is not dead.

MICCA CLUB Map pp106–7 Live Music

☎ 06 874 40 079; www.miccaclub.com; Via Pietra Micca 7a; ☺ 10pm-2am Mon, Tue & Thu, 10pm-4am Fri & Sat, 6pm-1am Sun Sep-May; Ⓜ Vittorio Emanuele; ⊠

At eclectic Micca, Pop Art and jelly-bright lighting fills ancient arched cellars, and the entertainment features burlesque, jazz, do-wop, glam rock and more, with loads of live gigs. There's an admission fee if a gig's on and at the weekend (€15). Register online for €5 discount. *Aperitivo* is from 7pm to 10pm from Thursday to Tuesday (€10; from 6pm Sundays), and there's a vintage flea market on Sundays.

CELIO HILL & LATERAN

COMING OUT Map p115 Bar

☎ 06 700 98 71; Via di San Giovanni in Laterano 8; ☺ 10.30am-2am; Ⓜ Colosseo

Spot this easygoing gay bar in the shadow of the Colosseum by the rainbow sign and the mixed, convivial crowds spilling out into the street. It's a popular pre-clubbing stop and features regular drag acts, DJs and live acts.

LAST NIGHT A DJ SAVED MY NIGHT

Pierandrea 'the Professor', so-named for his 60,000-strong record collection, runs the laidback Chiringuito (p231) and has DJed in Rome since the 1980s. Italo-Finnish Anja has DJed in Rome for two years, spinning minimal techno and electro house/wonk/UK funky at her night 'Dirty Stop Out' at Esc Atelier Occupato (p223) in San Lorenzo. Here they spill the disco-spangled beans on Roman nightlife.

Centro Storico

Anja There aren't really any clubs here – the centre's about bar culture. People tend to come here for *aperitivo* before going clubbing. The bars close at 2am, so people stay until 1am drinking, then move on to the clubs.

Monti

Anja Think bars for the young and wealthy; artists and media types live here, and it has a trendy, bohemian vibe.
Pierandrea Monti is a very typical central neighbourhood. There's an argument between here and Trastevere – each claims to be the oldest neighbourhood of Rome. It's particularly good in winter for the restaurants and *enoteche*.

Pigneto

Pierandrea Pigneto is really nice. But until a couple of years ago, this was a very dangerous area. Many people from northern Rome have recently moved to Pigneto, and now it's trendy. I always say to them: but a few years ago, it wasn't in your mind to go to Pigneto! As the city gets bigger, areas change. It's like in London: once Pimlico or Notting Hill Gate were considered dangerous areas, now they're expensive.
Anja Pigneto is similar to Shoreditch in London, full of immigrants, artists, students, and musicians. There are lots of bars here and cheap restaurants. It's the hub for underground international music scenes like dubstep, and close by there's the important club Circolo degli Artisti (p227).

Ostiense

Anja Ostiense has Rome's most famous clubs, like Goa (p228), Rashomon (p228), and La Saponeria (p228). During the winter season, from Thursday to Saturday, the area is packed.
Pierandrea The most popular club here is Goa. Personally I like the music (it's mainly techno) – but not the crowd – it's very young (the average age is 17 to 22).

Testaccio

Anja There are loads of small clubs here, playing music from electronic to rock. It's always busy and the clubs tend to be cheaper and more diverse than Ostiense.

GLADIATORI HOTEL TERRACE BAR

Map p115 Bar

☎ 06 775 91 380; Via Labicana 125; ☒ 4pm-midnight; Ⓜ Colosseo

A small flower-ringed terrace on the rooftop of the swish little Hotel Gladiatori, this bar is open to all. With 'marry-me' Colosseum views, it's perfect for a sundowner or an after-dark cocktail.

SKYLINE off Map p115 Club

☎ 06 700 94 31; www.skylineclub.it; Via Pontremoli 36; admission with Arcigay membership; ☒ 10.30pm-4am; Ⓜ San Giovanni; ☒

Gay bar-club Skyline is a popular spot for cruising and carousing, and the bright-walled warren gets very busy. There are bar areas, a video room, bustling dark areas and cubicles. Mondays is the popular 'naked party' night, and the second Saturday of the month is 'sexy night' when anything goes.

IL PENTAGRAPPOLO Map p115 Wine Bar

☎ 06 709 63 01; Via Celimontana 21b; ☒ noon-3pm & 6pm-1am Tue-Sun; Ⓜ Colosseo; ☒

A few blocks from the Colosseo, these mellow star-vaulted rooms offer 250 labels to choose from and about 15 wines by the glass. There's live jazz or soul from about 10pm and tasty aperitivo (6pm to 8.30pm). Equally splendid is the enoteca opposite,

Pierandrea Testaccio also has a few good clubs for live gigs: they work seven days per week, even in summer.

Trastevere

Anja This area comes into its own in the summer, when you'll find lots of places with tables outside. They have the same licensing laws as the *centro storico*, so bars close at 2am. Romans come here to eat or have an *aperitivo* before clubbing.

Ponte Milvio & Parioli

Anja Ponte Milvio has lots of bars and is always full of young people. It tends to be more commercial music-wise, and appeals to local models and footballers' wives. Parioli is an expensive area, and the home of Rome's oldest and most famous nightclub – Piper Club (p231), which is currently going through something of a renaissance.

San Lorenzo

Anja In the main university district you'll find lots of cheap bars and pubs with live music or DJs of various genres. There are also lots of great, cheap places to eat. It's hard to find a bad restaurant here! The bars are restricted by the 2am licensing law, but there are a couple of clubs open late, like the new Esc Atelier Occupato (p223) and Dimmidisi (p223).

Summertime

Pierandrea In summer, Romans move out to the beach. From the north it's easy to go to Fregene – from the south people go to Ostia. In Ostia there is a good nightlife scene with clubs all along the beach. Personally, I don't like it, because it's cheesy. I prefer to go to social centres (see the boxed text, p226).

Anja Clubs that have open-air facilities and gardens usually stay open in summer. One place that comes to life is the Lungotevere (the riverbank), where you'll find bars and music until 2am. All the open-air clubs in Rome are in EUR, where you'll find all the big-name DJs playing in fantastic venues, like Purple Club (www.purpleroma.it).

A good night out?

Pierandrea I'd say go for a meal at a good restaurant, and then, for clubbing I would always suggest Goa (p227), but also check what live music is playing at the Auditorium (p234).

Anja I recommend that tourists get *Zero* (www.zero.eu), which is a free guide found in most bars – you'll find what's going on, from nightclubs to live music and bars. Here it's not just the venue that counts, but who is organising the events, so you're best off checking the listings as to what music you prefer. But, as a rule, Testaccio is full of clubs and you'll probably find something to suit your taste!

CENTRI SOCIALI

Rome's *centri sociali* (social centres) are organised squats – centres of anti-establishment counterculture set up in the 1970s in disused public buildings, such as factories, garages or industrial estates. Then, squatters regularly battled with police, while nowadays most have been around long enough to be part of the establishment. However, they still offer Rome's most unusual and alternative entertainment, including gigs, club nights and exhibitions, and follow a left-wing political agenda. They're also a bargain, in accordance with their ethic of accessible culture.

Most important are Rialtosantambrogio (p220), Brancaleone (p232) and Villaggio Globale (below). There's also Forte Prenestino (Map pp106–7; ☎ 06 218 07 855; www.forteprenestino.net; Via F Delpino Centocelle), housed in a fort east of the city centre, where there are gigs, vintage markets and much more, including shiatsu massage (€15 one treatment) and a fantastic May Day festival (forget the famous mainstream concert at San Giovanni and head here).

Kottabus (☎ 06 772 01 145; Via Celimontana 32; ⊕ 7pm-1am).

AVENTINO & TESTACCIO

IL SEME E LA FOGLIA Map p120   Bar
☎ 06 574 30 08; Via Galvani 18; ⊕ 8am-2am Mon-Sat, 6pm-2am Sun; Ⓜ Piramide
It's an ordinary-seeming bar, but the position of this place at the edge of Testaccio's nightlife strip has seen it become a hip pre-club stop. It's tangerine and tiny inside, while outside has streetside seating where you can eavesdrop on conversations on topics as diverse as nihilism and where to go next.

L'OASI DELLA BIRRA
Map p120   Bar
☎ 06 574 61 22; Piazza Testaccio 41; ⊕ 7.30am-1.30pm & 4.30pm-2am Mon-Sat, 7.30pm-1am Sun; Ⓜ Piramide; ⊠
The Oasis of Beer is just that, and beer-lovers face a difficult decision between 500-plus varieties. But this isn't just a beer-lover's dream, it's charming, with intimate seating in the cellars beneath a well-stocked *enoteca* and lots of good food, such as hearty stews, or cheeses and cold cuts, to soak up the alcohol.

LINARI Map p120   Café
☎ 06 578 23 58; Via Nicola Zabaglia 9; ⊕ 6am-11pm Wed-Mon; 🚊 or 🚃 Via Marmorata
Spot this by the crowds of part-of-the-furniture locals. It has the busy clatter of a good bar, with excellent pastries, splendid coffee and barside banter. There are some outside tables, but you'll have to armwrestle the elderly ladies of the neighbourhood to get one.

AKAB Map p120   Club
☎ 06 572 50 585; www.akabcave.com; Via di Monte Testaccio 68-69; ⊕ 11pm-4am Tue-Sat, closed end Jun–mid-Sep; Ⓜ Piramide; ⊠
This eclectic former workshop has an underground cellar, an upper floor, a garden and a classically whimsical door policy. On Saturday the two levels get jiggy with R&B and house, while Friday nights Akab goes back to its roots with live music, usually local cover bands. Tuesdays it's L'Etrika, a must for house and electronica fans, with some big names. Entrance is €15 (one free drink).

CONTE STACCIO Map p120   Club
☎ 06 572 89 712; www.myspace.com\contestaccio; Via di Monte Testaccio 65b; ⊕ 11pm-4am Tue-Sat, closed end Jun–mid-Sep; Ⓜ Piramide
With an under-the-stars terrace, Contestaccio is a laidback cocktail bar with an arched white interior that hosts DJs and regular live gigs. Admission is usually free in the week.

L'ALIBI Map p120   Club
☎ 06 574 34 48; Via di Monte Testaccio 40; ⊕ midnight-5am Wed-Sun; Ⓜ Piramide
L'Alibi attracts a mixed gay and straight crowd. Spread over three floors, including a huge summer roof terrace, this sultry, cavernous club plays soulful commercial house to shake your ass to.

VILLAGGIO GLOBALE Map p120   Social Centre
☎ 334 179 00 06; www.vglobale.biz; Via di Monte Testaccio 22; ⊕ 10pm-4am, gigs usually 11pm, mid-Sep–Jun; Ⓜ Piramide
For an illegal-warehouse-party vibe, head to Rome's best-known *centro sociale*, originally a squat, occupying the city's former slaugh-

terhouse. Thirty years have passed and it's now part of the (anti-)establishment. Entrance is usually around €5, beer is cheap, and dreadlocks are the look; live sets and DJs focus on dancehall, reggae, dubstep, ska and drum'n'bass.

SOUTHERN ROME

The ex-industrial area of Ostiense is fertile clubbing land, with its many warehouses, workshops and factories just crying out for a new lease of life as pockets of nightlife nirvana. This is where Rome's serious clubbers lose countless hours worshipping at the shrines of electro, nu-house, nu-funk and all sorts of other eclectica. Nearby, the appealing suburb of Garbatella has long been undergoing trendification, and is a cool, boho district popular with left-leaning hipsters.

OSTIENSE, SAN PAOLO & GARBATELLA

DOPPIOZEROO Map pp124–5   Bar
☎ 06 573 01 961; Via Ostiense 68; ☽ 7am-2am Mon-Sat; Ⓜ Piramide; ▦

This easygoing bar was once a bakery, hence the name ('double zero' is a type of flour). But today the sleek, modern interior attracts hungry, trendy Romans like bees

---

DETOUR: PIGNETO & AROUND

Pigneto is emerging as Rome's nuovo-hip district, a rapid metamorphosis from the working-class rough-and-ready quarter that it has been for decades – immortalised by filmmaker Pasolini, who filmed *Accattone* around here. It has a small-town feel, with its decaying low-rise houses and narrow streets. The action is centred on Via Pigneto. The liveliest half is pedestrianised, and has a busy market during the day. It's where you'll find upmarket restaurant Primo (p208) and increasing numbers of bars with pavement tables in summer.

- Il Tiaso (Map pp106–7; ☎ 333 28 45 283; www.iltiaso.com; Via Perugia 20; ☽ 8am-2am; 🚊 Circonvallazione Casilina) Think living room, with zebra-print chairs, walls of indie art, Lou Reed biographies shelved between the wine bottles, and 30-something owner Gabriele playing his latest New York Dolls album to neo-beatnik chicks, corduroy professors and the odd neighbourhood dog. Wine is well priced, the vibe intimate and chilled, and there's regular live music, from jazz to funk.

- Vini e Olii (Map pp106–7; Via del Pigneto 18; ☽ 10.30am-2am; 🚊 Circonvallazione Casilina) Forget the other bars that line Pigneto's main pedestrianised drag, with their scattered outside tables and styled interiors. *This* is where the locals head, turning their noses up at newer interlopers. This traditional 'wine and oil' shop sells cheap beer and wine (bottles from €7.50), and you can snack on platefuls of antipasti and *porchetta* (pork roasted in herbs). It's outside seating only.

- Necci (off map pp106–7; ☎ 06 976 01 552; Via Fanfulla da Lodi 68; ☽ 8am-2am; 🚊 Circonvallazione Casilina) To start your exploration of this bar-studded area, try the iconic Necci, opened in 1924, where film director Pasolini used to hang out, and where he filmed some of *Accattone*. More recently it appeared in Francesca Archibugi's *Una questione di Cuore*. Gutted by fire in 2009, it was swiftly restored to how it was. It caters to an eclectic crowd of all ages, and has a lovely, leafy garden-terrace (ideal for families out for dinner, as the kids have some room to play). There's wi-fi.

- Circolo degli Artisti (Map pp106–7; ☎ 06 703 05 684; www.circoloartisti.it; Via Casilina Vecchia 42; ☽ 7pm-2am Tue-Thu, to 4.30am Fri-Sun; 🚊 Via Casilina; ▦) For the sound of the underground, Circolo is one of Rome's best nights out, serving up a fine menu of fun: there's Screamadelica on Saturday nights, with Italy's alternative music oracle Fabio Luzzietti, while Friday night cracks open the electronica and house for gay night Omogenic. Regular grunge-guitar-electronica gigs see big names: think Glasvegas and Cornershop. The large garden area is ideal for chilling out with a beer from the open-air bar, with a barbecue in summer. Admission is either free or a bargain. On Sunday there's usually a vintage market, sometimes curated by cutting-edge divas the Hysterics Fashion Network.

- Fanfulla 101 (off Map pp106–7; Via Fanfulla da Lodi 101; admission €5, free with Arci-card; ☽ 8pm-2am Mon-Sat, 7pm-1am Sun; 🚊 Circonvallazione Casilina) Hidden behind an unmarked workshop door, this is an underground cultural centre, a book-lined old hall that's all vintage chic and left-leaning punters. The look is bohemian, arty beards are plentiful, and drinks are dirt cheap. There are regular live indie, jazz, reggae and rock gigs, plus jam sessions, particularly from Monday to Thursday. Tuesday is the night for art-house films, documentaries and poetry readings.

to honey, all after the famously lavish, dinner-tastic *aperitivo* between 6.30pm and 9pm.

ALPHEUS Map pp124–5 Club

☎ 06 574 78 26; www.alpheus.it in Italian; Via del Commercio 36; ☽ 11pm-4.30am Tue-Sun Oct-May; Ⓜ Piramide; ♿

Alpheus has four halls hosting an eclectic array of sounds – from Argentine tango to Goldie – with plenty of live gigs. Saturday is the popular 'Gorgeous, I am' gay night, with lots of go-go dancers and guest DJs.

CAFFÈ LETTERARIO Map pp124–5 Club

☎ 338 802 73 17; www.caffeletterarioroma.it; Via Ostiense 83; ☽ 10pm-2am Mon-Fri, 3pm-2am Sat & Sun; 🚍 Via Ostiense; ♿

Garage-turned-cultural centre Caffè Letterario combines designer looks, bookshop, gallery, performance space and lounge bar. There are regular live gigs from indie folk to Indian dance. Check the website for upcoming events.

DISTILLERIE CLANDESTINE

Map pp124–5 Club

☎ 06 573 05 102; www.distillerieclandestine.com; Via Libetta 13; ☽ 11.30pm-4am Thu-Sun Sep-May; Ⓜ Piramide; ♿

One of Rome's umbrella venues, this funky place hauls in the hipsters. As well as a restaurant, there's a ship-shaped American bar with what look like light sabres suspended above it, a designer club that focuses on dance and house, and even a so-last-century smoking room.

GOA Map pp124–5 Club

☎ 06 574 82 77; Via Libetta 13; ☽ 11pm-4.30am Tue-Sun Oct-May; Ⓜ Garbatella; ♿

Goa is Rome's serious super-club, with international names (recent guests include 2ManyDJs), a dressed-to-the-nines crowd prancing like peacocks, and heavies on the door. The night to pick, though, is Thursday, when top Italian DJ Claudio Coccoluto ushers in the best of Europe's electronic music DJs. Goa also hosts a lesbian night, Venus Rising (www.venusrising.it), on the last Sunday of the month.

LA SAPONERIA Map pp124–5 Club

☎ 393 966 1321; Via degli Argonauti 20; ☽ 11pm-4.30am Tue-Sun Oct-May; Ⓜ Garbatella; ♿

Formerly a soap factory, nowadays La Saponeria lathers up the punters with guest DJs spinning everything from nu-house to nu-funk, minimal techno, dance, hip-hop and R&B.

RASHOMON Map pp124–5 Club

☎ 393 966 1321; www.myspace.com/rashomon club; Via degli Argonauti 20; ☽ 11pm-4.30am Tue-Sun Oct-May; Ⓜ Garbatella; ♿

Rashomon is sweaty, not posey, and where to head when you want to dance your ass off. Shake it to a music-lovers' feast of electro-rock, electronica, indie and new wave, plus occasional live acts

RISING LOVE Map pp124–5 Club

☎ 335 879 0428; www.risingrepublic.com; Via delle Conce 14; ☽ 11pm-4am Tue-Sun Oct-May; Ⓜ Piramide

For those who like their electronica, techno, funky groove and house, this white industrial space will tick all your boxes. Guest DJs such as DJ Falcon (Daft Punk), plus local talent, get the crowd rocking, and there are regular one-off nights.

LA CASA DEL JAZZ Map pp124–5 Live Music

☎ 06 70 47 31; www.casajazz.it; Viale di Porta Ardeatina 55; admission €5-10; ☽ 7pm-midnight; Ⓜ Piramide

In the middle of a 2500-sq-m park in the southern suburbs, the Casa del Jazz (House of Jazz) is housed in a three-storey 1920s villa that belonged to a Mafia boss. When he was caught, the Comune di Roma (Rome Council) converted it into a jazz-tastic complex, including a 150-seat auditorium, rehearsal rooms, café and restaurant, and it hosts regular shows by international jazz stars.

IL MELOGRANO Map pp124–5 Wine Bar

☎ 06 511 56 09; Via Guglielmo Massaia 9; ☽ 10.30am-3.30pm & 7pm-midnight Mon-Fri, 7pm-midnight Sat; Ⓜ Garbatella

A small, snug *enoteca*, this is run by two knowledgeable brothers who will suggest the best wines from their 300-strong list without making you feel like an ignoramus. There's a cheap set-dinner menu or you can choose dishes such as *bruschettine*, *crostini* and *carpacci* a la carte. Desserts are homemade, best accompanied by fragrant dessert wines.

TRASTEVERE & GIANICOLO

Enchantingly pretty, Trastevere is one of the city's most popular areas to wander, drink and decide what to do afterwards. Foreign visitors love it, as do those who love foreign visitors. The streets in summer are packed, with stalls, bars spilling into the street, and a carnival atmosphere – it's even a bit overcrowded and won't be to everyone's taste. To escape the throng, head to the bars on the outskirts of the area, where the vibe is gentler and the body count lower.

EAST OF VIALE DI TRASTEVERE

BIG MAMA Map pp132–3   Live Music
☎ 06 581 25 51; www.bigmama.it in Italian; Vicolo di San Francesco a Ripa 18; annual membership €13; ☒ 9.30pm-1.30am Tue-Sun Oct–mid-Jun; ☒ or ☒ Viale di Trastevere; ☒
To wallow in the Eternal City blues, there's only one place to go – this cramped Trastevere basement, which also hosts jazz, funk, soul and R&B. There are weekly residencies from well-known Italian musicians and songwriters, and frequent concerts by international artists.

LETTERE CAFFÈ GALLERY
Map pp132–3   Live Music
☎ 06 972 70 991; Via San Francesco a Ripa 100/101; ☒ 10am-2am winter, 6pm-2am summer, closed mid-Aug–mid-Sep; ☒ Piazza Trilussa; ☒
You like books? You like blues and jazz? Then you'll love this place, a clutter of barstools and books, where there are regular live gigs, poetry readings and comedy nights, followed by DJ sets playing indie and new wave.

WEST OF VIALE DI TRASTEVERE

BAR LE CINQUE Map pp132–3   Bar
Vicolo del Cinque 5; ☒ 6am-2am Mon-Sat; ☒ or ☒ Piazza Sonnino
There's no sign outside, and it looks like a run-down ordinary bar, but this is a long-standing Trastevere favourite, and always has a small crowd clustered around outside; they're here for the pivotal location, easy-going vibe and cheap drinks.

BAR SAN CALISTO
Map pp132–3   Bar
☎ 06 589 56 78; Piazza San Calisto; ☒ 6am-2.30am Mon-Sat; ☒ or ☒ Piazza Sonnino
Those in the know head to the down-at-heel 'Sanca' for its basic, stuck-in-time atmosphere and cheap prices (a large beer costs €2.50). It attracts everyone from intellectuals and pseudo-intellectuals to keeping-it-real Romans, alcoholics and American students. It's famous for its chocolate – drunk hot with cream in winter, eaten as ice cream in summer. We're reliably told that unless you have drunk a post-dinner coffee here, or a Sambuca con la Mosca ('with flies', with two or three raw coffee beans dropped in the drink), you will not truly know Trastevere.

BIG STAR Map pp132–3   Bar
☎ 339 764 45 75; Via G Mamelil 25; ☒ 6.30pm-2am, closed Aug; ☒ or ☒ Piazza Sonnino
If the scene in central Trastevere is feeling a bit too mainstream and trashy, head to the outskirts to find this unpretentious, grungy bar. It's a red-painted, rock-and-roll, pub-like place, with a cool studenty clientele and masses of beers on tap, from La Trappe to Sierra Nevada.

FRENI E FRIZIONI Map pp132–3   Bar
☎ 06 583 34 210; Via del Politeanna 4; ☒ 10am-2am; ☒ Piazza Trilussa; ☒
Everyone's favourite hip Trastevere hangout: in a former life, this bar/café was a garage, hence its name ('brakes and clutches'). The arty crowd flocks here to slurp well-priced drinks (especially mojitos) and pack the piazza in front. You can eat breakfast here, have lunch, munch brunch at the weekend, and feast on the good-value *aperitivo*. Hell, you could even move in here.

top picks

VIEWS

- Oppio Caffè (p217)
- Caffè Capitolino (p216)
- Gladiatori Hotel Terrace Bar (p225)
- Il Baretto (p230)
- Salotto 42 (p217)

OMBRE ROSSE Map pp132–3   Bar
☎ 06 588 41 55; Piazza Sant'Egidio 12; ☾ 8am-2am; ⛴ Piazza Trilussa; ✇
Another seminal Trastevere hang-out; grab a table on the terrace and watch the world go by. The cosmopolitan clientele ranges from elderly Italian wide boys to chic city slickers. Tunes are slinky and there's live music (jazz, blues, world) on Thursday and Sunday evenings from October to May.

LIBRERIA DEL CINEMA Map pp132–3   Café
☎ 06 581 77 24; Via dei Fienaroli 31d; ☾ 10am-9pm Sun-Fri, 11am-11pm Sat; ⛴ or ⛴ Piazza Sonnino; ✇
It's difficult to know in which category to put this place, as it's a bookshop-café, but we're putting it here as a perfect coffee-and-snack pitstop. There's *aperitivo* from 6pm. And, of course, you can browse the impressive cinema book collection too.

LA MESCHITA Map pp132–3   Wine Bar
☎ 06 583 33 920; Piazza Trilussa 41; ☾ 6pm-2am; ⛴ Piazza Trilussa
This tiny bar inside the entrance to up-market restaurant Enoteca Ferrara serves fantastic *aperitivo* and has a wide range of wines by the glass, from €7. Fancy an intimate tête-à-tête, with fine wines and snacks? This is your place.

GIANICOLO

IL BARETTO Map pp132–3   Bar
☎ 06 583 65 422; Via Garibaldi 27; ☾ 7am-2am Mon-Sat, 5pm-2am Sun; ⛴ or ⛴ Piazza Sonnino
Venture a little way up the Gianicolo, up a steep flight of steps from Trastevere. Go on, it's so worth it: you'll discover this truly hip cocktail bar, an architectural triumph. The bar is mostly huge plate-glass windows overlooking the district, and there's a garden terrace. *Aperitivo* is from 7pm to 10pm, the basslines are meaty, the interior mixes vintage with Pop Art, and it's genuinely cool.

VATICAN CITY, BORGO & PRATI

The quiet area around the Vatican harbours a few charming wine bars and splendid cafés and pastry stops. For nightlife there are a couple of live-music venues, including Italy's best jazz club.

CASTRONI Map pp138–9   Café
☎ 06 687 43 83; Via Cola di Rienzo 196; ☾ 8am-8pm; Ⓜ Ottaviano-San Pietro; ✇
This food shop (p185) harbours a great café with splendid coffee and snacks. You can stand at the busy bar or sit at outside tables; there are other branches at Via Ottaviano (Map pp138–9), Via Flaminio 28 (Map pp150–1) and Via Nazionale 71 (Map pp106–7).

ALEXANDERPLATZ Map pp138–9   Live Music
☎ 06 397 42 171; www.alexanderplatz.it; Via Ostia 9; admission with membership €10; ☾ 8pm-2am Sep-Jun; Ⓜ Ottaviano-San Pietro; ✇
The daddy of all jazz clubs in a city that loves jazz, Alexanderplatz attracts some huge international names. You'll need to book a table if you want dinner, and the music starts around 10pm. From July to September, the club moves outside to the grounds of Villa Celimontana (p116) for an enchanting, under-the-stars jazz festival.

FONCLEA Map pp138–9   Live Music
☎ 06 689 63 02; www.fonclea.it; Via Crescenzio 82a; ☾ 7pm-1.30am Sep-May; ⛴ Piazza del Risorgimento; ✇
Fonclea is a great little pub venue for live music, with bands playing anything from jazz to soul, funk to rockabilly, covers to African sounds (gigs start at 9pm). From June to August Fonclea moves outside – phone or check the website for the location.

MAKASAR Map pp138–9   Live Music
☎ 06 687 46 02; Via Plauto 33; ☾ 11am-1.30pm & 4-7.30pm Tue-Sat, 4-7.30pm Sun; ⛴ Piazza del Risorgimento; ✇
For a touch of tea-infused tranquillity pre or post Vatican, Makasar is ideal. It's an ochre-walled haven, with a Japanese vibe, featuring little wicker seats and tables, some beautiful teapots, lavish cookery books to browse, and a massive menu of teas with names like silvery fancy and Brasile bop

PASSAGUAI Map pp138–9   Wine Bar
☎ 06 874 51 358; Via Pomponio Leto 1; ☾ 10am-2am Mon-Sat; ⛴ Piazza del Risorgimento; ✇
A small, cavelike basement winebar, Passaguai has a few outdoor tables on the quiet street, and feels pleasingly off-the-radar. It boasts a good wine list and a range of artisanal beers, and the food – such as cheeses and cold cuts – is tasty too.

GAY & LESBIAN ROME

Rome has a well-established, if small, gay scene, despite the shadow of the Vatican. However, recent years have seen a few incidents of intolerance: two men were arrested for kissing outside the Colosseum in July 2007 (the following year a 'kiss-in' was held outside the monument to show solidarity with the couple), and there have been arson attacks on both Coming Out (p224) and Qube (below).

There's no openly gay part of town and only a few dedicated clubs and bars, though many clubs host regular gay and lesbian nights, listed throughout this chapter. However, Rome's pinker side is by no means invisible: there's a Gay Pride march annually in mid-June, and the 10-week Gay Village (www.gayvillage.it; admission €12; ☼ Jul–mid-Sep), a temporary complex of bars, clubs, cinema and even fitness areas, has run in different locations (usually in EUR) for more than five years.

For information on the local scene talk to the friendly folk at Libreria Babele (p174), and pick up the monthly magazine *AUT*, which has up-to-date listings and is published by Circolo Mario Mieli (p292). Lesbians can also find out more at Coordinamento Lesbiche Italiano (p292), which has a recommended women-only restaurant, Luna e L'Altra (men are allowed at lunch).

Most gay venues (bars and clubs) require you to have an Arcigay (www.arcigayroma.it) membership card. These cost €15/8 per year/month and are available from any venue that requires one.

Most gay saunas open from 2pm or 3pm until very late and admission is around €15 with a compulsory Arcigay card.

Apollion (Map pp106–7; ☎ 06 482 53 89; Via Mecenate 59a)

Europa Multiclub (Map p100; ☎ 06 482 36 50; Via Aureliana 40)

Mediterraneo (Map pp106–7; ☎ 06 772 05 934; Via P Villari 3)

Men and women carouse at Rome's gay beach, Il Buco, in the dunes 9km south of Lido di Ostia.

VILLA BORGHESE & NORTHERN ROME

Rome's genteel northern suburbs have various great places for a night out. The area around picturesque Ponte Milvio is hugely trendy with sashaying under-20s, dressed to the nines and driving tiny cars – it gets packed in summer, and has a carnival atmosphere. The wealthy district of Parioli is where the Ponte Milvio crew heads when they grow up.

PONTE MILVIO

CHIOSCHETTO DI PONTE MILVIO

Map pp150–1   Bar

☎ 06 333 34 61; Ponte Milvio 44; ☼ 5pm-2am Apr-Oct; ☒ Ponte Milvio

This tiny green kiosk next to the bridge has been open since the 1920s and is perennially popular, with lots of pavement tables. It might look like a shack, but the mojitos are the business and not too expensive either.

PARIOLI

CHIRINGUITO Map pp150–1   Bar

Viale Parioli 104; ☼ 6pm-2am; ☒ Viale Parioli

Pierandrea 'the Professor' (see p224) is currently running this summery kiosk bar in the centre of Parioli. With lots of pavement tables, it's a relaxed, inexpensive place to drink, watch the Pariolini play, and listen to some tunes on a summer's night.

PIPER CLUB Map pp150–1   Club

☎ 06 855 53 98; www.piperclub.it; Via Tagliamento 9; ☒ Via Salaria; ☒

Keeping Rome in the groove since 1965, Piper has worked through its midlife crisis and is starting to rediscover its mojo as the life and soul. As well as hosting some unfeasibly funky nights, it attracts big-name gigs (think Peaches, Babyshambles, the Fratellis).

TIBERTINA

QUBE off Map pp150–1   Club

☎ 06 438 54 45; www.qubedisco.com; Via di Portonaccio 212; Ⓜ Tiburtina; ☒

A taxi ride east of San Lorenzo, Rome's hugest disco offers Radio Rock night on Thursday and the superb gay night Muccassassina (Cow Assassin; www.muccassina.com) on Friday, hauling in a mixed crowd and run by Gay Pride organisers Circolo Mario Mieli. Saturday is Babylon, with regular international guest DJs. In July and August it moves outdoors (with live show and cruising garden). Check the website for details.

NOMENTANA

BRANCALEONE off Map pp150–1   Social Centre
☎ 06 820 004 382; www.brancaleone.eu; Via Levanna 11; admission usually €10; ☽ Oct-Jun; 🚌 Via Nomentana; ✕

The best is saved until last. Sure, it's a schlep, but this *centro sociale* is arguably Rome's finest club. It has blockbusting DJs – Miss Kitten and Jeff Mills, among others – who play every weekend, playing house, hip-hop, drum'n'bass, reggae and electronica to a young, alternative crowd. Thursday features the famous reggae and dancehall night, Friday minimal techno, and Saturday deep house. Everyone from serious musos to skate kids will be in their element.

THE ARTS

top picks

- Auditorium Parco della Musica (p235)
- Estate Romana (boxed text, p234)
- Isola del Cinema (boxed text, p237)
- Teatro dell'Opera di Roma (p236)
- Teatro Palladium (p238)
- Teatro Ghione (p238)
- Silvano Toti Globe Theatre (p238)

THE ARTS

Watching the world go by in Rome is often entertainment enough, but don't let that make you overlook the local arts scene. Rome's busy cultural calendar includes a host of amazing events, particularly when the Estate Romana (Roman Summer; boxed text, below) kicks off; it's an umbrella festival encompassing hundreds of theatre, cinema, opera and music events. Many performances take place in parks, gardens and church courtyards, with classical ruins and Renaissance villas providing atmospheric backdrops. Autumn also ushers in cultural feasts, with specialised shindigs dedicated to dance, drama and jazz.

In addition, a revolution has taken place in Rome, and it's all down to the Auditorium Parco della Musica (opposite). This otherworldly, beautiful, modernist arts centre hosts the majority of the city's important cultural events and attracts an extraordinarily eclectic mix of international stars in all musical genres, many of whom would previously have passed the city by.

Roma C'è (www.romace.it, in Italian; €1) is Rome's most comprehensive listings guide, and comes complete with a small English-language section; it's published every Wednesday. Another useful guide is *Trova Roma*, which comes as a free insert with *La Repubblica* every Thursday. The English-language magazine Wanted in Rome (www.wantedinrome.com; €1) contains listings in English, and is published every second Wednesday. Free listings booklet Zero (www.zero.eu) contains a wide range of entertainment. Useful websites include Comune di Roma (www.comune.roma.it, www.060608.it) and In Rome Now (www.inromenow.com).

MUSIC

Music in Rome is thriving, and the city's abundance of spectacular settings makes Rome a superb place to catch a concert. The Auditorium Parco della Musica is a state-of-the-art, modernist complex that combines architectural innovation with perfect acoustics. Free classical concerts are often held in many of Rome's churches, especially at Easter and around Christmas and New Year. Seats are available on a first-come, first-served basis, and the programmes usually feature beautiful renditions of classical music. The Chiesa di Sant'Ignazio di Loyola (p84) is a popular venue for choral masses, as are the Pantheon (p73) and Basilica di San Giovanni in Laterano (p116). The Basilica di San Paolo fuori le Mura (p127) hosts an important choral mass on 25 January and the hymn *Te Deum* is sung at the Chiesa del Gesù (p78) on 31 December.

Details are published in the daily newspapers, *Roma C'è* and *Trovaroma*. For more on pop, jazz, rock and world live-music gigs see the Drinking & Nightlife chapter (p216).

ACCADEMIA DI SANTA CECILIA
Map pp150–1

☎ 06 808 20 58; www.santacecilia.it; Auditorium Parco della Musica, Viale Pietro de Coubertin 10; 🚇 or 🚊 Viale Tiziano, or shuttle bus M from Stazione Termini

Rome's major classical-music organisation, the Accademia di Santa Cecilia dates back to the 16th century when it was founded by, among others, the Renaissance composer Palestrina. The academy's programme includes a world-class symphonic season – featuring superstar guest conductors – and short festivals dedicated to single composers. The inhouse orchestra is directed by London-born Italian Antonio

---

ROMAN SUMMER

Every August Romans pour out of the city, heading for the sea or the cool mountains. But if you can face the heat, Rome in summer is a buzzing place to be. Between June and September, the annual Estate Romana (www.estate romana.comune.roma.it) festival transforms much of the city centre into an open-air stage. Events include concerts, theatre performances, recitals, opera under the stars, exhibitions, DJ sets, contemporary dance, jazz festivals, book fairs, skateboard events and markets. Settings make full use of the city, ranging from Goran Bregovic playing in the Teatro Romano in Ostia, to Shakespeare in the Roman Forum, from concerts in parks to gigs and theatre on the banks of the Tiber. Check the website for details of what's on this year (the programme is usually posted in late spring).

Pappano, who is also musical director of London's Royal Opera House.

ACCADEMIA FILARMONICA ROMANA
Map pp150–1

☎ 06 320 17 52; www.filarmonicaromana.org, in Italian; Via Flaminia 118; 🚊 or 🚇 Piazza Mancini
The academy was founded in 1821 and its members have included Rossini, Donizetti and Verdi. It still attracts star performers, and its varied programme concentrates on classical and chamber music, but also includes opera, ballet and multimedia events. Concerts are held at the Teatro Olimpico (p236).

AUDITORIUM CONCILIAZIONE
Map pp138–9

☎ 899 50 00 55; www.auditoriumconciliazione.it; Via della Conciliazione 4; 🚇 Piazza Pia
Prior to the advent of the Auditorium Parco della Musica, this was Rome's premier classical music venue, and this recently renovated auditorium is still one to watch, hosting concerts, dance performances (featuring stars such as Baryshnikov) and film screenings. Specialist music bookshop on site.

AUDITORIUM PARCO DELLA MUSICA
Map pp150–1

☎ 06 802 41 281; www.auditorium.com; Viale Pietro de Coubertin 10; 🕚 11am 8pm; 🚊 or 🚇 Viale Tiziano, or shuttle bus M from Stazione Termini
Architect Renzo Piano's auditorium is just as audacious as his Pompidou centre in Paris. Three scarab-shaped buildings squat around a 3000-capacity amphitheatre, looking like alien spaceships landed in a northern Rome suburb. An amazing 2.5 million spectators flocked here in 2008, making it Europe's most popular arts centre. It's super-sleek and uber-chic, yet the excited throng is as wide a cross-section as you'd see on the Metro, a reflection of the democratic pricing (tickets cost from €5), and the programme, which encompasses anything from PJ Harvey to Puccini. Enter any of the halls (the largest is Sala Santa Cecilia, with 2756 seats), with their lipstick-red seating and billowing wooden interiors, and you're sold before anyone plays a note. The acoustics are amazing: Piano studied the interiors of lutes and violins as part of his design process. To get to the auditorium take tram 2 from Piazzale Flaminio or bus M from Stazione Termini, which departs every 15 minutes between 5pm and the end of the last performance.

top picks

ARTS FESTIVALS

The major festivals are outlined in the Festivals & Events section (p85), but here are a few more gems.

- Concerti del Tempietto (☎ 06 871 31 590; www.tempietto.it) The ancient Teatro di Marcello (p83) is the dramatic venue for a summer concert series in August and September, when piano and chamber music bounces off the rugged stone nightly from 8.30pm.
- Cosmophonies (☎ 06 565 16 89; www.cosmophonies.com in Italian) A short season (June to July) of theatre, music and dance held in the Roman theatre at Ostia Antica (p268).
- Festival Internazionale di Villa Adriana (☎ 06 802 41 281; www.auditorium.com/villaadriana/) Takes place in Tivoli (p278) with concerts, international theatre and dance in archaeological settings (June to July).
- Invito alla Danza (☎ 06 397 38 323; www.invitoalladanza.it) This mammothly popular modern-dance festival, which started in 1980, draws international performers (anything from tango to jazz) and passionate crowds to the beautiful parklands of Villa Doria Pamphilj (Map pp132–3; Via di San Pancrazio 10), south of the Vatican, in July. Tickets cost around €20.

ISTITUZIONE UNIVERSITARIA DEI CONCERTI Map pp106–7

IUC; ☎ 06 361 00 51; www.concertiiuc.it, in Italian; Piazzale Aldo Moro 5; 🚇 Castro Pretorio
The IUC organises a season of concerts in the Aula Magna of La Sapienza University, including many visiting international artists and orchestras. Held from October to May, performances cover a wide range of musical genres, including baroque, classical, contemporary and jazz – with anything from jazz quartets to Rachmaninov and Schumann.

OPERA

Rome's indoor opera season runs from December to June, then moves outside in summer, to the spectacular setting of the Terme di Caracalla (see p119).

Historically, opera in Rome was long opposed by the papacy. An opera house opened here in the 17th century, but it was only after independence that Rome's opera scene began

TICKETS & RESERVATIONS

Tickets for concerts and theatrical performances are widely available across the city. Prices range enormously depending on the venue and artist. Hotels can often reserve tickets for guests, or you can contact the venue or organisation directly. Otherwise there are a number of agencies you can try:

- Hellò Ticket (☎ 800 90 70 80, 06 480 78 400; www.helloticket.it in Italian)
- Orbis (Map pp106–7; ☎ 06 474 47 76; Piazza dell'Esquilino 37; ⏰ 9.30am-1pm & 4-7.30pm Mon-Fri, closed Aug) Near the Basilica di Santa Maria Maggiore.

You can also get tickets to concerts at major record outlets, including Messaggerie Musicali (p178).

to develop. Mascagni's *Cavalleria Rusticana*, Puccini's *Tosca* and Rossini's operas *Il Barbiere di Siviglia* and *La Cenerentola* all premiered here.

The opera house, Teatro dell'Opera di Roma, is a great grandiose venue but productions tend to be a bit hit-and-miss. But its finest hour is when the company moves outdoors for the summer season at the ancient Roman Terme di Caracalla, an unparalleled location. You can also see opera in various other outdoor locations, which vary from year to year: check current listings or at the tourist information kiosks (p300) for details.

TEATRO DELL'OPERA DI ROMA
Map pp106–7

IUC; ☎ 06 480 78 400; www.operaroma.it, in Italian; Piazza Beniamino Gigli; ⏰ box office 9am-5pm Mon-Sat, 9am-1.30pm Sun; Ⓜ Repubblica
It is functional and Fascist-era outside, but the interior of Rome's premier opera house – all plush red and gilt – is a stunning surprise. This theatre has an impressive history: it premiered Puccini's *Tosca*, and Maria Callas sang here. Built in 1880, it was given a Fascist makeover in the 1920s. Contemporary productions don't always match the splendour of the setting, but you may get lucky. Tickets for the ballet cost anywhere between €13 and €65; for the opera you'll be forking out between €30 and €140. First-night performances cost more. From July to mid-August, performances shift outdoors to the monumental setting of the old Roman baths, the Terme di Caracalla (p119).

TEATRO GHIONE Map pp138–9

☎ 06 637 22 94; www.teatroghione.it, in Italian; Via delle Fornaci 37; Ⓜ Piazza del Risorgimento Ⓜ Ottaviano-San Pietro
A former cinema, the Teatro Ghione is a small, beautifully restored theatre near St Peter's that offers a varied programme featuring major international performers. You can catch anything from Pirandello to opera arias, from Chopin to Sarah Kane.

TEATRO OLIMPICO Map pp150–1

☎ 06 326 59 91; www.teatroolimpico.it, in Italian; Piazza Gentile da Fabriano 17; Ⓜ or Ⓜ Piazza Mancini
The Accademia Filarmonica Romana holds its season here, and the programme features anything from classical soloists to opera performances, with some contemporary concerts and multimedia events, as well as regular ballet performances.

DANCE

Dance is not an art form that receives much patronage in Italy, and the best dancers tend to go abroad to work. But visiting dance companies are often class acts, and they're enthusiastically supported. See the daily papers and listings press for details.

TEATRO DELL'OPERA DI ROMA
Map pp106–7

☎ 06 480 78 400; www.operaroma.it; Piazza Beniamino Gigli; Ⓜ Repubblica
Home to Rome's official corps de ballet, the Teatro dell'Opera di Roma stages a number of ballet performances in its season (December to June). The repertoire is an interesting mix of classics and new work, but the standard is mixed. It's recommended when there is an important guest star.

TEATRO OLIMPICO Map pp150–1

☎ 06 326 59 91; www.teatroolimpico.it, in Italian; Piazza Gentile da Fabriano 17; Ⓜ or Ⓜ Piazza Mancini
The Teatro Olimpico keeps the Rome dance scene on its toes, with frequent world-class productions ranging from jazz to classical, ethnic to contemporary. Regular performances by big international stars – dancers, choreographers and companies – add to the glamour.

FILM

With such a backdrop, it's no surprise that Rome has a close relationship with the cinema. Rome's cinematic heyday was in the 1960s, with Fellini producing films like *La Dolce Vita* and *Roma,* and in the 1970s when Cinecittà (Film City) studios churned out enough spaghetti westerns to keep you entertained for life. But Rome's cinema scene has recently seen something of its former glory, even if it's not home-grown. Major international films recently produced at Cinecittà include *Ocean's Twelve, Mission Impossible 3* and the TV series *Rome* and *Dr Who.* The studios, built by Mussolini in 1937, suffered a setback in 2007, when around 3000 sq m of the complex were destroyed by fire – it actually started in storage lots for the *Rome* set, though no-one could confirm if Nero was fiddling as it burned.

In 2006, Rome began holding a star-studded international film festival, Festival Internazionale del Film di Roma (www.romacinemafest.it), which has continued to take place annually in November, despite concerns about its future.

Filmgoing has always remained popular, and there are some 80-odd cinemas dotted around the city. Many of these are small, single-screen affairs, although the number of multiscreen complexes is increasing. Most foreign films are dubbed into Italian; those shown in the original language are indicated in listings by *versione originale* or VO after the title – there are several cinemas that regularly show English versions.

Tickets cost between €5 and €8. Afternoon and early-evening screenings are generally cheaper, while all tickets are discounted on Wednesday. Check the listings press or daily papers for schedules and ticket prices.

A fantastic feature of Rome's cinema scene is the summer festival period, when films are shown outdoors at various locations.

ALCAZAR Map pp132–3

☎ 06 588 00 99; Via Merry del Val 14; 🚌 or 🚊 Viale di Trastevere
An old-style cinema with plush red seats. On Monday you can see films in their original language with Italian subtitles.

CASA DEL CINEMA Map pp150–1

☎ 06 42 36 01; www.casadelcinema.it; Largo Marcello Mastroianni 1; 🚌 Via Boncompagni
In Villa Borghese, the Casa del Cinema comprises an exhibition space, two projec-

tion halls, DVD room, café and bookshop. It sometimes screens films in their original language and has 24 computers on which you can watch a DVD from its large catalogue.

METROPOLITAN Map pp96–7

☎ 06 320 09 33; Via del Corso 7; Ⓜ Flaminio
This modern multiplex not 2m from Piazza del Popolo has four screens and the latest surround-sound audio technology. New releases, blockbusters and the more off-beat Hollywood films are regularly shown in the original language. For popular films it's best to book ahead.

NUOVO CINEMA AQUILA Map pp106–7

☎ 06 703 99 408; http://cinemaaquila.com; Via L'Aquila 68; ☽ Sep-May; 🚌 or 🚊 Via Prenestina
Pigneto's retro picture palace has had a makeover to go with the rest of the district. It's the neighbourhood's latest cultural hang-out, with three luxe cinemas, exhibition spaces, bar and bookshop.

NUOVO SACHER Map pp132–3

☎ 06 581 81 16; www.sacherfilm.eu; Largo Ascianghi 1; 🚌 or 🚊 Viale di Trastevere
Owned by cult Roman film director Nanni Moretti, this is the place to catch the latest European art-house flick. Originally designed to support home-grown film talent, it occasionally also shows films in their original language (English, French, Swedish etc). Summer screenings take place in the courtyard next to the cinema.

WARNER VILLAGE MODERNO Map pp106–7

☎ 892 111; Piazza della Repubblica 45; Ⓜ Repubblica
Film premieres are often held at this multiplex, which screens blockbusters from

CINEMA UNDER THE STARS

There are various wonderfully atmospheric outdoor summer film festivals; check current listings, but these take place annually.

- Isola del Cinema (www.isoladelcinema.com) Independent films in the romantic setting of the Isola Tiberina (Map pp74–5) in July and August.
- Notti di Cinema a Piazza Vittorio (☎ 06 444 04 31; www.agisanec.lazio.it in Italian) Italian and international releases at two open-air screens in Piazza Vittorio Emanuele II (Map pp106–7) in July and August.

Hollywood (both in English and Italian) and major-release Italian films.

THEATRE

It might be outdazzled by Broadway or London's West End, but Rome has a thriving local theatre scene. There are more than 80 theatres dotted across town, including an increasing number of smaller experimental places. In the larger city-centre venues the programmes tend to be conservative, and performances are usually in Italian.

Particularly wonderful are the summer festivals that make use of Rome's archaeological scenery – no city could be better suited to classic drama. Performances take place in settings such as Villa Adriana in Tivoli, Ostia Antica's Roman theatre and the Teatro di Marcello. In summer the Miracle Players (www.miracleplayers.org) perform classic English drama or historical comedy in English next to the Roman Forum and other open-air locations. Performances are usually free.

Further theatre information can be found online at www.tuttoteatro.com (in Italian).

ANFITEATRO DEL TASSO Map pp132–3

☎ 06 575 08 27; www.anfiteatroquerciadel tasso.com; Passagiata del Gianicolo; ☽ Jul & Aug; ⊟ Piazza Garibaldi
The setting is extraordinary: an amphitheatre overlooking Rome's rooftops that was built over 300 years ago. The productions are extraordinary too, for different reasons, featuring hammy turns in Greek and Roman comedy and the odd 18th-century drama, but they're always great fun.

ENGLISH THEATRE OF ROME Map pp74–5

☎ 06 444 13 75; www.rometheatre.com; Piazza Montevecchio 5; ☽ Oct-Jun; Ⓜ Cavour
The English Theatre of Rome stages a mix of contemporary and classic plays, stand-up comedians and bilingual productions, mainly at the Teatro L'Arciliuto, near Piazza Navona, and occasionally at other venues.

SILVANO TOTI GLOBE THEATRE Map pp150–1

☎ 06 06 08; www.globetheatreroma.com; Largo Aqua Felix, Villa Borghese; ⊟ Piazzale Brasile
Like London's Globe Theatre, but with better weather, this is an open-air Elizabethan theatre in the middle of Villa Borghese park. The season – mainly Shakespeare – includes occasional productions in English.

TEATRO AMBRA JOVINELLI Map pp106–7

☎ 06 443 40 262; www.ambrajovinelli.com, in Italian; Via G Pepe 43-47; Ⓜ Vittorio Emanuele
A home away from home for many famous Italian comics, the Ambra Jovinelli is a historic venue for alternative comedians and satirists. Between government-bashing, the theatre hosts productions of classics, musicals, opera, new works and the odd concert.

TEATRO ARGENTINA Map pp74–5

☎ 06 684 000 311; www.teatrodiroma.net, in Italian; Largo di Torre Argentina 52; ⊟ or ⓖ Largo di Torre Argentina
Rome's foremost theatre is one of the two official homes of the Teatro di Roma; the other is the Teatro India. Founded in 1732, it retains its original frescoed ceiling and a grand gilt-and-velvet auditorium. Rossini's *Barber of Seville* premiered here. Today it hosts major theatre and dance productions, with occasional performances in English. Book early for the dance productions, which often sell out.

TEATRO DELL'OROLOGIO Map pp74–5

☎ 06 683 92 214; www.teatroorologio.it; Via dei Filippini 17a; ⊟ Corso Vittorio Emanuele II
A well-known experimental theatre in the *centro storico,* the Orologio offers a varied programme, with works by contemporary authors (including theatrical dance pieces) and classic names such as George Bernard Shaw.

TEATRO INDIA Map pp124–5

☎ 06 442 39 286; www.teatrodiroma.net, in Italian; Lungotevere dei Papareschi; ⊟ Via Enrico Fermi
Inaugurated in 1999 in the postindustrial landscape of Rome's southern suburbs, the India is the younger sister of the Teatro Argentina. It's a starkly modern space in a converted industrial building, a fitting setting for its cutting-edge programme, with a calendar of international and Italian works.

TEATRO PALLADIUM Map pp124–5

☎ 06 57 33 27 68; www.teatro-palladium.it, in Italian; Piazza Bartolomeo Romano; Ⓜ Garbatella
Once at risk of being turned into a bingo hall, the wonderful Teatro Palladium was rescued for the residents of Garbatella and has been beautifully renovated. The 1920s interior houses an eclectic, fascinating

program of classical music (including the Roma Tre Orchestra), contemporary theatre, children's films and plays, and it's one of the venues for the Autumn RomaEuropa festival (www.romaeuropa.net).

TEATRO QUIRINO Map p100
☎ 06 679 45 85; www.teatroquirino.it, in Italian; Via delle Vergini 7; Ⓜ Via del Tritone
Within splashing distance of the Trevi Fountain, this grand 19th-century theatre produces the odd new work and a stream of well-known classics – expect to see works (in Italian) by Arthur Miller, Tennessee Williams, Shakespeare, Seneca and Luigi Pirandello.

TEATRO SISTINA Map p100
☎ 06 420 07 11; www.ilsistina.com, in Italian; Via Sistina 129; Ⓜ Barberini
Big-budget theatre spectaculars, musicals and comic star turns are the staples of the Sistina's ever-conservative, ever-popular repertoire.

TEATRO VALLE Map pp74–5
☎ 06 688 03 794; www.teatrovalle.it; Via del Teatro Valle 23a; Ⓜ or Ⓜ Largo di Torre Argentina
This perfectly proportioned 18th-century theatre is like a pocket opera house, with three levels of red-and-gold private boxes. There are occasional English-language works performed in English with Italian subtitles, as well as concerts from rock opera to recitals.

TEATRO VASCELLO Map pp132–3
☎ 06 588 10 21; www.teatrovascello.it; Via Giacinto Carini 72, Monteverde; Ⓜ Via Giacinto Carini
Left-field in vibe and location, this is an independent, fringe theatre that stages interesting, cutting-edge new work, including avant-garde dance performances, multimedia events and works by emerging playwrights.

240

SPORTS & ACTIVITIES

top picks

- Football at Stadio Olimpico (p243)
- Bike ride along the Appia Antica (p245)
- Six Nations rugby at Stadio Flaminio (p243)
- Swimming in Lago di Albano (p246)
- Ancient Roman-style steam bath at Acqua Madre Hammam (p245)

In this country of great passions, Il Calcio (football) is one of the greatest. After Italy won the World Cup in 2006, half a million people filled Circo Massimo to see the captain, Fabio Cannavaro, parade the trophy. From September to May, Romans flock to their largest temple of worship, the Stadio Olimpico (opposite).

Rome is a city split in two, with two Series A teams, Roma and Lazio. For more on the subject, and to work out who wears which colour scarf, see the boxed text, opposite.

Formula 1 is the only sport in Italy to challenge football in the glamour stakes, and Mayor Alemanno's proposal for a Grand Prix in the EUR district of Rome, possibly sometime after 2012, has caused great excitement.

Basketball (opposite) is fairly popular, but still trails football by a long way. Of late, rugby (opposite) has inspired a little more interest, the surge in support correlating with the Italian team doing slightly better in the Six Nations tournament, though recently poor form has seen them sink back to their previous level.

Romans do, as a rule, prefer watching to doing sport, but cycling is popular, and there are some attractive places around town to go running or horse riding, or play golf. During the long, hot summer, the pleasure of plunging into a pool, lake or the sea can't be beaten, so Rome's swimming options are well worth seeking out.

Also look out for opportunities to preen, indulge and pamper yourself – Rome has increasing numbers of fine spas, and beauty therapies, spas and plain-old barbers will make sure you can maintain the *bella figura* (beautiful look) despite all this activity.

SPECTATOR SPORT

FOOTBALL

In Rome you're either for AS Roma (*giallorossi* – yellow and reds) or Lazio (*biancazzuri* – white and blues). Both Rome's teams play in Serie A (Italy's premier league), at the Stadio Olimpico in the Foro Italico, north of the city centre. Both sides are considered solid, top-level performers, but Lazio has run into problems in recent years, while Roma has seen patchy success. Financial problems have beset both clubs, forcing them to sell top players and rely on one or two star performers.

Lazio's championship in 2000 broke a 26-year drought and was met with manic celebrations throughout the city, at least by the light-blue half. Representing the climax of Lazio's brief tour de force – they had previously won the European Cup Winners' Cup in 1999 – it was the club's finest moment. Basking in the glory were team coach Sven Goran Eriksson (who later became England's manager) and club president Sergio Cragnotti. However, it wasn't to last, and as Cragnotti's business empire crashed around him, the club's fortunes went from bad to worse and it had to sell many star players. In the 2004–5 season the side struggled to survive and finished in an ignominious 13th place. The one highlight for fans was the presence of

Paolo Di Canio, who had taken a 75% pay cut to join the cash-strapped club. Rome-born into a working-class, leftist neighbourhood, and a lifelong Lazio supporter, Di Canio provided some of the season's most controversial moments including his infamous Fascist salute following a derby game (see the boxed text, opposite). He later transferred to Cisco Roma, and has recently retired.

In 2007 Lazio was shamed as a result of its involvement in a match-fixing scandal, and it was announced that, after point deductions, they would be relegated to Serie B. After an appeal the punishment was reduced, but the team still lost its place in the following season's Union of European Football Association (UEFA; www.uefa .com) cup. However, they eventually recovered from the deduction to finish 3rd in Serie A in 2006–07. They thus qualified to the UEFA Champions League qualifying round, getting into the group phase but then ending up fourth in their group. They didn't fare much better in the league, finishing the Serie A season in 12th place. But the following season they put joy in the hearts of Rome's light-blue half, by winning the 2008–09 Coppa Italia for the fifth time (beating Sampdoria 6-5 on penalties).

Roma's fortunes have been similarly mixed. The club won the championship in 2001 and came second the following year. Manager Fabio Capello outraged the *giallorossi* fans and players

AS ROMA VS LAZIO

The Rome derby is one of the football season's highest-profile games. The rivalry between Roma and Lazio is fierce and little love is lost between the fans. The stereotype is that Lazio fans are right-wing and Roma fans are left-wing, but it's a good deal more complicated than that.

Lazio's fans traditionally come from the provincial towns outside Rome, although the team also has an unfortunate reputation for fascist sympathies – a reputation that key player Da Canio's regular 'Roman salutes' did nothing to dispel.

But AS Roma supporters have also been known to hang swastikas from their terraces. The AS Roma team was in fact founded in 1927 by Italo Foschi, a Fascist under Mussolini, merging three older Italian football clubs; Roman FC, SS Alba-Audace and Fortitudo-Pro Roma. Roma's supporters, known as *romanisti*, are historically working class, from Rome's Jewish community and from Trastevere, Testaccio and Garbatella.

Whatever the history and reputation of the clubs, you'll find plenty of different political persuasions among both sets of supporters. They are possibly united in only one thing: their dislike of the police.

If you go to the Stadio Olimpico, make sure you get it right – Roma fans (in deep red with a natty orange trim) flock to the Curva Sud (southern stand), while Lazio supporters (in light blue) stand in the Curva Nord (northern stand). If you want to sit on the fence, head to the Tribuna Tevere or Tribuna Monte Mario.

For more details on the clubs, check out www.asroma.it and www.sslazio.it (both in Italian).

by joining Juventus in 2004 (becoming England manager in 2007), and the club then struggled to find a suitable successor, with five changes of manager, until they settled on Luciano Spalletti, who has held the post since 2005. The public spats between Capello, subsequent managers, captain Francesco Totti and talented but impossible Antonio Cassano (who left for Real Madrid in 2006) were worthy of a soap opera. The 2004–05 season was disastrous, but in 2005–06 Roma fared better. They reached fifth place, but were bumped up to second when Juventus, Milan and Fiorentina lost points as a result of the match-fixing scandal. In the final of the Coppa Italia, AS Roma was beaten by Inter Milan – for the second year in a row.

In 2007 Roma won 2-1 against Manchester United, but sporting success was overshadowed by off-pitch violence. When Roma played Manchester United away, they lost a shameful 7-1. This meant they lost 8-3 on aggregate and were thus knocked out of the UEFA Champions League. They had better success at home, finally winning against Inter Milan in the final of the Coppa Italia (2006–07), giving Rome, or the yellow-and-red half of it, the chance to erupt with joy once again.

After a shaky start to the UEFA Champions League 2008–09, Roma managed to reach the knockout stage ahead of Chelsea in their group. They thus, for the first time in their history, emerged as winners of the group stage. However, their Champions League campaign ended when the *giallorossi* lost to Arsenal in the knockout stage on penalty kicks – cries of despair were heard all over Trastevere.

From September to June there's a game at home for Roma or Lazio almost every weekend and a trip to Rome's football stadium, the **Stadio Olimpico** (Map pp150–1; ☎ 06 368 57 520; Viale dei Gladiatori) is an unforgettable experience. Note that ticket purchase regulations are far stricter than they used to be. Tickets have to bear the holder's name and passport or ID number, and you must present a photo ID at the turnstiles when entering the stadium. Two tickets are permitted per purchase for Serie A, Coppa Italia and UEFA Champions League games – if you want to buy more, you can, but they will probably not be together. Tickets cost from €40 to €100. You can buy them from www.ticketone.it, www.listicket.it, from ticket agencies or at one of the AS Roma or Lazio stores around the city (see p173 and p184). To get to the stadium take metro line A to Ottaviano-San Pietro and then bus 32.

BASKETBALL

Basketball is a popular spectator sport in Rome, though it inspires nothing like the fervour of football. Rome's team, Virtus Roma, plays throughout the winter months at the **Palalottomatica** (Map p128; ☎ 199 12 88 00; Viale dell' Umanesimo; Ⓜ EUR Palasport) in EUR.

RUGBY UNION

Every time a Six Nations game gets played in Rome, the city fills with a swell of foreign spectators, easily discernable by their penchant for silly hats and beer.

Italy's rugby team, the Azzurri (the Blues), entered the Six Nations tournament in 2000, and has been the competition underdog ever since. There is a distinct lack of local media

FRANCESCO TOTTI

Modern-day gladiator and AS Roma captain Francesco Totti is a Roman god. He has played for AS Roma throughout his career, never being tempted away from his home town. It'd be hard to entice him: as well as being a Roma patriot, Totti is Italy's highest-paid footballer, apparently earning €6 million per season. It's not about money though – like any good Italian boy, Totti, with his strong Roman accent, has remained close to his family in Rome.

Born in 1976, he joined AS Roma in 1989, first playing for the side when he was only 16. He plays as a striker or attacking midfielder and has scored over 200 goals for the club – the most of any player in Serie A. Totti is famous for his chipping technique, called *er cucchiaio* (spoon) in the Roman dialect. Like David Beckham, he is at once derided for stupidity and hero-worshipped for his good looks and skill on the pitch.

A career low point came when he was expelled from Euro 2004 for spitting, but he is not always so unimaginative in his pitch behaviour. In 2005, after scoring at the Rome derby, as a tribute to his pregnant wife in the stands, he put the football up his shirt and pretended to give birth to it with the help of some other players. More recently, Totti has taken to sucking his thumb after he scores, apparently in honour of his young son.

Totti has played for the Italian national team since 2000, and was part of the victorious 2006 World Cup squad, but afterwards he announced his intention to retire from the national team so he could concentrate solely on playing for his beloved Roma. In June 2007, he was awarded the European Golden Boot, as the highest goal scorer across all European divisions, and in 2008 he was given the Pallone d'Argento (Silver Ball) for his sportsmanship.

As Rome's Beckham, he, of course, has his own clothing line ('Never without you'), fulfilling the needs of fans everywhere for Totti pencil cases and rucksacks.

His summer 2005 wedding to TV starlet Ilary Blassi in the Chiesa di Santa Maria in Aracoeli stopped traffic in Piazza Venezia as crowds formed to hail their king. They have two children, Cristian and Chanel.

interest in the game. Big matches might get a paragraph or two in national newspapers, while TV coverage is limited to the nation's smallest channel, La7. Public interest is further hampered by the complexity of the rules, which no-one quite understands, as Italian schools don't teach the game. However, in 2007 Italy won against both Scotland and Wales and finished in 4th place, which sparked an unprecedented wave of pride and coverage. In 2008 and 2009, they finished last.

The team plays home international games at Rome's Stadio Flaminio (Map pp150–1; www.federugby .it; ☎ 06 368 57 309; Viale Maresciallo Pilsudski).

TENNIS

Italy's premier tennis tournament, the Italian International Tennis Championships, is one of the most important events on the European tennis circuit. Every May the world's top players meet on the clay courts at the monumental, Fascist-era Foro Italico (Map pp150–1; ☎ 06 368 58 218; Viale del Foro Italico). Tickets can be bought at the Foro Italico each day of the tournament, except for the final days, which are sold out weeks in advance.

EQUESTRIAN EVENTS

Rome's top equestrian event is the Piazza di Siena showjumping competition (☎ 06 638 38 18; www .piazzadisiena.com), an annual event held in May,

gorgeously set in Villa Borghese (Map pp150–1). An important fixture on the high-society calendar, it attracts a moneyed Anglophile crowd.

ACTIVITIES
GOLF

To play golf you will usually have to show a membership card from your home club and proof of handicap. Rome's best golf course, in beautiful, cypress tree–dotted countryside close to the Appia Antica, is Circolo del Golf Roma Acquasanta (Map pp124–5; ☎ 06 780 34 07; www.golfroma .it; Via Appia Nuova 716; per day €100-120; ⏰ 8am-sunset Tue-Sun; ⓡ Via Appia Nuova).

HORSE RIDING

You can go on horse-riding excursions along and around Via Appia Antica. Call to book at Cavalieri dell'Appia Antica (Map pp124–5; ☎ 328 208 57 87; www .cavalieriappia.altervista.org; Via dei Cerceni 15; ⏰ 9am-1pm & 3-6pm Tue-Sun Oct-Apr, 9am-1pm & 4-7pm May-Sep; ⓡ Via Appia Antica); excursions cost around €25 per hour.

RUNNING

Good places to run include Circo Massimo, Villa Borghese, Villa Ada, Villa Doria Pamphilj, and along the banks of the Tiber. For those aspiring to more than a gentle jog, the Rome Marathon, which starts and finishes at the Colosseum, takes place in late March. No longer the long and colourful fun run it once was, it's now taken seriously and attracts some of the world's top marathon runners. If you're up to 42km on cobblestones, register your intentions well in advance with Italia Marathon Club (☎ 06 406 50 64; www.maratonadiroma.it).

CYCLING

Romans adore cycling, though they mostly head out of town in look-at-me lycra to mountain-bike in the hills. At certain times (check local press for details) Rome's *centro storico* is largely closed to traffic, which means you can glide around with relative ease. You can also participate in Rome's bike-sharing scheme (see p284), making it easier to cycle the city centre, though be aware that Roman motorists are not used to cyclists on the road.

There is a great cycle route alongside the river. The Tiber path runs from Castel Giubileo in the north to Mezzo Cammino in the south. To see this and other city routes, download the interactive map from Bici Roma (www.biciroma.it).

On Sundays the Via Appia Antica is closed to traffic, and bikes are available for hire (€3 per hour for first three hours, €10 per day) from the park information office. Two wheels is a great way to see the ancient road. At Parco Regionale dell'Appia Antica (www.parcoappiaantica.org) you can download five biking itineraries of 6km to 17km, taking beautiful routes through the regional park, past Roman ruins and through green countryside.

HEALTH & FITNESS
DAY SPAS & MASSAGE

ACANTO BENESSERE DAY SPA Map pp74–5
☎ 06 683 136 602; www.acantospa.it; Piazza Rondinini 30; ⏰ 10am-9pm Mon-Sat; 🚌 Corso del Rinascimento
This exquisite day spa near the Pantheon is the place for a divine designer detox. Settle back amid the mosaic mirrors, stained glass, soft lighting and curvaceous white seating, and get pampered. It offers a wide range of facials and massages – an hour-long massage costs around €90. Book ahead.

HOTEL DE RUSSIE WELLNESS ZONE
Map pp96–7
☎ 06 328 88 820; www.hotelderussie.it; Via del Babuino 9; ⏰ 9am-9pm; Ⓜ Flaminio

The admission charge of €45 is a bargain when you consider that this glamorous and gorgeous day spa is in one of Rome's best hotels, and factor in the remote possibility of bumping into Brad Pitt in the Turkish bath, sauna or gym. Treatments are also available, including shiatsu and deep-tissue massage; a 50-minute massage costs around €95.

ACQUA MADRE HAMMAM Map pp74–5
☎ 06 686 42 72; www.acquamadre.it; Via di Sant'Ambrogio 17; ⏰ mixed 2-9pm Tue, 11am-9pm Thu, Sat & Sun, women only 11am-9pm Wed & Fri; 🚌 🚊 Via Arenula
A chic new hammam in the Jewish Ghetto, where you can do-as-the-ancient-Romans-did and soak away your cares in the tepidarium (warm room), caldarium (hot room) and frigidarium (cold room), or indulge in massage and beauty treatments. First-timers can buy a bathing glove and slippers, and men/women can buy a bathing costume (€10/15).

BAAN THAI Map pp138–9
☎ 06 688 09 459; www.baanthai.it; Borgo Angelico 22a; ⏰ 11am-10pm; 🚌 Piazza del Risorgimento
Just the thing after a trip to the Vatican, this soothing centre offers Eastern-chic, heavenly scented oils and gracious masseurs. Treatments include soothing classic Thai massage (€60) and Ayurvedic massage (€60), and a half-hour foot massage is €35.

SWIMMING

On a smouldering summer's day, a dip in a swimming pool is just the ticket. Unfortunately, there are few public pools in Rome, and they are well outside the city centre, so if you want to swim without a trek you'll have to take the plunge and pay for a hotel pool.

Most public and private pools require a doctor's certificate before you are allowed to swim, so call first and ask '*serve un certificato medico?*' (do you need a medical certificate?). The pools reviewed in this section do not require a certificate.

For serious swimming, head to the two Olympic-sized pools at the Roman Sport Center (p246). The magnificent Fascist-era pools at the Foro Italico are not generally open to the public – these were the main venues for the World Swimming Championships in 2009.

As soon as the weather warms up, most Romans head straight for the coast to the

HAIR & NAILS

You might have noticed that Italians look better groomed than people of other nationalities. In Rome there are beauty parlours and barbers on almost every street helping to keep them that way. It's easy to take a break, pamper yourself and gain a little Italian style in the process. Most barbers look like they haven't changed their décor since they opened sometime in the mid-19th century; a standard cut will cost around €10.

For cool haircuts try Elleffe (Map pp132–3; ☎ 06 583 43 483; Via di San Calisto 6; haircut €55; 10am-6.30pm Tue-Sat), run by some uber-chic but unintimidating stylists in Trastevere. They also do reasonably priced manicures, pedicures and colouring.

A venerable ladies beauty salon that exudes old-fashioned class is Femme Sistina (Map pp96–7; ☎ 06 679 84 81; Via Sistina 75; 10am-7pm Mon-Sat, 11am-7pm Sun), which has been pampering and preening since 1951. It's more expensive than most – a pedicure with leg massage costs €50, a manicure is €25 – but you'll feel like Sophia Loren.

A swish nail bar near the Campidoglio, Gamax (Map pp74–5; ☎ 06 693 80 479; Via d'Aracoeli 35), with English-speaking staff, offers all sorts of nail treatments as well as a straightforward manicure (€20) or pedicure (€30 to €45). At less swish places around town these treatments will usually cost around €10 and €20 respectively.

seaside around Ostia (25km south of Rome), though few of them go in the water – it's unappealingly murky. You can reach Ostia Lido via a 30-minute train ride from Termini. If you have your own transport, you can also head out of town to the volcanic lakes dotted around the city – the water is much cleaner and the scenery enchanting. Lago di Albano (around 12km south of Rome), close to Castel Gandolfo, has lots of sunbeds set up around it in summer and is a good place for swimming, basking and taking out a pedalo.

GRAND HOTEL PARCO DEI PRINCIPI
Map pp150–1

☎ 06 85 44 21; www.parcodeiprincipi.com; Via G Frescobaldi 5; admission per day Mon-Fri €35 (€25 3-6pm), Sat & Sun €70 (€65 3-6pm); 10am-6pm May-Sep; Via Paisiello

On the edge of Villa Borghese, this hotel (p264) has a lovely pool shaded by tall trees and surrounded by flowers and rows of sun loungers. The daily rate means it's usually deserted, though weekends can be busier.

PISCINA DELLE ROSE Map p128

☎ 06 542 20 333; www.piscinadellerose.it; Viale America 20; admission from €7.50; 10am-10pm Mon-Fri, 9am-7pm Sat & Sun Jun-Sep; EUR Palasport

Out in the southern district of EUR, this open-air place is Rome's largest public swimming pool. It gets crowded, so get in early to grab a poolside deck chair, lie back and be entertained by the aqua aerobics.

RADISSON SAS Map pp106–7

☎ 06 44 48 41; www.radissonblu.com/eshotel-rome; Via Filippo Turati 171; May-Sep; Vittorio Emanuele

At this swish, cutting-edge hotel close to Termini, the sexy rooftop pool has a cocktail bar and restaurant alongside, and is open to nonguests for €40 per day.

GYMS

FARNESE FITNESS Map pp74–5

☎ 06 687 69 31; www.farnesefitness.com, in Italian; Vicolo delle Grotte 35; 9am-10pm Mon & Wed, 8am-10pm Tue & Thu, 9am-9pm Fri, 11am-7pm Sat, 10.30am-1.30pm Sun, closed Aug; Corso Vittorio Emanuele II

A handy city-centre gym in a historic building, with classes including fitness, dance, martial arts and pilates. It has a weights room and separate saunas for men and women. Day membership costs only €12.

ROMAN SPORT CENTER Map pp150–1

☎ 06 320 16 67; www.romansportcenter.com; Viale del Galoppatoio 33; 7am-10.30pm Mon-Fri, 7am-8.30pm Sat, 9am-3pm Sun; Spagna

This is Rome's largest gym, where you'll find squash courts, two Olympic-sized swimming pools, saunas and all the latest hi-tech gym equipment you could possibly need. It costs €30/180 per day/month to use the facilities.

lonely planet Hotels & Hostels

Want more sleeping recommendations than we could ever pack into this little ol' book? Craving more detail – including extended reviews and photographs? Want to read reviews by other travellers and be able to post your own? Just make your way over to **lonelyplanet.com/hotels** and check out our thorough list of independent reviews, then reserve your room simply and securely.

SLEEPING

top picks

SLEEPING

From opulent five-star palaces to chic boutique hotels, family-run *pensioni* (small hotels or guesthouses) and tranquil convents, Rome has accommodation to please everyone, from the fussiest prince to the most impecunious nun. Rates are relatively expensive, however, and you'll often pay more than for equivalent accommodation elsewhere. But (every global economic crisis has a silver lining) plenty of places have dropped their prices dramatically, and many rooms cost (depending on the time of year) around 30% less than they did a couple of years ago.

All the areas covered in this chapter are a bus ride or metro journey from Stazione Termini. If you come by car, be warned that there is a terrible lack of on-site parking facilities in the city centre, although your hotel should be able to direct you to a private garage. Street parking is not recommended.

Although Rome doesn't have a low season as such, many hotels offer large discounts from mid-July through August and from mid-November to mid-March (excluding the Christmas to New Year period). Expect to pay top dollar in spring (mid-March to mid-July) and autumn (September to mid-November) and over the main holiday periods (Christmas, New Year and Easter).

Most mid- and top-range hotels accept credit cards. Budget places might, but it's always best to check in advance. Many smaller places offer discounts of up to 10% for payment in cash.

In this book, reviews are in order of price, with the most expensive places listed first. Low-season and high-season rates have been provided, unless there's a single year-round price. See the inside front cover for a list of icons used.

The Comune di Roma (www.060608.it) publishes an extensive list of B&Bs, rooms and apartments to rent, and hotels, with prices.

Wherever you decide to stay and whenever you come, it's always a good idea to book ahead. For further details on reservations see opposite.

ACCOMMODATION STYLES

B&Bs

Alongside the hundreds of traditional B&Bs (private homes offering a room or two to paying guests), Rome has a burgeoning number of boutique-style guesthouses that offer up-market accommodation at mid- to top-end prices. You usually get your own keys and can come and go as you like. Note also that you're unlikely to be served a cooked breakfast; the usual offering is a continental combination of bread rolls, croissants, ham and cheese.

The following agencies specialise in B&B accommodation and offer online booking services:

Bed & Breakfast Association of Rome (Map pp124–5; ☎ 06 553 02 248; www.b-b.rm.it; Via A Pacinotti 73; ☺ 10am-2pm & 3-7pm Mon-Fri) Offers both rooms in B&Bs and short-term rentals of fully furnished flats.

Bed & Breakfast Italia (☎ 081 714 15 33; www.bbitalia .com) Rome's longest-established B&B network.

Cross Pollinate (www.cross-pollinate.com) An online agency.

Sleeping Rome (www.sleepingrome.com) Offers B&B and has good short-term flat rentals.

Hostels

Rome's hostels are smartening up their act. The number of private hostels is increasing and many now offer smart hotel-style rooms alongside traditional dorms. Curfews are rare and some even offer 24-hour receptions.

The central office of the Italian youth hostels association, the Associazione Italiana Alberghi per la Gioventù (AIG; Map pp106–7; ☎ 06 489 07 740; Piazza San Bernardo 107), has information about all the youth hostels in Italy. It will assist with bookings to stay at universities during summer, and you can also join Hostelling International (HI) here.

Pensioni & Hotels

The bulk of accommodation in Rome is made up of *pensioni* and *alberghi* (hotels).

A *pensione* is a small, family-run hotel. In Rome, they are usually housed in converted one- or two-floor apartments. Rooms tend to be simple, and although most now come with a private bathroom, those that don't will usually have a basin and bidet.

Hotels are bigger and more expensive than *pensioni,* although at the cheaper end of the market, there's often little difference between the two. All hotels are rated from one to five stars, although this rating relates to facilities only and gives no indication of value, comfort, atmosphere or friendliness. Most hotels in Rome's city centre tend to be three-star and up. As a rule a room in a three-star hotel will come with a hairdryer, minibar (or fridge), safe and air-conditioning. Many will also have satellite TV and internet connections.

A common complaint in Rome is that hotel rooms are small. This is especially true in the *centro storico* and Trastevere, where many options are housed in converted *palazzi* (mansions). Similarly, a spacious lift is a rare find, particularly in older *palazzi*, and you'll seldom find one that can accommodate more than one average-sized person with luggage.

Breakfast in cheaper hotels is rarely worth setting the alarm for, so, if you have the option, save a few bob and pop into a bar for a coffee and *cornetto* (croissant).

Religious Institutions

Unsurprisingly, Rome is well furnished with religious institutions, many of which offer cheap(-ish) rooms for the night. Bear in mind, though, that most religious institutions have strict curfews and the accommodation, while spotlessly clean, tends to be short on frills. Book well in advance. For a list of institutions, check out www.santasusanna.org/ comingToRome/convents.html.

CHECK-IN & CHECK-OUT TIMES

Hotels usually require you to check out on the day of departure between 10am and noon – check with individual hotels for specific regulations. Note also that some guesthouses require you to fix a time to check in. In addition, if you're going to arrive late in the day, it's probably best to mention this when you book your room.

Many hostels won't accept prior reservations for dorm beds, so arrive after 10am and it's first come, first served. Check-out times are often earlier in hostels, typically around 9am.

RESERVATIONS

It is always a good idea to book ahead, and it's essential if you're coming in high season or for a major religious festival (in particular Christmas or Easter). The easiest way is generally on the internet; otherwise, you'll probably be asked to fax confirmation of your reservation together with a credit-card number as deposit. If you don't have a credit card, you'll have to send a money order to cover the first night's stay. Note that although many budget hotels require a credit-card number to secure a booking, not all accept them as payment. To avoid embarrassing scenes when checking out, check in advance.

When reserving a room, make sure you ask for a *camera matrimoniale* if you want a room with a double bed. A *camera doppia* (double room) usually means a room with twin beds.

Arrive without a reservation, however, and all's not lost. There's a free hotel reservation service (Map pp106–7; ☎ 06 699 10 00; Stazione Termini; ☒ 7am-10.30pm) at the main train station (opposite platform 21); if you can, try to research the hotel they suggest before committing. Alternatively, the Enjoy Rome (p296) tourist office can sort you out with a room. Whatever you do, though, don't follow the people hanging around at the train station who claim to be tourism officials and offer to find you a room. Chances are they'll lead you to some dump for which you end up paying way over the official rates.

ANCIENT ROME

Stretching from the Campidoglio, down past the forums to the Colosseum and Palatino, Rome's ancient core is part of what makes this city so special. A busy area of ruins and roads, there's not that much accommodation around, and it tends to be expensive. That said, it's central and there's something magical about sleeping in the shadow of Italy's best-loved ruins.

PRICE GUIDE

The following is a guide to the pricing system used in this chapter. Unless otherwise stated, prices quoted are for a double room with private bathroom.

€	up to €120
€€	€120 to €250
€€€	€250-plus

HOTEL FORUM Map pp64–5 Hotel €€€

☎ 06 679 24 46; www.hotelforumrome.com; Via Tor de'Conti 25; s €130-420, d €180-420; Ⓜ Cavour; Ⓟ Ⓧ

A stately old pile, the Forum offers some of the best views in town. From the rooftop restaurant, you can look down on all of Ancient Rome, from Il Vittoriano on the right down to the forums and the Colosseum on the left. Inside, the look is olde-worlde, with antiques and leather armchairs strewn about the wood-panelled lobby, staff in ties and tails, and chandeliers a-dangling. Rooms are similarly styled, offering charm in place of hi-tech wizardry.

CAESAR HOUSE Map pp64–5 Hotel €€

☎ 06 679 26 74; www.caesarhouse.com; Via Cavour 310; d €140-220; Ⓜ Cavour; Ⓟ Ⓧ Ⓛ

Quiet, friendly, yet in the thick of it on busy thoroughfare Via Cavour, this has 11 rooms, terracotta floors, wi-fi, internet in the lounge, and even a tiny gym. The suite has a view over the Forum. The sunny rooms have a warm, peachy décor and small bathrooms, and are sparklingly clean.

HOTEL NERVA Map pp64–5 Hotel €€

☎ 06 678 18 35; www.hotelnerva.com; Via Tor de'Conti 3; s €70-150, d €90-220; Ⓜ Cavour; Ⓟ Ⓧ

Cheerful and family run, the Nerva is tucked away on a narrow road behind the Imperial Forums. A small place, it manages to squeeze 22 peach-coloured rooms onto its three floors (the stairs are among the steepest in Rome) as well as plenty of Roman paraphernalia – mosaic flooring in reception, an imperial bust halfway up the stairs, and mock frescoes. Rooms are not the biggest but they are quiet, carpeted and simply decorated; two have facilities for the disabled.

CENTRO STORICO

The *centro storico* is the best place to stay if you want to experience Rome to the hilt. An enthralling tangle of atmospheric squares, shadowy lanes, cafés and historic *palazzi*, this is the baroque heart of the city, the Rome of the Pantheon, Piazza Navona and Campo de' Fiori. Unsurprisingly, you pay more for such pleasures, and most hotels, *pensioni* and B&Bs are in the mid- to upper-price bracket. Be warned also that the area around Campo de'

Fiori is a popular nightlife spot, so it can be noisy after dark.

PANTHEON & AROUND

GRAND HOTEL DE LA MINERVE
Map pp74–5 Hotel €€€

☎ 06 69 52 01; www.grandhoteldelaminerve .it; Piazza della Minerva 69; d from €320; Ⓠ or Ⓠ Largo di Torre Argentina; Ⓧ Ⓛ

The grand old Minerve is one of Rome's historic hotels. Housed in an austere 17th-century *palazzo*, it's been in business since the late 18th century, but owes much of its current look, including the flamboyant Art Deco lobby, to architect Paolo Portoghesi's 1990 makeover. Rooms vary in size and look. Superior are smart but small, while deluxe are big, classic and classy. Some have original 17th-century wood-beamed ceilings, others have frescoes and four-poster beds. There's wheelchair access.

ALBERGO ABRUZZI Map pp74–5 Hotel €€

☎ 06 679 20 21; www.hotelabruzzi.it; Piazza della Rotonda 69; s €140-170, d €195-220; Ⓠ or Ⓠ Largo di Torre Argentina; Ⓧ

This popular three-star option is all about location, bang opposite the pockmarked façade of the Pantheon. But the small rooms are also attractive, with parquet, cherry wood furnishings and soft colour schemes, and the owners are a friendly bunch. The one problem is noise – double glazing will keep some of it out but a silent night is unlikely. Breakfast is served in a nearby café.

HOTEL MIMOSA Map pp74–5   Pensione €

☎ 06 688 01 753; www.hotelmimosa.net; Via di Santa Chiara 61, 2nd fl; s/d/tr/q €88/118/158/178, with shared bathroom €50/70/90/105; 🚇 or 🚋 Largo di Torre Argentina; ✇

This is one of the scarce budget choices in the historic centre. Imagine hard, and you'll experience a faint air of impecunious romance, but remove rose-tinted specs and you'll see basic accommodation in spartan rooms, some of which are cramped, but all of which are clean. To book a room you'll need to leave a credit-card number, though the hotel accepts payment in cash only.

PIAZZA NAVONA & AROUND

HOTEL RAPHAËL Map pp74–5   Hotel €€€

☎ 06 68 28 31; www.raphaelhotel.com; Largo Febo 2; d €200-300; 🚋 Corso del Rinascimento; Ⓟ ✇ 🖳

Peering out from behind a thick curtain of ivy, the much-loved Raphaël is striking inside and out. Art lovers can admire Picasso ceramics and Miro lithographs in the lobby while diners sit down to al fresco meals at the panoramic rooftop restaurant. The Richard Meier–designed executive rooms on the 3rd floor are sublimely minimalist and oak-lined, whereas those on other floors have an old-fashioned, gentlemen's-club feel, hung with Renaissance-style tapestries, but all have

top-end touches such as Bulgari toiletries in the bathrooms. Breakfast costs an extra €22 to €26. There's wheelchair access.

HOTEL DUE TORRI Map pp74–5   Hotel €€

☎ 06 688 06 956; www.hotelduetorriroma.com; Vicolo del Leonetto 23; s €100-150, d €170-230; 🚋 Via di Monte Brianzo; ✇

Tucked away at the end of a narrow side street, the Hotel Due Torri has always offered discretion – first as a residence for cardinals, then as a brothel, and now as a lovely, refined hotel. The look is classic, with huge gilt-framed mirrors, antiques, parquet floors, marble statuettes and plump pot plants, and the English-speaking staff are cordial and efficient. Rooms aren't huge, but they're bright; those with a balcony are best, on the 4th and 5th floors, with views over the rooftops.

TEATROPACE 33 Map pp74–5   Hotel €€

☎ 06 687 90 75; www.hotelteatropace.com; Via del Teatro Pace 33; s €120-160, d €150-250; ✇

Sublimely central, tucked in a lane beside Piazza Navona, this discreet, classy three-star is a top choice. In a former cardinal's residence, it has 23 beautifully appointed rooms decorated with parquet flooring, damask curtains and exposed wooden beams. There's no lift, just a monumental 17th-century stone staircase.

AT HOME IN ROME – APARTMENT RENTAL

Apartments in central Rome are not cheap, but they can nevertheless work out to be less expensive than a hotel. Bank on spending about €900 per month for a studio apartment or a small one-bedroom place, and, for longer-term stays, you may have to pay bills on top plus a condominium charge for the porter and building maintenance. A room in a shared apartment will cost from €600 per month, plus bills. You'll usually be asked to pay a deposit equal to one or two months' rent and the first month in advance.

Several English-language bookshops have noticeboards where people looking for accommodation or offering a room on a short- or long-term basis place messages. Try the Almost Corner Bookshop (p185) in Trastevere. Another option is to check the classified ads in *Wanted in Rome* (www.wantedinrome.com; or published fortnightly on Wednesday) or *Porta Portese* (published on Tuesday and Friday).

Rental agencies specialising in short-term rentals usually charge hefty commissions for their services – up to two months' rent in some cases. They are listed in the telephone directory under *Agenzie immobiliari*.

For a mini-apartment in a hotel block, go online at www.060608.it and check out the Sleeping section. Several hotels also offer apartment rental, such as the Beehive (p259), Hotel Campo de' Fiori (p252) and Residence Vittoria (p255). It's also worth checking the following websites:

Flat in Rome (www.flatinrome.it)

Flats in Italy.com (www.flatsinitaly.com)

Italy Accom (www.italy-accom.com)

Leisure in Rome (www.leisureinrome.com)

Rental in Rome (www.rentalinrome.com)

RELAIS PALAZZO TAVERNA

Map pp74–5   Hotel €€

☎ 06 203 98 064; www.relaispalazzotaverna.com;
Via dei Gabrielli 92; s €80-150, d €100-210; ☒ ⬛
A boutique hotel in a sensational location, the Relais Palazzo Taverna has 11
contemporary rooms that set a modernist
aesthetic (funky wallpaper, bright block
colour) against an ancient building. Ameni-
ties, such as plasma-screen satellite TVs
and tea- and coffee-making facilities, ice
the cake. Breakfast is served in your room.

HOTEL NAVONA Map pp74–5   Hotel €€

☎ 06 686 42 03; www.hotelnavona.com; Via dei
Sediari 8; s €100-125, d €135-155; ⬛ Corso del
Rinascimento; ☒
Spread over several floors of a 15th-
century *palazzo*, and set around a courtyard, Navona's rooms vary in quality: some
are big and bright, others are small, and
the décor is largely ad hoc (antique desks
mingle with plastic lamps). But what you're
really paying for here is the location, a skip
and a jump from Piazza Navona. The hotel
also offers nearby apartments sleeping two
for €145 to €250 per night including breakfast, and runs the also good, more upmarket, seven-room Residenze Zanardelli (see
the website for details) around the corner.

HOTEL PORTOGHESI Map pp74–5   Hotel €€

☎ 06 686 42 31; www.hotelportoghesiroma
.com; Via dei Portoghesi 1; s €130-160, d €160-200;
⬛ Via di Monte Brianzo; ☒ ⬛
This cosy, low-key hotel is on a picturesque
street near Piazza Navona. Rooms are
comfortable and have satellite TV and wi-fi,
though some (particularly the singles) are
small, with equally bijou bathrooms. Staff
are pleasant and the peaceful roof terrace
is a bonus.

CAMPO DE' FIORI & AROUND

HOTEL CAMPO DE' FIORI

Map pp74–5   Hotel €€€

☎ 06 688 06 865; www.hotelcampodefiori.com;
Via del Biscione 6; s €170-220, d €200-270, 2-person
apt €130-150, 4-person apt €180; ⬛ Corso Vittorio
Emanuele II
Here, red and flock walls are hung with gilt
mirrors and restored bric-a-brac, and facilities
include swish bathrooms, flat-screen satellite
TVs and wi-fi. They'll even loan you a laptop
if you so desire. It's close as can be to the

happening Campo, but double-glazing sorts
out the noise, and there is a wonderful roof
terrace with wicker sofas. The hotel also offers 13 comfortable apartments in the area.

RESIDENZA IN FARNESE

Map pp74–5   Hotel €€

☎ 06 682 10 980; www.residenzafarneseroma.it;
Via del Mascherone 59; s €140-290, d €160-290;
⬛ Via Giulia; ☒ ⬛
With its billiard table, pot plants and chessboard floor, this relaxed four-star resembles
a colonial club in the tropics. Rooms are
spread over two floors and decked out in
classical style – antique furniture, parquet
and floor-to-ceiling curtains. Pick of the
bunch is room 309, which retains its original 15th-century fresco.

HOTEL TEATRO DI POMPEO

Map pp74–5   Hotel €€

☎ 06 683 00 170; www.hotelteatrodipompeo.it;
Largo del Pallaro 8; s €140-160, d €180-210;
⬛ Corso Vittorio Emanuele II; ☒
Built on top of a theatre that Pompey constructed in 55 BC (now the breakfast room),
this family-run hotel is tucked away behind
the Campo de' Fiori. Rooms are comfortable, with a charmingly old-fashioned feel:
the pick are those on the 3rd floor, with
sloping wood-beamed ceilings.

CASA DI SANTA BRIGIDA

Map pp74–5   Religious Institution €€

☎ 06 688 92 596; www.brigidine.org; Piazza
Farnese 96, entrance Via di Monserrato 54;
s/d €110/190; ⬛ Via di Monserrato; ☒ ⬛
This isn't the cheapest convent in Rome,
but it's certainly one of the best. The location is superb, overlooking beautiful Piazza
Farnese, from this picturesque *palazzo*
(where the Swedish St Brigid died in 1373).
Rooms are pleasant and no-frills, the nuns
coolly cordial. No curfew! Meals cost €20.

CASA BANZO Map pp74–5   B&B €€

☎ 06 683 39 09; www.casabanzo.it; Piazza del
Monte di Pietà 30; r €100-200, apt €200-300;
☒ Via Arenula; ☒
Not an easy place to find (there's no sign),
Casa Banzo is stunningly close to Il Campo,
and has an eclectic mix of rooms – none
quite as grand as the 2nd-floor frescoed
reception hall. It's a European B&B, rather
than a hotel, with seven unique rooms on
different floors of the Renaissance *palazzo* (no lift), each with an independent

top picks

VIEWS

- Hotel Forum (p250) The forums, Colosseum and Campidoglio spread out before you.
- Hotel Scalinata di Spagna (p255) Soaring views over Roman rooftops, from the top of the Spanish Steps.
- Albergo Abruzzi (p250) Wake up to the Pantheon looming over vibrant Piazza della Rotonda.
- Portrait Suites (p254) The best roof terrace in town.
- Hotel Sant'Anselmo (p261) Rooms with terraces have dreamy rooftop views.

entrance and character. On the 4th floor, there is a light, bright two-bed apartment that sleeps up to six.

RELAIS GROUP PALACE
Map pp74–5   Hotel €€
☎ 06 976 01 286; www.relaisgrouphotel.com; Via dei Banchi Vecchi 115; d €80-230; 🚊 Via Arenula; 🛇
Handily set next door to the Libreria Babele (see p174), this is a gay-friendly place that has six rooms, rather sombrely decorated with lots of wood, wallpaper and oil paintings.

ALBERGO DEL SOLE Map pp74–5   Hotel €€
☎ 06 687 94 46; www.solealbiscione.it; Via del Biscione 76; s €100-125, d €120-160, s/d with shared bathroom €70-105; 🚊 Corso Vittorio Emanuele II
The oldest hotel in Rome, this place dates to 1462, and the complex warren of corridors and low wood-beamed ceilings give credence to its medieval roots, though the décor is standard hotel fare. Rooms are basic; some have more character than others. The 2nd-floor roof terrace is a definite plus, there's wi-fi, and the almost-on-the-Campo location is a lively spot. No credit cards.

HOTEL SMERALDO Map pp74–5   Hotel €€
☎ 06 687 59 29; www.smeraldoroma.com; Vicolo dei Chiodaroli 9; d €110-145; 🚊 Via Arenula; 🛇 🖳
Reasonable value and a central location are what you get at the Smeraldo. Just down the road from Campo de' Fiori, its rooms are simple and plain, in varying hues of beige, with tiled floors and small bathrooms. Up on the 5th floor, the rooftop garden is an added bonus. There's wi-fi in reception, and wheelchair access.

TRIDENTE

Rome's glossiest district is chock full of designer boutiques catering to high-rolling shoppers, and encompasses the Spanish Steps, Piazza di Spagna and Piazza del Popolo. There are lots of restaurants around here, but this is a district that's in its element during the day – after dark it's somewhat subdued. However, the Centro Storico is about a 10- to 15-minute walk away. Hotels tend to be upper range, though there are a few reasonably priced options.

PIAZZA DEL POPOLO & AROUND

HOTEL DE RUSSIE Map pp96–7   Hotel €€€
☎ 06 32 88 81; www.hotelderussie.it; Via del Babuino 9; s €270, d €390-410; Ⓜ Flaminio; Ⓟ 🛇 🖳
A favourite of Hollywood celebs, the historic de Russie is almost on Piazza del Popolo, and has exquisite terraced gardens. The décor is softly luxurious in many shades of grey, and the rooms offer state-of-the-art entertainment systems, massive mosaic-tiled bathrooms and the softest linen sheets. To wash away the stress of the city, the hotel's health spa is one of Rome's best, and organic toiletries are provided in the rooms. For more on the hotel's glittering past, see the boxed text, p254.

MARGUTTA 54 Map pp96–7   Hotel €€€
☎ 06 321 27 94; www.margutta54.it; Via Margutta 54; d from €290; Ⓜ Spagna; 🛇 🖳
Four suites, impeccably luxurious and decorated in sleek, lush Italian chic, are housed in former artists' studios, overlooking a courtyard off the criminally pretty Via Margutta, which is lined with upmarket galleries. The rooms are unusually huge for Rome, starting from 45 sq m. There's no restaurant, but the butler will bring breakfast to your room!

HOTEL LOCARNO Map pp96–7   Hotel €€€
☎ 06 361 08 41; www.hotellocarno.com; Via della Penna 22; s €130-200, d €200-320; Ⓜ Flaminio; 🛇 🖳
With its ivy-clad exterior, stained-glass doors and rattling cage-lift, the Locarno is an Art Deco classic – the kind of place Hercule Poirot might stay if he were in town. Rooms, spread over two sites – the main building and, over the road, the

SLEEPING TRIDENTE

THE DE RUSSIE – DEATH & GENIUS

For English Grand Tourists and regal Russians in the 19th century, there was only one hotel in Rome, the Hotel de Russie et des Iles Britanniques, as it was then known. Prince Napoleon-Jerome, nephew of the emperor, even died here in 1891, though this was no reflection of the service.

The royal death didn't put visitors off, and over the next decades, Picasso, Jean Cocteau and the entire Ballet Russes stayed here, while they were creating the ballet Parade, for which Picasso designed the décor and scenery. In a letter to his mother, Cocteau described how he could pick oranges from his hotel balcony. Stravinsky later joined the group, and he and Picasso explored Rome together. Picasso also met his first wife, Olga Khokhlova, while in Rome (she was a dancer with the ballet and daughter of a Russian colonel; he was desperate to get married, having already proposed to, and been rejected by, two different women that year).

Picasso's 10-week trip to Italy and consequent encounters with classical sculpture were to have a resounding impact on his work, and something of an impact on the Hotel de Russie, which later named a suite in his honour. With the outbreak of WWII, the party was over, and the hotel closed. Until 1993, it housed the RAI (Radiotelevisione Italiana) offices, until it was refurbished and reopened in 2000. Today it attracts contemporary glitterati such as Brad Pitt and George Clooney.

Anahi annex – vary in size and décor. Some have red silk wallpaper and period furniture, a bit tired but full of period charm, while others have light cream walls and wrought-iron beds. All have spotless bathrooms, many with vintage tiling. Rooms in the Anahi wing are nonsmoking and cheaper as there's no room service. There's a lovely roof garden and a restaurant, and guests have free use of bicycles. There's wheelchair access, too.

HOTEL FORTE Map pp96–7   Hotel €€
☎ 06 320 76 25; www.hotelforte.com; Via Margutta 61; s €125-176, d €85-220; Ⓜ Spagna; 🅧
Hotel Forte is a friendly little hotel in a lovely 17th-century *palazzo* around the corner from Piazza di Spagna. It's a bright place decorated in a cluttered, faux-classical style with fake columns in the corridors and antiques in every corner. The rooms are comfortable, if cramped. Some feature heavy fabrics and ornate wallpaper; others are done up in simpler white-and-beige colour schemes. Wi-fi is available.

OKAPI ROOMS Map pp96–7   Hotel €
☎ 06 326 09 815; www.okapirooms.it; Via della Penna 57; s €80-90, d €100-120; Ⓜ Flaminio; 🅧
Run by the owners of Pensione Panda (opposite), 20-room Okapi is housed in a town house in a great location close to Piazza del Popolo. Rooms are simple, small, airy affairs with cream walls, terracotta floors and double glazing. Some are decorated with ancient-style carvings and several have small terraces. Bathrooms are tiny but sparkling clean.

PIAZZA DI SPAGNA & AROUND

HASSLER VILLA MEDICI

Map pp96–7   Hotel €€€
☎ 06 69 93 40; www.hotelhassler.com; Piazza della Trinità dei Monti 6; s €440-470, d €550-850; Ⓜ Spagna; 🅧 🖵
Sumptuously surmounting the Spanish Steps, the Hassler is a byword for old-school luxury. It's the place for international blockbuster movie photocalls, and a long line of VIPs have stayed here, enjoying the ravishing views and sumptuous hospitality. Rooms, all unique, are mod-conned and opulent, and the service is slick and professional. The restaurant Imago serves fine food overlooking amazing panoramas. Under the same management is nearby boutique wonder Il Palazzetto (☎ 06 699 341 000; www.ilpalazzettoroma.com; Vicolo del Bottino 8), with views over the Spanish Steps, for those who want a more intimate experience.

PORTRAIT SUITES Map pp96–7   Hotel €€€
☎ 06 68 28 31; www.portraitsuites.com; Via Bocca di Leone, 23; r €300-690; Ⓜ Flaminio; Ⓟ 🅧 🖵
Owned by the Salvatore Ferragamo family – designer royalty – this is a discreet, exclusive boutique residence, designed by Florentine wonder-architect Michele Bonan. It's also something of a museum, filled with sketches and maquettes by Ferragamo. There are 14 suites and studios – as exquisitely styled as a Ferragamo suit – across six floors in a townhouse overlooking via Condotti, plus a dreamy 360-degree roof terrace and made-in-heaven staff. There's no restaurant, but you can have meals delivered, and breakfast is served in your room or on the terrace.

GREGORIANA Map pp96–7 Hotel €€€
☎ 06 679 42 69; www.hotelgregoriana.it; Via Gregoriana 18; d €228-248; Ⓜ Spagna; ⬛
This low-key, polished Art Deco hotel is fantastically set behind the Spanish Steps, and offers rooms with carved, curved maplewood headboards, lots of gleaming rosewood, and friendly, unpretentious service. Rather than being numbered, rooms are signified with letters by the 1930s French fashion illustrator Erté.

HOTEL SCALINATA DI SPAGNA
Map pp96–7 Hotel €€€
☎ 06 699 40 896; www.hotelscalinata.com; Piazza della Trinità dei Monti 17; d €130-370; Ⓜ Spagna; ⬛ ▣
Given its location – perched alongside the Spanish Steps – the Scalinata is surprisingly modestly priced. An informal and friendly place, it's something of a warren, with a great roof terrace and low corridors leading off to smallish, old-fashioned, yet romantic rooms (think plush furnishings and gilt-edged mirrors), the best with balconies. Book early for a room with a view.

CROSSING CONDOTTI
Map pp96–7 Pensione €€
☎ 06 699 20 633; www.crossingcondotti.com; Via Mario de' Fiori 28; r €180-280; Ⓜ Spagna; ⬛
A five-room place, this is one of Rome's new breed of upmarket guesthouses, where all the fittings, linen, and comforts are top of the range, but prices are kept lower than equivalent hotels because there is no restaurant, concierge etc. Rooms are character-filled, antique-furnished, stylish and comfortable, and it's smack bang in designer heaven. There's no breakfast, but there's a well-stocked kitchen with drinks and a Nespresso machine.

HOTEL MOZART Map pp96–7 Hotel €€
☎ 06 360 01 915; www.hotelmozart.com; Via dei Greci 23b; s €115-165, d €155-260; Ⓜ Spagna; ⬛ ▣
A credit-card's flick from Via del Corso, the Mozart has classic, immaculate rooms, decorated in dove greys, eggshell blues, and rosy pinks, with comfortable beds, gleaming linen and polished wooden furniture; deluxe rooms have Jacuzzi baths and small terraces. Upstairs, the roof garden is a memorable place for a sundowner in summer. It's opposite the Conservatorio Musica

di Roma, so you may hear classical strains drifting over the street. The lowest prices quoted are without breakfast.

RESIDENCE VITTORIA
Map pp96–7 Apartments €€
☎ 06 699 25 834; www.residencevittoria.com; Via Vittoria 64; per week d €550-850, 4-person apt €1000; Ⓜ Spagna; ⬛ ▣
This converted townhouse, bang in designer central on Via Vittoria, is not a hotel, but offers a range of luminous rooms and apartments, some with beamed or frescoed ceilings. The larger apartments are extremely spacious. Prices might appear steep but they compare well with local hotel rates.

PENSIONE PANDA Map pp96–7 Pensione €
☎ 06 678 01 79; www.hotelpanda.it; Via della Croce 35; s €75-80, d €98-108, tr €130-140, q €170-180; Ⓜ Spagna; ⬛
In an area of Rome where a bargain is a Bulgari watch bought in the sales, this lone *pensione* boldly flies the flag for the budget traveller. There really is nowhere else you can get a room this close to the Spanish Steps for so little. Rooms are small, basic, and clean, but it's really about the location. Air-con costs an extra €6 and wi-fi is available (reception only).

TREVI, QUIRINALE & VIA VENETO
TREVI FOUNTAIN TO THE QUIRINALE

CASA HOWARD Map p100 Hotel €€
☎ 06 699 24 555; www.casahoward.com; Via Sistina 149 & Via Capo le Case 18; s €140-220, d €190-250; Ⓜ Spagna; ⬛ ▣
This richly decorated boutique hotel, split between two nearby houses, has a great location and only 10 rooms, ranging from the funky Zebra room to the chinz-tastic Flower room. The Via Sistina rooms were designed by Tommaso Ziffer, also responsible for celebrity hotspot Hotel de Russie. Three of the rooms have private but not ensuite bathrooms. Both properties have Turkish hammams, which cost a cheeky €25/50 (Capo le Case/Sistina) to use. Continental breakfast, served in the rooms, also costs an extra €10 per person.

B&B 3 COINS Map p100 — B&B €€

☎ 06 446 06 34; www.3coinsbb.com; Via dei Crociferi 26; s €70-130, d €80-150, with shared bathroom s €60-90, d €90-100; Ⓜ Via del Tritone; ⌘
A coin's lob from the Trevi Fountain, this modest B&B is snug and quaint. A steep climb up to the 3rd floor and you'll find a warm, character-filled apartment full of family knick-knacks. No two of the seven rooms are alike – some are tiny, some bigger, some are carpeted and two have external bathrooms, but all are clean and cosy.

PIAZZA BARBERINI & VIA VENETO

HOTEL EDEN Map p100 — Hotel €€€

☎ 06 47 81 21; www.hotel-eden.it; Via Ludovisi 49; s €280-465, d €300-535; Ⓜ Barberini; Ⓟ ⌘ ⌘ ▣
Impeccable service, refined rooms and superb views are the deal at the Eden, one of Rome's most glamorous hotels. Rooms vary but most feature traditional antique furniture, thick carpets and gleaming marble-clad bathrooms, and there's a highly rated rooftop restaurant.

HOTEL MODIGLIANI Map p100 — Hotel €€

☎ 06 428 15 226; www.hotelmodigliani.com; Via della Purificazione 42; s €120-160, d €110-280; Ⓜ Barberini; ⌘
Run by an artistic couple, the 23-room Modigliani is all about thoughtful attention to detail and customer service. The dove-grey rooms are spacious and light, with rich red and gold bedspreads, and the best rooms have views and balconies, either outside, or over the quiet internal courtyard garden that's a lovely place for a drink. There are two apartments, one sleeping up to four, with a kitchenette, and another sleeping up to six. There's wi-fi too.

DAPHNE INN Map p100 — Hotel €€

☎ 06 478 23 529; www.daphne-rome.com; Via di San Basilio 55; d €130-220, with shared bathroom €90-160; Ⓜ Barberini; ⌘ ▣
Daphne is a gem, run by an American Italian couple, with chic, sleek, comfortable rooms. They come in various shapes and sizes but the overall look is minimalist modern with cooling earth tones and linear, unfussy furniture. The beds and linen are lovely, English-speaking staff are exceedingly helpful, and breakfasts are delicious. There are 15 rooms in two locations: this one off Via Veneto (the pick, and every room is ensuite) and a second one at Via degli Avignonesi 20, towards the Trevi Fountain. Wi-fi is available.

FELLINI B&B Map p100 — B&B €€

☎ 06 427 42 732; www.fellinibnb.com; Via Rasella 55; s €70-180, d €90-200, apt €200-370; Ⓜ Barberini; ⌘
A multistorey warren of bright, plain rooms, cheery, efficient Fellini is named for Italy's great director, who made an icon of the nearby Trevi fountain, and film posters along the hallways fit the theme. All the spic-and-span rooms have satellite TV, good beds and well-equipped bathrooms. The standout option here is the top-floor five-person apartment, which has a huge terrace with a view. It's always worth asking for discounts.

DOMUS JULIA Map p100 — B&B €€

☎ 06 474 57 65; www.domusjulia.it; Via Rasella 32; s €70-140, d €80-180, ste €90-240; Ⓜ Barberini; ⌘
The two large suites in this 18th-century palazzo are ideal for a stolen weekend with a loved one, fitting the romantic bill with their parquet floors, exposed wood-beamed ceilings and imposing antique furniture. The other four rooms are smaller and more modern but smart and spacious all the same.

HOTEL ERCOLI Map p100 — Pensione €

☎ 06 474 54 54; www.hotelercoli.com; Via Collina 48; s €60-90, d €70-110; Ⓜ Via Piave; ⌘
Old-fashioned and friendly, the 3rd-floor (there's an elderly cage lift) Ercoli is a straight-up pensione, renovated a couple of years back. It's popular with foreign students. The 14 rooms are functional rather than memorable, but they're all sparkling clean with tiled floors, breakfast is included and the air-con works.

MONTI, ESQUILINO & SAN LORENZO

The bulk of Rome's budget accommodation is concentrated in the Termini area, around the central station. It has its shady sides, but has been cleaned up in recent years and there are now some good places to stay. However, lone travellers, particularly women, should still take all the usual safety precautions, particularly around Via Giovanni Giolitti.

Monti, a wealthy yet bohemian district, sandwiched between Via Nazionale and Via Cavour, is a very attractive area, with some lovely *enoteche* (wine bars) and restaurants to keep you entertained in the evening, and boutiques to browse by day.

ESQUILINO

HOTEL COLUMBIA Map pp106–7   Hotel €€
☎ 06 488 35 09; www.hotelcolumbia.com; Via del Viminale 15; s €160-181, d €199-234; Ⓜ Termini or Repubblica; 🔀 🖳
In a workaday area that's a mere aria from the Opera House, the friendly Columbia sports a polished look with beamed or exposed stone ceilings, and dark-wood cabinets. The white-walled rooms are bright and surprisingly full of character, all have data plugs for laptop-toters and some have beautiful Murano crystal chandeliers. The breakfast is good, and in summer is served on the pretty roof terrace.

RADISSON SAS Map pp106–7   Hotel €€
☎ 06 44 48 41; www.radissonblu.com/eshotel-rome; Via Filippo Turati 171; s €130-150, d €150-220; Ⓜ Vittorio Emanuele; 🔀 🖳 🖳
The Radisson SAS is a swish, cutting-edge hotel unlike any other in Rome. Its location is not the best considering the price bracket, but it's a popular choice with business travellers and design-conscious customers who appreciate the minimalist sci-fi décor and hi-tech gadgetry. The poolside rooftop bar serves swell cocktails and offers views over Termini's busy rail tracks, and the pool is open to nonguests for €40 per day.

HOTEL BRITANNIA Map pp106–7   Hotel €€
☎ 06 488 31 53; www.hotelbritannia.it; Via Napoli 64; r €105-200; 🖳 Via Nazionale; 🔀
With the air of an overdecorated gentlemen's club, the Britannia is a popular four-star just off Via Nazionale. Dodgy frescoes and 19th-century horse-and-hound paintings hang on walls; floors are parquet one minute, inlaid marble or carpet the next; leather armchairs are tastefully arranged in the wood-panelled bar. The room décor is similarly ad hoc, with antique furniture, floral chintz and sparkling marble-clad bathrooms. Wi-fi is available. Check the website for last-minute offers.

FORUS INN Map pp106–7   Inn €€
☎ 06 478 24 745; www.forusinn.com; Via Cavour 194; s €100-120, d €120-160, tr €140-180, q €160-200; Ⓜ Cavour; 🔀
An elegant bolthole on busy Via Cavour, the Forus Inn offers discreet comfort, classical style and good soundproofing. The 10 rooms are small but prettily decorated with parquet floors, rich fabrics and framed prints; some even have their original wood ceilings. Mod cons include plasma TVs and broadband internet connections.

58 LE REAL DE LUXE Map pp106–7   B&B €€
☎ 06 482 35 66; www.lerealdeluxe.com; Via Cavour 58; r €110-170; Ⓜ Termini; 🔀
This cosy, peaceful 12-room B&B is on the 4th floor of a tall 19th-century town house on busy Via Cavour. Rooms are small, but a lot of care has gone into their decoration, especially the superior rooms: think leather armchairs and plasma TVs, crystal chandeliers, polished bedsteads and parquet floors. The sexy walk-in showers also merit a mention, as does the panoramic sun terrace.

NICOLAS INN Map pp106–7   B&B €€
☎ 06 976 18 483; www.nicolasinn.com; Via Cavour 295, 1st fl; s €90-150, d €100-180; Ⓜ Cavour; 🔀
This sunny B&B is at the bottom of noisy Via Cavour, a stone's throw from the Imperial Forums. Run by a welcoming young couple, it has four big guest rooms, each of which boasts homely furnishings with wrought-iron beds, colourful pictures and a large bathroom. For such a central place it's also remarkably quiet, and has a long line of satisfied customers.

66 IMPERIAL INN
Map pp106–7   B&B €€
☎ 06 482 56 48; www.66imperialinn.com; Via del Viminale 66; s €80-160, d €80-170; 🖳 Via Nazionale; 🔀
Sister of 58 Le Real De Luxe, this smart B&B, with a prettily green-and-grey frescoed reception, has only five cool cream rooms. With their high ceilings, lush green carpets and double glazing, they are airy, comfortable and quiet. The bathrooms are spotless and the Jacuzzi showers are a treat.

HOTEL DOLOMITI Map pp106–7   Hotel €€

☎ 06 495 72 56; www.hotel-dolomiti.it; Via San Martino della Battaglia 11; s €60-130, d €75-170, tr €95-210, q €120-250; Ⓜ Castro Pretorio; ✕ 🖳
Welcoming, family-run Dolomiti has rooms on the 4th floor of an apartment block. The rooms are colour-coordinated with cream walls, cherry-wood furniture, rich-red fabrics and prints of chubby-cheeked cherubs. The same family also manages the Hotel Lachea two floors below. The combined reception is on the 1st floor.

HOTEL & HOSTEL DES ARTISTES

Map pp106–7   Hostel €, Hotel €€

☎ 06 445 43 65; www.hoteldesartistes.com; Via Villafranca 20; dm €10-24, r €95-210, with shared bathroom €55-95; Ⓜ Castro Pretorio; ✕ 🖳
Rooms here are decked out in wood and gold, with faux-antique furniture, rich reds, and pink high-sheen bedspreads and curtains. There are also decent bathrooms and satellite TV. It offers discounts for longer stays and/or cash payment. There are some plain, four- to six-person dorm rooms on the 2nd floor, with a fan. The hotel runs the nearby clean and functional hostel Carlito's Way (☎ 06 444 03 84; www.rome-hotel-carlitosway. com; Via Villafranca 10), which also has some smart hotel-style doubles.

HOTEL GIULIANA Map pp106–7   Hotel €

☎ 06 488 07 95; www.hotelgiuliana.com; Via Agostino de Pretis 70; s €50-100, d €65-160; Ⓜ Termini; ✕
A cosy little hotel run by a jolly Londoner and her daughter, the Giuliana ticks all the right boxes. Its rooms, divided into standard and superior, are dapper; the location, near Via Nazionale, is convenient; and the service is cheery and efficient. Travellers for whom a holiday without tea is no holiday should ask for one of the three rooms with a tea service, while smokers can sneak a quick puff on the small internal balcony. There's a 5% discount for payments in cash.

HOTEL IGEA Map pp106–7   Hotel €

☎ 06 446 69 11; www.hoteligearome.com; Via Principe Amedeo 97; s €50-80, d €90-120; Ⓜ Termini; 🖳
The Igea has an old-fashioned air, right down to the staff with candy-floss hair. The rooms are spacious, plain, functional and extremely clean; some are a little gloomy and some feature 1970s tiling. There's a

preponderance of institutional green. Nods to modernity include satellite TV, hairdryers and free internet.

ROMAE Map pp106–7   Hotel €

☎ 06 446 35 54; www.hotelromae.com; Via Palestro 49; s €35-160, d €50-165; Ⓜ Castro Pretorio; ✕ 🖳
Run by the same folk who owned Yellow Hostel, this is the more grown-up version. It's a welcoming place, with English-speaking staff. None of the rooms are huge, but nab one of the renovated rooms, which are very sleek, white and bright, with nice rainfall showers. Many of the others have chequered tiled floors and large wooden bedsteads, and there are also larger rooms for families. Wi-fi is available and you can even rent a laptop.

HOTEL CONTINENTALE

Map pp106–7   Hotel €

☎ 06 445 03 82; www.hotel-continentale.com; Via Palestro 49; s €40-60, d €75-125; Ⓜ Castro Pretorio; ✕
One of several budget *pensioni* in the same building, the Continentale is a reasonable cheapie, with rooms on the 2nd and 3rd floors and its reception on the ground floor. If you've got a lot of luggage you might have trouble squeezing into the rattling old lift, but once up on your floor you'll find the pastel-coloured rooms are clean, if a tad drab. The staff are friendly and speak several languages, including English and French.

HOTEL D'ESTE Map pp106–7   Hotel €

☎ 06 446 56 07; www.hotel-deste.com; Via Carlo Alberto 4b; s €50-90, d €60-140, tr €80-160; Ⓜ Vittorio Emanuele
A charming 31-room hotel near the Basilica di Santa Maria Maggiore, Hotel d'Este is full of character. Chandeliers, wood panelling and brass banisters abound and the guest rooms are big and high-ceilinged, and some have small balconies. The quiet, old-fashioned atmosphere is a wonderful antidote to the frenzied noise outside. Breakfast is served on the 1st-floor terrace when it's warm and in a curious wood hut–like room when it's not.

HOTEL SWEET HOME

Map pp106–7   Hotel €

☎ 06 488 09 54; www.hotelsweethome.it, in Italian; Via Principe Amedeo 47; s €40-85, d €60-125, with shared bathroom s €30-65, d €45-95; Ⓜ Termini

A throwback to *nonna*'s day, this modest hotel is classic old school, with an air of fading gentility. Rooms have been spruced up and are pleasant, varying in size and comfort. Those facing away from the street are larger and quieter.

ALBERGO GIUSTI

Map pp106–7   Religious Institution €

☎ 06 704 53 462; s.annagiusti@tiscali.it; Via Giusti 5; s/d/tr €50/90/120; Ⓜ Vittorio Emanuele; ⊠

Run by the sisters of Sant'Anna, this spartan, spotlessly clean bed-and-breakfast option is in a convent in the side streets near the Basilica di Santa Maria Maggiore. Rooms are salmon-pink or minty-green and a few have small balconies. The nuns are hospitable, if rather stern, and it feels very safe – a tranquil haven close to Termini.

HOTEL CASTELFIDARDO

Map pp106–7   Hotel €

☎ 06 446 46 38; www.hotelcastelfidardo.com; Via Castelfidardo 31; s €40-90, d €50-120, tr €120-150, with shared bathroom s €40-60, d €60-100; Ⓜ Castro Pretorio; ⊠ ▢

Castelfidardo has high-ceilinged rooms that are not too cramped. These rooms are basic but reasonably smart and have swagged curtains, wallpaper borders and tiled floors. In the same building, and run by the same family, the Hotel Lazzari (☎ 06 494 13 78; www.hotellazzari.com; s €50-90, d €80-120, with shared bathroom s €40-60, d €60-100) offers more of the same.

THE BEEHIVE

Map pp106–7   Hostel €

☎ 06 447 04 553; www.the-beehive.com; Via Marghera 8; dm €20-30, d with shared bathroom €70-95, tr €95-120; Ⓜ Termini; ▢

More boutique chic than backpacker crash pad, the Beehive is one of the best hostels in town. Run by a southern Californian couple, it's an oasis of style with original artworks on the walls, funky modular furniture, a vegetarian café and a yoga studio. Beds are in a spotless, eight-person mixed dorm or in one of six private double rooms. Needless to say, it's popular, so make sure you book ahead. There's an on-site internet lounge, a book exchange and vegan and vegetarian café (breakfast €5, dinner dish of the day €6.50), garden courtyard and yoga studio. Massage costs €35.

WELROME HOTEL

Map pp106–7   Hotel €

☎ 06 478 24 343; www.welrome.it; Via Calatafimi 15-19; s €40-100, d €50-110, tr €105-148, q €120-187; Ⓜ Termini

The chatty owner of the seven-room Welrome has a personal mission to look after her guests: not only does she take huge pride in her small, spotless hotel but she enthusiastically points out the cheapest places to eat, tells you where not to waste your time and what's good to do. Families should go for the huge room named after Piazza di Spagna.

HOTEL CERVIA

Map pp106–7   Pensione €

☎ 06 49 10 57; www.hotelcerviaroma.com; Via Palestro 55; s €35-70, d €50-90, with shared bathroom s €25-55, d €40-65; Ⓜ Castro Pretorio

Run by two chatty, multilingual ladies, the Cervia, open since 1956, offers plain, high-ceilinged rooms and a warm welcome. There's nothing glamorous about the small rooms (the bathrooms are miniscule), with big windows and tiled floors, but it's a friendly, reasonable-value place. Children are welcome, with free cots available on request. On the 2nd floor (no lift) the Hotel Restivo (☎ 06 446 21 72; www.hotelrestivo.com) is run by the same people and has some modernised rooms in chocolate-brown hues, plus some old-style classics.

PAPA GERMANO

Map pp106–7   Hotel €

☎ 06 48 69 19; www.hotelpapagermano.it; Via Calatafimi 14a; dm €21-28, s €55-85, d €60-100, with shared bathroom s €35-50, d €55-85; Ⓜ Termini; ⊠ ▢

Easygoing and popular, Papa Germano is a budget stalwart. There are various sleeping options, ranging from four-person dorms to private rooms with or without private bathrooms. It's a bit institutional feeling, but the décor is plain and fairly smart, and all are clean. Breakfast is included, internet costs €2 per hour, and air-con is €5.

ALESSANDRO PALACE HOSTEL

Map pp106–7   Hostel €

☎ 06 446 19 58; www.hostelsalessandro.com; Via Vicenza 42; dm €18-35, d €70-110; Ⓜ Termini or Castro Pretorio; ⊠ ▢

This long-standing favourite appeals to both budgeting families and backpackers, and offers spic-and-span, terracotta-floored doubles, triples and quads, as well as dorms sleeping from four to eight, all with cheery-if-not-chic bedspreads. Every room has its own bathroom plus hairdryer. In some you can't open the windows. There's a bar downstairs, which has satellite TV. Internet and wi-fi are available, and there's 24-hour reception and no curfew. The same owners also run the less palatial, and thus cheaper, Alessandro Downtown Hostel (Map pp106–7; ☎ 06 443 40 147; Via Carlo Cattaneo 23).

HOTEL BEAUTIFUL Map pp106–7 Hotel €
☎ 06 447 03 927; www.solomonhotels.com; Via Milazzo 8; dm €16-27, s €25-40, d €45-80; Ⓜ Termini; 🏡

A hostel-hotel hybrid, this two-star place has 14 comfortable, clean, unexciting but bright rooms. There are doubles, triples and dorms, all with high ceilings and their own bathrooms. Reception is 24 hours. The same management also runs the popular Hostel Beautiful (Map pp106–7; ☎ 06 446 58 90; Via Napoleone III 35; dm €20-35; 🖳) on the other side of Stazione Termini.

FUNNY PALACE Map pp106–7 Hostel €
☎ 06 447 03 523; www.funnyhostel.com; Via Varese 33; dm €15-25, s/d €30/70, d with shared bathroom €55-100; 🖳

Run by a friendly international crew, with the Splashnet Laundry as their office-laundry-internet café, this great little back-packers hostel has doubles, triples and quads, with a comfortable, homey feel. Thoughtful touches such as clean towels, a bottle of wine on arrival and vouchers for breakfast in a nearby café make it an excellent choice. Wi-fi is available, as is Skype. No credit cards. Management also runs the similar Amazing Place, around the corner.

M&J HOSTEL Map pp106–7 Hostel €
☎ 06 446 28 02; www.mejhostel.com; Via Solferino 9; dm €10-35, s €50-70, d €60-100; Ⓜ Termini; 🏡 🖳

The long-established M&J is a hostel-cum-hotel run by two well-travelled brothers. There are a number of brightly painted dorms (up to 10 people), one of which is female-only and some of which have their own bathrooms. The doubles are more up-market, decorated in a chic, Zen style, and have air-con (dorms don't). There's 24-hour reception and a kitchen. The owners operate the Living Room bar downstairs, where breakfast is served as well as cheap meals, and which opens late. You can get deals if you book online. There's also wi-fi.

GAY STAYS

Rome's accommodation scene is fairly conservative but the following are all gay-friendly:
- 58 Le Real Deluxe (p257)
- Hotel Florida (p263)
- La Foresteria Orsa Maggiore (p262)
- Relais Group Palace (p253)
- La Casetta nel Bosco (www.lacasettanelbosco .com) Around 50km northwest of Rome, close to the Terme di Stigliano, this rurally set place has bright, simple rooms.

For more on gay and lesbian life in Rome, see p291.

THE YELLOW Map pp106–7 Hostel €
☎ 06 493 82 682; www.the-yellow.com; Via Palestro 44; dm €18-35; Ⓜ Castro Pretorio; 🏡 🖳

Popular Yellow caters to a youthful, party-loving crowd (there's even an age limit – 18 to 40). Décor is bright, clean and funky, featuring Starsky-and-Hutch stencils on the walls, and mixed dorms sleep between four and 12 people in basic bunks, with barracks-style showers and toilets (bigger dorms have bathrooms down the hall). Internet is free, there's wi-fi, and the bar downstairs (where you can buy breakfast), open till 2am, has outdoor tables. Reception is 24 hours.

PIAZZA DELLA REPUBLICA & AROUND

RESIDENZA CELLINI Map pp106–7 Hotel €€
☎ 06 478 25 204; www.residenzacellini.it; Via Modena 5; d €145-240, ste €165-280; Ⓜ Repubblica; 🏡 🖳

With grown-up furnishings featuring potted palms, polished wood, pale-yellow walls, oil paintings, and a hint of chintz, this charming hotel offers 11 spacious, elegant rooms, all with satellite TV and Jacuzzi or hydro-massage showers. There's wi-fi, too, and a sunny flower-surrounded terrace for summer breakfasts.

SUITE DREAMS Map pp106–7 Hotel €€
☎ 06 489 13 907; www.suitedreams.it; Via Modena 5; s €110-130, d €130-180, ste €200-250; Ⓜ Repubblica; 🏡 🖳

This popular place offers 15 rooms styled with expensive-looking neutrals, slate greys, chocolate-browns and contemporary art. Each has parquet floors, Frette linen and big wardrobes, and there's an impressive suite with a big round Jacuzzi. Check the website for special offers.

HOTEL OCEANIA Map pp106–7 Hotel €€
☎ 06 482 46 96; www.hoteloceania.it; Via Firenze 38; s €70-140, d €100-180, tr €125-215; Ⓜ Repubblica; ☐

The homely, quaint Oceania is a welcome break from the bustle of the streets five floors below. It's an intimate, old-fashioned hotel, with 15 bright-walled and colourfully curtained rooms spread over two adjacent apartments. Extras include satellite TV, modem plugs and free internet, excellent coffee and English newspapers. Book early.

HOTEL ANTICA LOCANDA
Map pp106–7 Hotel €€
☎ 06 478 81 729; www.antica-locanda.com; Via Boschetto 84; s €70-140, d €90-160; Ⓜ Cavour; ☒ ☐

In the wealthy-boho Monti district, with views over a narrow cobbled street that's one of the area's main drags, this little hotel has character-filled rooms of different shapes and sizes, all named after great composers. They're decorated with antiques and wooden furniture, with some carved wooden headboards and wood beams, and there are some family rooms.

TARGET INN Map pp106–7 Inn €€
☎ 06 474 53 99; www.targetinn.com; Via Modena 5, 3rd fl; s €70-100, d €100-150, ste €180-240; Ⓜ Repubblica; ☒

Sleek, minimalist Target combines red leather furniture, gleaming white walls, abstract art, black wardrobes and traditional parquet floors. Families should go for the suite, which sleeps four.

ABERDEEN HOTEL Map pp106–7 Hotel €€
☎ 06 482 39 20; www.travel.it/roma/aberdeen; Via Firenze 48; s €80-95, d €95-140, tr €130-160; Ⓜ Repubblica; ☒ ☐

For a decent, easygoing hotel in a well-connected central location, you could do a lot worse than this sparkling three-star. The spacious rooms feature chequered chessboard floors, comfy beds (orthopaedic mattresses are standard) and spotless mint-green bathrooms. Buffet breakfast is served under a charming coffered wood ceiling and everywhere you go the staff are cheerful, cordial and helpful.

CELIO HILL & LATERAN

HOTEL CELIO Map p115 Hotel €€
☎ 06 704 95 333; www.hotelcelio.com; Via dei Santissimi Quattro Coronati 35c; s €100-180, d €150-230; Ⓜ Colosseo; ☒ ☐

Not one for minimalists, this richly decorated small hotel crams in the kitsch, featuring mosaic floors with heavy baroque furnishings, frescoes and trompe l'oeil, no matter how snug the room. Equipped with flat-screen TVs and wi-fi, the rooms are each named for Renaissance artists. Upstairs on the roof there's a mini-gym with jogging machines and inspirational photos of Sophia Loren. Wheelchair access.

AVENTINO & TESTACCIO

The Aventino area (close to Circo Massimo) is a wonderfully peaceful and picturesque place to stay, a bit removed from the city centre. Testaccio, which has some excellent restaurants and happening nightlife, is a mere hip wiggle away.

HOTEL SANT'ANSELMO Map p120 Hotel €€
☎ 06 574 52 31; www.aventinohotels.com; Via S Melania 19; s €160-220, d €180-270; ☒ Via Marmorata; Ⓟ ☒

Enchanting, peaceful Aventine hill, all terracotta walls and umbrella pines, is one of Rome's most sought-after residential areas, and this 34-room hotel is wonderfully romantic and fantastically over the top, with modern twists giving the design a sassy edge. Rooms have carved beds or four-posters, and many have frescoed walls and chandeliers. There are either claw-foot baths or Jacuzzi baths or showers, and some rooms have terraces with dreamy views.

TRASTEVERE & GIANICOLO

Trastevere is beautiful: cobbled narrow streets, ivy-coated terracotta buildings, graceful piazzas – this is the Roman Holiday of your dreams. It's also thick with restaurants, pubs and cafés, and gets mind-bogglingly busy, especially on hot summer nights, when in some streets you can hardly move for crowds. So, not a good choice for light sleepers. Its tightly packed streets are dotted by hotels in historic *palazzi*, although note that space is tight and rooms tend to be small (a common feature of many city-centre lodgings).

EAST OF VIALE DI TRASTEVERE

RESIDENZA ARCO DE' TOLOMEI

Map pp132–3   Hotel €€

☎ 06 583 20 819; www.bbarcodeitolomei.com; Via Arco de' Tolomei 27; d €160-220; 🚇 or 🚋 Viale di Trastevere; 🖧

Upstairs from Arco del Lauro (below), this gorgeous place has a completely different feel, decorated with polished antiques and rich chintzes. It's a lovely place to stay, and the owners are friendly and helpful.

ARCO DEL LAURO

Map pp132–3   B&B €€

☎ 06 978 40 350 9am-2pm, 346 244 3212; www .arcodellauro.it; Via Arco de' Tolomei 29; s €75-125, d €95-145, tr €120-165, q €135-180; 🚋 Viale di Trastevere; 🖧

With only six rooms, this fab B&B in an ancient *palazzo* is a find, through a large stone arch and on a narrow cobbled street, with gleaming white rooms which combine rustic charm with minimalist simplicity. The largest room has a high wood-beamed ceiling.

WEST OF VIALE DI TRASTEVERE

BUONANOTTE GARIBALDI

Map pp132–3   Guesthouse €€

☎ 06 583 30 733; www.buonanottegaribaldi.com; Via Garibaldi 83; r €220-280; 🚇 or 🚋 Piazza Sonnino; 🚇

With only three rooms, this is a haven, an upmarket B&B in a divinely pretty inner-city villa, set around a courtyard. The rooms, themed Green, Orange and Blue, are beautifully decorated and there are works of art and sculpture all over the place – this is an artist's house. The elegant Luisa Longo has her studio in one corner of the courtyard. Pick of the rooms is Blue, upstairs, which opens onto a greenery-shaded terrace.

HOTEL SANTA MARIA

Map pp132–3   Hotel €€

☎ 06 589 46 26; www.hotelsantamaria.info; Vicolo del Piede 2; s €160-190, d €175-230; 🚇 or 🚋 Piazza Sonnino; 🅿 🖧 🚇

Walk along the ivy-lined approach and you'll enter a tranquil haven. Housed in a spacious modern cloister (a former con-

vent site), the Santa Maria has 19 rooms around an orange tree–shaded courtyard garden. Rooms are cool and comfortable, with slightly fussy décor and terracotta floors. There are some much larger family rooms. Staff are helpful and professional, and it's wheelchair-friendly. Its appealing, smaller, sister property is Residenza Santa Maria (www.residenzasantamaria.com), just around the corner.

VILLA DELLA FONTE

Map pp132–3   Hotel €€

☎ 06 580 37 97; www.villafonte.com; Via della Fonte d'Olio 8; s €110-130, d €135-150; 🚇 or 🚋 Piazza Sonnino; 🖧

A lovely terracotta-hued, ivy-shrouded gem, Villa della Fonte occupies a 17th-century building in a street off Piazza Santa Maria in Trastevere. It only has five rooms, all of which are simply decorated but have pretty outlooks, good bathrooms and comfortable beds covered with lovely linen. The sunny garden terrace (for breakfast in warm weather) is a plus.

HOTEL CISTERNA

Map pp132–3   Hotel €€

☎ 06 581 72 12; www.cisternahotel.it; Via della Cisterna 7-9; d €100-140; 🚇 or 🚋 Piazza Sonnino; 🖧

Cisterna is a modest three-star on a pretty cobbled street, close to Trastevere's focal Piazza Santa Maria in Trastevere. It offers 20 presentable, sunny rooms with creamy yellow walls. There's a small internal courtyard for early-evening drinks.

HOTEL TRASTEVERE

Map pp132–3   Hotel €

☎ 06 581 47 13; www.hoteltrastevere.net; Via Luciano Manara 24a-25; s/d/tr/q €80/103/130/155; 🚇 or 🚋 Viale di Trastevere

Overlooking the market square of San Cosimato (think noise), this is a reasonable, cheap Trastevere option, with basic, no-frills rooms. There's a bit of a run-down feel about the place but the rooms are large, clean and fine for the money, and it's completely unpretentious.

LA FORESTERIA ORSA MAGGIORE

Map pp132–3   Guesthouse €

☎ 06 689 37 53; www.casainternazionaledelle donne.org/foresteria; Via di San Francesco di Sales 1a; dm €26, s/d €75/110, with shared bathroom €52/72; 🚇 Piazza Trilussa; 🖧

This lesbian-friendly, predominantly women-only guesthouse (boys aged 12 or younger are welcome to accompany their mums) is housed in a restored 16th-century convent. It is run by the Casa Internazionale delle Donne (International Women's House) and offers safe and well-priced accommodation in a quiet corner of Trastevere. The 13 simple rooms sleep two, four, five or eight on rather hard beds, and some have views onto the attractive internal garden. There's a 3am curfew. Wheelchair accessible.

VATICAN CITY, BORGO & PRATI

Long a haven for pilgrims, the Vatican and the neighbouring districts of Borgo and Prati are well set up with accommodation. In the streets north and northeast of St Peter's Basilica you'll find everything from cheerful old-school *pensioni* to smart three-stars, B&Bs and tranquil convents. It's a popular area, though, and you'll need to book ahead, especially if you're staying during the big religious holidays (Christmas and Easter). Busy during the day, these areas are well connected and quiet at night.

VILLA LAETITIA Map pp138–9   Hotel €€
☎ 06 322 62 26; www.villalaetitia.com; Lungotevere delle Armi 22; d from €190; Ⓜ Lepanto; Ⅺ
Owned by the Fendi family, this boutique residence has 14 rooms and suites in a graceful riverside mansion. Much of the furniture has been collected by Anna Fendi on her travels, and, as you might expect from one of the world's most famous design families, the rooms look amazing, from fabulously stylised Art Deco to Asian. The look is divine, darling, and it's not all that expensive, either. When staying in the Garden Suite, choosing between your private terrace and the wonders of the Rome will be a tough call.

HOTEL BRAMANTE Map pp138–9   Hotel €€
☎ 06 688 06 426; www.hotelbramante.com; Vicolo delle Palline 24; s €100-160, d €150-240; 🚇 Piazza del Risorgimento; Ⅺ
Set in one of the narrow streets of the medieval Borgo district, Bramante feels like a country house in the city, full of rustic elegance, oriental rugs, beams and antiques. It's housed in the 16th-century building that was home to architect Domenico Fontana before Pope Sixtus V banished him from Rome, and has just 16 rooms, filled with character.

HOTEL LADY Map pp138–9   Pensione €€
☎ 06 324 21 12; www.hotelladyroma.it; Via Germanico 198, 4th fl; d €100-130, with shared bathroom s €50-65, d €70-95; Ⓜ Lepanto
A homey old-school *pensione* on one floor of an apartment block, the Hotel Lady is a quiet and inviting place. The eight rooms are snug, comfortable and spotless, and 4 and 6 have wood-beamed ceilings. The owner and his wife don't speak English, but will merrily chat to you in Italian and serve you breakfast (€10) in the attractive salon.

HOTEL FLORIDA Map pp138–9   Hotel €
☎ 06 324 18 72; www.hotelfloridaroma.it; Via Cola di Rienzo 243; s €40-150, d €50-170, tr €65-200, q €80-185; 🚇 Piazza del Risorgimento; Ⅺ
This has fussily wallpapered, old-fashioned rooms, decorated with solid wooden furniture. New refurbished rooms on the 2nd and 3rd floors are much more minimalist, with wooden floors and big beds, but all have small bathrooms. There's a 5% discount for cash payment.

HOTEL GIUGGIOLI Map pp138–9   Hotel €
☎ 06 360 05 389; www.hotelgiuggiolirome.com; Via Germanico 198; s €60-120, d €70-140; Ⓜ Ottaviano-San Pietro; Ⅺ
The Giuggioli's nine 1st-floor rooms sport a dapper, pearl-grey look with a minimum of furniture and large, comfortable beds. There's nothing large about the bathrooms, though; they're tiny. It's in the same block as its sister hotel, the more old-fashioned Hotel dei Quiriti, which is reasonable, but not as good.

COLORS HOTEL & HOSTEL
Map pp138–9   Hotel, Hostel €
☎ 06 687 40 30; www.colorshotel.com; Via Boezio 31; dm €23-27, s €50-90, d €100-135; 🚇 Piazza del Risorgimento; Ⅺ 🖳
This hostel-hotel is a relaxed place, with seven sunny, brightly painted dorms that can be noisy when windows are left open. It has a fully equipped kitchen, spotlessly clean shared bathrooms, and a small roof terrace. The doubles are simple, bright and attractive, with comfortable beds, high ceilings and modern bathrooms. Note that there's an age limit for the dorms: 18 to 35. There are singles and doubles with shared bathrooms that are around €10 to €15 cheaper.

HOTEL JOLI Map pp138–9   Pensione €

☎ 06 324 18 93; www.hoteljoliroma.com; Via Cola di Rienzo 243; s €40-77, d €60-115; 🚇 Piazza del Risorgimento; 🎦

Family-run, unpretentious and a little tatty around the edges, the Joli is a popular *pensione* six floors above busy Via Cola di Rienzo. There are few frills but rooms are bright and the décor is harmless. Bathrooms, while clean enough, could do with a little attention – the addition of shower curtains would be a good start. Air-con costs an additional €10; some rooms have fan only.

PENSIONE PARADISE

Map pp138–9   Pensione €

☎ 06 360 04 331; www.pensioneparadise.com; Viale Giulio Cesare 47; s €52-62, d €85-98, tr €110-125, q €135-150, with shared bathroom s €42-52; Ⓜ Lepanto

Perhaps not paradise, but rooms are simple and bright, and have terracotta-tiled floors and basic furniture. It's handily near Lepanto metro station, and the owner amiably greets all his guests in English or Italian.

BIBI E ROMEO'S HOME Map pp138–9 Hotel €

☎ 346 965 69 37; Via Andrea Doria 36; s €50-80, d €60-100; Ⓜ Ottaviano-San Pietro; 🎦

The area has a nice neighbourhood feel, with cafés along the broad avenue and a handy food market opposite. This peaceful, welcoming B&B has rooms that are a cut above. They're decorated in stylish mixes of white, brown and grey, with quotes written on the walls by the authors they're themed for: Pablo Neruda, Pessoa, Tersani and Santagostino. Bibi and Romeo are charming and helpful, and Bibi bakes great cakes.

HOTEL SAN PIETRINO Map pp138–9 Hotel €

☎ 06 370 01 32; www.sanpietrino.it; Via Giovanni Bettolo 43; d €75-118, with shared bathroom s €60-85, d €60-85; Ⓜ Ottaviano-San Pietro; 🎦 🖳

In peaceful Prati, not far from Ottaviano-San Pietro Metro, San Pietrino is a fab choice. Its 16 rooms are prettily decorated, with terracotta floors, some with statuary, and carvings in the hallways. Features are the comfortable beds, wi-fi and helpful staff.

CASA DI ACCOGLIENZA PAOLO VI

Map pp138–9   Religious Institution €

☎ 06 390 91 41; casapaolovi@tiscalinet.it; Viale Vaticano 92; s/d/tr/q €35/60/78/90; Ⓜ Ottaviano-San Pietro; 🎦

A lovely, palm-shaded convent, right opposite the entrance to the Vatican Museums, where the welcoming sisters offer small, sunny rooms that are so clean they gleam. Book way ahead. There's no breakfast, but you get a discount if you stay more than one night. There's a midnight curfew.

VILLA BORGHESE & NORTHERN ROME

Stretching outwards from Piazza del Popolo and Villa Borghese, northern Rome is affluent and smart. It's here you'll find some of the city's most expensive real estate as well as a number of fascinating museums. However, you're more likely to gravitate towards the centre to explore, eat and drink, though there are some lively pockets of nightlife around Parioli and Ponte Milvio.

VILLA BORGHESE & AROUND

GRAND HOTEL PARCO DEI PRINCIPI

Map pp150–1   Hotel €€€

☎ 06 85 44 21; www.parcodeiprincipi.com; Via Frescobaldi 5; s €260-480, d €300-620; 🚇 Via Giovanni Paisiello; 🅿 🎦 🖳

With one of the best outdoor swimming pools in central Rome, this luxury hotel perches on the edge of Villa Borghese. Decidedly traditional in look, it features wood-panelled walls, marble columns, chandeliers, swagged heavy drapes and gilt-framed paintings. Upstairs, the terrace restaurant commands some wonderful treetop views over to St Peter's Basilica. The swimming pool is open to nonguests for €35 to €75.

CASA MONTANI Map pp150–1   Hotel €€

☎ 06 326 00 421; www.casamontani.com; Piazzale Flaminio 9; d €140-240; Ⓜ Popolo; 🎦 🖳

Run by an Italian-French couple, this is another lovely, upmarket guesthouse with just five rooms. Fixtures and fittings are of the utmost quality, with custom-made furniture and contemporary art. Prices are low considering the level of comfort and the position, overlooking the Porta del Popolo, and it's a specially good deal if you book for three nights in low season (€120 per night). Nab the larger rooms if you can because the smallest, though a tad bijou, is the same price.

EXCURSIONS

If you have enough time, you should definitely do as the Romans do and explore the country-side around the city. Locals pour out of Rome every weekend into the jewel-green landscape of unsung Lazio, into criminally pretty nearby Umbria, or even into Tuscany – a short trip on a fast train. You have an amazing choice of beaches, extraordinary hilltop towns, volcanic lakes and stupendous ancient sites. One of the wonderful things about Rome is just how easy it is to leave it behind.

Lazio, easily overlooked in the stampede towards its capital, is a region that's not only beau-tiful – green and hilly in the north, parched and rugged in the south – but also rich in history and culture. In ancient times the wealthy built villas in the countryside, and towns developed as fiefdoms of noble Roman families, and today Lazio's landscape is freckled with reminders of its ancient past. The most obvious place to start is Ostia Antica, imperial Rome's port. On the other side of Rome, to the east, are the awe-inspiring ruins of Emperor Hadrian's Villa Adriana complex in Tivoli.

To see something *really* old, however, head northwest to Etruria, the ancient land of the Etruscans. Cerveteri and Tarquinia were important centres between the 8th and 4th centuries BC and are today famous for their Etruscan treasures. Nearby, Viterbo retains enough of its medieval core to evoke its 13th-century golden age.

In summer, overheated Romans cool down by heading to the Castelli Romani, the green hills south of Rome, or by driving north to Bolsena, a charming medieval lake town. For the sea, the beaches at Sabaudia and Sperlonga are among the region's best.

Further afield, beautifully preserved Orvieto in Umbria looks like it sprang from an illumi-nated manuscript and makes for a great weekend break. Even Tuscany – namely Florence – is an easy day trip from Rome, though undoubtedly you'll want to stay longer.

All the places mentioned in this chapter are accessible by public transport, although getting to some of the smaller towns will require patience. Your own wheels will make life a lot easier (see p287 for details on car hire in Rome), though beware the traffic flowing back into Rome on Sunday evenings.

HILLS, LAKES & THE SEA

Just 20km south of the city, the Castelli Romani (p279) is a picturesque area of lush vine-covered hills and pretty towns. The best known are Frascati, a smart wine town with a lively *centro storico* (historic centre), and Castel Gandolfo, perched on a hill overlooking Lago di Albano, one of the area's two volcanic lakes (the other being Lago di Nemi).

Lazio's largest lake, Lago di Bolsena (p273), lies in the very north of the region. It takes too long to reach to merit a day trip, but the lake-side town of Bolsena has a pretty medieval centre and plenty of accommodation.

If the idea of splashing around in fresh water doesn't appeal, head for the beach. The best of Lazio's beaches are about two hours south of Rome, near the border with Cam-pania. Whitewashed Sperlonga (p280) is ideal for an evening stroll after a soothing day on the sand. Nearby, the Parco Nazionale del Circeo at Sabaudia (p280) is perfect for those who prefer watching birds to people.

ANCIENT WONDERS

You might be surprised at just how many clas-sical monuments dot the Lazio countryside. Chief among these are the ruins of Ancient Rome's port Ostia Antica (p268) and Villa Adriana in Tivoli (p278). The ruins at Ostia have been remarkably well preserved and are among the most impressive in the country. They are easily explored in a day and are easy to interpret – as you walk down the skeletal streets you really can imagine how the town must once have looked.

Villa Adriana, Emperor Hadrian's enor-mous palace complex, is more like a town than a mere mansion, and provides a staggering example of the scale on which the Roman emperors operated.

Predating the Romans, the Etruscans were a highly civilised people who provided many of the artistic and architectural techniques that the Romans subsequently adopted as their own. According to the Greek historian Hero-dotus, they originated in Asia Minor, moving

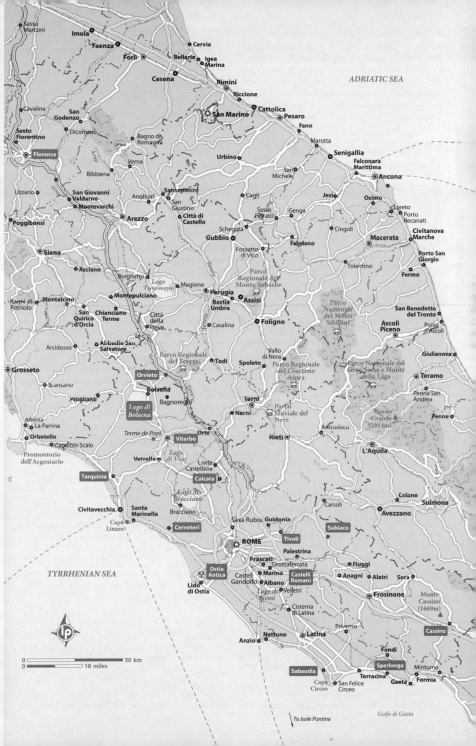

to Italy in about 1000 BC. They were at their strongest between the 8th and 4th centuries BC, before being incorporated into the expanding Roman Republic in the 3rd century BC. Two of Etruria's major centres were Cerveteri (opposite) and Tarquinia (p270). Both towns boast fascinating Unesco-listed tomb complexes that count among Lazio's most haunting sights.

MEDIEVAL & RENAISSANCE MARVELS

The Middle Ages was an ugly period for Rome. Fighting among the city's aristocrats reduced much of the city to rubble, while church feuding culminated in Pope Clement V transferring to Avignon in 1309. But while Rome floundered, many of the hilltop towns in the surrounding areas flourished. In the north of Lazio, Viterbo (p271) became an important medieval centre and in the 13th century the popes established a residence there. Before that it had already established a reputation as a thermal town and today its therapeutic hot springs still have an invigorating effect.

Over the regional border, in neighbouring Umbria, Orvieto (p273) owes its stunning Gothic cathedral, one of Italy's finest, to the munificence of a 13th-century pope who wanted to celebrate a miracle in Bolsena. At the same time, the Medici family were beginning to find their groove in Florence (p275), and Cosimo de'Medici began a tradition of artistic patronage that would go on for generations, and which saw the Tuscan city become one of Italy's most beautiful and masterpiece-packed.

OSTIA ANTICA

With a level of preservation that in places matches that of Pompeii, the ancient Roman port of Ostia Antica deserves more visitors than it gets. But its relatively undiscovered feel can only work to your advantage: you'll get the site largely to yourself.

Founded in the 4th century BC, Ostia (named for the mouth or *ostium* of the Tiber) became a great port and later a strategic centre for defence and trade. In the 5th century AD barbarian invasions and the outbreak of malaria led to its abandonment followed by its slow burial – up to 2nd-floor level – in river silt, hence its survival. Pope Gregory IV reestablished the town in the 9th century.

The ruins (Scavi Archeologici di Ostia Antica; ☎ 06 563 52 830; www.ostiantica.info, in Italian; Viale dei Romagnoli 717;

adult/child €4/free, car park €2.50; ☉ 8.30am-7pm Tue-Sun Apr-Oct, to 6pm Mar, to 5pm Nov-Feb, last admission 1hr before closing) are spread out and you'll need at least a few hours. You can buy a handy site map from the ticket office (€2).

Ostia was a busy working port until 42 AD, and the town is made up of restaurants, laundries, shops, houses and public meeting places, giving a good impression of what life must have been like when it was at its busiest. The main thoroughfare, the Decumanus Maximus, runs over 1km from the city's entrance (the Porta Romana) to the Porta Marina, which originally led to the sea.

At one stage, Ostia had 20 baths complexes, including the Terme di Foro – these were equipped with a roomful of stone toilets (the *forica*) that remain largely intact.

The most impressive mosaics on site are at the huge Terme di Nettuno, which occupied a whole block and date from Hadrian's renovation of the port. Make sure you climb the elevated platform and look at the three enormous mosaics here, including Neptune driving his seahorse chariot, surrounded by sea monsters, mermaids and mermen. In the centre of the baths complex you'll find the remains of a large arcaded courtyard called the Palaestra, in which athletes used to train. There's an impressive mosaic here depicting boxing and wrestling.

Next to the Nettuno baths is a good-sized amphitheatre, built by Agrippa and later enlarged to hold 3000 people. By climbing to its top and looking over the site, you'll get a good idea of the original layout of the port and how it would have functioned.

Behind the amphitheatre is the Piazzale delle Corporazioni (Forum of the Corporations), the offices of Ostia's merchant guilds, which sport well-preserved mosaics depicting the different interests of each business.

Further towards the Porta Marina is one of the highlights of the site: the Thermopolium (the equivalent in contemporary Rome is the *tavola calda* – 'hot table'), an ancient café that's breathtakingly similar to our modern-day versions. Check out the bar counter, surmounted by a frescoed, pictorial menu, the kitchen to the right and the small courtyard at the rear, where customers would have sat next to the fountain and relaxed with a drink.

The site has a complex comprising a cafeteria/bar (but a picnic is always a good idea), toilets, gift shop and museum, which houses statues and sarcophagi excavated on site.

Near the entrance to the excavations is the Castello di Giulio II (☎ 06 563 58 024; Piazza della Rocca; ✆ free guided tours 10am & noon Tue-Sun, plus 3pm Tue & Thu), an impressive example of 15th-century military architecture.

INFORMATION

Ostia Antica (www.ostiaantica.net)

EATING

Ristorante Monumento (☎ 06 565 00 21; Piazza Umberto I 8; meals €26; ✆ Tue-Sun) A historic restaurant near the ruins, this place specialises in homemade pasta and fish.

CALCATA

Medieval Calcata is storybook pretty, perched above dense forest. It was first famed as a pilgrimage site due to its possession of the Holy Foreskin, one of Italy's more discomforting relics. To find out more about the town and the relic, check out David Farley's book, *An Irreverent Curiosity: In Search of the Church's Strangest Relic in Italy's Oddest Town* (2009).

In the 1930s, the village was condemned because the cliffs beneath it were thought to be unstable. Thirty years later, artists began to take over the disused buildings. The town was reborn, the condemnation notice was withdrawn and now Calcata is packed with artists, bohemians, galleries and hordes of day-tripping Romans on a Sunday afternoon.

INFORMATION

Calcata Info (www.calcata.info)

EATING & DRINKING

If you want to stay a while, you can rent simple rooms or houses – check Calcata Info (www.calcata .com) – and there are some good restaurants.

La Latteria del Gatto Nero (☎ 0761 58 80 15) This cluttered, cavelike eatery serves up memorable *fettucine al ragù di Nonna.*

CERVETERI

Outside Rome lies an extraordinary, Unesco-listed Etruscan burial complex, a haunting town of tombs.

Cerveteri, or Kysry to the Etruscans and Caere to Latin-speakers, was one of the most important commercial centres in the Mediterranean from the 7th to the 5th centuries BC. As Roman power grew, however, so Cerveteri's fortunes faded, and in 358 BC the city was annexed by Rome.

After the fall of the Roman Empire, the spread of malaria and repeated Saracen invasions caused further decline. In the 13th century there was a mass exodus from the city to the nearby town of Ceri, and Caere became Caere Vetus (Old Caere), from which its current name derives. The early 19th century saw the first tentative archaeological explorations in the area, and in 1911 systematic excavations began in earnest.

You can get an hourly shuttle bus from the tourist information point to the Necropoli di Banditaccia (☎ 06 399 67 150; www.pierrici.it; Via del Necropoli; admission €6, incl museum €8; ✆ 8.30am until 1hr before sunset), the tomb complex 2km out of town. The bus leaves seven to nine times per day starting at 8.20am and finishing at 6pm (earlier in winter). The trip takes five minutes and costs €1. Alternatively, follow the well-signposted road – it's a pleasant 15-minute walk.

The 10-hectare necropolis is laid out as an afterlife townscape, with streets, squares and terraces of 'houses'. The most common type

TRANSPORT – CALCATA
Distance from Rome 45km
Direction north
Travel time 45 minutes
Car Take either Via Flaminia (SS3) or Via Cassia (SS2) northwards.
Train Take a train from Rome Ferrovia Nord to Saxa Rubra, then a bus from outside the train station.

TRANSPORT – CERVETERI

Distance from Rome 35km

Direction Northwest

Travel time 40 to 90 minutes

Bus Cotral bus (€3.50, 65 minutes, 19 daily from 6.25am) from outside the Cornelia metro stop on metro line A. Buses leave Cerveteri for Rome from the main square. The last return bus is at 8.05pm.

Car Take either Via Aurelia (SS1) or the Civitavecchia autostrada (A12) and exit at Cerveteri-Ladispoli.

of tomb is the tumulus, a circular structure cut into the earth and crowned by a cumulus – a topping of turf. Signs indicate which path to follow, and some of the major tombs, including the 6th-century-BC Tomba dei Rilievi, are decorated with painted reliefs of figures from the underworld, cooking implements and other household items.

In Cerveteri's medieval town centre is the splendid Museo Nazionale di Cerveteri (Piazza Santa Maria; admission €6, incl necropolis €8; ☾ 8.30am-7.30pm Tue-Sun), where treasures taken from the tombs help to bring the dead to life.

INFORMATION

Tourist information point (☎ 06 995 52 637; Piazza Aldo Moro; ☾ 9.30am-12.30pm)

EATING

Antica Locanda le Ginestre (☎ 06 994 06 72; Piazza Santa Maria 5; meals €45; ☾ Tue-Sun) This top-notch family-run restaurant offers delicious food, prepared with organically grown local produce and served in the elegant dining room or flower-filled courtyard garden. Book ahead.

Cavallino Bianco (☎ 06 994 36 93; Piazza Risorgimento; ☾ Wed-Sun) A cheaper alternative.

TARQUINIA

A long day trip from Rome, Tarquinia is nevertheless worth the effort, with beautiful painted tombs, a wonderful Etruscan museum and an evocative medieval quarter. Legend suggests that the town was founded towards the end of the Bronze Age, in the 12th century BC. It was home to the Tarquin kings of Rome before the creation of the Roman Republic, and it reached its prime in the 4th century

BC before a century of struggle ended with surrender to Rome in 204 BC.

On the edge of the *centro storico* lies the exquisite 15th-century Palazzo Vitelleschi, which houses the Museo Nazionale Tarquiniese (☎ 06 399 67 150; Piazza Cavour; adult/child €6/3, incl necropolis €8/4; ☾ 8.30am-7.30pm Tue-Sun). Highlights of its collection include a breathtaking terracotta frieze of winged horses (the Cavalli Alati); a room full of painted tomb friezes; displays of sarcophagi, jewellery and amphorae; and some remarkably saucy ceramics in ground-floor Sala VI. Also on the ground floor, in Sala IX, the *Sarcofogo con cerbiatto* is a model of 4th-century BC workmanship, showing a half-naked reclining woman holding a plate from which a long-necked dog (the *cerbiatto*) is drinking.

To see the famous painted tombs *in situ*, head for the necropolis (☎ 06 399 67 150; adult/child €6/3, incl museum €8/4; ☾ 8.30am until 1hr before sunset Tue-Sun), 2km from town. Almost 6000 tombs, of which 60 are painted, have been excavated since the first digs in 1489 – only a tiny section of the original burial area, which stretched all the way to the coast. The tombs have suffered centuries of exposure and are maintained at constant temperatures, and are visible only through glass partitions. There are some beautiful hunting and fishing scenes in the Tomba della Caccia e della Pesca; scenes featuring dancers, she-lions and dolphins in the Tomba delle Leonesse; and a surprising S&M scene of a man whipping a woman in the Tomba della Fustigazione (Tomb of the Flogging), as well as hetero and homosexual scenes on the Tomb of the Bulls. Erotica was a common artistic theme for the open-minded Etruscans.

To get to the necropolis from the tourist office, walk up Corso Vittorio Emanuele and turn right at Piazza Nazionale into Via di Porta Tarquinia. Continue past the Chiesa di San Francesco and then down Via Ripagretta until you see the necropolis on your left. Alternatively, a shuttle bus (€0.60) leaves from outside the tourist office every 30 to 45 minutes from 9am to 11.45am and from 3pm to 6.15pm, returning to town five minutes after it arrives at the necropolis.

INFORMATION

Tourist information office (☎ 0766 84 92 82; info@ tarquinia@apt.it; Piazza Cavour 1; ☾ 8am-2pm Mon-Sat) On your left as you walk through the town's medieval gate (Barriera San Giusto).

TRANSPORT – TARQUINIA

Distance from Rome 90km

Direction Northwest

Travel time 1½ hours

Bus From Rome, take a Cotral bus from Cornelia Metro A station. You'll have to change at Civitavecchia (€4.50, about hourly) for a bus to Tarquinia (€2, 25 minutes). The last bus leaves Tarquinia for Rome at 8.45pm.

Car Take the Civitavecchia autostrada (A12) then Via Aurelia (SS1).

Train By train, catch the Pisa Centrale train from Termini (€6.20, every one to two hours). Buy a return ticket as the ticket office in Tarquinia only operates in the morning. After getting off at Tarquinia station, catch the line BC shuttle bus to the centre of town.

EATING & SLEEPING

Il Cavatappi (☎ 0766 84 23 03; Via dei Granari 19; meals €25; ✆ Thu-Tue) In the *centro storico*, this family-run trattoria specialises in dishes made with local products.

Re Tarquinio (☎ 0766 84 21 25; Alberata Dante Alighieri 10; ✆ Wed-Mon) Highly rated, this occupies an ancient frescoed cellar in the medieval centre, and serves dishes such as *fettucine con ragout di cervo e salsa di lamponi* (pasta with venison ragu with raspberry sauce).

Hotel San Marco (☎ 0766 84 22 34; www.san-marco .com; Piazza Cavour 18; d €80-90) If you need to stay over, friendly little San Marco, opposite the Museo Nazionale Tarquiniese, has light, unfussy rooms with tiled floors. Noise from the downstairs American-style bar can be a nuisance.

VITERBO

Viterbo is a medieval gem, despite having sustained WWII bomb damage. It makes a good base for exploring Lazio's rugged north, or it can be visited on a day trip.

Founded by the Etruscans and eventually taken over by Rome, Viterbo developed into an important medieval centre, and in the 13th century it became the residence of the popes. Papal elections were held in the Gothic Palazzo dei Papi, where in 1271 the entire college of cardinals was briefly imprisoned. The story goes that after three years of deliberation the cardinals still hadn't elected a new pope. Mad with frustration, the Viterbesi locked the dithering priests in a turreted hall and starved them into electing Pope Gregory X.

Apart from its historical appeal, Viterbo is famous for its therapeutic hot springs. The best known is the sulphurous Bulicame pool, mentioned by Dante in the *Divine Comedy*.

Viterbo's walled *centro storico* is small and best covered on foot. The focal square, the Renaissance Piazza del Plebiscito, is dominated by the imposing Palazzo dei Priori (Piazza del Plebiscito; admission free; ✆ 10am-1pm & 4-7pm). Now home to the town council, it's worth venturing inside for the 16th-century frescoes that colourfully depict Viterbo's ancient origins – the finest are in the Sala Regia on the 1st floor. Outside, the elegant courtyard and fountain were added two centuries after the *palazzo* (mansion) was built in 1460.

For an idea of how rich Viterbo once was, head southwest to Piazza San Lorenzo, the medieval city's religious heart. It was here that the cardinals came to vote for their popes and pray in the 12th-century Cattedrale di San Lorenzo.

Built originally to a simple Romanesque design, it owes its current Gothic look to a 14th-century makeover; damage by Allied bombs meant the roof and nave had to be rebuilt. Next door, the Museo del Colle del Duomo (admission incl Sala del Conclave in Palazzo dei Papi €3 or €5 incl guided visit to Palazzo dei Papi; 🕑 10am-1pm & 3-8pm Tue-Sun, to 6pm winter €5 Loggia) displays a small collection of religious artefacts, including a reliquary said to contain the chin of John the Baptist.

The oldest church in Viterbo, the 11th-century Romanesque Chiesa di Santa Maria Nuova (Piazza Santa Maria Nuova; 🕑 10am-1pm & 3-5pm), was restored to its original form after WWII bomb damage. The cloisters, believed to date from an earlier period, are particularly lovely.

South of here lies the remarkably well-preserved medieval quarter. Wander down Via San Pellegrino with its low-slung arches and claustrophobic grey houses to pint-sized Piazza San Pellegrino.

For a shot of Etruscan culture, head to the Museo Archeologico Nazionale (☎ 0761 32 59 29; Piazza della Rocca; admission €6; 🕑 8.30am-7.30pm Tue-Sun), housed in an attractive *palazzo* by the northern entrance to the town. It's small, but has an interesting collection of artefacts discovered locally and, on the 1st floor, an impressive series of statues dedicated to the Muses.

A short walk away is the Chiesa di San Francesco (☎ 0761 34 16 96; Piazza San Francesco; 🕑 8am-6.30pm), a Gothic church containing the tombs of two popes: Clement IV (d 1268) and Adrian V (d 1276). Both are attractively decorated, notably that of Adrian, which features Cosmati work (multicoloured marble and glass mosaics set into stone and white marble).

On the other side of town, the Museo Civico (☎ 0761 34 82 75; Piazza Crispi; admission €3.10; 🕑 9am-7pm Tue-Sun summer, to 6pm winter) features more Etruscan goodies, as well as curious fake antiquities created in the 15th century by Annius

of Viterbo, a monk and forger trying to boost Viterbo's reputation. There's also a small art gallery, the highlight of which is Sebastiano del Piombo's *Pietà*.

In its eponymous piazza, the Fontana Grande (Big Fountain) lives up to its name, and is also the oldest of Viterbo's Gothic fountains.

For a High Renaissance spectacle, head to the wonderful Villa Lante, 4km northeast of Viterbo at Bagnaia. This mannerist drama of terraces, water cascades and gaily waving statues, forms part of the bucolic park (☎ 07612 88 008; admission €2; 🕑 8.30am-1hr before sunset Tue-Sun) that surrounds the 16th-century villa. To get to Bagnaia from Viterbo, take the bus from Viale Trieste (€1).

INFORMATION

Tourist information office (☎ 0761 32 59 92; www .provincia.vt.it, in Italian; Via Filippo Ascenzi; 🕑 10am-1pm & 3-6pm Tue-Sun)

EATING & SLEEPING

Agriturismo Antica Sosta (☎ 0761 25 13 69; s/d €50/75) Five kilometres from Viterbo, on SS Cassia Nord, is this mansion set in pea-green countryside, with spacious, simple rooms and a delicious restaurant (meals €25), serving tasty dishes such as *strozzapreti al radicchio gorgonzola e noci* ('priest-strangler' pasta with red chicory, gorgonzola cheese and nuts).

Ristorante Enoteca La Torre (☎ 0761 22 64 67; Via della Torre 5; meals €55; 🕑 lunch Thu-Tue, dinner Thu-Wed) Viterbo's best restaurant is a dream date for foodies: the Japanese chef combines precision and delicacy of presentation with innovative uses of fresh seasonal produce, and the sommelier here really knows his stuff.

Ristorante Tre Re (☎ 0761 30 46 19; Via Macel Gattesco 3; meals €25; 🕑 Fri-Wed) Tre Re reigns as a historic trattoria, dishing up steaming plates of tasty local specialities and seasonally driven dishes. None is more typical than the *pollo alla Viterbese*, roast chicken stuffed with spiced potato and green olives. Heartwarmingly cheap and palate-pleasingly fantastic.

Tuscia Hotel (☎ 0761 34 44 00; www.tusciahotel.com; Via Cairoli 41; s €44-50, d €68-76; Ⓟ 🅧) The best of the city's midrange options, this central, spic-and-span place is leagues ahead of the competition in cleanliness and comfort. The rooms, some with air-con, are large and light, and there's a sunny roof terrace.

DETOUR: THERMAL SPRINGS

Originally used by both the Etruscans and the Romans, Viterbo's famous thermal springs are concentrated in an area 3km west of town.

The easiest to reach are the Terme dei Papi (☎ 0761 35 01; www.termedeipapi.it; Strada Bagni 12; pool Wed-Sat €12, Sun €25; 🕑 9am-7pm Wed-Mon, 9.30pm-1am Sat), where you can swim in the sulphurous pool, get a massage (from €55 for 50 minutes) or treat yourself to a gloopy mud bath (from €10). Take the bus from Viterbo's Viale Trento (€1).

LAGO DI BOLSENA

Surrounded by lush rolling countryside a few kilometres short of the regional border with Umbria, Lago di Bolsena is the largest and northernmost of Lazio's lakes. The lake's main town is Bolsena, a charming, low-key place that, despite a heavy hotel presence, retains its medieval character.

Like many Italian towns, Bolsena has its own miracle story. In 1263 a priest who had been tormented by doubts about the veracity of transubstantiation (the transformation of wine and bread into the blood and body of Christ) was saying mass, when he noticed blood dripping from the bread he was blessing. The bloodstained cloth in which he wrapped the bread may be seen in Orvieto's cathedral (right), which was built to commemorate the miracle. Pope Urban VII also founded the festival of Corpus Domini to celebrate it – each June the townspeople hold a 3km procession and decorate the town with flowers. The story is famously depicted in Raphael's *Messa di Bolsena* (Mass of Bolsena) in the Vatican Museums' Stanze di Raffaello (p144).

Bolsena's few specific sights are in the medieval centre. In the 11th-century Basilica di Santa Cristina (☎ 0761 79 90 67; www.basilicasantacristina .it; Piazza Santa Cristina; ☽ 7.15am-12.45pm & 3.30-7.45pm Easter-Sep, 7.15am-12.30pm & 3-5.30pm Oct-Easter) you'll find four stones stained with miraculous blood. The church is named for the martyr, who was daughter of the local prefect and yet was tortured and finally killed for her faith – her story is re-enacted annually on July 23 and 24. Beneath the basilica are a series of catacombs (admission €4; ☽ 9.30am-noon & 3.30-6.30pm Easter-Sep, 9.30-11.30am & 3-4.30pm Oct-Easter), noteworthy for the number of tombs that are still sealed.

For dizzying lake views climb up to the hilltop Castello Monaldeschi (☎ 0761 79 86 30; admission castle €3.50, panoramic walkway €2; ☽ 10am-1pm & 4-8pm).

INFORMATION

Tourist office (☎ 0761 79 99 23; Piazza Matteotti; ☽ 9.30am-12.30pm & 3.30-6.30pm daily May-Sep, 9.30am-12.30pm Mon-Sat Oct-Apr)

EATING & SLEEPING

Trattoria Pizzeria del Moro (☎ 0761 79 88 10; Piazza Dante Alighieri 5; meals €25) With a fantastic setting on a pier jutting into the lake, this trattoria specialises in local wines and fresh lake fish: pike, perch and eel. Lake Bolsena eels are mentioned in Dante's *Divine Comedy*.

Hotel Columbus (☎ 0761 79 90 09; www.atihotels.it; Viale Colesanti 27; s €47-72, d €65-94) Value for money and a central lakeside location are what you get at this modern three-star. Rooms are comfortable, carpeted and a bit bland.

ORVIETO

Crowning a steep hill, beautiful medieval Orvieto is dominated by its awe-inspiring humbug-striped *duomo* (cathedral). Unsurprisingly, it's a tourist honeypot and gets crowded, particularly in summer. But don't let that deter you. This is a wonderful place to wander and makes a perfect day trip from Rome. Perched precariously on a cliff made of the area's tufa stone, it also houses an important collection of Etruscan artefacts, and the cliff beneath is riddled with a fascinating series of ancient underground caves.

A good investment is the Carta Unica (adult/concession €18/15), which includes five hours' free parking, a return trip on the cable car, free bus transport, and admission (only once) to the Cappella di San Brizio in the cathedral, Museo Claudio Faina e Civico, Orvieto Underground, Torre del Moro, Museo dell'Opera del Duomo and the Crocifisso del Tufo necropolis (the last is at the foot of the rock massif on which Orvieto stands). It's available at participating sites, the Campo della Fiera car park, the tourist office and the funicular car park.

Confoundingly beautiful, the cathedral (☎ 0763 34 11 67; www.opsm.it, in Italian; Piazza Duomo; ☽ 7.30am-12.45pm & 2.30-7.15pm Apr-Sep, 7.30am-12.45pm & 2.30-6.15pm Mar & Oct, 7.30am-12.45pm & 2.30-5.15pm Nov-Feb) is otherworldly in its striped magnificence. Started in 1290, it was originally planned in the Romanesque style, but as work proceeded and architects changed, it became more Gothic. The black-and-white marble banding of the main body of the church is surpassed and complemented by the dancing polychrome colours of the façade.

Pope Urban IV commissioned the cathedral to celebrate the Miracle of Bolsena (see opposite) in 1263, but it took 30 years to plan and three centuries to complete. It was probably started by Fra Bevignate and later additions were made by Lorenzo Maitani, Andrea Pisano and his son Nino Pisano, Andrea Orcagna and Michele Sanicheli. The great bronze doors, the work of Emilio Greco, were added in the 1960s.

Inside, Luca Signorelli's fresco cycle, *Il Giudizio Universale* (The Last Judgment), shimmers with life in the Cappella di San Brizio (admission incl museum adult/concession €6.5/5; 9am-12.45pm & 2.30-5.15pm Nov-Feb, 9am-12.45pm & 2.30-6.15pm Mon-Fri, 2.30-5.45pm Sat & Sun Mar & Oct, 9am-12.45pm & 2.30-7.15pm Mon-Fri, 2.30-5.45pm Sat & Sun Apr-Jun, 9am-12.45pm & 2.30-7.15pm Mon-Fri, 2.30-6.45pm Sat & Sun Jul-Sep), to the right of the altar. Signorelli began work on the series in 1499. Michelangelo is said to have taken inspiration from it for the Sistine Chapel. Indeed, to some, Michelangelo's version runs a close second to Signorelli's work.

The Cappella del Corporale houses the blood-stained altar linen from Bolsena, and features frescoes by Ugolino di Prete Ilario that depict the miracle.

Next to the cathedral is the Museo dell'Opera del Duomo (0763 34 35 92; www.opsm.it; Palazzo Soliano & Palazzi Papali, Piazza Duomo; adult/concession incl Cappella di San Brizio €6.50/5; 9.30am-1pm & 3-7pm Wed-Mon Nov-Feb, 9.30am-1pm & 2-6pm Wed-Mon Mar & Oct, 9.30am-7pm daily Apr-Sep), housed in the former papal palaces, with a clutter of religious relics, as well as Etruscan antiquities and paintings by artists such as Simone Martini, Arnolfo di Cambio, and the three Pisanos: Andrea, Nino and Giovanni.

Around the corner in the Palazzo Papale, you can see one of Italy's most important collections of Etruscan archaeological artefacts in the Museo Archeologico Nazionale (/fax 0763 34 10 39; Piazza Duomo; adult/concession €3/1.50; 8.30am-7.30pm) and the more interesting Museo Claudio Faina e Civico (0763 34 15 11; www.museofaina.it; Piazza Duomo 29; adult/concession €4.50/3; 9.30am-6pm daily Apr-Sep, 10am-5pm Tue-Sun Oct-Mar), where you'll find some significant Greek ceramic works, mostly found near Piazza Cahen in tombs dating to the 6th century BC.

Head northwest along Via del Duomo to Corso Cavour and the Torre del Moro (Moor's Tower;

0763 34 45 67; Corso Cavour 87; adult/concession €2.80/2; 10am-8pm May-Aug, 10am-7pm Mar, Apr, Sep & Oct, 10.30am-1pm & 2.30-5pm Nov-Feb). Climb all 250 steps and you're rewarded with sweeping city views. Nearby, in Piazza della Repubblica , once the site of Orvieto's Roman Forum and later the heart of the medieval city, stands the 12th-century Chiesa di Sant'Andrea (8.30am-12.30pm & 3.30-7.30pm) with its curious decagonal bell tower. Continue west and you come to the 11th-century Chiesa di San Giovenale (Piazza Giovenale; 8am-12.30pm & 3.30-6pm), its interior brightened by 13th- and 14th-century frescoes.

Standing watch at the town's easternmost tip is the 14th-century rock fortress, La Rocca, part of which is now a public garden. To the north of the fortress, the Pozzo di San Patrizio (St Patrick's Well; 0763 34 37 68; Viale Sangallo; adult/concession €4.50/3.50; 9am-7.45pm May-Aug, 9am-6.45pm Mar, Apr, Sep & Oct, 10am-4.45pm Nov-Feb) is a 60m-deep well, lined by two spiral staircases for water-bearing mules.

The coolest place in Orvieto, in degrees and atmosphere, is Orvieto Underground (0763 34 48 91; Parco delle Grotte; adult/concession €5.50/3.30; tours 11am, 12.15pm, 4pm & 5.15pm daily Mar-Jan, more frequent in busy periods, Sat & Sun only Feb). Underneath the city, the rock is riddled with 440 caves, which have been used for millennia for various purposes. Tours (with English-speaking guides) take you through caverns variously used as WWII bomb shelters, refrigerators, wells and, during many a siege, dovecotes to trap pigeons for dinner (still seen on local restaurant menus as *palombo*).

There's a pleasant, tranquil walk around Orvieto's walls (5km) – pick up a map at the tourist office, where you can also enquire about wine tours in the Umbrian countryside. To find out more information on local wine trails, contact Associazione Strada dei Vini Etrusco Romana in provincial di Terni (0763 306508; www.stradadeivinietruscoromana.it).

TRANSPORT – ORVIETO

Distance from Rome 120km

Direction Northwest

Travel time 1¼ to 1½ hours

Bus Bargagli (057 778 62 23; www.bargagliautolinee.it) runs a daily bus service to Rome (€8, 8.10am and 7.10pm). From Rome, buses depart from Stazione Tiburtina twice daily, at 3.15pm and 9pm.

Car The city is on the A1 north-south autostrada. There's plenty of parking space in Piazza Cahen and in several designated areas outside the old city walls.

Train Hourly trains depart from Rome's Stazione Termini (€7.10 to €13). Take the funicular up to Piazza Cahen at the eastern end of the old town, from where there's a shuttle bus to the Piazza del Duomo (otherwise it's a 20-minute walk uphill).

DETOUR: CIVITA DI BAGNOREGIO

Around 25km south of Orvieto lies *il paese che muore* (the dying town) of Civita di Bagnoregio. This dramatically scenic hilltop town is accessible via a long bridge from handsome Bagnoregio, the town built to replace it. Already on the decline, Civita's future was sealed after a serious 17th-century earthquake. Set on a piece of crumbling volcanic tuff, its buildings are gradually collapsing. The permanent population numbers around 12, though it multiplies in summer. On May 31 and September 13, an alternative to Siena's Il Palio (horserace in the main square) is held here, using donkeys; it's called La Tonna di Civita (www.latonnadicivita.it). It's also magical around Christmas, when there is a *presepe vivente* (living nativity).

For more info, check www.civitadibagnoregio.it. Bagnoregio is accessible via regular Cotral buses from Viterbo (€2.50, 40 minutes). It's a walk of about 2km from Bagnoregio to the old town.

To reach Bagnoregio from Orvieto, take the SS71 south and turn left onto the SP130.

INFORMATION

Information office (☎ 0763 30 23 78; Piazza della Pace; ☺ 10am-6pm) At the bottom of the funicular.

Tourist office (☎ 0763 34 17 72; info@iat.orvieto.tr.it; Piazza Duomo 24; ☺ 8.15am-1.50pm & 4-7pm Mon-Fri, 10am-1pm & 3-6pm Sat, Sun & holidays)

EATING

Cantina Foresi (☎ 0763 34 16 11; Piazza del Duomo 2; snacks from €4; ☺ 10am-8pm) Under the shadow of the *duomo*, yet surprisingly reasonable, this family-run *enoteca* (wine bar) serves simple *panini* (bread rolls) and sausages, washed down with local wine.

L'Asino d'Oro (☎ 0763 34 44 06; Vicolo del Popolo 9; meals €28; ☺ Tue-Sun) Innovative yet thoroughly Umbrian food at affordable prices in the speciality of the house, with dishes such as *cinghiale in agridolce* (sweet-and-sour boar).

Ristorante La Pergola (☎ 0763 34 30 65; Via dei Magoni 9b; meals €35; ☺ Thu-Tue) Intimate and elegant, with a flower-filled garden, this serves great Umbrian cuisine, with plenty of 'hunter-style' chicken, lamb and boar dishes.

Ristorante Zeppelin (☎ 0763 34 14 47; Via Garibaldi 28; meals €25) With high, arched ceilings and an old-fashioned feel, this jazz-cool restaurant produces creative Umbrian food. Expect delicate ravioli combined with ingredients such as sage and almonds, and a dazzling array of rich, meaty *secondi* (second courses).

SLEEPING

Hotel Maitani (☎ 0763 34 20 11; www.hotelmaitani.com; Via Lorenzo Maitani 5; s/d €79/130; P) Polished parquet floors, sober antique furnishings, and cathedral views (in some rooms) are a winning combination at this thoughtful hotel. Prices quoted are without breakfast.

Hotel Corso (☎ 0763 34 20 20; www.hotelcorso.net; Corso Cavour 343; s €70-92, d €83-118; ☒ ☐) This restructured medieval building overlooks a small piazza, and offers snug rooms with wooden-beamed ceilings, terracotta bricks and antique cherry-wood furniture.

B&B Valentina (☎ 0763 34 16 07; www.bandbvalentina .com; Via Vivaria 7; s €45-60, d €65-90, tr €65-129, apt €130-180) On a cobbled alley, Valentina offers casually elegant, spacious rooms, a couple with kitchen facilities, and also has an apartment sleeping four.

Hotel Piccolomini (☎ 0763 34 17 43; www.hotel piccolomini.com; Piazza Ranieri 36; s €97, d €154; ☒ ☐) A boutique hotel in a restructured Renaissance building, this has beautifully decorated rooms in pared-down modern style. Room 311 is the pick, with great piazza views.

FLORENCE

With fast trains zipping between Rome's Termini and Florence, it's tempting to take a trip to this most romantic, if perennially packed, Renaissance city, sometime home to Machiavelli, Michelangelo and the Medici.

It's thought that Julius Caesar founded Florentia in 59 BC. In the 12th century Florence became a commune (town council), and agitation between factions led to centuries of power struggles from which the Medici family emerged as top dogs in the 15th century, partly because they were the papal bankers. Cosimo de'Medici became Florence's ruler, and a host of master artists flourished, such as Donatello, Fra Angelico and Fra Filippo Lippi. The rule of Cosimo's grandson Lorenzo il Magnifico (r 1469–92) later ushered in the most glorious period of the Italian Renaissance. Shortly before Lorenzo's death, the papal bank failed and the family was driven from Florence, returning to regain power in 1569.

In 1737 the French House of Lorraine took control and retained it (apart from a brief incursion by Napoleon) until Italy's independence in 1860. Florence was briefly made capital before Rome took over in 1870.

Ever beautiful, the city has been buffeted by the modern age. During WWII the Germans blew up all Florence's bridges apart from Ponte Vecchio. Floods ravaged the city in 1966 and a huge Mafia car bomb in 1993 killed five people, injured 37 and destroyed part of the Uffizi.

Dominating the city skyline is the russet-domed Cattedrale di Santa Maria del Fiore (☎ 055 21 53 80; www.duomofirenze.it; ☀ 10am-5pm Mon-Wed & Fri, to

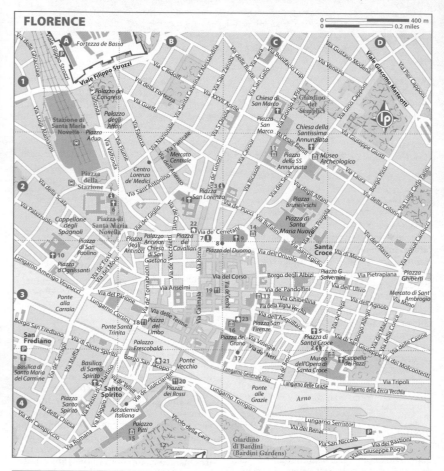

FLORENCE

3.30pm Thu, to 4.45pm Sat, to 3.30pm 1st Sat of month, 1.30-4.45pm Sun), with its furiously pretty façade in pink, white and green marble. Begun in 1296 by Arnolfo di Cambio, the world's fourth-largest cathedral took almost 150 years to complete. The restrained interior is a surprise after the tumultuous decoration of the façade. It's also surprisingly secular in places (a sizeable chunk of the cathedral was not paid for by the church).

It's a must to scale the 463 steps to the Brunelleschi-designed dome (☎ 055 230 28 85; admission €8; ⓨ 8.30am-7pm Mon-Fri, 8.30am-5.40pm Sat) for unforgettable panoramas, and you can also climb the Giotto-designed, 82m campanile (ⓨ 8.30am-7.30pm). The 11th-century Romanesque baptistry has three sets of doors, executed by Pisano and Ghiberti, the finest being the latter's *Gates of Paradise*. The originals are in the Museo dell'Opera del Duomo (Piazza del Duomo 9; www.operaduomo.firenze.it; admission €6; ⓨ 9am-6.50pm Mon-Sat, 9am-1pm Sun); those *in situ* are copies.

For Italy's most comprehensive collection of Tuscan Renaissance sculpture, head to Museo del Bargello (ⓨ 8.15am-1.50pm Tue-Sat, to 5pm Jul), with some fine works by Michelangelo.

To see the city's political heart, seek out Piazza della Signoria, surrounded by some of Florence's most celebrated buildings, including Palazzo Vecchio (☎ 055 276 82 24; www.palazzovecchio-museoragazzi.it; Piazza della Signoria; adult/18-25yr/3-17yr €6/4.50/2; ⓨ 9am-7pm Fri-Wed, to 2pm Thu) crowned by the 94m-tall Torre d'Arnolfo. Once the seat of Florentine government, then the Medici residence, it's now the mayor's office. It's best visited via guided tour (€2).

Florence also contains the incredible Uffizi (☎ 055 238 86 51; Piazzale degli Uffizi 6; adult/concession €6.50/3.25, 85min audioguide for 1/2 €5.50/8; ⓨ 8.15am-6.35pm Tue-Sun, to 9pm Tue Jul-Sep), currently undergoing a facelift that should be completed in 2013. It contains the Medici family's private art collection, with masterpieces from medieval, Renaissance, Mannerist, Baroque and neoclassical schools, including works by Giotto, Michelangelo, Raphael, Titian, Tintoretto and many more.

Florence's glorious churches include the 13th-century Chiesa di Ognissanti (ⓨ 7am-12.30pm & 4-8pm Mon-Sat, 4-8pm Sun), featuring paintings by Botticelli and Ghirlandaio; Basilica di Santa Maria Novella (☎ 055 21 59 18; Piazza di Santa Maria Novella; admission €2.50; ⓨ 9am-5pm Mon-Thu, 1-5pm Fri); and the never-finished Basilica di San Lorenzo (Piazza San Lorenzo; admission €3.50; ⓨ 10am-5pm Mon-Sat, 1.30-5pm Sun).

In the San Marco area lies the excellent Galleria dell'Accademia (☎ 055 29 48 83; Via Ricasoli 60; adult/

TRANSPORT – FLORENCE

Distance from Rome 284km

Direction North

Travel time 1 hour 40 minutes

Train From Stazione Termini (€40, hourly).

concession €6.50/3.25; ⓨ 8.15am-6.50pm Tue-Sun), which contains Michelangelo's *David*, plus masterpieces by artists such as Botticelli. Designed by Arnolfo di Cambio, the Basilica di Santa Croce (☎ 055 246 61 05; adult/concession incl Museo dell'Opera €5/3; ⓨ 9.30am-5.30pm Mon-Sat, 1-5.30pm Sun), with its Giotto frescoes and Brunelleschi cloisters, so dazzled Stendhal that he nearly fainted.

You can cross over to the Oltrarno via the Ponte Vecchio, the 14th-century bridge laden with jewellery shops, the only bridge to escape destruction by the Nazis in 1944. On the other side lie the Brunelleschi-designed Palazzo Pitti (☎ 055 94 48 83; Piazza de' Pitti 1), another former home of the Medici, and the Boboli Gardens (ⓨ 8.15am-7.30pm Jun-Aug, to 6.30pm Mar-May & Sep, to 5.30pm Oct, to 4.30pm Nov-Feb, closed 1st & last Mon of month).

INFORMATION

Comune di Firenze tourist office train station (☎ 055 21 22 45; www.comune.fi.it, in Italian; Piazza della Stazione 4; ⓨ 8.30am-7pm Mon-Sat, to 2pm Sun); Santa Croce (☎ 055 234 04 44; Borgo Santa Croce 29r; ⓨ 9am-7pm Mon-Sat & 9am-2pm Sun Mar–mid-Nov, 9am-5pm Mon-Fri & 9am-2pm Sun mid-Nov–Feb)

Provincia di Firenze Tourist Office (☎ 055 29 08 32; www.firenzeturismo.it; Via Cavour 1r; ⓨ 8.30am-6.30pm Mon-Sat, 8.30am-1.30pm Sun)

EATING

Cantinetta dei Verrazzano (☎ 055 26 85 90; Via dei Tavolini 18-20; dishes €3-12; ⓨ noon-9pm Mon-Sat) A *forno* (bakery) and *cantinetta* (small cellar) create alchemy here, with focaccia fresh from the oven, perhaps topped with caramelised radicchio or porcini mushrooms, perfectly accompanied by Chianti.

Cantinetta Antinori (☎ 055 26 85 90; Via de' Tornabuoni 7; meals €55; ⓨ noon-9pm; ⓨ Mon-Fri) A small cellar on a completely different scale, this occupies a 1502 *palazzo* and serves classic Tuscan cuisine together with fine local wines.

Le Volpe e l'Uva (☎ 055 239 81 32; Piazza dei Rossi 1; cheese or meat platter €7; ⓨ noon-9pm; ⓨ Mon-Fri)

Over in Oltrarno, this could be Florence's finest *enoteca*: intimate, with wine by the glass and antipasti galore, such as juicy *prosciutto di parma* and boutique Tuscan cheeses.

SLEEPING

Hotel San Giovanni (☎ 055 28 83 85; www.hotelsangiovanni .com; Via Cerretani 2; d €45-60, with bathroom €85) This no-frills place is nonetheless one of the city's best deals, as many rooms here have views of the cathedral, campanile and baptistery.

In Piazza della Signoria (☎ 055 239 95 46; www.in piazzadellasignoria.com; Via dei Magazzini 2; d €160-280) A central and intimate B&B. Rooms here have high ceilings and lots of polished wood, and some have piazza views.

Hotel Lungarno (☎ 055 272 64 000; www.lungarnohotels .com; Borgo San Jacopo 14; r from €370) Romantic, riverside Lungarno has suntrap terraces and around 450 original artworks on the walls. It was designed by Florentine wonder-designer Michel Bonan and is owned by the Ferragamo family (of high-fashion fame).

TIVOLI

For millennia, the hilltop town of Tivoli has been a summer escape for rich Romans, as amply demonstrated by its two Unesco World Heritage sites, both breathtaking hedonistic playgrounds. Villa Adriana was the mammoth country estate of Emperor Hadrian, and the 16th-century Villa d'Este is a wonder of the High Renaissance. You can visit both in a day, though you'll have to start early.

Emperor Hadrian's summer residence Villa Adriana (☎ 06 399 67 900; adult/child €6.50/3.25, possible €3.50 for exhibition, car park €2; ⏰ 9am until 1hr before sunset), 5km outside Tivoli, set new standards of luxury when it was built between AD 118 and 134, even given the excess of the Roman Empire. A model near the entrance gives you an idea of the scale of the original complex, which you'll need several hours to explore. Consider hiring an audioguide (€4), which gives a helpful overview. There's a small cafeteria next to the ticket office, but bringing a picnic would be nicer.

A great traveller and enthusiastic architect, Hadrian himself designed much of the complex, taking inspiration from his travels. The pecile, a large porticoed pool area where the emperor used to stroll after lunch, was a reproduction of a building in Athens. Similarly, the canopo is a copy of the sanctuary of Serapis near Alexandria, with a long canal of water, originally surrounded by Egyptian statues, representing the Nile.

To the east of the *pecile* is one of the highlights, Hadrian's private retreat, the Teatro Marittimo. Built on an island in an artificial pool, it was originally a mini villa accessible only by swing bridges, which the emperor would have raised when he felt like a dip. Nearby, the fish pond is encircled by an underground gallery where Hadrian liked to wander. There are also *nymphaeums*, temples and barracks, and a museum with the latest discoveries from ongoing excavations, which is often closed.

In Tivoli's hilltop centre, the gardens of Villa d'Este (☎ 199 76 61 66, 0445 23 03 10; www.villadestetivoli .info; Piazza Trento; adult/child €6.50/free; ⏰ 8.30am until 1hr before sunset Tue-Sun) have an *Alice in Wonderland* magic, and are a superlative example of a High Renaissance garden. The villa was once a Benedictine convent, converted by Lucrezia Borgia's son, Cardinal Ippolito d'Este, into a sumptuous pleasure palace in 1550. From 1865 to 1886 it was home to Franz Liszt and inspired his compositions *To the Cypresses*

TRANSPORT – TIVOLI

Distance from Rome 30km

Direction East

Travel time 30 minutes to one hour

Bus Cotral buses depart at least every 20 minutes and the one-hour journey costs €1.60 (€3.20 return). However, it's best to buy a Zone 3 BIRG ticket (€6), which will cover you for the whole day. The easiest way to visit both sites via public transport is take a bus or train to Tivoli and visit the Villa D'Este first. Then take the CAT bus 4 or 4X (www.cattivoli.com; €1, 10 minutes, half hourly Monday to Saturday, every 70 minutes Sunday) from Largo Garibaldi, asking the driver to stop at Villa Adriana. To return, you can then take a bus (€2, 50 minutes) to Tiburtina from outside the site.

Car Take either Via Tiburtina (SS5) or the faster Rome-L'Aquila autostrada (A24).

Train From Stazione Tiburtina (€2.50, 50 minutes, hourly).

of the Villa d'Este and Fountains of the Villa d'Este.

The rich Mannerist frescoes of the villa interior merit a glance, but it's the garden that you're here for: terraces with water-spouting gargoyles, fountains powered by gravitational force, elaborate avenues lined with deep-green, knotty cypresses. One fountain (designed by Gianlorenzo Bernini) used its water pressure to play a concealed organ, another imitated the call of birds. One of the highlights is the 130m-long path of the Hundred Fountains, which joins the Fountain of Tivoli to the Fountain of Rome. Don't miss the Rometta fountain, with reproductions of the landmarks of Rome.

The villa is a two-minute walk north from Largo Garibaldi. Picnics are forbidden, but there's a stylish café.

Nearby is Villa Gregoriana (☎ 06 399 67 701; Piazza Tempio di Vesta; adult/child €5/2.50; ☼ 10am-6.30pm Tue-Sun Apr–mid-Oct, 10am-2.30pm Mon-Sat, 10am-4pm Sun Mar & mid-Oct–Nov, by appointment Dec-Feb), a 19th-century park laid out by Pope Gregory XVI in 1834. The park descends down a steep gorge, over which water crashes to the bottom of the canyon more than 100m below; the highlight is the 120m-high Cascata Grande (Great Waterfall).

INFORMATION

Tourist information point (☎ 07 743 13 536; ☼ 10am-1pm & 4 6.30pm, shorter hrs in winter) On Piazza Garibaldi, where the bus arrives.

EATING & SLEEPING

Villa d'Este (☎ 0774 31 17 65; Villa d'Este, Piazza Trento; set menus €16) In Villa d'Este, this is a stylish café-restaurant for a drink or lunch.

Hotel Adriano (☎ 0774 38 22 35; www.hoteladriano.it; Largo Yourcenar; s €90-100, d €100-120) A smart three-star opposite the entrance to Villa Adriana. Its excellent restaurant (meals €45) has served Federico Fellini and Queen Elizabeth II.

CASTELLI ROMANI

About 20km south of Rome, the Colli Albani (Alban hills) and their 13 towns are collectively known as the Castelli Romani. For millennia they've provided Romans with a green refuge on hot summer weekends. The most famous towns are Castel Gandolfo, where the pope has his summer residence, and Frascati, famous for its crisp white wine. The other towns are Monte Porzio Catone, Montecompatri, Rocca Priora, Colonna, Rocca di Papa,

Grottaferrata, Marino, Albano Laziale, Ariccia, Genzano and Nemi.

Frascati is an easy bus or train ride from Rome and makes a rewarding day trip. A villa perches over the town above ornamental gardens, its flat-fronted façade like an expensive stage set. It's the 16th-century Villa Aldobrandini, designed by Giacomo della Porta and built by Carlo Maderno.

If you have a car head up to the ruins of ancient Tusculum. All that remains of this once-imposing 4th-century-BC town is a small amphitheatre, a crumbling villa and a small stretch of road leading up to the city, but it's a lovely spot for a walk, and the views are stupendous.

Villas and views are all very well, but most people come to Frascati for the food and fresh white wine. You can pick up a porchetta panini (sandwich made of pork roasted with herbs) from one of the stands that do a brisk weekend trade around Piazza del Mercato, or head to the cantinas that dot the town, which usually sell porchetta, olives, salami and cheeses plus jugs of wine.

A short drive away at Grottaferrata there's a 15th-century abbey (abbazia; ☎ 06 945 93 09; Viale San Nilo; admission free; ☼ 7am-12.30pm & 3.30pm until 1hr before sunset), founded in 1004. The church interior resembles an incense-perfumed jewellery box, and Mass is particularly atmospheric. The congregation of Greek monks wear distinctive flat-topped black caps.

Continuing southwest brings you to Castel Gandolfo, an impressive, dome-capped hilltop borgo (small village) overlooking Lago di Albano. This is the pope's summer residence, which, although closed to the public, still attracts hordes of tourists to the impressive town square. Lago Albano, a great azure expanse, is simply glorious for a summer swim, and cafés and boating-hire places dot its banks.

The smaller of the two volcanic lakes in the Castelli Romani, Lago di Nemi was the centre of a cult to the goddess Diana in ancient times, and favourite holiday spot of the emperor Caligula. The Museo delle Navi Romani (☎ 06 939 80 40; Via Diana; admission €2; ☼ 9am-7pm) on the shore was built by Mussolini to house two Roman boats salvaged from the lake in 1932. These dated from Caligula's time but were tragically destroyed by fire in 1944 – what you see now are scale models.

INFORMATION

Frascati Point (☎ 06 940 15 378; ☼ 10am-4pm Mon-Wed & Fri, 10am-3pm Thu, 10am-7pm Sat) Here you can access information about local wines, vineyards and

TRANSPORT – CASTELLI ROMANI

Distance from Rome 20km

Direction Southeast

Travel time 20 to 50 minutes

Bus To reach Frascati, take a bus (€2, 25 minutes, 35 per day weekdays, fewer on weekends) from Anagnina Metro station. To get from Frascati to Grottaferrata (€1, 15 minutes, every 30 to 40 minutes), catch a Cotral bus from Piazza Guglielmo Marconi. To reach Lago di Nemi, catch a Velletri-headed bus and get off at Genzano di Roma (€1, 30 minutes, infrequent), from where you'll need to catch another bus to the lake (€1, 10 minutes, infrequent). To reach Castel Gandolfo (€1, 30 minutes, hourly), catch the Pomezia bus from Piazza Guglielmo Marconi.

Car For Frascati and Grottaferrata take Via Tuscolana (SS215); for Castel Gandolfo and Albano Laziale take Via Appia Nuova (SS7) south, following signs for Ciampino Airport.

Train Trains leave from Stazione Termini for Frascati (€1.90, 30 minutes, about hourly Monday to Saturday, every two hours Sunday), Castel Gandolfo (€1.90, 40 minutes, hourly, every two hours Sunday) and Albano Laziale (€1.90, 50 minutes, hourly, every two hours Sunday), from where you can catch a bus to Nemi.

---

cantinas (wine cellars). The building is the former stables of the Villa Aldobrandini and owes its makeover to Italy's hippest architect, Massimiliano Fuksas.

EATING & SLEEPING

Antico Ristorante Pagnanelli (☎ 06 936 00 04; Via A Gramsci 4, Castel Gandolfo; meals €55; ☺ Wed-Mon year-round plus Tue May-Oct) With high-class cuisine, a 3000-label wine list and a terrace with spectacular lake views, this restaurant is the business.

Trattoria la Sirena del Lago (☎ 06 936 80 20; Via del Plebiscito 26, Nemi; meals €25; ☺ Tue-Sun) Here the local game and trout are excellent and the local wine refreshing. Nemi is also famous for its wild strawberries – sprinkled over almost everything (especially ice cream) in season.

Le Vie dei Canti (☎ 06 940 104 13; Via G D'Estouteville 3, Frascati; ☺ 7.30pm-midnight) A rustic enoteca, softly lit and wood-lined, tucked down a cobbled alleyway (off Piazza Paolo III), serving up plates of delicious cheeses, salami, carpacci (thin slices of raw meat or fish) and crostone (toasted bread brushed with olive oil and toppings such as olive paste or truffles).

Hotel Pagnanelli Lucia (☎ 06 936 14 22; www.albergo pagnanelli.it; Via A Gramsci 2, Castel Gandolfo; d €100) A modest two-star hotel, where rooms have wrought-iron beds and lake views.

SPERLONGA & SABAUDIA

The best of Lazio's beaches are south of Rome, near the regional border with Campania.

Fashionable coastal town Sperlonga is all about tourism. Its whitewashed centro storico buzzes in summer and there are two inviting, sandy beaches either side of a rocky promontory. The town is divided into two parts: medieval Sperlonga Alta on top of the promontory, and modern Sperlonga Bassa at sea level.

Other than the beach, the town's main attraction is the Museo Archeologico di Sperlonga (☎ 07 715 48 028; Via Flacca, km1.6; admission €4; ☺ 8.30am-7.30pm), home to sculptures and masks dating from the 2nd century BC and a cave with a circular pool used by the emperor Tiberius. The remains of his villa are in front of the cave.

Developed on reclaimed land by sun-worshipping Fascists, Sabaudia, 120km southeast of Rome and 43km west of Sperlonga,

---

TRANSPORT – SPERLONGA & SABAUDIA

Distance from Rome 120km

Direction Southeast

Travel time 1½ to two hours

Bus Cotral buses leave from outside the Laurentina station on metro line B heading for Terracina and pass by Sabaudia en route (€5.50, two to three hours depending on traffic).

Car Take Via Pontina (SS148) south to Terracina and then the SS213.

Train Take a regional train (not the intercity) from Stazione Termini to Fondi (€6.20, 1¼ hours, about 20 daily). From the Fondi train station, you can catch the connecting Piazzoli Giorgio bus (☎ 07 715 19 067) to Sperlonga (€1, 15 minutes, hourly). Returning from Sperlonga, the bus to Fondi leaves from the main road in the lower town.

DETOUR: SUBIACO & CASSINO

Founder of the Benedictine order, St Benedict is regarded to be the father of Western monasticism. He is also the patron saint of engineers and speleologists, an accolade that he owes to three years he spent holed up in a cave in Subiaco. Fleeing the vices that had so disgusted him as a student in Rome, he sought the gloom of the grotto to meditate and pray. During this time he attracted a large local following that eventually provoked the ire of his fellow friars and forced him onto the road.

Remote-feeling and dramatic, Subiaco is well worth the trip to see its wonderful monasteries and impressive abbey, with breathtaking cross-country views. The Monastery of St Benedict (☎ 07 748 50 39; ☽ 9am-12.30pm & 3-6.30pm) is carved into the rock over the saint's former cave. It has a stunning setting, described by Petrarch as 'the edge of Paradise', and is adorned with rich 13th- to 15th-century frescoes. Halfway down the hill from St Benedict is the Monastery of St Scholastica (☎ 07 748 55 25; ☽ 9am-12.30pm & 3.30-7pm), the only one of the 13 monasteries built by St Benedict still standing in the Valley of the Amiene. It has a restaurant offering set menus for €18 and €26. Its Foresteria (☎ 07 748 55 69; www.benedettini-subiaco.it; per person B&B €36, half board €45, full board €55) is a great place to spend a comfortable and contemplative night, but book ahead, as Benedictine clergy often make the pilgrimage here to work in the monastery's famous library and archive (☽ 9am-6pm Mon-Fri, 9am-12.30pm Sat).

From Subiaco, St Benedict headed south until, it's said, three ravens led him to the top of Monte Cassino. Here, in AD 529, he founded the abbey that was to be his home until he died in AD 547. One of the medieval world's most important Christian centres, the monumental abbey (☎ 0776 31 15 29; parking €2; ☽ 9am-12.30pm & 3.30-6pm) has been destroyed and rebuilt several times throughout its history, most recently in 1953. During WWII the abbey was central to German efforts to stop the Allied push north. After almost six months of bitter fighting, the Allies finally bombed the abbey in May 1944 in a desperate attempt to break through.

In Cassino, there's a helpful tourist office (☎ 0776 2 12 92; www.apt.frosinone.it; Via G Di Biasio; ☽ 8.30am-1.30pm & 3-6pm Mon-Fri, 9am-1pm Sat).

To get to the monasteries in Subiaco from Rome by public transport, take a Cotral bus to the Subiaco bus station (€6.30, 50 minutes to 1¼ hours, every 15 to 30 minutes weekdays, less frequently weekends) from Ponte Mammolo on metro line B. The shorter trip takes the A24; the longer trip is via Tivoli. The bus stops a little way from the Monastery of St Scholastica – it's a 3km scenic, if demanding, uphill walk.

For Cassino, take one of the regular trains from Stazione Termini (€7.40, 2¼ hours). Some trains take around 1¾ hours and cost a little more. Then take one of the shuttle buses (€2 return) from Piazza San Benedetto up to the abbey. These leave at 9.45am (return at noon) and at 3.30pm (return 5pm). If you walk, it'll take around two hours to get up the hill and 1½ hours to walk back down!

is a stark 1930s curiosity rather than picturesque, but it's also the launchpad for the Parco Nazionale del Circeo (www.parcocirceo.it; Via Carlo Alberto 107; ☽ 10am-1pm & 2.30-6pm), a lovely 800-hectare area of sand dunes, rocky coastline, forest and wetlands. The visitor centre (☎ 0773 51 13 85) can provide details on local activities, including fishing, bird-watching, walking and cycling.

EATING & SLEEPING

Gli Archi (☎ 0771 5 43 00; Via Ottaviano 17; meals €35) Rustic and set in the medieval quarter, Gli Archi offers seafood so fresh it virtually wriggles off the plate. Signature dishes include *linguine agli scampi* (long pasta with scampi) and *zuppa di cozze* (mussel soup). It's worth eating fresh buffalo mozzarella in town – it's super fresh because there are many producers in the area.

Hotel Mayor (☎ 0771 54 92 45; www.hotelmayor.it; Via 1 Romita 4; s €65-140, d €80-140; P ☒) Just off the main seafront road into town, with plain, clean rooms, some with balconies, and excellent facilities for beach bunnies: tone up on your tan in the solarium before heading to the hotel's private beach area. In high season you must book for three nights or more.

ISOLE PONTINE

This group of small islands between Rome and Naples serves as an Italian Hamptons. Roman weekenders descend in droves to eat shellfish at little terrace restaurants, swim in emerald coves, and take boat trips around the craggy coast. Few foreigners have discovered this idyllic archipelago, though this is slowly changing. Be warned that Ponza and Ventotene – the only two inhabited islands – get crowded during holiday periods, and they're not cheap. It's best to visit in spring or autumn.

The islands have long been a favoured getaway. Homer refers to Ponza in the *Odyssey*,

TRANSPORT – ISOLE PONTINE

Distance from Rome 135km

Direction Southeast

Travel time Three hours

Car Take the SS138 southwards, then take the exit for Anzio and follow the SS07.

Ferry Ponza and Ventotene are accessible by car ferry or hydrofoil from Anzio. Some services run year-round but others run only from late June to the start of September. The major company is Vetor (www.vetor.it), and the trip takes 1 hour 10 minutes.

Train Trains for Anzio leave from Termini about hourly and take one hour (€3.20).

while in Roman times emperors and courtiers came here for some downtime. But as the Roman Empire declined, the islands were left vulnerable to violent attacks by the Saracens and by groups from mainland Italy and the nearby Aeolian Islands. During this period the island's main visitors were exiled outcasts from society: unfaithful wives, promiscuous daughters and persecuted Christians.

A golden age came in the 18th century, but commerce flourished at the expense of the natural habitat. Today Ponza is ecologically still in poor shape: there's a lot of erosion caused by terraced farming, and migrating birds would do well to find a different route between Europe and Africa, as hunting is hugely popular. Fortunately, the islands are now under national park protection.

Cars and large motorbikes are forbidden on Ponza in summer, but there's a good local bus service (tickets €1). Otherwise, you can rent a scooter or even a golf buggy to get around.

INFORMATION

Ponza Online (www.ponza.it, in Italian) Online information about Ponza.

Pro Loco tourist office (☎ 0771 8 00 31; www.proloco diponza.it)

SLEEPING

Many of the locals rent rooms to tourists; you'll find them touting at the port. Otherwise, the tourist office will help you out. The following places are on Ponza.

Villa Ersilia (☎ 0771 8 00 97; www.villaersilia.it) Rents out a variety of simple rooms, studios and apartments. Prices range from €35 to €100 per person per night.

Villa Laetitia (☎ 0771 985 10 03; www.villalaetitia .com; Salita Scotti; d €150-230) Book ahead for this haven of chic, a residence owned by the Fendi family, with just three rooms with views, exquisitely decorated with fabulous artefacts.

Grand Hotel Santa Domitilla (☎ 0771 80 99 51; www .santadomitilla.com; Via Panoramica; d €280-390; 🍴 🖥 🛋) Divinely light, chic rooms offer space and tranquillity. Make like the beautiful people and book this swish four-star, which has three pools.

TRANSPORT

Rome is an easy place to get to. It's served by direct flights from across the world and hundreds of European connections. Once you're in the city, there's a comprehensive public-transport system, which makes getting around pretty simple.

If you wish to book flights, tours and rail tickets online, you can do so at www.lonely planet.com/travel_services.

AIR
Airlines

Rome is served by most of the world's major international airlines and a host of low-cost carriers – check out www.flycheapo.com for details of budget airlines. Many airlines have counters in the departure hall at Fiumicino airport (Leonardo da Vinci Airport; p284).

Domestic flights are operated by a number of international companies, including Ryanair (☎ 899 678 910; www.ryanair.com) and easyJet (☎ 899 678 990; www.easyjet.com), and Italy's big two domestic airlines: Alitalia (☎ 06 22 22; www.alitalia.it) and Meridiana (☎ 89 29 28; www.meridiana.it).

International airlines with direct connections to Rome include the following:

THINGS CHANGE...

The information in this chapter is particularly vulnerable to change. Check directly with the airline or a travel agent to make sure you understand how a fare (and any ticket you may buy) works, and be aware of the security requirements for international travel. Shop carefully. The details given in this chapter should be regarded as pointers and are not a substitute for your own careful, up-to-date research.

Air Berlin (AB; ☎ 199 400 737; www.airberlin.com)

Air Canada (AC; ☎ 06 835 14 955; www.aircanada.com)

Air France (AF; ☎ 848 88 44 66; www.airfrance.com)

Alitalia (AZ; ☎ 06 22 22; www.alitalia.it)

American Airlines (AA; ☎ 06 660 53 169; www.aa.com)

British Airways (BA; ☎ 199 71 22 66; www.britishairways.com)

Brussels Airlines (SN; ☎ 899 80 09 03; www.brussels airlines.com)

Delta Air Lines (DL; ☎ 848 390 256; www.delta.com)

EasyJet (U2; ☎ 899 678 990; www.easyjet.com)

CLIMATE CHANGE & TRAVEL

Climate change is a serious threat to the ecosystems that humans rely upon, and air travel is the fastest-growing contributor to the problem. Lonely Planet regards travel, overall, as a global benefit, but believes we all have a responsibility to limit our personal impact on global warming.

Flying & Climate Change

Pretty much every form of motor transport generates CO_2 (the main cause of human-induced climate change) but planes are far and away the worst offenders, not just because of the sheer distances they allow us to travel, but because they release greenhouse gases high into the atmosphere. The statistics are frightening: two people taking a return flight between Europe and the US will contribute as much to climate change as an average household's gas and electricity consumption over a whole year.

Carbon Offset Schemes

Climatecare.org and other websites use 'carbon calculators' that allow travellers to offset the greenhouse gases they are responsible for with contributions to energy-saving projects and other climate-friendly initiatives in the developing world – including projects in India, Honduras, Kazakhstan and Uganda.

Lonely Planet, together with Rough Guides and other concerned partners in the travel industry, supports the carbon offset scheme run by climatecare.org. Lonely Planet offsets all of its staff and author travel.

For more information check out our website: www.lonelyplanet.com.

Emirates (EK; ☎ 06 452 06 060; www.emirates.com)

Iberia (IB; ☎ 199 101 191; www.iberia.com)

KLM (KL; ☎ 199 414 199; www.klm.com)

Lufthansa (LH; ☎ 199 40 00 44; www.lufthansa.com)

Malaysia Airlines (MH; ☎ 06 42 15 41; www.malaysia airlines.com)

Qantas (QF; ☎ 848 35 00 10; www.qantas.com)

Ryanair (FR; ☎ 899 678 910; www.ryanair.com)

Singapore Airlines (SQ; ☎ 06 478 55 360; www.singapore air.com)

Thai Air (TG; ☎ 06 47 81 31; www.thaiair.com)

Vueling (VY; ☎ 199 30 88 30; www.vueling.com)

Travel websites worth checking for tickets:

Cheap Tickets (www.cheaptickets.com)

Expedia (www.expedia.com)

Flightbookers (www.ebookers.com)

Opodo (www.opodo.com)

Skyscanner (www.skyscanner.net)

Note that some low-cost airlines, most notably Ryanair, only accept bookings made on their own website.

Airports

Rome is served by two airports: the main international airport Leonardo da Vinci (FCO; ☎ 06 6 59 51; www.adr.it), better known as Fiumicino, and Ciampino (CIA; ☎ 06 6 59 51; www.adr.it).

Thirty kilometres from the centre of town, Leonardo da Vinci is divided into five terminals: Terminals A and AA for domestic flights, Terminal B for international flights to Schengen countries, Terminal C for all other international flights, and Terminal 5 for flights to the USA and Israel. Terminals A, B and C are within easy walking distance of each other in the main airport building. Terminal 5 is accessible by shuttle bus from Terminal C.

Facilities at the airport include a post office, internet access, some 140 shops, and a left-luggage office (⏱ 6.30am-11.30pm) on the ground floor of Terminal C. To leave a bag costs €6 per 24 hours.

Ciampino, 15km southeast of the city centre, is used by low-cost airlines and charter operators. It's not a big airport but there's a steady flow of traffic and at peak times it can get extremely busy. Facilities are limited but you'll find a post office, banks and ATMs.

Travellers with disabilities should contact ADR Assistance (www.adrassistance.it) for assistance at either Fiumicino or Ciampino.

BICYCLE

The centre of Rome doesn't lend itself to cycling: there are steep hills and treacherous cobbled roads, and the traffic is terrible. However, if you want to pedal around town, pick up *Andiamo in Bici a Roma* (€7), a useful map published by L'Ortensia Rossa, which details Rome's main cycle paths.

On Sunday, and weekdays after 9pm, you can take your bike on the metro and the Lido di Ostia train, although you'll have to buy a separate ticket for it.

You can also carry bikes on bus No 791 and on some regional trains, paying a €3.50 supplement. On Intercity and Eurocity/Euronight services the supplement is €5 on national routes and €10 on international journeys.

As an alternative to hiring, Rome now offers a bike-sharing scheme with 200 bikes available at 19 stands in the historic centre. On signing up to the scheme you're provided with a rechargeable smartcard that allows you to pick up a bike and use it for up to 24 hours within a single day. You can sign up at the ATAC ticket offices at Termini, Spagna and Lepanto metro stations. There's a €5 signing on fee and a €5 minimum charge. On the road, you'll pay €0.50 for every 30 minutes. For further information see www.atacbike sharing.com or call ☎ 06 5 70 03.

Hire

Appia Antica Regional Park Information Point (Map pp124–5; ☎ 06 513 53 16; www.parcoappiaantica.org; Via Appia Antica 58-60; per hr/day €3/10)

Bici e Baci (Map pp106–7; ☎ 06 482 84 43; www .bicibaci.com; Via del Viminale 5; per hr/day €4/11)

Eco Move Rent (Map pp106–7; ☎ 06 447 04 518; www .ecomoverent.com; Via Varese 48-50; per hr/day €6/11)

Treno e Scooter (Map pp106–7; ☎ 06 489 05 823; www .trenoescooter.com; Piazza dei Cinquecento; per hr/day €4/10)

Villa Borghese (Map pp150–1; Via delle Belle Arti; per hr €3)

BUS & TRAM

Rome's buses and trams are run by ATAC (☎ 06 5 70 03; www.atac.roma.it). The main bus station (Map pp106–7) is in front of Stazione Termini on Piazza dei Cinquecento, where there's an information booth (☉ 8am-8pm). Other important hubs are at Largo di Torre Argentina, Piazza Venezia and Piazza San Silvestro. Buses generally run from about 5.30am until midnight, with limited services throughout the night.

Useful routes:

H Stazione Termini, Via Nazionale, Piazza Venezia, Largo di Torre Argentina, Ponte Garibaldi, Viale Trastevere and into the western suburbs.

3 Stazione Trastevere, Testaccio, Circo Massimo, Colosseo, San Giovanni, Porta Maggiore, Policlinico, Villa Borghese.

8 Tram Largo di Torre Argentina, Trastevere, Stazione Trastevere and Monteverde Nuovo.

23 Piazzale Clodio, Piazza Risorgimento, Ponte Vittorio Emanuele II, Lungotevere, Ponte Garibaldi, Via Marmorata (Testaccio), Piazzale Ostiense and Basilica di San Paolo.

40 Express Stazione Termini, Via Nazionale, Piazza Venezia, Largo di Torre Argentina, Chiesa Nuova, Piazza Pia (for Castel Sant'Angelo) and St Peter's.

64 Stazione Termini to St Peter's Square. It takes the same route as the 40 Express but is more crowded and has more stops.

GETTING INTO TOWN

Fiumicino

The easiest way to get to and from Fiumicino is by train. The efficient *Leonardo Express* leaves from platform 24 at Stazione Termini and travels direct to the airport every 30 minutes from 5.52am until 10.52pm. It costs €11 (children under 12 free) and takes about 30 minutes. From Fiumicino, trains start at 6.36am and run half-hourly until 11.36pm.

If you want to get to Termini, don't take the FM1 train for Orte or Fara Sabina. These slower trains stop at Trastevere, Ostiense and Tiburtina stations but not Termini. They cost €5.50 and run every 15 minutes (half-hourly on Sundays and public holidays) from 5.57am to 11.27pm, and from Tiburtina from 5.05am until 10.33pm. Journey time is 30 minutes to/from Ostiense and 45 minutes to Tiburtina.

Train tickets can be bought from vending machines in the arrivals hall and train station, from ticket offices, and from *tabacchi* (newsagents).

Cotral (☎ 800 15 00 08; www.cotralspa.it in Italian) runs eight daily buses from Stazione Tiburtina via Stazione Termini to Fiumicino, including night services at 12.30am, 1.15am, 2.30am and 3.45am, returning at 1.15am, 2.15am, 3.30am and 5am. Tickets, available on the bus, cost €4.50. Note that Tiburtina is not a safe place to hang around at night.

By car, follow signs for Roma out of the airport complex and onto the autostrada. Exit at EUR, following signs for the *centro,* to link up with Via Cristoforo Colombo, which will take you directly into the centre.

Official taxis leave from outside the arrivals hall. The set fare to the city centre is €40, which is valid for up to four passengers and includes luggage.

Several private companies run shuttle services. Airport Connection Services (☎ 06 338 32 21; www.airportconnection.it) charges from €37 per person to or from the city centre. Airport Shuttle (☎ 06 420 14 507; www.airportshuttle.it) operates minibus transfers to/from Fiumicino for €28/35 one way for one person then €6 for each additional passenger up to a maximum of eight. A 30% surcharge is added between 9pm and 7am. You need to book in advance.

All major car-hire companies are present at Fiumicino.

Ciampino

For Ciampino your best bet is to take a shuttle bus. Terravision (☎ 06 454 41 345; www.terravision.eu) buses depart from Via Marsala outside Stazione Termini every 20 minutes between 4.30am and 9.20pm and from Ciampino between 8.15am and 12.15am. Buy tickets (single/return €4/8) for the 45-minute journey from Terracafè at Stazione Termini or at Ciampino airport. Alternatively, SIT (☎ 06 591 68 26; www.sitbusshuttle.com) covers the same route, with regular departures from Termini between 4.30am and 9.45pm, and from Ciampino between 7.45am and 11.45pm. One-way tickets, available on the bus, cost €6 from Termini, €4 from Ciampino.

Schiaffini (☎ 800 700 805; www.schiaffini.com) runs up to 20 daily services to and from Via Giovanni Goilitti outside Stazione Termini. Tickets are available from sellers outside the bus (€4.50) or on board (€6.50).

Otherwise, local orange buses run from the airport to Ciampino train station from where regular trains run to Termini.

Airport Connection Services (☎ 06 338 32 21; www.airportconnection.it) and Airport Shuttle (☎ 06 420 14 507; www.airportshuttle.it) also operate transfers. With the former you'll pay from €37; with the latter €42 for one or two people, then €6 for each extra passenger.

By taxi the set rate to or from Ciampino is €30.

If you wish to hire a car, you'll find all the major rental companies in the arrivals hall.

170 Stazione Termini, Via Nazionale, Piazza Venezia, Via del Teatro Marcello and Piazza Bocca della Verità (then south to Testaccio and EUR).

175 Via del Teatro di Marcello, Via del Circo Massimo, Aventino Hill and Stazione Ostiense.

492 Stazione Tiburtina, San Lorenzo, Stazione Termini, Piazza Barberini, Piazza Venezia, Corso Rinascimento, Piazza Cavour, Piazza Risorgimento and Cipro-Vatican Museums (metro line A).

590 Follows the route of metro line A and has special facilities for disabled passengers.

660 Largo Colli Albani, Via Appia Nuova and Via Appia Antica (near Mausoleo di Cecilia Metella).

714 Stazione Termini, Piazza Santa Maria Maggiore, Piazza San Giovanni in Laterano and Viale delle Terme di Caracalla (then south to EUR).

910 Stazione Termini, Piazza della Repubblica, Via Piemonte, Via Pinciana (Villa Borghese), Piazza Euclide, Palazzetto dello Sport and Piazza Mancini.

Rome's night bus service comprises more than 25 lines, many of which pass Termini and/or Piazza Venezia. Buses are marked with an n before the number and bus stops have a blue owl symbol. Departures are usually every 30 minutes, but can be much slower.

The most useful routes:

n1 Follows the route of metro line A.

n2 Follows the route of metro line B.

n7 Piazzale Clodio, Via Zanardelli, Corso Rinascimento, Corso Vittorio Emanuele II, Largo di Torre Argentina, Piazza Venezia, Via Nazionale and Stazione Termini.

Long-distance national and international buses use the bus terminus on Piazzale Tiburtina, in front of Stazione Tiburtina.

CAR & MOTORCYCLE
Driving

Most of the *centro storico* (historic centre) is closed to normal traffic. You're not allowed to drive in the centre from 6.30am to 6pm Monday to Friday and 2pm to 6pm Saturday unless you're a resident or have special permission. Further limits are also in place in Monti, Testaccio, Trastevere and San Lorenzo between 11pm and 3am on Friday and Saturday nights.

All streets accessing the 'Limited Traffic Zone' (ZTL) are equipped with electronic-access detection devices. If you're staying in this zone, contact your hotel, which will fax the authorities with your number plate, thus saving you a fine. For further information, check www.atac.roma.it or call ☎ 06 57 003.

Driving out of town can be costly. Tolls apply on *autostradas* and petrol and diesel are expensive.

All EU driving licences are valid in Italy, except for the old-style green UK licences. If you have one of these, or a licence from a non-EU country, you'll need an International Driving

---

TICKETS, PLEASE

Public-transport tickets are valid on all Rome's bus, tram and metro lines, except for routes to Fiumicino airport. They come in various forms:

BIT (*biglietto integrato a tempo,* a single ticket valid for 75 minutes and one metro ride) €1

BIG (*biglietto integrato giornaliero,* a daily ticket) €4

BTI (*biglietto turistico integrato,* a three-day ticket) €11

CIS (*carta integrata settimanale,* a weekly ticket) €16

Abbonamento mensile (a monthly pass) €30

Children under 10 travel free.

To travel in Lazio your best bet is a daily BIRG (*biglietto integrato regionale giornaliero*) ticket. This allows unlimited travel on all city and regional transport, including buses, trains, trams and, in Rome, the metro. It's priced according to zones: the most expensive, zone 7, costs €10.50; the cheapest, zone 1, is €2.50.

You can buy tickets at *tabacchi,* at newsstands and from vending machines at metro, bus and train stations. They must be purchased before you get on the bus or train and then validated in the yellow machine once on board, or at the entrance gates for the metro. You risk a €50 fine if you're caught without a validated ticket.

Note that the Roma Pass (p291) comes with a three-day travel pass valid on all transport (except for Cotral buses and national trains) within the city boundaries. The Vatican and Rome card (1/3 days €19/25) provides unlimited travel on all public transport within the city and on the Open buses operated by Roma Christiana (see p295).

Permit (IDP). Valid for a year, they're available from national motoring associations.

To ride a moped, motorcycle or scooter up to 125cc, the minimum age is 16 and a licence (a car licence will do) is required. For anything over 125cc you need a motorcycle licence. Helmets are compulsory.

Remember to drive on the right and overtake on the left, to wear seat belts and turn your headlights on outside built-up areas. It's also compulsory to carry a warning triangle and fluorescent waistcoat in case of breakdown. The blood-alcohol limit is 0.05%.

A good source of information is the Automobile Club d'Italia (ACI; www.aci.it in Italian), Italy's national motoring organisation.

Hire
CAR

Avis (www.avisautonoleggio.it in Italian; per day €56-166) Ciampino airport (☎ 06 793 40 195); Fiumicino airport (☎ 06 650 11 531); Stazione Termini (Map pp106–7; ☎ 06 481 43 73)

Europcar (www.europcar.com; per day €56-188) Ciampino airport (☎ 06 793 40 387); Fiumicino airport (☎ 06 657 61 211); Stazione Termini (Map pp106–7; ☎ 06 488 28 54)

Hertz (www.hertz.it in Italian; per day €53-218) Ciampino airport (☎ 06 793 40 616); Fiumicino airport (☎ 06 650 11 553); Stazione Termini (Map pp106–7; ☎ 06 474 03 89)

Maggiore National (central bookings ☎ 199 151 120; www.maggiore.it in Italian; per day €50-167) Ciampino airport (☎ 06 793 40 368); Fiumicino airport (☎ 06 650 10 678); Stazione Termini (Map pp106–7; ☎ 06 488 00 49)

MOTORCYCLE & SCOOTER

Bici e Baci (Map pp106–7; ☎ 06 482 84 43; www .bicibaci.com; Via del Viminale 5; scooters per day €19-80)

Eco Move Rent (Map pp106–7; ☎ 06 447 04 518; www .ecomoverent.com; Via Varese 48-50; scooters per day €40-80)

Treno e Scooter (Map pp106–7; ☎ 06 489 05 823; www .trenoescooter.com; Piazza dei Cinquecento; scooters per day €34-70)

On Road (Map pp106–7; ☎ 06 481 56 69; www.scooterhire. it; Via Cavour 80; scooter/motorbike per day €47-80/€85-160)

Parking

Blue lines denote pay-and-display spaces with tickets available from meters (coins only) and *tabacchi*. Costs vary but in the centre expect to pay €1 per hour (€1.20 in the ZTL) between 8am and 8pm (11pm in some parts). Traffic wardens are vigilant and fines are not uncommon. If your car is clamped or towed away, contact the municipal police (☎ 06 676 91).

The most convenient car park is at Villa Borghese (Map pp150–1; per hr/day €1.30/16); entry is from Piazzale San Paolo del Brasile. There are also car parks at Stazione Termini (Map pp106–7; 1st 2hr €5 then per hr/day 1.50/28.40); at Piazzale dei Partigiani (Map pp124–5; per hr/day €0.77/9.30), just outside Stazione Roma-Ostiense; and at Stazione Tiburtina (off Map pp106–7; per day €2).

METRO

Rome's metro (☎ 06 5 75 31; www.metroroma.it) has two lines, A (orange) and B (blue), which traverse the city in an X-shape. They cross at Stazione Termini, the only point at which you can change from one line to the other. Trains run approximately every five to 10 minutes between 5.30am and 11.30pm (to 1.30am on Friday and Saturday).

All the metro stations on line B have wheelchair access, except for Termini, Circo Massimo, Colosseo, Cavour and EUR Magliana. On line A Cipro-Musei Vaticani station is one of the few stations equipped with lifts.

For ticket details, see the boxed text opposite.

TAXI

Always make sure your taxi is licensed (it'll be white with a TAXI sign on the roof and an identifying number on the doors), and always go with the metered fare, never an arranged price (the set fares to and from the airports are an exception to this rule). In town (within the ring road) flag fall is €2.33 (Sundays/10pm to 7am €3.36/4.91), then it's €0.78 per km. If you have a problem, get the driver's name and licence number from the plaque on the inside of the rear door and call the Comune di Roma (☎ 06 06 06) or the central taxi office (☎ 06 671 070 844).

You can hail a cab in Rome, but it's often easier to wait at a taxi rank or telephone for one. You'll find ranks at Stazione Termini, Largo di Torre Argentina, the Pantheon, Corso Rinascimento, Piazza Navona, Piazza di Spagna, Largo Goldoni, Piazza del Popolo, Piazza Venezia, the Colosseum, Piazza GG Belli in Trastevere and near the Vatican at Piazza Pio XII and Piazza Risorgimento. To book a phone taxi, try the following:

La Capitale (☎ 06 49 94)

Pronto Taxi (☎ 06 66 45)

Radio Taxi (☎ 06 35 70)

Samarcanda (☎ 06 55 51)

Tevere (☎ 06 41 57)

Note that if you phone for a taxi, the meter is switched on immediately and you pay from wherever the driver receives the call.

TRAIN

Rome's main train station and transport hub is Stazione Termini (Map pp106–7; Piazza dei Cinquecento), from where there are regular trains to other European countries, all major Italian cities and many smaller towns.

Opposite platform 5, the train information office (Map pp106–7; ☽ 7am-9.45pm) is helpful, though often crowded. It cannot, however, make reservations. These must be made at the main ticket and reservation windows in the front hall or through the automatic ticket machines. Alternatively, go online at www.trenitalia.com

or find one of the many travel agencies with an FS or *biglietti treni* (train tickets) sign. Further train info is available at www.trenitalia.com or, if you speak Italian, by calling ☎ 89 20 21.

The station has the usual assortment of shops, snack bars and ATMs, plus a tourist office and a hotel reservation service (see p249). The left-luggage office (☽ 6am-11.50pm) is on the lower ground floor under platform 24. To leave an item costs €4 for the first five hours, then €0.60 for each additional hour.

Rome's second train station is Stazione Tiburtina (off Map pp106–7), a short ride away on metro line B. Of the capital's eight other train stations, the most important are Stazione Roma-Ostiense (Map pp124–5) and Stazione Trastevere (Map p120).

Apart from connections to Fiumicino airport, you'll probably only need the overground rail network if you head out of town to the Castelli Romani (p279), Ostia (p268) or Florence (p275).

BUSINESS HOURS

Most shops in central Rome open between 9am and 7.30pm (or 9.30am and 8pm) Monday to Saturday. Some larger stores and supermarkets also open on Sundays, typically from 11am to 7pm. Many smaller, family-run shops open from 9am to 1pm and 3.30pm to 7.30pm (or 4pm to 8pm) Monday to Saturday. Many food shops close on Thursday afternoons (winter) and Saturday afternoons (summer), while other shops stay closed on Monday mornings. Many shops also close for two weeks in August.

Banks generally open from 8.30am to 1.30pm and from 2.45pm to 4.30pm Monday to Friday. In the centre some also open from 8.30am to 12.30pm on Saturday mornings. However, it's always possible to find an exchange office open (see p294).

Bars and cafés usually open from about 7.30am to 8pm. Some then stay open until 1am or 2am, catering to a nocturnal crowd. Many pubs open around noon for lunch and close at about 2am. Clubs (known as *discoteche* in Italian) open at about 10pm but the action rarely starts before midnight. Restaurants open noon to 3pm and 7.30pm to 11pm (later in summer). Most restaurants close for one day each week.

Opening hours of the major sites vary enormously. Many of the big archaeological sites open from 9am until an hour before sunset. The big museums tend to open from around 9.30am to 7pm, although some might stay open later in summer or close earlier in winter (generally October to March). Note also that last admission to museums is generally an hour before the stated closing time and that many museums are closed on Mondays.

CHILDREN

Romans love children, and even if there are few child-friendly facilities in town, your little 'uns will be welcome just about everywhere. Restaurants, for example, are very laid-back when it comes to accommodating children and will happily serve a *mezza porzione* (child's portion) and provide *seggioloni* (highchairs). Some hotels can supply a *culla* (cot) on request.

Rome's museums and galleries are not ideal for rampaging toddlers, but many of the bigger ones now offer educational services and children's workshops. Some even host kid-friendly events.

In Villa Borghese, Casina di Raffaello (Map pp150–1; ☎ 06 428 88 888; www.casinadiraffaello.it; Viale della Casina di Raffaello) is a well-equipped daycare centre with a nice little playground, a small library and a soft play area. Accessing the facilities costs €3 per child.

Museums, galleries and archaeological sites are generally free for EU citizens under 18, and children under 10 years old travel free on all public transport. Major car-rental firms can provide children's safety seats on request.

See the boxed text, p102, for a list of child-friendly sites and activities. For information about children's events, check out *Roma C'è* or *Trovaroma*, the Thursday supplement to *La Repubblica* newspaper.

Useful websites include http://piccolituristi .turismoroma.it, which has loads of practical information and provides a three-day child-friendly itinerary, and www.romemama.com, an English-language forum with articles, details of forthcoming events and classified ads. *Rome with Kids* by JM Pasquesi is another useful resource. For more general information, see Lonely Planet's *Travel with Children* by Brigitte Barta et al.

You can buy baby formula and sterilising solutions at all pharmacies. Disposable nappies (diapers; *pannolini* in Italian) are available from supermarkets and pharmacies.

Babysitting

Many top-end hotels provide child-minding facilities and most others can arrange babysitters. If you want an English-speaking sitter, contact Angels (Map pp64–5; ☎ 06 678 28 77; staffin italy@yahoo.co.uk; Via dei Fienili 98), which charges €14 per hour plus an agency fee of €25.

For longer-term residents, the English All Saints Church (Map pp96–7; ☎ 06 360 01 881; www .allsaintsrome.org; Via del Babuino 153) runs a parent-toddler group called Ladybirds, which meets on Wednesday mornings between 10am and noon. The church noticeboard is also a good place to look for messages from babysitters seeking work.

CLIMATE

Rome enjoys a typically Mediterranean climate. Summers (from June to September) are hot and dry with temperatures often soaring to 35°C. High humidity is also common, particularly in July and August. Winter tends to be moderate, with temperatures averaging around 10°C to 15°C between December and February. Spring (March to June) and early autumn (September and October) are the best times to visit Rome, with lovely blue skies and mild temperatures. November and December are the two wettest months. For more on when to visit, see p16.

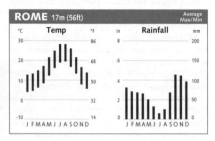

COURSES

Rome is a popular destination for foreign students. But even if you're not reading for a degree, there are loads of courses available for enthusiastic amateurs.

Cooking

Cookery writer Diane Seed (*The Top One Hundred Pasta Sauces*) runs her Roman Kitchen (Map pp74–5; ☎ 06 678 5759; www.italiangourmet.com) several times a year from her kitchen in Palazzo Doria Pamphilj (p93). There are one-day, two-day, three-day and week-long courses costing €200 per day and €1000 per week, and a combined Tuesday-morning market visit and class for €180.

The Italian gastronomic organisation Gambero Rosso organises a range of cooking courses at its Rome complex, Città del Gusto (Map pp124–5; ☎ 06 551 12 211; www.gamberorosso.it; Via Enrico Fermi 161). Three- or six-hour courses (in Italian) focus on a particular dish or ingredient such as pasta, pizza or seafood. Lessons cost from €65 for three hours.

Language

There are hundreds of schools offering language courses. Costs range from around €350 for a 40-hour, two-week course to about €3840 for a one-year course. Some schools also offer accommodation packages. Reputable schools include:

Arco di Druso (Map pp138–9; ☎ 06 397 50 984; www.arcodidruso.com; Via Tunisi 4)

Centro Linguistico Italiano Dante Alighieri (Map pp150–1; ☎ 06 442 31 400; www.clidante.it; Piazza Bologna 1)

DILIT International House (Map pp106–7; ☎ 06 446 25 93; www.dilit.it; Via Marghera 22)

Italiaidea (Map pp96–7; ☎ 06 699 41 314; www.italiaidea.com; Via dei Due Macelli 47)

Torre di Babele Centro di Lingua e Cultura Italiana (Map pp150–1; ☎ 06 442 52 578; www.torredibabele.com; Via Cosenza 7)

Mosaic-Making

Turn your hand to mosaic-making at Art Studio Café (Map pp138–9; ☎ 06 326 09104; www.artstudiocafe.it; Via dei Gracchi 187a), a café, exhibition space and mosaics school. One-day classes cost €50, two-day classes €80 and an intensive six-day course costs €200.

Wine Tasting

Refine your palate at a course run by the International Wine Academy of Roma (Map pp96–7; ☎ 06 699 08 78; www.wineacademyroma.com; Vicolo del Bottino 8). Learn about Italy's wine regions and tone up your tasting skills on the €155 half-day (two-hour) course, which includes lunch or dinner. There are also one-day tours (from €300) to local vineyards, and tastings (€25) on Thursdays and Saturdays. Bookings essential.

CUSTOMS REGULATIONS

If entering Italy from another EU country you can bring, duty-free: 800 cigarettes, 10L of spirits (more than 22% alcohol by volume), 20L of fortified wine or apéritif, 90L of wine, 110L of beer, and unlimited quantities of perfume.

If you're arriving from a non-EU country the limits are 200 cigarettes, 1L of spirits, 2L of fortified wine or apéritif, 4L of wine or 16L of beer. On top of this you can also carry goods, including perfume and electronic devices, up to a value of €430 for air and sea travellers, €300 for land travellers. On leaving the EU, non-EU residents can reclaim value-added tax (VAT) on expensive purchases (see p298). You can bring up to €10,000 into Italy.

DISCOUNT CARDS

There's a range of combination tickets available for serious sightseeing.

Appia Antica Card (adult/EU 18-24yr €6/3, valid 7 days) Entrance to the Terme di Caracalla, Mausoleo di Cecilia Metella and Villa dei Quintili.

Archaeologia Card (adult/EU 18-25yr €23.50/13.50, valid 7 days) Entrance to the Colosseum, Palatino, Terme di Caracalla, Museo Nazionale Romano (Palazzo Altemps, Palazzo Massimo alle Terme, Terme di Diocleziano, Crypta Balbi), Mausoleo di Cecilia Metella and Villa dei Quintili.

Roma Pass (www.romapass.it; €23, valid 3 days) Includes free admission to two museums or sites (you choose from a list of 38) as well as reduced entry to extra sites, unlimited public transport within Rome, access to the bike-sharing scheme, and reduced-price entry to other exhibitions and events. If you use this for more expensive sights such as the Capitoline Museums and the Colosseum you'll save a considerable amount of money. There's also a Roma & Più pass (€25) which extends to the surrounding province.

Vatican & Rome Pass (www.josp.com; 1/3 days €19/25) Provides unlimited public transport within Rome and on the Roma Cristina Open bus (see p295). It's available from ATAC ticket offices.

The cards can be purchased at any of the monuments or museums listed. The Roma Pass is also available at tourist information points.

Note that EU citizens aged between 18 and 25 generally qualify for a discount at most galleries and museums, while those under 18 and over 65 often get in free. In both cases you'll need proof of your age, ideally a passport or ID card.

ELECTRICITY

The standard voltage in Italy is 230V, 50Hz, although some older buildings still use 125V. Power points have two or three holes and do not have their own switches; plugs have two or three round pins. Adaptors are available from electrical shops. For further electrical information log onto www.kropla.com, where you'll find loads of useful tips on plugs, adaptors, transformers and other gizmos.

EMBASSIES & CONSULATES

Australia (Map pp150–1; ☎ 06 85 27 21, toll-free emergency number 800 87 77 90; www.italy.embassy.gov.au; Via Antonio Bosio 5; ☽ 9am-5pm Mon-Fri)

Austria Embassy (Map pp150–1; ☎ 06 844 01 41; www.bmeia.gv.at/it/ambasciata/roma; Via Pergolesi 3);

Consulate (Map pp150–1; ☎ 06 841 82 12; Viale Liegi 32; ☽ 9am-noon Mon-Fri)

Canada (Map pp150–1; ☎ 06 854 442 911; www.canada.it; Via Zara 30; ☽ 9am-noon Mon-Fri)

France Embassy (Map pp74–5; ☎ 06 68 60 11; www.ambafrance-it.org; Piazza Farnese 67); Consulate (Map pp74–5; ☎ 06 68 60 11; Via Giulia 251; ☽ 9am-12.30pm Mon-Fri)

Germany (Map pp106–7; ☎ 06 49 21 31; www.rom.diplo.de; Via San Martino della Battaglia 4; ☽ consular section 8.30am-11.30am Mon-Fri)

Ireland (Map pp74–5; ☎ 06 697 91 21; www.ambasciata-irlanda.it; Piazza Campitelli 3; ☽ 10am-12.30pm & 3-4.30pm Mon-Fri)

Netherlands (Map pp150–1; ☎ 06 322 86 001; www.olanda.it; Via Michele Mercati 8; ☽ 8.30am-5pm Mon-Fri)

New Zealand (Map pp150–1 ☎ 06 853 75 01; www.nzembassy.com; Via Clitunno 44; ☽ 8.30am-12.45pm & 1.45-5pm Mon-Fri)

Switzerland (Map pp150–1 ☎ 06 80 95 71; www.eda.admin.ch/roma; Via Barnaba Oriani 61; ☽ consular section 9am-noon Mon-Fri)

UK (Map pp106–7; ☎ 06 422 00 001; www.britishembassy.gov.uk/italy; Via XX Settembre 80a; ☽ consular section 9.15am-1.30pm Mon-Fri)

USA (Map p100; ☎ 06 46 741; http://rome.usembassy.gov; Via Vittorio Veneto 119/A; ☽ emergency services 8.30am-12.30pm Mon-Fri)

EMERGENCY

Ambulance (☎ 118)

Fire (☎ 115)

Police (☎ 113)

GAY & LESBIAN TRAVELLERS

Although it's no shining light on the international gaydar, Rome has a thriving gay scene. It's fairly low-key and much smaller than those in many other European capitals, but it is out there and the big annual events – Gay Pride in June, Gay Village in the summer – are colourful crowdpleasers. In clubland, gay nights are a regular fixture and mixed venues are 'in'.

In terms of gay rights, Italy is a late developer. Homosexuality is legal (over the age of 16) and even widely accepted, but it is publicly frowned on by the government, the views of which largely coincide with the Vatican's. And with the Catholic hierarchy decidedly against same-sex marriages and rights for common-law couples, both straight and gay, changes to the statute books are unlikely any time soon.

The main cultural and political organisation is the Circolo Mario Mieli di Cultura Omosessuale (Map pp124–5; ☎ 06 541 39 85; www.mariomieli.it, in Italian; Via Efeso 2a), which organises debates, cultural events and social functions. It also runs free AIDS/HIV testing and a care centre. Its website has info and listings of forthcoming events.

The national organisation for lesbians is the Coordinamento Lesbiche Italiano (CLI; Map pp132–3; ☎ 06 686 42 01; www.clrbp.it, in Italian; Via San Francesco di Sales 1b). Weekly political meetings of the Centro Femminista Separatista are held here, as well as conferences and literary evenings. There is also a women-only hostel, La Foresteria Orsa Maggiore (p262).

An excellent source of information is the Libreria Babele (Map pp74–5; ☎ 06 687 66 28; www.libreria babeleroma.it; Via dei Banchi Vecchi 116), a gay and lesbian bookshop in Trastevere, which stocks listings guides such as the free monthly *AUT* and *Pride*.

Other useful listings guides include *Clubbing* and the international gay guide *Spartacus*, available at gay and lesbian organisations and in bookshops. You can also go online at www.gayrome.it or www.gayfriendlyitaly .com, both of which carry listings for Rome.

The following might also be of help:

Arcigay Roma (Map p120; ☎ 06 645 01 1 02; www .arcigayroma.it; Via Nicola Zabaglia 14) The Roman branch of the national Arcigay organisation. Offers counselling, phone lines and general information.

Arcilesbica (off Map pp106–7; ☎ 06 418 02 11; www .arcilesbica.it; Viale Stefanini 15) Organises social outings.

Zipper Travel Association (Map pp106–7; ☎ 06 443 62 244; www.zippertravel.it; Via del Castro Pretorio 30) A specialist gay and lesbian travel agency.

HOLIDAYS

Most Romans take their annual holiday in August. This means that many businesses and shops close for at least part of the month, particularly around Ferragosto (Feast of the Assumption) on 15 August. Surprisingly, though, August is not considered high season by Rome's hoteliers, many of whom offer discounts to avoid empty rooms.

Italian schools close for three months in summer (from mid-June to mid-September), for three weeks over Christmas (generally the last two weeks of December and the first week of January) and for a week at Easter.

Public holidays:

Capodanno (New Year's Day) 1 January

Epifania (Epiphany) 6 January

Pasquetta (Easter Monday) March/April

Giorno della Liberazione (Liberation Day) 25 April

Festa del Lavoro (Labour Day) 1 May

Festa della Repubblica (Republic Day) 2 June

Festa dei Santi Pietro e Paolo (Feast of St Peter & St Paul) 29 June

Ferragosto (Feast of the Assumption) 15 August

Festa di Ognisanti (All Saints' Day) 1 November

Festa dell'Immacolata Concezione (Feast of the Immaculate Conception) 8 December

Natale (Christmas Day) 25 December

Festa di Santo Stefano (Boxing Day) 26 December

For further details of Rome's holiday calendar, see p85 and p16.

INTERNET ACCESS

The easiest way to access the internet is at an internet café, and there are plenty to choose from.

Internet Café (Map pp106–7; ☎ 06 478 23 051; Via Cavour 213; per hr €2-2.90; ☺ 11am-1am Mon-Fri, 3pm-1am Sat & Sun) Rates vary according to the time of day; they're cheapest before 4pm.

Internet Café (Map pp106–7; ☎ 06 445 49 53; Via dei Marrucini 12; per hr €3; ☺ 9am-midnight Mon-Fri, 10am-midnight Sat, 2pm-midnight Sun) East of Termini.

Internet Point (Map pp132–3; ☎ 06 583 33 316; Piazza Sonnino 27; per hr €4; ☺ 8.30am-10pm) In Trastevere.

Splashnet (Map pp106–7; ☎ 06 493 82 073; Via Varese 33; per hr €1.50; ☺ 8.30am-midnight) One of several laundrette-cum-internet points in the Termini area.

Tritone Internet Point (Map pp96–7; ☎ 06 478 26 180; Via Zucchelli 1d; per hr €2.50; ☺ 10am-10.30pm Mon-Thu, to 9.30pm Fri & Sat, 11.30am-9pm Sun) An international phone centre just off Via del Tritone.

Yex Internet Point (Map pp74–5; Piazza Sant'Andrea della Valle 1; per hr €4.50; ☺ 10am-10pm) Near Piazza Navona. All terminals have webcams.

Many hostels and hotels also provide a computer for internet access and wi-fi is becoming more common – see the boxed text, opposite.

If you're travelling with a notebook or handheld computer, be aware that your modem may not work once you leave your home country.

WI-FI ACCESS

Free wi-fi access is available in much of central Rome. There are hotspots in all the major parks as well as Piazza Navona, Campo de' Fiori, Piazza di Spagna, the Pantheon, Campidoglio, the Trevi Fountain and Largo di Torre Argentina. It's free (for an hour a day) but you will need to register and to do that you'll need an Italian mobile-phone number. If you've got one, you can sign on by filling in the registration form that appears when you open your browser in a hotspot and validating the account with a quick phone call (from the mobile whose number you've provided).

Many hotels, bars and cafés also offer wi-fi access, although it's rarely free.

Telecom Italia (www.187.it, in Italian) sells prepaid wi-fi cards for €3 (one hour), €5 (five hours), €15 (24 hours) and €40 (seven days).

The safest option is to buy a reputable 'global' modem before you leave home, or a PC-card modem with one of the Italian mobile-phone operators, which gives wireless access through the mobile telephone network.

To plug your modem into a fixed phone line, note that you might need a power transformer if your laptop isn't set up for dual voltage, an RJ-11 telephone jack that works with your modem, and a plug adaptor. Most electrical shops in Rome sell adaptors that convert from RJ-11 to the local three-pinned plug variety; many modern phone lines take the RJ-11 jack directly.

LEGAL MATTERS

The most likely reason for a brush with the law is to report a theft. If you do have something stolen and you want to claim it on insurance, you must make a statement to the police as insurance companies won't pay up without official proof of a crime.

The Italian police is divided into three main bodies: the *polizia*, who wear navy-blue jackets; the *carabinieri*, in a black uniform with a red stripe; and the grey-clad *guardia di finanza* (fiscal police), responsible for fighting tax evasion and drug smuggling. If you run into trouble, you're most likely to end up dealing with the *polizia* or *carabinieri*.

If you are detained for any alleged offence, you should be given verbal and written notice of the charges laid against you within 24 hours. You have no right to a phone call upon arrest but you can choose not to respond to questions without the presence of a lawyer. For serious crimes it is possible to be held without trial for up to two years.

Rome's Questura (police headquarters; Map pp106–7; ☎ 06 4 68 61; Via San Vitale 15) is just off Via Nazionale.

The voting age in Italy is 18, the age of consent is 16 (homosexual and heterosexual) and you can drive at 18. Minors under 16 can buy wine and beer but not *superalcolici* (spirits).

Drink & Drugs

Rome is not a good place to be caught with dope. Under Italian law there's no distinction between hard and soft drugs, so cannabis is effectively on the same legal footing as cocaine, heroin and ecstasy. If you're caught with what the police deem to be a dealable quantity, you risk heavy fines or prison sentences of between six and 20 years. In practice, these draconian punishments are rarely enforced, and if you can prove you're a Rastafarian, you should get off scot-free – in July 2008 the Italian Supreme Court ruled that it was OK for Rastas to smoke cannabis, as it's part of their religion.

The legal limit for a driver's blood-alcohol reading is 0.05%.

MAPS

You can buy a useful *Public Transport Map* (€2.50) at the tourist office in Termini station. Tourist information kiosks around town also hand out *Charta Roma,* an A3-sized stylised map with the major sights and their opening hours. Plenty of maps are also available at newsstands and bookshops.

Editrice Lozzi (www.editricelozzi.it) publishes various city maps, including the pocket-sized *Roma Map Bus* (€2.50), which lists all major streets and bus/metro routes, and *Roma* (€5), a fold-out map with a street directory and an enlarged plan of the city centre.

For maps of Ancient Rome try the Lozzi *Archaeo Map* (€4), with a plan of the Roman Forum, Palatino and Colosseum, or *Ancient Rome* (€3.50), published by Electa.

The best road map is the 1:12,500 *Pianta Roma* (€7), published by the Touring Club Italiano.

MEDICAL SERVICES

Italy has a public health system that is legally bound to provide emergency care to everyone. EU nationals are entitled to reduced-cost, sometimes free, medical care with a European Health Insurance Card (EHIC), available from your home health authority; non-EU citizens should take out medical insurance.

For emergency treatment, go to the *pronto soccorso* (casualty) section of an *ospedale* (public hospital), where it's also possible to receive emergency dental treatment. For less serious ailments call the Guardia Medica (☎ 06 57 06 00). You can also call a private doctor to come to your hotel or apartment. The callout/treatment fee will probably be around €130, but it's worth it if you have insurance. Try Roma Medica (☎ 338 622 48 32; ☻ 24hr). Pharmacists will serve prescriptions and can provide basic medical advice.

If you need an ambulance, call ☎ 118.

Emergency Rooms

Ospedale Bambino Gesù (Map pp132–3; ☎ 06 6 85 91; Piazza di Sant'Onofrio 4) Rome's premier children's hospital; on the Gianicolo.

Ospedale di Odontoiatria G Eastman (Map pp106–7; ☎ 06 84 48 31; Viale Regina Elena 287b) Specialist dental care.

Ospedale Fatebenefratelli (Map pp74–5; ☎ 06 6 83 71; Piazza Fatebenefratelli, Isola Tiberina)

Ospedale San Camillo Forlanini (off Map p120; ☎ 06 5 87 01; Circonvallazione Gianicolense 87)

Ospedale San Giacomo (Map pp96–7; ☎ 06 3 62 61; Via A Canova 29)

Ospedale San Giovanni (Map p115; ☎ 06 7 70 51; Via Amba Aradam 9)

Ospedale Santo Spirito (Map pp138–9; ☎ 06 6 83 51; Lungotevere in Sassia 1)

Policlinico Umberto I (Map pp106–7; ☎ 06 4 99 71; Viale del Policlinico 155)

Pharmacies

Marked by a green cross, *farmacie* (pharmacies) open from 8.30am to 1pm and 4pm to 7.30pm Monday to Friday and on Saturday mornings. Outside these hours they open on a rotational basis, and all are legally required to post a list of places open in the vicinity. Night pharmacies are listed in daily newspapers and in pharmacy windows.

If you think you'll need a prescription while in Rome, make sure you know the drug's generic name rather than the brand name.

There's a 24-hour pharmacy (Map pp106–7; ☎ 06 488 00 19; Piazza dei Cinquecento 51) on the western flank of Piazza dei Cinquecento near Stazione

Termini. In the station, you'll find a pharmacy (☻ 7.30am-10pm) next to platform 1.

In the Vatican, the Farmacia Vaticana (Map pp138–9; ☎ 06 698 905 651; Palazzo Belvedere; ☻ 8.30am-6pm Mon-Fri Sep-Jun, 8.30am-3pm Mon-Fri Jul & Aug, plus 8.30am-1pm Sat year-round) sells certain drugs that are not available in Italian pharmacies, and will fill foreign prescriptions (something local pharmacies can't do).

MONEY

Italy's currency is the euro. The seven euro notes come in denominations of €500, €200, €100, €50, €20, €10 and €5. The eight euro coins are in denominations of €2 and €1, and 50, 20, 10, five, two and one cents.

Exchange rates are given inside the front cover of this book. For the latest rates, check out www.xe.com. For a guide to costs, see p18.

ATMs

ATMs (known in Italy as *bancomat*) are widely available in Rome and most will accept cards tied into the Visa, MasterCard, Cirrus and Maestro systems. As a precaution, though, check that the appropriate logo is displayed on the ATM before inserting your card. The daily limit for cash withdrawal is €250.

Remember that every time you withdraw cash, you'll be charged a transaction fee (usually around 3% with a minimum of €3 or more) as well as a 1% to 3% conversion charge. Check with your bank to see how much this is.

If an ATM rejects your card, don't despair. Try a few more before assuming the problem lies with your card.

Changing Money

You can change your money in banks, at post offices or at a *cambio* (exchange office). There are exchange booths at Stazione Termini (Map pp106–7) and at Fiumicino and Ciampino airports. In the centre, there are numerous bureaux de change, including American Express (Map pp96–7; ☎ 06 6 76 41; Piazza di Spagna 38; ☻ 9am-5.30pm Mon-Fri, 9am-12.30pm Sat). Post offices and banks tend to offer the best rates. A few banks also provide automatic exchange machines that accept notes from most major currencies.

Always make sure you have your passport, or some form of photo ID, at hand when exchanging money.

Credit Cards

Credit cards are widely accepted but it's still a good idea to carry a cash back-up. Virtually all midrange and top-end hotels accept credit cards, as do most restaurants and large shops. You can also use them to obtain cash advances at some banks. Some of the cheaper *pensioni* (guesthouses), trattorias and pizzerias accept nothing but cash.

Major cards such as Visa, MasterCard, Eurocard, Cirrus and Eurocheques are widely accepted. Amex is also recognised, although it's less common than Visa or MasterCard.

Note that using your credit card in ATMs can be costly. On every transaction there's a fee, which with some credit-card issuers can reach US$10, as well as interest per withdrawal. Check with your issuer before leaving home.

If your card is lost, stolen or swallowed by an ATM, telephone to have an immediate stop put on its use.

Amex (☎ 06 729 00 347)

Diners Club (☎ 800 86 40 64)

MasterCard (☎ 800 87 08 66)

Visa (☎ 800 819 014)

The Amex office (opposite) can issue customers with new cards, usually within 24 hours and sometimes immediately, if they have been lost or stolen.

If you're not a regular traveller, it pays to let your credit-card company know of your travel plans. Otherwise the bank might block the card when it sees your unusual spending.

NEWSPAPERS & MAGAZINES
English

English-language newspapers and magazines are available from many city-centre newsstands. For magazines try Feltrinelli International (p183) or Messaggerie Musicali (p178), both of which have excellent selections.

British papers are generally available around lunchtime on the day of publication; for the Sunday papers you'll have to wait until Monday. American publications usually appear a day after printing. The major German, French and Spanish dailies and some Scandinavian papers can also be found.

Two local publications worth a look are Wanted in Rome (www.wantedinrome.com; €1), a fortnightly news and listings magazine aimed at Rome's foreign residents, and The Roman Forum

(www.theromanforum.com; €3), which has news about Rome and a useful classifieds section. Both have good websites.

Italian

Italian newspapers are long on domestic politics and tend to assume the reader is well versed in current affairs.

Rome's two main newspapers are *Il Messaggero,* a daily broadsheet good for news about the capital, and *La Repubblica,* a slightly left-of-centre national that publishes an excellent listings guide, *Trovaroma,* every Thursday. Italy's leading broadsheet is the Milan-based *Corriere della Sera,* which has in-depth foreign and political coverage. The voice of the Vatican, *L'Osservatore Romano,* is published daily in Italian with weekly editions in English and other foreign languages.

Italy's biggest-selling weekly magazine is *Famiglia Cristiana,* a predictably conservative periodical produced by a Catholic publishing house. The two top current-affairs magazines are *L'Espresso* and *Panorama,* both of which provide in-depth analysis of domestic and international affairs.

Rome's best listings guide is *Roma C'è* (€1), which comes out every Wednesday. For classified ads, check out *Porta Portese* (€1), which comes out on Tuesdays and Fridays. Both are available at newsstands across the city.

ORGANISED TOURS
Boat

BATTELLI DI ROMA Map pp138–9

☎ 06 977 45 498; www.battellidiroma.it; adult/6-12yr & over 65yr/under 5yr €12/8/free

This outfit runs 70-minute hop-on hop-off boat tours along the Tiber between Ponte Sant'Angelo and Ponte Cavour. Trips depart at 10am from Ponte Sant'Angelo, and then every half hour until 6.30pm.

There are also dinner cruises (€54, 2¼ hours) and wine-bar cruises (€35, 2¼ hours) at 9pm on Thursday, Friday and Saturday. Tickets are available online or at the embarkation points on Molo Sant'Angelo and Isola Tiberina.

Bus

ARCULT Map pp106–7

☎ 339 650 3172; www.arcult.it; Via Grosseto

Arcult offers excellent tours focusing on Rome's contemporary architecture. Run by architects, the customisable tours visit sites such as EUR, the Auditorium Parco della Musica, the Chiesa Dio Padre Misericordioso and the Ara Pacis. A half-day tour starts at €200 for two to 10 people, so it makes sense to get a like-minded group together.

ROMA CRISTIANA Map pp138–9

☎ 06 69 89 61; www.romacristiana.orpnet.it; adult/7-12yr/under 7yr 1 tour €12/7.50/free, 24hr ticket for both tours €15/7.50/free; ☺ tours every 15min 8am-7pm

Operated by the Vatican-sponsored Opera Romana Pellegrinaggi, this hop-on-hop-off open bus service runs two lines, both departing from Via della Conciliazione. Line A (San Pietro; 1¾ hours) follows a circular route up to Stazione Termini and back by way of the major churches and sites, including Santa Maria del Popolo, Museo e Galleria Borghese, Santa Maria degli Angeli, Santa Maria Maggiore, San Pietro in Vincoli, SS Cosma e Damiano, Santa Sabina, Santa Maria in Cosmedin, San Marco, the Pantheon and Chiesa Nuova. Line B (San Paolo; 2¼ hours) stops off at 22 sites in Trastevere, Gianicolo, Via Ostiense, Via Appia Antica and San Giovanni before returning to the Vatican.

There's a multilingual commentary and tickets are available online or on board.

TRAMBUS OPEN Map pp106–7

☎ 800 281 281; www.trambusopen.com; Piazza dei Cinquecento

Trambus operates two tour buses: the 110open and the Archeobus.

The 110open (adult/6-12yr/under 5yr €20/15/free; ☺ every 20min 8.30am-8.30pm) is an open-top double-decker bus, equipped with an audioguide in eight languages, that departs from the bus terminus outside Termini and stops at the Quirinale, Colosseum, Bocca della Verità, Piazza Venezia, Piazza Navona, St Peter's, Piazza Cavour, Ara Pacis, Trevi Fountain and Via Veneto. The entire tour lasts two hours, but the tickets, available on board, from the Info Boxes on Piazza dei Cinquecento and at the Colosseum, are valid for 24 hours and allow you to hop off and on as you please.

Archeobus (adult/6-12yr/under 5yr €15/10/free; ☺ half-hourly 8.30am-4.30pm) is another stop-and-go bus, which takes sightseers down Via Appia Antica, stopping at 16 points of archaeological interest along the way. These include Piazza Venezia, Bocca della Verità, Circo Massimo, Terme di Caracalla, Porta

San Sebastiano, Catacombe di San Callisto and San Sebastiano, Mausoleo di Cecilia Metella and Villa dei Quintili. Buses, which depart from Termini bus station, Piazza Venezia, and the Colosseum, are single-deck and open, equipped with an audioguide in eight languages. Tickets are available in the same places as for the 110open service.

You can buy a joint ticket to both the 110open and Archeobus for €30/20 for adult/six to 12 years old (valid 48 hours). If you have a Roma Pass (p291), you qualify for a €5 discount on each of the bus tours.

Bike & Scooter

BICI E BACI Map pp106–7

☎ 06 482 84 43; www.bicibaci.com; Via del Viminale 5

Bici & Baci runs daily bike tours of central Rome, taking in the historic centre and the Colosseum. Departure is at 10am, 3pm and 8pm daily between March and October, by request only from November to February; the cost is €35 plus tax. It also offers tours of Rome on vintage Vespas – the best and most authentic way to travel in the city. You'll need to book 24 hours ahead. Routes and prices vary according to your requests.

Walking & Running

DARK ROME

☎ 06 455 50 015; www.darkrome.com

Dark Rome runs a range of themed tours, costing between €39 and €59 per person. Popular choices include the Crypts and Catacombs tour, which takes in Rome's buried treasures, and the afternoon Best of Rome tour, a 3½ hour stroll through the city centre.

ENJOY ROME Map pp106–7

☎ 06 445 18 43; www.enjoyrome.com; Via Margherita 8

Enjoy Rome organises various walks for the budget traveller. Three-hour tours cover Ancient Rome (by day or night, April to October), the Vatican (under/over 26 €25/30), Trastevere, the Jewish Ghetto, and the Catacombs and Via Appia Antica (€40). Unless otherwise indicated tours cost under/over 26 €22/27. Note that the Vatican tour does not cover entrance charges and the Ancient Rome tour does not enter the Colosseum. All guides are native or fluent English speakers.

FRIENDS IN ROME

www.friendsinrome.com

A social networking group, Friends in Rome organises occasional walking tours around central neighbourhoods. These are as much about meeting fellow foreigners as discovering the city and are usually cheerful affairs. They generally cost €8 and are followed by drinks in a local bar. See the website for upcoming tours and events.

SIGHTJOGGING

☎ 347 335 31 85; www.sightjogging.it

If you're fit and in a hurry, sightjogging is for you. As the name suggests, it consists of seeing the sights on the run. A trainer collects you from your hotel and runs you round one of 15 routes, each centred on a specific area. The routes are graded for difficulty and are all between 8.5km and 10.5km. Prices range from €70 for a solo tour to €140 for a group of four. Booking is essential.

THROUGH ETERNITY CULTURAL ASSOCIATION Map p115

☎ 06 700 93 36; www.througheternity.com; Via Sinuessa 8

Another reliable operator offering various itineraries led by English-speaking experts. Walks include a group twilight tour of Renaissance and baroque Rome (€27, 2½ hours), the Vatican Museums and St Peter's Basilica (€39, five hours), and an Angels and Demons tour (€32, 3½ hours) based on Dan Brown's bestselling book.

PHOTOGRAPHY

Rome's historic cityscape, bright light and hilly terrain make it a photographer's dream. Make sure you have enough memory to store your snaps – two 128MB cards will probably be enough – but if you do run out your best bet is to burn your photos onto a CD, something that many processing labs and internet cafés will do for you.

As a general rule, the soft light in the late afternoon photographs better than the sharp glare in the morning. For more photo tips check out Lonely Planet's *Travel Photography* by Richard I'Anson.

Although you'd never know it from the flashes going off around you, flash photography is banned at most museums, galleries and churches.

POST

Italy's postal system, Poste Italiane (☎ 803 160; www.poste.it) is not the world's best, but nor is it as bad as it's often made out to be. The Vatican postal system, on the other hand, has long enjoyed a reputation for efficiency.

Stamps (*francobolli*) are available at post offices and authorised tobacconists (look for the official *tabacchi* sign: a big 'T', usually white on black).

There are local post offices in every district of the city. Opening hours vary but are typically 8.30am to 6pm Monday to Friday and 8.30am to 1pm on Saturday. All post offices close two hours earlier than normal on the last business day of each month.

Main post office (Map pp96–7; ☎ 06 697 37 213; Piazza di San Silvestro 19; ☻ 8am-7pm Mon-Sat)

Vatican post office (Map pp138–9; ☎ 06 698 83 406; Piazza San Pietro; ☻ 8.30am-6.30pm Mon-Sat) Letters can be posted in blue Vatican post boxes only if they carry Vatican stamps.

Rates

Letters up to 20g cost €0.65 to Zone 1 (Europe and the Mediterranean Basin), €0.85 to Zone 2 (other countries in Africa, Asia and America) and €1 to Zone 3 (Australia and New Zealand). For more important items, use registered mail (*raccomandata*), which costs €4.80 to Zone 1, €5.60 to Zone 2 and €6 to Zone 3.

RELOCATING

When you relocate to Rome there's a certain amount of paperwork you'll need to deal with; exactly what depends on whether you're an EU citizen or not.

For information regarding visas and the *permessio di soggiorno* (permit to stay), see p301.

On arrival in Rome you'll need to get a tax number (*codice fiscale*). Surprisingly, these are very easy to get – simply go to your nearest tax office (*ufficio delle entrate*) with your passport and *permesso di soggiorno*, and fill in a form. The number will then be issued within a few days.

To get residency (*residenza*), for which you'll need an address, take your passport and *permesso di soggiorno* to the registry office (*ufficio anagrafe*) at your local council office (*comune*) and complete a residency request form. A few days later you'll be visited by a

STOP, THIEF

The greatest risk visitors face in Rome is from pickpockets and thieves. There's no reason for paranoia but you need to be aware that the problem exists.

Pickpockets follow the tourists, so watch out around the Colosseum, Piazza di Spagna, Piazza San Pietro and Stazione Termini. Be particularly vigilant around the bus stops on Via Marsala, where thieves prey on disorientated travellers fresh in from Ciampino airport. Crowded public transport is another hot spot – the 64 Vatican bus is notorious. If travelling on the metro, try to use the end carriages, which are usually less crowded.

A money belt with your essentials (passport, cash, credit cards) is a good idea. However, to avoid delving into it in public, carry a wallet with a day's cash. Don't flaunt watches, cameras and other expensive goods. If you're carrying a bag or camera, wear the strap across your body and away from the road – moped thieves can swipe a bag and be gone in seconds. Be careful when you sit down at a streetside table – never drape your bag over an empty chair by the road or put it where you can't see it.

Beware of gangs of dishevelled-looking kids waving newspapers and demanding attention. If you notice that you've been targeted, either take evasive action or shout 'va via!' ('go away!') in a loud, angry voice. Remember also that some of the best pickpockets are well dressed.

Cars, particularly those with foreign numberplates or rental-company stickers, also provide rich pickings for thieves. Try removing or covering the stickers or leaving a local newspaper on the seat. Never leave valuables in your car – in fact, try not to leave anything on display if you can help it and certainly not overnight. It's a good idea to pay extra to leave your car in supervised car parks.

A more insidious form of theft to watch out for is short-changing. One popular dodge goes as follows: you pay for a €4 *panino* (bread roll) with a €20 note. The cashier then distractedly gives you a €1 coin and a €5 note before turning away to carry on their conversation. The trick here is to wait and chances are that the €10 note you're owed will appear without a word being said.

In case of theft or loss, always report the incident to the police within 24 hours and ask for a statement.

traffic warden *(vigile urbano)* to check that you're living at your stated address.

To enrol in the national health system *(servizio sanitario nazionale)* and be assigned a doctor, you'll need to go to your nearest ASL *(azienda sanitaria locale)*. See http://italy .angloinfo.com/countries/italy/healthinsure .asp for further details.

If you're planning to drive, you'll need to sort out your driver's licence. EU licence-holders can use their home licence for a year, after which they'll need to convert it to an Italian licence. Holders of non-EU licences will need to get theirs converted straightaway and might have to sit a driving test. It's quite a process converting your licence, involving long queues at the traffic-control authority *(motorizzazione)* and plenty of head-scratching. Rather than go it alone, you'd be well advised to do it through an ACI (Automobile Club d'Italia; www .aci.it, in Italian) branch office, although this does cost more.

Finding somewhere to live can be hard work. Rental accommodation is much in demand and competition for flats is fierce. The best way is through a friend or contact. If you don't have anyone who can help, look out for *affitasi* (to rent) signs or check out the local press. For more information, see the boxed text, p251.

For further tips check out www.just landed.com or http://italy.angloinfo.com, both of which have loads of concise, clear information.

SAFETY

Rome is not a dangerous city but petty crime is rife (see the boxed text, above).

Road safety is also an issue. The highway code is obeyed with discretion, so don't take it for granted that cars and scooters will stop at pedestrian crossings, or even at red lights. The only way to cross the road is to wait for a suitable gap in the traffic and then walk confidently and calmly across, ideally with a group of local nuns.

For issues facing lone women travellers, see p301.

TAXES & REFUNDS

A value-added tax of 20%, known as IVA (Imposta di Valore Aggiunto), is slapped on just about everything in Italy. If you are a non-EU resident and you spend more than €155 on a purchase, you can claim a refund when you leave the EU. The refund only applies to purchases from affiliated retail outlets that display a 'Tax Free' sign. When you make your purchase ask for a tax-refund voucher, to be filled in with the date of your purchase and its value. When you leave the EU, get this voucher stamped at customs and take it to the nearest tax-refund counter where you'll get an immediate refund, either in cash or charged onto your credit card. If there's no refund counter at the airport or you're travelling by sea or overland, you'll need to get the voucher stamped at the port or border crossing and mail it back for refund.

Note that under Italian tax law you are legally required to get a receipt for any purchase you make. Although it's highly unlikely, you could be asked by an officer of the *guardia di finanza* (fiscal police) to produce one immediately after you leave a shop. Without one, you risk a fine.

TELEPHONE
Domestic Calls

Rome's area code is 06. Area codes are an integral part of all Italian phone numbers and must be dialled even when calling locally. Mobile-phone numbers are nine or 10 digits long and begin with a three-digit prefix starting with a 3. Toll-free numbers are known as *numeri verdi* and usually start with ☎ 800. Some six-digit national-rate numbers are also in use (such as those for Alitalia and Trenitalia).

For directory inquiries, dial ☎ 1240.

International Calls

To call abroad from Italy dial ☎ 00, then the relevant country and area codes, followed by the telephone number.

Try to avoid making international calls from a hotel, as you'll be stung by high rates. It's cheaper to call from a private call centre or from a public payphone with an international calling card. These are available at newsstands and tobacconists, and although they can be hit-and-miss, are often good value. Another alternative is to use a direct-dialling service such as AT&T's USA Direct (access number ☎ 800 172 444) or Telstra's Australia Direct (access number ☎ 800 172 610), which allows you to make a reverse-charge call at home-country rates. Skype is also available at many internet cafés.

To make a reverse-charge (collect) international call from a public telephone, dial ☎ 170. All phone operators speak English.

Mobile Phones

Italian mobile phones operate on the GSM 900/1800 network, which is compatible with the rest of Europe and Australia but not with the North American GSM 1900 or Japanese systems (although some GSM 1900/900 phones do work here).

If you have a GSM dual- or tri-band phone that you can unlock (check with your service provider), it can cost as little as €10 to activate a prepaid *(prepagato)* SIM card in Italy. TIM (Telecom Italia Mobile; www.tim.it), Wind (www.wind.it) and Vodafone (www.vodafone.it) all offer SIM cards and have retail outlets across town. Note that by Italian law all SIM cards must be registered in Italy, so make sure you have a passport or ID card with you when you buy one. Also, if you're buying a SIM card abroad, check that the provider offers a registration service.

Public Phones

Despite the fact that Italy is one of the most mobile-saturated countries in the world, you can still find public payphones around Rome. Most work and most take telephone cards *(schede telefoniche)*, although you'll still find some that accept coins or credit cards. You can buy phonecards (€5, €10 or €20) at post offices, tobacconists and newsstands. Before you use them you need to break off the top left-hand corner of the card.

Fax

Major post offices offer fax services; otherwise, there are numerous private services, usually in tobacconists and stationery stores.

TIME

Italy is in a single time zone, one hour ahead of GMT. Daylight-saving time, when clocks move forward one hour, starts on the last Sunday in March. Clocks are put back one hour on the last Sunday in October.

Italy operates on a 24-hour clock, so 6pm is written as 18:00.

TOILETS

Rome is not a good place to get caught short. Public toilets are not widespread and those that do exist are often closed. The best thing to do is to nip into a café or bar, all of which are required by law to have a loo. The law doesn't extend to loo paper, though, so try to have some tissues to hand. There are toilets at the following places:

Colosseum (Map pp64–5; ☺ 9am-6.40pm)

Giardini di Castel Sant'Angelo (Map pp138–9; ☺ 10am-4.40pm)

Piazza di San Pietro (Map pp138–9)

Piazza di San Silvestro (Map pp96–7; ☺ 10am-7.40pm)

Piazza di Spagna (Map pp96–7; ☺ 10am-7.40pm)

Stazione Termini (Map pp106–7; admission €0.80; ☺ 6am-1am)

TOURIST INFORMATION
Telephone & Internet Resources

Comune Call Centre (☎ 06 06 06; ☺ 24hr) Very useful for practical questions such as: where's the nearest hospital? Where can I park? When are the underground trains running? The centre is staffed 24 hours and there are staff who speak English, French, Arabic, German, Spanish, Italian and Chinese available from 4pm to 7pm.

Tourist Information Line (☎ 06 06 08; www.060608 .com; ☺ 9am-9pm) A free multilingual tourist information line and website providing information on culture, shows, hotels, transport, etc; you can also book theatre, concert, exhibition and museum tickets on this number. The website is similarly comprehensive and easy to use.

Turismo Roma (www.turismoroma.it) The official website of Rome Tourist Board with accommodation and restaurant lists, as well as details of upcoming events, museums and much more.

Tourist Offices

Centro Servizi Pellegrini e Turisti (Map pp138–9; ☎ 06 698 81 662; Piazza San Pietro; ☺ 8.30am-6.15pm Mon-Sat) The Vatican's official tourist office.

Enjoy Rome (Map pp106–7; ☎ 06 445 18 43; www.enjoy rome.com; Via Marghera 8a; ☺ 8.30am-7pm Mon-Fri & 8.30am-2pm Sat Apr-Sep, 9am-5.30pm Mon-Fri & 8.30am-2pm Sat Oct-Mar) A private tourist office that arranges guided tours and books accommodation.

Meridiana Information Point (Map pp150–1; ☎ 06 853 04 242; www.villaborghese.it; Viale dell'Uccelliera 35; ☺ 9am-5pm daily year-round, to 7pm Fri-Sun Apr-Sep) For information on Villa Borghese.

Rome Tourist Board (APT; ☎ 06 06 08; www.turismo roma.it; Terminal B, International Arrivals; ☺ 9am-6pm) At Fiumicino airport.

The Comune di Roma also runs tourist information points throughout the city:

Castel Sant'Angelo (Map pp138–9; Piazza Pia; ☺ 9.30am-7pm)

Ciampino airport (International Arrivals, baggage reclaim area; ☺ 9am-6.30pm)

Fiumicino airport (Terminal C, International Arrivals; ☺ 9am-6.30pm)

Piazza Navona (Map pp74–5; ☺ 9.30am-7pm) Near Piazza delle Cinque Lune.

Piazza Santa Maria Maggiore (Map pp106–7; Via dell'Olmata; ☺ 9.30am-7pm)

Piazza Sonnino (Map pp132–3; ☺ 9.30am-7pm)

Stazione Termini (Map pp106–7; ☺ 8am-8.30pm) Next to platform 24.

Trevi Fountain (Map p100; Via Marco Minghetti; ☺ 9.30am-7pm) Nearer to Via del Corso than the fountain.

Via Nazionale (Map pp106–7; ☺ 9.30am-7pm)

At these kiosks pick up the useful monthly what's-on pamphlet *L'Evento* as well as *Un Ospite a Roma* (A Guest in Rome; www.aguestinrome.com).

TRAVELLERS WITH DISABILITIES

Rome isn't an easy city for travellers with disabilities. Cobbled streets, blocked pavements and tiny lifts are difficult for the wheelchair-bound, while the relentless traffic can be disorientating for partially sighted travellers or those with hearing difficulties.

Getting around on public transport is difficult, although efforts are being made to improve accessibility. On metro Line B all stations have wheelchair access except for Termini, Circo Massimo, Colosseo, Cavour and EUR Magliana, while on Line A few of the central stations have facilities except for Cipro-Musei Vaticani. Note that bus 590 covers the same route as metro Line A and is wheelchair-accessible. Rome's newer buses and trams can generally accommodate wheelchairs.

If travelling by train, ring the national helpline ☎ 199 30 30 60 to arrange assistance. At Stazione Termini, the Sala Blu Assistenza Disabili (Map pp106–7; ☎ 06 488 17 26; ☺ 7am-9pm) next to platform 1 can provide information on wheelchair-accessible trains and help with transport in the station. Contact the office 24 hours ahead if you know you're going to need assistance. There's a similar office at Stazione Tiburtina.

Airline companies should be able to arrange assistance at airports if you notify them of your needs in advance. Alternatively, contact ADR Assistance (www.adrassistance.it) for assistance at Fiumicino or Ciampino airports.

Some taxis are equipped to carry passengers in wheelchairs; ask for a taxi for a *sedia a rotelle* (wheelchair). For contact numbers, see p287.

Organisations

The best point of reference is CO.IN (off Map pp106–7; www.coinsociale.it, in Italian; Via Enrico Giglioli 54/A), an umbrella group for associations and cooperatives across the country, which can provide useful information and local contacts.

Other useful resources:

Handy Turismo (☎ 06 350 75 707; www.handyturismo .it) A comprehensive and easy-to-use website with information on travel, accommodation and access at the main tourist attractions.

Roma per Tutti (☎ 06 571 77 094; www.romapertutti.it, in Italian) A council-backed venture to provide assistance and free guided museum visits.

VISAS

EU citizens do not need a visa to enter Italy. Nationals of some other countries, including Australia, Canada, Israel, Japan, New Zealand, Switzerland and the USA do not need a visa for stays of up to 90 days.

Italy is one of the 15 signatories of the Schengen Convention, an agreement whereby participating countries abolished customs checks at common borders. The standard tourist visa for a Schengen country is valid for 90 days. You must apply for it in your country of residence and you can not apply for more than two in any 12-month period. They are not renewable inside Italy.

Technically, all foreign visitors to Italy are supposed to register with the local police within eight days of arrival. However, if you're staying in a hotel you don't need to bother as the hotel does this for you.

Up-to-date visa information is available on www.lonelyplanet.com – follow links through to the Italy destination guide.

Permesso di Soggiorno

A *permesso di soggiorno* (permit to stay, also referred to as a residence permit) is required by all non-EU nationals who stay in Italy longer than three months. In theory, you should apply for one within eight days of arriving in Italy. EU citizens do not require a *permesso di soggiorno* but are required to register with the

local registry office (*ufficio anagrafe*) if they stay for more than three months.

To get one, you'll need an application form; a valid passport, containing a stamp with your date of entry into Italy (ask for this, as it's not automatic); a photocopy of your passport with visa, if required; four passport-style photographs; proof of your ability to support yourself financially (ideally a letter from an employer or school/university); and a €14.62 official stamp.

Although correct at the time of writing, the documentary requirements change periodically, so always check before you join the inevitable queue. Details are available on www.poliziadistato.it – click on the English tab and then follow the links.

To apply pick up an application kit at the main post office at Piazza San Silvestro 19 or go to the Ufficio Immigrazione (off Map pp106–7; Via Teofilo Patini; ⏰ 8.30-11.30am Mon-Fri & 3-5pm Tue & Thu) in the city's eastern suburbs.

Study Visas

Non-EU citizens who want to study at a university or language school in Italy must have a study visa. These can be obtained at your nearest Italian embassy or consulate. You will normally require confirmation of your enrolment, proof of payment of fees and proof that you can support yourself financially. The visa only covers the period of the enrolment. This type of visa is renewable within Italy but, again, only with confirmation of ongoing enrolment and that you are still financially self-supporting.

Work Visas

To work in Italy all non-EU citizens require a work visa. Apply to your nearest Italian embassy or consulate. You'll need a valid passport, proof of health insurance and a work permit. The work permit is obtained in Italy by your employer and then forwarded to you prior to your visa application. For more on work permits, see p302.

WOMEN TRAVELLERS

Rome is not a dangerous city for women, but lone women might want to avoid the area around Termini late at night.

The most common source of discomfort is harassment. Staring is much more overt in Rome than in more reticent northern parts, and although it is almost always harmless, it can become annoying. If you find yourself being pestered by local men and ignoring them isn't working, tell them that you are waiting for your husband (*marito*) or boyfriend (*fidanzato*), and if necessary, walk away. Avoid becoming aggressive, as this may result in an unpleasant confrontation.

Gropers, particularly on crowded public transportation, can also be a problem. If you do feel someone start to touch you inappropriately, make a fuss – a loud '*che schifo!*' (how disgusting!) should do the job. If a more serious incident occurs, report it to the police, who are then required to press charges.

WORK

EU citizens can legally work in Italy with nothing more than a tax number (*codice fiscale;* see p297). Non-EU nationals require a work permit. This should be organised by your prospective employer in Italy and forwarded to the Italian consulate in your country, enabling you to apply for the relevant work visa. If you intend to work for a non-Italian company or plan to go freelance, you must organise the permit in your country of residence through an Italian consulate. This process is complicated and can take many months.

Casual work in Rome is not always easy to find but you might strike it lucky in bars or hostels, au pairing or tour-guiding. Teaching English is another option, although to secure a place at a reputable school you'll need a Teaching English as a Foreign Language (TEFL) certificate. It's best to apply for teaching work in September, in time for the beginning of courses in October.

Teaching and other jobs are advertised in *Porta Portese* (weekly) and *Wanted in Rome* (fortnightly). You could also look in *Il Messaggero* and the *Herald Tribune* for job ads, and on the bulletin boards of English-language bookshops. A useful guide is *Living, Studying and Working in Italy* by Travis Neighbour Ward and Monica Larner (2003).

Online, you could try the following:

British School (www.britishschool.it) A private English-language organisation with various schools across Rome.

International House (www.ihromamz.it) One of Rome's best-known English language schools.

Roma Au Pair (www.romaaupair.it) An organisation that arranges short-term positions for au pairs with Italian families.

Volunteer Abroad (www.volunteerabroad.com) Lists volunteer opportunities in Rome and Italy.

Doing Business

There are no special issues in doing business in Rome. However, an awareness of Italian business etiquette always helps. Some basic tips:

Contacts If you know someone who can help you, have no qualms about using them.

Formalities Courtesy counts and formalities are observed. Italian speakers should use the formal third person *lei* rather than the informal *tu*.

Punctuality It might not always be reciprocated, but punctuality is appreciated.

Socialising Expect to be invited to lunch or dinner; the host pays.

Many of the smarter hotels have business centres or secretarial assistance for guests. Otherwise try the following:

Executive Services Business Centres (Map pp150–1; ☎ 06 85 23 71; www.executivenetwork.it; Via Savoia 78) Secretarial services, video-conferencing facilities, interpreters and other services.

World Translation Centre (Map pp106–7; ☎ 06 488 10 39; www.wtcsrl.com; Via Merulana 259) Can provide sworn translations for legal and corporate needs.

LANGUAGE

It's true – anyone can speak another language. Don't worry if you haven't studied languages before or that you studied a language at school for years and can't remember any of it. It doesn't even matter if you failed English grammar. After all, that's never affected your ability to speak English! And this is the key to picking up a language in another country: you just need to start speaking.

Learn a few key phrases before you go. Write them on pieces of paper and stick them on the fridge, by the bed or even on the computer – anywhere that you'll see them often.

You'll find that locals appreciate travellers trying their language, no matter how muddled you may think you sound. So don't just stand there, say something! If you want to learn more Italian than we've included here, pick up a copy of Lonely Planet's comprehensive but user-friendly *Italian Phrasebook* or *Fast Talk Italian*.

SOCIAL
Meeting People
Hello.
Buongiorno.
Goodbye.
Arrivederci.
Please.
Per favore.
Thank you (very much).
(Mille) grazie.
Yes./No.
Sì./No.
Do you speak English?
Parla inglese?
Do you understand (me)?
(Mi) capisce?
Yes, I understand.
Sì, capisco.
No, I don't understand.
No, non capisco.

Could you please …?
Potrebbe …?
  repeat that   ripeterlo
  speak more   parlare più lentamente
  slowly
  write it down   scriverlo

Going Out
What's on …?
Che c'è in programma …?
  locally   in zona
  this weekend   questo fine settimana
  today   oggi
  tonight   stasera

Where are the …?
Dove sono …?
  clubs   dei club
  gay venues   dei locali gay
  places to eat   posti dove mangiare
  pubs   dei pub

Is there a local entertainment guide?
C'è una guida agli spettacoli in questa città?

PRACTICAL
Question Words
Who?   Chi?
What?   Che?
When?   Quando?
Where?   Dove?
How?   Come?

Numbers & Amounts
1	uno
2	due
3	tre
4	quattro
5	cinque
6	sei
7	sette
8	otto
9	nove
10	dieci
11	undici
12	dodici
13	tredici
14	quattordici
15	quindici
16	sedici
17	diciasette

18	diciotto
19	dicianove
20	venti
21	ventuno
22	ventidue
30	trenta
40	quaranta
50	cinquanta
60	sessanta
70	settanta
80	ottanta
90	novanta
100	cento
1000	mille
2000	duemila

Days

Monday	lunedì
Tuesday	martedì
Wednesday	mercoledì
Thursday	giovedì
Friday	venerdì
Saturday	sabato
Sunday	domenica

Banking

I'd like to …
Vorrei …

cash a cheque	riscuotere un assegno
change money	cambiare denaro
change some travellers cheques	cambiare degli assegni di viaggio

Where's the nearest …?
Dov'è il … più vicino?

| automatic teller machine | bancomat |
| foreign exchange office | cambio |

Post

Where is the post office?
Dov'è la posta?

I want to send a …
Voglio spedire …

fax	un fax
parcel	un pachetto
postcard	una cartolina

I want to buy a/an …
Voglio comprare …

aerogram	un aerogramma
envelope	una busta
postage stamp	un francobollo

Phone & Mobile Phones

I want to buy a phonecard.
Voglio comprare una scheda telefonica.

I want to make …
Voglio fare …

| a call (to …) | una chiamata (a …) |
| reverse-charge/ collect call | una chiamata a carico del destinatario |

Where can I find a/an …?
Dove si trova …?
I'd like a/an …
Vorrei …

adaptor plug	un addattatore
charger for my phone	un caricabatterie
mobile/cell phone for hire	un cellulare da noleggiare
prepaid mobile/ cell phone	un cellulare prepagato
SIM card for your network	un SIM card per vostra rete telefonica

Internet

Where's the local internet café?
Dove si trova l'internet point?

I'd like to …
Vorrei …

| check my email | controllare le mie email |
| get online | collegarmi a internet |

Transport

What time does the … leave?
A che ora parte …?

bus	l'autobus
plane	l'aereo
train	il treno

What time's the … bus/passenger ferry?
A che ora passa … autobus/batello?

first	il primo
last	l'ultimo
next	il prossimo

Is this taxi free?
È libero questo taxi?
Please put the meter on.
Usa il tassametro, per favore.
How much is it to …?
Quant'è per …?
Please take me to (this address).
Mi porti a (questo indirizzo), per favore.

FOOD

breakfast	prima colazione
lunch	pranzo
dinner	cena
snack	spuntino/merenda
eat	mangiare
drink	bere

Can you recommend a ...?
Potrebbe consigliare un ...?

bar/pub	bar/pub
café	bar
restaurant	ristorante

Is the service/cover charge included in the bill?
Il servizio/coperto è compreso nel conto?

For more detailed information on food and dining out, see p187.

EMERGENCIES

It's an emergency!
È un'emergenza!
Could you please help me/us?
Mi/Ci può aiutare, per favore?

Call the police/a doctor/an ambulance!
Chiami la polizia/un medico/
un'ambulanza!
Where's the police station?
Dov'è la questura?

HEALTH

Where's the nearest ...?
Dov'è ... più vicino?

dentist	il dentista
doctor	il medico
hospital	l'ospedale
(night) chemist	la farmacia (di turno)

I need a doctor (who speaks English).
Ho bisogno di un medico (che parli inglese).

Symptoms

I have (a) ...
Ho ...

diarrhoea	la diarrea
fever	la febbre
headache	mal di testa
pain	un dolore

GLOSSARY

ACI – Automobile Club Italiano (Italian Automobile Association)
alimentari – grocery shop
alta moda – high fashion
ambasciata – embassy
anfiteatro – amphitheatre
aperitivo – aperitif, pre-meal drink with snacks
ATAC – Agenzia per i Trasporti Autoferrotranviari del Comune di Roma (Rome's public transport company)
autostrada – motorway, highway

baccalà – salted cod
bancomat – ATM
benzina senza piombo – unleaded petrol
biancazzurri – 'white and blues'; Lazio fans and players
biglietteria – box or ticket office
biglietto – ticket
birreria – pub

calcio – football (soccer)
cambio – exchange office
cappella – chapel
carabinieri – police with military and civil duties
casa – house, home
castello – castle
catacomba – catacomb, underground tomb complex

centro sociale – social club; organised squat
centro storico – historic city centre
chiesa – church
cimitero – cemetery
colonna – column
commissariato (di polizia) – police station
comune – municipality; town or city council
coperto – cover charge in most restaurants
cornetto – a croissant filled with chocolate, marmalade or custard cream

enoteca, enoteche (pl) – wine bar
ES – Eurostar train
est – east

fornaio, forni (pl) – bakery

gelateria – ice-cream parlour
gelato – ice cream
giallorossi – 'yellow and reds'; AS Roma fans and players
giardino – garden

IC – Intercity train
IVA – Imposta di Valore Aggiunto (value-added tax)

Laziali – Lazio fans
libreria – bookshop

macchiaioli – 'dabbers'; the late-19th-century Italian version of the Impressionists

mezza porzione – half or child's portion

motorino – moped

nord – north

numero verde – toll-free number

ospedale – public hospital

osteria – neighbourhood inn

ovest – west

palazzo – mansion

panino – bread roll

pasquinades – anonymous messages posted around 17th-century Rome

pasticceria – cake/pastry shop

pensione – small hotel or guesthouse

permesso di lavoro – work permit

permesso di soggiorno – permit to stay in Italy for a nominated period

piazza – square

pinacoteca – art gallery

piscina – pool

pizza al taglio – pizza by the slice

polizia – police

ponte – bridge

porta – city gate

posta – post office

primo – first course

profumeria – perfume shop

pronto soccorso – first aid; *(riparto di) pronto soccorso* is a casualty/emergency ward

questura – police headquarters

Regionale – slow local train

Rinascimento – Renaissance

rione – a historic district of central Rome

Risorgimento – late-19th-century movement led by Garibaldi and others to create a united, independent Italian state

ristorante – restaurant

romanesco – Roman dialect

Romani – Romans

Romanisti – AS Roma fans

sala – room in a museum or a gallery

saldi – sales (ie with price reductions)

secolo – century; as in XV sec = 15th century

secondo – second course

sedia a rotelle – wheelchair

seggiolone – child's high chair

servizio – service charge in restaurants

sindaco – mayor

SPQR – Senatus Populusque Romanus (the Senate and People of Rome; symbol of the Roman Republic)

stazione – station

tabaccheria – tobacconist's shop

tavola calda – literally 'hot table'; a cheap, self-service eatery

teatro – theatre

terme – baths, hot springs

torre – tower

trattoria – cheap restaurant

ufficio postale – post office

ufficio stranieri – foreigners bureau (in police station)

via – street, road

vicolo – alley, alleyway

ZTL – Zone a Traffico Limitato (limited traffic zones)

BEHIND THE SCENES

THIS BOOK

This is the 6th edition of *Rome*. Duncan Garwood and Abigail Hole wrote the previous edition. This guidebook was commissioned in Lonely Planet's London office, and produced by the following:

Commissioning Editor Paula Hardy

Coordinating Editors Kate James, Simon Williamson

Coordinating Cartographers Andras Bogdanovits, Mark Griffiths

Coordinating Layout Designer Jacqui Saunders

Senior Editors Helen Christinis, Katie Lynch

Managing Cartographers David Connolly, Owen Eszeki, Alison Lyall

Managing Layout Designer Sally Darmody

Assisting Editor Joanne Newell

Assisting Cartographers Ross Butler, Csanad Csutoros, Hunor Csutoros, Corey Hutchison, Peter Shields

Cover Yukiyoshi Kamimura, lonelyplanetimages.com

Internal Image Research Sabrina Dalbesio, lonelyplanetimages.com

Project Manager Rachel Imeson

Language Content Robyn Loughnane

Thanks to Shahara Ahmed, Lucy Birchley, Annelies Mertens, Trent Paton, Herman So

Cover photographs Garden detail, Villa Lante, northeast of Viterbo at Bagnaia, Christopher Wood, Lonely Planet

Images (top). Statues at the Colosseum, Rome, Italy, Jeffery Titcomb/Stock Connection/ Aurora Photos (bottom).

Internal photographs Bryan Busovicki/Dreamstime p7 (#4); P Deliss/Godong/Corbis p85, p88 (bottom); Franco Origlia/Getty Images p89; Osservatore Romano/epa/Corbis p88 (top); Picture Media/Paolo Cocco/Reuters p90; Radius Images/Corbis p5 (#3); Riccardo Spila/Grand Tour/Corbis p86; Michael S Yamashita/Corbis p12 (#1). All other photographs by Lonely Planet Images: Glenn Beanland p4 (#1), p8 (#2); Tony Burns p10 (#1), p11; Paolo Cordelli p6 (#2), p8 (#1); Jon Davison p5 (#5); Guylain Doyle p7 (#5); Krzysztof Dydynski p9 (#3); Greg Elms p2; Simon Foale p7 (#3); Martin Moos p5 (#5), p9 (#5), p87, p92; Russell Mountford p3, p6 (#1); Will Salter p9 (#4), p12 (#2); Neil Setchfield p10 (#2); Jonathan Smith p4 (#2).

All images are the copyright of the photographers unless otherwise indicated. Many of the images in this guide are available for licensing from Lonely Planet Images: www.lonelyplanetimages.com.

THANKS
DUNCAN GARWOOD

As always, I owe a lot of thanks for the help, support and encouragement I received on this job. At Lonely Planet, thanks to CE Paula Hardy and mapping maestro Herman So. In Rome, I'd like to thank Valentina Moncada, Leonetta Bentivoglio, Corrado Augias and Patrizia Notarnicola for their time and helpful insights. Thanks also to Richard McKenna for his company and fellow author Abi Hole for her support and valuable suggestions. On the home front,

THE LONELY PLANET STORY

Fresh from an epic journey across Europe, Asia and Australia in 1972, Tony and Maureen Wheeler sat at their kitchen table stapling together notes. The first Lonely Planet guidebook, *Across Asia on the Cheap*, was born.

Travellers snapped up the guides. Inspired by their success, the Wheelers began publishing books to Southeast Asia, India and beyond. Demand was prodigious, and the Wheelers expanded the business rapidly to keep up. Over the years, Lonely Planet extended its coverage to every country and into the virtual world via lonelyplanet.com and the Thorn Tree message board.

As Lonely Planet became a globally loved brand, Tony and Maureen received several offers for the company. But it wasn't until 2007 that they found a partner whom they trusted to remain true to the company's principles of travelling widely, treading lightly and giving sustainably. In October of that year, BBC Worldwide acquired a 75% share in the company, pledging to uphold Lonely Planet's commitment to independent travel, trustworthy advice and editorial independence.

Today, Lonely Planet has offices in Melbourne, London and Oakland, with over 500 staff members and 300 authors. Tony and Maureen are still actively involved with Lonely Planet. They're travelling more often than ever, and they're devoting their spare time to charitable projects. And the company is still driven by the philosophy of *Across Asia on the Cheap*: 'All you've got to do is decide to go and the hardest part is over. So go!'

SEND US YOUR FEEDBACK

We love to hear from travellers – your comments keep us on our toes and help make our books better. Our well-travelled team reads every word on what you loved or loathed about this book. Although we cannot reply individually to postal submissions, we always guarantee that your feedback goes straight to the appropriate authors, in time for the next edition. Each person who sends us information is thanked in the next edition and the most useful submissions are rewarded with a free book.

To send us your updates – and find out about Lonely Planet events, newsletters and travel news – visit our award-winning website: lonelyplanet.com/contact.

Note: We may edit, reproduce and incorporate your comments in Lonely Planet products such as guidebooks, websites and digital products, so let us know if you don't want your comments reproduced or your name acknowledged. For a copy of our privacy policy visit lonelyplanet.com/privacy.

a huge *grazie di cuore* to Lidia, without whose support I couldn't do the job, to my mother-in-law Nicla, and to my two little rascals, Ben and Nick.

ABIGAIL HOLE

Molto grazie to all at Lonely Planet, especially to Paula Hardy and to fellow author, Duncan. *Tante grazie* to my

LONELY PLANET AUTHORS

Why is our travel information the best in the world? It's simple: our authors are passionate, dedicated travellers. They don't take freebies in exchange for positive coverage so you can be sure the advice you're given is impartial. They travel widely to all the popular spots, and off the beaten track. They don't research using just the internet or phone. They discover new places not included in any other guidebook. They personally visit thousands of hotels, restaurants, palaces, trails, galleries, temples and more. They speak with dozens of locals every day to make sure you get the kind of insider knowledge only a local could tell you. They take pride in getting all the details right, and in telling it how it is. Think you can do it? Find out how at **lonelyplanet.com**.

interviewees Anja Petitto, Pierandrea Righetti and Mariantonietta Caraccio. *A le mie famiglie a Roma*: Marcello, Anna, Carlotta, Alessandro, Paolo, Clemente e Simone. *Grazie* in Rome especially to Paola Zaganelli, and to her friends Manuela and Lorenzo, to Stephanie Santini for making research much more fun, to Barbara Lessona for showing me her shopping secrets, and to Benjamin Holmes. Many, many thanks to the bidgie-carers: Marcello, Anna, Mum, Ant, Karen, Esme, Jack Lula, Mel, Gracie May and Chrissy; and to Luca, Gabriel and Jack Roman for being so *fighi*.

OUR READERS

Many thanks to the travellers who used the last edition and wrote to us with helpful hints, useful advice and interesting anecdotes:

Ingrid Anastasiu, Sarwat Bakhsh, Matthew Belmonte, David Bloustein, Mark Broadhead, Marian Brooks, Michelle Caldwell, Lacey Chong, Severine Covens, William Deering, Meltem Demirkan, Malvina Diletti, Libero Dipensare, Janice Furphy, Matthew Keogh, Audun Lem, Jenny Little, Corneliu Mantescu, Antonio Mar, Massimo Marchesani, Rajiv Mitra, Daniel Piggott, Arnaud Pitois, Shane Radbone, Bob Spiegel, Piero Spinelli, Alona Tatarsky, Adan Varela, Henrik Von Maltzahn, Jenny Ward, Rachel Wood

Notes

Notes

lonelyplanet.com

INDEX

000 map pages
000 photographs

INDEX

GOING GREEN

The following sights, accommodation options, restaurants and courses have been selected because they meet our criteria for sustainable tourism. While many restaurants in Rome serve seasonal, locally sourced produce, we've highlighted those that choose to go that extra mile and are accredited by the Italian Slow Food movement. We've also included Rome's colourful produce markets. Accommodation options make it if they show a real commitment to recycling or energy conservation, while attractions are listed if they are Unesco-listed World Heritage sites.

We want to keep developing our sustainable travel content, so if you think we've left someone or something out, contact us at www.lonelyplanet.com/feedback and set us straight for next time.

For more information about sustainable travel, check out our website at www.lonelyplanet.com/responsibletravel.

MAP LEGEND

ROUTES

............Freeway ....Mall/Steps
............Primary ....Tunnel
............Secondary ....Pedestrian Overpass
............Tertiary ....Walking Tour
............Lane ....Walking Trail
............Unsealed Road ....Walking Path
............One-Way Street ....Track

TRANSPORT

............Ferry ....Rail
............Metro ....Rail (Underground)
............Monorail ....Tram
............Bus Route ....Cable Car, Funicular

HYDROGRAPHY

............River, Creek ....Water

BOUNDARIES

............International ....Regional, Suburb
............State, Provincial ....Ancient Wall

AREA FEATURES

............Airport ....Land
............Building ....Mall
............Campus ....Park
............Cemetery, Christian ....Sports
............Forest ....Urban

POPULATION

○ CAPITAL (NATIONAL)   ◉ CAPITAL (STATE)
● Large City   ○ Medium City
○ Small City   ○ Town, Village

SYMBOLS

Information
⊖ ....Bank, ATM
⊘ ....Embassy/Consulate
⊕ ....Hospital, Medical
⊖ ....Information
@ ....Internet Facilities
⊕ ....Police Station
⊗ ....Post Office, GPO
⊕ ....Telephone
⊕ ....Toilets

Sights
🏰 ....Castle, Fortress
✝ ....Christian
▯ ....Monument
🏛 ....Museum, Gallery
● ....Point of Interest
⊠ ....Ruin
🐦 ....Zoo, Bird Sanctuary

Shopping
🛍 ....Shopping

Eating
🍴 ....Eating

Drinking & Nightlife
🍷 ....Drinking
☕ ....Café

Arts
🎭 ....Arts

Sports & Activities
🏊 ....Pool
● ....Point of Interest

Sleeping
🛏 ....Sleeping
⛺ ....Camping

Transport
✈ ....Airport, Airfield
🚌 ....Bus Station
🅿 ....Parking Area

Geographic
📷 ....Lookout
▲ ....Mountain
🏞 ....National Park
⬤ ....Waterfall

Published by Lonely Planet Publications Pty Ltd
ABN 36 005 607 983

Australia (Head Office)
Locked Bag 1, Footscray, Victoria 3011,
☎ 03 8379 8000, fax 03 8379 8111,
talk2us@lonelyplanet.com.au

USA 150 Linden St, Oakland, CA 94607,
☎ 510 250 6400, toll free 800 275 8555,
fax 510 893 8572, info@lonelyplanet.com

UK 2nd fl, 186 City Rd, London, EC1V 2NT,
☎ 020 7106 2100, fax 020 7106 2101,
go@lonelyplanet.co.uk

© Lonely Planet 2010
Photographs © As listed (p307) 2010

Printed by Hang Tai Printing Company,
Hong Kong.
Printed in China.

Mixed Sources
Product group from well-managed
forests and other controlled sources
www.fsc.org Cert no. SGS-COC-005002
© 1996 Forest Stewardship Council